Sixth Canadian E

Feminist Issues: Race, Class, and Sexuality

Nancy Mandell
York University

Jennifer L. Johnson
Thorneloe University, federated with Laurentian University

Toronto

Editorial Director: Claudine O'Donnell
Acquisitions Editor: Matthew Christian
Marketing Manager: Christine Cozens
Program Manager: Madhu Ranadive
Project Manager: Pippa Kennard
Developmental Editor: Keriann McGoogan
Production Services: Garima Khosla, iEnergizer Aptara®, Ltd.
Permissions Project Manager: Kathryn O'Handley
Photo Permissions Research: Navinkumar Srinivasan
Text Permissions Research: Renae Horstman
Interior Designer: Anthony Leung
Cover Designer: Anthony Leung
Cover Image: Clivewa/Fotolia

Vice-President, Cross Media and Publishing Services: Gary Bennett

Credits and acknowledgments for material borrowed from other sources and reproduced, with permission, in this textbook appear on the appropriate page within the text.

10 9 8 7 6 5 4 3 2 1 [V0RY]

Library and Archives Canada Cataloguing in Publication

Feminist issues : race, class, and sexuality / [edited by] Nancy Mandell (York University), Jennifer Johnson (Laurentian University). — Sixth Canadian edition.

Includes bibliographical references and index.
ISBN 978-0-13-514668-2 (paperback)

1. Feminism—Canada. 2. Women—Canada—Social conditions. I. Mandell, Nancy, editor II. Johnson, Jennifer (Jennifer L.), editor

HQ1206.F445 2015 305.4 C2015-906618-2

ISBN 978-0-13-359366-2

Dedication

Micah, Eli, Charlotte, Brooke, and Emily

and

Leandré, Rhys, and Maël

Brief Contents

Contents

Notes on Contributors

Carrie Bourassa is Professor of Indigenous Health Studies at First Nations University of Canada. She is proud to be the successful Nominated Principal Investigator on a Canada Foundation for Innovation Grant that funded the Indigenous Community–based Health Research Labs at FNUniv. She is a member of the College of New Scholars, Artists and Scientists of the Royal Society of Canada. Carrie's research interests include the impacts of colonization on the health of Indigenous people; creating culturally safe care in health service delivery; Indigenous community–based health research methodology; Indigenous HIV/AIDS research; Indigenous end-of-life care and Indigenous women's health. Carrie is Métis, belonging to the Regina Riel Métis Council #34.

Shana L. Calixte is a PhD candidate in Gender, Feminist and Women's Studies at York University. Her teaching and research include critical race and sexuality studies in the history of the Caribbean Girl Guides movement. She teaches courses such as Girl Cultures, Female Sexualities, Hip-Hop Feminisms and Reproduction and Mothering at Thorneloe University federated with Laurentian University. She is also the full time Executive Director of NISA/Northern Initiative for Social Action, a peer-led mental health organization serving thousands of Northern Ontarians. Recent publications include articles in the *Journal of Mental Health*, and in *Difficult Dialogues About 21st Century Girls* (forthcoming).

Ann Duffy is a Professor at Brock University in Sociology and Labour Studies. Her research interests focus on the intersections between women, work (paid and unpaid), social inequality, and the economy. She has co-authored and co-edited a variety of books on the sociology of work, sociology of the family and family violence. With Professors Daniel Glenday and Norene Pupo, she is presently co-authoring a book on the crisis in Canadian employment. Having just completed a SSHRC-funded project on deindustrialization with Professors June Corman and Norene Pupo, she is also co-authoring a book on the collapse of manufacturing in Niagara Region.

Amber Gazso is Associate Professor of Sociology, York University. She holds a PhD in Sociology (University of Alberta, 2006). Her current research interests include citizenship, family and gender relations, poverty, research methods, and social policy and the welfare state. Her recent publications focus on low income mothers on social assistance and Canadians and Americans' experiences of midlife. Her current research explores how diverse families make ends meet by piecing together networks of social support such as government and community and informal supports. Another ongoing and comparative project explores the relationship between health and income inequality among Canadians and Americans in midlife.

Christopher J. Greig is Associate Professor at the University of Windsor, in the Faculty of Education and Women's and Gender Studies Program, Canada. His research is focused on historical perspectives on Canadian men, boys, and masculinities. Feminist analyses of social, political and economic periods and contexts inform Greig's research, which appears in journals such as *Educational Review, Discourse: Studies in the Cultural Politics of Education*, and the *Alberta Journal of Educational Research* and include a co-edited book, *Canadian Men and Masculinities: Historical and Contemporary Perspectives* (2012) and *Ontario Boys: Masculinity and the Idea Boyhood in Postwar Ontario, 1945–1960* (2014).

Jennifer L. Johnson is Associate Professor of Women's, Gender and Sexuality Studies at Thorneloe University federated with Laurentian University. Her research and teaching include feminist geographical approaches to the study of social reproduction and global economies; gender, race and racism, and feminist pedagogy. She sits on the editorial board of *Atlantis: Critical Studies in Gender, Culture & Social Justice/Études critiques sur le genre, la culture, et la justice*. Her current research explores how gender and race are socially constructed through the spatialization of work, and in particular, the nuclear family home.

Susanne Luhmann is Associate Professor in the Department of Women's and Gender Studies at the University of Alberta. Her teaching/research interests and published work concern feminist and queer pedagogies, sexuality studies, the formation of Women's and Gender Studies, and German cultural memory. She is currently finishing a book manuscript tentatively entitled "Domesticating the Nazi Past: Familial Legacies of Nazi Perpetration in Contemporary German Memory," which examines representations that restage, recover, and narrate legacies of perpetration from within the space of private and family life in Germany.

Nancy Mandell is a Professor in the Department of Sociology, York University. She is a faculty associate at the Centre for Feminist Research (CFR) and the Centre for Excellence for Research on Immigration and Settlement (CERIS). Her research and teaching interests include gender, aging, qualitative methods, schooling, and family. Recently she has published on life course analysis of midlife Canadian women, senior immigrants, and transnational family patterns, gendered and racialized forms of carework, and academic-community research partnerships. She is completing a SSHRC grant entitled "Worked to Death," which examines patterns of economic security among aging immigrant families.

Corinne L. Mason is Assistant Professor of Sociology and the Coordinator of Gender & Women's Studies at Brandon University. She conducts transnational critical-race feminist analyses of development discourses and popular news media, focusing specifically on representations of LGBT rights, violence against women, reproductive justice, and foreign aid. Her work has been published in *Feminist Formations*, *International Feminist Journal of Politics*, *Critical Studies in Media Communication*, *Surveillance & Society*, *and Canadian Journal of Communication*. She is currently working a book-length project on sexuality rights and development, and exploring the connections between race, social media, and humanitarianism.

J. Maki Motapanyane is Associate Professor of Women's & Gender Studies in the Department of Humanities, Mount Royal University. She teaches courses on global gender issues and transnationalism; colonialism and de-colonization; Hip-Hop culture;

environmental justice; and liberation ecology. Her research spans the fields of feminist theory, motherhood, and cultural studies. She has published on feminist theory, transnational feminist research methods, racialized comedy in Canada, and gender in Hip-Hop culture. She is the editor of *Mothering in Hip-Hop Culture: Representation and Experience* (Demeter Press, 2012), as well as the forthcoming *Motherhood and Lone/Single Parenting: A 21st Century Perspective* (Demeter Press, 2015).

Carmela Murdocca is Associate Professor in the Department of Sociology at York University, where she is also appointed to the graduate programs in Sociology, Socio-Legal Studies, and Social and Political Thought. Her work has appeared in Law and Social Inquiry, Social and Legal Studies, the Australian Feminist Law Journal, and the Canadian Journal of Law and Society. She is the author of *To Right Historical Wrongs: Race, Gender and Sentencing in Canada* (2013) and co-editor (with D. Brock and A. Glasbeek) of *Criminalization, Representation, Regulation* (2014).

Barbara A. Pollard is a PhD candidate in the Faculty of Education at the University of Windsor, Canada. Her research interests focus on critical literacy and critical pedagogy as it is practised across educational contexts. Pollard draws on feminist and other critical theoretical frameworks in order to explore how culture, ideology, knowledge, and identity are linked to social justice. Her research examines factors such as gender and social class under circumstances of oppression and resistance in the lives of students and teachers. Pollard has presented her research at numerous peer-reviewed conferences and was recently published in *Critical Literacy: Theories and Practices*.

Katherine McKenna is an Associate Professor jointly appointed in the Departments of History and Women's Studies and Feminist Research at the University of Western Ontario. Her publications in the area of gender-based violence include a co-edited volume *Violence Against Women: New Canadian Perspectives* (2002) and co-authored reports *The Economic Costs and Consequences of Child Abuse in Canada* (2003) for the Law Commission of Canada and *Measuring the Economic Costs of Violence Against Women: An Evaluation of the Literature* (2005) for the Division for the Advancement of Women of the United Nations.

Carla Rice is a Canada Research Chair at University of Guelph. A leader in the field of embodiment studies, Dr. Rice is founder and former director of the Body Image Project at Women's College Hospital in Toronto and the National Eating Disorder Information Centre. Her research explores representations and narratives of body and identity. Rice has published in widely in international journals including *Feminism & Psychology*, *Women's Studies International Forum*, and *Cultural Studies <=> Critical Methodologies* among others. Books include *Gender and Women's Studies in Canada: Critical Terrain* (2013), and *Becoming Women: The Embodied Self in Image Culture* (2014).

Katie Warfield is faculty in the Department of Journalism and Communication at Kwantlen Polytechnic University, Surrey, British Columbia. She is an authority on selfies and director of the Making Selfies/Making Self Research Project, which explicates visual presentations of gender and subjectivities via social media. She is also the director of the Visual Media Workshop, a centre for research and learning into digital visual culture.

She teaches classes in communication theory, popular culture, media and diversity, and social media; and is interested in phenomenology, new materialism, gender theory, and digital humanities. She has worked in the realms of media, cultural policy, and fashion design.

Michelle Webber is an Associate Professor in the Department of Sociology at Brock University and is affiliated with the Centre for Labour Studies, also at Brock University. Her research interests lie in the sociology of labour, education, and gender. Her current research is an investigation of faculty associations and the politics of accountability governance in Ontario universities (with Larry Savage and Jonah Butovsky—both at Brock University).

Fiona Whittington-Walsh is Chair of the department of Sociology at Kwantlen Polytechnic University in British Columbia. She teaches in the area of media, disability, and gender. Her research examines beauty, the body, disability and difference, media, and popular culture. Her current research is exploring the history of disability representation in film using participant action research methodology. She is a member of the Board of Directors for Inclusion BC, a nonprofit organization dedicated to the full inclusion of people with disabilities in every facet of society. She resides in British Columbia with her partner, daughters, and grandchildren.

Preface

We are very pleased and proud to bring forward the 6th edition of *Feminist Issues*. Significantly revised, the new edition provides an in-depth analysis of key issues facing women in Canada. Politics, sexuality, social media, intimate relationships, life course challenges, and institutional barriers are some of the issues the authors address. While the text is aimed at the new undergraduate reader, seasoned students and practitioners of feminism(s), anti-oppression, and related areas of study will also find rich and engaging discussions of current feminist topics. No matter who you are, where you are or what your life circumstances, young girls and women experience oppression and omission. Sensitive to differences in age, gender, sexuality, language, region, and ethnicity, in this book our authors examine both continuing and new challenges facing women.

Since the 5th edition, there has been a veritable groundswell of media interest in feminist issues in Canada and transnationally. The continued widespread existence of sexual assault on university and college campus campuses, ongoing sexual harassment in workplaces, unyielding calls by Indigenous people and allies that challenge Canadian society to account for literally hundreds of missing and murdered Indigenous women, ongoing violence against women transnationally, and genuine engagement from feminist men's groups in shifting dominant ideas about masculinity have all come to the forefront of popular discussions about feminism. In order to ensure that media interest is more than fleeting, students of feminist ideas need to continue to build capacity for action. Whether your feminist action happens in your teaching, on social media, at your child's daycare, in the streets, at the kitchen table, or on the floor of the House of Commons, we think it is important that readers continue to have access to in-depth feminist discussion of the topics addressed in this book as a part of their/our reason to act.

The 6th edition includes nine new authors from across Canada who have singly or collaboratively authored new material for this introductory text. These wonderful new contributors broach the topics of critical race and Indigenous feminisms, transnational feminist theory, critical masculinity studies, sexuality and gender identity, violence against women, and health. Returning contributors have substantially revised and updated five chapters within the thematic areas of education, aging, beauty culture, mothering and work, education, and historical trajectories of select types of feminism. Every chapter is theoretically grounded and contains contemporary examples.

With the writing of this preface, we have also to mark the passing of our colleague, friend, and previous contributor, Dr. Sharon Rosenberg (July 31st, 2010). We remember Sharon as an internationally recognized, controversial, challenging, and well-loved theorist of cultural and feminist studies. We also remember her as a mentor of new feminist thinkers.

As always, we have sought contributors who are both seasoned academics as well as new-entry scholars in an effort to further collaborative research and teaching about feminism. We have done this by reaching out to scholars in universities of all sizes across Canada, who have deep commitments to the intellectual communities they work within.

The production of knowledge about feminism can be a minefield of politics, social tensions, and debate, both within communities that already consider themselves "feminist" (and there are many) and those who baldly oppose gender, racial, class, and sexual equality (and sadly, there still exist some of those as well). In other words, the production of knowledge about feminism is messy and often partial and incomplete. One of the most important features of this book is that authors write the material for this collection, drawing upon their own original research and assessment of their fields as they stand today. They have sifted through mountains of literature, firsthand interviews, popular media, policy and legal documents, and records of individual/collective experiences to distill for the reader some key ideas about their topic. Authors have been asked to present answers to the following questions: Why is the topic an issue for feminism? Why discuss it now? How have some of the core issues for feminists been taken up within this topic? How would/how do feminists working on this topic define problems that exist for women?, and: What solutions does are posed for these problems? In their answers, authors challenge our ideas about what topics feminism can be applied to and where feminist understandings of these issues still need to grow.

Putting together this collection of ideas, arguments, and research has been a privilege and a pleasure. The contributors and peer reviewers of this text have been generous with their time, constructive criticism, and written work. We thank each one of them for their work. For one of us—Jen Johnson—work on this collection represents a full circle return to a text that was first introduced to her as a student in 1995. Working with Nancy Mandell, the originator and editor of this text, has been a privilege and a tremendous learning experience. For Nancy, bringing Jen on board was an inspired choice as she has completely revitalized the discussion and moved it in new and fascinating directions. We each do our part in the ongoing struggles for women's equality in Canada. We the editors and the contributors are very proud to offer this edition as our small contribution to these movements.

Acknowledgements

Numerous people have read versions of these chapters and generously offered rigorous and thoughtful critiques. Given their attention to peer review, we are confident that these chapters represent the best possible versions of the contributors' work and for this we are extremely grateful. We thank also the seven anonymous reviewers of the previous edition, feminist scholars from all over Canada who teach about feminism to 'new' audiences and to those students who have given invaluable feedback over the years—we are listening. At Pearson we would like to thank Madhu Ranadive, Matthew Christian, and Keriann McGoogan for their guidance and timely suggestions on the composition and framing of the collection. To Pearson's staff and copy editors, especially Ruth Chernia and Garima Khosla, we are grateful for your attention to detail and for bringing this collection to fruition.

Nancy would like to welcome Jennifer Johnson on board and thank her for agreeing to co-edit *Feminist Issues*. Jen's lively sense of humour and her considerable energy and enthusiasm for the project have made her an ideal collaborator. The sixth edition is markedly stronger because Jen has joined the team. Nancy also thanks the people from whom she gains strength and affection: her long time partner Lionel; her 'boys'—Jeremy, Ben, and Adam—and their partners—Marissa, Caroline, and Jamie—and now their children—Micah, Eli, Charlotte, Brooke, and Emily. As *Feminist Issues* has grown, so too has Nancy's family!

Jen is very thankful to Nancy for the opportunity to join her in co-editing this text—thank you for taking a chance on me! Working with you afforded me the opportunity to learn far more than I ever could have on my own. I am extremely thankful also to my research assistant, Taynia Rainville: thank you for your exceptional work ethic and ability to ask good questions fearlessly. To Shana, thank you for your patience into the many months of drafts and editing. My hope is that this book is one small part of shifting our culture to allow our trio of proto-feminists: Leandré, Rhys, and Maël, a chance at living in a more just society.

Chapter 1

Theorizing Women's Oppression and Social Change: Liberal, Socialist, Radical, and Postmodern Feminisms

Shana L. Calixte, Jennifer L. Johnson, and J. Maki Motapanyane

INTRODUCTION

Although feminism has come to mean many things to many people, we prefer the words of bell hooks who wrote: "Simply put, feminism is a movement to end sexism, sexist exploitation, and oppression" (2000, p. 1). Feminism begins with the premise that women's and men's positions in society are socially, economically, culturally, and historically shaped, not biologically predetermined. It is also premised on the idea that not all women experience gender inequalities in the same way. An understanding of this unequal distribution of power inevitably exposes other oppressions based on factors such as race, sexuality, class, dis/ability, and nationhood (St. Denis, 2007, p. 47). Feminism is political in that it aims to achieve gender equity in all spheres—social life, politics, economic conditions, language, culture, and many other areas. But feminists remain unclear about how best to achieve both general and specific redistribution of social and economic power.

In this chapter, we outline several historical and contemporary approaches to defining women's oppression, their means for remedying this oppression, and the ways in which each perspective judges whether equity has been achieved. The first three of these theories are decidedly modernist and challenge oppression within the framework of gender dichotomies, while the fourth theory presented—postmodern feminism—attempts to shatter these altogether. Although not exhaustive, this chapter follows several historical trajectories of feminism in Western nations revealing how fundamental assumptions and ideas about gender have emerged and changed over time.

LIBERAL FEMINISM: KEY HISTORICAL POINTS, PRINCIPLES, AND GOALS

Liberalism is a philosophy of politics and scientific inquiry developed in the 17th and 18th centuries during a period of European social change called the "Enlightenment" or the "Age of Reason." Liberal feminists use the core principles of liberalism to insist that women be integrated into existing social, political, religious, and economic institutions in order to achieve equality with men. Specifically, liberal feminists use liberal ideas of rationality, meritocracy, equality of opportunity, and freedom of choice as core principles on which to achieve women's equality.

First, liberal feminists emphasize women's capacity for rational thought and thus their shared humanity with men. Early feminist thinkers argued strenuously that women's capacity for reason was the same as that of men. Mary Wollstonecraft, in *A Vindication of the Rights of Woman* (1792) scandalized her contemporaries by refuting the widely held idea that women were inherently simple, irrational, and emotional. Through formal education, Wollstonecraft claimed, women can develop their innate capabilities for intellectual thought and thus become better wives and mothers. Wollstonecraft's ideas anticipated arguments put forward by women in later centuries.

Second, liberal feminists endorse the concept of meritocracy. This principle emerges clearly in the works of Harriet Taylor Mill (1807–1858) and her long-time companion, the political philosopher John Stuart Mill (1806–1873). Harriet Taylor Mill argued radically for the desirability of women to earn and have control of their own property and money that she saw as the basis for achieving equality between the sexes. Only by earning their own status (instead of relying upon a man for their keep) and controlling their own property would women have a chance of realizing equality of opportunity with men in other spheres.

These two principles—rationality and meritocracy—have been particularly important in facilitating women's access to formal education. Early liberal feminists understood that, without a formal education, women could not advance in social status or political participation, and could not acquire other social and legal rights unless they held educational credentials equal to those of men. But in 19th century Canada, women faced many challenges in this regard. First, women who wanted further education found themselves up against the view that educated women compromised their natural roles as child-bearers (Garvie & Johnson, 1999). Second, some 19th century white women who wanted an education, particularly married women, were accused of "racial suicide" because the racial theories of the time presumed the moral superiority of white people and women's obligation to reproduce that "race" instead of going to university (Valverde, 1992). As well, some ethnic minorities and people of colour, such as members of the Black communities of eastern Canada and southern Ontario, found themselves unwelcome in white Protestant or Catholic schools. Black women were key in establishing separate schools as early as 1830, even prior to the formal abolition of slavery in Canada. Separate schools were not only a site of women's education but also a form of resistance to the racism Black people experienced from white Canadians (Kelly, 1998; Sadlier, 1994). In Canada West (now Ontario) and East (now Quebec), female teachers proliferated throughout the 1850s, providing what little education was considered necessary for girls, such as writing, reading, and needlework (Prentice et al., 1996). In 1858, Canada's first female university students studied at Mount Allison University in New Brunswick. They studied a limited range of topics that typically included literature, languages, rhetoric, history, and home economics (developed specifically for female students' entry into post-secondary education). Typically, women students were segregated in all-female classrooms and required to sit apart from male students in adjoining rooms where they could hear the lecture but not be seen by the men (Garvie & Johnson, 1999). By the early 1900s in Canada, through informal but highly effective networks of women graduates, education for women came to be thought of as an enhancement of the young middle-class woman's "natural" qualities (Garvie & Johnson, 1999). The principles of rationality and meritocracy were thus exercised incrementally in the fight for early access to education.

Third, liberal feminists advocate equality of opportunity for women in all areas of social, economic, legal, and political life. This principle was critical in shaping liberal feminists' goal of getting women in Canada the vote. Between 1850 and 1920 liberal feminists pushed for women's suffrage.[1] Feminists lobbied the state, held demonstrations, and staged mock parliamentary debates to ridicule the men who upheld women's political and legal inequality. Suffragists used a variety of tactics to challenge the familiar dichotomy of "passive" femininity versus the "active" and political masculinity thought appropriate for political decision-making (Roome, 2001). Some felt that petitioning, letter-writing, and public speaking were the best tactics to achieve their goals. The work of maternal feminist and journalist Nellie McClung (1875–1951) in Manitoba is a good example of effective public speaking; she used wit to ridicule male politicians in the press. Maternal feminists argue that women's essential role as mothers imbues them as moral and caring people who have the best interests of children and communities at heart, thus making them well-suited to political participation.

Canadian women gained equality of opportunity to participate politically unevenly. Although most women were granted the federal vote in 1918, this still excluded most Indigenous people and people of Chinese origin (Cleverdon, 1974, p. 108). After 1918 the federal government divested itself of responsibility for granting the provincial franchise, so while some Manitoban women could vote provincially in 1916, others, such as their Québécoise counterparts, had to mobilize to bring 14 separate bills in 13 years to the Quebec legislature. Finally, under the leadership of Thérèse Casgrain (1896–1981) they enjoyed success in 1940. For Status Indian women, enfranchisement under the Indian Act required that they give up their association with a band, their status, and any land or property entitlements, a deeply unjust trade. Status Indian women achieved the vote in 1960 when the universal right to vote was introduced, though this cannot be attributed to the legacy of liberal feminism.

The movement for universal suffrage was often combined with women's attempts to correct other social inequities such as poverty. Maternal feminists and liberal feminists worked together along with socialist and conservative women toward the goals of social reform and, ultimately, the vote (Roome, 2001). Led by Dr. Emily Howard Stowe (1831–1903), the Toronto Women's Literary Club (established in 1876) reorganized as the Canadian Women's Suffrage Association in 1883 when some minor rights for women to vote in municipal elections were won (Prentice et al., 1996). In Quebec, women's organizing around suffrage and social problems such as poverty and health took place largely through women's Roman Catholic organizations, reflecting the appeal of Christian-based public service organizations such as the Women's Christian Temperance Union (WCTU) and the Young Women's Christian Association (YWCA). Their work centred on providing shelter and educational programs for young, single, and poor women. With the slight increase in women's access to formal education and legislation such as the 1884 Married Women's Property Act (allowing married women to hold property exclusive of their husbands' ownership), feminists built the capacity for their movement (Prentice et al., 1996). Social reformers and religious organizations such as the WCTU were concerned about the state of urban dwellers, reacting to the poverty and malnutrition of the masses that came with urbanization and industrialization. In Western Canada, for example, where milk was more costly than alcohol, women began to make the connections between poverty, the availability of alcohol, and the violence of men toward women and children (McClung, 1915/1972).

While a national women's movement advocated for the vote for women, it did not advocate for every women to have the right to vote. Social Darwinist ideas of racial purity as the basis for building a strong nation meant that Indigenous peoples, people of Chinese origin, and new immigrants from Eastern and Southern Europe were viewed as biologically inferior and denied the vote (Strong-Boag, 1998). Even social reformers argued for white women's superiority. Flora MacDonald Denison, a Canadian suffragist, was particularly critical of the morals of recent male immigrants (Prentice et al., 1996), while Emily Murphy (1868–1933), one of the "famous five" women who won women's right to take up public offices, such as appointment to the Senate of Canada in 1929 (Cleverdon, 1974, p. 149), wrote extensively on the threat of Chinese and Black men's corruptive tendencies to the moral purity of white women (Valverde, 1992). The white ribbons worn by WCTU activists signified white racial purity as much as they did the purity of milk over alcohol (Valverde, 1992). Despite the extensive political organizing of Black women such as Harriet Tubman (1820–1913) in the suffrage movement and of other women of colour in organizations such as the WCTU, white suffragists and social reformers persisted in the belief that their participation was additional, not central, to its eventual success (Sadlier, 1994; Valverde, 1992). Maternal feminists in particular embraced and applied the principles of equal opportunity and meritocracy but felt that white women had a superior moral and racial integrity, indicating white female suitability for political participation (Roome, 2001; Valverde, 1992).

Fourth, freedom of choice is a principle of liberal feminism. Freedom of choice is often understood as being closely related to the concept of equal opportunity, for without the opportunity to do so, you cannot freely *choose* anything. For example, the question of whether to stay home and care for your children or seek paid work is often understood as a question of choice for liberal feminism, a choice that requires equal opportunity in order to be exercised. The federal government had briefly empowered women to join the paid workforce during the Second World War by investing in subsidized daycare and encouraging women to join the war effort in traditionally male forms of employment (Timpson, 2001). After the war, women were encouraged by the media, religious institutions, and school systems to go back to the role of homemaking. In addition to the existence of sexist job descriptions and the lack of labour laws to prohibit sexist hiring practices in most fields, the post-war welfare state did not include a national daycare program (nor has any federal government since then), so many women had little choice but to fulfill their unpaid roles as mothers and wives. Women, who had previously worked outside the home, and even those who had not, became increasingly focused on exercising their freedom of choice to engage in paid labour.

Liberal feminist principles and, in particular, equality of opportunity are evident again in the Royal Commission on the Status of Women, 1970 (RCSW), which is a benchmark moment of Canadian women's rights. It is important to understand the groundswell of activism leading up to the RCSW was not only an undertaking of liberal feminists but also included the efforts of many involved in other inter-related struggles, such as new immigrant activist networks (Brown, 1989; Calliste, 2001); renewed challenges to the federal Indian Act raised by First Nations, Métis, and Inuit peoples; and the revitalization of Indigenous women's leadership in their communities (Maracle, 2003, p. 71). Simultaneously, the gay and lesbian liberation movement was challenging the criminalization of homosexuality and in 1969 achieved its decriminalization (Kinsman, 1987). As well, gender-based labour organizing was gaining strength (Luxton, 2006). These movements provided a new base of women dissatisfied with their relationship to the state and ready to do something about it.

Strategically, the RCSW proposed a human rights framework that had equal opportunity as its goal (Timpson, 2001, p. 29). Headed by Florence Bird (1908–1998), the RCSW spent over a year touring the country receiving briefs and hearing presentations from individuals and groups that had something to say about the status of women in Canadian society. The entire process was televised so that the nation watched; feminists were hopeful that the public nature of the RCSW would help them hold the federal government to carrying out the recommendations.

Based on the input of more than 300 women's organizations across the country and many more individuals, the RCSW identified four major areas of importance for Canadian women: the right to choose homemaking or paid employment; the shared responsibility for child care among mothers, fathers, and society at large; the special treatment of women relating to their maternity; and the special treatment of women to help them overcome the adverse effects of discriminatory practices in Canadian society (Paltiel, 1997, p. 29). These recommendations supported the central liberal feminist principle of equality of opportunity for women. The RCSW made 167 specific recommendations to the federal government as to how the social, political, and economic status of women could be improved. Some were implemented; many more were not. For example, Canada still lacks a national daycare program that would allow more women equal participation in the labour force. Many liberal-feminist organizations, although recognizing that many more issues have been added to the agenda, still use the RCSW recommendations as a measuring stick for women's equality with men in Canada.

Contemporary and Global Dimensions of Liberal Feminist Thought

Perhaps surprisingly, Canada is a global leader in supporting women's equality in some areas to the exclusion of others. In education it is certainly a leader in most fields. Women were rare in Canadian university programs in medicine, the sciences, and engineering until the

1940s, when Canada's participation in the Second World War necessitated more doctors. Although some female physicians did practice medicine in Canada before the Second World War, the number of female students did not immediately approach the number of male students. After the Second World War the number of women seeking higher education in general arts increased dramatically. Women have worked their way slowly into universities and colleges and into traditionally male-dominated areas of study, such as the sciences and engineering, such that their numbers have begun to approach those of men or exceed them in some fields, such as in the arts and in the study of law at some universities. Access to education is one of the major accomplishments of liberal feminism.

As a result of high levels of education, Canadian girls and women enjoy high overall labour force participation (62%) when you consider that in many countries women over the age of 15 account for far less than half of the active labour force (for example, 15% in Algeria and 40% in Italy) (World Bank, 2014). In contrast to Canada's relatively stable paid labour force access for women, current trends tell another story. In fact, Canada now ranks 19th in a measure called the Global Gender Gap set out by the World Economic Forum, where it lags behind countries that have experienced major wars and social upheavals in the late 20th century, such as Nicaragua (6th), Rwanda (7th), or large economic crises that have necessitated periodic mass migration, such as the Philippines (9th). Whereas in the 1990s it ranked among the top countries in the world according to the United Nations Gender Equality Index, Canada now ranks 23rd globally (Prasad & Freeman, 2015).

Why the change? Among many other factors, these statistical tools look at the significance of persistent gender wage gaps as a main indicator of equality between men and women in the prime of their work lives. Statistics Canada reports that the percentage of women ages 25 to 54 years old in the paid workforce was 81% in 2005 and has approached that of men, which was 91% in that same year (Statistics Canada, 2006b). Whereas women's earnings relative to men even narrowed until the late 1990s, their average hourly wage rate has stayed consistent at 82 to 83% of men's average wage, where it appears to be stuck (Drolet, 2011, pp. 6, 14). Of course, women cannot choose the average wage they'd prefer—the *male* dollar ($1.00) versus the *female* dollar ($0.82)—so the wage gap continues to be a liberal feminist issue.

It is also quite remarkable that despite women's achievements in the labour force, Canada has not been able to elect equal numbers of men and women to the House of Commons. Canada currently lags behind other Western nations with comparable advantages in the global economy including the United States (43%) and New Zealand (40%). By comparison, countries such as the Philippines (55%) and St. Lucia (52%) surpass gender parity among elected legislators (United Nations, 2012). At a very basic level, outright sexism is still actively directed at female Members of Parliament, the most evident of these being through social media (Ryckewaert, 2015). Green Party leader Elizabeth May noted, "Our looks are attacked more, our clothing is attacked, the notion of sexual attractiveness and sexual violence . . . some of it is quite vile," and MP Megan Leslie reports tweets made by members of the public on official social media for their offices, referring to sexual violence against female MPs of all political backgrounds: "'CPC skank

Michelle Rempel needs to eat a dick,' read one example. 'Eve Adams is a skanky-ass bitch, a younger Playboy version of Belinda Stronach'," read another (Ryckewaert, 2015). Others suggest these sexist attitudes extend to their daily participation in the House of Commons with MP Laurin Liu observing that her party's finance critic was heckled during one speech with comments such as "learn to read" (Ryckewaert, 2015).

Unfortunately, if standards for gender equality are taken to mean that governments should continuously protect and support gender equality, then Canada has recently been set on a very different path. The 1990s saw repeated cuts to social funding under a Liberal government and the eventual dissolution of the National Action Committee on the Status of Women, then Canada's only national feminist lobby group. In 2006 Status of Women Canada had its operating budget reduced by 43% by a Conservative federal government. Ironically, the responsibility of announcing and carrying out the extraordinary cuts fell to a woman, then Minister Bev Oda, responsible for Status of Women, who also removed the word "equality" from the agency's main goals (Brodie, 2008).

Critiques of Liberal Feminism

It is important to understand that equality of opportunity, meritocracy, and freedom of choice have not been advanced equitably for all women. White women in Europe and the Americas might have seen hope in liberal ideas, but the status of Indigenous women within their own communities was particularly compromised by those acting on liberal democratic—but patriarchal and racist—ideas (Maracle, 2003, p. 74). Enakshi Dua outlines many forms of political action that Indigenous, Black, and immigrant women have taken to challenge their exclusion. These focused on women's roles in treaty negotiations, (sometimes armed) Indigenous resistance to colonization, resistance to racist immigration and settlement policies, and access to democratic rights (Dua, 1999, pp. 11–12). Indigenous people in Canada have suffered a diminished economic, political, and social status under a significant piece of legislation called the Indian Act (1876). Among the goals of land appropriation and racial assimilation, a major intention of the Act was for Indigenous women and children to become subject to their husbands and fathers just as European women were. Furthermore, Article 86 of the Act forbade Indians from obtaining a formal education unless they gave up Indian Status and any land or property they might have access to, making it impossible for both men and women be both "educated" and "Indian" at the same time (Downe, 2005). Canadians viewed these measures as a path to "civilizing" Indigenous people, when in fact it was an aggressive and nonsensical destruction of the diverse and strong family structures already in place throughout Indigenous societies (Stevenson, 1999). Women who enjoyed meaningful political participation and high status in their societies before the arrival of Europeans actually had their status reversed by the presence of European liberal democratic rule (Lawrence 2004, p. 46). Furthermore, the implementation of Indian residential schools as a tool of assimilation (from 1884 to 1996) meant that generations of Indigenous children experienced devastating repression of language and culture within the formal education system. People's experience of equality of opportunity, meritocracy, and freedom of choice is therefore heavily mediated by the ways in which their legal and political history are gendered and racialized.

A primary criticism of liberal feminist theory is its selectivity and privileging of the objectives of white middle- or upper-class women. In the past, women's equality with men has not always been the primary consideration of women whose social class was far removed from that of the average middle- or upper-class wife. If a person is subject to legislation such as the Indian Act, arguing for gender equality with men makes little difference without racial and class equality (Arneil, 2001, p. 54). This short-sightedness is demonstrated by the argument of some early Canadian feminists that only white women of Canadian birth should be allowed the vote (Prentice et al., 1996).

At the same time, liberal feminism has often been written about without attention to the contributions made by Indigenous women and women of colour whose participation in equality-seeking activism is significant (Dua, 1999). Acknowledging the complexity of obtaining goals for *all* women, such as equal access to education and political and labour force participation, is necessary. Liberal feminist understanding of women's oppression and methods of social change incorporate women into existing political and economic institutions without necessarily transforming the relations of power between men and women within those organizations or even in society at large.

SOCIALIST FEMINISM

Defining Socialist Feminism

Socialist feminism originates in Marxist theory and uses class and gender as central categories of analysis in its explanation of women's oppression. Socialist feminism has several key goals in its analyses and activism. First, socialist feminism relates the oppression experienced by women to their economic dependence on men. One of the goals of socialist feminism is therefore to advocate for women's economic independence. In addition, socialist feminism provides a materialist analysis of gender inequality by identifying the relationship between systems of patriarchal oppression in which women are subordinated to men, and class relations in capitalist economic systems in which the working classes are subordinated to the upper classes. A second goal of socialist feminism is to expose and challenge the devaluation of women's unpaid labour in the home. In doing so, socialist feminists advocate for the acknowledgement of the value of women's domestic work, a sharing of domestic responsibilities in the home, and state involvement (financial and legislative) in creating a society that is equitable and just for everyone. A third, related goal of socialist feminism is to highlight and do away with continuing gendered pay inequality (a major contributor to women's financial dependency on men and the over-representation of women among the total number of poor), as well as the gendered division of labour within the wage labour market (which is responsible for the over-representation of women in service industries and feminized employment). Socialist feminism uses analyses of class to explain the ways in which social, economic, and political power is distributed in varying amounts to members of society, and how this process is influenced by factors such as gender, racialized and ethnic identity, age, sexual orientation, and ability.

Historical Background: Marxist and Socialist Feminism

Karl Marx (1818–1883) and Friedrich Engels (1820–1895) were influential in the development of socialist feminist thought. Their *Communist Manifesto* (1848/1998) outlines the relationship of human beings to the ways in which we produce and reproduce for survival as a central factor in understanding the socio-political characteristics of any particular historical period. Individuals consciously and socially manipulate our environments in particular ways in order to feed, clothe, and house ourselves (Tong, 1998).

In *The German Ideology* (1932/1968), Marx and Engels advance an analysis of capitalist oppression that features the family as the original site of an inequitable division of labour, later to be reflected in the capitalist labour market. Marx and Engels argued that wives and children constituted a "first property" for men, to whom they provided labour, and men exerted control over the context, conditions, and environment in which this labour took place. Although gender and the oppression of women were not a focus for much of early Marxist thought, in *The Origin of the Family, Private Property and the State* (1884/1972), Engels did venture an examination of the sources of women's inequality (Somerville, 2000). Engels linked the economic conditions of people to the ways in which the family is organized as a productive and reproductive unit. The change in modes of production, which saw men in charge of the domestication and breeding of animals, was, according to Engels, a major factor in the unequal shifting of power between men and women. With men predominantly in charge of the family, the work and the material contributions of women to the community were devalued. Men became the owners of private property (women, land, family resources), and inheritance tended to flow downward, from husbands to sons. Individuals and individual units became more important than communities or collective acts.

Concern over inheritance led to the patriarchal formalization of the nuclear family unit as a method of ensuring the passing down of private property and wealth from father to children of his own blood (Somerville, 2000). Engels advanced this as simply a reflection of the inequalities perpetuated by the capitalist labour market, with the husband representing the "bourgeoisie" (owners) and the wife taking the role of the "proletariat" (workers). Therefore, the source of women's oppression, according to Engels, lay in the fact that they did not own or have control over private property. As such, the liberation of women could be ensured only by the eradication of capitalism and the reintroduction of women on an equal footing in the economic production process (Brenner, 2000).

By locating women's oppression as rooted in capitalism, women's economic dependence on men is defined as the source of their inequality. Only paid work is valued within a capitalist system that equates the value of an individual to paid work. As unpaid family workers, women are not valued. The capitalist economic system works simultaneously with a patriarchal socio-political system to divide and relegate certain types of work, and, consequently, certain levels of pay, to individuals based on their gender. The result is a society in which men are over-represented in the highest-paying professional jobs, women's (unpaid) domestic contributions are not regarded as work, and women are over-represented in service-oriented jobs at lower pay. These hierarchies have an impact on women's ability to achieve economic independence, pay for health care, receive pensions, exercise child care and maternity leave options, and make them susceptible to violence (among other factors).

Marx's discussion of the process of industrialization and the concentration of the production of goods outside the home is used by Marxist feminists to expose a shift in the popular understanding of what constitutes productivity. Working in a factory producing goods is viewed by capitalist states as productive but cooking, cleaning, doing laundry, and taking care of children are not (Waring, 1999). Value is judged by wages. Women's inability to turn their work in home into a marketable product makes it less economically valued even through their work is socially necessary (Tong, 1998). Furthermore, as Mariarosa Dalla Costa and Selma James (1975) have suggested, to argue for the equal inclusion of women within the labour force (as liberal feminists have done), without socializing or making a public responsibility of child care and housework, will only increase the oppressive conditions under which women live. The result is that waking up in the morning to prepare breakfast and lunch for the kids and husband, going to the office, and returning home in the evening only to cook dinner, finish the laundry, and clean, means a double day of work for women (Mitchell, 1971). In order for women to be liberated, domestic labour must be equalized.

Socialist feminists, like Marxist feminists, consider capitalism a significant factor in the oppression experienced by women. They also consider the oppressive role of patriarchy. Patriarchy is an analytic category and system of distributing power in society that hierarchically ascribes importance to all things male or masculine over all things female or feminine. Socialist feminists find Marxist feminism problematic in that it locates most aspects of women's oppression within the bourgeoisie/proletariat (owner/worker) paradigm, neglecting the more complex aspects of relationships between women and men. Using an intersectional analysis that considers the interplay of gender, racialized and ethnic identity, sexuality, and age (among other factors), socialist feminists have also looked to the ways that women participate in the oppression of other women in the context of capitalist economies. In Canada, for instance, the persistent need for child care and the government's failure to adopt universal child care are key reasons that so many middle- and upper-class women rely on the exploited labour of racialized women from developing countries.

Two foundational concepts to social feminist thought are unpaid labour and the feminization of poverty. In the case of unpaid labour, socialist feminist analysis has provided important insights into the fundamental contribution of housework done predominantly by women to the unfolding of the daily activities of individuals. Current statistical trends on this topic are reviewed in Chapter 10 of this book (Gaszo). As housewives and workers in the home, women contribute to the profits of the capitalist economy by ensuring that present-day and future workers in the paid labour force, be they teenagers or adults, are cared for in the home in ways that prepare and support them in their positions within the paid labour force (Morris, 2000). Whether by doing family laundry, preparing meals, cleaning, and maintaining organization in the home; or transporting household members to and from school, work, and play, women provide an important service—not only to their families, but also to a capitalist patriarchy that benefits from the present and future labour of these family members. By seeing housework as women's expression of their love for their families, capitalist and state institutions can enjoy benefit and profits from women's unpaid labour. These benefits include the reproduction of members of the future workforce and the maintenance of their physical, emotional, and mental health allowing them to continue to be productive. Despite an increase in men's participation in unpaid domestic work over the last three decades, 2011 Statistics Canada data indicate that Canadian women continue to do the majority of household work and feel more time-stressed as a result than their male counterparts (Milan, Keown, & Urquijo, 2011).

The *feminization of poverty* is a term used by socialist feminists to identify the disproportionate majority of women who are poor, linking their poverty to patriarchal and capitalist sexist and profit-based initiatives that segregate the labour market. This segregation is carried out based on constructed notions of gender ("women's work" vs. "men's work"); by devaluing labour in the home; by not factoring home work into official national labour-based calculations such as the Gross Domestic Product (GDP)[2]; and by reinforcing notions of household labour as a "natural" consequence of a woman's love for her family. Canadian women are the majority of part-time workers (Canadian Women's Foundation) and continue to outnumber men in the Canadian population of low-income earners (Employment and Social Development Canada).

Since women's responsibilities for and within the home are not recognized as "real" work, women are not compensated by the state for reducing their wage labour to part-time work in order to take care of children, or for losing job training and seniority upon taking maternity leave from waged work. The relegation of women to lower-paying employment sectors, long accepted as more suited to women's "feminine" characteristics (teaching, nursing, cleaning, cooking, typing), has contributed to women's disproportionate poverty while maintaining the wage gap between men and women. Canadian women not only earn less on average than their male counterparts, but also continue to earn less than their male peers in full-time positions of comparable or same professional training (Morissette, Picot, & Lu, 2013).

The increased presence of women in the paid labour force and in post-secondary education, along with the increase in single-parent homes led by women (Statistics Canada, 2012), highlight the complicated constraints that wage working women continue to negotiate outside of adequate state and social support. It is important to note that an increase in women's wage labour participation is not an indication of equitable labour relations as a whole. Statistics Canada data indicate that, despite their increased participation in the wage labour market, women continue to do the majority of unpaid work in the home, at an average of 50.1 hours per week compared to Canadian men at 24.4 hours per week (Milan, Keown, & Urquijo, 2011). For socialist feminists, eradicating poverty and the oppression of women involves not only the equal sharing of domestic responsibilities between men and women, but also policies that create flexibility in determining when and under what conditions one re-enters employment (Harman, 2000).

Poverty does not affect all women in the same way. Indigenous women, non-white women, and women with dis/abilities are particularly vulnerable to poverty. According to a 2011 Statistics Canada report, First Nations girls and women disproportionately live in substandard housing compared to non-First Nations women and girls. Furthermore, First Nations women consistently earn less than non–First Nations women in Canada (O'Donnell & Wallace, 2011). The history of the Live-In Caregiver Program in Canada also reflects the ways in which women's experiences of oppression differ within the capitalist system. The interconnectedness of "race" and racism, gender, class, and sexuality—all in relation to labour—is visible in the disproportionately large number of immigrant and non-white women occupying low-wage, non-unionized jobs with no benefits (Citizenship and Immigration Canada, 2007). With limited childcare spaces and a general increase in the working hours and responsibilities of employees, resorting to privatized domestic service becomes one way Canadian women manage the responsibilities of a household and employment in the labour market (Morris, 2002).

The Contemporary and Global Landscapes

Contemporary socialist feminist analyses, particularly produced by women of colour, have expanded the boundaries of materialist deconstructions of gender-based oppression, by revealing the ways in which "race," racism, colonialism/neo-colonialism, class, gender, dis/ability, and sexuality work simultaneously to differentiate women's experiences of oppression. Globalization and the role of gender in transnationalism have also found a place within the work of some contemporary socialist feminist theorists (Ault & Sandberg, 2001; Dua, 1999; Sparr, 1994). This stretching of the boundaries of early socialist feminist theory to more adequately reflect the complexities and shifts of gender relations in a global economy is extremely valuable. It illustrates an understanding of the connection between, for example, an unemployed inner-city youth of colour with $200 Nike sneakers and the employed but overworked and underpaid Indonesian woman who sews these sneakers, yet can barely afford to feed herself (Human Rights Watch, 2002). Global economic restructuring has led many Canadian and American companies to downsize their operations and make use of the inexpensive labour available in non-Western countries. This downsizing has resulted in increased layoffs, increased workloads for those still employed, and increased part-time, temporary, low-security, low-wage, no-benefits, non-unionized jobs, largely worked by immigrants, particularly women of colour (Morris, 2000).

Two overarching observations have been made by contemporary feminist scholars of political economy in capitalist democracies of the global North. First, feminists have questioned current neo-liberal policies that advocate unconstrained market economics, which claim that open market competition on a global scale is likely to improve living and labour conditions for marginalized groups (Cohen & Brodie, 2007). Socialist feminists have pointed to the failure of laissez-faire market economics in pressuring large-scale employers (through the principle of open competition) to value the labour of their employees through improved pay, working conditions, and benefits. Instead, an oppressive "global care chain" (Hochschild, 2000) thrives, shaped significantly by the negative consequences of the structural adjustment programs (SAPS) and lending conditions to which many developing nations find themselves tied. This global care chain is characterized by the migration of women from lesser economically developed regions of the world to the wealthiest countries. Canada, for example, remains dependent on female migrant labour for its agricultural, sex, and domestic service industries. A complicated set of dynamics, involving rigid immigration and labour rights restrictions, perpetuates and compounds the vulnerability of women in these domains.

Second, socialist feminists have highlighted the transformation of the industrial economy of the 20th century into service and information-oriented economies. Developments in technology and a shift toward information-based work has introduced greater flexibility into the labour market, leading to what some political economy feminists (Fudge & Owens, 2006) call "precarious work" (lack of income and job security, part-time employment, temporary work, home work, on-call work, low wages, few benefits, and absence of union representation). However, it is not only technological development that is influencing labour trends and shifts. The historically feminine and domesticated work responsibilities of women have a sharply increased presence in the paid labour market. Indeed, political economy feminists have noted a new economy of women's work (in which working-class men are now also increasingly participating). Hence, the increase of service-oriented jobs, many of which are precarious in nature, is termed the *feminization of work* (Fudge & Owens, 2006). As socialist feminists indicate, responsibility for domestic work has not decreased as more women have entered the wage labour market. The burden of an increased number of obligations without (any or in-) adequate state support in wealthy countries is negotiated at the expense of more vulnerable women (Thistle, 2006).

Critiques of Socialist Feminism

Socialist feminism's use of a materialist analysis as the basis of its deconstruction of oppression leaves some questions unanswered. Critiques from other feminist quarters, such as those of radical feminists regarding the root of male dominance, propelled socialist feminists to consider the ways in which a gender-based materialist analysis that is focused on capitalism alone is insufficient in addressing the problem of sexist oppression. For example, should some measure of equitable redistribution of power and wealth in society actually occur, and economic systems find themselves operating outside of or beyond the parameters of capitalism, gendered and exploitative social relations, as well as masculinist approaches to the natural world and governance would not necessarily cease (Gordon, 2013). Therefore, socialist feminism has been continuously challenged to grapple with the ways in which economics and class alone are insufficient in explaining and challenging the problem of gender inequality and oppression. The theoretical engagement of radical feminism with other social realities, such as family forms outside of the heterosexual, nuclear family model (such as queer-identified, non-white, immigrant, Indigenous, and single-parent), has also provided legitimate critiques of socialist feminist texts and forms of activism that have used the "ideology of separate spheres for men and women" (Mandell & Elliot, 2001) as a key component of materialist analyses of oppression.

RADICAL FEMINISM

Defining Radical Feminism

Have you ever wondered when women started to "Take Back the Night," rallying for safer streets and demanding that violence against women be stopped? These demonstrations, along with demonstrations for abortion rights as well as anti-violence protests, sprang from radical feminism. Radical feminists have contributed much to feminist theory by concentrating on sexuality, control, and violence, and by making clear the ways in which men's power over women can be seen in all areas of women's lives.

Many scholars attribute the rise of radical feminism to New York–based groups such as the Red Stockings, the Furies, and the Radicalesbians, yet Canadian-based radical feminist groups such as the New Feminists of Toronto are also important to the development of radical feminist action in Canada (Echols, 1989). Groups like these organized around many issues through consciousness-raising (CR) sessions where women came together to share stories of sexist oppression and gendered exploitation to discover that "the personal is political" (Crow, 2000, p. 6). The CR group or "rap session" appealed to many women. They could share accounts of oppression across class and race lines, link those accounts to a larger theoretical framework in order to build critical organizing skills, and publicly air their goals. Radical feminists active in the 1960s and 1970s also used manifestos as a revolutionary method to "speak bitterness" (Freeman, 1975, quoted in Crow, 2000, p. 6). Collectively, radical feminist activities seek to form the basis for a global sisterhood, spreading feminism internationally and building alliances around concrete concerns such as violence and pornography (Morgan, 1970).

Sites of Oppression: Patriarchy, the State, and the Family

Radical feminists argue that the key to deconstructing women's oppression lies in discovering an explanatory theory. In the earliest attempts to theorize women's oppression, radical feminists identified sex oppression as the first and most fundamental oppression from which all other areas of repression sprang (Crow, 2000, p. 2). By sex oppression, radical feminists mean that women's oppression is based on the relations of domination and subordination between the sexes, in which women are seen as a sex class whose sexuality is directly controlled by men. Radical feminists insist that, in order for women to understand their inferior roles in patriarchal society, they must look at how men have come to hold and wield power over women in all social relationships.

Radical feminists identify three main areas that shape women's oppression: the state, the family, and motherhood. Unlike liberal feminists who focus on the legal status of women, radical feminists theorize from women's everyday lives. They believe that patriarchy, a "sexual system of power in which the male possesses superior power and economic privilege," is what shapes everyday life and what specifically affects women, for the benefit of men (Eisenstein, 1979, p. 17). Patriarchy, they argue, is constituted in and through various social structures and is reproduced and activated in everyday relations, having impacts on a global scale. It can be found in all aspects of society, including the state, the family, and other institutions, such as schools, the media, and religious institutions. In order to free themselves from the "Father Land" of patriarchy, an autonomous social, historical, and political force created by men for their own benefit, women must resist and undermine this system (Daly, 1978, p. 28; Donovan, 2000, p. 156).

Radical feminists argue that the state (which includes political institutions, the legal system, and elected representatives) is founded on, and is emblematic of, male interests. Therefore, radical feminists believe that entrusting women's liberation to the state will result in their being taken for granted. Although the state assumes objectivity as its norm, in practice, "women are raped by the state just as they are raped by men" (Andersen, 1997, p. 359). Engaging with the state through state-sponsored initiatives is seen as futile. Violence against women has not diminished despite considerable state-funded initiatives.

Male power and control also resides in the family, which represents another site of oppression for women. Radical feminists see the sexual, social, and economic energy women provide to reproducing the family as sustaining their oppression. Ideologies of romance and love and heterosexual marriage function as "opiates," keeping women drugged and under male control. Romantic love, beauty, dieting, and other cultural practices are seen as tools used by patriarchy to uphold and support heteronormativity, keeping women reliant on men's sexual attention and affection and by making women promote and service the desires of men (Firestone, 1970, pp. 131, 146). Ti-Grace Atkinson (1970), an early radical feminist, stated that love, as an institution of male power and control, supports violence and also "promotes vulnerability, dependence, possessiveness, susceptibility to pain, and prevents the full development of a woman's potential" (p. 117).

Traditional mothering ideology and practice also come under radical feminist scrutiny. As Rich has argued, mothering under patriarchy is an exploitative responsibility (Rich, 1976). The seeming naturalness of motherhood and its institutionalization has become a normative obligation for women in patriarchal society. In the 1960s and 1970s, radical feminists pointed to the idea that women were supposed to be on the mothering job 24 hours a day, every day, with no outside contacts (Tong, 1998, p. 83). Patriarchal order dictates that women's ability to mother becomes conflated with their worthiness as women. If you are not a good mother, you are not a good woman (Kreps, 1973, p. 236). Radical feminist analyses of motherhood have been critiqued, especially by feminist theorists who have formulated mothering as an empowering feminist enterprise. Many feminists have reclaimed motherhood as an important step in the formation of their feminism. As Andrea O'Reilly (2000) states, "[t]hough I had identified myself as a feminist for a number of years; motherhood made feminism real for me and radically redefined it" (pp. 182–183).

Women's Bodies: Reproduction, Pornography, and Violence

Many early radical feminist theorists looked to women's reproductive roles to discover the root problem of women's oppression (Firestone, 1970). Biology separates the sexes, a division that relegates an enormous amount of reproductive labour to women. As women nurture and care for children, men are free to participate in public life and in social institutions, where they can acquire power, privilege, and property which emboldens their superior social status (Hamilton, 1996, p. 20). This seemingly "natural" sexual division of public from private labour (men in the public, women in the private) means that women are at the mercy of their biology (Firestone, 1970). Within this sexual division of labour, women's bodies become objects, passed down from father to husband, placing the ownership of their sexuality squarely in the hands of men (Hamilton, 1996, p. 65). According to radical feminists, the only way to end women's oppression is to end these types of exploitative relationships.

In order to dismantle patriarchy, some radical feminists call for a re-evaluation of women's reproductive roles and an elimination of the traditional family. Women had little control over their reproductive functions because abortion was illegal in Canada until 1988[3] and birth control was hard to acquire in the early phases of the women's movement in the 1960s and 1970s. Many, therefore, suggested that freeing women from the "tyranny of reproduction" and relying on technological advances would diminish clearly marked and oppressive gendered differences (Firestone, 1970). As a remedy, some radical feminists believed that in vitro fertilization, artificial insemination, and eventually cloning would separate women from their wombs, therefore breaking the oppressive tie of women to biology. Others countered that although women would be liberated from reproduction through new reproductive technologies, these new techniques would only lead to male control as men tended to own the technologies. Margaret Atwood's famous novel *The Handmaid's Tale* (1985) tells a story of a dystopian future where women become uniquely defined and controlled by their reproductive roles.

Radical feminists question the meaning of masculinity and femininity, arguing that masculinity is linked to dominance and that femininity is linked to subordination. These unequal relations of power are eroticized in traditional heterosexual relations in which women are positioned as objects of male pleasure, constantly available, constantly ready, and constantly scrutinized. Anne Koedt (1970), in her well-known article "The Myth of the Vaginal Orgasm," says that a male defined view of sexuality assumes women can only achieve orgasm through male penetration and that those who cannot must be frigid. Clearly this model ignores women's needs and desires (MacKinnon, 1989).

In popular media and online pornography, the male gaze further constructs women's sexuality and structures male and female sexual relations. As a result, many young people define their own ideas around sexuality and sexual relations only through these sources. Some radical feminists think that male violence against women stems from an intake of violent pornography, making it acceptable to see women as purely objects of sexual gratification rather than as mutual players of love and intimacy (Tong, 1998). Popular feminists such as Eve Ensler, author of *The Vagina Monologues* (1996), argue that these relations of power can be linked to global violence against women, such as incest, honour killing, and rape as a war crime.

Radical feminist theories have been successful in providing a framework for understanding what is and is not considered criminally obscene in Canada. In 1992, a landmark Supreme Court decision in *Butler v. the Queen* brought into debate the definition of what constitutes criminal obscenity (Donald Butler was arrested for selling hard-core pornographic videos in his Manitoba store). Catherine MacKinnon (1946–) and Andrea Dworkin (1946–2005), two very famous radical feminists from the United States, along with the Canadian organization Women's Legal Education and Action Fund (LEAF), were instrumental in shaping the Canadian obscenity law. These anti-pornography proponents used earlier radical feminist ideas that viewed pornography as essentially violent and degrading to women and a facet of the patriarchal order. The court found that any images that portrayed "degrading" sex, especially of women, could be criminalized (Cossman, Bell, Gotell, & Ross, 1997, p. 18). This was seen as a victory for many anti-pornography feminists, who insisted that these images were detrimental to women. According to the 1992 decision, the goal of outlawing certain types of material and defining them as obscene was to protect people, most notably women, from harm. What is considered pornographic and what is considered obscene is decided through one simple test: whether or not images are degrading to women. Obscenity laws were no longer seen as a matter of public morality or decency, but were evaluated according to questions of harm, especially harm to women (Cossman et al., 1997).

This 1992 judgment also affected gay and lesbian materials in unforeseen ways. What is considered "obscene" in a homophobic society, critics argue, often means demonizing images, ideas, and texts that transgress the normative bounds of heterosexual sex. Many gay and lesbian bookstores across Canada (for example, Little Sister's Book and Art Emporium in Vancouver and Glad Day Books in Toronto) maintained that Canadian customs officials were more heavily scrutinizing, seizing, and destroying shipments intended for their stores, searching for contraventions to the 1992 ruling. A small victory occurred in 2000 when the courts agreed that customs officials were overwhelmingly heavy-handed in their appraisal of lesbian and gay material (McCann, 2007a).

Radical feminist theorists have also spoken strongly against rape, seeing it as a crime resulting from, and maintaining, male power. If domination and subordination are the basis for unequal sexual relations between men and women and if these unequal sexual relations go unchallenged, what is the difference between sex and rape? (Brownmiller, 1976; Dworkin, 1974; MacKinnon, 1989). If women and men are not equals in society, and if men wield power over women, then loving and sexual relationships between the two are always mediated by unequal power exchanges, where one person (man) controls the other (woman). Radical feminists conclude that women cannot experience their sexuality as pleasurable, because sexuality is male-coded and controlled. How then, they ask, do women construct their own sexuality? What would woman-defined sexuality look like?

Female Separation: Lesbian Feminism and Cultural Feminism

Lesbian feminism sprang from radical feminists' desire to discover and value women's contributions to society. Lesbian feminists shifted the debate from analyzing and reacting to male structures of power to focusing on how passionate bonds between women can foster a politics of emancipation. Lesbianism connotes sexual relations between women. But it also represents a political stance, a support system that allows women to turn to other women to escape from an oppressive male-dominated world. Lesbian feminists argue that every culture is infused with phallocentric social and cultural values forcing women to live lives geared toward men and heterosexual and monogamous pairings (Rich, 1980). In part, women are taught that self-worth comes from heterosexual marriage and mothering. The idea of compulsory heterosexuality—where women are understood to be naturally sexually oriented toward men—restricts women socially and economically. Originally, alternatives to this model, such as lesbian sexuality, were not well received by mainstream society and cast aside as deviant (Rich, 1980, p. 4).

Lesbian feminism suggests that the main way women can resist male domination and power is to refrain from having sexual relations with men. Arising from this idea is the famous slogan "feminism is the theory and lesbianism is the practice." Or, as Catherine MacKinnon said, "feminism is the epistemology of which lesbianism is ontology" (quoted in Heller, 1997, p. 22). Adrienne Rich, a well-known American lesbian feminist, advanced the idea of the lesbian continuum in order to operationalize that slogan. In order to separate lesbianism from being solely a sexual relation between women, Rich (1980) described a continuum, a position of compromise where all relations between women (friendships and caring relationships such as elder care) can be placed within the definition of lesbian and lesbian feminist politics. Not all feminists were comfortable with Rich's suggestion that lesbian be adopted as a political slogan. In Canada particularly, homophobic responses led to the ejection of many lesbians from feminist organizing groups, as some believed that the prominent presence of lesbians would undermine the movement (Grant, 1998; Ross, 1995).

Radical cultural feminists, successors of radical feminists in the 1970s and 1980s, banded together and mobilized around what they see as women's uniqueness: their femaleness. Cultural feminists espouse a "politics of disengagement," a breaking out of a male-dominated society by providing women-only cultural spaces (Adamson, Briskin, & McPhail, 1988, p. 192; Donovan, 2000, pp. 255–256). By concentrating on the positive features of women-only cultural spaces—care, sympathy, and nurturance—women would be able to promote and celebrate these relationships. Often seen as the "separatists" in the feminist movement, cultural feminists believe that valuing women demands a woman-centred culture, where goddesses are worshipped, and bookstores, co-ops, and centres—run by women for women—can counter the negative effects of a male-dominated society.

Global and Contemporary Dimensions of Radical Feminist Thought

Radical feminists argue that the sexual dominance of men over women stretches around the world. Globally it is estimated that 79% of all human trafficking is done for the purposes of sexual exploitation and that the majority of those exploited were women and children; 18% were trafficked for the purposes of other labour (United Nations Office on Drugs and Crime 2009, p. 57). Despite the adoption of the Protocol to Prevent, Suppress and Punish Trafficking in Persons, Especially Women and Children (United Nations, 2003) that 117 out of 167 member nations have signed, human trafficking persists. The Protocol seeks to "suppress, prevent and punish trafficking in persons specifically women and children" (Dozema, 2005, p. 62). With 44 000 victims of trafficking being identified in a single year, an estimated 20 million more may have been missed (United States Department of State, 2014). This complex and illegal industry generates an estimated US$7 to 12 billion per year (United Nations Development Fund for Women [UNIFEM], 2007; Valenta, 2007). Radical feminists often focus on sex trafficking over other forms of human trafficking and argue that these industries thrive on an international capitalist system based on sexist and racist ideas about women and sexuality. The sex industry and sex tourism are profitable international businesses founded on exploiting women and girls (Barry, 1984).

Radical feminists believe an international or global feminism is needed in order to combat sex trafficking. Global feminism would link actions of women around the world in challenging patriarchal and sexual exploitation of women that crosses state and national borders (Barry, 1995; Jeffreys, 1999; Morgan, 1984/1996). Global feminist views of prostitution and human trafficking have been heavily influenced by radical feminist thought and have played a pivotal role in some countries' adoption of laws that criminalize the purchasers of sex (primarily men) and recognize the sellers of sex as victims (Jeffreys, 2009). Although cross-border movement often comes to mind, it is important to note that a large portion of victims are often trafficked regionally or domestically (United Nations Office on Drugs and Crime, 2009, p. 57), making this an issue that women's organizations also act locally upon. In comparison to other countries, Canada is not considered to have high rates of sex trafficking (United States Secretary of State, 2014) but radical feminists have agitated for it to adopt much tighter legislation and policy that attempt to combat these problems. Inevitably, recent contemporary shifts in Canadian laws on trafficking and prostitution have come to reflect deep conflicts between sex worker advocacy groups and radical feminist opponents of sex trafficking.

In 2007, some Canadian sex workers[4] sought the outright decriminalization of prostitution in Ontario on the basis that existing laws force sex workers into dangerous and criminalized environments and inhibit sex workers from seeking resources they are otherwise entitled to. In 2010, the challenge launched by Terri Jean Bedford, Amy Lebovitch, and Valerie Scott enjoyed partial success at Ontario's Superior Court. It was then appealed and sent to Canada's highest court where three provisions of Canada's Criminal Code were struck down. These included: s. 210 (keeping or being found in a bawdy house),

s. 212(1)(j) (living on the avails of prostitution), and s. 213(1)(c) (communicating in public for the purpose of prostitution). The Supreme Court of Canada struck down the three laws as unconstitutional because they violate section 7 of (the right to security of the person) of the Canadian Charter of Rights and Freedoms (Canada v. Bedford, 2013).

Radical feminist organizers responded with swift intervention at the level of the then federal Conservative government. They partnered widely with organizations such as the Native Women's Association of Canada, the Elizabeth Fry Society, and others. Their interventions made a lasting impression that resulted in the development of a new law on prostitution that criminalized the purchasers of sex, but not the prostitute, Bill C-36. Although sex worker organizations and women's legal and health organizations also intervened, arguing for the complete decriminalization of prostitution as a harm reduction approach to sex work, these were largely excluded from the development of new legislation.

Radical feminist ideas have provided a theoretical framework for understanding women's everyday lives and continue to be relevant to contemporary theorizing. Organizations such as The Sisterhood Is Global Institute (sigi.org), Women Against Pornography (WAP), Always Causing Legal Unrest (ACLU), and the RadFems conference in the United States; popular media interveners such as Europe-based Stop Porn Culture (stoppornculture.org); and journals such as *Off Our Backs* continue to uphold radical-feminist theoretical tenets. Taking up similar topics to those of 40 years ago, contemporary radical feminists remain committed to providing an analytical framework around women's oppression as a result of patriarchal domination. It is significant that even after the advent of Slutwalk (Teekah, Scholz, Friedman, & O'Reilly, 2015), which has connected these issues for new generations of young feminists, many women and allies still gravitate to "Take Back the Night" in order to demand safer streets and harsher penalties for sex offenders.[5] Across Canada in the 2010s, a spate of public accusations of sexual assault against male celebrities and public figures, including music and radio celebrities, football players, and even some Members of Parliament, seems to have re-ignited popular interest in the issues highlighted by radical feminists.

Critiques of Radical Feminism

Strategically radical feminists insist that the category of "woman" is needed for women to truly rally around, for if *we* do not, how do we then establish a basis for feminist action and organizing (Thompson, 2001, p. 69)? Charges of "essentialism" haunt radical feminists as they are brought to task for generalizing about the fundamental nature of each sex. First, discourses of victimization pervade radical feminist theory. Theoretical writings by radical feminists assume that men are inherently violent and aggressive, while women are nurturing and caring. Where are the spaces for resistance? Many postmodern feminists claim that radical feminist theory suffers not only from essentialism but also from romanticism, ethnocentrism, and historicism (Mandell & Elliot, 2001). They argue that definitions of patriarchy and women given by radical feminists are homogenizing and limiting and do not account for the diversities offered by class, race, sexuality, age, history, and other aspects of women's lives that make them unique and multiple.

Many women of colour challenge white radical feminists on their imperialist and universalizing notions of women under the banner of "global sisterhood," in which women of colour and Third-World women are often cast as "backward" and in need of "saving." Black American feminist Angela Davis has taken white radical feminists to task for writing about non-white communities as deviant, writing about Black men and rape, and naturalizing the myth of the Black rapist, so prevalent during and after slavery (Tong, 1998, p. 223). Others also argue that the radical feminist attacks on the family are Euro- and ethnocentric and undermine the importance of family for many non-white people. As Linda Carty states, "[f]or Black people and people of colour, the family served as protection against, and a central source of resistance to, racist oppression" (Carty, 1999, p. 42).

Transgender feminists argue that gender becomes politically problematic when it is defined through biology alone (MacDonald, 2000, p. 289; Stone, 1991). They respond in part to radical and cultural feminists who question the "dangers" of transgendered people in general and of transsexual women in particular, invading women's spaces and bodies. Rather than broaden their ideas about gender, a vocal minority of radical feminists consider transsexual women to be committing violence: Janice Raymond (1998) says, "Rape . . . is a masculinist violation of bodily integrity. All transsexuals rape women's bodies by reducing the female form to an artifact, appropriating this body for themselves . . . Rape, although it is usually done by force, can also be accomplished by deception" (p. 308). This idea underpins resistance to the inclusion of trans people in some types of feminist organizing. Not all self-proclaimed radical feminists uphold transphobic ideas, but are perceived as doing so on the basis of high profile cases such as that of Kimberly Nixon. In 1995 the Vancouver Rape Relief and Women's Shelter refused to let Nixon, a transsexual woman, become a rape crisis counsellor out of the conviction that being born a woman is the basic and primary definition of being a woman (Wente, 2000). Initially, Nixon was awarded $7500 by the BC Human Rights Tribunal on the basis that she had been discriminated against. The case was appealed and finally taken to the Supreme Court of Canada in 2007, where it was refused a hearing (McCann, 2007b). On this landmark case and so many instances of trans people's rights activism since then, radical feminism has largely failed to work through its essentialism, sometimes garnering the largely pejorative term TERF (a trans-exclusive radical feminist) (Goldberg, 2014).

POSTSTRUCTURAL AND POSTMODERN FEMINISM

Defining Poststructural and Postmodern Feminism

Poststructural and postmodern feminist approaches seek to move beyond what are perceived to be the grand narratives of modernist perspectives on women's oppression offered by Liberal, Socialist, and Radical feminism. Specifically, postmodern feminists tend to concentrate on the nature and function of *power* in interpersonal relationships and in our societies more broadly. Postmodern feminist analysis involves the *deconstruction of assumed* "*truths*," including the deconstruction of identities assumed to be stable such as that of "woman" and "man." Instead of assuming that sex (female/male) is a fixed biological identity, postmodern feminism deconstructs sex (and our assumptions about biology), placing all of human identity in the domain of social construction. This means that in postmodern feminist theory, all identities and any "truths" are regarded as already implicated in, if not products of, a person's culture. It also means that postmodern feminism seeks to challenge sexism and gender-based oppression by questioning all dominant cultural norms and accepted truths, including taken-for-granted norms of feminist thinking and practice.

Postmodern feminism challenges the idea of analyzing social relations according to simplistic oppressor/oppressed models: for example, men oppress women, the rich oppress the poor, white people oppress Black people, and so on. Rather, postmodern feminists suggest that people in positions of vulnerability are not in a permanent state of victimhood. We are invited to reject the idea of utter victimhood, and encouraged to consider and recognize the many ways in which the oppressed have the capacity for and often exercise their own oppositional/alternative gaze, voices, and forms of resistance. In considering the issue of power, we are also asked to think about the ways in which power is not something people hold in measurable quantities. Those in positions of power may exercise certain forms of power even as they embody a marginalized identity marker (e.g., a gay white man who benefits from the privileges afforded by whiteness and maleness at the same time as he experiences homophobia, a heterosexual black man who experiences daily racism even as he benefits from straight male privilege), and members of marginalized groups can exercise agency as well as power over others in certain circumstances (e.g., women who are invested in patriarchal ideology in ways that support their own oppression or the oppression of other women).

An important example of this is postmodern feminism's engagement with sex work. The landscape of contemporary postmodern feminism and its global dimensions reveals an on-going set of debates surrounding the international realm of sex work, where "choice," autonomy, and victimhood remain key points of contention (Dozema, 1998, 2002; Kempadoo, 2005), as discussed in the previous section. Postmodern feminist perspectives consider sex work as neither a wholly empowered choice or form of sexual expression, nor a completely victimizing and inherently oppressive experience. While a radical feminist perspective might argue that objectification and the predominance of women in the sex industry in the context of sexist heteropatriarchal culture makes the exchange of sex for money fundamentally oppressive, from a postmodernist view, there is nothing *inherently* oppressive in the exchange of sex for money. Sex work can be a subversive alternative to heteropatriarchal sexual scripts that serve to direct women's sexuality toward the gendered norms of monogomous marriage (Scoular, 2004). Postmodern feminism contemplates the multiple points of meaning making related to a subjective experience, as well as the possible points of agency for sex workers. Postmodern perspectives on sex work resist the broad stroke meta-narrative of victimization and oppression that modernist feminist approaches present, yet must simultaneously contend with a context of unequal relations between gendered human beings and countries, a context that visibly places women, children, and a range of marginalized people in a position of marked vulnerability to sexual exploitation.

Historical Influences

Although they are often used interchangeably, there are some distinctions to be made between poststructuralism and postmodernism. Poststructuralism developed out of inquiry into the relationship between language, reality, and what and how we know things. This work is credited to structural anthropologist Claude Levi-Strauss (1908–2009), philosopher Jacques Derrida (1930–2004), and psychoanalyst Jacques Lacan (1901–1981). Their insights into the symbolic order of the human mind have been applied in theories of language, knowledge production, and literary criticism. Postmodernism has tended to occupy the interdisciplinary domain of cultural and social philosophy, history, and sociology (Agger, 1991). The rejection of meta-narratives that seek to explain history and social relations in broad strokes, for instance, is evident in French philosopher and sociologist Jean-Francois Lyotard's (1924–1998) rejection of German philosopher Karl Marx's theory of historical materialism, on the basis that it reduces and over-simplifies dynamic historical events; such a critique is typical of postmodernist interventions.

In *Discipline and Punish* (1979) postmodern French philosopher Michel Foucault (1926–1984) proposes that a core characteristic of the development of modern societies and the associated major social institutions with which we are accustomed (schools, medicine, the military, the media, organized religion, and law enforcement and courts) is that they are deeply invested in cultures of *discipline*. These cultures of discipline reflect the particular power dynamics and social trends of any specific historical period. According to Foucault, the main function of discipline in modern societies is to produce obedient and compliant bodies. Note here the connection to postructuralism—Foucault's obedient bodies are enacting their compliance to fit into Derrida's or Lacan's notion of a "symbolic order." The function of discipline in modern (Western) societies is thus linked to Foucault's analysis of power as diffuse, being everywhere and nowhere at once. Examples of this include means by which we are under constant real and perceived regulatory surveillance (e.g., street/traffic cameras and lights, sexual objectification, and body judgment) to the point that we self-regulate/self-discipline even when no one is looking. This self-discipline is a reaction to the diffuse operation of power, to not knowing for sure whether one is or is not being watched. We comply with what we are "supposed" to do because the penalties for non-conformity to established norms are made clear over and over again (receiving a speeding ticket in the mail; or, in the case of bodily discipline, romantic rejection, not getting a job or promotion, and so on). According to Foucault, it is the scattered operation of power that encourages individuals to impose forms of self-discipline (e.g., stopping at a red light in the middle of the night even though no one else is around; starving oneself or obsessive exercise in order to be thin even though no one is explicitly demanding this of that individual), the ultimate function of which is to meet the regulatory blueprint of that society at that particular historical moment.

Poststructural and postmodern feminism reveal a number of influences, including existential and deconstructionist (early poststructuralist) philosophy; and psychoanalytic, linguistic, and literary theory. Links to existential philosophy, particularly the work of existential feminist philosopher Simone de Beauvoir are readily evident in postmodern feminist theory. De Beauvoir's assertion in *The Second Sex* (1949/1973, 301) that "one is not born, but rather becomes, a woman," is a consistent theme in contemporary postmodern feminist writing and is clearly evident in one of postmodern feminism's most applauded publications, Judith Butler's *Gender Trouble* (1990). Moreover, the deconstruction of sex itself, and not only ascribed gender, harkens? back to the work of deconstructionist philosophers, among them Jacques Derrida (1967/1980), who questioned the existence of a unified "Self" and the ability of language to tell us anything "true" about what it describes (Tong, 1998). If we examine the identity "woman" from a postmodern feminist perspective, we are called to see that there is nothing essentially/biologically "true" in the identity "woman." To the extent that we use gendered and essentialist language to describe the existential realities of womanhood, we further reproduce the socially constructed norms and fictions that present "woman" as a stable and fixed identity.

Indeed, Butler proposes deconstructing and destabilizing the very identity of "woman" as a unified subject; hers is one of the best-known feminist contributions to postmodern theory. Butler (1990) reads gender identity as unstable, maintained only by a series of stylized repetitive acts that have no basis in a profoundly rooted biology. She states, there is "nothing about femaleness that is waiting to be expressed; there is, on the other hand, a good deal about the diverse experiences of women that is being expressed and still needs to be expressed," asserting that language sets out the very conditions for one's experience of the world as a "woman" (Butler, 2010, p. 429). This proposition raises important questions for feminists. If, as Butler suggests, the identity "woman" is grounded in a series of repetitively performed acts rather than in biology, can *anyone* claim to be a woman? What are the political implications of accepting the instability of "woman" as an identity, while still attempting to organize collectively against the real material consequences of sexist oppression? How is the subject of these collective political efforts to be represented and talked about in matters of policy and electoral politics? Who, exactly, is the subject of these collective efforts? We see these matters manifested in the realm of day-to-day relations all the time. For instance, should a women's shelter accommodate female-to-male or woman-to-man transsexual and transgender persons in crisis?[6] In fact, since the case of Kimberly Nixon, referred to above, many now do either include women and trans people or all women, including trans women, in their scope of service and employment. This shift marks a tremendous incursion of postmodern thinking and trans feminist activism into women's organizations, many of which were established under the strategically essentialist goal of "serving women only." Serving women "only" was a strategic goal that met a desperate need for disproportionately female survivors of sexual and physical violence, but from a postmodern feminist perspective, this goal was never meant to further oppress other marginalized groups and thus it has shifted slowly. This is just one example of the ways in which the postmodern question of what and who constitutes a "woman" plays out in our day-to-day relations with one another.

A poststructuralist understanding of the relationship between language and reality is also visible in the work of postmodern feminists such as Hélène Cixous, who critiques the exclusion of "the feminine" from Western language (Tong, 1998). Here we find feminist critique directed at a male-centred, or phallocentric, language that excludes feminine expression, or écriture feminine (Cixous, 1976). Included in this vein of postmodern feminist writing is the work of Julia Kristeva, who also critiqued the phallocentrism of language while cautioning against the essentialist tendencies reflected in Cixous's writing (i.e., assuming a fixed definition of the feminine that is always tied to female biology). In the realm of psychoanalysis, engagement with and critique of the work of Sigmund Freud and Jacques Lacan are also observable in Luce Irigaray's *This Sex Which Is Not One* (1977). Irigaray challenges Freud's male-centred and sexist assertions regarding women's "penis envy," arguing the plurality of women's sexuality, and that women have many sexes (the clitoris, vagina, breasts). Irigaray insists that this multiplicity in women's sexual pleasure, or "homo-sexuality," should not be regarded as a pathological sexual fragmentation, as is often done when human sexuality is read from a heterosexist point of view.

Postmodern feminist work also highlights the gaps in postmodern theory more broadly when gender is left out of accounts of discipline, discourse, and power in modern societies. Postmodern feminist philosopher Sandra Lee Bartky (2010), for instance, has contributed insightfully to the expansion of Foucauldian theories of discipline and power by pointing out that gender is key to distinguishing the ways in which women and men experience established cultures of discipline. Bartky points out that in the larger scheme of the overarching symbolic order, men and women are expected to manifest their corporal docility in different ways; that there are particularly feminine forms of discipline that differ from those more specifically directed at producing a certain type of masculine subject. Bartky calls attention to a specifically feminine "disciplinary project of bodily perfection" (p. 407). Aside from the gendered and anxiety ridden practices of dieting, exercise, and costly beauty regimes evident in many women's routines, the disciplinary project of perfection to which Bartky refers can also be observed in the trained physical gestures, postures, and movements of women as they attempt to take up as little space as possible in both public and private places. Minimizing one's girth on subway trains and buses, keeping one's arms close to the body and giving way while walking down the street, and lowering one's gaze/avoiding direct eye contact when passing others, particularly men, are, according to Bartky, all manifestations of a specifically feminine culture of discipline. These behaviours manifest in the context of a sense of being under constant surveillance, or what Bartky describes as women's sense of being under constant and inescapable (sexist) *judgment*. The resulting self-imposed disciplinary behaviours on the part of women are encouraged and sustained by "technologies of femininity" (Bartky, 2010, p. 410) such as media, the beauty industry, and social pressure that often produce a condition of *alienation from the self* and varying degrees of self-hate in women (Bartky, 1990). It is interesting to note here the combination of both postmodern analyses of power and discipline, with the Marxist concept of alienation (see the preceding section in this chapter on Marxist/Socialist feminism) to produce a specifically feminist postmodern theory of gendered oppression.

Feminist Critiques of Poststructural and Postmodern Feminism

A key challenge to feminism posed by postmodern approaches, therefore, is that an unequivocal rejection of broad identity categories makes it difficult to organize collectively for a change in the inequitable material conditions that are a real consequence of the function of identity categories as social constructions embedded in power relations. One such critique is that postmodern feminism borrows from more politicized bodies of feminist theory such as critical-race and anti-racist feminist frameworks, with little to no commitment to the politics corresponding to the material realities represented by these frameworks. For example, postmodern feminism has absorbed theories of intersectionality coming out of critical race and anti-racist feminism, these being theories that have long troubled simplistic definitions of "woman" and "man," particularly when these definitions ignore intersection with other markers of identity such as "race," class, sexual orientation, and ability. Yet, postmodernism's categorical rejection of unified subject positions ("woman," "Black"), even where intersectionality is taken into account (*Black* woman on *disability* benefits; middle income, *gay* white man etc.), begs the question of how the social realities of inequality and discrimination experienced by people in such subject positions might be articulated in concrete terms within the realms of law, public policy, and government legislation.

Postmodernism problematically threatens to do away with feminism within a broader social context in which feminism and its main political subjects "women" are still very much needed (Di Stefano, 1989). Sandra Harding, a feminist philosopher, further argues that "socially situated knowledge" or a feminist standpoint theory (2005, p. 218) endangers the social justice objectives of feminism. The tendency, then, of postmodern theory to veer into relativist stances (i.e., there is not one, but many "truths"; bodies are the stuff of performance, not grounded "truth") can present particular challenges for feminist efforts to directly attend to the material realities of sexist power dynamics. In the face of this, and to the extent that postmodernism gives rise to unyielding relativism, feminist scholars such as Seyla Benhabib, Susan Bordo, and Nancy Harstock have maintained that just "as human bodies cannot be understood as endlessly mobile and flexible, so human understanding also possesses necessary boundaries and rigidities" (Nicholson, 1989, p. 9). A related critique of postmodernism is that its advocates deconstruct ad infinitum while offering no concrete solutions to pressing social and political problems (e.g., concrete action plans).

CONCLUSION

This chapter provides an introduction to liberal, socialist, radical, and postmodern feminist theoretical approaches to understanding women's and gender oppression. The theories are examined in terms of their central principles, their methods of challenging women's oppression, their practical goals, and their achievements.

Liberal feminism is based on the principles of women's capacity for rationality, meritocracy, equal opportunity, and freedom of choice. From the application of liberal philosophy to inequalities between men and women, we learn that at the source of women's oppression is an inequitable integration of women into society's institutions such as schools and universities, government, professions, and economic organizations. Liberal feminists have thus concentrated on achieving equal opportunity for women by ensuring that all the rights, benefits, and responsibilities that accrue to men also accrue to women.

Socialist feminists explain and advocate for women's liberation through a theoretical framework that places the interconnectedness of capitalism, patriarchy, and more recently, race, sexuality, and globalization, at the centre of its analyses of women's oppression. Socialist feminists challenge women's oppression through unions, advocating for equal pay for work of equal value, increased state investment in social services, and the eradication of poverty. The theoretical and activist contributions of socialist feminists have been instrumental in influencing the Canadian state to include, for the first time in the 1996 census, questions on unpaid labour. In addition, many workplaces have passed paternity-leave provisions (although women continue to take the majority of parental leaves).

Radical feminists investigate what they believe to be the root cause of women's oppression: that is, sex oppression of women by men. They argue that sex oppression can be found in social structures such as the state and the family. Radical feminists identify how women's sexuality is directly controlled by men, through an analysis of reproduction, pornography, and rape, but also through other institutions of social control in everyday relations such as heterosexual love, marriage, and motherhood. Lesbian and cultural feminists argue that women need to break free from patriarchal culture, through an endorsement of lesbian relationships and women-only cultural spaces. Radical feminist theorizing has been influential, bringing to light issues such as rape, pornography, and violence against women in a misogynist society.

Poststructural and postmodern feminist approaches have contributed important critical tools to feminist theory, particularly in the areas of deconstructive and anti-essentialist critique. They have elaborated on the notion of power as diffuse, and have applied gender-based analysis to illustrate the ways in which power is not only visible through obvious brute force, but also through the use of language and the ways in which the symbolic realm creates the possibilities and limitations of our reality. These theories have also, importantly, suggested that language presents opportunities for agency and resistance. Yet, these theoretical contributions have also presented particular challenges for feminism, for, if "strictly speaking, 'women' cannot be said to exist" (Kristeva quoted in Butler 2005, p. 145), what is the basis of the subject identity that feminist politics seeks to represent? Postmodern feminist approaches do not deny sexist inequality and exploitation but consider spaces of subversion and agency simultaneously, and generally avoid the unified, broad sweeping explanations of sexist oppression that are more suited to pushing for concrete legal reforms within modernist state structures.

Endnotes

1. It should be noted that most suffragists did not actually call themselves feminists until the early twentieth century (Roome, 2001).
2. The GDP is a calculation of the total economic value of a country's yearly output of goods and services.
3. Abortion was first decriminalized in 1969, yet initially access was only granted by committees composed usually of men who had to determine if the procedure would preserve a woman's

"health," an ill-defined term. The full decriminalization of abortion occurred in 1988, although accessibility across the country is limited due to geography, provincial underfunding, and a limited number of physicians willing to provide the service.

4. Sex worker, advocate, and organizer Carol Leigh of COYOTE (Call Off Your Old Tired Ethics) has been acclaimed as the creator of the term "sex worker" as opposed to prostitute, which has been seen to have "connotations of shame, unworthiness or wrongdoing" (Bernstein, 1999). "Sex worker" is seen by many feminist thinkers as a more useful term, as it promotes a sex-positive politic in its attempt to normalize those involved in the industry as simply "service workers and care-giving professionals" who require rights similar to others as workers (Bernstein, 1999).
5. Slutwalk is a sex-positive contemporary protest march that originated in response to the rape victim–blaming of a Toronto police officer in 2011 (see www.slutwalktoronto.com).
6. See, for example, the article, "Transsexual and Transgender Women Denied Access to Shelters as Temperatures Drop in Montreal" (February 6, 2013), by Sherbrooke-based non-profit organization Head & Hands.

Discussion Questions

1. Define each of the four theories (liberal, socialist, radical, and postmodern feminism) in your own words. Which one do you most identify with, if any?
2. Discuss how each theory defines the source of women's oppression and their approaches to social change.
3. Identify an accomplishment or goal of each group of feminists. How did theory inform their actions?
4. What are the main criticisms of each theory? Are they valid critiques? Why or why not?
5. Do you see evidence of these theories at work today? Give examples.

Bibliography

Adamson, N., Briskin, L., & McPhail, M. (1988). *Feminist organizing for change: The contemporary women's movement in Canada*. London, England: Oxford University Press.

Agger, B. (1991). Critical theory, poststructuralism, postmodernism: Their sociological relevance. *Annual Review of Sociology, 17*, 105–131.

Andersen, M. L. (1997). *Thinking about women: Sociological perspectives on sex and gender*, 4th ed. Boston, MA: Allyn & Bacon.

Arneil, B. (2001). Women as wives, servants and slaves: Rethinking the public/private divide. *Canadian Journal of Political Science, 34*(1), 29–54.

Atkinson, T.-G. (1970). The institution of sexual intercourse. In S. Firestone (Ed.), *Notes from the Third Year*. New York, NY: Random House.

Atwood, M. (1985). *The handmaid's tale*. Toronto, ON: McClelland & Stewart.

Ault, A., & Sandberg, E. (2001). Our policies, their consequences: Zambian women's lives under structural adjustment. In I. Grewal & C. Kaplan (Eds.), *An introduction to women's studies: Gender in a transnational world* (pp. 469–473). New York, NY: McGraw-Hill.

Barry, K. (1984). *Female sexual slavery*. New York: New York University Press.

Barry, K. (1995). *The prostitution of sexuality: The global exploitation of women*. New York, NY: New York University Press.

Bartky, S. L. (1990). *Femininity and domination: Studies in the phenomenology of oppression*. New York, NY: Routledge.

Bartky, S. L. (2010). Foucault, femininity, and the modernization of patriarchal power. In C. R. McCann & S.-K. Kim (Eds.), *Feminist theory reader: Local and global perspective* (2nd ed., pp. 404–418). New York, NY: Routledge.

Bernstein, E. (1999). What's wrong with prostitution? What's right with sex work? Comparing markets in female sexual labor. *Hastings Women's Law Journal, 91*, 91–117.

Bird, F., MacGill, E., Lange, L. M., Lapointe, J., Ogilvie, D., Henripin, J., & Humphrey, J. P. (1970). Commissioners' list of recommendations. In *Report on the Royal Commission on the status of women in Canada*. Ottawa, ON: Government of Canada.

Brenner, J. (2000). *Women and politics of class*. New York, NY: Monthly Review Press.

Brodie, J. (2008). We are all equal now: Contemporary gender politics in Canada. *Feminist Theory* 9(2): 145–164.

Brown, R. (1989). *Being Brown: A very public life*. Toronto, ON: Random House.

Brownmiller, S. (1976). *Against our will: Men, women and rape*. Toronto, ON: Bantam.

Butler, J. (1990). *Gender trouble: Feminism and the subversion of identit*y. London, England: Routledge.

Butler, J. (2005). Subjects of sex/gender/desire. In A. E. Cudd & R. O. Andreasen (Eds.), *Feminist theory: A philosophical reader* (pp. 145–153). Malden, MA: Blackwell Publishing.

Butler, J. (2010). Performative acts and gender constitution: An essay in phenomenology and feminist theory. In C. R. McCann & S.-K. Kim (Eds.), *Feminist theory reader: Local and global perspectives* (2nd ed., pp. 419–430). New York, NY: Routledge.

Calliste, A. (2001). Immigration of Caribbean nurses and domestic workers to Canada, 1955–1967. Retrieved from www.chinookmultimedia.com/poccd/registered

Canada (Attorney General) v. Bedford. (2013). SCC 72, [2013] 3 S.C.R. 1101. Date: 20131220. Docket: 34788.

Canadian Women's Foundation. The facts about women and poverty. Retrieved from http://www.canadianwomen.org/facts-about-poverty.

Carty, L. (1999). The discourse of empire and the social construction of gender. In E. Dua & A. Robertson (Eds.), *Scratching the surface: Canadian anti-racist feminist thought* (pp. 35–48). Toronto, ON: Women's Press.

Citizenship and Immigration Canada. (2007). Working temporarily in Canada: The live-in caregiver program. Retrieved from www.cic.gc.ca?ENGLISH/work/caregiver/index,asp

Cixous, H. (1976). The laugh of the Medusa (K. Cohen & P. Cohen, Trans.). *Signs, 1.4* (Summer), 875–893.

Cleverdon, C. (1974). *The women suffrage movement in Canada*. Toronto, ON: University of Toronto Press.

Cohen, M. G., & Brodie, J. (Eds.). (2007). *Remapping gender in the new global order*. London, England: Routledge.

Cossman, B., Bell, S., Gotell, L., & Ross, B. L. (1997). *Bad attitude/s on trial: Pornography, feminism, and the Butler decision*. Toronto, ON: University of Toronto Press.

Crow, B. A. (Ed.). (2000). *Radical feminism: A documentary reader*. New York: New York University Press.

Dalla Costa, M., & James, S. (1975). *The power of women and the subversion of the community*. Bristol, England: Falling Wall.

Daly, M. (1978). *Gyn/ecology, the metaethics of radical feminism*. Boston, MA: Beacon Press.

De Beauvoir, S. (1949/1973). *The Second Sex*. New York, NY: Vintage Books.

Derrida, J. (1967/1980). *Writing and Difference* (A. Bass, Trans.). Chicago, IL: University of Chicago Press.

Di Stefano, C. (1989). Dilemmas of difference Feminism, modernity, and postmodernism. In L. Nicholson (Ed.), *Feminism/Postmodernism* (pp. 63–82). New York, NY: Routledge.

Donovan, J. (2000). *Feminist theory: The intellectual traditions* (3rd ed.). New York, NY: Continuum Publishing.

Downe, P. (2011). Excerpts from the Indian Act of Canada. In L. Biggs & P. Downe (Eds.), *Gendered intersections: An introduction to women's and gender studies* (pp. 103–106). Halifax, NS: Fernwood Press.

Dozema, J. (1998). Forced to choose: Beyond the voluntary v. forced prostitution dichotomy. In K. Kempadoo & J. Doezema. (Eds.), *Global sex workers: Rights, resistance, and redefinition* (pp. 34–50). New York, New York,: Routledge.

Dozema, J. (2002). Who gets to choose? Coercion, consent, and the UN trafficking protocol. *Gender and Development: Trafficking and Slavery, 10*(1), 20–27.

Dozema, J. (2005). Now you see her, now you don't: Sex workers at the UN trafficking protocol negotiation. *Social Legal Studies, 14*, 61–89.

Drolet, M. (2001). *The persistent gap: New evidence on the Canadian gender wage gap.* Business and Labour Market Analysis Division, No. 157. Ottawa: Statistics Canada.

Drolet, M. (2011). Why has the gender-wage gap narrowed? *Perspectives on Labour and Income*, Spring. Ottawa, ON: Statistics Canada.

Dua, E. (1999). Canadian anti-racist feminist thought: Scratching the surface of racism. In *Scratching the surface: Canadian anti-racist feminist thought*, Dua, E., & Robertson, A. (Eds.). (7–31) Toronto, ON: Women's Press.

Dworkin, A. (1974). *Woman hating*. New York, NY: E. P. Dutton.

Dworkin, A. (1981). *Pornography: Men possessing women*. New York, NY: Perigee Books.

Echols, A. (1989). *Daring to be bad: Radical feminism in America 1967–1975*. Minneapolis: University of Minnesota Press.

Eisenstein, Z. R. (1979). *Capitalist patriarchy and the case for socialist feminism*. New York, NY: Monthly Review Press.

Employment and Social Development Canada. Financial security – low income incidence. Retrieved from http://well-being.esdc.gc.ca/misme-iowb/.3ndic.1t.4r@-eng.jsp?iid=23.

Engels, F. (1884/1972). *The origin of the family, private property and the state*. New York, NY: Pathfinder Press.

Ensler, E. (1996). *The vagina monologues*. New York, NY: Random House.

Firestone, S. (1970). *The dialectic of sex: The case for feminist revolution*. New York, NY: William Morrow.

Foucault, M. (1979). *Discipline and punish* (A. Sheridan, Trans.). New York, NY: Vintage Books.

Fudge, J., & Owens, R. (Eds.). (2006). *Precarious work: Women and the new economy*. Oxford, ENGLAND: Hart Publishing.

Garvie, M. McCallum, & Johnson, J. L. (1999). *Their leaven of influence: Deans of women at Queen's University, 1916–1996*. Kingston, ON: Queen's Alumni Association Committee on Women's Affairs.

Goldberg, M. (2014, August 4). What is a woman? The dispute between radical feminism and transgenderism. *The New Yorker*. Retrieved from www.newyorker.com/magazine/2014/08/04/woman-2?src=mp

Gordon, L. (2013). Socialist feminism: The legacy of the "second wave." *New Labor Forum 22*(3), 20–28.

Grant, A. (1998). UnWomanly acts: Struggling over sites of resistance. In R. Ainley (Ed.), *New frontiers of space, bodies and gender*. New York, NY: Routledge.

Hamilton, R. (1996). *Gendering the vertical mosaic: Feminist perspectives on Canadian society*. Toronto, ON: Copp Clark.

Harding, S. (2005). Rethinking standpoint epistemology: What is "strong objectivity?" In A. E. Cudd & R. O. Andreasen (Eds.), *Feminist theory: A philosophical reader* (pp. 218–236). Malden, MA: Blackwell Publishing.

Harman, H. (2000). An urgent case for modernization: Public policy on women's work. In A. Coote (Ed.), *New gender agenda: Why women still want more* (pp. 109–116). London, England: Biddles.

Head & Hands. (2013, February 6). *Transsexual and transgender women denied access to shelters as temperatures drop in Montreal*. Retrieved from http://headandhands.ca/2013/02/trans-women-denied-shelter/

Heller, D. A. (1997). *Cross-purposes: Lesbians, feminists, and the limits of alliance*. Bloomington: Indiana University Press.

Hochschild, A. (2000). The nanny chain. American Prospect II 4. Retrieved from www.prospect.org

hooks, b. (2000). *Feminism is for everybody: Passionate politics*. Cambridge, MA: South End Press.

Human Rights Watch. (2002). Sex discrimination in the maquiladoras. In I. Grewal & C. Kaplan (Eds.), *An introduction to women's studies: Gender in a transnational world* (pp. 467–468). New York, NY: McGraw-Hill.

Irigaray, L. (1977). *This sex which is not one* (C. Porter with C. Burke, Trans.). New York, NY: Cornell University Press.

Jeffreys, S. (1999). Globalizing sexual exploitation: Sex tourism and the traffic in women. *Leisure Studies 18*(3), 179–196.

Jeffreys, S. (2009). Prostitution, trafficking and feminism: An update on the debate. *Women's Studies International Forum*, *32*(4), 316.

Kelly, J. (1998). *Under the gaze: Learning to be Black in white society*. Halifax, NS: Fernwood Press.

Kempadoo, K. (2005). Victims and agents of crime: The new crusade against trafficking. In J. Sudbury & J. Chinyere Oparah (Eds.), *Global lockdown: Race, gender and the post-industrial complex* (pp. 35–56). New York, NY, and London, England: Routledge.

Kinsman, G. (1987). *The regulation of desire: Sexuality in Canada*. Montreal, QC: Black Rose Books.

Koedt, A. (1970). The myth of the vaginal orgasm. In *Notes from the first year*. New York: New York Radical Women. Retrieved from http://scriptorium.lib.duke.edu/wlm/notes/#myth

Kreps, B. 1973. Radical feminism 1. In A. Koedt, E. Levine, & A. Rapone (Eds.), *Radical feminism* (pp. 234–239). New York, NY: Quadrangle Books.

Kristeva, J. (1980). *Desire in language*. New York, NY: Columbia University Press.

Lawrence, B. (2004). Regulating native identity by gender. *"Real Indians" and others: Mixed-blood urban native peoples and indigenous nationhood* (pp. 44–63). Vancouver, BC: UBC Press.

Luxton, M. (2006). Feminist political economy in Canada and the politics of social reproduction. In K. Bezanson & M. Luxton (Eds.), *Social reproduction: Feminist political economy challenges neo-liberalism* (pp. 11–44). Montreal, QC, & Kingston, ON: McGill-Queen's University Press.

MacDonald, E. 2000. Critical identities: Rethinking feminism through transgender politics. In B. A. Crow & L. Gotell (Eds.), *Open boundaries: A Canadian women's studies reader* (2nd ed., pp. 381–389). Toronto, ON: Prentice Hall.

MacKinnon, C. 1989. *Towards a feminist theory of the state*. Cambridge, MA: Harvard University Press.

Mandell, N., & Elliot, P. 2001. Feminist theories. In N. Mandell (Ed.), *Feminist issues: Race, class, and sexuality* (3rd ed., pp. 23-48. Toronto, ON: Prentice Hall.

Maracle, S. 2003. The eagle has landed: Native women, leadership and community development. In K. Anderson & B. Lawrence (Eds.), *Strong women stories: Native vision and community survival* (pp.70-84). Toronto, ON: Sumach Press.

Marx, K., & Engels, F. (1848/1998). *The communist manifesto* (S. Moore, Trans.). Halifax, NS: Fernwood Press.

Marx, K., & Engels, F. (1932/1968). *The German ideology*. S. Ryazanskaya (Ed.), Moscow, Russia: Progress Publishers.

McCann, M. (2007a, January 19). Little Sister's declares defeat in the wake of 7–2 Supreme Court ruling: With no money to fight censorship, bookstore says seizures will go unchecked. Retrieved from www.xtra.ca/public/viewstory.aspx?SESSIONID=nzvhqtqryza2q145zfb0lbic&STORY_ID=2583&PUB_TEMPLATE_ID=2

McCann, M. (2007b, February 1). Supreme Court of Canada won't hear Kimberly Nixon case: Case put trans discrimination on the map. Retrieved from www.xtra.ca/public/viewstory.aspx?AFF_TYPE=2&STORY_ID=2632&PUB_TEMPLATE_ID=2

McClung, N. (1915/1972). *In times like these*. V. Strong-Boag (Intro.). Toronto, ON: University of Toronto Press.

Milan, A., Keown, L.-A., & Urquijo, C.R. (2011). Families, living arrangements and unpaid work. Ottawa, ON: Statistics Canada. Retrieved from http://www.statcan.gc.ca/pub/89-503-x/2010001/article/11546-eng.pdf

Mill, H. Taylor. (1998). *The complete works of Harriet Taylor Mill*. J. E. Jacobs (Intro.). Bloomington, Indiana: Indiana University Press.

Mitchell, J. (1971). *Woman's estate*. New York, NY: Pantheon Books.

Morgan, R. (1970). *Sisterhood is powerful: An anthology of writings from the women's liberation movement*. New York, NY: Random House.

Morgan, R. (1984/1996). *Sisterhood is global: The International Women's Movement anthology.* New York, NY: Feminist Press, City University of New York.

Morris, M. (2000). *Women, poverty and Canadian public policy in an era of globalization*. Ottawa, ON: Canadian Research Institute for the Advancement of Women.

Morris, M. (2002). *Women and poverty*. (Factsheet). Ottawa, ON: Canadian Research Institute for the Advancement of Women.

Morissette, R., Picot, G., & Lu, Yuqian. (2013). The evolution of Canadian wages over the last three decades. Ottawa, ON: Statistics Canada. Retrieved from http://www.statcan.gc.ca/pub/11f0019m/11f0019m2013347-eng.pdf

Nicholson, L. (1989). Introduction. In L. Nicholson (Ed.), *Feminism/Postmodernism* (pp. 1–18). New York, NY: Routledge.

O'Donnell, V. & Wallace, S. (2011). First Nations, Métis and Inuit women. Ottawa, ON: Statistics Canada. Retrieved from http://www.statcan.gc.ca/pub/89-503-x/2010001/article/11442-eng.pdf

O'Reilly, A. (2000). A mom and her son: Thoughts on feminist mothering. *Journal of the Association for Research on Mothering 2*(1), 179–193.

Paltiel, F. L. (1997). State initiatives: Impetus and effects. In C. Andrew & S. Rodgers (Eds.), *Women and the Canadian state/Les femmes et l'état canadien*. Montreal, QC, and Kingston, ON: McGill-Queen's University Press.

Prasad, S., & Freeman, M. (2015). Opinion: Twenty years after the Beijing Declaration on women's rights, progress remains slow. *Montreal Gazette*. Retrieved from http://montrealgazette.com/

news/world/opinion-twenty-years-after-the-beijing-declaration-on-womens-rights-progress-remains-slow

Prentice, A., Bourne, P., Cuthbery Brandt, G., Light, B., Mitchenson, W. & Black, N. Eds. (1996). *Canadian women: A history*. Toronto, ON: Harcourt Brace.

Raymond, J. (1998). Sappho by surgery: The transexually constructed lesbian-feminist. In P. D. Hopkins (Ed.), *Sex/machine: Readings in culture, gender and technology*. Bloomington: Indiana University Press.

Rich, A. (1976). *Of woman born: Motherhood as experience and institution*. New York, NY: W.W. Norton.

Rich, A. (1980). Compulsory heterosexuality and lesbian existence. *Signs: Journal of Women in Culture and Society, 5*(4), 3–32.

Roome, P. (2001). Women's suffrage movement in Canada. In *Canada, Confederation to the present.* Edmonton, AB: Chinook Multimedia.

Ross, B. (1995). *The house that Jill built: A lesbian nation in formation*. Toronto, ON: University of Toronto Press.

Ryckewaert, L. (2015, April 6). Negative online comments about female MPs often sexualized, say political veterans. *The Hill Times*. Retrieved from www.equalvoice.ca/speaks_article.cfm?id=972

Sadlier, R. (1994). *Leading the way: Black women in Canada*. Toronto, ON: Umbrella Press.

Scoular, J. (2004). The 'subject' of prostitution: Interpreting the discursive, symbolic and material position of sex/work in feminist theory. *Feminist Theory 5*(3), 343–355.

Sommerville, J. (2000). *Feminism and the family: Politics and society in the UK and USA*. London, England: MacMillan.

Sparr, P. (Ed.). (1994). *Mortgaging women's lives: Feminist critiques of structural adjustment*. London, England: Zed Books.

St. Denis, V. (2007). Feminism is for everybody: Aboriginal women, feminism and diversity. In J. Green (Ed.), *Making space for indigenous feminisms* (pp. 33–52). Halifax, NS: Fernwood Press.

Statistics Canada. (2000). *Women in Canada 2000: A gender-based statistical report*. Ottawa, ON: Statistics Canada.

Statistics Canada. (2006a). *Women in Canada: A gender-based statistical report* (5th ed.). Ottawa, ON: Statistics Canada.

Statistics Canada. (2006b, July 19). General social survey: Paid and unpaid work. *The Daily*. Retrieved from www.statcan.gc.ca/daily-quotidien/060719/dq060719b-eng.htm

Statistics Canada. (2012). Portrait of families and living arrangements in Canada. Ottawa, ON: Statistics Canada. Retrieved from http://www12.statcan.gc.ca/census-recensement/2011/as-sa/98-312-x/98-312-x2011001-eng.pdf

Status of Women Canada. (2003a). What do you mean women couldn't vote? Women's history month in Canada. (Factsheet). Ottawa, ON: Status of Women Canada.

Status of Women Canada. (2003b). Women and education and training—Canada and the United Nations Assembly: Beijing+5 (Factsheets). Ottawa, ON: Status of Women Canada.

Stevenson, W. (1999). Colonialism and First Nations women in Canada. In E. Dua & A. Robertson (Eds.), *Scratching the surface: Canadian anti-racist feminist thought* (pp. 49–80). Toronto, ON: Women's Press.

Stone, S. (1991). The "empire" strikes back: A posttranssexual manifesto. In K. Straub & J. Epstein (Eds.), *Body guards: The cultural politics of gender ambiguity* (pp. 280–304). New York, NY: Routledge.

Strong-Boag, V. (1998). "A red girl's reasoning": E. Pauline Johnson constructs the new nation. In V. Strong-Boag, S. Grace, A. Eisenberg, & J. Anderson (Eds.), *Painting the maple: Essays on race, gender, and the construction of Canada* (pp. 130–154). Vancouver, BC: University of British Columbia Press.

Teekah, A., Scholz, E. J., Friedman, M., & O'Reilly, A. (Eds.). (2015). *"This is what a feminist slut looks like": Perspectives on the SlutWalk movement*. Bradford, ON: Demeter Press.

Thistle, S. (2006). *From marriage to the market: The transformation of women's lives and work*. Berkeley, CA: University of California Press.

Thompson, D. (2001). *Radical feminism today*. London, England: Sage.

Timpson, A. M. (2001). *Driven apart: Women's employment equality and child care in Canadian public policy*. Vancouver, BC: University of British Columbia Press.

Tong, R. Putnam. (1998). *Feminist thought: A more comprehensive introduction* (2nd ed.). Boulder, CO: Westview.

United Nations. (2012). Statistics and indicators on women and men: Table 5f—Women legislators and managers. Retrieved from http://unstats.un.org/unsd/demographic/products/indwm/

United Nations Development Fund for Women (UNIFEM). (2007). Facts & figures on VAW. Retrieved from www.unifem.org/gender_issues/violence_against_women/facts_figures.php United Nations. 2003. Protocol to Prevent, Suppress and Punish Trafficking in Persons, Especially Women and Children, supplementing the United Nations Convention against Transnational Organized Crime. United Nations, *Treaty Series*, vol. 2237, p. 319; Doc. A/55/383. New York, NY: United Nations.

United Nations Office on Drugs and Crime. (2009). *Global Report on Trafficking in Persons. Policy Analysis and Research Branch UNODC*. Retrieved from www.unodc.org/documents/Global_Report_on_TIP.pdf

United States Department of State. (2014). *Trafficking in Persons Report, 2014*. Retrieved from www.state.gov/j/tip/rls/tiprpt/2014/index.htm

Valverde, M. (1992). "When the mother of the race is free": Race, reproduction and sexuality in first-wave feminism. In F. Iacovetta & M. Valverde (Eds.), *Gender conflicts: New essays in women's history* (pp. 3–28). Toronto, ON: University of Toronto Press.

Valenta, M. (2007). *Argentina: Recruiting celebs against trafficking in women.* InterPress Service News Agency. Retrieved from www.ipsnews.net/news.asp?idnews=36936

Waring, M. (1999). *Counting for nothing: What men value and what women are worth* (2nd. ed.). Toronto, ON: University of Toronto Press.

Wente, M. (2000, December 14). Who gets to be a woman? *Globe and Mail*. Retrieved http://www.theglobeandmail.com/news/national/who-gets-to-be-a-woman/article771473/

Wollstonecraft, M. (1792/1982). *A vindication of the rights of woman.* Hardmondsworth, England: Penguin Books.

World Bank. (2014). Table: Labor force participation rate, female (% of female population ages 15+) (modeled ILO estimate). International Labour Organization, Key Indicators of the Labour Market database. Catalog Sources World Development Indicators. Retrieved from http://data.worldbank.org/indicator/SL.TLF.CACT.FE.ZS

World Economic Forum. (2014). Global gender gap index 2014. Retrieved from http://reports.weforum.org/global-gender-gap-report-2014/rankings/

INTRODUCTION

Feminism has a *race* problem. Who counts as a "woman" in the women's movement? How have women of colour and Indigenous women been included and excluded in feminist movements and feminist theorizing? What are the particular issues faced by women of colour and Indigenous women? What would it mean to write the history of Black feminism or Indigenous feminism as the history of the women's movement? What would it mean to build a solidarity movement across the lines of gender, sexuality, class, and race; and include a framework of decolonization? What are the tensions between different approaches to feminism? These are the kinds of questions that challenge the history of feminism and women's movements in Western Europe and North America. Indeed, the fact that these issues are framed as questions suggests a history of contestation within the women's movement and within feminist theorizing. In this chapter, I explore some of the debates raised by these questions. The chapter prioritizes contributions to feminist theorizing made by Indigenous women and women of colour.

In the first section, I outline connections between the concept of race within historical processes of colonialism and slavery. The politics of race and representation and the relationship between race and ideas about "culture" are explored. The representation of race and notions of culture have different implications for Indigenous women and women of colour. In the second section, I situate the feminist concept of intersectionality as one of the most significant contributions that feminist theorists of colour have made to the women's movement and to feminist theorizing. I also explore Indigenous feminist challenges to the concept of intersectionality. As fair warning to the reader, this chapter contains disturbing material about historical and contemporary events. Legacies of colonialism and racism are, of course, in themselves disturbing. I urge readers to reflect on and share their thoughts with other trusted readers. Specifically, I ask readers to think about the reasons why it has been so important for feminism to engage directly with these events and ideas.

This chapter draws upon the fields of feminist theory, critical race theory, Indigenous theory, post-colonial theory, and cultural studies in order to provide insights into how the historical processes of colonialism and racialization have contributed to feminist theorizing. Scholarly and activist interventions about race, Indigeneity,[1] and feminism use different categorizations. Some of these descriptions include critical race feminism, Indigenous feminism, Native feminism, anti-racist feminism, post-colonial feminism, transnational feminism, and global feminism, among other formulations. Each of these descriptions signals distinct points of entry into the debates concerning race, Indigeneity, colonialism, imperialism, and feminism. Drawing on these contributions, this chapter prioritizes the substantive engagements of these fields rather than tracing their distinct and overlapping genealogies.

In prioritizing contributions by feminists of colour and Indigenous feminists, certain challenges and tensions arise. The historical context of the approach of feminist theorists of colour, Black feminists, and Indigenous feminists emerges from different historical and experiential processes and are distinct bodies of work. Indigenous feminists, for example, often examine experiences of genocide, forced assimilation, dehumanization, colonial violence, and land theft. Black feminists often write through histories of enslavement, dehumanization, anti-Black racism, and particular forms of exploitation in the context of capitalism. Other feminists of colour may focus on forced migration; indentured labour; and experiences and processes of immigration that result from histories of colonialism, imperialism, and capitalism. In addition, where Black feminists and other feminists of colour often use the category of "race" as a starting point in their feminist analysis, Indigenous feminists "often spend less time focussing on questions of race and racism *per se*, and more on issues of land and sovereignty" (Emphasis in original. Stewart, 2013, p. 50). These approaches are therefore distinct in terms of orientation to gender and feminism. Rather than resolving these tensions, the chapter attempts to keep these complexities alive.

RACE, COLONIALISM, MODERNITY

Race is one of the defining ideas of modern Western societies. Post-colonial and critical race scholars argue that race and racism are modern, European inventions. During the 18th century, the Enlightenment produced a set of philosophical, cultural, economic, and political ideas that were central to the development of the concept of race. Some of the characteristics of Enlightenment thinking include the rise of empiricism and science, the importance of reason, the idea of progress (i.e., the notion that the human condition can be improved), universalism (i.e., the idea that general rules and laws apply to all people), and the belief in freedom. The ideas that are central to the Enlightenment emerged from specific political, economic, and cultural processes that began in Europe and proliferated throughout the world. Colonialism (from the 15th century to the present day) gave rise to the political and geographical context within which many Enlightenment ideas about the category of human, gender, and race proliferated. The transatlantic slave trade contributed to the globalization of markets, economies, and political projects. The impact of these world-defining and world-changing events has implications for our current understandings of race, Indigeneity, gender, and sexuality.

Many Enlightenment thinkers were invested in the idea of the "human"; the category of "human" came to be an important signifier of ideas related to race and racialization. Critical race scholar David Theo Goldberg argues that the more universal and abstract the idea of the human became during this period, the more the historical record reveals that a notion of difference, categorization, classification, value, and hierarchy came to be associated with distinctions between human beings (Goldberg, 1993). These representations were made possible through European scientific racism (an insistence on identifying inherent biological differences between human beings) and anthropological observations and cultural forms (including art and visual representation). These significant historical, political, economic, and cultural processes produced the ideas concerning race that we are familiar with today. To indicate that race is an idea is to suggest that it is a created concept, a constructed concept, with a history and a past. Most critical race scholars maintain that race is a social, political, and cultural construction. Race is not biologically determined nor is race an objective social or political fact. Race, therefore, is a social construction (Dei, 2012; Kelly, 1998). For example, as Walcott observes: "Located between the U.S. and the Caribbean, questions of Blackness (in Canada) far exceed the categories of the biological and the ethnic (2009, p. 27). To understand race as a social construction means that social, historical, political, and economic processes shape the meaning that is given to race over time and in different geographical areas.

Some Definitions: Colonialism, Imperialism, and Race

To understand the impact of colonialism on feminist theorizing of race and Indigeneity, it is important to begin with some definitions. Colonialism and imperialism are terms that are often used interchangeably but it is helpful to distinguish them geographically and politically. Colonialism is a political "project that extends a nation's sovereignty over territory beyond its borders by the establishment of either settler colonies or administrative dependencies in which indigenous populations are directly ruled, displaced" and murdered.[2] Imperialism refers to the project of extending the dominance of an empire, national, and metropolitan centre over foreign entities, or of acquiring colonies (Loomba, 1998). Imperialism can be exercised without the creation of formal colonies. Colonialism requires the establishment of formal colonies secured by military force and governance through colonial administration.

Alongside distinct colonial projects, the transatlantic slave trade, indentured servitude, the rise of industrialization, and capitalism together produced particular forms of racialization in Western nations. Indentured servitude or indentureship refers to the practice of a worker being under contract to work for a period of time, usually without pay. In North America (particularly in the 16th and 17th centuries), indentured servants were usually migrants who could not afford the cost of travelling. Indentureship and slavery were ultimately systems of labour that operated together to support the project of colonization. The transatlantic slave trade, colonization, and the rise of capitalism structured what critical race theorist Howard Winant describes as the "modern world system." For Winant, the "modern world system" is characterized by increased globalization, specifically, global economic integration that links economic markets around the world. This global economic integration was assisted and animated by Enlightenment ideals and carried out through processes such as the conquest of Indigenous people in North and South America and the transatlantic slave trade (Winant, 2000, p. 172).

Colonization and slavery are predicated on extreme forms of racialized and sexualized violence and were accomplished through the genocide of Indigenous people. These historical processes suggest a profound and complicated genealogy for the idea of race. Colonization and slavery were not simply top-down processes; the colonized, the enslaved, and the exploited were not merely passive victims of economic and political exploitation. Colonization and slavery are dynamic in form and spawned complex practices of survival and resistance, as a few historical Canadian examples reveal.

Marie-Joseph Angélique was an enslaved Black woman who was owned by Thérèse de Couagne de Francheville of Montréal. In *The Hanging of Angélique: The Untold Story of Canadian Slavery and the Burning of Old Montréal*, Afua Cooper tells the story of a fire that burned Montréal in April 1734. Marie-Joseph Angélique was the main suspect although she maintained her innocence throughout the two-month trial. She was found guilty and was sentenced to torture and death. On the day of her execution, she suffered brutal torture ("the hangman applied a gruesome torture, in which her legs were squeezed tight between planks of wood and then smashed with a heavy iron" [Cooper, 2006, p. 6]). The brutal torture was meant to extract a confession. Angélique broke down under the torture and confessed to setting the fire. She was subsequently hanged. In telling the story of the murder of Angélique, Cooper shows how the history of Black slavery has disappeared from Canada's history books, which is striking since "the enslavement of Black people was institutionalized and practised for the better part of three centuries" (2006, p. 7). As Cooper maintains, the evidence against Angélique was circumstantial at best and no one truly knows whether she set fire to Montréal. Cooper, however, believes that Angélique set the fire in an act of great resistance against the conditions of her enslavement (2006, p. 9). The story of Angélique is "dramatic and extraordinary" and starkly reveals part of the untold story of slavery, violence, and resistance in Canada. It is also a story about how the history of colonialism and slavery in the West instituted a distinct racial hierarchy that marked enslaved people as subhuman (Cooper, 2006, p. 9).

Bonita Lawrence has explored the history of warfare and resistance between Indigenous people, English and French settlers, *and* the "large scale intertribal" warfare that marked early settler colonialism (Lawrence, 2002, p. 27). Mercantile colonialism (an early version of international trade) was a type of colonialism that assisted the establishment of settler colonialism in Canada. Mercantile colonialism facilitated by the European invasion of markets, in the 16th and 17th centuries was "instrumental in destabilizing existing intertribal political alliances in eastern North America" (Lawrence, 2002, p. 27). For example,

> the Mi'maq people of Gaspé began killing the Iroquians who crossed within their trade territories . . . Meanwhile the Innu nation in the sixteenth century became embroiled in two different trade wars—the Naskapi fought the Inuit for access to furs in Labrador while the Montagnais fought the Iroquois for control of the rich Saguenay River route to James Bay and the Great Lakes. (Lawrence 2002, p. 27)

The trade wars and the diseases brought by Europeans devastated populations in Ontario and Québec (Lawrence, 2002, p. 27). The chilling example of the murder of Angélique and the intertribal warfare spawned by European disruption of tribal societies challenge the simple binaries of colonizer/colonized, oppressor/oppressed, and demonstrates that the brutality and progression of slavery and colonization resulted in complex social and political processes.

There are different kinds of colonialism and each emerged in distinct ways in different geographical locations and in different historical periods around the globe. In Canada, for example, settler colonialism proliferated along with the emergence of a new nation and continues apace today. Settler colonialism is a racial project that is dependent upon the usurpation of land and the administrative and bureaucratic governance of Indigenous populations. As Sherene H. Razack explains:

> A white settler society is one established by Europeans on non-European soil. Its origins lie in the dispossession and near extermination of Indigenous populations by the conquering of Europeans. As it evolves, a white settler society continues to be structured by a racial hierarchy. In the national mythologies of such societies, it is believed that white people came first and it is they who principally settled the land; Aboriginal people are presumed to be mostly dead or assimilated. European settlers thus *become* the original inhabitants and the group most entitled to the fruits of citizenship. A quintessential feature of white settler mythologies is, therefore, the disavowal of conquest, genocide, slavery, and the exploitation of the labour of peoples of colour. In North America, it is still the case that European conquest and colonization are often denied, largely through the fantasy that North America was peacefully settled and not colonized. (2002, pp. 1–2)

In North America, settler colonialism is predicated on land theft, genocide, and slavery. These practices formed the basis of Canadian nationalism. Nationalism can be defined as an "imagined community" of a collectivity of individuals with a shared common culture (Anderson, 2006). Nationalism consists of the stories that we tell about our countries and ourselves. In Canada, the story of nationalism promotes a white settler (European) version of history and ultimately constructs the history of the *nation* through the categorical exclusion of Indigenous sovereignty and entitlement to the land. At the heart of stories of nationalism, Sunera Thobani suggests, are "exalted subjects" or noble subjects, who "having overcome great adversity in founding the nation . . . face numerous challenges from outsiders—'Indians,' immigrants and refugees who threaten their collective welfare and prosperity" (2007, p. 4). Today, these deeply rooted conflicts continue to manifest themselves in governmental refusal to support Indigenous claims to the land as well as in the context of immigration. As Himani Bannerji explains, "immigration" is most often "a euphemistic expression for racist labour and citizenship policies"—policies that have been shaped through racial hierarchies (2000, p. 4). The complex histories of land theft, genocide, migration, and immigration have posed challenges to feminists seeking to find a place to stand within and outside of the politics of nationalism in Canada and around the world. For example, in the 20th century, Indigenous people re-initiated active and distinct practices of self-determination, anticolonial nationalist movements, and decolonial movements. Resistance has been ongoing. Consider earlier cultural and military rebellions such as the Red River Rebellion (1869) and the North West Rebellion (1885) led by the Métis Louis Riel. Lina Sunseri defines decolonization as "the process by which longstanding colonial relations between Aboriginal and non-Aboriginal people are abolished and new relations are formed (2000, p. 146). Recently, the decolonial Idle No More movement is an example of a social movement with the goal of securing Indigenous sovereignty and the protection of land and water.[3] Each of these initiatives—self-determination, anti-colonial nationalist movements, and decolonial movements—are distinct and come with pitfalls and promises for women. Social movements, for example, that "fail to combine a gender analysis with an anti-colonial one can only increase the chances that colonized women's lives will not be improved" (Sunseri, 2000, p. 146). On a broader scale, however, the challenge has always been, as Audra Simpson demonstrates, "how to proceed as a nation if the right to the terms of legal belonging, a crucial component of sovereignty, has been dictated by foreign governments" (2014, p. 10). Indeed, the ultimate goal is "the choice of Aboriginal peoples to determine which course to take rather *than having one imposed on them*, as has been the case with the Canadian state" (Emphasis in original. Sunseri, 2000, p. 145).

Feminists of colour have similarly demonstrated the role that nationalism has played in women's lives. For example, women have often been positioned as the "producers and reproducers of the national culture" (Sunseri, 2000, p. 144; see also McClintock, 1995). There is also a significant body of feminist scholarship that demonstrates the central role that women have played in nationalist, anti-colonial, and revolutionary movements (Ranchod-Nilsson & Tétreault, 2000). Some feminist scholars have argued that nationalist frameworks are incompatible with strategies of decolonization and liberation hence signalling some of the tensions between aspects of Indigenous theorizing and anti-racist theorizing (Sharma & Wright, 2009).

Settler colonialism (and the lack of attention to the effects of settler colonialism in feminist and critical race feminist theorizing) has had deleterious effects on Indigenous women. Existing feminist frameworks for understanding the effects of settler colonialism on Indigenous women are insufficient and often reinforce racism against Indigenous women. As Haudenosaunee scholar Patricia Monture explains: "I have a hard time understanding again how my experience is an experience of disadvantage. Disadvantage is a nice, soft, comfortable word to describe dispossession, to describe a situation of force whereby our very existence, our histories, are erased continuously before our eyes. Words like disadvantage conceal racism" (Monture-Angus, 2003, pp. 3–4). Indigenous feminists insist that considerations of race and gender are only possible if we understand how white supremacy and heteropatriarchy are organized through the techniques of settler colonialism—land theft, violence, cultural genocide (Arvin, Tuck, & Morrill, 2013; Smith, 2005). The yardstick of discrimination does not address a needed focus on genocide, land theft, sovereignty, and practices of decolonization in settler colonialism.

Andrea Smith eschews the idea of discrimination and suggests, instead, that we must focus on three "logics" that structure North American culture: "anti-Black racism, which anchors capitalism," "genocide, which anchors colonialism," and "orientalism, which anchors war" (Smith, 2010). These three historical process—not discrimination or exclusion or prejudice—give rise to white supremacy in Western culture. These three logics have particular implications for differently situated women of colour. In Black communities, for example, anti-Black racism is manifest in disproportionate incarceration in prison, which is a reality that can be traced through the legacy of criminalization and slavery (Davis, 2003). The processes of genocide and colonialism ensure that Indigenous women continue to experience violence with impunity and are denied sovereignty (Simpson, 2008). For other women of colour, Western forms of orientalism have provided the imperial rationale for war in order to, paraphrasing Gayatri Spivak, save brown women from brown men (Spivak, 1980).

Many feminist scholars of race and Indigenous feminists show how ideas about race are *material* and *symbolic*. In other words, race and forms of racialization are sustained and produced through political, economic, legal, and social structures, and proliferate through symbolic cultural representations of the racialized Other. The theories of these feminist scholars can be traced using Edward Said's ideas concerning colonial discourse and colonial racism that draw from his ground-breaking work *Orientalism*.

Race and Representation

Edward W. Said (1935–2003) is a central thinker in the development of the field of post-colonial studies.[4] In *Orientalism*, Said uses Michel Foucault's notion of discourse to argue that the *idea* of the Orient was produced "politically, sociologically, militarily, ideologically, scientifically, and imaginatively" through European colonial projects and conversely, "European culture gained in strength and identity by setting itself off against the Orient" (1979, p. 11). The significance of Edward Said's work for the social sciences and humanities rests on the connection that he establishes between the economic, political, *as well as* cultural process of colonial projects. As Said argues, colonialism and imperialism do not only require military and governmental power but also an *idea of empire*. In other words, colonialism, imperialism, and empire-building need to be understood not only for the accumulation of capital but also as cultural manifestations concerning the production of *ideas and representations* about race. In short, Said's path-breaking work reveals how colonialism is structural (political and economic) as well as cultural.

In her famous essay "Under Western Eyes," Chandra Mohanty relies on a *discursive* definition of colonization (which follows from Said's writing) in order to examine representations of the category "third world women" in Western feminist writing. In particular, Mohanty challenges how the feminist concept of the orientalized "sexually oppressed woman" is attached to non-Western women.

> When the category of "sexually oppressed women" is located within particular systems in the third world which are defined on a scale which is normed through Eurocentric assumptions, not only are third-world women defined in a particular way prior to their entry into social relations, but since no connections are made between first- and third-world power shifts, it reinforces the assumption that people in the third world just have not evolved to the extent that the west has. This mode of feminist analysis, by homogenizing and systematizing the experiences of different groups of women, erases all marginal and resistant modes of experiences. (Mohanty, 1988, p. 80)

Mohanty is concerned with how, and to what extent, representations of third world women are ideological, legitimating economic and political interests that contribute to the "latent economic and cultural colonization of the 'non-Western' world" (Mohanty, 1988, p. 82). The incorporation of "third world women" into Western/white feminist discourse has the effect of categorical silencing of women of colour as representational veneers in mainstream feminist discourse. These forms of representation spawned one of the most important contributions by women of colour to feminist theorizing—writing against the silencing of women of colour. Mohanty's contributions emerge from what has been described as transnational feminism or global feminism. At stake in this qualification of feminism is the necessity to reject the universalization of the category of "woman" (predominant in mainstream white feminism) and to address the links between women's struggles beyond the confines of the nation-state. The universalizing impulse of white Western feminism "reproduces the paradigmatics of imperialism wherein colonizers speak for all humanity and the colonized simply talk about their own condition" (Johar Schueller, 2005, p. 64).

In *Woman, Native, Other,* Trinh T. Minh-ha explores the challenges faced by women writers of colour: "Neither black/red/yellow nor woman but poet or writer . . . Writer of color? Woman writer? Or woman of color? Which comes first? . . . writing weaves into language the complex relations of a subject caught between the problems of race and gender" (Minh-Ha, 1989, p. 6). Gayatri Spivak's classic text "Can the Subaltern Speak?" similarly advances the idea that Western philosophical writing (from the French philosophers Derrida, Deleuze, and Foucault to the German philosopher and revolutionary socialist Marx) serves economic and political interests (Spivak, 1980). In this sense, knowledge is a commodity that serves dominant interests. Spivak is particularly wary of feminist and post-colonial scholars who are invested in attempts to allow the subaltern (a person who holds a subordinate position) to "speak." Such benevolent attempts at inclusion, Spivak argues, works to reassert what she describes as "epistemic violence" or colonial racism that is at the root of forms of knowledge production (Spivak, 1980). As Said, Spivak, Minh-Ha, and others demonstrate, the figure of the racialized colonial subject is/was made through anthropological, scientific, and cultural representations and discourses that constructed race as a fixed, biological, and hierarchical category.

The category of race was further consolidated through colonial projects of the 18th and 19th centuries. For example, in the 18th century and onward, African and Indigenous peoples were often perceived and represented by colonizers as "savage," "barbaric," and subhuman. Racialized representations of Indigenous people had particular implications for Indigenous women since "strategies of colonization were gendered purposefully to undermine and remove Indigenous women's traditional authority and agency" (NWAC, 2010, p. 11; see also Anderson, 2000).

These strategies of colonization systematically devalued, undermined, and subjugated Indigenous women in every way: mentally, emotionally, physically, spiritually, economically, and politically. Women who resisted were put in their place or punished through ridicule, exclusion, and violence (Anderson, 2000; Monture & McGuire, 2009; NWAC, 2010, p. 12; Smith, 2000).

Racialization

Racialization is a word that is often used to describe the *process* through which ideas about race are constructed and the idea of race becomes meaningful in socio-political, legal, economic, and cultural formations. The word racialization can be traced to the writings of the anti-colonial revolutionary writer Frantz Fanon (1925–1961). Born in Martinique, Fanon was a psychiatrist and a philosopher. He supported the Algerian resistance movement against colonizer France. His writings have influenced the fields of critical race studies, post-colonial studies, and social movement studies. In *Black Skin, White Masks*, Fanon explores the psychological and social effects of living as a Black man in a colonial world. His theory argues that European colonialism created a binary world, whereby sharp and distinct categories of domination and subjection structure social, political, and economic relations. Fanon described this binary world as a Manichean world; Manichean refers to religious or philosophical dualism (Fanon, 2008). The binary pairing of colonizer/colonized, Black/white, civilized/barbaric, and respectable/degenerate became profound psychic and social orders of domination for colonized people in a colonized world. These sharp distinctions have the effect, Fanon argues, of splitting humanity into two categories: human and subhuman. Fanon first uses the phrase "to racialize" when contrasting it with the phrase "to humanize," thereby signalling the ways in which processes of racialization eject certain peoples from the very category of the human (Fanon, 2008). In this sense, racialization can be viewed as assisting processes of domination, oppression, subjugation, violence, and marginalization.

This genealogy of racialization echoes the analysis advanced by many women writers of colour, including Audre Lorde. In her path-breaking essay "Age, Race, Class and Sex: Women Redefining Difference," Lorde writes:

> Much of western European history conditions us to see human differences in simplistic opposition to each other: dominant/subordinate, good/bad, up/down, superior/inferior. In a society where the good is defined in terms of profit rather than in terms of human need, there must always be some group of people who, through systemized oppression, can be made to feel surplus, to occupy the place of the dehumanized inferior. Within this society, that group is made up of Black and Third World people, working-class people, older people, and women. (1984, p. 114)

Ideas about race and processes of racialization are interwoven into institutions, social structures, and systems of representation. Race is a polyvalent concept that changes over time and through geographical places. In our contemporary world, we see the residues of 18th- and 19th-century views on race in that we often consider racial difference as biologically fixed. The legacy of scientific or biological racism supports the view that race largely and exclusively, refers to phenotype (observable traits such as skin colour). Following critical race and post-colonial scholarship, the concept of racialization challenges this view. Focusing on the *process* of racialization helps us to see how what we know about the concept of "race" comes from the stories that we tell about race and the forms of governance that assist in the organization of knowledge about race. Whether these stories are derived from popular media, such as television shows, movies, newsfeeds, Twitter, or Facebook; or through formal governmental and legal processes, they rely on ideas about race that have a long history in Western culture.

Race and Culture

Scholars of race, Indigeneity, and colonialism address how, and to what extent, the concept and the idea of culture is a harbinger for racism and racialization. Sherene Razack describes this process as the "culturalization of racism" and shows how in cases of sexual violence against women of colour and gender-based asylum cases, ideas about the culture and religion of non-white people often "pre-empt both racism and sexism" in the legal process (Razack, 1998, p. 60). The "culturalization of racism" refers to the ways in which the idea of "culture" is used as a euphemism for insidious forms of racism. The challenge is to ensure that when the language of culture enters the social, political, and legal sphere, it is not concealing or masking women's real experiences of racism and sexism. Today, cultural sensitivity training for workers (such as teachers, police officers, judges, health-care workers, and others) or books and training sessions that assist with "cross-cultural" communications are just a few examples of *how* race relations are often managed through a language of culture. While these kinds of strategies seek to address an increasingly diverse workforce, for example, and are viewed as progressive strategies to assist with relations among diverse people, we need to pay attention to the very real ways in which these strategies can promote new kinds of racism and sexism.

The "culturalization of racism" is also used in the service of settler colonialism. Indigenous scholars have long demonstrated the ways in which ideas about Indigenous "culture" and "tradition" work to sustain and enact forms of racism against Indigenous women, men, and children (Anderson, 2010; Smith, 2005; St. Denis, 2011). In Canada, the establishment of reserves and residential schools was inspired by colonial and racist ideas about inferior Indigenous cultures and civilizing "the Indian." Ultimately, these representational ideas about race and Indigenous culture provided the underlying rationale for genocide and land theft. These forms of racialized violence were further sustained legally through the establishment of the Indian Act in 1876. For example, ideas about "Indian culture" were reinforced by legal prohibitions criminalizing Indian cultural ceremonies and dance (Backhouse, 1999). Today, as incarceration rates for Indigenous women and men are at an all-time high in Canada, criminal justice processes, such as restorative justice and "cultural sensitivity" training for criminal justice officials, often fail when they are framed through ideas about cultural difference (Murdocca, 2013).

Cultural approaches to addressing racism and sexism also fail when invoked through stereotyped narratives about non-white people and cultures. Razack argues,

> [C]ulture talk is clearly a double-edged sword. It packages difference as inferiority and obscures both gender-based and racial domination, yet cultural considerations are important for contextualizing oppressed groups' claims for justice, for improving their access to services, and for requiring dominant groups to examine the invisible cultural advantages they enjoy." (Razack, 1998, p. 59)

The complexity of the real-world experiences of women of colour, Indigenous women, and other marginalized women led many feminist theorists of colour to develop new conceptual and analytic tools to "voice" everyday and historical realities and to account for the exclusion of their experiences by mainstream women's movements.

TRACING INTERSECTIONALITY

Intersectionality is one of the main contributions that feminists of colour have made to feminist theorizing. Intersectionality refers to the study of the interconnections between different systems, social processes, and representations of discrimination and oppression. As social and cultural forms, race, gender, sexuality, dis/ability, and other forms of social identification shape these systems, processes, and representations. Intersectionality largely emerges from the United States feminist context. This section charts the emergence of intersectionality in United States scholarship and provides examples of the use of intersectionality (the "how" of intersectionality) when analyzing torture in the context of war and violence against Indigenous women. Finally, this section also addresses some critiques of intersectionality (limitations and possibilities) made by Indigenous and other scholars of colour.

In the United States, feminist approaches to race coalesce around three social and political processes: 1. The exclusion of Black women and other women of colour in the first and second waves of feminism; 2. Black lesbian feminist writings in the 1970s and 80s; and 3. An emerging Black feminist critique of civil rights and discrimination laws. Pre-dating these interventions is a much longer Black female intellectual history that emerged out of survival and resistance to slavery and its attendant forms of discipline and control dating back to the work of Sojourner Truth (c.1797–1883), an abolitionist and women's rights activist. Lee Maracle's celebrated *I Am Woman* was partly inspired by Truth's anti-slavery feminist speech "Ain't I a Woman?" suggesting historical links between ideas that inspired reclaiming women's knowledge across racial lines and differently situated women (Maracle, 2003; see also Stewart, 2013).

Jennifer Nash suggests that intersectionality has advanced feminist theorizing in three ways: 1. Intersectionality challenges dichotomous and binary thinking of the race/gender systems of domination and subordination; 2. "Intersectionality seeks to demonstrate the racial variation(s) within gender and the gendered variation(s) within race" through a focus on recognizing the complexity of subjects and identities (2008, 2); and 3. Intersectionality challenges the legacy of excluding racialized and marginalized subjects from anti-racist and feminist work (2008). One could argue that feminist theory *is* a theory of intersectionality. Or, as Leslie McCall explains: "One could even say that intersectionality is the most important theoretical contribution that women's studies, in conjunction with related fields, has made so far" (2005, p. 1771). Indeed, the related fields—Black feminist theory, critical race theory, anti-racist feminist theory, Indigenous theory, Latina/Chicana feminist theory, post-colonial feminist theory—have made the most significant contributions to a theory of intersectionality.

Legal scholar Kimberlé Crenshaw is often regarded as the first to develop a theory of intersectionality (first published in 1989). However, Angela P. Harris's important work similarly used "a racial critique to attack gender essentialism in feminist legal theory" (1990, p. 585). Harris proposed an analysis that recognizes the complexity and relationality of identity categories: "In constructing knowledge and theory about the nature and causes of women's oppression, we must account for simultaneity; we must ask: "[H]ow do they combine with and/or cut across one another? How does racism divide gender identity and experience? How is gender experienced through racism? How is class shaped by gender and 'race'?" (1990, p. 123).

Similar to Harris's work, Crenshaw's theory of intersectionality emerged out of an attempt to address the mutual conditioning of race and gender in Black women's lives in relation to civil rights law in the United States. Crenshaw's theory of intersectionality emerged out of a critique of law's purported objectivity, colour blindness, and neutrality. For Crenshaw (and other feminists of colour, and anti-racist and critical race scholars), intersectionality is also a historical indictment of the exclusion of women of colour from the mainstream feminist movement. As Crenshaw explains:

> Because the intersectional experience is greater than the sum of racism and sexism, any analysis that does not take intersectionality into account cannot sufficiently address that particular manner in which Black women are subordinated. Thus . . . the entire framework that has been used as the basis for translating "women's experience" or the "Black experience" into concrete policy demands must be rethought and recast. (2011, p. 26; 1991)

Crenshaw uses the analogy of the traffic accident to consider the real world consequences of the concept of intersectionality:

> The point is that black women can experience discrimination in a number of ways and that the contradiction arises from our assumptions that their claims of exclusion must be unidirectional. Consider an analogy to traffic in an intersection, coming and going from all four directions. Discrimination, like traffic through an intersection, may flow in one direction, and it may flow in another. If an accident happens in an intersection, it can be caused by cars traveling from any number of directions and, sometimes, from all of them. Similarly, if a black woman is harmed because she is in the intersection, her injury could result from sex discrimination or race discrimination. (2011, p. 29)

For women of colour, intersectionality accounts for the experience of "double discrimination" or the "double bind" of discrimination. Importantly, J. Kéhaulani Kauanui examines how this civil rights genealogy of intersectionality does not address the issues of "territory, sovereignty and nationhood (that) structure colonized peoples' relationship to the nation-state" (2008, p. 635–636). Furthermore, Kauanui argues that "conflating race with indigeneity" is another symptom of a civil rights or legal framework that makes it difficult, if not impossible, for Indigenous people to advance claims of sovereignty to the land (2008, p. 635). This is an important illustration of where Black feminist or critical race feminist approaches to civil rights, for example, may be complicit with the ongoing project of settler colonialism.

In the Canadian context, feminists of colour also began to respond to the exclusion of Black women and other women of colour from the mainstream feminist movement and feminist legal scholarship. For example, the first issue of the journal *Canadian Journal of Women and Law* was an indictment of Black, Indigenous, and other women of colour exclusion from mainstream feminism. In particular, Esmeralda Thornhill's article "Focus on Black Women" argued "that if the experiences of all oppressed women are to be understood, addressed, and incorporated, then all must participate in the building of theory" (Thornhill in Kline 1989, p. 117). Drawing on Thornhill, Marlee Kline began the task of documenting the ways in which Canadian feminist analysis of child custody, a feminist review of Canadian criminal law, and the radical feminist theory of Catherine MacKinnon failed to take into consideration how race and racism structures the experience of women of colour (Kline, 1989). Patricia Monture also reflects on the use of law and education as a tool of subjugation and racism for Indigenous people (Monture, 1990).

Although Crenshaw uses the word "intersectionality" (and is generally identified as the first to do so), Black feminist activists and other activists and artists of colour had already developed a legacy of anti-racist feminist action and theorizing that advanced what might be called an "intersectional critique." These scholars, poets, and writers had long established a legacy where ideas about intersectionality, double discrimination, and difference were central themes. Concerned with advocating for the eradication of forms of exclusion, violence, and war, these writings are directly connected to political action and solidarity among different kinds of women globally. Revisiting these works today, their collective visions seem ever more relevant.

For example, the Combahee River Collective, a collective of Black and lesbian feminist activists in Boston who were committed to the idea that "the liberation of all oppressed people necessitates the destruction of the political-economic systems of capitalism and imperialism as well as patriarchy" (1977).

In advocating an intersectional analysis of the connection between individual identities, local struggles and global relations, the Combahee River Collective advocates a version of a historicized transnational feminist analysis that is propelled by an intersectional approach.

The Combahee River Collective traces the origins of Black feminism in the historical legacy of slavery, global feminist movements, *and* the historical forms of exclusion and sexism experienced by Black women in the mainstream/white feminist movement, the Civil Rights movement and Black nationalist movements. Significantly, the Combahee River Collective's approach in 1977 ultimately challenges later feminist theorizing (into the 80s, 90s, and 2000s) to advance a global and historicized approach to understanding the politics of subordination and domination.

Similarly, the path-breaking collection *This Bridge Called My Back: Writings By Radical Women of Color* (1984) advocates for the development of a global feminist analysis that addresses questions of solidarity for different groups of women.

This Bridge prioritizes the experiential knowledge of women of colour and advances an anti-racist and critical race approach by "draw[ing] explicitly on the person of color's lived experiences by including such methods as storytelling, family history, biographies, scenarios, parables, cuentos, chronicles, and narratives" (Solorzano, 1998, p. 133).

These writings offer a vision of what we might call intersectionality politics—an analysis of the world and social life that is rooted in experiential knowledge across women's diverse experiences. It is rooted in solidarity and action in relation to experiences of violence, exclusion, and exile. Sarah Hunt describes how *This Bridge*, in its focus on building solidarity movements across Indigenous, Black, Chicana, queer, and Asian women, opens up a radical politics that aims to dissolve identity categories (Hunt, 2007). Similarly, there have been attempts in Canada to consider collaborative work between Black and Indigenous feminists with the view of thinking through Indigenous relations to the land and Black Canadians who experience diaspora realities of settlement in the context of histories of enslavement and migration (Amadahy & Lawrence, 2010).

These works echoed contemporaneous writings on women of colour and Black women's exclusion and disillusionment with the white women's movement. bell hooks's classic book *Feminist Theory: From Margin to Center* (2000), for example, is an indictment of the white mainstream women's movement in the United States. "Feminism in the United States has never emerged from the women who are most victimized by sexist oppression . . . Racism abounds in the writings of white feminists, reinforcing white supremacy and negating the possibility that women will bond across ethnic and racial lines" (hooks, 2000, pp. 1, 3). Patricia Hill Collins called attention to the suppression of Black women's intellectual traditions in her ground-breaking book *Black Feminist Thought* (Collins, 2000). She argues that African-American women's oppression is/was organized by a triangulated web of exclusion that includes labour ("Black women's long-standing ghettoization in service professions" [2000, p. 3]), legal rights (inequitable treatment in the criminal justice system as well as the history of denying African-American women the vote and the opportunity to hold public office [2000, p. 4]), and significantly, visual representation and cultural ideology ("from the mammies, jezebels and breeder women of slavery to the smiling Aunt Jemimas on pancake mix boxes, ubiquitous black prostitutes and ever-present welfare mothers of contemporary popular culture, negative stereotypes applied to African American women have been fundamental to Black women's oppression" [2000, p. 4]).

In Canada, feminist work that attempts to address the intersections between race, class, and gender has been described as anti-racist feminist thought (Calliste & Dei, 2003; Dua & Robertson, 1999). Inspired by a political economy approach and a critical race critique of liberalism and multiculturalism, some of the issues that anti-racist feminist thought has explored concern immigration, labour, reproduction, building solidarity with Indigenous women, and the role of "culture" in structuring women's lives (Agnew, 2007; Bannerji, 2000; Monture, 2003; Philip, 1992). In this sense, Canadian anti-racist feminist thought challenges the Black/white dichotomy that structures some strands of United States–based feminism. Significantly, there have also been debates in the Canadian context concerning the possibility of "decolonizing anti-racism" and the challenge this poses to building solidarity between anti-racist feminism and Indigenous feminism (Lawrence & Dua, 2005).

Collectively, these scholars unsettled the white women's movement and academic feminism and contributed to the development of an intellectual tradition in the writing of women of colour concerning what we have now come to call *intersectionality*—a theoretical, activist, and literary tradition that recognizes that all aspects of our identity and experience (racial, sexual, class, religious, migratory, dis/ability, cultural, religious, etc.) are inherently and necessarily interconnected. Intersectionality demands recognition that our identities and experiences are complex. If we accept (as I do) that feminist theory *is*, at its core, a theory of intersectionality, then it follows—as these writings demonstrate—that feminist theory is a theory that has been made possible by the writings and experiences of Indigenous women and women of colour.

The "How" of Intersectionality

Despite efforts to examine the rich genealogy of the concept of intersectionality and its different iterations across feminist writing and differently situated women, few feminist scholars have turned their attention to addressing the *how* of intersectionality. That is to say, *how do we accomplish an intersectional analysis in our feminist work and political goals* (McCall, 2005, p. 1771)? *How* does intersectionality account for experiences of exclusion and discrimination? What does intersectionality do as a theory and, perhaps more importantly, what does it offer methodological approaches used by feminist, critical race, and Indigenous scholars?

There have been several revisions to the concept of intersectionality that have attempted to show the limits of the concept when mobilized to explain particular social, political, or legal phenomena. For example, in the Canadian context, echoing the Combahee River Collective, Sherene Razack prioritizes the word interlocking rather than intersecting in order to address the relationships between race, gender, class, sexuality, disability, and other axes of identity. "I use the word interlocking rather than intersecting to describe how the systems of oppression are connected. Intersecting remains a word that describes discrete systems whose paths cross. I suggest that the systems *are* each other and that they give content to each other" (Emphasis in original. Razack, 2008, p. 62). Significantly, Razack describes how to advance an interlocking approach through an analysis of the torture and prisoner abuse scandal at Abu Ghraib Prison in Iraq (now Baghdad Central Prison).

During the 2003 United States–led invasion of Iraq, the Abu Ghraib prison located just west of the Baghdad city centre was seized and became a United States military prison. Most of the prisoners in Abu Ghraib were civilians, and women and children (Hersh, 2004). In 2004, *The New Yorker* obtained a report written by Major General Antonio M. Taguba (which was not intended for public release) and the CBS television program 60 *Minutes* released photos depicting widespread abuse and torture of prisoners in Abu Ghraib prison by United States soldiers. The report stated that between October and December of 2003 there were numerous instances of "sadistic, blatant, and wanton criminal abuses" at Abu Ghraib (Hersh, 2004). Soldiers perpetuated these abuses. The widely circulated photos taken by fellow soldiers depicted horrific acts of racialized, sexualized, and gendered violence. The report describes one of the photos in the following manner:

> The photographs tell it all. In one, Private England, a cigarette dangling from her mouth, is giving a jaunty thumbs-up sign and pointing at the genitals of a young Iraqi, who is naked except for a sandbag over his head, as he masturbates. Three other hooded and naked Iraqi prisoners are shown, hands reflexively crossed over their genitals. A fifth prisoner has his hands at his sides. In another, England stands arm in arm with Specialist Graner; both are grinning and giving the thumbs-up behind a cluster of perhaps seven naked Iraqis, knees bent, piled clumsily on top of each other in a pyramid. There is another photograph of a cluster of naked prisoners, again piled in a pyramid. Near them stands Graner, smiling, his arms crossed; a woman soldier stands in front of him, bending over, and she, too, is smiling. Then, there is another cluster of hooded bodies, with a female soldier standing in front, taking photographs. Yet another photograph shows a kneeling, naked, unhooded male prisoner, head momentarily turned away from the camera, posed to make it appear that he is performing oral sex on another male prisoner, who is naked and hooded. (Hersh, 2004)

In seeking to analyze the events at Abu Ghraib, and the thousands of photos that circulated, some scholars and mainstream analysts sought to "exceptionalize" the violence and torture committed by male and female soldiers who were portrayed by Western media as being on the "right" side of the war (Puar, 2005a; Razack, 2008). For example, commentators suggested that the torture was just the result of a "few bad apples" in the army (Puar, 2005b; Razack, 2008). As Puar explains, these accounts viewed the racialized and sexualized torture as rare, extreme bodily and sexual violence ("the site of violation as extreme in relation to the individual rights of privacy and ownership accorded to the body within liberalism") (Puar, 2005a, p. 14).

Razack asks the following questions of the torture at Abu Ghraib: 1. Why take photos to record the torture and prisoner abuse? (And, why did soldiers send nearly 2000 photos to their families?); 2. "Why record evil?"; 3. "Why the sex? (This last question is often connected to the women's participation)" (2008, p. 67). Razack proposes that an interlocking approach facilitates an analysis of how we each, individually and collectively, come to participate in racialized and historical processes of subordination and domination. Razack advances an interlocking analysis of the torture at Abu Ghraib in the following way:

> The fact that the status of Iraqis is so evidently subhuman, so *culturally different*, and so in need of discipline, crowds our newsreels. Unless we have become numb to it all, we will need to find an explanation for the sexualized terror and for the ways that ordinary people participate in it. Pyramids of naked men forced to simulate having sex should not baffle us, but neither should we believe they are trivial or exceptional moments in a giant clash of civilizations. To grasp their import, we will have to attend to prisoner abuse as a publicly enacted, sexualized ritual of racial violence and track the trade in mythologies signalled by our persistent marking of ourselves as modern and the non-West as culturally different . . . We will need to consider how race, class, gender, and sexuality give each other meaning [in the context of racialized and gendered violence],

> structuring desire and producing men and women whose sense of coherency rests on anxiously drawing the line between those who are abandoned and those who are to remain members of political community. (Razack, 2008, p. 80)

Several features of this analysis are significant. Razack seeks to historicize the sexualized racialized violence enacted at Abu Ghraib. In so doing, historical processes of sexualized racialization (human/subhuman) coupled with particular forms of Enlightenment thinking (pre-modern/modern, civilized/uncivilized) make the torture possible. The potency of the images of torture from Abu Ghraib is rendered "coherent" through historical and transnational processes of imperialism, racialization, and sexualization.

Of particular interest in analyses of the torture was the participation of female soldiers. As noted in the Abu Ghraib memo, Private Lyndie England was depicted in photos smiling and giving a "thumbs-up" to the camera next to naked prisoners piled in a pyramid and pointing to a man's genitals. Some white liberal feminist scholars and commentators were bewildered by the presence and active participation of female soldiers. As Puar explains:

> The picture of Lyndie England, dubbed "Lyndie the Leasher," leading a naked Iraqi on a leash (also being referred to as "pussy whipping") has now become a surface on which fundamentalism and modernization, apparently dialectically opposed, can wage war. One could argue that this image is about both the victories of liberal feminists, who claim that women should have equal opportunities within the military, and the failures of liberal feminists to adequately theorize power and gender beyond male-female dichotomies that situate women as less prone toward violence and as morally superior to men. (Eisenstein in Puar, 2005a, p. 20)

Puar suggests that the failure to adequately account for gendered racial violence is part of a version of white liberal feminism that is rooted in binary gender categories and essentialist ideas about women (i.e., women are less prone to violence). A more complex account of the violence and torture at Abu Ghraib would reveal the ways in which forms of subordination and domination travel transnationally across geopolitical space in order to position certain bodies in historical hierarchies racialization and sexualization.

In the Canadian context, the murder of an Indigenous woman is another violent episode that can be examined through an intersectional analysis. Razack's analysis of the brutal murder in Regina of Pamela George, an Indigenous woman and mother from the Saulteaux nation who was working as a sex worker on the night of her murder, provides another example of the possibilities of an intersecting analysis. In particular, the case of Pamela George demonstrates the ways in which the law fails to adequately address violence against Indigenous women. George was murdered by two young white university students who "took turns brutally beating her and left her lying with her face in the mud" (Razack, 2002, p. 121). Razack argues that George's murder should be understood as gendered racial violence where "the racial or colonial aspects of this encounter are more prominently brought into view by tracing two inextricably linked collective histories: the histories of the murderers, two middle-class white men, and of Pamela George, a Saulteaux woman" (Razack, 2002, p. 126). By reviewing the transcripts from the murder case, Razack asks the following questions: How does the history of colonialism and racism in Canada directed at Indigenous people help us to shed light on Pamela George's murder? What is it about the biographies of George and her murderers that brought them into a violent encounter with each other? What about the histories of the white men made it possible to brutally murder George? Why must the violence directed at George be understood as racialized gendered violence? What was it about Pamela George that not only made her especially vulnerable but also made her a target? Razack insists that to fully comprehend the enormity of the violence directed at George, and the law's response to violence against Indigenous women, a historical view of gendered racial violence must be advanced. Razack writes:

> I deliberately write against those who would agree that this case is about an injustice but who would de-race the violence and the law's response to it, labelling it as generic patriarchal violence against women, violence that the law routinely minimizes. While it is certainly patriarchy that produces men whose sense of identity is achieved through brutalizing a woman, the men's and the court's capacity to dehumanize Pamela George came from their understanding of her as the (gendered) racial Other whose degradation confirmed their own identities as white—that is, as men entitled to the land and the full benefits of citizenship. (Razack 2002, p. 126)

Through analyzing the court transcripts, Razack's analysis concludes that forms of racialization, representation, and regulation resulted in George's "absence" from her own murder trial: "If this exploration of Pamela George's murder trial, does anything at all, my hope is that it raises consciousness about how little she mattered to her murderers, their friends and families, and how small a chance she had of entering the court's and Canadian society's consciousness as a person" (Razack, 2002, p. 156).

The murder of Pamela George is one episode in a long history of violence against Indigenous women. According to the Native Women's Association of Canada (NWAC), "approximately 60% of 3000 women that have gone missing or been murdered in Canada since 1980 are Native, with approximately 500 cases outstanding in BC alone . . . The discrepancy between these numbers can be attributed to a lack of funding for widespread research, most recently manifest in the government's cutting of funds to NWAC's Sisters in Spirit campaign" (NWAC, n.d.). Many Indigenous and non-Indigenous advocacy groups, including Amnesty International, are calling on local, provincial, and federal governments to address these cases. The *Stolen Sisters* report, produced by Amnesty International calls upon the state to address the following root causes of violence in the lives of Indigenous women in Canada:

1. The role of racism and misogyny in perpetuating violence against Indigenous women;
2. The sharp disparities in the fulfillment of Indigenous women's economic, social, political, and cultural rights;
3. The continued disruption of Indigenous societies caused by the historic and ongoing mass removal of children from Indigenous families and communities;
4. The disproportionately high number of Indigenous women in Canadian prisons, many of whom are themselves the victims of violence and abuse; and

5. The inadequate police response to violence against Indigenous women as illustrated by the handling of missing persons cases (Amnesty International, 2004).

Recently, the Indigenous Nationhood Movement, a movement described as a people's movement which includes a diverse group made up of Indigenous people and their allies, has launched a Twitter and social media initiative to address the continued violence experienced by Indigenous women in Canada. This solidarity movement aims to include the diverse realities of all of the Indigenous peoples. "#ItEndsHere Confronting the Crisis of Colonial Gender Violence" is a campaign dedicated to eliminating violence, including violence based on gender, sexual identity, and orientation.[5] In order to comprehend the scale of the violence against Indigenous women in Canada (violence that the law routinely ignores and authorizes), an intersectional analysis that attends to the historical dimensions of race, sexuality, gender, and territory, and sovereignty and decolonization must be advanced. For example, the remarkable collection inspired by the Idle No More Movement, *The Winter We Danced* (2014), demonstrates the imaginings that are possible when solidarity movements are advanced to prioritize a decolonizing approach to social, political, and economic subjugation.

Some Possibilities and Limitations of Intersectionality

The theory of intersectionality is not without its critics (Nagarajan, 2014; Wiegman, 2012). Although it has been heralded as the most significant contribution of feminist theory to the social sciences and humanities, it is nevertheless a contribution that is mired in intellectual and popular culture debate. In addition, as evidenced by Razack's interlocking analysis above, theorists seeking to find an analytic basis for capturing theoretical, methodological, and tactical ways to address global and transnational formations have further developed the concept of intersectionality. Jasbir Puar has proposed the idea of the assemblage, for example, as an effort to push against the tendency in feminist theorizing to exalt intersectionality as a "shorthand to diagnose difference" rather than attending to historical, geographical, and global social movement specificities (Q&A with Jasbir Puar [Interview] | *Darkmatter Journal*, 2014). Puar derives the concept of assemblage from the French philosopher Gilles Deleuze. Puar further describes the limitations of intersectionality in the following manner:

> The theory of intersectionality argues that all identities are lived and experienced as intersectional—in such a way that identity categories themselves are cut through and unstable—and that all subjects are intersectional whether or not they recognize themselves as such. But what the method of intersectionality is most predominantly used to qualify is the specific "difference" of "women of color", a category that has now become, I would argue, simultaneously emptied of specific meaning on the one hand and overdetermined in its deployment on the other. In this usage, intersectionality always produces an Other, and that Other is always a Woman Of Color (WOC), who must invariably be shown to be resistant, subversive, or articulating a grievance. (Puar, 2005b)

Puar argues that the additive approach of intersectionality, where race, gender, and sexuality are viewed as separate components of identity, fails to ultimately demonstrate how multiple forces (within and beyond identity) produce lived experiences. For example, Puar suggests that human rights (and feminist approaches to human rights) are "globalized, sometimes problematically, whereby the terrain of the U.S.-centric frame is transposed onto other regional and national locations without sufficient attention to differing epistemological category formations" (Q&A with Jasbir Puar [Interview] | *Darkmatter Journal*, 2014). Therefore, the idea of assemblage, unlike intersectionality, advocates for an approach that recognizes how global processes are particularized in local sites. An assemblage locates identity within the changing patterns of other social, cultural, and political formations (like nationalism, religion, war, militarization).

In her view, an assemblage addresses the "interwoven forces that merge and dissipate time, space, and body against linearity, coherency, and permanency" (Puar, 2005b, p. 128). Puar's idea of assemblage carries particular importance in our neo-liberal era concerned with securitization, counterterrorism, and nationalism. In *Queer Assemblages*, for example, Puar argues that the incorporation of the queer subject into liberal politics (through the legalization of gay marriage, the overturning of anti-sodomy laws, and through increased popular cultural representation) has depended upon the concomitant representations of certain populations (i.e., racialized Muslim and Arab communities) as "orientalized terrorists" (Puar, 2005b). Puar combines transnational feminist theory and queer theory (along with Foucaultian and Deleuzian insights) in order to address the ways in which transnational flows of capital, knowledge, and people have legal and disciplinary consequences for those marked as the "racialized Other" in a particular historical period. For example, in the context of the post–9/11 global war on terror, the Western world has witnessed the increased racial profiling, surveillance, and criminalization of Muslims and "Arab-looking" individuals.

One of the challenges of intersectionality as an analytic tool, derived from a distinctly United States context, is its applicability in other geographical and political spaces. Transnational feminist scholars examine the organization and politicization of the role of race, class, gender, and sexuality beyond the confines of the nation-state. The phrase "transnational feminism" points to the "position that feminists worldwide have taken against the process of globalization of the economy, the demise of the nation state, and the development of a global mass culture as well as pointing to the nascent global women's studies research into the ways in which globalization affects women around the globe" (Mendoza, 2002, p. 314; see also Grewal & Kaplan, 2005; 1994). Gail Lewis describes the "unsafe travel" of intersectionality to contexts other than the United States. For example, she explores the unwillingness of European feminists to mobilize an analysis of race when advancing an intersectionality framework. Lewis explains: "how intersectionality travels suggest that there is a deep anxiety traceable in the reception of, and debates about, intersectionality that have arisen as it has traveled from the feminism that black women and other women of color have fashioned in the United States" (2013, p. 873). There are other "travels" that intersectionality has made that are equally concerning. The influence of intersectionality as a Western analytic tool is evident in its increasing depoliticization and its "co-optation . . . in the corporate university" evidenced by new research institutes dedicated to intersectionality, thematic conferences in a number of disciplines, dedicated journals, and mission statements of women's and gender studies programs (Nash, 2014, p. 45). These forms of institutionalization highlight how intersectionality fails to live up to the political goals of feminist movements. Robin Wiegman describes this process as the temporal impossibility of intersectionality. She argues that "intersectionality will always disappoint, since the 'political desires' that animate intersectionality are always greater than the analytic's ability to enact social justice" (Wiegman, 2012, p. 240). The depoliticization of intersectionality is arguably intensified in the context of social media where direct political interventions are mediated by online environments.

For example, one of the main critiques of intersectionality has been that it offers little utility for direct political action and solidarity movements, a problem intensified by the use of social media. As Nagarajan explains:

> Increasing our collective vocabulary alone is not a sign of success. What matters is the impact this has on the movement and through this on wider society as a whole. Yet, many of us seem to have decided to prioritise tweeting about or writing about or talking about theoretical concepts instead. Social media creates a tendency to be sucked away into discussions rather than making conscious decisions to do so. I cannot be the only person to have become engrossed in writing or tweeting only to realise that it is 3am in the morning, I have not done the activist work I planned to do and I have to be up in a few hours. What are we not doing because so many of our resources as a movement are taken up with this? There has not been enough of a coherent, concerted feminist response to closures of violence against women services, the removal of legal aid, the conditions in factories overseas where the clothes and equipment we use are made, attacks on the rights of immigrants, or changes in the benefits system. (Nagarajan, 2014)

Indeed, Indigenous feminists have long demonstrated the fault lines inherent in an intersectional approach. In the Canadian context, there has been a robust dialogue concerning the relationship between Indigenous knowledge and the feminist concept of intersectionality. Although some Indigenous people find that "intersectionality has been useful for making connections between Indigenous knowledge and other epistemologies, or for making sense of colonial ideologies and institutional frameworks" (Intersectionality Research and Social Policy, 2012, p. 3; see also Simpson, 2009), others suggest that "academic terms such as 'intersectionality' should not be needed to legitimize Indigenous knowledge, particularly as the revitalization of Indigenous language and concepts are integral to self-determination (Intersectionality Research and Social Policy, 2012, p. 3). Indigenous women have expressed how an idea of intersectionality has always been a part of Indigenous ways of knowing: "this is a new term, but I've been living it since I was a child" (p. 2–3). In addition, many Indigenous feminists and activists experience a large gulf between the priorities of academic feminism and the real issues in the lives of Indigenous women and other women of colour.

> We are not equal when initiatives to achieve gender equality have reverted yet again to "saving people" and making decisions for them, rather than supporting their right to self-determination, whether it's engaging in sex work or wearing a niqaub. So when feminism itself has become its own form of oppression, what do we have to say about it? Western notions of polite discourse are not the norm for all of us, and just because we've got some new and hot language like "intersectionality" to use in our talk, it doesn't necessarily change things in our walk (i.e., actually *being* anti-racist). (Emphasis in original. Yee, 2011, p. 12)

Indigenous feminists prioritize the goal of decolonization. Intersectionality may be an insufficient framework for addressing the issues of land theft, sovereignty, and decolonization of Indigenous communities in colonization (see also Canon & Sunseri, 2011).

As previously explored, intersectionality emerged from Black feminist theorizing in the United States and has proliferated to include an approach where race, class, gender, sexuality, dis/ability (and sometimes nation, in the context of transnational feminism) are incorporated into a theoretical and methodological approach. As Smith states:

> Because the United States is balanced upon notions of white supremacy and heteropatriarchy, everyone living in the country is not only racialized and gendered, but also has a relationship to settler colonialism. Indigenous feminist theories offer new and reclaimed ways of thinking through not only how settler colonialism has impacted Indigenous and settler communities, but also how feminist theories can imagine and realize different modes of nationalism and alliances in the future. (Smith in Arvin, Tuck, & Morrill, 2013, p. 9)

The challenge is to advocate for an approach to intersectionality (and feminism in general) that takes into consideration the paradigmatic nature of colonialism, and settler colonialism in particular, in structuring power relations (for all women, including Indigenous women) in the Western world. As Tiffany Lethabo King suggests, "Black Feminist Studies have developed rigorous modes of inquiry and analysis that result in multiple theorizations of how Black female gender formation occurs during slavery. Seldom do [we] consider the Black female figure in relation to settler colonial power" (King, 2013, pp. 2–3). Similarly, white feminist theorizing does not position whiteness in relation to, and as a construction of, settler colonialism. Maile Arvin, Eve Tuck, and Angie Morrill (2013) argue that Native feminism (which they define as "as those theories that make substantial advances in understandings of the connections between settler colonialism and both heteropatriarchy and heteropaternalism" [p. 11]) poses five distinct challenges to mainstream feminist and gender and women's studies. Indeed, these challenges can also be directed at certain strands of critical race and anti-racist feminism.

1. "To problematize and theorize the intersections of settler colonialism, heteropatriarchy, and heteropaternalism" (p. 14);
2. "To refuse the erasure of Indigenous women within gender and women's studies and reconsider the implications of the end game of (only) inclusion" (p. 17);
3. "To actively seek alliances in which differences are respected and issues of land and tribal belonging are not erased in order to create solidarity, but rather, relationships to

settler colonialism are acknowledged as issues that are critical to social justice and political work that must be addressed" (p. 19);

4. "To recognize the persistence of Indigenous concepts and epistemologies, or ways of knowing" (p. 21);

5. "To question how the discursive and material practices of gender and women's studies and the academy writ large may participate in the dispossession of Indigenous peoples' lands, livelihoods, and futures, and to then divest from these practices" (p. 25).

These challenges represent not only goals for the future of feminist theorizing but also deep fractures in contemporary feminist movements. What would it mean to address sovereignty and land in feminist struggles over reproduction and child care? What would it mean address the structure of settler colonialism and heteropatriarchy in the context of labour, migration, and immigration? What would it mean to think about Indigenous ways of knowing that does not descend into tokenized inclusion or New Age symbols for white consumption? How to keep the history of anti-Black racism at the forefront of feminist theorizing without subsuming Indigenous feminists concerns about land, sovereignty, and decolonization? How does the history of forced migration and immigration relate to Black enslavement and Indigenous genocide? What does it mean to work toward a feminist future that is motivated by the goal of decolonization?

CONCLUSION

This chapter has addressed some of the ways in which feminist interventions about race, Indigeneity, and colonialism challenge, rearticulate, and redirect feminist theory and feminist projects. Identifying race and Indigeneity through a historical framework that considers the emergence of race through colonization and slavery in the Western world permits and compels an analysis of the centrality of the writing of women of colour and Indigenous women to feminist projects. Intersectionality is a paradigmatic feature of feminist concerns about race (The Combahee River Collective, 1977; Crenshaw, 2011; Puar, 2005; Razack, 2008). Yet, intersectionality fails in its obfuscation of settler colonialism and processes of globalization. The writers and theorists in the chapter inspire a reconsideration of feminist engagement with social, legal and political struggles.

Endnotes

1. The word Indigeneity is derived from the word Indigenous. Legally, politically, socially, and culturally, Indigenous peoplehood is generally based on: 1. "Self-identification as indigenous peoples at the individual level and accepted by the community as their member;" 2. "Historical continuity with pre-colonial and/or pre-settler societies;" 3. "Strong links to territories and surrounding natural resources;" 4. "Distinct social, economic or political systems;" 5. "Distinct language culture and beliefs;" 6. "Form non-dominant groups of society;" 7. "Resolve to maintain and reproduce their ancestral environments and system as distinctive peoples and communities." (United Nations Permanent Forum on Indigenous Peoples, n.d.)

2. Retrieved from *New World Encyclopedia*, Definition "Colonialism."

3. www.idlenomore.ca/
4. Post-colonial theory is an interdisciplinary field of study that focuses on the historical, political, economic, cultural, legal, and social effects of colonialism. Although the "post" in post-colonialism carries the connotation of *after* colonialism, "it has been suggested that it is more helpful to think of post-colonialism not just as coming literally after colonialism and signifying its demise, but more flexibly as the contestation of colonial domination and the legacies of colonialism." (Loomba, 1998, p. 16)
5. See http://nationsrising.org/tag/itendshere/

Discussion Questions

1. What are "race" and racialization? What are colonialism and imperialism? What is settler colonialism? Why are land and sovereignty central to Indigenous women's lives and resistance strategies?
2. What is intersectionality? What is the genealogy of the concept of intersectionality in feminist theorizing? What are some of the critiques of intersectionality?
3. What challenges does Indigenous women's theorizing pose for mainstream feminism and for critical race and anti-racist feminism?
4. Look for images in the dominant culture that depict particular ideas about race and racialization, or ideas about Indigenous people. How might some of the ideas advanced in this chapter assist in analyzing these images? How can feminist perspectives on race, Indigeneity, and colonialism assist with providing an analysis of these images?

Bibliography

Agnew, Vijay. (2007). ***Interrogating race and racism***. Toronto, ON: University of Toronto Press.

Amadahy, Z. & Lawrence, B. (2010). Indigenous peoples and black people in Canada: Settlers or allies? In A. Kempf (Ed.). ***Breaching the Colonial contract: Anti-colonialism in the US and Canada*** (pp. 105–136). New York, NY: Springer Publishing.

Amnesty International. (2004). ***Stolen sisters: A human rights response to discrimination against Indigenous women in Canada***. Retrieved from www.amnesty.ca/research/reports/stolen-sisters-a-human-rights-response-to-discrimination-and-violence-against-indig

Anderson, B. (2006). ***Imagined communities: Reflections on the origin and spread of nationalism***. London, UK; New York, NY: Verso.

Anderson, K. (2000). ***Recognition of being: Reconstructing native womanhood***. Toronto, ON: Second Story Press.

Anderson, K. (2010). Native women, the body, land, and narratives of contact and arrival. In H. Lessard, J. Webber, & R. Johnson, (Eds.), ***Storied communities: The role of narratives of contact and arrival in constituting political community***. Vancouver, BC: UBC Press.

Arvin, M., Tuck, E., & Morrill, A. (2013). Decolonizing feminism: challenging connections between settler colonialism and heteropatriarchy. ***Feminist Formations***, ***25***(1), 8–34.

Backhouse, C. (1999). ***Colour-coded: A legal history of racism in Canada, 1900–1950.*** Toronto, ON: University of Toronto Press, Scholarly Publishing Division.

Bambara, T. C., Moraga, C., & Anzaldua, G. (1984). ***This bridge called my back: Writings by radical women of color*** (2nd ed.). New York, NY: Kitchen Table/Women of Color.

Bannerji, H. (2000). ***Dark side of the nation: Essays on multiculturalism, nationalism, and gender***. Toronto, ON: Canadian Scholars' Press Inc.

Calliste, A. & Dei, G. (2003). *Anti-racism feminism: critical race and gender studies.* Halifax, NS: Fernwood Publishing.

Cannon, M. & Sunseri, L. (Eds.). (2011). *Racism, colonialism and indigeneity in Canada: A reader*. Toronto, ON: Oxford University Press.

The Combahee River Collective. (1977). The Combahee River Collective Statement. Retrieved from www.sfu.ca/iirp/documents/Combahee%201979.pdf

Collins, P. H. (2000). *Black feminist thought: Knowledge, consciousness, and the politics of empowerment*. New York, NY: Routledge.

Crenshaw, K. W. (2011). Demarginalizing the intersection of race and sex: A black feminist critique of antidiscrimination doctrine, feminist theory, and antiracist politics. In H. Lutz, M. Vivar, & L. Supik, (Eds.), *Framing intersectionality: debates on a multi-faceted concept in gender studies.* (pp. 25–42). Surrey, England: Ashgate Press.

Cooper, A. (2006). *The hanging of Angelique: The untold story of Canadian slavery and the burning of old Montreal.* Toronto, ON: Harper Perennial Canada.

Crenshaw, K. (1991). Mapping the margins: Intersectionality, identity politics, and violence against women of color. *Stanford Law Review*, *43*(124), 1241–1299.

Davis, Angela Y. (2003). *Are prisons obsolete?* New York, NY: Seven Stories Press, 2003.

Dei, G. (2012). Revisiting the intersection of race, class, gender in anti-racism discourse. In V. Zawilski (Ed.), *Inequality in Canada: A reader on the intersections of gender, race and class* (2nd ed.). Toronto: Oxford University Press.

Dua, E. & Robertson, A. (1999). *Scratching the surface: Canadian anti-racist feminist thought*. Toronto, ON: Women's Press.

Fanon, F., & Philcox, R. (2008). *Black skin, white masks*. New York, NY; Berkeley, CA: Grove Press.

Goldberg, D. T. (1993). *Racist culture: Philosophy and the Politics of meaning*. Oxford UK; Cambridge, MA: Wiley-Blackwell.

Grewal, I., & Kaplan, C. (1994). *Scattered hegemonies: Postmodernity and transnational feminist practices*. Minneapolis, MN: University of Minnesota Press.

Grewal, I., & Kaplan, C. (2005). *An introduction to women's studies: Gender in a transnational world* (2nd ed.). Boston, MA: McGraw-Hill Humanities/Social Sciences/Languages.

Harris, A. P. (1990). Race and essentialism in feminist legal theory. *Stanford Law Review*, 581–616.

Hersh, S. M. (2004, May 3). Torture at Abu Ghraib. *The New Yorker*. Retrieved from www.newyorker.com/magazine/2004/05/10/torture-at-abu-ghraib

hooks, b. (2000). *Feminist theory: From margin to center*. Pluto Press.

Hunt, S. E. (2007). Excerpt from Trans/formative identities: Narrations of decolonization in mixed-race and transgender lives. MA Thesis, University of Victoria. Retrieved from www.sfu.ca/iirp/documents/Hunt%202007.pdf

Institute for Intersectionality Research and Policy (2012). Summary of themes: Dialogue on intersectionality and indigeneity. April 26, 2012. Retrieved from www.sfu.ca/iirp/documents/Indigeneity%20dialogue%20summary.pdf

Johar Schueller, M. (2005). Analogy and (white) feminist theory: Thinking race and the color of the cyborg body. *Signs 31*(1), 63–92.

Kauanui, J. Kēhaulani. (2008). Colonialism in equality: Hawaiian sovereignty and the question of U.S. civil rights. *South Atlantic Quarterly 107*(4), 635–36.

Kelly, J. (1998). *Under the gaze: Learning to be black in white society.* Halifax, NS: Fernwood Publishing.

King, T. L. (2013). *In the clearing: Black female bodies, space and settler colonial landscapes*. PhD Dissertation. Retrieved from http://drum.lib.umd.edu/handle/1903/14525

Kino-nda-niimi Collective. (Ed.). (2014). *The winter we danced: Voices from the past, the future, and the idle no more movement*. Winnipeg, MB: Arbeiter Ring Publishing.

Kline, M. (1989). Race, racism, and feminist legal theory. *Harvard Women's Law Journal*, *12*, 115.

Lawrence, B. (2002). Rewriting histories of the land: Colonization and indigenous resistance in eastern Canada. In S. Razack. (Ed.). *Race, space, and the law: Unmapping a white settler society*. Toronto, ON: Between the Lines.

Lawrence, B. & Dua, E. (2005). Decolonizing antiracism. *Social Justice 32*(4), 120–143.

Lewis, G. (2013). Unsafe travel: Experiencing intersectionality and feminist displacements. *Signs*, *38*(4), 869–892.

Loomba, A. (1998). *Colonialism/postcolonialism*. London, UK; New York, NY: Routledge.

Lorde, A. (1984). Age, race, class and sex: Women redefining difference. In *Sister outsider: Essays and speeches* (pp. 114–123). Freedom, CA: Crossing Press.

Maracle, L. (2003). *I am woman*, (2nd ed.). Vancouver, BC: Press Gang.

McCall, L. (2005). The complexity of intersectionality. *Signs*, *30*(3), 1771–1800.

McClintock, A. (1995). *Imperial leather: Race, gender, and sexuality in the colonial contest*. New York, NY: Routledge.

Mendoza, B. (2002). Transnational feminisms in question. *Feminist Theory*, *3*(3), 295–314.

Minh-Ha, T. T. (1989). *Woman, native, other: Writing postcoloniality and feminism*. Bloomington, IN: Indiana University Press.

Mohanty, C. T. (1988). Under Western eyes: Feminist scholarship and colonial discourses. *Feminist Review*, (30), p. 61–88.

Monture, P. (1990). Now that the door is open: First Nations and law school experience. *Queen's Law Journal 15*(2), 179–216.

Monture, P. & McGuire, P. (Eds.) (2009). *First voices: An aboriginal women's reader*. Toronto, ON: Inanna Publications.

Monture-Angus, P. (2003). *Thunder in my soul: A Mohawk woman speaks*. Halifax, NS: Fernwood Books Ltd.

Murdocca, C. (2013). *To right historical wrongs: Race, gender, and sentencing in Canada*. Vancouver, BC: UBC Press.

Nagarajan, C. (2014, February 24). Enough talk about intersectionality. Let's get on with it. openDemocracy. Retrieved from www.opendemocracy.net/transformation/chitra-nagarajan/enough-talk-about-intersectionality-lets-get-on-with-it

Nash, J. C. (2008). Re-thinking intersectionality. *Feminist Review*, *89*(1), 1–15.

Nash, J. C. (2014). Institutionalizing the margins. *Social Text*, *32*(1 118), 45–65.

Native Women's Association of Canada. (n.d.). *Fact sheet: missing and murdered Aboriginal women and girls*. Retrieved from www.nwac.ca/wp-content/uploads/2015/05/2010-Fact-Sheet-Atlantic-MMAWG

Native Women's Association of Canada. (2010). Culturally relevant gender based models of reconciliation. Retrieved from www.nwac.ca/files/reports/Culturally%20Relevant%20Gender%20Based%20Models%20of%20RECONCILIATION.pdf

Philip, Nourbese M. (1992). *Frontiers: Essays and writings on racism and culture 1984–1992.* Stratford, ON: Mercury Press.

Puar, J. K. (2005a). On torture: Abu Ghraib. *Radical History Review*, *93*, 13–38.

Puar, J. K. (2005b). Queer times, queer assemblages. *Social Text, 3–4*(84–85), 121–139.

Puar, J. K. (2 May 2008). Q&A with Jasbir Puar [Interview]. *Darkmatter Journal*. Retrieved from www.darkmatter101.org/site/2008/05/02/qa-with-jasbir-puar/

Ranchod-Nilsson, S. & Tetreault, M. A. (2003). *Women, states and nationalism: At home in the nation?* London, England: Routledge.
Razack, S. (1998). *Looking white people in the eye: Gender, race, and culture in courtrooms and classrooms*. Toronto, ON; Buffalo, NY: University of Toronto Press, Scholarly Publishing Division.
Razack, S. (2002). *Race, space, and the law: Unmapping a white settler society*. Toronto, ON: Between the Lines.
Razack, S. (2008). *Casting out: The eviction of Muslims from western law and politics*. Toronto, ON: University of Toronto Press, Scholarly Publishing Division.
Razack, S. (2014). Equality is not a high standard Patricia Monture: 1958–2010. [Editorial] *Canadian Journal of Women and the Law/Revue Femmes et Droit*, *26*(1), i–iii.
Said, E. W. (1979). *Orientalism*. New York, NY: Vintage.
Sharma, N. & Wright, C. (2009). Decolonizing resistance, challenging colonial states. *Social Justice 35*(3), 120–138.
Simpson, A. (2014). *Mohawk interruptus: Political life across the borders of settler states*. Durham, NC: Duke University Press.
Simpson, J. (2009). *Everyone belongs: A toolkit for applying intersectionality*. Ottawa: CRIAW/ICREF. Retrieved from http://criaw-icref.ca/sites/criaw/files/Everyone_Belongs_e.pdf
Simpson, L.B. (2008). *Lighting the eighth fire: The liberation, resurgence, and protection of indigenous nations*. Winnipeg, MB: Arbeiter Ring Publications.
Smith, A. (2005). *Conquest: Sexual violence and American Indian genocide*. Cambridge, MA: South End Press.
Smith, A. (2010). Indigeneity, settler colonialism, white supremacy. *Centre for World Dialogue: Global Dialogues*. *1*(2). Retrieved from www.worlddialogue.org/content.php?id=488
Solorzano, D. G. (1998). Critical race theory, race and gender microaggressions, and the experience of Chicana and Chicano scholars. *International Journal of Qualitative Studies in Education*, *11*(1), 121–136.
Spivak, G. C. (1980). Can the subaltern speak? In C. Nelson & L. Grossberg (Eds.), *Marxism and the interpretation of culture*. Chicago, IL: University of Illinois Press.
Stewart, F. E. (2013). (Doctoral Dissertation). *Naturalizing Canada: Settler colonial "wilderness" and the making of race and place.* Toronto, ON: Social and Political Thought, York University.
St. Denis, V. (2011). Rethinking cultural theory in Aboriginal education. In M. Cannon & Sunseri, L. (Eds.), *Racism, colonialism and indigeneity in Canada: A reader*, (pp. 163–182). Don Mills, ON: Oxford University Press.
Sunseri, L. (2000). Moving beyond the feminism versus nationalism: An anti-colonial feminist perspective on aboriginal liberation struggles. *Canadian Woman Studies 20*(2), 143–148.
Thobani, S. (2007). *Exalted subjects: Studies in the making of race and nation in Canada*. Toronto, ON: University of Toronto Press.
United Nations Permanent Forum on Indigenous Peoples, (n.d.) Factsheet: Who are Indigenous Peoples? Retrieved from www.un.org/esa/socdev/unpfii/documents/5session_factsheet1.pdf
Walcott, R. (2009). *Black like who?: Writing black Canada*. London, ON: Insomniac Press.
Wiegman, R. (2012). *Object lessons*. Durham, NC: Duke University Press Books.
Winant, H. (2000). Race and race theory. *Annual Review of Sociology*, *26*, 169–185.
Yee, J. (2011). *Feminism for real: Deconstructing the academic industrial complex of feminism*. Canadian Centre for Policy Alternatives. Retrieved from www.policyalternatives.ca/publications/ourschools-ourselves/feminism-real

INTRODUCTION

The late 20th century saw a global explosion of attention to women's rights. In 1975, the United Nations announced the United Nation's Decade for Women to raise awareness of international women's rights. Four world conferences were held between 1975 and 1985 during which women from all over the world gathered to discuss such issues as gender discrimination, violence against women, poverty, health, armed conflict, the economy, the rights of girls, and the environment. Since these initial meetings, research on global gender inequality has increased immensely. Of women worldwide 35% have experienced gendered violence in their lives (UN Women, 2014). Of all women who are employed, 50% work in vulnerable employment in the informal economy where there are no working regulations or protections for workers, such as sexual harassment policies and the range of other workplace protections from injury and exploitation that some take for granted (UN Women, 2014). There is now growing consensus around the world that mobilizing for gender equality is a global project for the 21st century as well.

Transnational feminism constitutes a framework that can be used to address the challenges of working toward gender equality globally. Transnational feminism can be thought of as a two-pronged approach that analyzes shifts and changes in gender relations globally and builds feminist communities of resistance across and against borders. As a theoretical paradigm, transnational feminism examines how gender equality is manifested geographically (in various locations), and also traces historical structures of inequality.

Transnational feminism is specifically concerned with how colonialism and imperialism map onto current forms of global gender inequality. According to Ania Loomba (2005), colonialism can be defined as "conquest and control of other people's lands and goods" (p. 8). It may include the direct or indirect control of land and people by foreign occupiers, and in some cases, the settling of foreign populations and the displacement of those indigenous to the land (for example, Canada). Imperialism can be understood as the cultural and economic dependency and control over people and land that ensures that labour and markets are opened to imperial powers (p. 11). Transnational feminists work from the assumption that colonial and imperial projects have and continue to alter gender relations in significant ways that intersect with issues of health, poverty, the economy, and the environment (for more on colonialism and imperialism, please refer to chapter 2). They also acknowledge that colonial and imperial projects have an impact on how these global issues are represented and discussed in feminist scholarship. Transnational feminists contend that current imperial projects, including dominant forms of economic globalization, affect women's lives and the ways in which feminists can align themselves in acts of global solidarity against systems of oppression.

This chapter offers an introduction to transnational feminist theories and activisms. First, this chapter will explain the concept of "transnational" by distinguishing transnational feminism from the terms "global" and "international" feminism. Second, this chapter will explore the differences between "global feminism" and transnational feminism. Third, the chapter will outline three issues of global significance where transnational feminists have made specific interventions: migration, representation of global women's issues, and violence against women. Fourth, feminist mobilizations across borders will be explored. By working through these key questions and issues, this chapter focuses on how power operates transnationally and how—with both successes and failures—transnational feminists are organizing and agitating for gender equality across borders.

GLOBALIZATION, LOCAL/GLOBAL, AND THE TRANSNATIONAL

Globalization is a highly contested term and yet an essential one for transnational feminists.[1] Globalization can be described as the increased movement and flows of peoples, information, and consumer culture across borders (Naples, 2002, p. 8). For many, the term globalization might conjure images of the United States' companies such as McDonald's opening in Tanzania and Starbucks serving its coffee in Shanghai. The term might also evoke images of people crossing borders for holiday travel, of bananas from Latin America being imported into Canada, and of receiving cold calls from a United States' company that has outsourced its work to India. The term globalization appeals to people's optimistic visions of an interconnected world, where national identities and borders are becoming less important to the ways in which individuals move and interact, the services and goods people can access, and how companies do business. The largest corporations in the world, including Nestlé and Shell, are called multinational corporations (MNCs) or transnational corporations, meaning that these companies spread their work around the world, which is facilitated by processes of globalization.

Importantly, globalization has winners and losers. Critics of globalization say the costs outweigh the benefits since the benefits are not equally distributed. For Marchand and Runyan (2011), the term "globalization" is coded language that gives a positive spin on projects and processes that are actually imperialist in nature. They use the term "globalization-cum-imperialism" to denote the ways in which the term globalization masks the powerful forces behind changes in economies and cultures that create conditions in which some win and some loose. For example, while goods may flow across national borders more frequently, these flows are unequal in their volume and the profits are not shared in equitable portions with producers. For example, many Northern governments are known to subsidize domestic farmers in their agro-industries. Government subsidies, or small amounts of money distributed in various ways to local producers, allow domestic farmers to sell their goods on the global economy at lower costs. These cheaper goods can then flood Southern markets and push domestic farmers in poorer countries out of business because they were produced at a much lower cost by the original producer. This situation likely means that a Jamaican farmer is more vulnerable to unemployment while a farmer in the United States can be more assured of a market for her product, due to the ways that food production is now globally orchestrated.

Globalization has shifted cultures, social interactions, political structures, and national economies. Taken together, the complex processes of globalization have resulted in jobs for women opening up worldwide. Unfortunately, the most under-paid, under-valued, and exploitative jobs seem to be designated for women. A feature of current forms of globalization is that it is highly gendered, in that many women around the world, who are formally employed, work in export manufacturing and/or must migrate for work and leave their families behind. Feminist scholars use the term "feminization of labour" to mark this shift in the global economy. The pressure to reorient national economies to manufacture for export has feminized the global labour force. International financial institutions, including the International Monetary Fund and World Bank, often require poorer countries to gain capital through a reorientation of their economies for the export of goods and services. Low wages are attractive to investors in export-oriented economies because more profit can be derived if lower wages are paid. Given that many export-dependent countries are located in the Southern Hemisphere, these economic advantages come through the increasing exploitation of racialized women as the employees of choice in manufacturing and low-paid service and informal economies. The stereotype of nimble-fingered, inherently docile, and hardworking Third-World[2] women is used to justify their suitability for repetitive and monotonous work (Bergeron, 2006; Eisenstein, 2009; Erevelles, 2006; Fernandez-Kelly, 1983).

For feminists concerned with the negative impact of globalization on gender relations and on women in particular, globalization is neither inevitable nor unchanging, but rather a project shaped by social and political forces. In other words, globalization is a process, and therefore, it can be resisted. Marchand and Runyan (2011) find the term "global economic restructuring" a more accurate and effective one to describe the project of globalization-cum-imperialism. This process generally includes the dismantling of nationally funded social services and health care in favour of putting these services into an open market for private sector companies to own, deliver, and profit from. By seeing globalization through the lens of economic restructuring, the gendered impacts are more visible for study and can be challenged. For example, a major impact of globalization has been the increase in women's unpaid labour. Women do about 70% of the household work globally (Desai, 2002). Due to global economic restructuring, women are doing more unpaid care work than ever before. When countries liberalize their economies, many state supports for reproductive labour are effectively removed and women end up picking up the slack. Feminists have termed this the "double-burden" or "triple-burden" of labour where they perform not only paid work in the market and unpaid work for their families, but also the caregiving and domestic labour that might otherwise have been subsidized by the state. Among the impacts of global economic restructuring is also the increase in the price of goods, including food, that makes women more vulnerable to malnutrition as they often eat last after providing for family members (Desai, 2002, p. 20).

Transnational feminists conceptualize global economic restructuring as a useful way of understanding global power systems and cultural flows—and as a starting point for enacting change. This way of thinking about globalization is important for transnational feminist theories because scholars are interested in mapping changing politics, cultures, and economies and contributing to positive change.

Transnational feminist theory invites people to think differently about how culture is also subject to globalizing forces. Globalization has not meant that cultures have become homogeneous nor has it meant that the flow of Western products, services, and ideas proceed uniformly from the West to other countries (Marchand & Runyan, 2011). Certainly, colonialism and imperialism shape the ways in which culture and capital flow, and it is important for transnational feminists to map how this happens as well as to note resistance to it. One way to think about how culture flows unpredictably under globalization is to take the example of the Mattel toy, the Barbie doll. In their canonical text *Scattered Hegemonies: Postmodernity and Transnational Feminist Practices*, Grewal and Kaplan (1994) use the example of the consumption of Barbie in India to describe the globalization of culture. Challenging the assumption that cultural flows are unidirectional (i.e., from the West to "the rest"), Grewal and Kaplan ask where, by whom, and for what reason some elements of culture are consumed and not others. Since Barbie is sold in India dressed in a sari while Ken is dressed in "American" clothes, some American culture is being consumed, but India's culture is also changing Barbie. Grewal and Kaplan ask that people think about what a Barbie dressed in a sari might communicate about the interplay between the global and the local, suggesting that although an American multinational corporation can impose culture, so can the recipient influence its production to a certain extent.

More than Barbie's dress, Grewal (2005) notes that most Barbie dolls sold in the United States in the 1990s were made in China, Malaysia, and Indonesia. The plastics of the doll were made in Taiwan from oil bought from Saudi Arabia. Her hair was made in Japan and the packaging was made in the United States. According to Grewal, the labour cost associated with Barbie was about 35 cents per Barbie and the labour was performed primarily by poorly paid Asian women in assembly line work. Most of the cost of Barbie is associated with shipping, marketing, and profit for Mattel. The example of Barbie demonstrates that the globalized production and consumption of Barbie is multidirectional and gendered in both labour and consumption. It also shows that the poor, Southern nations are positioned as sites of resources for the West where captive labour and markets are opened to Western powers through the project of globalization-cum-imperialism.

Local/Global

Transnational feminists are particularly concerned with the terms "local" and "global." Global is often used to denote the workings of globalization at a level that is supra-national, or transgresses state borders. You may have heard the phrase "think global, act local," which promotes resistance to globalization. Resisting the harmful effects of globalization has involved taking local action, such as purchasing food at farmer's markets or checking the labels on clothing to ensure it has been traded fairly. These are complex consumer practices, and transnational feminists help us understand that the local and the global are not two distinct entities; instead, they are mutually constitutive spaces that cannot be separated (Grewal & Kaplan, 1994). In other words, the local and global are two interconnected aspects of the same phenomenon.

The division between thinking globally and acting locally makes little sense to many people who are already integrated into structures of globalization in their locality. For example, in 2013, a garment factory (Rana Plaza) in Bangladesh collapsed killing over 1000 people and injuring thousands of others (BBC, 2013; Uddin, 2013). Although a crack in the building was known to be dangerous, workers were encouraged to return to work after being evacuated a few days before the collapse. Over 4 million people work in clothing factories in Bangladesh. According to the Bangladesh Garment Manufacturers and Exporters Association, 85% of the workers are women and over four-fifths of its $20 billion in production is sent to the West (NBC News, 2013; The Guardian, 2013). The collapsed Rana Plaza building paints a disastrous but informative example of the interplay between local, national, and global events. Indeed, the Rana Plaza buildings were due for upgrades and structural renovations that were put off by the local companies overseeing the manufacturing of garments. Afterwards, numerous local people were arrested on charges of negligence. Nationally, the government of Bangladesh closed 18 other factories due to safety issues (BBC, 2013). Transnationally, activists called for boycotts of multinational corporations working in Bangladesh, such as The Gap and Canadian retailer Joe Fresh. Since the collapse of Rana Plaza, almost 200 transnational garment retailers have signed the Accord on Fire and Building Safety in Bangladesh (2013). This disaster, and the response to it, involves global economic systems, multinational corporations, national policies and legislation, local and global patriarchies (especially since most precarious work in this industry is done by women), historical forms of colonialism, imperialism, and consumer culture in the West. For transnational feminists, the collapse of Rana Plaza and the response to its collapse are indeed *transnational* since they cannot be made sense of without an understanding that the local and global are interconnected.

Transnational

According to Swarr and Nagar (2010), transnational feminist theory has grown out of two interconnected dialogues in the field of feminist studies: first, it has been employed by those seeking to question globalization and neo-liberalism, and to underscore social justice issues, including the creation of alliances across borders; and second, it has been used in feminist debates about Eurocentrism since the 1980s in feminist theory and writing, especially regarding issues of how stories of Other women lives (including questions of voice, authority, identity, and representation) cross borders. But the very meaning of the term transnational is contested among scholars in the fields of postcolonial, Third World, and international feminisms. Laura Briggs, Gladys McCormick, and J. T. Way (2008) suggest that transnationalism is an overused term, taking on very different meanings in multiple disciplines (p. 625). For example, the term transnational can indicate migratory processes and capital circulations, or transnational flows of people and goods. The term is sometimes used to signal the apparent powerlessness of the state to control trade and flows of people across its own borders. The term is also used to describe the world as borderless and interconnected. In fact, in the post–9/11 period especially, borders are very real and worthy of attention. Since passengers on commercial airlines attacked the New York World Trade Center on September 11, 2001, the way in which individuals cross some borders has changed dramatically. Some argue that in contrast to opening, borders are more entrenched and closed to some people than ever, and yet more open to capital. As Walia (2013) writes: "Capital, and the transnationalization of its production and consumption, is freely mobile across borders, while the people displaced as a consequence of the ravages of neoliberalism and imperialism are constructed as demographic threats and experience limited mobility" (p. 4). Border crossings, and our varied experiences with crossing borders based on gender, race, class, sexuality, ability, and citizenship status, can tell us how borders continue to matter under globalization. Feminist interpretations of the transnational that do not take borders, boundaries, and inequalities seriously risk hollowing out the concept. So rather than abandoning the term on account of its multiple and often conflicting usages, the term allows its users to challenge the flattening of power relations between states.

The use of the term "transnational," instead of "international" or "global," marks some feminist theorists' refusal to valorize inequitable global systems. International usually refers to relations *between* nations. Transnational does a better job of getting at the social, economic, cultural, and political flows that *transcend* the boundaries of the nation-state (Mann, 2012, p. 356). Karen Booth (1998) suggests that the term international denotes Western power systems founded by global inequalities, including the United Nations. As Radika Mongia (2007) argues, the term "international" denotes equality between nations and does not take into account the power differentials between nations. Nor, I would add, can it adequately acknowledge cases where multiple nations (some acknowledged, some unacknowledged) may exist within a single state, as in the case of many Indigenous nations. Using an anti-colonial analysis, she argues that the term international does not allow scholars to take into account the way in which nation-states are "co-produced through a complex array of related and relational historical events" (p. 384). Mongia (2007) sheds light on the inadequacy of the term international by exploring the work of the United Nations. At the United Nations (UN) only recognized sovereign nations can negotiate with other nations that are understood to be "equivalent" to one another. The UN and its many agencies, as an example of the "international," have a membership of only recognized sovereign nation-states. The functioning of the UN ahistoricizes the uneven co-production of nations in the post–Second World War period. Importantly, many former colonies and occupied territories were not sovereign at the time that the United Nations was established and could not obtain membership. Significantly, the UN Security Council is an unequal space where the United States has the power of a veto vote, and where the Western world holds the most power (Mongia, 2007, p. 410).

For many transnational feminists, the term "transnational" is also a corrective term for the "global" in some feminist studies. According to Naples (2002), the term "transnational" intertwines the global and the local and pays attention to the interplay between both sites, paying specific attention to how power operates within and between nations, and among and between women. "Global," on the other hand, has come to represent theorizing and political organizing that assumes natural and inevitable solidarities among women globally. For transnational feminists Grewal and Kaplan, "global feminism has elided the diversity of women's agency in favor of a universalized Western model of women's liberation that celebrates individuality and modernity" (1994, p. 17). In other words, global feminism has come to represent a kind of theorizing and organizing among feminists that presents Western women as more advanced, modern, and liberated than their Third World sisters, and enables them to "save" their sisters from backward, patriarchal, and traditional men. Post-colonial theorist Gayatri Chakravorty Spivak (1988) coined the phrase, "White men saving brown women from brown men" to describe the ways in which Third World women are too often positioned in Western scholarship as agentless and waiting to be rescued. While the term "global" is not always understood so negatively, transnational feminists have chosen the word "transnational" to repair what they see as the failures and shortcoming of global feminism, as discussed below.

To review, while a variety of scholars use the terms global, international, and transnational in many different ways, transnational feminists use the term transnational because they find it useful for feminist theorizing and organizing across and against borders, and for understanding globalization. Importantly, transnational feminist theorists continually reflect on the term transnational itself, especially its usage, and what it communicates.

GLOBAL FEMINISM AND TRANSNATIONAL FEMINISM: KNOWING THE DIFFERENCE

Transnational feminism is often conceptualized as an alternative to global feminism, and has come to dominate Western feminist interventions into issues related to globalization. In 1984, Robin Morgan published *Sisterhood Is Global: The International Women's Movement Anthology*. Morgan envisioned a global sisterhood as a network of women from around the world, working together to address women's issues. While this text is not representative of all global feminist theorizing, and Morgan is not the only scholar I might cite here, this book demonstrates the most problematic aspects of global feminism that transnational feminists aim to address. In the text, Morgan suggests that because women from many countries around the world contributed to the anthology, it represents the state of women's issues globally. Significantly, each chapter is devoted to women's issues in different countries but there is little analysis of the connections and power differentials between women and countries. The anthology implies that if feminists know more about women's issues nation by nation, they can see that women around the world have connections to one another on the basis of their shared experiences under patriarchy. Learning about experiences of oppression other than your own is clearly a very desirable political goal, but Morgan, as the anthology editor, invited certain women to publish in the text and had control over the publishing of the anthology. A Western feminist, she collected and controlled women's stories for the anthology and provided the language of sisterhood to bring the chapters together, thus allowing it to be framed through a Western lens. This is significant because transnational feminists not only question what stories about Other women are being told, but who has the power to tell these stories.

Transnational feminists are concerned with how stories are told. According to Chandra T. Mohanty (2003), academic curricula—including the very text you are reading—"tell[s] a story—or tells many stories" (p. 238). As already explored in this chapter, how feminists think about the local and the global, and think about, or do not think about, the connection between these two sites, matters. In the classroom, these stories matter as much as academic research on globalization. In her chapter "Under Western Eyes Revisited" from *Feminism without Borders: Decolonizing Theory, Practicing Solidarity*, Chandra T. Mohanty (2003) criticizes the process of "internationalizing" the gender and women's studies curriculum (p. 238). As demonstrated in the first section of this chapter, globalization, or what Marchand and Runyan (2011) call "global economic restructuring," has had a negative impact on women's lives transnationally. In the 1980s, gender and women's studies programs in the United States and Canada shifted their focus from centralizing North America to examining the impact on women of globalization. While the geographical focus of many classrooms changed during this period, global feminism often dominated studies of global women's issues.

The "internationalizing" of gender and women's studies curricula has often meant a narrow focus on a set of topics including garment export factories and female genital mutilation, and a destabilization of dominant subject positions, but through inclusion frameworks that stabilize almost everything else (Fernandez, 2013). This restricted outlook in feminist classrooms reflects some of the most troubling aspects of global feminism according to transnational feminists. Global feminist scholarship on the body and sexuality, and specifically on what in the West is commonly described as "female genital mutilation," is routinely embedded in what Grewal and Kaplan (2001) call "the binary axis of tradition-modern" (p. 669). In other words, scholarship on this subject habitually produces "traditional" subjects that are agentless in a backward culture in order to establish more "modern" Western subjects. For the authors, "the global feminist is one who has free choice over her body and a complete and intact, rather than a fragmented or surgically altered body, while the traditional female subject of patriarchy is forcibly altered . . . and deprived of choices or agency"(Grewal & Kaplan, 2001, pp. 669–670).

Mohanty's (2003) and Fernadez's (2013) analyses about how feminists teach and learn about Other women is a central feature of transnational feminism.[3] As a way of decolonizing curriculum, Mohanty offers a "comparative feminist studies" or "feminist solidarity" model for the classroom. To understand why this model is most successful for teaching and learning through a transnational feminist lens, it is important to first explore two less nuanced pedagogical models that are based on the premise that the student of gender and women's studies is universally white, middle class, and Western. What Mohanty calls the "Feminist as Tourist Model" involves "forays into non-Euro-American cultures" and showcases particularly sexist practices in those cultures. In this global feminist approach, students are encouraged to metaphorically travel around the world and learn how patriarchal, misogynist, and backward Other cultures are when compared with their own. In this model, it becomes the "white women's burden" to liberate her 'sisters' from oppression (Mohanty, 2003, p. 239). Difference and distance between women in the West and the "Third World" are solidified, and Western women confirm themselves as powerful, modern, and progressive. A second pedagogical model is the "Feminist as Explorer Model," wherein Other women are both the object and subject of knowledge, and the entire curriculum is devoted to countries other than the one in which the classroom is located. For example, a class using this model would teach about Latin America and Latin American women, but would not discuss the connections between where students are located and the places and people they are studying. This pedagogical strategy "internationalizes" the curriculum by emphasizing "distance from home" (Mohanty, 2003, p. 240).

Transnational feminist teaching practices suggest instead that a learning and teaching model based of feminist solidarity is desirable. Beginning from the premise that the local and global are defined as interconnected, rather than separate geographical territories, means that curriculum can help students discuss commonalities and difference among and between women. This pedagogical strategy also foregrounds the women's and gender studies classroom as a possible site for transnational solidarity and creates a space for teacher activism—by centring mutual responsibility to ending transnational oppressions, defining what Mohanty (2003) calls "common interests" around which feminists? globally can rally, and anchoring action in solidarity (and not saving, as is often the goal of global feminist curriculum).

The difference between global and transnational feminism might be best understood by looking at scholarship and claims for women's rights during the so-called War on Terror. In the aftermath of the attack on the New York World Trade Center, global feminism has been particularly occupied with the "binary axis of traditional-modern" that Grewal and Kaplan (2001) identify. Some Western feminists have concerned themselves with the alleged subordination of women under Islamic laws and governance, focusing specifically on women's bodily autonomy and even more specifically on veiling practices. Using the hijab, burqa, and niqab as a stand-in for nuanced analyses of women's lives, and specifically their religious and cultural practices, some Western feminists claim that "Eastern" women are pawns in a grand patriarchal scheme. Muslim women, especially those who wear the hijab, burqa, and niqab, are used as symbols for the cultural backwardness, social conservatism, and extremism of Islamic fundamentalism of the "East."

Jennifer Fluri (2009) uses the term "corporal modernity" to describe the ways in which the visibility of the female body has become a yardstick to measure a nation's level of modernity or "progress" in the post–9/11 era. She critiques the association of visibility of the female body with power, suggesting instead that lack of cultural and historical context ignores the ways in which the War on Terror has provided a political context for using the body and its coverings or lack thereof as a measure of liberation. In other words, women living in cultures that glorify the uncovering of the body are considered progressive, while those that support the covering of the body are regressive. This is a problematic and oversimplified formula for understanding gendered relations of power and women's agency. Fluri's work can be read as a criticism of global feminism's inattention to geography and history, and the lack of attention paid to the interplay between "home" and "abroad." Fluri and other scholars including Mahmood (2005), Thobani (2007), and Moallem (2005) maintain that what some Western feminists ignore is that the burqa and other veiling practices provide corporeal privacy in public space, and have allowed women to resist public patriarchal structures in their lives. Isolating veiling practices as symbolic of oppression does not accurately trace the cultural and political changes that lead women to wear, or take off, burqas, niqabs, and hijabs. Ignoring contextual analyses and the voices of Muslim women, global feminists have overwhelmingly argued that Muslim women are forced to act against their own human agency, or the innate sense of individual autonomy and desire for freedom against the weight of custom and tradition. Muslim women in this strand of global feminist theorizing are thought of as living with false consciousness or internalized patriarchy, and in need of saving by their liberated Western sisters (Abu-Lughod, 2002; Razack, 2008).

What is also missing from this global feminist discourse is an acknowledgment of the United States' role in women's loss of freedom in Taliban-controlled Afghanistan—a regime they supported during the Soviet occupation of the 1980s. In feminist rescue narratives, no mention is made of the Revolutionary Association of Women of Afghanistan (RAWA) that was established in 1977 and remains active in promoting human rights, health care, education, and democratic and secular rule in Afghanistan (Naples, 2002, p. 267). Instead, by employing the "traditional-modern binary axis," global feminist scholarship assumes that women are waiting to be saved (Grewal & Kaplan, 2001).

Given that transnational feminism is often presented as a reparative theoretical framework for "previous" feminisms (including global feminism), it is important to acknowledge the limits of this framework. While transnational feminist theory emerged out of theories from women of colour feminisms, third world feminisms, multicultural feminisms, and international feminisms, a variety of deployments of transnational feminism both continue and depart from these political and intellectual histories. Transnational feminist theorists often reflect on the field, how the term "transnational" is deployed, and the kinds of analyses and activism that the term transnational makes possible. As Swarr and Nagar (2010) maintain, transnational feminism is an unstable field that is critical of its own definitions and practices. Desai, Bouchard, and Detournay (2011) offer one such critique. They suggest that transnational feminism "is often seen to subsume women of color feminism" (p. 49). As explored briefly in Chapter 2, transnational feminism pays attention to the role of race, class, gender, and sexuality beyond the confines of the state borders. However, transnational feminists note that it is incorrect to assume that transnational feminism resolves racism and/or transcends the contributions of critical race or postcolonial feminisms. Some argue that transnational feminism removes the emphasis on race altogether. This critique has led scholars, including Adrien K. Wing (2000) to claim their work as "transnational critical race feminism" as a way to ensure that their scholarship is read and located within critical race *and* transnational feminist theoretical traditions.

Although the field is too broad to outline extensively here, this chapter turns now to sketch three focal issues of transnational feminism: migration, representation, and violence against women.

MIGRATION

The movements of culture, capital, and people under globalization are contradictory and complex. The tension between opening borders for the flows of global capital and culture and the desire of states to protect their borders from immigration is a major concern (Harvey, 2003; Walia, 2013). For transnational feminists, the increasing security measures at borders, especially in the post–9/11 period, is a concern. They argue that there are racist and imperialist dimensions to border security and control of individuals' movements, and a lack of justice-based responses to the effects of globalization (Magnet, 2011; Puar, 2007; Walia, 2013). While border crossings may be increasingly restricted by Western states, globalization simultaneously displaces people from poorer Southern regions due to instability, violence, and poverty. Migration has been and will likely continue to be a survival strategy for many.

"Care work" provides a good example of the ways in which migration is gendered and racialized. Care work is labour that is reproductive in nature, namely childrearing, elder care, and home care. One of the impacts of global economic restructuring has been the movement of women into the global workforce. These movements have resulted in a "crisis of care" that affects women around the world in different ways. In poorer Southern countries, global economic restructuring has pushed women into the workforce, and in the Western world, more women are working than ever before. While this represents increased economic independence for women, household duties have not been redistributed among members. In her foundational work, Arlie Hochschild (1989) found that women in the United States were working, on average, a full extra month above and beyond their productive duties. Calling this phenomenon the "second shift," Hochschild showed that unequal distribution of workload within households falls on women, or their community and family networks. When women are unable to work this "second shift," households seek employees to do this work for them. Families often hire low-paid child-care, home-care, and elder-care workers who are often un-unionized and have very few working rights and protections. Many women, in addition to taking care of their own children, provide child care for other families in their own homes because child care is un- or under-subsidized. Since most child care occurs within private homes, this issue remains a "private" issue and is considered a woman's personal responsibility. In Canada, this idea is reinforced by the fact that the Canada Revenue Agency (2015) provides a meagre universal child care benefit to individual families so they can choose their own child care options, rather than subsidize public child care across the country.

Global economic restructuring in the United States and Canada shapes the transnational migration patterns of women. Welfare state retrenchment in both countries means most families lack an adequate social safety net. In the United States, there is no guarantee of paid maternity or paternity leave, no public child care, and no universal health care system. In Canada, women working in the most precarious, piecemeal labour do not qualify for paid maternity leave, while paternity leave is often less valued, and women spend upwards of 30% of their annual income on publically available child care due to the lack of subsidized child care nationally (with the exception of the province of Quebec) (Macdonald & Friendly, 2014). Under increasing pressure from work and household-related needs, middle-class families have the option of hiring migrant workers to care for their children, especially relatively inexpensive live-in caregivers provided through the Canadian government's Live-in Caregiver Program (Citizenship and Immigration Canada, 2014).

Some families in economies like those of Canada and the United States find that public child care is too expensive, and they can only afford to hire private caregivers as long as they are inexpensive. Less privileged women from the poorer Southern nations are called on to fill this gap. Migration, according to Marchand and Runyan (2011), is "fashioned as the solution to child-care, eldercare, and healthcare crises in the North and un- and- under employment in the South" (p. 14). Ehrenreich and Hochschild (2003) use the phrase "global care chain" to denote the migration of women from poor, developing countries to developed ones as maids and nannies. Many countries, due to global economic restructuring and national debts, depend on remittances as a way to further develop their own economies (Rodriquez, 2008). Remittances are monetary transfers from foreign workers to their home country. For example, the Philippine state relies on the export of labour through national migration apparatuses. As Rodriquez (2008) suggests, "brokering workers" in this way ensures remittances; women who leave poorer countries for richer ones, as caregivers, send money home to their families, especially to their own children and to bolster their nation's economy. However, this leaves a major care gap in their home nations and households.

As I alluded to, the global care chain is not an informal network of gendered and racialized labour. Rather, governments in the West are responding to the known crisis of care by investing in transnational recruitment of women as maids and nannies. Ehrenreich and Hochschild (2003) call this the "female underside of globalization," where women in poorer countries migrate to do what is considered women's work in richer countries. The state is involved in this aspect of migration as governments, such as in the Philippines, for example, train women for "women's work" outside of the country, which includes training to conform to norms of gender and sexuality (Rodriquez, 2008). While care work is available transnationally, poorer nations must promote and market their women as the best in the field, and often the cheapest, to compete on a global scale. For Ehrenreich and Hochschild (2003), the international division of labour is about more than reproductive labour such as caring for infants and children. In fact, they claim that *feelings* are "distributive resources" (p. 23). In other words, migrant domestic workers also engage in emotional labour. Similar to women workers in export processing zones who are expected to perform a "docile and dexterous" femininity along the global assembly line, nannies and maids are expected to perform femininity by nurturing and acting lovingly.

REPRESENTATION

Transnational feminists emphasize the study of representation as a key site of feminist thought and activism. As Swarr and Nagar (2010) remind us, transnational feminism is a theoretical framework that intervenes in feminist debates about the issues of how stories of Other women's lives cross borders. Transnational feminists concerned with representation are particularly interested in questions of voice, authority, and identity since Western feminists are often telling stories of Other women's lives in their scholarship and in classrooms. They borrow from cultural studies theorist Stuart Hall (2013) and agree that studying representation is about understanding how "the words we use about them, the stories we tell about them, the images of them we produce, the emotions that we associate with them, the ways we classify and conceptualize them, and the values we place on them" give meaning to things (Hall, 2013, p. xix). To study the "production and circulation of meaning" of text, talk, and images about global women's issues, and more specifically Third World women, is important, particularly as certain types of research and media coverage may have harmful results. As such, they understand the study and use of representation as a very useful political strategy to effect change as well as an important practice in and of itself.

Decolonizing Feminist Thought

First published in 1984, Chandra Talpade Mohanty's canonical "Under Western Eyes: Feminist Scholarship and Discourses" critiqued Western feminist scholarship as misrepresenting Other women. In 2003, Mohanty republished the essay in her book *Feminism without Borders: Decolonizing Theory, Practicing Solidarity* and re-visited the original article to respond to the huge scholarly attention it had received. This text is now considered a "signal piece" in transforming the global frameworks of many United States feminists (Mann, 2012, p. 365). Mohanty's aim was to deconstruct United States feminist discourses, although it has been taken up in many other contexts. In other words, she was concerned with how Other women's stories were being represented in United States scholarship. She was particularly concerned with what she called the "third world woman" who appeared in most texts as a "singular monolithic subject" (Mohanty, 2003, p. 372). To use Mohanty's term, Third World women are often presented as part of a coherent group with similar interests and desires, regardless of their class, ethnic, or racial location. While marginal in the academy, Mohanty (2003) argues that feminist theory has "political effects and implications beyond the immediate feminist or disciplinary audience" (p. 21). She therefore challenges the way in which Third World women have historically been represented in Western feminist scholarship as homogeneously oppressed. Mohanty argues that representing Third World women as lacking agency is ineffectual for designing strategies to combat oppression globally.

Transnational feminist scholars concerned with representation attend to the kinds of language, storytelling practices, and images that circulate in a variety of areas. These include feminist scholarship, as well as popular media, humanitarian and international development campaigns, and global feminist activisms. As Mohanty maintains in "Under Western Eyes," Western feminist scholarship too often engages in representational practices that collapse differences between Third World women and erase their agency. In particular, she argues that women's experiences of oppression in specific contexts are erased in favour of more simplistic renderings of their lives. She terms this overused representational practice "third world difference." Here, Western women are represented as secular, modern, and in control of their bodies and lives in contrast to Third World women who are represented as traditional, backward, and oppressed by patriarchal culture and violent men. Third World women are rarely represented as resisting oppression from multiple levels and sites of power, and it is often traditional and patriarchal culture (embodied by men) that stands in for women's subordination, rather than deep analysis of global structures of power.

Mohanty is also concerned with how this category of Third World women allows Western feminists to assume expertise in Third World women's issues. Often, feminist scholars assume that all Third World women have common experiences, problems, and needs, and so, they must have similar goals. Western feminist scholarship needs to be historically specific and take into account the differences between Third World women and the concrete reality of their lives. She writes: "These arguments are not just against generalization as much as they are for careful, historically specific generalizations responsive to complex realties" (Mohanty, 2003, p. 377). For Mohanty, the first prong of a two-pronged project toward liberating all women from oppression globally is "deconstructing and dismantling" representations and the second is "building and constructing" new coalitions of feminists across borders (Mohanty, 2003, p. 17).

Decolonizing Feminist Research

As a response to what Mohanty calls colonized Western feminist discourses, transnational feminists aim to produce better, more accurate, and more ethical research. But Mohanty's call for careful, historically accurate representations that account for the differences among and between women and the realities of women's lives is difficult to produce. Some say that this caution has led to less cross-border research by feminists. Staeheli and Nagar (2002) argue that many Western feminists became overwhelmed with questions of representation, essentialisms, universalisms, power and privilege, and were at a loss when conducting fieldwork across borders. Richa Nagar (2003) charges that transnational feminist's focus on the study of representation at the expense of other types of empirical work has led to widening the gulf between Western academic theory and the "on-the-ground" priorities of Southern subjects (p. 359). In other words, Western feminists have become overly cautious of cross-border research, and this critical analysis of colonized representations has made many researchers anxious about how to tell Other women's stories. Briggs et al. (2008) claim that transnational feminist scholarship has the potential for transformative politics through "collaboration among academics and intellectuals located in publishing's First World (the United States and Europe, with access to international publics) and Third World (where knowledge, however erudite, seems to be of strictly "local" provenance)" (p. 44). This kind of collaboration would dramatically change the relationship of women to knowledge production across borders, and help to build solidarities among women while paying attention to power and privilege differentials.

One powerful quality of transnational feminism is the scholar's dedication to reflexivity. Feminist reflections have frequently revolved around questions of how feminists produce knowledge through research, how researchers can be accountable to those they study, and how to represent these stories ethically and within a social justice framework when academics publish their work. In the academy, researchers often use the "grassroots" or the "local" as sites of knowledge to be excavated. Transnational feminists complicate the term "grassroots" to constantly decolonize representations of women's issues transnationally. Naples (2002) argues that the idea of the grassroots is too often romanticized as a site where individuals are always resisting and never desiring or benefiting from globalization. The grassroots is also largely defined as a site for intervention by Western experts. For Priti Ramamurthy (2003), the grassroots is a site of both agency and contradiction. Using the term "perplexity," she maintains that desire, benefit, and resistance are all experienced by those who inhabit this site.

As Mohanty (2003) maintains, "testimonials, life stories and oral histories are a significant mode of remembering and recording experience and struggles" (p. 77). However, she warns that the current diversification of the Eurocentric canon by publishing culturally diverse stories—a marked academic trend—can contribute to an exoticization (the process of making something or someone seem different, alien, or Other) of "different" stories from women who write as "authentic truth-tellers." Thus, the mere presence of more writings from Other women within the academy does not mean a de-centring of knowledge production. The ways in which stories are shared, heard, read, and institutionally located are critical for scholarly interrogation. Mohanty argues that the point of transnational feminist praxis is not only to record Other women's stories in order to create cross-border connections. Rather, it is to take seriously how stories and memories are recorded, the way they are shared and read, and the way in which they are disseminated to a broad audience (2003, p. 78).

Sangtin Yatra/Playing with Fire: Feminist Thought and Activism through Seven Lives in India (2006) outlines some of the problems and possibilities of cross-border collaborations between Third World grassroots activists and Western academics. With few exceptions, Nagar (2003) claims that there are very few tools to execute transnational feminist projects, and thus, she proposes collaborative border crossings. *SangtinYatra/Playing with Fire* is set in Uttar Pradesh, India. It involves workers of a non-governmental organization with the pseudonym Nari Samata Yojana (NSY) who came together to write about their experiences of their individual social locations and their work. The Sangtin Collective brought together eight community-based activists with Richa Nagar, a women's studies scholar from the University of Minnesota. The writers composed autobiographies about issues such as childhood, womanhood, and sexuality in an intersectional analysis of class, caste, regional inequalities, and gender (Mohanty, 2006).

When the collective decided to publish their stories as *Sangtin Yatra* in India in 2004, the stories were braided together to avoid collapsing the stories into a singular narrative. The collective claims that the book represents a "blended but fractured 'we'" (Nagar, 2006, p. xxxiv). Nagar (2006) writes: "The chorus of nine voices does not remain constant throughout the book. As one speaks, the voice of the second or third suddenly blends in to give an entirely new and unique flavour to our music" (p. xxiv). Nagar (2006) notes that the process of sharing, braiding, and editing was often bitter and caused anger, suspicion, and conflict within the collective. The members assumed no shared experience of womanhood and "collectively crafted individual stories shaped through painful dialogue" (Mohanty, 2006, p. xiii). Working with and through difference was essential to the collective's success in producing a collection of individual but connected stories and to building solidarity with one another.

Sangtin Yatra is one example of transnational methodology that has aimed to disrupt dominant ways of coming to know about Other women. And yet, as Nagar (2006) claims, "no act of translation is without problems of voice, authority and representation and no act of publication comes without risk and consequences" (p. xxiii).

VIOLENCE AGAINST WOMEN

Another issue that is often covered by transnational feminist research is violence against women. Globally, violence against women is a major problem. According to the United Nations' *In-depth Study on All Forms of Violence against Women*, "violence against women persists in every country in the world as a pervasive violation of human rights and a major impediment to achieving gender equality" (2006, p. 9). The Declaration on the Elimination of Violence against Women (1993) defines violence against women as: "any act of gender-based violence that results in, or is likely to result in, physical, sexual or psychological harm or suffering to women, including threats of such acts, coercion, or arbitrary deprivation of liberty, whether occurring in public life or in private life" (United Nations, 1993, n.p.).

In 2006, the UN Secretary-General launched an in-depth study on violence against women. According to the corresponding UN campaign entitled UNITE, violence against women is a universally unjustifiable crime that exists in every corner of the world. UNITE maintains that persistent discrimination against women lies at the root of the issue, and violence against women is unconfined to any culture, region, or country (UNITE, 2012). This in-depth study revealed that up to 70% of women globally experience violence in their lifetime. In Canada, a study of adolescents ages 15 to 19 found that 54% of girls had experienced "sexual coercion in a dating relationship" (UNITE, 2012). The United Nations includes forced marriages, human trafficking, dowry murders, and honour killings in its report on global violence against women. It also includes issues of violence against women in war and conflict situations. The United Nations reports that in the Democratic Republic of Congo, over 200 000 women have suffered from sexual violence during conflict. In Rwanda, between 250 000 and 500 000 women were raped during the 1994 genocide (UNITE, 2012).

Globalization and Violence against Women

As noted at the outset of this chapter, globalization has meant an increase in women's paid employment in a range of sectors, including in the informal sector and in export manufacturing. Export processing zones (EPZ) are contradictory sites for women. While they may provide women with income, and perhaps more economic autonomy within the household, they are connected to violence against women in complicated ways. One of the most well-known EPZs is the *maquiladoras* of the borderlands between the United States and Mexico. The majority of maquiladora employees are young women. According to scholar Kathleen Staudt (2008), who studies EPZs near Ciudad Juarez, this city and women's work here are situated within a matrix of "femicide" (the killing of women).

The Mexican government's Programa industrial fronterizo (border industrialization program) was established in 1960 to facilitate foreign direct investment and global free trade regimes to be globally competitive and to develop. In 1994, Canada and the United States solidified the North American Free Trade Agreement (NAFTA) with Mexico. One of many results of these two major trade programs is the growth of Ciudad Juarez, which has become home to hundreds of factories employing more than 200 000 workers, over half of them women (Staudt, 2008, p. 7). Although profitable for factory owners and investors, feminists have argued that the workers experience structural violence at the hands of "a global economy that has shrunk the real value of earnings in the export-processing economic development model that dominates in Juarez" (Staudt, 2008, pp. 7–8). Although there are more jobs in the city, they have come at a high price. On top of inadequate shelter, food, and wages, the fact that over 370 women have been murdered since 1993 within and around the EPZ has inflicted terror on the population (Staudt, 2008, p. x). While families of those missing, raped, and/or murdered in Juarez have rallied for justice, there has been little response nationally or internationally by governments, global institutions, or the development community. Serial killers and drug cartels are popular explanations among some scholars, and yet, violence within the home has simultaneously become commonplace. This suggests feminists should broaden their understanding of the systemic causes of violence in a community where gender conflicts have been sparked by changing patterns of labour for meager wages—all of which is couched in the heavily increased security of the United States and Mexican borders (Staudt, 2008, p. 143).

Since transnational feminists are interested in understanding the negative effects of global economic restructuring on women, they pay attention to the manifestations of violence. In particular, the example of violence in Ciudad Juarez connects the local and global since the violence experienced in the site is not one or the other, but rather connected to local manifestations of patriarchy, as well and transnational economic and political forces that are also deeply invested in maintaining these interlocking systems of oppression.

Representing Violence against Women

Given the pervasiveness of gender violence globally, violence against women is a crucial issue for feminists. Still, feminist scholars commonly misrepresent violence against Other women in problematic ways (Narayan, 1997). Uma Narayan, a self-identified Third World feminist, has made foundational contributions to transnational feminism. Using the concept of "border crossing," Narayan suggests that information about dowry murders in India is shaped, distorted, and decontextualized when it crosses borders. The practice of dowry (transferring parental property to a daughter at the time of her marriage), and the violence associated with dowry (the abuse by husbands and in-laws related to this property exchange), is both complicated and changing, and yet, it is represented in Western contexts as a traditional and static practice that occurs regardless of class and caste. Narayan argues that only certain kinds of information about dowry and dowry-related violence is passed through a filter when it crosses borders, producing simple, quick facts and media-friendly sound bites. There is little coverage of violence against women in India in North American media, and dowry-related violence is rarely framed in terms of the general issue of domestic violence. This means that stories of dowry murder tend to cross borders with more frequency and currency than more complicated and nuanced reports of violence against women.

Narayan maintains that while dowry is a social, economic, political, religious, and cultural practice that varies over time and space, a "cultural explanation" is most often given when women experience violence related to this exchange (Narayan, 1997, p. 101). Western media's focus on widow/wife burning, and even on the dowry itself—a relatively lesser-known or misunderstood practice—as "alien," codes the practice as "Indian," and therefore Other. For Narayan, phenomena that seem "different," "alien," and "Other" cross borders with more regularity than do problems that seem to also affect so-called Western women. Unlike dating violence or domestic abuse, for example, dowry murders are misrepresented as foreign and unlike anything "at home" (Narayan, 1997, p. 102).

In Canada, popular discourse does not often represent violence against women as a cultural issue, even though the issue is systemic, as discussed further in Chapter 8. According to Statistics Canada (1993), half of all women in Canada have experienced at least one incident of physical or sexual violence.[4] In Canada, approximately 1200 Indigenous women have been murdered or gone missing since 1999, and over 200 of these cases remain unsolved (RCMP, 2014). With the exception of Indigenous communities and anti-violence advocates, popular discourse has not framed the violence as an issue of Canadian culture. While systemic in nature and related to gender and racial inequality, media reports of violence against women use individualized explanations related to mental health, stress, alcohol and drug abuse, or provocation. While these explanations are problematic in their own right and are complicated by feminist theorizing on the issue, it is important to contrast this framing of the issue in Canada with "cultural explanations" offered in regard to violence against Indian women.

In all social justice organizing, certain issues are highlighted over others in order to mobilize attention and resources. In the case of dowry murders, the United States and Indian women's anti-violence movements focused their attention in asymmetrical ways, leading to Western feminists' over-emphasis of dowry deaths as *the issue* of Indian women. More recently Elora Halim Chowdhury (2011) has mapped the activism around, and transnational representation of, acid attacks in Bangladesh. Chowdhury describes the complicated relationship between anti-violence organizing in Bangladesh and the ways in which this issue is taken up transnationally. Borrowing from Elizabeth Friedman's (1999) phrase "transnationalism reversed," Chowdhury is specifically concerned with local or grassroots organizing against acid attacks and its transnational affects. Similar to Narayan (1997), Chowdhury's (2011) extensive analysis points to the ways in which rhetoric around violence against women, including how violence is made visible and mobilized by activists in the locality, has global resonance. These scholarly works demonstrate how misrepresentations of violence against women create opportunities for feminist saviour narratives, but also feminist mobilizations across borders that are based on the misunderstanding that Western women need to save their sisters.

ACTIVISM AND SOLIDARITY

Transnational feminists examine the negative effects of globalization on women's lives while also taking account of women's resistances. While recognizing the limitations of resistances, transnational feminists explore the possibilities of generating transformative change through solidarity activism. Transnational feminists, as they seek solidarity practices, are particularly critical of global feminism's assumption that women are natural or inevitable sisters in struggle. Much transnational feminist literature considers how to collaborate and resist structures of oppression globally, while also recognizing the differences among women. Feminist scholarship on globalization has too often focused on global economic, social, and political change without taking into account the way in which women's daily lives are shaped by globalization—outside of women's labour force participation and the feminization of poverty in the Third World. Through providing various case studies of women organizing against local, national, and transnational forces, transnational feminist scholars aim to demonstrate the power of women's activism and the potential of transnational feminist practices, without romanticizing grassroots resistance. Transnational feminist scholars, including Grewal and Kaplan (1994), use transnational feminism both as a theoretical and activist framework that aims to avoid "the old sisterhood model of intervention and salvation that is clearly tied to older models of center-periphery relations" (p. 19). Yet, "old sisterhood models" continue to shape mobilizations of feminists globally, especially in response to violence against women as I offer in the final discussion.

SAVING OTHER WOMEN

In 2012, a 23-year-old female paramedic was gang raped by six men in a moving bus in South Delhi.[5] She died in a Singapore hospital two weeks later (*Times of India*, 2014). The gang rape received widespread coverage by international media; so much, in fact, that the phrase "the Indian gang rape" became a shorthand descriptor for the event. Importantly, this violent crime provoked discussion among anti-violence advocates and feminist scholars about how to intervene in a so-called culture of rape in India.

As feminist author and activist Jaclyn Friedman argued on TVO's current affairs program *The Agenda with Steve Paikin* (TVO, 2013), while individuals talk about "rape culture" in North America, popular discourse does not often include the phrase "culture of rape," and yet, this is the phrase circulated about India in light of the gang rape in 2012.

These two terms are distinctive, and the difference is telling. When feminists speak and write about rape culture, they often refer to the ways in which sexual violence against women is explicitly and tacitly accepted in Western culture. This may include representations of violence in movies, jokes, and even colloquial ways of speaking (e.g., "I just raped that exam"). When feminists and others speak and write about "cultures of rape," as they did in the case of India following the 2012 gang rape, anti-violence advocates drew on stereotypes of Indian culture as inherently hyper-violent, misogynist, backward, and traditional. As in the discussion of dowry murder from earlier in this chapter, the 2012 gang rape that happened on a bus in South Delhi was given a cultural explanation.

In practice, cultural explanations of sexual or domestic violence do not allow for women to build solidarities transnationally. In the case of "the Indian gang rape" as it is ubiquitously known, a cultural explanation disallowed for connections to be made between North American and Indian women, in particular, about the different manifestation of gendered violence at a local level. As Mohanty (2003) articulates, solidarities among and between women require the mapping of power and difference, and an exploration of common interests. When "the Indian gang rape" was described as a cultural issue, many feminists in North America positioned themselves as saviours.

One of the most explicit examples of Western feminist attempts to "save their global sisters" comes from the Harvard College Women's Center when it announced a policy task force entitled "Beyond Gender Equality" just following the highly publicized rape and murder in South Delhi. The Harvardites presumed a stance of superior knowledge and, implicitly, culture, as they offered "recommendations to India and other South Asian countries." Understandably angered by the assumption that Indian feminists needed North American expertise, the following letter was written to the Harvard task force and published online on the blog *Kafila* by Nivedita Menon (2014):

Letter from Indian feminists VRINDA GROVER, MARY E JOHN, KAVITA PANJABI, SHILPA PHADKE, SHWETA VACHANI, URVASHI BUTALIA and others, to their siblings at Harvard

We're a group of Indian feminists and we are delighted to learn that the Harvard community—without doubt one of the most learned in the world—has seen fit to set up a Policy Task Force entitled 'Beyond Gender Equality' and that you are preparing to offer recommendations to India (and other South Asian countries) in the wake of the New Delhi gang rape and murder. Not since the days of Katherine Mayo have American women—and American feminists—felt such concern for their less privileged Third World sisters. Mayo's concern, at that time, was to ensure that the Indian State (then the colonial State) did not leave Indian women in the lurch, at the mercy of their men, and that it retained power and the rule of the just. Yours, we see, is to work towards ensuring that steps are put in place that can help the Indian State in its implementation of the recommendations of the Justice Verma Committee, a responsibility the Indian State must take up. This is clearly something that we, Indian feminists and activists who have been involved in the women's movement here for several decades, are incapable of doing, and it was with a sense of overwhelming relief that we read of your intention to step into this breach.

You might be pleased to know that one of us, a lawyer who led the initiative to put pressure on the Justice Verma Committee to have a public hearing with women's groups, even said in relief, when she heard of your plans, that she would now go on holiday and take a plane ride to see the Everest. Indeed, we are all relieved, for now we know that our efforts will not have been in vain: the oral evidence provided by 82 activists and organizations to the Justice Verma Committee—and which we believe substantially contributed to the framing of their report—will now be in safe American hands!

Perhaps you are aware that the Indian State has put in place an Ordinance on Sexual Assault that ignores many recommendations of the Justice Verma Committee? If not, we would be pleased to furnish you a copy of the Ordinance, as well as a chart prepared by us, which details which recommendations have been accepted and which not. This may be useful in your efforts to advise our government. One of the greatest things about sisterhood is that it is so global, feminism has built such strong international connections—such that whenever our first world sisters see that we are incapable of dealing with problems in our countries, they immediately step in to help us out and provide us with much needed guidance and support. We are truly grateful for this.

Perhaps you will allow us to repay the favour, and next time President Obama wants to put in place legislation to do with abortion, or the Equal Rights Amendment, we can step in and help and, from our small bit of experience in these fields, recommend what the United States can do.

Vrinda Grover (mere lawyer)

Mary E. John, Senior Fellow, Centre for Women's Development Studies, New Delhi

Kavita Panjabi, Professor of Comparative Literature, Jadavpur University, Kolkata

Shilpa Phadke, Assistant Professor, School of Media and Cultural Studies, Tata Institute of Social Sciences, Mubmai

Shweta Vachani, Senior Editor, Zubaan

Urvashi Butalia, Director, Zubaan

And many others.

Adding to the conversation, United States feminist scholar Carol Vance (2013) asks:

> What lessons can be learned from feminist organizing and activism in India in the wake of the Delhi rape (especially since it could be said that feminist activism is much more vibrant and effective in India)? What reforms in law and its implementation are effective, given different legal systems and historical contexts? How do we understand the (relative) lack of response to horrific rapes in the US? (n.p.)

What this case demonstrates is how global solidarity cannot be assumed. Instead, global solidarity must be built through negotiations of power and difference across borders.

It should go without saying that Third World women, to use Mohanty's (2003) term, are not waiting to be saved.

The United Nations As a Site for Advocacy

At the transnational level, the United Nations has provided a complicated venue for feminist organizing (Desai, 2005; Ferree & Tripp, 2006; Freeman, 1999). Since the United Nations Decade for Women (1975–1985), women have used the United Nations to gather and discuss women's issues around the globe. However, Manisha Desai's (2005) *Transnationalism: The Face of Feminist Politics Post-Beijing* questions whether the United Nations as a site of transnational feminist practice enables the latest incarnation of global feminism, or if such spaces allow for a transformative feminist politic.

Since the field of transnational feminism emerged in United States academic discourse, Western notions have played a heavy hand in shaping as well as describing transnational feminist movements (Desai, 2005). Desai explains how this comes to be a problem as she explores the United Nations Fourth Women's World Conference in Beijing. She explains that as sites of transnational feminist organizing "across national borders as well as framing local, national, regional and global activism [through] activist discourse" (p. 319), global conferences are still power-laden spaces, where structural resources and inequalities within and between countries in the First and Third World shape which feminist activists are able and allowed to participate. Using Desai's analysis, feminists might think of current forms of transnational activism as "globalization from the middle" since it is often middle-class, educated people who circulate from the academy to UN agencies to international NGOs (Waterman, 2000, as cited in Desai, 2005, p. 321). Since NGOs have to be registered as a credible party to participate in such conferences, there is an increasing depoliticization or de-radicalization of transnational feminist movements (Desai, 2005).

Additionally, critics of such practices suggest that transnational feminist movements are uneven, with many First World countries overrepresented and many Third World advocates uninvolved in collaborative efforts, though Southern NGOs often receive their funding from First World donors. Given the history of UN political manoeuvres outside of feminist initiatives, this tension should not be surprising. After all, many member states see UN forums as aiming to *develop* Third World countries—hardly a viable starting point for a transnational feminist exchange. As a result, transnational feminist movements tend to mirror previous forms of global feminism, where middle-class, educated women from the West see themselves as helping desperate, poor, marginalized Third World women, rather than seeking transformative gender justice (Desai, 2005).

Worker Solidarity

While criticizing global feminist saviour models and international organizing that remains inequitable, transnational feminism also provides a renewed hope in feminist organizing though solidarity movements. Transnational feminist scholars stress the myriad of ways that women who may never meet "can draw strength from each other and organize across differences" (Naples, 2002, p. 270). For example, Mohanty's (2003) chapter, "Women Workers and the Politics of Solidarity," in *Feminism without Borders: Decolonizing Theory, Practicing Solidarity* sheds a positive light on transnational feminist organizing by underscoring solidarity through common interests rather than assume common experiences.

Solidarity organizing through common interests takes into account women's varied desires and needs while acknowledging women's social circumstances as workers. Both the Working Women's Forum (WWF) and the Self Employed Women's Association (SEWA) in India are examples of successful organizations of women workers. The Self Employed Women's Association was one of the first organizations to conceptualize women's informal work as work—that is, work done in the private or outside formal working regulations, including vegetable vending and producing goods from home. In 1972, SEWA unionized informal women workers and formed cooperatives to share resources. The women have formed support networks, trained community health workers, and established a SEWA university, where women are trained in production and managerial skills (Desai, 2002, p. 19). SEWA not only provides leadership training, but also has women's banks and producer cooperatives (Mohanty, 2003, pp. 164–65). By defining common interests, sites of power, and complicity, as well as the needs of Third World women as workers, SEWA provides a transformative basis for collective struggles (Mohanty, 2003).

In addition to mapping the negative effects of globalization, feminists are also concerned with mapping women's resistances to globalization, even if they may seem small. Scholars, including Fernandez-Kelly (1983) and Ong (1987), have traced resistances in workplaces by women organizing in solidarity. Although women surely have been exploited by labour conditions in EPZs, they have also been active resisters, engaging in work stoppages, resisting long hours without breaks, and using religious or cultural celebrations to refuse work and to organize workers in these areas (Ong, 1987; Fernandez-Kelly, 1983). These local actions have transnational effects, and can lead to larger transformative solidarity actions among workers (Mendez, 2002). For example, the Central American Network for Women in Solidarity with Women Workers in the Maquilas ("The Network") has utilized communication technologies to launch national and international campaigns pressuring factory owners to sign codes of ethics. Their media campaign, "Jobs, Yes . . . but with dignity," has helped to decrease what is known as shop-floor violence, and has in turn helped The Network to negotiate with factory owners to monitor conditions for workers. It is important to note that most of The Network's funding has come from non-governmental organizations in Northern countries. This means that The Network's activism is funded by, and therefore partly accountable to, Northern countries, which may affect how they do their work.

CONCLUSION

Transnational feminist theories aim to repair the failures and shortcomings of global feminism and the "internationalization" of gender and women's studies curriculum. Western feminism has too often homogenized all Third World women as an uncivilized Other, in need of empowerment and saving. For transnational feminists, representing women's issues within ongoing global economic restructuring, attending to the nuanced facets of women's lives, is necessary for cross-border coalitions. While global feminism tends to assume that women are natural and inevitable sisters in struggle against a universal form of patriarchy, transnational feminism uses a framework of analysis that emphasizes power and differences among women within the context of shifting global power relations, in addition to paying attention to gender inequalities within localities.

This chapter has outlined some of the major concerns for transnational feminists including the concept of globalization and flows of culture and capital; the mutually constitutive relationship, or the interplay, between the local and the global; the politics of representing the stories of "Third World women" in scholarship and in classrooms; collaborating across borders in research practices; migration and the international division of care labour; violence against women; and women's organizing. It is important to remember that transnational feminism is not a homogenous subfield of feminist theory with shared values, meaning, ideas, and languages (Swarr & Nagar, 2010, p. 3). Instead, transnational feminism is a diverse field of study in which theorists have intervened in a variety of questions pertaining to global women's issues. It is a field of inquiry into globalization and its effects, with no single, coherent position or strategy. As scholars remain reflexive and the flow of goods and cultures shift and transform, the field shifts and changes. As global economic restructuring continues to alter transnational systems of oppression, new opportunities for solidarity open up. Transnational feminists concerned with solidarity at the global level will continue to reframe their analyses of the world and women's place within it.

Endnotes

1. Watchel (2001) has collected over 450 definitions of the term (as cited in Desai, 2002, p. 15).
2. The term "Third World" originated during the Cold War, a conflict that occurred between capitalist and communist states after the Second World War. Countries that had been previously colonized by European or North American countries were constructed as a third world in reference to the inequalities between them. Third world countries may have found formal independence from colonial powers during this period but colonialization left profound disparities in wealth, capacity to compete in a globalizing economy, the health and life expectancy of populations, and the political status of these nations. The comparable wealth and status of "First World" countries, such as Canada, Great Britain, and the United States, led these types of countries to exercise a great deal of power globally. The "Second World" referred to the Communist countries (Union of Soviet Socialist Republics, Cuba, China, and others), although this term was only meant by implication, as it was with these countries that the United States and its allies were silently engaged in a major nuclear arms struggle. The term "Fourth World" has also emerged to refer to Indigenous societies that may be geographically and politically located in any of these countries. The term Third World has been problematized and also periodically reclaimed. Where Third World is used in this article, it appears as the language used by scholars under discussion.

3. Put simply, to "other" someone is to distinguish "them" from "us." It is a process of demarcating difference, but also superiority and inferiority among groups of people. In this case, Other women are understood to be different and inferior to Western women.
4. Although more up-to-date data would be preferable, no Statistics Canada surveys since 1993 have asked women about their lifetime experience of violence.
5. In compliance with Indian law, the real name of the victim was initially not released to the media.

Discussion Questions

1. What are two major critiques of global feminism offered by transnational feminism? How are global feminist frameworks replicated in the classroom?
2. Manisha Desai suggests that at UN conferences first world delegates outnumber third world women. If there were more third world women at the table, would women's organizing at this forum be different? If so, how?
3. Since the events of September 11, 2001, how have Muslim women been represented by the popular and news media? How could you use a transnational feminist framework to challenge these portrayals?
4. The Canadian Live-in Caregiver program is controversial, with some transnational feminists claiming that the "global care chain" is exploitative. How might someone who is not a migrant worker advocate for this group in solidarity with them?
5. Taking into consideration the response of Indian anti-violence advocates to the Harvard Policy Task Force, how might transnational feminists concerned about global violence against women approach this issue differently?

Bibliography

Abu-Lughod, L. (2002). Do Muslim women really need saving? Anthropological reflections on cultural relativism and its others. ***American Anthropologist 104***(3), 783–790.

Accord on fire and building safety in Bangladesh. (2013). Retrieved from http://bangladeshaccord.org/about/

Alexander, J. (2005). ***Pedagogies of crossing: Meditations on feminism, sexual politics, memory, and the sacred***. Durham, NC: Duke University Press.

Alexander, J., & Mohanty, C. T. (2010). Cartographies of knowledge and power: Transnational feminism and radical praxis. In A. Swarr & R. Nagar (Eds.), Critical transnational feminist praxis, (pp. 23–45). Albany, NY: SUNY Press.

BBC. (2013, May 10). Bangladesh factory collapse toll passes 1,000. Retrieved from www.bbc.com/news/world-asia-22476774

Bergeron, S. (2006). ***Fragments of development: Nation, gender and the space of modernity***. Ann Arbor, MI: The University of Michigan Press.

Briggs, L., McCormick, G., & Way, J. T. (2008). Transnationalism: A category of analysis. ***American Quarterly 60***(3), 625–648.

Burke, J. (2013, June 6). Bangladesh factory collapse leaves trail of shattered lives. Retrieved from www.theguardian.com/world/2013/jun/06/bangladesh-factory-building-collapse-community

Canada Revenue Agency. (2015). Universal child care benefit (UCCB). Retrieved from www.cra-arc.gc.ca/bnfts/uccb-puge/menu-eng.html

Chowdhury, E. H. (2011). *Transnationalism reversed: Women's organizing against gendered violence in Bangladesh.* Albany, NY: SUNY Press.

Citizenship and Immigration Canada. (2014). Live-in Caregiver Program. Retrieved from www.cic.gc.ca/ENGLISH/work/caregiver/index.asp

Desai, M. (2002). Transnational solidarity: Women's agency, structural adjustment, and globalization. In N. Naples & M. Desai (Eds.), *Women's activism and globalization: linking local struggles and transnational politics* (pp. 14–31). New York, NY: Routledge.

Desai, M. (2005). Transnationalism: The face of feminist politics post-Beijing. *International Social Science Journal 57*(184), (319–330).

Desai, J., Bouchard, D., & Detournay, D. (2011). Disavowed legacies and honorable thievery: The work of the 'transnational' in feminist and LGBTQ studies. In A. L. Swarr, & R. Nagar (Eds.), *Critical transnational feminism praxis* (pp. 46–54). New York, NY: SUNY Press.

Ehrenreich, B., & Hochschild, A. R. (2003). *Global economy of care: Nannies, maids, and sex workers in the new economy*. London, UK: Sage Publications.

Eisenstein, H. (2009). *Feminism Seduced: How global elites use women's labor and ideas to exploit the world*. London, UK; Boulder, CO: Paradigm Publishers.

Erevelles, N. (2006). Disability in the new world order. In INCITE! Women of Color Against Violence (Ed.), *Color of violence: The INCITE Anthology* (pp. 25–31). Cambridge, MA: South End Press.

Ferree, M. Marx, & Tripp, A. M. (2006). *Global feminism: Transnational women's activism, organizing, and human rights*. New York, NY: New York University Press.

Fernadez, L. (2013). *Transnational feminism in the United States: Knowledge, ethics, and power*. New York, NY: New York University Press.

Fernandez-Kelly, M. P. (1983). *For we are sold, I and my people: Women and industry in Mexico's frontier.* Albany, NY: SUNY Press.

Fluri, J. (2009). The beautiful 'other': A critical examination of 'western' representations of Afghan feminine corporeal modernity. *Gender, Place and Culture 16*(3), 241–257.

Freeman, E. J. (1999). The effects of "transnationalism reversed" in Venezuela: Assessing the impact of UN Global Conferences on the women's movement. *International Journal of Feminist Politics 1*(3), 357–381.

Grewal, I. & Kaplan C. (2001). Global identities: Theorizing transnational studies of sexuality. *GLQ: A Journal of Lesbian and Gay Studies 7*(4), 663–679.

Grewal, I. (2005). *Transnational America: Feminisms, diasporas, neoliberalisms*. Durham, NC: Duke University Press.

Grewal, I., & Kaplan, C. (Eds.). (1994). *Scattered hegemonies: Postmodernity and transnational feminist practices.* Minneapolis, MN: University of Minnesota Press.

Hall, S. (2013). *Representation: Cultural representations and signifying practices* (2nd ed.). London, UK: Sage Press.

Harvey, D. (2003). *The new imperialism*. Oxford, UK: Oxford University Press.

Hochschild, A. R. (1989). *The second shift: Working parents and the revolution at home*. New York, NY: Viking Press.

Loomba, A. (2005). *Colonialism/postcolonialism* (2nd ed.). London, UK; New York, NY: Routledge.

Macdonald, D., & Friendly, M. (2014). The parent trap: Childcare fees in Canada's big cities. Centre for Policy Alternatives. Retrieved from www.policyalternatives.ca/sites/default/files/uploads/publications/National%20Office/2014/11/Parent_Trap.pdf

Magnet, S. A. (2011). *When biometrics fail: Gender, race and the technology of identity.* Durham, NC: Duke University Press.

Mahmood, S. (2005). *The politics of piety: Islamic revival and the feminist subject.* Princeton, NJ: Princeton University Press.

Mann, S. Archer. (2012). *Doing feminist theory: From modernity to postmodernity*. Oxford, UK: Oxford University Press.

Marchand, M., & Runyan, A. (Eds.). (2011). *Gender and global restructuring: Sightings, sites and resistances* (2nd ed.). New York, NY: Routledge.

Menon, N. (2014). Dear sisters (and brothers?) at Harvard. Kafila. Retrived from http://kafila.org/2013/02/20/dear-sisters-and-brothers-at-harvard/

Mendez, J. (2002). Creating alternatives from a gender perspective: Transnational organizing for maquila workers' rights in Central America. In N. Naples, & M. Desai (Eds.), *Women's activism and globalization: Linking local struggles and transnational politics* (pp. 121–141). New York, NY: Routledge.

Moallem, M. (2005). *Between warrior brother and veiled sister: Islamic fundamentalism and the politics of patriarchy in Iran*. Berkley, CA: University of California Press.

Mohanty, C. T. (2003). *Feminism without borders: Decolonizing theory, practicing solidarity*. Durham, NC: Duke University Press.

Mohanty, C. T. (2006). *Playing with fire: Feminist thought and activism through seven lives in India* Sangtin Writers Collective & Richa Nagar (Eds.). (Forward, pp. ix–xvi). Minneapolis, MN: University of Minnesota Press.

Mongia, R. (2007). Historicizing state sovereignty: Inequality and the form of equivalence. *Comparative Studies in Society and History 49*(2), 384–411.

Morgan, R. (Ed.). (1984). *Sisterhood is global: The International Women's Movement anthology.* New York, NY: Anchor Press/Doubleday.

Nagar, R. (2002). Footloose researcher, 'traveling' theories, and the politics of transnational feminist praxis. *Gender, Place And Culture 9*(2), 179–186.

Nagar, R. (2003). Collaboration across borders: Moving beyond positionality. *Singapore Journal of Tropical Geography 24*(3): 356–372.

Nagar, R. (2006). *Playing with fire: Feminist thought and activism through seven lives in India* Sangtin Writers Collective & Richa Nagar (Eds.). (Introduction, pp. xxi–xlvii). Minneapolis, MN: University of Minnesota Press.

Nagar, R., & Swarr, A. L. (Eds.). (2010). *Critical transnational feminist praxis.* Albany, NY: SUNY Press.

Naples, N., & Desai, M. (Eds.). (2002). *Women's activism and globalization: Linking local struggles and transnational politics*. New York, NY: Routledge.

Narayan, U. (1997). *Dislocating cultures: Identities, traditions, and third world feminism*. New York, NY: Routledge.

Ong, A. (1987). *Spirits of resistance and capitalist discipline.* Albany, NY: State of New York Press.

Puar, J. (2007). *Terrorist assemblages: Homonationalism in queer times.* Durham, NC; London, UK: Duke University Press.

Ramamurthy, P. (2003). Material consumers, fabricating subjects: Perplexity, global connectivity discourses, and transnational feminist research. *Cultural Anthropology 18*(4), 524–550.

Razack, S. (2008). *Casting out: The eviction of Muslims from western law and politics*. Toronto, ON: University of Toronto Press.

Royal Canadian Mounted Police (RCMP). (2014). Missing and murdered aboriginal women: A national operational overview. Retrieved from www.rcmp-grc.gc.ca/pubs/mmaw-faapd-eng.pdf

Sangtin Writers Collective, & Nagar, R. 2006. *Playing with fire: Feminist thought and activism through seven lives in India.* Minneapolis, MN: University of Minnesota Press.

Spivak, G. C. (1988). Can the subaltern speak? In C. Nelson & L. Grossberg (Eds.), *Marxism and interpretation of culture* (pp. 271–313). Chicago, IL: University of Illinois Press.

Staeheli, L. A., & Nagar, R. (2002). Feminists talking across worlds. *Gender, Place and Culture 9*(2), 167–172.

Statistics Canada. (1993). The violence against women survey. Retrieved from www23.statcan.gc.ca/imdb/p2SV.pl?Function=getSurvey&SDDS=3896&lang=en&db=imdb&adm=8&dis=2

Staudt, K. (2008). *Violence and activism at the border: Gender, fear, and everyday life in Ciudad Juarez.* Austin, Texas: University of Texas Press.

Swarr, A. L., & Nagar, R. (2010). *Critical transnational feminist praxis*. New York, NY: SUNY Press.

Thobani, S. 2007. White wars: Western feminisms and the 'War on Terror.' *Feminist Theory, 8*(2), 169–185.

Times of India. 2014. SC stays death penalty of 2 in Nirbhaya case. Retrieved from http://timesofindia.indiatimes.com/india/SC-stays-death-penalty-of-2-in-Nirbhaya-case/articleshow/38398073.cms

TVO. The Agenda with Steve Paikin. (2013, January 8). Jaclyn Friedman: A culture of rape? Retrieved from http://tvo.org/video/186821/jaclyn-friedman-culture-rape

Uddin, S. (2013, May 26). Bangladesh factory collapse: Why women endure danger to make clothes for the West. Retrieved from http://worldnews.nbcnews.com/_news/2013/05/26/18447688-bangladesh-factory-collapse-why-women-endure-danger-to-make-clothes-for-the-west

United Nations. (1993). Declaration on the elimination of violence against women. Retrieved from http://www.un.org/documents/ga/res/48/a48r104.htm

United Nations. (2006). In-depth study on all forms of violence against women. Report of the Secretary-General. Retrieved from www.un.org/womenwatch/daw/vaw/SGstudyvaw.htm

United Nations. (2012). UNITE to end violence against women. Retrieved from http://endviolence.un.org/

UN Women. (2014). Facts and figures: Ending violence against women. United Nations Entity for Gender Equality and the Empowerment of Women. Retrieved from www.unwomen.org/en/what-we-do/ending-violence-against-women/facts-and-figures

Vance, C. (2013, February 18). What is wrong with this picture? http://kafila.org/2013/02/18/what-is-wrong-with-this-picture-carole-vance-2/

Walia, H. (2013). *Undoing border imperialism.* Oakland, CA: AK Press/Institute for Anarchist Studies.

Wing, A. K. (2000). *Global critical race feminism: An international reader* (2nd ed.). New York, NY: New York University Press.

#INTRODUCTION

On October 9, 2012, while riding home from a school exam in the Swat Valley of Pakistan, a Taliban soldier boarded the bus carrying a young, girl's rights and social media activist. He called out her name and said if she didn't identify herself, he would shoot everyone on the bus. Malala Yousafzai identified herself, and the soldier shot her in the head. One day later, on October 10, 2012, halfway around the world, a teenager from British Columbia, Canada, Amanda Todd, took her own life after an extensive period of stalking, sexual exploitation, and cyberbullying.

Malala survived, Amanda did not.

Two moments of physical violation and two turning points in the narrative of girls' rights globally. After Malala's shooting and recovery, her continued legacy has affected United Nations policy on girls' right to education. After Amanda's death, the Canadian government passed a federal bill to regulate cyberbullying and expand police contacts at high schools throughout Canada to report instances of unwanted cyber activities.

Further and most significantly for this current work, two days after Malala's shooting, and one day after Amanda's death, on October 11, the world celebrated the first anniversary of the UN's freshly inaugurated International Day of the Girl.

Amanda and Malala's stories reveal the complexity of theorizing about "girlhood" in an age of social media. The stories of these plugged-in girls are extraordinary but, when we pore over them and listen to them, the stories reveal the many forces that play upon girls as they attempt to construct their identities simultaneously offline and online through various forms of social media. For those girls, life is mediated, meaning girlhood is mediated.

Some of these forces have a long history: the gaze, objectification, patriarchy, institutionalized oppression, lack of rights, gender norms, and control and power dynamics. Many of the forces still play out online. Social media have contributed to a re-negotiation of our relationship to these forces, our command of the medium, and an ontological rethinking of our conception of girlhood and the lived experiences of girls in all their diversity, including race, sexuality, dis/ability, body size, and nationhood. Even though the media of communication change, every time the language we use to conceptualize its components and our interaction with media remains the same. Technology changes quickly, but how we talk about it does not. Online space is conceived of as different, separate from, and less valuable than offline space. Layered on this divide are discourses that cleave and subordinate women from the masculine high ground of technology and the public arena. Online communication is reinforced as being textual and disembodied rather than lived and embodied, which shapes the manner in which online violence is addressed—as symbolic and not real.

The Canadian Oxford Dictionary defines *cyberspace* as "the forum in which the global electronic communications network operates." Interestingly, early discourses about cyberspace presented it as a playful realm of science fiction and gaming, therefore shaping online space as "unreal" and unimportant. Until recently in media discourse, online space continued to be treated as less serious, less real, with less impact than offline space and offline interactions (Robins, 1995).

Mary Anne Franks states the following about the paradoxical "realities" of online exploration:

> Cyberspace idealism often produces conflicting accounts of the "realness" of cyberspace. On the one hand, cyberspace is often regarded as more real than real life—that is, the ability to control the terms of representation makes cyberspace existence more genuine. On the other hand, harms committed in cyberspace are often dismissed as "not really real," as they are by their nature not physical, bodily harms. The way this tension plays out in terms of the law's recommended role in cyberspace can yield schizophrenic results: freedom of speech, for example, in cyberspace is "really real" and must be vigorously protected; harassment in cyberspace is not "really real" and thus should not be taken very seriously. (Franks, 2011, p. 226)

Franks maintains that the virtual self-representation central to digital media sets women and young girls up to be targets for sexual predators by having their images manipulated. Franks refers to this process of *identity sextortian* as being an "unwilling avatar," an avatar being a person's virtual self-representation. Despite its liberatory promise, much of the public discourse surrounding the online world paints cyberspace as a new public place only men can handle and inhabit. This masculinization of cyberspace through discourse reinforces classic notions that men can manage the public realm and women should be relegated to the domains of the private (like the home) (Bailey & Steeves, 2013).

Contemporary research on women and technology sees emancipatory potential in the future of mobile technologies. Lee and Sohn's study (2004) reveals that young women are active in adopting new multimedia functions with mobile phones. Some feminists see media products as empowering and liberating for young women (Kearney, 2006). Amy Shields Dobson (2014) argues that social media can act to challenge Judith Butler's (1990) and Angela McRobbie's (2009) notion of *gender melancholia*[1] by providing space for girls to show agency through "shameless" photos or sexy activities that challenge gender norms.

These efforts are often met with mixed reactions as they unwittingly align closely with the sex-positive versus anti-pornography feminist sex wars of the 1980s. The same critiques from the 1980s can be applied to the representations of sexiness online through social media. On the one hand you can argue that girls taking control of their bodies and showing themselves as sexually liberated and exposed could be sex-positive and progressive as Gayle Rubin (1987) and Wendy McElroy (1996) advocated. On the flip side, however, you can also argue that the patriarchic lens remains so embedded within all media that any woman who presents herself sexually through any medium will, by default, be objectified by the lens of the medium designed for the pleasure of men (Greer, 1999; Levy, 2005; MacKinnon, 1987). Recent research on SMS (short message service) and digital imaging of a person's body has further attempted to delineate discourse from reality. The research shows the complicated and nuanced relations girls have with technology and subjectivity (Hasinoff, 2012; Ringrose, 2011).

Cyberspace has been described as a pastiche of fabricated ideas torn and recycled from previous ideas. We like this metaphor. Metaphors of fabric, quilting, stitching, and sewing seem poetically fitting for a discussion of girls and social media. Interestingly, one of the earliest computers was a programmable weaving loom developed by Joseph Marie Jaquard in the 1700s. The idea that weaving, a traditional practice of women, was one of the inspirations of Charles Babbage's computers, is a discursive lineage we hope to revive in order to reconnect the natural connection between fractured discourses like women and technology.

This chapter discusses how patriarchy, capitalism, and Cartesian dualism reinforce these longstanding embedded discourses that have come to shape our contemporary ideas about social media and girls. Drawing on Marx's explanations of ideology and Foucault's conception of discourse, we propose that these dominant ideologies have shaped the constellation of dualistic and oppressive discourses concerning technology, online visibility, women, agency, and the body. Before we explore any of this, however, we insist on recognizing (as perhaps you have already) that not all girls are plugged in. And moreover, we remind you that girls and girlhood are experienced from diverse subject positions in different social contexts with disparate levels of access to technology. The study of girls, culture, and social media can involve an examination of gender, class, race, and disability as key variables (Alper, 2014; Gajjala, 2012; Kolko & Nakamura, 2000; Marciano, 2014). This means that a certain amount of privilege situates our starting point for this chapter. Our focus is on girls and social media. Our starting point is girls who have access to social media or girls who exist on and through social media. Drawing on the postmodern work of Donna Haraway (1991), we also encourage a discussion around the idea that perhaps being mediated could be part and parcel of anyone connected or not who identifies or aligns with being a woman.

danah boyd (2007) lists three components of social networking sites (SNS). Social networking sites are "web-based services that allow individuals (1) to construct a public or semi-public profile within a bound system; (2) articulate a list of other users with whom they share a connection; and (3) view and traverse their list of connections and those made by others in the system" (boyd & Elison, 2007, p. 2).

Furthermore, we recognize that the stories of Malala and Amanda are exceptional. Alongside these anomalous stories, gleaming with asterisks, we will also unfold the stories of ordinary, plugged-in Canadian girls from the west coast of Canada whom we interviewed in the fall of 2014.[2] These few stories are not cited to propose a universality of experience online (not at all!). Rather, they attempt to listen to the mediated nature of the lives of plugged-in girls. In this chapter, cut, pasted, stitched, and stapled through these stories will be the theories of past and contemporary scholars from discourse theory, feminist theory, and social media studies. Their ideas will be integrated in a way that reflects the postmodern quilt-like nature of cyberspace itself.

#MEDIA#IDEOLOGY

Karl Marx argued that the ideas that form the foundation of capitalist society are culturally created by powerful elites. These ideas represent ideology and are produced through a socially constructed system of reification whereby abstract concepts are given causal powers and subjectivity. As Marx[3] contends in *The German Ideology*, one of the most important aspects in the production of ideology is a belief in the separation of mental and physical labour. This belief is rooted in the practical and actual historical division of labour, which determines social relationships. The division of labour implies a "contradiction between the interests of the separate individual or the individual family and the communal interest of all individuals who have intercourse with one another" (Marx, 1998, p. 52).

Under a capitalist economic foundation the ruling class controls not only the material conditions of society but also the intellectual conditions, which solidify their hold on power. The goal of the ruling class is to create conditions whereby abstract concepts that support and maintain their position of power are seen and understood to be not only universal but also to belong to the *natural world* while at the same time being divine.[4] This concept of the natural world gives us the belief that we are powerless to interfere in the actual domination that is based upon this false consciousness. Through this system of ruling ideas, abstract concepts such as gender are given subjectivity, appearing real and possessing causal powers, while we lose subjectivity.

Mass media is perhaps one of the most influential and important institutions governing our lives and has become one of the key means for the delivery and acceptance of ideology. As a key hegemonic and economic force, the mass media engage in the production of commodities and services and are the major thrust behind the invention and advancement of communication technologies. Jackson, Nielsen, and Hsu argue that while we cannot claim that there is one global "mediated society," the media as powerful, ideological tools dictate certain cultural values that have a "normalizing impact" on us and affect "the type of citizenship that is practiced" (Jackson, et al., 2011, p. 2).

Bagdikian maintains that capitalists who own and control media are the new "lords of the global village . . . penetrat[ing] the world with messages" that reflect their interests (1989, p. 805). Bagdikian cites Rupert Murdoch and his NewsCorp Empire as an example of a "Lord" with dominating, global power. Since the publication of Bagdikian's seminal piece, the new Lords[5] of the village are now the CEOs behind social media networks. These young, white, male heads of the global state reign from newly constructed empires such as Facebook, Instagram, Twitter, and YouTube.

#NATURE#BODY VERSUS #MIND#TECHNOLOGY

A second key dualistic assumption—the notion of the body somehow being separate from experience—originates in Cartesian dualism or the notion that the mind is separate from the body. This disembodied thinking subject is believed to be found within the essence of men, whose ideal task is to rule the mind/body relationship. Under this dualism, men were considered to be the thinkers, all that was pure. Women were relegated to a secondary, subservient subjectivity under the control and domination of men. In Western history, dating from the ancient Greeks, women were positioned as matter, unclean, on a level on par with slaves (who were of course women too!). Their bodies were to be controlled and contained (Lloyd, 1984).

In the *Dialectic of Enlightenment*, Theodor Adorno and Max Horkheimer (1972) contend that out of enlightenment philosophy, such as the Cartesian separation of mind and body, women became represented both as fascinating and repulsive to men who were told to limit their contact with natural forces including those located within their own being, in order to ensure the evolution of the human spirit. The main proposition in Adorno and Horkheimer's work is that under the enlightenment philosophical tradition, men negate the sacred/profane essence of their connection with nature and begin to represent nature as *anti*-reason, therefore, the enlightenment tradition "aims above all at the *domination of nature*" (Vogel, 1996, p. 52).

Under this ideological system, to conquer nature is to conquer the body and to symbolically eradicate all that is female. In her critique of post-structuralism and postmodernist thought, Dorothy E. Smith adds that such thinking reinforces the Cartesian philosophy of disembodying human subjectivity because it separates the "bases of consciousness from the local historical activities of people's everyday lives" (1999, p. 98). Smith introduces a new "materialist analysis of social consciousness" from the "standpoint of women." Smith's contention is that women have been excluded from sociological inquiry that subsequently has created an "externalized body of knowledge based on an organization of experience that excludes ours" (1990, p. 21). Women and young girls are generally understood to be a reminder of this dualism. They are seen as unwilling avatars, victims, passive, disembodied bodies and objects, with no active subjectivity.

A further dualistic discourse, and one key to any discussion involving social media and cyberspace, is the divide between notions of public and private realms. Rooted in both patriarchy and Marx's notions of ideology, men historically have been situated in the public arena reaping all the benefits it offers while women have been confined to the private sphere. This is the foundation of gender inequality and the ideology of patriarchal capitalism. Dorothy E. Smith further adds to Marx's conception that the production of ideology is duplicated in the gendered realm of capitalist society:

> Men have functioned as subjects in the mode of governing; women have been anchored in the local and particular phase of the bifurcated world. It has been a condition of man's being able to enter and become absorbed in the conceptual mode, and to forget the dependence of his being in that mode upon his bodily, that he does not have to focus his activities and interests upon his bodily existence. (1990, p. 18)

At the centre of this female oppression is patriarchy, dominating fathers and men in general, all of whom are seen as deeply connected with material power relationships that flourish and take shape under a capitalist economic system. Under this oppressive system and the ruling relations that organize it, men are positioned as rather abstract "knowers" alienated from corporeal subjectivity. Women are relegated to all things irrational and involving the body. Under the ideology of the beauty ideal, women lose their subjectivity and are viewed as mere objects. Smith concludes that the "gendered organization of subjectivity" creates a crevasse between men and women and ultimately "silences women" (1990, p. 19).

The ideological propositions set up within the logics of patriarchy, capitalism, and Cartesian dualism leave little room for conceptualizing women as capable, agency-filled, and savvy media consumers. The next section delineates how the above-mentioned ideological frameworks have come to shape discourses on women and technology and subsequent interpretations of major news events concerning girls and social media.

#SOCIAL#MEDIA

There are several ways SNS, or the more contemporary and comprehensive term "social media" differ from older media:

1. by reconfiguring the relationships between message maker, message, and audience;
2. by being multimedia; and,
3. by reconfiguring conceptions of public and private space.

Stuart Hall (1973) argued that when it came to broadcast media (TV, radio, and newspapers), major media conglomerates *encoded*, imbued, or authored mainstream, normalized, hegemonic ideas into the messages broadcast on these media. Once the message reached the audience, the audience could make sense of or "decode" the message in different ways: *hegemonically* (where the audience aligns with the ideologies of the message producer); *oppositionally* (where the audience directly challenge the ideologies); and *mixed* (where the audience negotiates the ideologies).

Although Hall argued that the audience was active in the act of decoding and could challenge and negotiate the hegemonic messages of media producers, what the audience lacked was the force to make those oppositional readings known by a larger audience. This is not the case with social media and it's exactly the power of broadcasting coupled with the back and forth dialogic nature of social media communication that differentiates social media from the old broadcast media (Fuchs, 2014).

At the point when Stuart Hall introduced the encoding/decoding model, individuals couldn't just buy a newspaper, a TV, or radio station and get their opinions out to the world. Only a privileged group could—an economically privileged elite group—and so the power of broadcasting rested in a few hands. However, widespread broadcast ability is possible with social media. Founded on the dialogic, bullet-proof, multi-modal, and hub-based system of the internet, any member of the "audience" is also a potentially powerful "broadcaster."

With the diversification of messengers and media messages also comes a diversification of audiences. Not only can media messages be tailored to a wide variety of niche groups perhaps not previously recognized as financially worthy in the heyday of classic media, but previously powerful media outlets also become audiences to—and co-dependent upon—citizen journalists, independent bloggers, and instagramers whose cameras were in the right or wrong place at the right time. The typical person can now, with enough followers, become what Theresa Senft (2008) calls a "microcelebrity" in cyberspace.

Rather than a linear relationship from producer to audience, messages flow dynamically and cyclically among a variety of messengers and a variety of audiences. We have had new messengers and audiences since the emergence of the internet but what really differentiates social media are contemporary new media and new messages. Social media outlets permit people to connect and to share both newsworthy events and the banality of everyday life (Beer, 2008, p. 522). Borrowing the term "the spaces in-between" from urbanist Jan Gehl (1987), we can think of the relationship between broadcast media and the ubiquity of social media in this way: if old media shared news about high rises and civic masterpieces, social media share news about the spaces in-between those buildings such as the alleys, the curbs, the street corners, and the hideaways. Many social media outlets evolved from texting platforms (e.g., the social media platform QQ) and so the communication shared over these forums evolved to concern people's everyday lives.

Whereas broadcast media uphold the classic notion of "objectivity" in news and a disembodied presentation of the world devoid of a bias-filled author, social media *embrace* the subjectivity of experience and draw attention directly to the embodied emotional experiences of online narrators. Status updates on Facebook and Twitter can highlight and chronicle a person's mood through emoji, and Twitter hashtags textually label one's feelings #sad, #happy, and #grateful.

The messages we share are also increasingly multi-sensed, appealing to our eyes, ears, emotions; and arrive in different forms: text, photograph, video, and audio. As a result we can share richer snapshots of our lives than those that could be shared through text alone. Instagram and Snapchat images, Vines, gifs, the plethora of apps introduced to capture the perfect selfie or edit your photos all provide a variety of ways to mediate ourselves and "experience" others.

Apart from providing a voice/eye/ear to the heterogeneous audience, users of social media are also more integrated into social media infrastructure. When you sign up for a social media profile, you are required to provide a fair amount of information such as your name, location, and email. Not only are we users of social media but also fundamentally we *are* social media (Deuze, 2013). In most user agreements, we trade the privilege of a profile for our right to privacy. The information we provide is often tracked and saved for commercial and advertising purposes. Kenneth Werbin (2012) describes these qualities of online governance as the *regime of surveillance and the regime of commodification*. The information we provide is used to track us (surveillance) and to turn our aggregated data into *meta-data* that can be sold and shared for market purposes (commodification). It is not the individual bits of data that we share that are valuable but rather it is the aggregated data that paint an "expected profile" of our consumer habits.

Another force shaping our actions on social media is the reconfiguration of *space*. Offline, we have learned various codes that dictate what is public space (the park, a school, the library) and what is private space (your bedroom, a bathroom, the home) Drawing on theatre terms, Erving Goffman called these spaces the "front stage" and "back stage" that regulate the performance of one's identity (Goffman, 1959). danah boyd coined the term *context collapse* when describing how space is reshaped online (boyd, 2001). She argued that those visual and material borders that exist in the real world to delineate and separate the public spaces from the private—and thus dictate where public and private activities ought to take place—are erased online. The public and the private collapse in on each other and this leads to seeing activities that, offline, would normatively be considered private in public media. There are many examples of these collapses of the public and private: a Tumblr page called #postsexselfies (n.d.) is the product of trolling Instagram for images people have taken or seem to have taken of themselves after sex. Several contexts are collapsed in this instance. The public conception of sex as a private act is challenged when people provide a visual image of the privacy of their bedroom in a state of post-coital bliss.

boyd expanded her theory of "context collapse" in a blog post in 2006 in which she explores the term "superpublics":

> In talking about "super publics," I want to get at the altered state of publics—what publics look like when they are infused with the features of digital architectures. What does it mean to speak across time and space to an unknown audience? What happens when you cannot predict who will witness your act because they are not visible now, even though they may be tomorrow? How do people learn to deal with a public larger and more diverse than the one they learned to make sense of as teenagers? How are teenagers affected by growing up in an environment where they can assume super publics? I want to talk about what it means to speak for all time and space, to audiences you cannot conceptualize. (boyd, 2006)

#PLUGGED-IN#GIRLS

Teens have historically looked for the convergence of back and front stages; social media is the perfect medium. One of our plugged-in girls said the following about how space is experienced online:

> I feel like on Facebook and Instagram, I am always in front of an audience or like on stage to be judged? It feels like I'm performing almost. Every move seems critical. Twitter feels like I'm in front of a panel and the panel consists of professionals—writers, professors, people from the media.[6]

The essence of adolescents in Western, capitalist society is the drive and desire to be both independent and autonomous, resulting in a "healthy self-governance" including the ability for decision-making, self-reliance, and conformity (Russell & Bakken, 2002). Central to this desire is securing "space" in which teens can stake ownership claims away from the prying eyes of parents and other adults. Digital social media sites have finally offered teens a space that, for the most part, is condoned by adults with minimal contact or interference. In this virtual world, teens are actually engaging more but these interactions are mediated through technology. Warnings have emerged claiming that over-use of digital media is somehow associated with higher rates of suicide, substance abuse, depression, hyper-sexuality, and anti-social behaviour (Frank, et al., 2010; Leena, 2005; Yen et al., 2009; Yuan-Sheng, et al., 2010).

However, the now portable, online world is all about shaping reputations, managing networks, and masking information (Madden et al., 2013). According to Duggan (2013), teens share a wide range of information about themselves on SNS. The popularity of each site depends on the type of interaction the teen is seeking. As of this writing, the four most popular sites are Facebook, Twitter, Snapchat, and Google Plus (Madden, et al., 2013). Madden et al. found that teens are keeping their Facebook accounts, but find too much "drama" (negative interactions and too much disclosure) involved so they are turning to other media such as Twitter and Instagram. Twitter's attraction is that the 140-character limit prevents the drama found on Facebook but still allows for personal information sharing. Snapchat's appeal is the ability to share photos and videos quickly. The images are only displayed for a few seconds and then disappear.

One of our plugged-in girls said the following about why she abandoned Facebook and her desire to find and secure a space that is free of hate:

> [Going] to my Instagram account gives me a safe feeling almost, it comforts me in seeing people with similarities to me post it's like a meeting ground. All social media give off a different vibe to me personally. I don't go on Facebook too often anymore because most the posts are cruelty toward another person, lots of 'slut shaming' and people nursing fights, the same goes for Twitter, while I'm on those sites the environment that I'm becoming consumed it may as well be my high school. Instagram is different for me because I don't follow as many people who attend my school. I've met the people I follow through that site, I find people with similar interests to my own, things in common to me and it grows from there.[7]

Youth are becoming the main consumers of SNS with young women more active users than men (Duggan, 2013). According to a recent United States study, 95% of youth aged 12 to 17 are avid internet users, and 80% of those are using SNS with Facebook and Twitter being the most popular (Madden et al., 2013). The same study found that girls (aged 14 to 17) are highly engaged users with 93% vs. 85% of boys using Facebook and 31% vs. 21% using Twitter. Similarly in Canada, 32% of students in grades 4 to 6 (approximate age 9 to 11 years) have Facebook accounts and 16% use Twitter[8] (Steeves, 2014a; 2014b). Facebook gains popularity by grade 11 (16 years) with 95% of students having accounts while just under 47% of students in grades 7 to 11 have Instagram and Twitter accounts (Steeves, 2014a). Little gender variation exists in younger students (grades 4 to 6), but by the time students are in grade 11, more girls are using Twitter (53% vs. 41%) and Instagram (55% vs. 32%). Facebook remains at 83% for both boys and girls (Steeves, 2014a).

But the online world is far from easily malleable and controlled. Seventeen percent of teens report being "approached" by unknown persons who triggered uncomfortable feelings and fears about safety (Madden, et al., 2013). Mirroring or perhaps acting as an extension for the real embodied world, the online experience seems more dangerous for girls as they are more than twice as likely as boys (24% vs. 10%) to experience interactions with strangers that cause them to feel uncomfortable and scared (Madden, et al., 2013). There is a lure, or perhaps a belief, for teens that somehow the online world is a private, easily controlled world where its virtual nature allows for more and more freedom in order to develop an autonomous identity free from parental and/or adult control. According to Madden et al. (2013) only 9% of teens report being "very concerned" about the possibility of third-party access to their data in comparison to their parents of whom 81% stated they were "very" or "somewhat" concerned about how much information about their children is online.

When asked about interacting with strangers online, one of our plugged-in girls said:

> I do chat with them. I've been on social media for a long time so chatting with strangers (only if we've followed each other for a while) doesn't seem strange to me. I've made a lot of good friends through chatting. Of course, I have received negative remarks as well. Especially with the 'anonymous' feature on Tumblr Ask.[9]

#IAM#AMANDA

Perhaps one of the most compelling life stories exemplifying these concerns is the story of Amanda Todd, a 15-year-old teen from Port Coquitlam, British Columbia, who experienced all aspects of the negative side of SNS. Her poignant story is often used as a cautionary tale for teens. Her story also points to the importance of feminism for young girls and how feminist inquiry and theory need to adapt to a rapidly changing social

Source: Todd, A. (2011). A still from Amanda Todd's YouTube video telling the story of years of bullying after having a nude photo sent to classmates. [Online Image]. Retrieved from http://cnews.canoe.ca/CNEWS/Canada/2014/04/17/21611366.html

world—a social world dominated by digital technology. Here is Amanda's story, written and narrated by Amanda and shared via an uploaded video on YouTube on September 7, 2012. The title of her video is "My *Story: Struggling, bullying, suicide, and self-harm.*"

> Hello!
>
> I've decided to tell you about my never ending story In 7th grade I would go with my friends on webcam To meet and talk to new people. Then got called stunning, beautiful, perfect etc . . . Then wanted me to flash . . . So I did . . . 1 year later . . . I got a message on facebook from him . . . Don't know how he knew me . . . It said . . . If you don't put on a show for me I will send ur boobs . . . He knew my address, school, relatives, friends family names . . . my photo was sent to everyone . . . I then got really sick and got . . . Anxiety, major depression and panic disorder . . . I then moved and got into Drugs & Alcohol . . . My anxiety got worse . . . couldn't go out
>
> A year past and the guy came back with my new list of friends & school. But made a facebook page . . . My boobs were his profile pic . . . Cried every night, lost all my friends & respect people had for me . . . again . . . Then nobody liked me name calling, judged . . . I can never get that Photo back . . . Its out there forever . . . I'm not constantly crying now . . . Everyday I think why am I still here . . . cant go to school . . . Meet or be with people . . . constantly cutting. I'm really depressed . . . I overdosed . . . in hospital for 2 days . . . I'm stuck . . . what's left of me now . . . nothing stops . . . I have nobody . . . I need somebody | |
>
> My name is Amanda Todd . . . [10]
>
> Underneath her video she has the following disclaimer:
>
> "I'm struggling to stay in this world, because everything just touches me so deeply. I'm not doing this for attention. I'm doing this to be an inspiration and to show that I can be strong. I did things to myself to make pain go away, because I'd rather hurt myself then someone else. Haters are haters but please don't hate, although im sure I'll get them. I hope I can show you guys that everyone has a story, and everyone's future will be bright one day, you just gotta pull through. I'm still here aren't I?"[11]

On October 10, 2012, 33 days after posting her story, Amanda took her own life. The now famous video (to-date there have been over 9 million downloads) is filmed in black and white and shows a partially hidden Todd holding up her hand-written message on numerous pieces of paper. Her young age is apparent by the slightness of her build, her long hair curled at the ends, and the numerous string bracelets, ironically referred to as friendship bracelets, adorning her wrists.[12] The film is silent, or rather Amanda is silent with just the soundtrack she chose herself: "Hear You Me," by Jimmy Eat World. Amanda's silence is understood to somehow be a projection of the debilitating, gendered-based violent attacks she experienced at the hands of sexual exploiters and schoolyard bullies.

Although Amanda's story is tragic on so many levels, her story also points to the major negative aspect of social media: the sexual exploitation of young women and girls and the growing phenomenon of cyber bullying. Michelle Dean (2012) brilliantly connects Amanda's story to Franks's by maintaining that she was an unwilling avatar. As previously introduced, Franks documents the fact that in many cases of online harassment sexually explicit images are used without consent as revenge or for blackmail purposes as was demonstrated in Amanda's testimonial[13]: "In stark contrast to the way users exert control over their online identities, the creation of unwilling avatars involves invoking individuals' real bodies for the purpose of threatening, defaming, or sexualizing them without their consent" (2011, pp. 226–227).

Central to becoming an unwilling avatar is the camera and how women and young girls are so easily victimized by the ever-present male gaze. Women and young girls have historically been objects of a patriarchal gaze. As John Berger (1972) contends, this desire to objectify women as lifeless objects of male sexual fantasy first became entrenched in representation during the European art tradition of the nude. This is symbolic violence where women are represented as objects without life, agency, and will. Laura Mulvey similarly argues the male gaze is found within mainstream films and has become part of the camera work. Mulvey (1975) contends that the "controlling and curious gaze" of the "fetishistic, scopophillic" spectator not only turns the person being observed into an object of both fear and desire but also actually requires an active participation by the spectator (pp. 28–29). The spectator is not only consumed by his anxiety about his own identity, but intermixed with these anxieties is desire. So as not to be dangerous, the spectator turns the object into a fetish, which creates a power imbalance.

Since Mulvey's initial work, many scholars have agreed with her psychoanalytical interpretation of women's experience in film (Cooper, 2000; Kaplan, 1997; Ussher, 1997), while others argue that this psychoanalytic reading negates female sexuality and ignores any issues regarding race and class (Arbuthnot & Seneca, 1990; Gamman, 1989; Mayne, 1993; Stacey, 1991; Studlar, 1990). Some of these critics maintain that psychoanalytic theories investigating female subjectivity in film do not sufficiently address the "complexities of female experience with the cinema" (Studlar, 1990, p. 74) and ignore the cultural and social dimensions that are behind the production of patriarchal narratives (Stacey, 1991).

Michel Foucault (1979) argues that the gaze is connected to power and surveillance, giving the bearer of the gaze empowerment over those who are gazed upon. However, Foucault did not extend his analysis to examine how gender is enacted through the gaze. Both Susan Bordo (1993) and Sandra L. Bartky (1997) expand Foucault's analysis to incorporate gender relationships and its impact upon female embodiment. Bordo utilizes Foucault's methodology arguing that power is a "dynamic or network of non-centralized forces" (p. 26) that are maintained through individual "self-surveillance and self-correction" (p. 27). Bartky contends that disregarding the "feminine body" perpetuates the "silence and powerlessness . . . and as a whole reproduces the sexism which is endemic throughout Western political theory" (1997, p. 132).

Similar critiques are presented within the realm of online gendered relations. Whittington-Walsh (2006) explains the presence of online hate websites such as the user-generated site uglypeople.com as extensions of the tyrannical male, patriarchal, colonial gaze. This gaze involves both embodied and virtual experiences of young girls and women with physical disabilities/differences who experience *attitudinal violence* toward their physical appearance and beauty. Online, attitudinal violence merges physical and symbolic forms of violence in which people enact hatred toward physical difference by posting images of everyday people and celebrities. Using Mulvey's analysis of the gaze and cinematic spectatorship, Whittington-Walsh maintains that the spectator of those hate sites is simultaneously using an active "controlling and curious gaze" (Whittington-Walsh, 2006, p. 20) by turning the person on display (usually female) into an object of both desire and fear. The ultimate power imbalance lies in the fact that the active spectator can post "unwilling avatars" onto the site and rate each image on a score of 1 to 10 for "ugliness" and even have the option of "putting this ugly on a t-shirt" (2006, p. 20). Here, as mentioned in our analysis of Hall's media model, previous categories between audience and producer break down. Furthermore, embodied reactions to online textual violence challenge the reinforced dualistic separation between mind and body and thus online and offline selves.

Similarly, Franks's research also draws attention to the fallacies of the dualism between offline and online lives by arguing that women are often victimized online similar to the extent they experience in the offline, so-called embodied world. The online world denies women the opportunity to become fully embodied citizens with all rights afforded by law that "amplifies the sexual stereotypes and discrimination women experience in the offline world" (2011, p. 260). Franks refers to this as a new form of "social tyranny" (p. 251) in the fact that most retractors argue that rather than enforcing regulations and laws governing behavior in the online utopia women should not participate. However, this view only seems to recreate and reinforce traditional gendered relations and minimizes women's ability to benefit from engagement in this new frontier.

It is within this discourse that Amanda is positioned. We are told to see her as an unwilling avatar, as numerous studies and media accounts testify—she is a victim of a form of technology that she was somehow too naïve to handle. But this discourse must be separate from her actual *embodied* offline lived reality, Amanda is not alone. Hinduja and Patchin (2009) coined the term cyberbullicide to capture the growing phenomenon of predominantly youth committing suicide after being victimized from aggressive online bullying. Seeking to determine if suicidal ideation was linked to cyberbullying, Hinduja and Patchin surveyed 2000 randomly selected middle school–aged students (in the United States) and found that 20% (19.7% girls, 20.9% boys) had seriously thought about attempting suicide, while 19% (17.9% girls, 20.2% boys) reported attempting suicide. Youth who were victimized online were twice as likely to attempt suicide compared to youth who had not experienced cyberbullying. Although youth may have been experiencing other emotional and social issues at the time of their deaths, cyberbullying exasperated feelings of "instability and hopelessness."

Similar patterns have been detected in Canada. In a national survey of 5436 Canadian students in grades 4 to 11, Steeves (2014a) found that 23% had been mean to someone online while 37% of students had been victims of mean or cruel behavior. Among grade 4 students, 6% had been bullied, with grade 8 (31%) and grade 11 (38%) students experiencing even more. The most common forms of cyberbullying were the following:

- harassment
- spreading rumours
- posting embarrassing photos

- making fun of someone's race, ethnicity, or sexual orientation
- saying something about someone's sexual activity

According to Hinduja and Patchin (2010) the most common social media sites for cyberbullying to occur are through email (18%), instant messaging (18%), MySpace (14%), and chat rooms (10%). As with all areas of our social world, girls are more likely than boys to have something mean said about them and boys are more likely to engage in mean or cruel behavior toward someone online (Steeves, 2014a).

Another key aspect to Amanda's story is the fact that she engaged in self-harming behaviour (suicide) but also non-suicidal self-harm. Amanda refers to this in her story as "constantly cutting" (Todd, 2012) referring to intentional self-poisoning or other forms of self-injury behaviour, which is widely believed to be a coping device when experiencing high levels of stress. Deliberate self-harm (DSH) is very common in adolescents with younger females (12 years) engaging in higher rates than males at 12:1. By 18 years of age the rate becomes 2:1 (Hawton, et al., 2012). Most significantly, DSH is an important risk factor for future suicide (Hawton, et al., 2012). Cutting is the most commonly used technique, although Amanda engaged in all forms of self-injurious behaviour: self-poisoning (drinking bleach), self-injury (cutting), and suicide.

Non-suicidal self-harming behaviours have moved out of the shadows of clinical diagnosis (such as border-line personality disorder) and are now beginning to be conceptualized as a social phenomenon. James (2013) found in her survey of 387[14] girls aged 13 to 16 in New Zealand that self-harming is more normalized than previously thought and is being heavily influenced by peers. Most significantly, 23% of girls who engaged in self-harming had done so in front of other people, most notably peers and a shocking 12% had harmed together. Interestingly, self-harming girls are more likely to be popular at school, which further dispels another image and discourse—that harmers are believed to be highly troubled (James, 2013).

In Canada, self-harming behaviours, most commonly cutting, are also on the rise. According to the division chief of community-based psychiatry at the Children's Hospital of Eastern Ontario in Ottawa, teens aged 12 to 17 are engaging in cutting behaviours at twice the rate as seen in previous years. Kim St. John, divisional head of child and adolescent psychiatry at the Janeway Children's Hospital in St. Johns, Newfoundland, contends that cutting has become "almost a fad . . . And many of the young people that I see that cut do it to belong to a group or to stay within a group. They post it on Facebook" (The Canadian Press, 2014). Social media has become a key medium in which self-harming behaviours occur and are documented and shared. Young girls are reported to be engaging in what is being referred to as copy-cat behaviour where they send a video to YouTube and/or photo-sharing sites of self-harming, causing self-harming competitions (Adams, 2013). Further, there is a correlation between the amount of time spent online with self-harming (Mitchell & Ybarra, 2007). Self-harmers have higher rates of online use, and most significantly, online use that exceeds five hours per day was associated with suicidal ideation and planning (Kim et al., 2006; Lam et al., 2009; Messias, et al., 2011; Mitchell & Ybarra, 2007).

Another contradiction in the discourse surrounding Amanda's story is that she did not see herself as a helpless victim. In a 2013 edition of *The Fifth Estate* documentary show, The Sextortian of Amanda Todd,[15] her story is explored and a thorough examination of her computer reveals further details of her online activity. While the beginning of her "never-ending" nightmare (it did in fact end with the taking of her life) occurred online with the sextortian she experienced while interacting on BlogTV,[16] she eventually found another supportive online community where she could discuss the issues she was experiencing. By creating and posting her video, *My Story: Struggling, bullying, suicide, and self-harm*, Amanda became a *willing* avatar. She decided to use the very medium that was used against her, the site of so much of her vulnerability and pain, namely social media. The very last image she posted is the image she wanted seen. It is an image of a young woman returning the gaze, not an unwilling avatar.

The popularization of the correlation between cutting, mental health, and social media usage has led to the presumption that correlation means causation. To return to Stuart Hall's (1973) analysis, to reinforce this understanding is to encourage a decoding, or reading, that girls bodies online are ripe for victimization. Hegemonic discourse suggests that social media and technology in general is separate from bodies and quite beyond the capacities of young women. The logic of this storyline, as we've narrated until now, reinforces classic dualistic divides between women/Nature/Body/private versus Men/Mind/Technology/public.

#IAM#MALALA

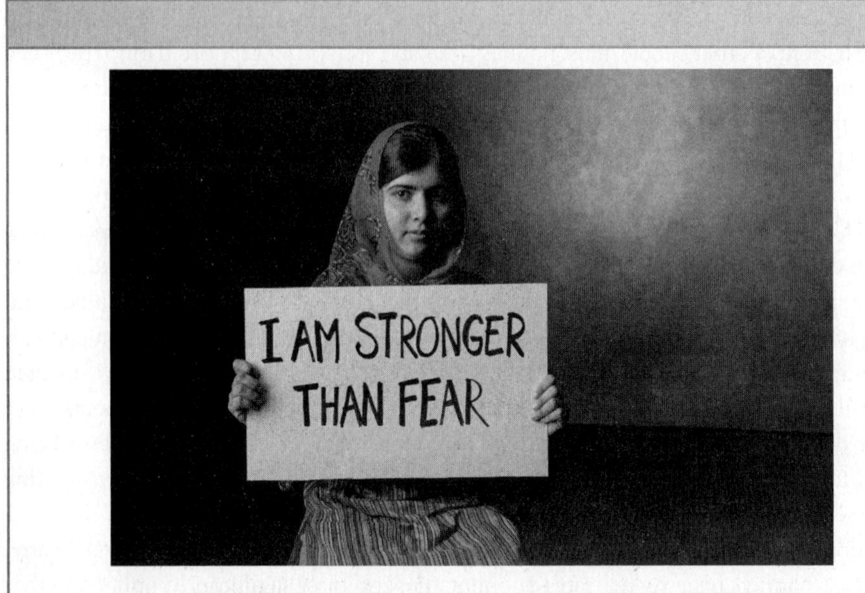

Source: Global Partnership for Education. [Online Image]. https://www.facebook.com/globalpartnership/photos/a.247464265289994.53377.247459801957107/700417876661295/

> I come from Swat Valley, Pakistan. A region where rifles are fired to celebrate the birth of a son, but daughters are hidden away behind a curtain. Where I grew up girls were afraid to go to school. But I'm not afraid. I believe that education is a universal human right. I believe that one child, one teacher, one book, one pen, can change the world. Schools were attacked. I still went and I spoke out. We realize the importance of our voices only when we are silenced. I was shot on a Tuesday, at lunchtime. One bullet, one gunshot, heard around the world. But here I stand; I am Malala.[17]

While Amanda's story is read and positioned as a cautionary tale of either shameful behaviour (as wanton as Lolita's) or victimization by sexual predators, Malala Yousafzai's story is based on a survival narrative. Malala was born the same year as Amanda but in a vastly different country. Malala was born in the Swat Valley of Pakistan. Her father was a huge proponent of girls' right to education and owned and operated a school for both boys and girls. Malala's first contact with the media was in 2008 at the age of 11 (Ellick, 2012). The Taliban, an Islamic fundamentalist political movement, had already banned TV and music (Peer, 2012) and a website for the BBC Urdu was interested in presenting a novel way of covering the Taliban's increasing presence. The BBC contacted Malala's family and she posted her first blog post January 3, 2009, under the pseudonym "cornflower" (Boone, 2012). Malala narrated her thoughts about everyday life under the Taliban and in her blog under the name Gul Makai, she began to focus on the on again, off again availability of education for girls in the region. The Taliban originally closed girls' schools but then boys' schools closed their doors in solidarity. Local boys returned to school and girls were permitted to attend co-ed classes but not girls' only schools. When tensions and Taliban control of the region increased, Malala's blog went silent mid-March 2009.

After the publication of the blog posts, *New York Times* reporter Adam B. Ellick approached Malala and her father to produce a documentary. The film recounts Malala's vision of education for all girls. Following the documentary, Malala began to gain traction in mainstream media as a political figure. She was interviewed locally by several national news stations as well as internationally by the *Toronto Star*. She received several awards for her efforts for girl's education.

Not all the attention she received, however, was positive. Malala began to experience harassment both on- and offline. Similar to Amanda, Malala was an active user of Facebook and several anonymous users created fake profiles for her (Peer, 2012). The harassment escalated and she started receiving threatening messages, including death threats. Local police communicated to her that the Taliban were targeting Malala and two other female activists. Strangers were constantly seen outside the family's house, lurking in the shadows despite nightly police patrols. Malala recalls this general, day-to-day fear by describing what happens while the bus they were riding hit a large pothole jerking her sleeping brother awake. Startled, his first question was "Was that a bomb blast? This was the fear that filled our daily lives. Any small disturbance or noise could be a bomb or gunfire." (Yousafzai & Lamb, 2012, p. 84).

Although Malala never admitted to being frightened by the rising threats and the daily fears, she began to take precautionary measures to assure her safety and the safety of her family.

> At night I would wait until everyone was asleep—my mother, my father, my brothers, [. . .] then I'd check every single door and window. I'd go outside and make sure the front gate was locked. Then I would check all the rooms, one by one. My room was at the front with lots of windows and I kept the curtains open. I wanted to be able to see everything." (Yousafzai & Lamb, 2012 p. 118)

On October 9, 2012, the online threats and the offline fears were realized. While riding a bus home from a school exam, a Taliban soldier boarded and called out her name. Threatening to kill all girls on the bus if she did not identify herself, Malala stood up and was shot. One bullet went through her head and neck and became lodged in her shoulder. She went through intense medical treatment, which included temporarily removing part of her skull, but her recovery was relatively quick, given the nature of the injury, and by October 17, she emerged from a coma.

Media outlets around the world covered the shooting. The United Nations, the United States government, celebrities all proclaimed their hope for Malala's recovery and their support for her causes. In October of 2012, the UN Special Envoy for Global Education Gordon Brown launched a petition in her name and using the slogan "I am Malala." The petitions demanded that no child be left out of school by 2015.

At the outset, Malala's words, then her image, and then her body, became the site of political debate. The words of her blog were used to add a personal connection to the political turmoil in the Swat Valley. The BBC Urdu service reporter responsible for setting up Malala's first blog, said that in choosing her name "corn flower," which harkens to a traditional Swat Valley folk tale, he "wanted to give an indigenous, symbolic attachment to Swat so that people could own it journalistically" (Rahman, 2014). It also meant that they could own or at least attach themselves directly and rhetorically into Malala's plight. Her face and her body on the screen of the documentary became the embodiment of her political motives that quickly, through other media outlets, began to network amid more global political motives and movements. She was reproduced and rebroadcast through global media outlets, which individually curated and manicured her words, image, and body in different ways.

Malala's words, image, and body were copied and redistributed digitally around the world. Did she become a *willing* avatar because her body became a symbolic site for the battle over girls' right to education? In a post-colonial analysis of Malala's story, author Fauzia Rahman wrote, "The message around her was always, imagine: if a girl can rise out of their current contents of patriarchy, repression, cultural backwardness, and poverty, and claim their rights not only as Pakistani citizens, but also global citizens for the 21st century?" (Rahman, 2014). Her narrative, when retold in Canada and the United States, presented her as an example of the plight of a girl who represented a struggling but hopeful developing nation.

The image of Malala watching TV and fighting with her brothers over the remote control was never a part of the public discourse that surrounded her, but was a key part of her autobiography, being mentioned several times. Malala's favorite show was *Ugly Betty*, and she wrote the following in her autobiography, *I am Malala*, about the show and what it means to be female in Western society: "Although Betty and her friends had certain rights, women in the United States were still not completely equal; their images were used to sell things. In some ways, I decided, women are showpieces in American society too" (Yousafzai & Lamb, 2013).

The embeddedness of colonial discourses in Malala's narrative is illustrated by a statement by United States Senator Dianne Feinstein in the *Huffington Post* and reprinted in her newsletter: "The barbaric attack on this brave girl should be condemned by the civilized world" (Feinstein, 2012). *Civilized world* is key. Malala's story highlights the emancipatory potential of social media for girls around the world (Clinton, 2010; MacKinnon, 2012). Implicit in this logic is the idea that without technology, girls are helpless. Technology and its power usurp the individual capacity of girls—a logic that is opposite of the dystopian projection of girls with technology implicit in the discourse surrounding Amanda Todd. In both cases girls, on their own, are unable to wield and manage the overwhelming potential of social media and technology that can be used for us vs. them.

Interestingly, Malala's feelings about herself, her *body*, changed when she started seeing herself through the media gaze. While on the one hand Malala understands the complexity involving the media's representation of women (as demonstrated in her discussion of *Ugly Betty*) she, similar to Amanda, saw her media-self through the male gaze: "I suddenly noticed all kinds of things about my looks—things that had never much bothered me before. My skin was too dark. My eyebrows were too thick. One of my eyes were smaller than the other. And I hated the little moles that dotted my cheek" (Yousafzai & Lamb, 2013).

Through the global reach of her words, images, and body, Malala's online presentation of herself spread globally. But her post-attack vision did not align with the vision of powerful groups who began to see the power of her online identity and influence. She had been violated verbally online for quite a time before she was shot. She was depicted negatively in anger, and finally action when the bullet pierced her skull on October 9, 2012. At that point there no longer existed a separation of online and offline space. Malala's online and offline selves became one. Her attack became a spark that catalyzed the future of online/offline communication, online/offline advocacy, and online/offline reality.

Amanda Hess (2014) further documents this private-public collapse. Documenting her story (she was threatened with beheading and rape), she maintains that "on the internet women are overpowered and devalued" and that instances of cyber violence have transferred into actual in-person violence. Hess states the following:

"Ignore the barrage of violent threats and harassing messages that confront you online everyday." That's what women are told. But these relentless messages are an assault on women's careers, their psychological bandwidth, and their freedom to live online. We have been thinking about internet harassment all wrong.

Significantly, the stories Hess recounts all involve women who are speaking and writing publically in cyberspace about gender equality. Of victims of online harassment, 60% are female and within the total harassment cases reported, 76% saw an escalation of violence and 25% saw offline threats of violence (WHOA, 2013). Another major study reported that 5% of female internet users reported that online harassment led to offline "physical danger" (Hess, 2014).

#BACKLASH

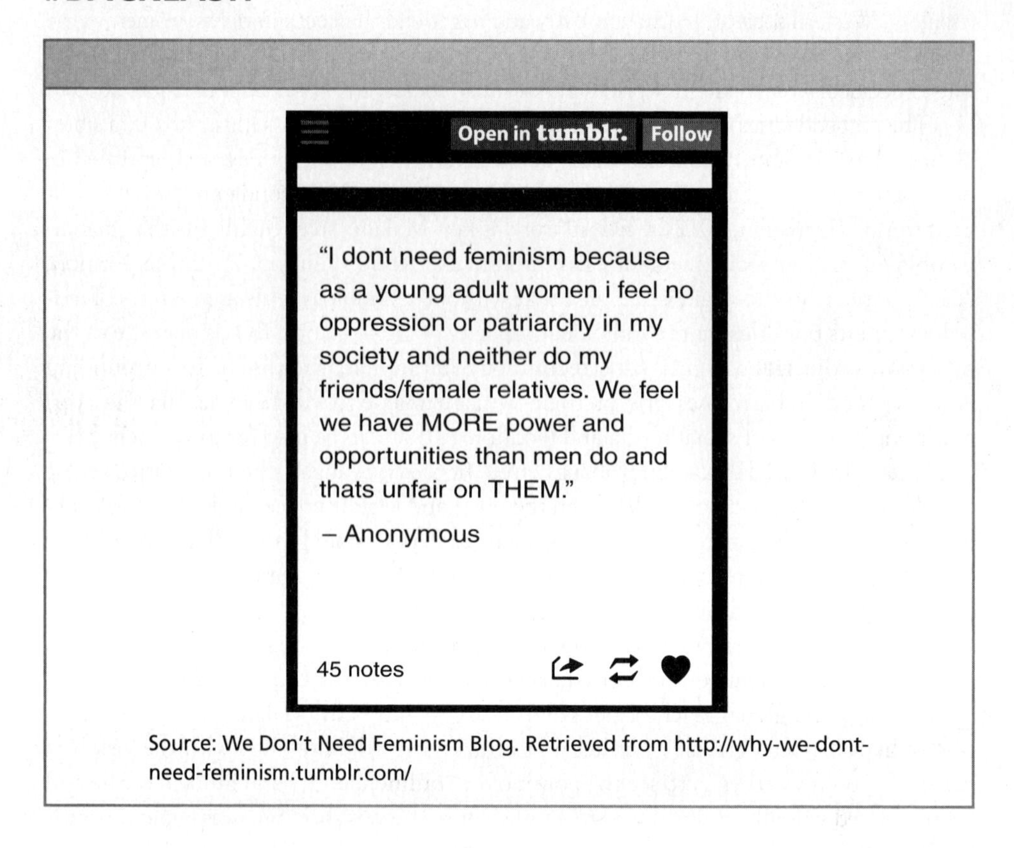

Source: We Don't Need Feminism Blog. Retrieved from http://why-we-dont-need-feminism.tumblr.com/

In April 2012, just months before both Malala and Amanda's online identities went viral, on the Duke University campus in North Carolina, 16 young women enrolled in a "Women in Public Space" class as part of their women's studies course. Inspired by feminist theory and history, they decided to use social media as a way to "fight back against popular misconceptions surrounding feminist movement" and created an online media campaign to expose stereotypes surrounding feminism and challenge the belief that feminism is no longer needed (Beattie et al., 2012). Through interactive social media sites such as Twitter, Facebook, and Tumblr they launched a campaign that showcased young women holding up hand-written signs stating "I need feminism because . . ." finished with a personalized reason why they needed feminism to draw attention to issues at the heart of gender ideology. A year later the Duke University group had 29 000 Facebook likes and universities across the United States, Canada, the United Kingdom, Australia, and even Pakistan quickly followed and started their own campaigns taking over cyberspace (Seidman, 2013).

Young women and girls who attempt to claim an equal amount of space in the public/private realms experience backlash, which demonstrates why feminism is necessary and how the collapse between cyber- and offline space is complete. For example, a group of 16-, 17-, and 18-year-old young women from Altricham Grammar School in Cheshire, England, created their own Who Needs Feminism Society with school approval. As in the other campaigns, they made posters showing themselves holding up signs stating why they needed feminism. Each poster had a deeply personal reason. They found that the more they voiced their right to openly discuss gender issues, the "more vitriolic the boys' abuse became" (Younis, 2013). Jinan writes the following:

> We were told that our "militant vaginas" were "as dry as the Sahara desert", girls who complained of sexual objectification in their photos were given ratings out of 10, details of the sex lives of some of the girls were posted beside their photos. And others were sent threatening messages warning them that things would soon "get personal."

The school issued a statement similar to Franks' contentions: women who experience harassment need to leave the site. The blame lies solely on the young women for daring to claim space, any space in the name of equality:

> We are committed to protecting the safety and welfare of our students, which extends to their safety on-line. We consider very carefully any society that the school gives its name to and support to. As such, we will take steps to recommend students remove words or images that they place online that could compromise their safety or that of other students at the school. (Younis, 2013)

In the summer of 2014, another online campaign trended and served as a backlash to the *I Need Feminism Because . . .* campaign.[18] *#WomenAgainstFeminism* and *#idontneedfeminism* started on Tumblr but soon took over other SNS including Facebook and Twitter. Stuart Hall could not have anticipated how his encoding/decoding model could be reconfigured in the age of social media. The messages produced by the originators of the *#idontneedfeminism* meme suggested that certain young girls believed that "feminism" was not necessary anymore because women are equal. Furthermore, these authors conceived of "feminism" as reinforcing gender inequalities and continuing to position women as less than men. Some of the most popular #idontneedfeminism memes showed selfies with girls holding up signs that read:

"#idontneedfeminism because they reject femininity but try to feminize men and demand equality but ask for special treatment."

"#idontneedfeminism because it demonizes traditional family constructs, because I do not blame men for an action I am responsible for, and being whistled at or complimented on the street is not oppression.

"#idontneedfeminism I am not a target of violence and there is not war against me."

Although the meme garnered enough hegemonic followers for it to gain traction,[19] the majority of the news coverage and public uproar was a result of oppositional readings. Many girls, vehemently challenged the original viral message by creating the oppositional hashtag *#idoneedfeminism*. These hashtags reminded girls that they wouldn't have the privilege they have right now had it not been for the hard work and history of feminism that came before them.

"I do need feminism because who do you think fought for our right to vote? Feminists! Feminism = equal rights. #idoneedfeminism."

Several memes pointed out the misconstrued definitions the original producers had of "feminism," equating feminism with militancy, anger, and man-hating. They commented that these girls saw feminism through the lens of dominant discourses and not reality. Perhaps this was made most visible by the number of male allies who took to the campaign holding signs such as the following:

"I need feminism because men of quality support women's equality #idoneedfeminism."

"I need feminism because I know I hold gender biases and I don't want to #idoneedfeminism."

Other commentators considered the need for feminism on a global scale.

"I need feminism because 1 woman dies every 7 minutes due to an unsafe and illegal abortion. Our struggle for equality is far from over. Women's rights = human rights. #idoneedfeminism."

Paralleling some of the intersectional demands of third-wave feminists such as Rebecca Walker, the oppositional #solidarityisforwhitewomen hashtag pointed a finger at the privileged position of the white middle-class population of faces who predominantly tended to colour (or not colour) the selfies of both the "I do" and I don't" side of the debate. Some oppositional tweets highlighted the "compassion gap" (Kristof, 2014) between the white middle-class privileged youth of America and other oppressed groups. Other oppositional tweets highlighted the neo-liberal agenda embedded in the stereotype of girl-power feminism that argues if a girl wants it, it's a matter of her and her hard work against the world (McRobbie, 2009).[20]

"#solidarityisforwhitewomen when poc [people of colour] are angry for no reason but white women are 'passionate crusaders for justice.'"

"#solidarityisforwhitewomen when convos about the gender pay gap ignore that white women earn more than black, latino, and Native American men."

"#solidarityisforwhitewomen when Rihanna is criticized for wearing a carnival outfit bt Lena Dunham is praised for going topless."

Another important movement launched in reaction to the #idontneedfeminism movement meme was the hashtag #notyourasiansidekick, a product of freelance writer and activist Suey Park. In support of Asian American feminism, Park said she started the hashtag because, as a Korean-American, she was "tired of the patriarchy in Asian American spaces and sick of the racism in white feminism" (Kim, 2013). Many of her tweets and the tweets of others under this hashtag listed media stereotypes and personal experiences of gender or racial prejudice and ignorance.

"Not all #indians are engineers and doctors. And the rest of us don't answer phones for a living. #notyourasiansidekick."

"'Do you know Korean?' 'No I speak Japanese.' 'they're pretty similar right?' THEY ARE LITERALLY DIFFERENT LANGUAGES! #notyourasiansidekick."

This case illustrates how feminists, discussions about feminism, and the principles behind the ideology are being reshaped through social media. The #idontneedfeminism movement embodies the conclusion of this chapter where we suggest that the reshaping of the medium—from broadcast media to social media—could be leading to a reshaping of the relationship among bodies, discourses, and ideologies that, instead of being fixed for long periods of time and controlled by a limited set of voices, are now being hacked through a perpetual digitally mediated living and fluid conversation.

#CYBORG

In the face of a waning period of social feminism in the 1970s, Donna Haraway, a critic of power constructs in the natural sciences, penned an ironic paper chastising the Cartesian, patriarchic, and capitalist dualisms that shape the oppressive structures in which feminism operates. Rather than suggesting working within the existing systems, Haraway proposed an ironic linguistic ontological paradigm shift. She said that the way we think about and conceive of concepts like nature/technology and man/woman shape the way we talk about and treat them in their material forms. She clearly lays out the relationship—as we have throughout this chapter—how ideology shapes discourse that then controls bodies in the material world.

The power of her ironic propositions is evident when she says that high-tech culture (cyberspace before cyberspace existed) could help in erasing, discursively, and thus ideologically, the borders between these dualisms:

> High-tech culture challenges these dualisms in intriguing ways. It is not clear who makes and who is made in the relation between human and machine. It is not clear what is mind and what is body in machines that resolve into coding practices. In so far as we know ourselves in both formal discourse (for example, biology) and in daily practice (for example, the homework economy in the integrated circuit), we find ourselves to be cyborgs, hybrids, mosaics, chimeras. Biological organisms have become biotic systems, communications devices like others. There is no fundamental, ontological separation in our formal knowledge of machine and organism, of technical and organic. (Haraway, 1991, p. 179)

We can apply this idea to the real dynamics of social media today. Whereas broadcast media (a major manufacturer of dominant discourse) is so deeply rooted in a capitalist, patriarchal, and Cartesian dualistic matrix that its ideology and discourses seem immovable and fixed, the fluid and dialogic nature of social media changes these dynamics. If, in the traditional model, dominant ideology (e.g., capitalism) shaped dominant discourses (e.g., public/private domains), which in turn orders bodies (e.g., women in private abode and men in the public arena), in the realm of social media the model is reversed. Without sounding too utopian in our own proclamations, we must fully acknowledge that major conglomerates still do control SMSs and mine our conversations, status updates, tweets, and tags for metadata to sell to advertisers. But unlike broadcast media, the gatekeeper sits more at the point of the medium and less at the point of the message.

The mass of people (bodies) who have access to social media perpetuate a mass of voices, chatter, and talk (discourse) that at least sit alongside and at most challenge the hegemonic voices (dominant discourses) on the same terrain. This mass of voices, such as those from #solidarityisforwhitewomen and #notyourasiansidekick, flood our eyes and ears with oppositional and negotiated readings of original texts. Oppositional discourses hold a mirror up to privilege and control and give rise to a backlash of voices from *real bodies* of those who are marginalized and located beyond the focused lens of the majority. This constant, forceful nattering turns ossified dominant discourse into living discourse and in that process makes embedded ideology visible and potentially accountable. Whereas the ideological foundation to the commercial broadcast media system perpetuates discourse, which affects and shapes bodies, the potential to reverse this pattern lies in social media. The mass of diverse, marginalized, and real bodies shapes discourse, which in turn exposes dominant ideological standpoints. This in turn has the potential to come full circle by even shaping our bodies.

Social media provides a stage for women to write, post, and update ourselves into being. On social media, we work in and through what we "ought to be"—the structures that have determined us for so long—to find, figure out, and broadcast "who we really are," and in those digital instances the lines between ideology/discourse/text and body collapse too because with every Instagram image, tweet, and Tumblr post we are re-presenting and making "women" anew. To quote Hélène Cixous in *the Laugh of Medusa*,

> She must write her self, because this is the invention of a new *insurgent* writing which, when the moment of her liberation has come, will allow her to carry out the indispensable ruptures and transformations in her history . . . It is by writing, from and toward women, and by taking up the challenge of speech which has been governed by the phallus, that women will confirm women in a place other than that which is reserved in and by the symbolic, that is, in a place other than silence . . . (1976, pp. 880–881).

In the constantly connected lives of plugged-in girls who are adding to online discourse and challenging ideological structures, under this new operative system, text is not static and disconnected. Text is reconnected to producer and to a physically embodied, living being. The dualism between body and technology is erased and a new accountability and respect for text is absolute and necessary. Under this paradigm shift, we can see how the textual and symbolic violence against Amanda is simply violence like any other kind that occurs in the offline world. We can also understand how the physical violence against Malala's body is also symbolically important because it relates not to just one girl but to the integrated circuit of all the bodies labelled as "female."

Haraway suggests that cyborgs are a product of the imagination and flesh, a substance in the material world. She says that women are cyborgs—a combination of the imaginary and the real. "By the late twentieth century, our time, a mythic time, we are all chimeras, theorized and fabricated hybrids of machine and organism; in short, we are cyborgs" (1991, p. 150).

Haraway suggests that women have always been mediated. We have always been part flesh and part imaginary, part media construction and part lived flesh. She proposes a fracturing of boundaries and binaries, suggesting there is no distinction between natural life and artificial machine because discourses that reinforce these binaries also reinforce the structures that have historically oppressed "women, people of color, nature, workers, animals . . . all [those] constituted as others" (p. 178).

Social media and the lives of plugged-in girls must be considered in this manner if we are to attempt to understand what they are really like. We must rethink an ontology that stitches back together cleaved dichotomies, which control, organize, and oppress. We are nature and we are technology. We are public and we are private. We are text and we are body. We are objectified and subjectively embodied.

Endnotes

1. In ***The Aftermath of Feminism***, McRobbie (2009) explains how melancholia, illness, and discontent have become key identifying elements of contemporary girlhood. Embodying this melancholy doesn't challenge norms; rather, we are melancholically accepting of our place within the heterosexual matrix.
2. The research for this chapter involved in-depth narrative interviews with four cisgender girls, with a variety of different gender expressions, who were between the ages of 13 and 16 all located on the west coast of Canada. Ethics approval of this research was granted by Kwantlen Polytechnic University in August of 2014.
3. We are utilizing D. E. Smith's contention that despite co-writing ***The German Ideology*** with Friedrich Engels, the work is most notably that of Marx. See Smith, 1987.
4. For a thorough discussion of this please see D. E. Smith, 1990.
5. Most significant that they are Lords not Ladies.
6. Interview, Plugged-in Girl One, September 16, 2014.
7. Interview, Plugged-in Girl Two, September 24, 2014.
8. Steeves (2014) notes that both Facebook and Twitter have age restrictions of 13+ but the restrictions are ignored, as the statistics suggest.
9. Interview, Plugged-in Girl One, September 16, 2014.
10. Published on September 7, 2012 under the YouTube username TheSomebodytoKnow
11. Published on September 7, 2012 under the YouTube username TheSomebodytoKnow
12. Bracelets are also used to hide self-injurious behaviours such as cutting and are sometimes worn as act as inspirations to not self-harm. Retrieved from https://self-injury.net/self-injurers/in-their-own-words/how-do-you-hide-your-self-harm/bracelets-help-hide
13. In April 2014, a 35-year-old man living in the Netherlands was arrested and charged with extortion, internet luring, criminal harassment, and child pornography in connection to Amanda's suicide and in dozens of other cases involving the sextortian of underage girls. See Culbert & Hager, 2014; White, 2014a, 2014b.
14. 303 non self-harmers and 84 self-harmers.

15. Original Broadcast date, November 15, 2013.
16. BlogTV is a live-streaming video website where people, generally youth, express their talents and ideas.
17. #wearesilent Campaign. April, 2014. www.youtube.com/watch?v=8Se1MpgdN-0.
18. At the time of writing this chapter, on September 22, 2014, British actress and United Nations Women's Goodwill Ambassador Emma Watson gave a speech at the UN in New York to launch her #HeForShe campaign for gender equality. Watson's plea included the argument that women should have the right to make choices about their bodies. Her speech went viral and within a few hours a website was created, "Emma You Are Next," threatening to leak nude photos of the feminist/celebrity. This is another example of the online backlash against girls and young women who speak out against gender inequality.
19. To date, the Women Against Feminism Facebook page has 23 913 likes.
20. McRobbie, 2009.

Discussion Questions

1. Watch Amanda Todd's YouTube video and Malala Yousafzai's *New York Times* documentary. What do you think about the way the two women are portrayed in the different styles of videos: one camgirl-style and one documentary style?
2. We suggest that all women are mediated and have always been mediated. Discuss this statement. Do you believe it's true? How do you see media affecting you?
3. Discuss the concept of the "unwilling avatar." Can you think of a case in the news where a person has become an unwilling avatar or turned into a meme?
4. Do you have different personae for different social media accounts? What are your different personae?

Bibliography

Adams, S. (2013, January 29). Teens using mobile for self-harming competitions: children are using smartphones to film themselves self-harming before sending pictures to their friends in new trend, parents and teachers have warned. *The Telegraph*. Retrieved from www.telegraph.co.uk/health/healthnews/9835457/Teens-using-mobiles-for-self-harming-competitions.html?mobile=basic

Adorno, T., & Horkheimer, M. (1972). *Dialectic of enlightenment*. New York, NY: Herder and Herder.

Alper, M. (2014). *Digital youth with disabilities*. Cambridge, UK: The MIT Press.

Arbuthnot, L., & Seneca, G. (1990). Pre-text and text in gentlemen prefer blondes. In P. Erens (Ed.), *Issues in Feminist Film Criticism*, (pp. 112–125). Bloomington, IN: Indiana University Press.

Bailey, J., & Steeves, V. (2013). Will the real digital girl please stand up? Examining the gap between policy dialogue and girls' accounts of their digital existence. In G. Wise and H. Koskela (Eds.) *New visualities, new technologies: The new ecstasy of communication.* New York, NY: Ashgate Publishing. Retrieved from http://ssrn.com/abstract=2316907

Bartky, S. L. (1997). Foucault, femininity and the modernization of patriarchal power. In K. Conboy, N. Media, & S. Stanbury (Eds.), *Writing on the Body: Female embodiment and feminist theory* (pp. 129–154). New York, NY: Columbia University Press.

Beattie, A., Burrows, M., Gadsden, K., Kendrick, S. (2012, April 12). Who needs feminism? Retrieved from www.dukechronicle.com/articles/2012/04/12/who-needs-feminism#.VawnnLVUDm4

Before, during and after sex selfies. (n.d.) Retrieved from *aftersexselfiesofficial.tumblr.com/*

Berger, J. (1973). *Ways of seeing*. London, UK: BBC and Penguin.

Boone, J. (2012, October 9). Malala Yousafzai: Pakistan Taliban causes revulsion by shooting girl who speaks out. *The Guardian*. Retrieved from www.theguardian.com/world/2012/oct/09/taliban-pakistan-shoot-girl-malala-yousafzai

Bordo, S. (1993). *Unbearable weight: Feminism, western culture, and the body*. Los Angeles, CA: University of California Press.

boyd, d. (2006). Super Publics [blog post]. Retrieved from www.zephoria.org/thoughts/archives/2006/03/22/super_publics.html

boyd, d., & Ellison, N. (2007). Social network sites: Definition, history, and scholarship. *Journal of Computer-Mediated Communication, 13*(1), pp. 210–230.

Butler, J. (1990). *Gender trouble: Feminism and the subversion of identity*. London, England: Routledge.

Canadian Centre for Child Protection. (2014, September 4). Alert for parents: Sextortionists targeting teens. In News and Media. Retrieved from https://protectchildren.ca/app/en/media_release_201409_sextortionists_teens

The Canadian Press. (2014, March 15). Canadian hospitals stretched as self-harming teens seek help. Retrieved from www.cbc.ca/news/canada/canadian-hospitals-stretched-as-self-harming-teens-seek-help-1.2574316

Cixous, H. (1976). The laugh of medusa. *Signs*, *1*(4), pp. 875–893.

Cooper, B. (2000). "Chick Flicks" as feminist texts: The appropriation of the male gaze in Thelma & Louise. *Women's Studies in Communication*, *23*(3), 277–306.

Courtesy of Free The Children's We Are Silent campaign (www.freethechildren.com), for which Malala Yousafzai is a 2014 Ambassador.

Culbert, L., & Hager, M. (2014, June 27). Dutch Man charged in Amanda Todd online blackmail case. *The Vancouver Sun*. Retrieved from www.vancouversun.com/life/Dutch+charged+Amanda+Todd+online+blackmail+case/9749151/story.html

Dobson, A. S. (2014) Performative shamelessness on young women's social network sites: Shielding the self and resisting gender melancholia. Feminism & Psychology, 24(1) 97–114.

Dobson, K., boyd, d., Ju, W., Donath, J., & Ishii, H. (2001). *Creating visceral personal and social interactions in mediated spaces*. Interactive Poster at Conference on Human Factors and Computing Systems (CHI 2001). Seattle, Washington: ACM, March 31–April 5, 2001.

Duggan, M. (2013, September 12). It's a woman's social media world. *FactTank: PEW Research Centre*. Retrieved from www.pewresearch.org/fact-tank/2013/09/12/its-a-womans-social-media-world/

Essinger, J. (2007). *Jacquard's web: How a hand-loom led to the birth of the information age*. Oxford, England: Oxford University Press.

Feinstien, D. (2012, October 17). Malala tragedy reveals plight of Afpak girls. Retrieved from www.feinstein.senate.gov/public/index.cfm/op-eds?ID=9559984e-6c38-4433-941d-15ea18fa4356.

Frank, S., Dahler L., Santurri L. E., & Knight K. (2010, November 6–10). Hyper-texting and hyper-networking: A new health risk for teens? Paper presented at the 138th American Public Health Association's Annual Meeting and Expo, Denver, Colorado.

Franks, M. A. (2011). Unwilling avatars: Idealism and discrimination in cyberspace. *Columbia Journal of Gender and Law*, *20*, 224–248.

Fuchs, C. (2014). *Social media: A critical introduction*. London: Sage.

Gajjala, R. (2012). *Cyberculture and the subaltern*. Plymouth, UK: Lexington Books.

Gamman, L. (1989). Watching the detectives: The enigma of the female gaze. In L. Gamman & M. Marshment (Eds.), *The female gaze: Women as viewers of popular culture* London, UK: The Women's Press.

Gehl, J. (1987). *Life between buildings: Using public space*. (Jo Koch, trans.). New York, NY: Van Nostrand Reinhold.

Goffman, E. (1959). *The presentation of the self in everyday life*. New York, NY: Anchor Press.

Greer, G. (1999). *The whole woman*. London, England: Black Swan.

Hall, S. (1973). Encoding and decoding in the television discourse. In *Centre for Cultural Studies* CCS Stenciled Paper no.7. Birmingham, UK: University of Birmingham, Centre for Cultural Studies.

Haraway, D. (1991). A cyborg manifesto: Science, technology, and socialist-feminism in the late twentieth century. In *Simians, Cyborgs, and Women: The Reinvention of Nature* (pp. 149–181). New York: Routledge.

Hasinoff, A. (2012). Sexting as media production: Rethinking social media and sexuality. *New Media and Society* [On-line]. Retrieved from http://nms.sagepub.com/content/early/2012/09/23/1461444812459171

Hawton, K., Hall, S., Simikin, S., Bale, E., & Bond, A. (2012). Self-harm and suicide in adolescents *The Lancet*, *379*, 2373–2382.

Hess, A. (2014, January/February). The next civil rights issue: Why women aren't welcome on the internet. *Pacific Standard: The Science of Society*. Retrieved from www.psmag.com/navigation/health-and-behavior/women-arent-welcome-internet-72170/

Hinduja, S., & Patchin, J. W. (2009). *Bullying beyond the school yard: Preventing and responding to cyberbullying.* Thousand Oaks, CA: Sage Publications (Corwin Press).

Hinduja, S., Patchin, J. W. (2010). Bullying, cyberbullying, and suicide. *Archives of Suicide Research*, *14*(3), 206–221.

James, S. A. (2013). *Has cutting become cool? Normalizing, social influence and socially-motivated deliberate self-harm in adolescent girls* (doctoral dissertation, Massey University, Albany, New Zealand. Retrieved from http://mro.massey.ac.nz/bitstream/handle/10179/4671/02_whole.pdf?sequence=1&isAllowed=y

Kaplan, E. A. (1997). *Looking for the Other: Feminism, Film, and the Imperial Gaze*. New York: Routledge.

Kim, K., Ryu, E., Chon, M. Y., Choi, S. Y., Seo, J. S., & Nam, B. W. (2006). Internet addiction in Korean adolescents and its relation to depression and suicidal ideation: A questionnaire survey. *International Journal of Nursing Studies*, *43*(2), 185–192.

Kim, Y. (2013, December 17). #NOTYOURASIANSIDEKICK is a civil rights movement for Asian American women. Retrieved from, www.theguardian.com/commentisfree/2013/dec/17/not-your-asian-sidekick-asian-women-feminism

Kolko B. & Nakamura, L. (2000). *Race in cyberspace*. New York: Routledge.

Kristof, N. (2014, March 1). The compassion gap. *The New York Times*. Retrieved from www.nytimes.com/2014/03/02/opinion/sunday/kristof-the-compassion-gap.html?_r=0

Lam, L. T., Peng, Z., Mai, J., & Jing, J. (2009). The association between internet addiction and self-injurious behavior among adolescents. *Injury Prevention*, *15*(6), 403–408.

Lee, D.-H. and Sohn, S.-H. (2004, October). *Is there a gender difference in mobile phone usage?* In S. D. Kim (Ed.), Mobile Communication and Social Media Conference Proceedings, South Korea, pp. 243–259.

Leena, K., Tomi, L., & Arja, R. R. (2005). Intensity of mobile use and health-compromising behaviours: How is information and communication technology connected to health-related lifestyle in adolescence? *Journal of Adolescence*, *28*(1), 35–47.

Levy, A. (2005). *Female chauvinist pigs: Women and the rise of raunch culture*. New York: Simon and Shuster.

Lloyd, G. (1984). *The Man of Reason: 'Male' and 'Female' in Western Philosophy*. London: Methuen.

MacKinnon, C. (1987). *Feminism Unmodified*. Cambridge, MA: Harvard University Press.

Madden, M., Lenhart, A., Cortesi, S., Gasser, U., Duggan, M., Smith, A., & Beaton, M. (2013). *Teens, Social Media and Privacy*. Beckman Center for Internet Research: Harvard University: Pew Research Center. Retrieved from www.pewinternet.org/files/2013/05/PIP_TeensSocialMediaandPrivacy_PDF.pdf

Marx, K. (1998). *The german ideology*. New York, NY: Prometheus Books.

Mayne, J. (1993). *Cinema and spectatorship*. New York, NY: Routledge.

McElroy, W. (1996). *Sexual correctness: The gender-feminist attack on women*. Jefferson, NC: McFarland & Company Inc. Press.

McRobbie, A. (2009). *The aftermath of feminism: Gender, culture, and social change*. London, UK: Sage.

Messias, E., Castro, J., Saini, A., Usman, M., & Peeples, D. (2011). Sadness, suicide, and their association with video game and internet overuse among teens: Results from the youth risk behavior survey 2007 and 2009. *Suicide Life Threat Behavior*, *41*(3), 307–315.

Mitchell, K. J., & Ybarra, M. L. (2007). Online behavior of youth who engage in self-harm provides clues for preventative intervention. *Preventative Medicine*, *45*, 392–396.

Mosco, V. (2009). *The political economy of communication*. (2nd ed.). London, England: Sage Publishing.

Mulvey, L. (1975). Visual pleasure and narrative cinema. *Screen*, *16*(3), 6–18.

Oxford Dictionary of English (3rd ed.). (2010). Oxford, UK: Oxford University Press.

Peer, B. (2012, October 10). The Girl who wanted to go to school. *The New Yorker*. Retrieved from www.newyorker.com/news/news-desk/the-girl-who-wanted-to-go-to-school

Rahman, F. (2014). We are not all Malala! In L. Herrera (Ed.), *Wired Citizenship: Youth Learning and Activism in the Middle East* (pp. 99–116). New York, NY: Routledge.

Ringrose, J. (2011). Are you sexy, flirty or a slut? Exploring "sexualisation" and how teen girls perform/negotiate digital sexual identity on social networking sites. In *New Femininities: Postfeminism, Neoliberalism and Identity* (99–116). London, UK: Palgrave.

Robins, K. (1995). Cyberspace and the world we live in. *Body & Society*, *1*(3–4), 135–155.

Rubin, G. (1987). Misguided, dangerous and wrong. In A. Assiter (Ed.), *Bad Girls and Dirty Pictures* (pp. 18–40). London, England: Pluto Press.

Russell, S., & Bakken, R. (2002). Development of autonomy in adolescents. In *NebGuide*. Lincoln: University of Nebraska. Retrieved from www.ianrpubs.unl.edu/epublic/archive/g1449/build/g1449.pdf

Seidman, R. (2013). Who needs feminism? One year and going strong. *Women AdvaNCe*. Retrieved from http://womenadvancenc.org/who-needs-feminism-one-year-and-going-strong-2/

Senft, T. M. (2008). *Camgirls: Celebrity & community in the age of social networks.* New York: Peter Lang Publishing, Inc.

Smith, D. (1987). *The everyday world as problematic: A feminist sociology*. Toronto: University of Toronto Press.

Smith, D. (1990). *The conceptual practices of power: A feminist sociology of knowledge*. Toronto: University of Toronto Press.

Smith, D. (1999). *Writing the social*. Toronto: University of Toronto Press.

Stacey, J. (1991). Feminine fascinations: Forms of identification in star-audience relations. In Gledhill, C. (Ed.), *Stardom: Industry of desire* (141–163). New York: Routledge.

Steeves, V. (2014a). *Young Canadians in a wired world, Phase III: Cyberbullying: Dealing with online meanness, cruelty and threats*. Ottawa: Media Smarts.

Steeves, V. (2014b). *Young Canadians in a wired world, Phase III: Life online*. Ottawa: Media Smarts.

Studlar, G. (1990). Reconciling feminism and phenomenology: Notes on problems and possibilities, texts and contexts. *Quarterly Review of Film & Video*, *12*(3), 69–78.

Text from Youtube.com video; "My Story: Struggling, bullying, suicide, and self-harm." Used with permission of the Amanda Todd Legacy Society.

Ussher, J. M. (1997). *Fantasies of femininity: Reframing the boundaries of Sex*. New Brunswick, NJ: Rutgers University Press.

Vogel, S. (1996). *Against nature: The concept of nature in critical theory.* Albany, New York: State University of New York Press.

Werbin, K. C. (2012). Autobiography: on the immanent commodification of personal information. International Review of Information Ethics *17*(July), 46–53.

White, P. (2014a, May 31). On the trail of Amanda Todd's alleged tormentor/*The Globe & Mail*, Retrieved from www.theglobeandmail.com/news/world/on-the-trail-of-amanda-todds-alleged-tormentor/article18935075/?page=all

White, P. (2014b, June 25). Dutch police used controversial software in Amanda Todd case. *Globe & Mail.* Retrieved from www.theglobeandmail.com/news/world/dutch-police-used-contentious-software-in-amanda-todd-case/article19345909/

Whittington-Walsh, F. (2006). The broken mirror: Young women, beauty, and facial difference. *Women's Health and Urban Life* (Special Issue), *6*(2), 7–24.

WHOA. (2013). Cyberstalking Statistics. *Working to halt online abuse*. www.haltabuse.org

Yen, C. F., Tang, T. C., Yen, J. Y., Lin, H. C., Huang, C. F., Liu, S. C., & Ko, C. H. (2009). Symptoms of problematic cellular use: Functional impairment and its association with depression among adolescences in southern Taiwan, *Journal of Adolescence*, *32*(4), 863–873.

Younis, J. (2013, June 20). What happened when I started a feminist society at school. *The Guardian Blogging Students*. Retrieved from www.theguardian.com/education/mortarboard/2013/jun/20/why-i-started-a-feminist-society

Yousafzai, M. & Lamb, C. (2013). *I am Malala: The girl who stood up for education and was shot by the Taliban.* New York: Little, Brown and Company.

Yuan,-Sheng, Y., Ju-Yen, Y., Chih-Hung, K., Chung-Ping, C., & Cheng-Fang, Y. (2010). The association between problematic cellular phone use and risky behaviors and low self-esteem among Taiwanese adolescence. *BMC Public Health*, *10*, 217.

Chapter 5

Constructing Gender, Regulating Sexuality

Susanne Luhmann

INTRODUCTION

Sex always makes the news. As I am writing this, in Alberta in the summer of 2014, a hotly debated news topic is: Who should teach sex ed in high school and what should it entail? Earlier in the summer, Edmonton teenager Emily Dawson and her mother successfully filed a complaint with the Alberta Human Rights Commission after Emily's public high school, like many others in Edmonton, invited a Christian fundamentalist organization to teach sex ed. Although, according to Dawson, the organization's instructors more accurately taught "anti–sex ed," as they emphasized abstinence as the only viable option for young people. According to Emily, the instructor emphasized the dangers of sexuality, shamed girls and held them responsible for keeping boys' supposedly unbridled sexual urges at bay, refused to talk about LGBTQT2-S issues, and bashed single parent families. (CBC, 2014).

Learning about Sex—Constructing Sexuality

Does this sound familiar to you? Take a moment to reflect upon your own sex education, both inside and out of school. Where did you learn about sex: at home, at school, from the media, on the internet? Who taught you, where, and what did you learn? What did that education feel like: Did it make you feel afraid, nervous, curious, giggly, informed, proud, empowered, blasé, bored? What counts as "having sex"? What did you learn about different genders and sexual orientations? Do you feel your sex ed constructed sex as dangerous or pleasurable? Did it emphasize risk and violence?

Most likely, your school-based sex education stressed the risks of unplanned pregnancy, sexually transmitted infections, exploitation, and emotional heartbreak. Did you learn about pleasure or how to figure out what you do and don't like sexually? Did you learn about how to ask for and give (enthusiastic) consent? Did your sex ed class entail relevant information for students who identify as lesbian, gay, bisexual, asexual, intersex, trans, queer, or two-spirit? Most likely the answer to these latter questions is "No." Generally speaking, adults and educators tend to talk to young people primarily in terms of sex as dangerous, as something to be avoided or at least to be carefully regulated. Educators tend to speak very little about sexual pleasure, fearing that "all hell will break loose" if they do. This mode of emphasizing sex as hazardous, while downplaying the role of pleasure, is a central mode of regulating sexuality in the wider culture—with serious consequences, especially for people who already face sexism, homophobia, and/or transphobia. For students who don't identify as heterosexual and/or cisgendered, most school-based sex ed has nothing to offer beyond feeling alienated. By cisgendered I am referring to everybody whose sex assignment at birth (female or male) matches their gendered presentation (feminine or masculine) and their identity (woman or man).

In this chapter I explore how the regulation of sexuality works historically and in the contemporary moment and how feminist analyses and activisms both intervene in this regulation, as well as participate in it, at times. This chapter contests the assumption of a predestined "natural" sexuality; even though feminists and queers (these terms are not mutually exclusive) have often argued that repression of sexuality is a major problem in society. Instead I demonstrate how and where sexuality is socially constructed. I turn to feminist and queer scholarship to argue that policing, regulation, and resistance to/of sexuality, are part of the ongoing construction of sexuality. Everybody's sexuality is regulated in some form or other. Some modes of sexuality are privileged, socially valued, and rewarded while others are deemed "unnatural" and "immoral" and are subject to various forms of punishment. I also explore in detail how the regulation of sexuality works centrally through the policing of gender.

FIRST THOUGHTS ON SEX AND SEXUALITY (AND ON GENDER TOO)

Before we talk further about sex and sexuality—and feminism—I should perhaps introduce myself: I am a professor in the Department of Women's and Gender Studies at the University of Alberta and have been teaching a course on feminisms and sexualities for about 15 years. By addressing you the reader directly throughout this chapter, I hope that we can get a bit of an (imaginary) dialogue going: I hope you will speak back as you are reading this chapter.

So let's develop some common language. How do you define sex? Or, alternatively, what do popular sex surveys mean when they ask "how often do you have sex?" (Note that the "how often" question really seems to matter to people much more than the question of how good or enjoyable it was.) When does "having sex" begin: with a thought, a bodily response, an action? And when is sex "over": with an orgasm or ejaculation (his or hers)? Reflecting on this you see pretty quickly that the popular understanding of what "having sex" means is really quite unimaginative: usually it refers to heterosexual penetrative intercourse, which supposedly begins with his erection and ends with his ejaculation. (This should make you wonder: what about her? Is there always a her? Is there always a him?) The widely used definition of what counts as sex is androcentric,[1] organized around cismen, and nearly always heteronormative. By heteronormative, I refer to both beliefs and institutionalized practices that make heterosexuality the norm, essential, and "natural"; mostly by marginalizing everything else as "abnormal," as unimportant, inauthentic, or deviant. Heteronormative understandings of sex, for example, make same-sex sexual practices seem unimaginable. (Indeed, lesbians often find themselves confronted with the question of "what do lesbians do in bed?".) But the heternormative understanding of what counts as sex also makes a whole range of practices between heterosexuals not seem to be sex either.

Maybe you are old enough to remember former United States President Bill Clinton infamously declaring publicly that he "did not have sexual relations with that woman" in the aftermath of his affair with Monica Lewinsky? By reducing sex to heterosexual penetrative intercourse, many folks can maintain that they are not having sex, thus are "not cheating," or are "saving sex" for marriage and are still "virgins,"—even if they engage in all kinds of sexual activities, including oral and anal sex, and affairs like Clinton's. (Note: virginity and "saving sex for marriage" also seem highly prized by a lot of folks, as is having only one partner.) So let's summarize: "Having sex" obviously involves a wider spectrum of practices than generally is recognized; some of these practices are physical, while others are primarily or exclusively mental, like fantasizing or sex talk. Having sex usually involves one or more people. Let's keep in mind that having sex with oneself is a common sexual practice and some people like to have sex with more than one person. Let's also remember that the very limited understanding of what "counts" as having sex is already a mode of regulation.

Why Have Sex?

In my class, when we make a list of why people have sex, usually the first response is: "to make babies." This response reveals something about the popular imagination and discourse of sex: obviously reproduction often, but certainly not always, involves penile/vaginal penetrative sex. (Think of modes of reproduction such as insemination, adoption, surrogate pregnancies, and so on.) Clearly in sheer quantity, most sex is not about having babies. Quite the opposite, it's mostly about avoiding getting pregnant—at least among straight people of a certain age in North America. However, culturally (and unfortunately also in evolutionary psychology classes) sex tends to be reduced to reproduction. Indeed, for many, sex is only legitimate if it is about love and family. Sex for pleasure, which is arguably a primary reason for having sex, is still somewhat suspect. Eventually in my class discussions, we create a long list of why people have sex. It usually includes: for money; against loneliness and boredom; for fun; for love; to create or express intimacy and connection; as a competition ("scoring"); to feel desired; to relax; to guilt trip; to make up; for self-esteem; for mental health reasons; for power; as a form of violence; and so on. So, there is much more at stake in having sex than reproduction or even love. In the Western world today, the most acceptable and idealized context for socially approved sex is within a committed, monogamous, ideally married (heterosexual) adult relationship, as an expression of love, for reproductive purposes, and in the privacy of one's home. The most idealized version is certainly not the most frequent scenario.

Sex vs. Gender

The English language complicates matters because sex always potentially refers to two different things that are often confused: "having sex," but also as "being" a sex—as in female, male, intersex, or transsexual. I am writing this with some trepidation because an important critical contribution of feminist gender studies has been to focus on gender more so than on sex. Gender studies broadly build on the idea that gender refers to the socially constructed, historically and culturally specific expectations attached to being female and male. Sex was long understood to refer to the presumed biological and physical differences between female and male, such as genitals, anatomy, and chromosomes. (We will see later in this chapter that these biological differences might not be as clear-cut as commonly assumed.) The initial idea was that sex is biological, while gender is social. Distinguishing biological sex from social gender meant, for example, to recognize that many (but not all) women have the ability to get pregnant and give birth, which is biological and related to their sex.

However, the ideas that women by and large are the primary caregivers of children, both at home and professionally, and are considered more nurturing, are entirely social and related to their gender. Who carries a pregnancy and gives birth is biological and one marker of sex; who nurtures and raises the kids and is considered more suited to this complex task is socially constructed and relates to socially defined genders. This means that different cultures might construct very different parenting roles. One example is the parenting practices of the Aka Pygmy people, a traditionally nomadic people who live in both the Central African Republic and the Republic of the Congo. Among them, mothers and fathers share parenting nearly equally, including men suckling the infants (Hewlett, 1991; Moorhead, 2005).

You probably can already see why the insight that gender is socially constructed has appealed to feminists for a very long time. The possibility that vastly unequal shares of work and social and political status could be re-distributed among men and women is repeatedly proven by this and many other examples. Feminists have thus long argued against biological determinism, which is the idea that a woman's biology, her sex, predetermines her behaviour, temperament, abilities and justifies a second-class social status.

Gender Differences in Cultural Context

The distinction of sex from gender was informed by early 20th century anthropological field research that found that the organization of gender differs drastically across different cultures. Although nearly all societies have some form of gender differentiation, how gender is organized and what count as "natural" traits of a gender varies greatly. The work of United States anthropologist Margaret Mead was ground-breaking in this regard. Mead (1935/1963) described diverse patterns of gendered behaviour she observed during her field research in the Sepik region of Papua New Guinea. Among the Arapesh she found both women and men to be gentle, sensitive, and cooperative—attributes frequently associated with femininity in the West. Among the Mundugumor (now Biwat), both women and men were violent, selfish, and aggressive, behaviour often associated with masculinity in the West. Mead found Tchambuli (now Chambri) women and men had distinct temperaments, but roles were reversed: women were dominant and managerial and men were emotionally dependent and rarely in charge.

Although some of Mead's findings and descriptions have been modified and her reference to "primitive societies" speaks to a problematic colonial mindset, cross-cultural and cross-historical research continues to be an important source of knowledge for understanding how gender (and sexuality) is constructed and experienced very differently in specific historical and cultural contexts.

Studying Gender Cross-Culturally

Cross-cultural gender studies research prompts critical reflection upon the specific constructions of gender within a person's own culture, including questioning the limits of the categories "woman" and "man" as the two and only two genders that structure Western Eurocentric thinking. Why accept these as given and natural when other cultures, elsewhere and within North America, acknowledge more variation, sometimes three or four genders? Multiple gender systems have been documented as existing in 110 to 150 Native American societies prior to colonization (Nanda, 2014) and some of this history allowed Indigenous lesbian, gay, bisexual, and trans folks to re-claim the term "two-spirit." Gender anthropologist Sabine Lang (1990/1998) mapped four genders: woman, man, woman-man, and man-woman. A woman-man would have been identified as male at birth but later took up the culturally defined role of a woman; a man-woman was assigned female at birth and, usually during adolescence, felt inclined to take up the social role defined for men.[2] Indigenous people prior to colonization are not the only cultures who acknowledged gender variance.[3] As part of the violent legacy of settler colonialism these traditions were largely eradicated or forced underground, as missionaries and other settlers took the less rigid gender system of many Indigenous societies as indication of their allegedly more "primitive" and less evolved state. Or, as Andrea Smith argues quite forcefully, colonial domination sought to instil a gender-binary system, often by way of sexual violence, since it remains foundational to heteropatriarchy that, in turn, "is the logic that makes hierarchy seem natural" (2011, p. 59). More broadly speaking, derogatory sexualized depictions of Indigenous peoples—ranging from images of sexual licentiousness to sexual brutality—play a central role in settler colonialism. They serve, as Joanne Nagle has shown, to justify "military, political, and economic policies, and ultimately, these images provided a rational for seizing native resources"—and for other programs aimed at the "civilisation and assimilation" of Indigenous peoples (2000, p. 122). In the face of this long repression, assimilation, and often problematic naming and categorization by Western anthropologists, some queer Indigenous people began to reclaim a range of culturally specific gender and sexual identities in the 1990s. Specifically the identity of "two-spirit" emerged to describe non-normative sexual, gender, and other social roles within many Indigenous societies (Thomas & Jacobs, 1999). By looking cross-culturally, we begin to get a glimpse of sexuality as not just a "private issue." Instead what counts as "normal" or "civilized" sexuality plays a central role in historical and contemporary modes of oppression and in the constructions of national and racial self and Other.

In the next section, we question mainstream Canadian culture's investment in a developmental model that neatly lines up birth sex with gender identity and sexual desire. The foundational (albeit wrong) assumptions of this model are that every child is born male or female, will develop a gender identity coherent with their sex, ideally will desire a person of the other gender, and will come to understand themselves as heterosexual. Judith Butler (1990) critically calls this "the heterosexual matrix": a dominant and coercive meaning making system that assumes, even demands, a coherence between sex, gender, and desire/sexuality. Butler turns this model on its head to argue that in order to maintain the vision of a supposedly "natural" reproductive heterosexuality, gender identity is both enforced and enacted, which retrospectively serves to make sex assignment seem natural and biological.

The Coherence of Sex, Gender, and Sexuality As Heterosexual Matrix

Of course, you already know that this "coherence" of sex, gender, and desire may be frequent, but it certainly is not the only form that gender and sexual attraction take. Just because a majority of people in Canada today may identify as heterosexual—understanding themselves to be attracted to another sex than the one they identify with—does not make heterosexuality more "normal" or "natural" than other sexual identities. Certainly you are aware of human sexual variation beyond heterosexual, such as lesbian, gay, bisexual, and asexual, to name a few. Indeed, same-sex sexual behaviour is frequently found not only within human but also among nonhuman animals (Roughgarden, 2004). The question of how societies respond to human sexual variation beyond heterosexuality is social—not biological—and varies greatly across history and cultures.

Today social anxiety still surrounds human sexual variation. Witness the ongoing debates about gay marriage and the outlandish arguments of gay marriage opponents, including the idea that the legalization of same-sex marriage will "destroy the family" and end civilization as we know it. Ten years into same-sex marriage in Canada, many lesbians and gays are getting married, having children, and are divorcing too, "just like heterosexuals." And the institution of "the family" seems alive and well, or, at least as well as it had been for decades before gay marriage became legal.

Binary Gender Constructions

Beyond noting variation in sexual attraction and practices, we certainly also see lots of variation in gender. Indeed, when it comes to behaviour, skills, temperaments, and identifications, the binaries of feminine and masculine and women and men are not exhaustive. Think of masculine women and soft or more feminine men. Consider the enormous physical strength and muscularity of many female athletes or the grace of male dancers. In mainstream Canadian culture, we use rather blunt categories to distinguish girls from boys and women from men. If you are familiar with queer culture, you may be familiar with a much more nuanced and elaborate gender and sexual identity vocabulary that includes butch lesbian, faerie, femme dyke, tomboi, lipstick lesbian, bear, butch bottom, femme top, stone femme—each term denoting more finely tuned articulations of gender identity, sexual preferences, and erotic attraction.

Based upon the problematic reduction of human variation to only two sexes, our culture largely insists on recognizing only two binary genders. This has grave consequences for anybody who does not fit this neat binary system—boys who don't measure up to the "toughness" required to pass as "male" and girls who are regarded as "too" assertive and strong. Girls and boys and women and men who don't fit the stereotypes associated with their gender face near daily homophobic name calling ("sissy," "pussy," "dyke," "lesbian") and all too often, physical violence, not only from their peers but also, too frequently, from their own families. It is worth noting that gender non-conformity is policed by way of sexual shaming.

Gender non-conforming and queer youth face immense risks. They constitute as much as 25 to 40% of all homeless youth (Abramovich, 2012). Gender non-conforming youth and adults attempt suicide in much higher numbers than any other population—41% as compared to 4.6% of the overall United States population and 10 to 20% among lesbian, gay, and bisexual adults (Grant et al., 2011). Life is dangerous for gender non-conforming people and even more so if the person is young, not white, Indigenous, has little education, and/or is poor.

Part of the problem is the misguided assumption of the "natural" coherence of sex and gender, namely that the sex assignment at birth or in utero can correctly predict the gender identity and behaviour of kids as they grow up. Privileging heterosexual sexual orientation and condoning homophobia doesn't make things better. The boy who plays with dolls is "feared" to be gay; the girl who refuses to wear dresses and is tough is "feared" to be lesbian. As long as gayness and lesbianism are considered undesirable in children and adults, or are merely "tolerated," rather than celebrated and welcomed as part of human sexual variation, gender non-conforming kids are gravely at risk not only for social pressures to "conform," but also for physical violence. An alternative view would be to see gender on a much wider spectrum beyond masculine and feminine, boy and girl, man and woman, beyond a binary construction of supposedly oppositional differences. There is no knowing what range of gender expression we might see if children and adults alike were encouraged to express their gender in any way they want.

The policing of gender-conforming behaviour is not just problematic for trans folk, but for nearly everybody. Think of the female politician or businesswoman who gets called aggressive and power hungry for behaviour that is acceptable in men. Consider the boy who is not allowed to cry or is shamed for wanting to take ballet rather than play hockey. While those of us who are most gender conforming do reap some benefits, such as social acceptance, to do gender normatively requires a lot of "gender work." Gender work could include dieting and grooming regimes and other exhausting activities involved in producing, meeting, and maintaining the standards set for conventional femininity and masculinity. So most of us "fail" in some way at doing gender, as long as we still "pass," we are much safer than those who don't. (Although of course, another argument is that inhabiting conventional femininity poses other dangers.) But given the work involved in getting gender "right," the often violent efforts at gender patrolling, and the increasing number of children, some as young as three and four years old, who actively challenge their assigned gender, we should question whether the assignment of sex at birth or in utero is a reliable indicator of the future gender identity of the child. Still, the guiding assumption is that the presence or absence of a penis in utero indicates the sex of the embryo and, in turn, the future gender of the child and the eventual adult. Think of pink and blue cribs, names, outfits, nursery colours, baby toys, baby showers, and pronouncements about what the child will be when they grow up. Indeed, shopping for any baby or kids' item that is not gender colour-coded has become close to impossible. The intense need to gender children from a young age should make us question how natural the division into female and male really is. If it were a purely biological division, as many still claim, why spend so much effort on reinforcing it through symbols, language, and social structure and demanding that children and adults get it right? Beyond the intense gendering to which children and adults are exposed, even from before birth, sex assignment in utero or at birth is not always correct or successful in forecasting the gender identity a person might develop over the life course.

We might want to ask why human gender variation beyond girl/boy or woman/man is such a site of anxiety. What is at stake when we accept that there are more than two genders, that a person's gender identity might not neatly match their genitals and chromosomes, that over the life-course an individual's gender identity may change? Besides challenging some fundamental assumptions about the relationship between bodies and identities, accepting more than two genders and some fluidity in gender identities centrally challenges the "naturalness" of heterosexuality.

A few years ago, after asking my class to imagine a world in which gender identities would not exist or would be truly fluid and changeable, a rather panicky-sounding (male) student interjected, "I would not know who to be attracted to!" This seems a telling response that affirms Judith Butler's (1990) more analytical claim that the construction and policing of binary genders, whether done violently or in seemingly more benign modes, is ultimately about solidifying and securing the presumed "naturalness" of heterosexuality.

A (BRIEF) HISTORY OF SEXUALITY

Students are sometimes surprised when I assert that sexuality has a history. Their surprise is grounded in their acceptance of a natural reproductive heterosexuality. Indeed, if sexuality is biological and "natural," as many assume, how can it have a history? History usually suggests some kind of change over time—think about rapid technological changes and how technology has profoundly affected our modes of transportation and communication, from the invention of the steam engine to space rockets. Think about the first telegraphic message sent in 1844, and compare this to emailing, texting, and tweeting today.

Biological matters on the other hand, unless we take the long view of evolution, do not seem to change that much. Sexuality certainly has a biological, or at least physiological, component. Think, for example, of the lubrication of the vagina, the enlargement of the clitoris and penis during arousal; the release of oxytocin during orgasm; or female and male ejaculation. These physiological aspects are not unrelated to social and discursive constructions of sexuality. What counts as sexual and as erotic, as appropriate or inappropriate sexual feelings and behaviour, is certainly socially defined—and thus varies drastically across various historical (and cultural) contexts. Your own family's social expectations regarding appropriate sexual behaviour (who, when, with whom, where, at what age, in what kind of context, what kinds of practices) have changed significantly from your grandparents, to your parents, to you. If in the 1950s oral sex was scandalous, and one step away from being a Communist, today it might be regarded as good sexual etiquette—or not as sex at all. In the late 19th to early 20th century, women who showed their ankles were considered indecent. Today short skirts and hot pants seem de rigueur for many young women. On the other hand, until quite recently nude baby pictures were considered cute and were widely shared. Now in the context of rising anxieties around sexual abuse and child pornography, these no longer seem innocent. Sexual mores not only change across time, they are always profoundly *gendered,* meaning they differ for women and men. And sexual mores do *gender*: they are a mode by which gender is produced and maintained.

Cross-historical and cross-cultural comparisons allow us to see variations in how sexuality is lived and experienced. For example, many take it to be a biological "fact"—and evidence of a "natural sexual difference"—that men desire sex frequently and with various partners. Women are often described as desiring intimacy, closeness, connection, and friendship. Indeed, socio-biology claims that women's monogamy and men's promiscuity are natural imperatives, all allegedly driven by different strategies required for securing the survival of their respective genetic material. Assuming that the survival of genetic material is what drives humans—and thus their sexual behaviour—the argument is that men seek "to spread their seed," while women seek a single male protector around for their offspring. Note that sexual behaviour in this explanation is once again directly tied to reproduction. All the other motivations for sex seem to fall by the wayside. But also note how sexuality is profoundly linked to reproducing gender.

Interestingly enough, ideas about women's and men's "nature" were distinctly different in earlier centuries. The European Renaissance (1440–1680), for example, prized friendship as the most valued relationship. Only men were deemed mentally equipped for such important and demanding connections. Women, understood to be intellectually inferior to men, were deemed incapable of such an evolved relationship form. Instead women were seen as driven by insatiable sexual appetites. Marriage and motherhood were deemed appropriate ways for controlling these inclinations. And men were seen as being in need of protection from being lured by women's sexual urges (Fone, 2000). Even though we continue to see resonances of the contemporary image of the female seductress or the sexually controlling woman, these ideas differ radically today. All of these changing constructions are deeply shot through with gendered expectations.

One-Sex and Two-Sex Model

Another important and perhaps even more surprising difference to contemporary views can be found in the medieval period. According to Thomas Laqueur (1990), early medical knowledge insisted that male and female genitalia were practically the same. Laqueur calls this the "one-sex model," as compared to our "two-sex model." Today medical textbooks present entirely different female and male bodies. My students are incredulous as to how early anatomists could have seen similarities. But perhaps they were onto something.

According to Laqueur, women's genitals were understood as corresponding with male genitalia, only less developed. Thus the vagina was described as an inverted penis folded up inside the body, while men's had dropped down. The clitoris was presumed to be a shrunken, external penis. The notion that women were really underdeveloped males corresponded with women's inferior social status, confirmed somatically by their supposedly immature genitalia. Women, like young boys, were seen as lacking sufficient heat to make the genitals drop down. Did the early anatomists deliberately misinterpret what they saw in dissections in order to maintain the belief of women's inferiority? The one-sex view was the dominant model for understanding sexual difference for hundreds of years. It was not until the discoveries of Gabriel Fallopius (1523–1562), after whom the fallopian tubes are named, that this model was seriously challenged.

The insistence on absolute sexual difference and absolutely distinct sexes, which may be taken as a biological "truth" grounding gender difference and all it stands for ("boys will be boys"), is not quite scientifically accurate either. Distinct genitals (penis and vagina/clitoris) are seen as indication and proof of dimorphism.[4] How does the "truth" of natural absolute sex and gender difference shift when we understand that these different external genitals develop from the same tissue? The insistence on the absolutely dimorphic body is foundational to naturalizing heterosexuality. Here penis and vagina are constructed in a "key-lock analogy" (Valverde, 1985), according to which the key (penis) is presumed to be a "natural" fit for the lock (vagina). This is a problematic construction in many different ways, not least because it ignores the role of the clitoris for sexual pleasure. So we also have to consider, what difference does it make to understand the clitoris, as opposed to the vagina, as the penis equivalent?

THE PERILOUS ROUTE OF SEXUAL DIFFERENTIATION

For the first two or two-and-a-half months after fertilization of the human egg cell, embryos look exactly the same. This is called the state of sexual *undifferentiation*, meaning all of us start out the same and the tissue from which the external genitals later develop are the same. They initially look closer to what eventually leads to the sex assignment as female: two folds (inner and outer) with a small protuberance in the middle. All human fetuses have the potential for this tissue to develop either into a clitoris, vagina, and vulva; penis, urethra, and scrotum; or into something in between. What makes the difference is the level of exposure to hormones, more specifically androgens and testosterone. A specific gene, usually located on the Y chromosome, activates the development of the undifferentiated gonads into testes. If this gene is missing, the gonads develop into ovaries. If the fetus has testes, if the testes produce a certain level of testosterone, and if the tissue responds to the testosterone, the outer two folds will swell and fuse to grow into the scrotum. The protuberance in the middle grows to form the penis, with the inner folds fusing around the penis to form the penile urethra. Without exposure to certain levels of testosterone the tissue develops into clitoris, vagina, and vulva. So genital development is shaped both by chromosomal makeup (XX or XY combinations in the fertilized egg cell) and the exposure to in utero hormones.

Needless to say, there are a lot of "ifs" involved, as hormone levels vary. Thus there are instances in which despite an XY chromosome makeup, the tissue does not develop into a penis or does not develop in ways that are seen as sufficient for what is considered "normal" penis size—meaning the tissue turns into what can variously be identified as a micro-penis or a large clitoris.

There is some evidence that exposure to high levels of chemicals or artificial hormones during pregnancy may affect birth outcomes, resulting in higher than statistically expected ratios of babies born with a clitoris and a vagina, assigned as girls (Lean, 2006; McDonald et al., 2014). Exposure to environmental pollutants can affect genital development. However, to determine gender identity based upon visual impressions of the genitals is always problematic, since not everybody's genitals match their gendered self-understanding.

Given that female and male genitals develop from the same tissue and genital structure, perhaps the early anatomists and their one-sex body model were not so wrong after all. Seeing women as underdeveloped males, as they did, and using this to justify women's social inferiority is certainly not something to embrace today; however, the later move to the two-sex model did not alleviate women's social inferiority and secondary status. From then on, women's alleged "absolute" difference to men and male bodies became justification for inequality. But the notion of the "absolute" difference of women and men does not hold at the level of genital structures. As we have seen, bodies are not as dimorphic as many believe, thus confirming once more that gender equality or inequality is not a biological but a social issue. Throughout history, social and discursive constructions of male and female bodies have been mobilized to justify social status differences between women and men.

Intersex and Human Variation

Somatic dimorphism, the idea of two and only two sexes, is a social ideal rather than a biological reality. It is biologically more accurate to think of a range of bodies and somatic differences. Not all babies are born with clearly identifiable female or male external genitalia. Approximately one of about 1500 to 2000 babies (or 0.15 to 0.2%) have ambiguous or atypical genitalia at birth, and are then identified as intersex (Intersex Society of North America, 2008a). It's a small number. But in addition to visibly ambiguous birth genitalia, a wide range of other sex anatomical variations exist. Conte and Grumback (1989) list more than 25 different ones, not all of which are discovered at birth. Some only become noticeable later in life, others never. The most frequent is chromosomal make-up other than XX or XY (variations such as XXY, XO, XYY, XXYY, and XX males or XXX females). Altogether, based upon their extensive survey of the medical literature from 1955 to 1998, Blackless et al. (2000) note that up to 2% of the population deviate from the "ideal" female or male. This number is still small, but not insignificant, especially when we compare it to some other anatomical variations. For example, 2% of the world's population has green eyes or red hair. While red-haired or green-eyed humans are a minority globally, we see these as "normal" human variations rather than as pathologies in need of fixing. So why is intersex considered a "condition"?

In fact which sex anatomical variations are considered "intersex" is up for debate, as people, even in the medical community, disagree.[5] The disagreement is rooted in the fact that what counts as "intersex" and what counts as "female" or "male" is humanly defined. These are socially constructed categories, based upon an ancient Platonic ideal "that for each sex there is a single, universally correct developmental pathway and outcome" (Blackless et al., 2000, p. 151).

By deviating from the imagined ideal female and male developmental pathway, intersex challenges this Platonic ideal. Understood as a "condition" in need of "medical intervention," an intersex "diagnosis" also confirms the ideal of absolute difference. Alice Dreger (1995) has shown that since the late Victorian period, medical professionals have been hard at work to keep women and men distinct and to settle once and for all everybody's "true sex." This also means an attempt at settling, once and for all, the question of what makes a person female or male. Intersex interrupts the desire to settle these questions. How can we know women's place in society when we don't even know what makes one a woman? And how does one distinguish "normal" (aka heterosexual) relations from same-sex relations, if one cannot clearly distinguish woman from man? These are especially pertinent issues at a time when feminists as well as lesbians and gays (not mutually exclusive) are challenging their respective secondary social status. Ambiguous genitalia throw social certainties into relief and thus contest the social order. The social epitome of the two-sex body requires the assimilation of every body into this ideal, through whatever surgical or medical interventions are deemed necessary.

In the 21st century, visibly ambiguous genitalia are still seen as pathological and in need of "fixing." The "fix it" approach is based on the assumption that both the parents and the child will not be able to cope with genitalia that don't match the ideal. While ambiguous genitalia are not medical problems in most cases, they are considered a "psychosocial emergency" by the medical profession, potentially leading to depression, suicide, and possibly "homosexuality." (Note here that same-sex sexuality is seen as a problem.) The common practice since the 1950s has been early medical intervention: genital surgery and hormone treatment. The decision on what genitalia to create has been based on ideal penis size and heterosexuality: to be assigned male, the penis at birth must be larger than 1 cm; smaller size leads to female assignment. A clitoris regarded as too large may be surgically altered, again, to fit the female ideal, often with negative consequences for the experience of sexual pleasure later in life not to mention immediate surgical trauma to the infant. Since constructing a sizeable penis is more difficult, "normalizing" surgery often involves creating "female" genitalia (Fausto-Sterling, 2000).

A major problem is that these assignments are not always correct, grounded as they are in "genital ideals" and a presumed heterosexuality, leading to enormous pain and suffering for those who find themselves at odds between their assignment sex and their own gender identity. Moreover, genital surgery can lead to loss of genital sensitivity and seriously impede the ability to experience sexual pleasure. Since the 1990s, intersex activists have lobbied fiercely against current treatment protocols, especially against surgical intervention during infancy. Arguing that ambiguous birth genitalia constitute a crisis primarily for the parents and not, at least initially, for the child, the Intersex Society of America (ISSA) offers a distinctly different treatment protocol. Citing the baby's inability to grant surgical consent, ISSA's protocol forgoes irreversible genital cosmetic surgery during infancy in favour of assigning a social gender initially, while leaving any later medical intervention to the purview of the intersex person.

Mainstream treatment protocols tell us something about the ways in which sex difference is surgically manufactured in cases when genitals do not fit an imaginary ideal and when somatic differences are not as clear as our culture presumes them to be. Intersex understood as a form of human variation, on the other hand, challenges the deeply rooted belief in absolute dimorphism and absolute differences between female and male anatomy.[6]

The Invention of Heterosexuality

Gender identity is often confused with sexual identity. Perhaps it helps to remember that gender identity is about *who* I go to bed *as* (woman, man, gender queer), while the sexual identity (lesbian, gay, straight, bisexual, asexual) is defined by *whom* I go to bed *with*. To organize sexuality in distinct identity groups is a 20th century, Western approach. Historian Jonathan Katz (1990) shows that the terms "heterosexuality" and "homosexuality" were first coined in the late 19th century. Originally both terms named sexual deviance. Heterosexuality referred to the *excessive* attraction to the other sex or sexual relations outside of reproduction (Katz, 1990). Siobhan Somerville (1994) shows how the invention and determination of "the homosexual body" as distinct from heterosexuality borrows heavily from dominant racial ideologies and scientific racism at the time. Late 19th century racism assumed somatic differences between different races and between different sexualities, promoting the idea that both miscegenation (interracial relations) and same-sex relations were inherent and deviant sexual orientations. Only in the 20th century did heterosexuality become the term used to describe what is now considered "normal" sex: sex between adults with different sex assignments.

Much of contemporary sexuality studies is informed by Michel Foucault's (1976/1978) *The History of Sexuality*. He describes the process through which married adults having sex in the privacy of their bedroom became established as the only "normal" form of sexuality. This happened by way of intense social scrutiny and moral regulation of all other sexual practices, especially the sexuality of children, sex in public, sex between adults of the same sex, and masturbation (which in the Victorian era at least was considered cause for medical concern). Foucault also suggests that this structuring of "normal" and "deviant" sexual relations is central to the emergence of the middle class. The middle class defines itself *against* the presumed sexual excesses of the upper class as well as against the supposed sexual disorders of the working class, and against what was considered the uncivilized, licentious sexual abandon of non-white and non-Western people.

Charting Human Sexual Diversity

Across cultures, we find immense differences in the ways in which sexuality is organized and what is labelled as "normal." Evelyn Blackwood (2000) offers a useful distinction between two versions of social constructionism: weak and strong. The "weak" social constructionist view assumes the existence of "natural desires" that are then shaped and constrained by societies according to specific social and cultural values and beliefs. This construction might entail the learning of specific gendered scripts in a given historical and cultural context. The strong social constructionist view assumes a very general and somewhat vague "sexual potential" that societies then construct into what counts as sexual desires, behaviours, and meanings. The main difference between these two social constructionist positions is that the weak view presumes a pre-existing sexuality, which is culturally shaped and regulated. The strong social constructionist view proposes that what counts as sexual is socially determined by a wide variety of factors such as religious ideologies, ethnicity, class, gender, family, everyday life, and material and social conditions.

Thinking about sexuality as socially and discursively constructed is challenging, in part, because to many of us, our sexual attractions, desires, pleasures, distastes, and sexual identities feel deeply rooted inside ourselves, maybe even like something that we can't help but feel and want. Just because something is deeply felt as authentic doesn't mean that it is not socially constructed. To say something is socially constructed does not mean that it is trivial, easily changed, or not real.

Looking at sexuality cross-culturally we see immediately that the present dominant Western way of thinking and organizing sexuality in terms of identities based upon "sexual orientation" is far from universal. Katz's and Foucault's work cited earlier charted the historical process by which different sexual "types" emerged in the process of inventing hetero- and homosexuality. So, currently in the West, somebody who identifies as a woman and is attracted to other women is considered a lesbian. A woman who is attracted to both women and men is considered bisexual, a woman attracted to men is considered heterosexual. Sounds reasonable, yes? Except of course, that things tend to be more complicated than this categorical organizing proposes. Obviously, lesbians are not attracted to all women, just as heterosexual women are not attracted to all men; heterosexually identified women might find themselves attracted to women too, might have erotic fantasies about women, just as lesbians might fall in love with a specific man. And bisexual women at any given moment might be either in a heterosexual or lesbian relationship or the gender of their partner might not be relevant. All of this suggests that the notion of stable "sexual types" or inherent sexual identities might not be as stable as is often presumed. How people identify sexually in public or to themselves does not always capture the complexities of their attractions, desires, and behaviours.

Constructing Sexuality Cross-Culturally

Looking cross-culturally, Blackwood's (2000) anthropological survey of women's sexualities demonstrates that various "sociocultural factors . . . *produce* sexual beliefs and practices" ([emphasis added] p. 224), including but not limited to: gender, religion, age, marriage, and family systems. Blackwood offers examples of socially sanctioned same-sex practices and relationships between girls and women in various non-Western cultural contexts. These range from intimate erotic and educational friendships between girls in rural Lesotho, a small country surrounded by South Africa, to erotic ritual practices during initiation into adult womanhood among Australian Aborigines prior to colonization, as well as adolescent sex play among the !Kung San of the Kalahari Desert of Southern Africa. Each of these are culturally distinct and complex formations of sexuality; some may be surprising and challenging to current Western assumptions about sexuality, especially to the presumption of stable sexual identities and concerns about the sexuality of young people.

The so-called "mummy-baby" relations among younger and older girls in Lesotho are a socially sanctioned context for girls to experience their first romantic and sexual encounters with each other. They precede heterosexual marriage and are the site of a practical sex education. According to Blackwood, mummy-baby relations are the result of a cultural negotiation between Indigenous pro-sex views that value women's sexual agency, and the Roman Catholic instance on girls' virginity. They emerge out of older Indigenous traditions, such as both married women and men having sex with people other than their spouses and intense, long-lasting affective partnerships between women alongside heterosexual marriage.

Other examples of quite "practical" sex education could be found among Australian Aboriginal women prior to colonization when adult women taught girls about sexuality by way of homoerotic dances and movements during erotic initiation rituals. The !Kung of Southern Africa constructed adolescence as a phase of sexual experimentation with both same-sex and other-sex partners, as a time of exploration and learning about sexual feelings and desires, prior to heterosexual marriage.

These brief examples entail very different constructions of sexuality, shaped by factors such as age, gender ideologies, religion, marriage, and family. My students are frequently surprised by the centrality of women's sexual agency in these examples and by the sex-positive views concerning young people in these cultures. This surprise arises from the ethnocentric assumption that women and girls in the West are the most "liberated"; but also, from students' experiences with (anti-sex) education in high school, which does not sanction sexual experimentation.

The most challenging example Blackwood raises concerns the Sambia people of Papua New Guinea for whom femininity is something inherent and stable with which girls are born, while masculinity and manhood must be acquired. Masculinity is understood as unstable and in constant threat of being overtaken by women, who are perceived as dominant. Masculinity is acquired through rituals that involve ingesting adult men's semen.

My students respond with shock when they learn about this ritual production of masculinity. For the Sambia this is a necessary practice for becoming a man and for accomplishing and maintaining masculinity. In a Western cultural context, these practices are understood as pedophilia and sexual abuse. We usually have very lively discussions around this practice, because it raises complex questions about how different cultures construct what counts as sexual. These examples also raise interesting questions about how our understanding and assumptions about gender shape constructions of sexuality in Canada today.

Blackwood's second example of gender ideologies shaping sexuality are the Chinese marriage resisters of the 19th century. Young women working in the silk factories achieved economic independence that allowed them to postpone heterosexual marriage indefinitely. Instead of marrying men, they lived in sisterhoods with other women. They vowed publicly to remain unwed and to not engage in sex with men. They lived together and formed sexual relationships with each other, including "ménage à trois" (Sankar cited in Blackwood, 2000, p. 279). The Chinese marriage resisters were responding to gender ideologies in ways that shaped their sexual practices. Chinese men at the time were granted a wider range of sexual options, including male lovers. Women's sexuality was subordinated to men's desires. This inequality also produced the kind of resistance that sisterhood represented. (Sisterhoods were banned after the victory of the Red Army in 1949.)

Another example given by Blackwood are the tombois in West Sumatra, who are physically female but see themselves as men attracted to normatively feminine women. Tombois behave in the manner of the men in West Sumatra culture. They smoke, play cards, drive motorcycles, and model themselves in all aspects in terms of the constructions of masculinity. They love feminine women; in couples tombois and their lovers refer to each other as *mami* and *papi*. The tomboi identity is a blended sexual and gendered construction that is grounded in a gender ideology that sees women and men as inherently different. It is also a construction grounded in a matrilineal Muslim culture, meaning that people trace their family line through the mother rather than the father. While men in this cultural context enjoy different rights and privileges, they are not considered superior. Instead, women are traditionally the leaders and reproducers. Within a pretty strict two-gender order, tomboi as an appropriation of the masculine gender is the only alternative for girls who do not conform to the standards of conventional femininity. Being called tombois by others becomes an explanation for their own behaviour. Tomboi is a blended gendered and sexual identity. Gendered behaviour preferences come to determine sexual identity.

The point of these cross-cultural examples is not to idealize "non-Western" sexualities and genders as somehow "freer," "more authentic," or unfettered by social regulation. Rather, the point is to show that while all cultures construct—and regulate—sexuality and gender, they do it uniquely. The categorization used in the West today to organize sexuality, namely by discrete sexual categories (hetero-, bi-, and homosexuality) does not hold in other cultural contexts. Indeed in the examples above, same-sex and different-sex relations exist in parallel. Same-sex sexual practice in adolescence does not preclude heterosexual relations in adulthood—in some cultures it is seen as making them possible. In some contexts same-sex sexual practices continue alongside heterosexual marriage.

Sexual monogamy is not a universal cultural value; neither is limiting sex to reproduction. Cross-cultural comparative studies show a range of human sexual diversity.

Local concepts of sexuality, however, are changing with globalization. Prior to the internationalization of lesbian and gay discourses, for example, tombois did not easily translate into any Western category. They seem neither clearly lesbian, butch, transgender, woman, nor man. Now they are increasingly seen as only a sexual orientation. This changing understanding of tomboi in West Sumatra today is an example of how local, national, and transnational discourses shape the construction of sexuality, constructions that certainly are shifting over time and across different contexts.

The Strong Social Constructionist View

Gender ideologies, religion, tradition, economics, age, and other factors shape how sexuality is constructed, lived, understood, and responded to in specific cultural and historical contexts. The strong social constructionist view goes beyond this by suggesting that the very definition of what counts as sexual is socially defined. These social definitions are pretty powerful—they shape how we experience ourselves, our bodies, our desires, and others. They shape what we consider appropriate or unacceptable and how we construct our identities and that of others. That is not to say that we are "brain washed" and experience and believe all the same things. Social definitions, or discourses, of sex give us a language through which we make sense of what we feel, see, and experience. That can also entail experiencing and defining oneself against dominant ways of thinking about sex and gender. Think about the tombois, for example. They certainly define themselves in opposition to the constructions of conventional femininity in their cultural context. However, they do so by appropriating and modifying dominant constructions of masculinity for themselves. We can also see that social constructions of gender and sexuality affect what is seen as sexual and what is seen as violent. Semen ingestion as a means to acquire and stabilize masculinity, as practised among the Sambia, is hardly imaginable in a context in which this would be considered sexual abuse.

Cross-cultural variations regarding sexuality lend support to Gayle Rubin's (1984) conclusion that "sexuality is as much a human product as are diets, methods of transportation, systems of etiquette, forms of labor, types of entertainment" (p. 277). Like other human products, sexuality is profoundly structured by modes of regulation and policing. Sexual norms and expectations are frequently justified through the language of the "normal," "moral," and "acceptable." Rubin (1984) maps a detailed "sex hierarchy" of different sexual practices and the ongoing social struggles over where to "draw the line" between sex deemed "good, normal, natural, holy" and sex deemed "bad, abnormal, unnatural, sinful, sick" (p. 281). In the "good sex" category, Rubin situates heterosexual, married, monogamous, reproductive sex at home. Sex deemed "bad" includes sex for money, sadomasochism, fetishism, and intergenerational sex. Under contestation are unmarried heterosexual couples, promiscuous heterosexuals, with long-time stable lesbian and gay couples inching their way into respectability.

CONSTRUCTING SEXUAL NORMALCY

At this point, I hope you have become suspicious of the concept of "normal" sex—and its "second cousin," "healthy sex." Sexual regulation in the West today works perhaps less through the moral terms of "good" and "bad" and more often as "healthy" or "unhealthy." But there is really very little that is inherently "healthy" or "unhealthy" about sex. Whether kissing is a "normal" and important part of sexuality and intimacy or regarded as unhygienic and disgusting as in Burma (Levine, 2002), whether intergenerational sex is deviant and abusive or an accepted precursor to adult heterosexuality (as in mummy-baby relationships in Lesotho or in man-boy marriage among the Azande) is not universal but culturally specific. Thus our sexuality and our sexual behaviour, like many other aspects of our daily life, such as what we wear, eat, do for entertainment, and find beautiful, is shaped by what our culture deems appropriate and normal. Our sexuality is not just individual and unique to each of us. Instead it is profoundly shaped by the world around us by books, art, movies, television, advertising, what our friends and family say, social institutions (church, school, legal system). I suggest then that sexuality is shaped, not determined, by the discourses that circulate around us.

Feminist Challenges to "Sexual Normalcy"

Feminist and lesbian/gay movements of the late 20th century have been on the forefront of questioning what long had been accepted as sexual "normalcy" and "deviance." Central to this questioning was an analysis of questions of power and the political nature of sexual regulation. One starting point for doing so was Anne Koedt's (1970) widely circulated political pamphlet "The Myth of the Vaginal Orgasm." A scathing critique of the ways that, at least since Freud, penile vaginal penetration has been misconstrued as "mature" heterosexual sex, Koedt describes vaginal orgasms as "a myth," an androcentric construction, organized around men's sexual pleasure that ignores the reality of women's bodies and the role of the clitoris in women's orgasm. Koedt argued that penile vaginal intercourse leaves women sexually unsatisfied, while the vaginal orgasm myth blames women for their alleged "inability" to orgasm, misconstruing this as a sign of their alleged "sexual immaturity" and "frigidity." Recognizing the clitoris as the centre of women's sexual pleasure threatens men, as it renders men "sexually expendable." Ultimately, the myth of the vaginal orgasm anchors the normalization and naturalization of heterosexuality.

While there is lot to be said about the assumptions that guide Koedt's critique, including her ethnocentric statements about women in "backwards nations," her deconstruction of the idealized vaginal orgasm was a huge relief to many women. Realizing its unattainability helped women to feel less like sexual failures. Koedt's critique also opened a door to challenging not only normalized sex acts such as heterosexual penetration but also institutionalized heterosexuality and men's power. Nearly twenty years later, Nancy Tuana (2004) shows that the role of the clitoris as the "seat of women's pleasure" is not new knowledge. Its role for sexual pleasure was recorded as early as 1559, when within the one-sex model discussed earlier, the clitoris was understood as analogous to the penis. Tuana demonstrates that throughout the history of anatomy, the clitoris gets discovered and forgotten over and over again. By calling this a "strategic forgetting," Tuana argues that knowledge of the role of the clitoris "gets lost" intentionally rather than accidentally. The attention to the clitoris distracts from the cultural narrative of sex being about reproduction. Ignoring the clitoris in favour of a supposedly "natural fit" of penis and vagina, on the other hand, aids the cultural construction of reproductive (hetero)sex.

Sadly, even four decades after Koedt's analysis, the rates of women not achieving orgasm during partner sex continue to be high. Vaginal orgasms, preferably simultaneous with a person's lover, continue to be mythologized and idealized. Think about representations of orgasm in mainstream movies and on TV. Here clitoral stimulation, for example by way of oral sex, is represented as foreplay at best, while "real" sex still means penile vaginal penetration with no clitoral stimulation involved. (How often is the role of the clitoris for women's sexual pleasure mentioned in sex ed curricula?)

The Compulsory Institution of Heterosexuality

Feminists do not always agree on how to think about sexuality. For example, during the early second feminist wave, lesbians, who were very active in the emerging women's movement, found themselves asked by heterosexual feminists to keep their sexual orientation hidden so as to not give feminism a bad name. Outraged by such silencing of their voices and experiences, radical feminists made lesbianism a central political issue (Jackson & Scott, 1996). Some lesbians argued that they focused their energies on other women instead of on the oppressor—men. Many feminists began to think of lesbianism as political resistance to patriarchy and male dominance.

Germinal to this debate was an article published in 1978 by the American poet and essayist Adrienne Rich (1978/1996). Entitled "Compulsory Heterosexuality and Lesbian Existence," the text challenged the common beliefs that heterosexuality is natural and that women voluntarily engage in heterosexual relations. Instead, Rich provocatively suggested that across history and cultures heterosexuality has been forced upon women. One way to do so is through male violence. Another one is withholding or demonizing alternative options such as love between women. Rich urged feminists to make the critique of compulsory heterosexuality a pivotal political issue for feminism. Feminists, she insisted, should not only address gender inequality or the taboos surrounding homosexuality, but must also understand "the enforcement of heterosexuality for women as a means of assuring male right of physical, economic, and emotional access [to women]" (1978/1996, p. 135). Feminism must understand heterosexuality as a social institution, not a natural order. As social institution, rather than inherent orientation and identity, heterosexuality is similar to the education system, organized religion, and the family opening up heterosexuality to the same kind of scrutiny for how it benefits men and disadvantages women.

Rich urged women to dis-identify with heterosexuality and men—and to *identify* as lesbians instead. "Lesbian identification," as Rich called it, does not necessarily mean to engage in sexual relationships with other women. For Rich lesbianism is not primarily about sex or desire. Instead, "lesbian" means making other women an emotional and political priority in your life. Lesbian identification is a consciously chosen bond, something that allegedly all women already experience in their deep emotional connection with each other as sisters, mothers, best friends, teachers, and so on. Lesbian *identification* then becomes a choice: to honour and make legible the ways women bond with each other.

Leaving aside for a moment that Rich takes deep bonds between cisgendered women as a given, the text is radical, provocative, and strategic all at once. Rich called out straight feminists for their homophobia. She strategically challenged a feminist movement that had become deeply divided over the issue of lesbianism by asking straight women to identify politically *with* and *as* lesbians—instead of telling lesbians to shut up. Rich called out to feminists to critically analyze heterosexuality, question its naturalness—even when it may feel natural and normal—and begin to understand how heterosexuality benefits (most) men and hinders (many) women. Within feminist communities, this evoked lively, even divisive debates, which arguably are ongoing.

By suggesting women can choose to *identify as lesbian*, rather than "being born that way," Rich introduced the radical notion of political choice into sexual identity discourses and moved away from what Eve Sedgwick (1990) later would call a "minoritizing" view. Within a minoritizing view only a "distinct population 'really are' gay." A minoritizing view assumes that one either *is* or *is not* lesbian/gay. Contrary to this, a universalizing view, like that of Rich, recognizes that anybody could engage in homo or heterosexual *acts* and that sexual desire is much more fluid and not easily predictable. Rich endorses lesbianism as a universalizing position, one that anybody can choose to take up. Understanding lesbianism as a radical (political) choice as compared to an inherent condition of a distinct population, while simultaneously daring to question the naturalness of heterosexuality, Rich's text became an important building block for queer theory—albeit one frequently unacknowledged.

Thoroughly productive as Rich's text has been, it also garnered well-deserved criticism. Her political, non-sexual lesbianism makes erotic desire between women invisible once more. She implied that lesbians are all political freedom fighters against patriarchy. She failed to outline how compulsory heterosexuality does not benefit all men, but oppresses gay men too. She made problematic use of transhistorical and transcultural evidence to demonstrate heterosexuality's compulsory and violent nature (Sullivan, 2003).

Heterosexual Privilege

One critical and productive response to Rich is the concept of "heterosexual privilege," an analytical term that suggests that heterosexuality does not only limit women as Rich had claimed. Instead, heterosexual privilege names the benefits straight people accrue when complying with the compulsory nature of heterosexuality. Privileges associated with heterosexuality may include the right to have a person's relationship socially and economically recognized and supported; never having "to come out" to friends, family, and co-workers; not being discriminated against for being straight; access to varied and many positive representations in the media of your relationship; never having to hide your partner for fear of discrimination. (Of course, heterosexual privilege does not necessarily protect a person from discrimination and violence on the basis of race, ethnicity, class, or religion. Thus not all heterosexuals accrue the same privileges.)

For many straight-identified feminists, then and now, to question heterosexuality poses personal and political dilemmas. Particularly troubling is the suggestion that heterosexuality supports male dominance. Many straight women ask themselves how to love men and be a feminist committed to gender justice. Canadian Christine Overall (1990) proposes a "feminist heterosexuality." Refusing to accept heterosexuality as either innate, which is the popular view, or as forced upon women, which is Rich's suggestion, Overall argues that heterosexuality can also be a choice you make without just "acquiescing in it, or benefiting from heterosexual privilege, but actively tak[ing] responsibility for being heterosexual" (p. 266).

Overall encourages moving beyond a demoralizing choice according to which heterosexual feminists either have to feel guilty about loving men or accept that heterosexual desire and attachment are always already anti-feminist. Instead, Overall, with other feminists, paves the path to changing both the institution and the ways in which heterosexuality is lived. Recognizing its privileged position and the rewards attached to heterosexuality is a first step. The next step may be to "queer" heterosexual norms.

Queering Heterosexuality

For Lynn Segal (1994) queering heterosexuality involves challenging traditional understandings of gender and sexuality. This includes looking at how women's and men's bodies are coded in ways that support a binary model of oppositional genders that are then supposedly attracted "naturally" to each other. Segal encourages us to recode bodies differently so as to move away from an understanding of (heterosexual and cisgender) women's bodies as only "passive," "receptive," "penetrable," and "vulnerable" and of (heterosexual cisgender) men's bodies only as "active," "determined," "penetrating," and "impenetrable." (Keep in mind that lesbian and gay bodies and practices have always included both sexual receptivity and penetration.)

If we stop and think about this for a moment, we can perhaps begin to imagine talking about women's and men's bodies during heterosexual penetrative sex quite differently—not in terms of a "quasi militarized invasion and occupation of the female body" (Sullivan, 2003, p. 130) in which the aggressor/penis pushes its way into a defenceless but fortified vagina.[7] Maybe instead we can see the vagina as actively pulling in and enfolding a penis, as holding it and pushing it in and out.

To learn how to recode bodies in ways that veer away from a conventional gendered and naturalized script, straight folks might learn from queer folks. Within butch/femme culture, femme femininity and sexuality has long been celebrated as active and aggressive rather than merely passive and receptive. Within trans communities and among lovers of trans women and men[8] it is common to recode bodies too, especially pre-operative bodies that don't match normative and idealized cis-male or cis-female genitalia. For example pre- or non-operative trans men (and their lovers) may produce *male bodiedness* when speaking of their pre-operative genitalia, particularly those changed by testosterone, in their difference in size rather than structure from cis-male genitalia. This focus on size and structural similarity invokes the anatomical continuum between clitoris and penis we discussed earlier. What would be identified as clitoris, breasts, and vaginal opening respectively in cis-female identified humans, by way of vernacular may be recoded by trans men as dick, man boobs, and bonus hole, respectively.[9] This recoding is part of discursively producing bodies that match gender identity.

If we understand that all bodies are coded through language, we can see that coding plays a central role in the construction of gendered and sexual difference. If trans and queer folks can recode bodies, then straight and cis-bodied folks should be able to do the same. In so doing they may be able to unsettle the unequal discursive constructions of cis-male and cis-female bodies in ways that allow for less restrictive gender roles, both sexually and in the world. Such unsettlement also might undo the transphobic distinction between bodies and genders that pass as "real" and those considered "unreal," by showing that all bodies and genders are discursive and linguistic constructions.

When we talk about such queering of bodies, my feminist, cis-female, and heterosexually identified students are quite intrigued. They want to think about ways to expand and undermine restrictive gender scripts, knowing how these limit their own sexuality and pleasure. (After all, how pleasurable is it to always imagine sex as a militaristic male invasion of female defences?) However, they have a hard time imagining how to win over their cisgendered boyfriends. Indeed, imagining male bodies as vulnerable, receptive, and penetrable is deeply threatening to many cis men—and to many cis women too.

This anxiety tells us how deeply rooted homophobia still is in our culture, despite the increased tolerance towards LGBTQT2-S people and despite the wider recognition of same-sex relationships. Penetrability of men continues to signify gay masculinity in our culture and thus is something that most straight men seek to distance themselves from, even if they tolerate gayness in others. The fear of being read as gay may well be at the heart of sex that is not only heterosexual but heteronormative, sex constrained in the name of reproducing normatively gendered sexual practices.

Such constraint tells us something else. Sadly conventional sex is rarely just about pleasures. Nor is sex "just" an expression of some inherent orientation. Instead, sex practices play a central role in the *production* and *consolidation* of coherent identities (for example as heterosexual, as "normal" woman and man, as cisgendered). Calvin Thomas (2000) critically calls this "fucking to assert identity." That is, sex that seeks to assert the unequal construction of sex, gender, and sexuality, and the privileges associated with these subject positions. Such sex cannot tolerate how during consensual sex the boundaries of gendered subjectivities are often transgressed. "Fucking to assert identity" cannot bear that one of the pleasures of sex might precisely be the loss, rather than the assertion, of a self, of boundaries and dichotomies of self and other, of supposedly complementary bodies, of active/passive, and of inside and outside (Bersani, 1987; Segal, 1994; Thomas, 2000). That is to say, sex itself has *queer potential*, if we understand "queer" not just as a convenient short form for the identity diversity that the acronym LGBTQT2-S represents. Instead, "queer" here represents a move to undermine the normative and coercive coherence of sex, gender, and sexuality—and the violent efforts involved in producing such coherence.

Accordingly, sex's potential to *undo* us can be queer even when it involves cisgendered and heterosexually identified women and men. Sex is "queer" when it is not about the assertion of straight identities. But, similarly, sex can be straight and heteronormative, even if it involves same-sex lovers. Indeed, for Thomas (2000) sex is *heteronormative* when it is "teleologically narrativized sex: sex with a goal, a purpose, a product" (p. 33); when it is reproductive, with the product being an identity, a sense of self, or a child. Merri Lisa Johnson (2002, p. 49) provides us with a quite concrete list of what *queering heterosexuality* might entail: sex with less restrictive gender roles; pleasure; recognition of heterosexuality and the nuclear family as one relationship/family form among many; body integrity; and sexual practices that are less coitus, penetration, and penis-centred.

While many of my students can see the value of opening up a wider spectrum of gender and sexual practices for everyone, they often voice concerns that identifying as "queer" when one is not *really* lesbian, gay, bisexual, trans, or intersex is an appropriation of somebody else's identity in ways that does not acknowledge sufficiently the discriminations that *real* queer folks experience. Ultimately, they argue identifying as a *queer straight* person is just about being trendy, and this *straight queerness* only gets articulated in contexts where being queer is cool. I think their concerns are legitimate. However, these are based upon notions of stable identities and assume that *real* queers are somehow unified in their experience of similar hardships. But are they really?

If we think about progress and equality, lesbian and gays in North America certainly have had much to celebrate over the last two decades as access to marriage, adoption, military service, and survivors' benefits have been won. These are significant accomplishments that extend social recognition and human rights protection. However, these equality measures have in common that they were won by insisting that lesbians and gays are "just like straight people." And that claim is the crux. Basically, these equality measures are for those same-sex couples who most closely resemble straight folks in terms of their gender, their relationship model, and their modes of reproduction. Rather than challenge the heteronormative institutions of marriage, monogamy, procreation, and gender, recently won gay rights simply assimilate and sustain them. Calling this critically "homonormativity," queer theorists and activists, following Lisa Duggan (2000) and Martin F. Manalansan (2005), have argued that these socio-legal successes ultimately benefit only that small segment of queer communities who are in monogamous relationships and can afford weddings and property, who have access to pension and health care plans, and who wish to procreate. Indeed, Duggan argues that these rights ultimately depoliticize gay culture by reducing equality to equal access to "domesticity and consumption" (p. 50). Similarly, Manalansan offers the criticism that these kinds of rights put queer communities "to sleep," after having recoded "freedom" and "liberation" to mean merely "freedom and liberty to consume" (p. 142).

These are harsh critiques and in my class we have lively discussions about whether these rights constitute progress of some sort or not. Certainly, for (some) students who grew up lesbian and gay and suffered from social exclusion and violence, the idea of finding true love, getting married, having a family, and getting recognition for being "just like everybody else" is very appealing. Yet others recognize that the right to marry will not fix economic or racial injustices or lessen the harassment they may experience for not "doing gender" conventionally. Indeed, the right to marry and other equality measures might most benefit white and middle-class lesbian women and gay men, while it does not end homelessness for poor queers, provide trans-specific health care options, or decrease violence against gender-nonconforming queers. Then again, marriage might give some queers access to benefits and immigration, the kinds of security that might otherwise remain unattainable.

More broadly speaking, we can conclude that constructions of sexuality in the contemporary moment are wildly contradictory. On the one hand, we note more cultural visibility of lesbians, gays, bisexuals, and, to a lesser degree, of trans folk, intersex folk, and other queers. At the same time, marginalization, violence, and homo- and transphobia persist raising the question of whether visibility really equals legal protection and greater safety.

CONCLUSION: THE ANTINOMIES OF YOUNG PEOPLE'S SEXUALITY

As I am finishing this chapter during the winter of 2015,[10] the Conservative majority in the Alberta legislature just stopped an opposition bill that would have enshrined the right for students to create Gay-Straight Alliances (GSAs) in high schools, no matter what principals, school boards, or parents might think about them. This bill also would have stripped from the Alberta Human Rights Act a provision that allows parents to remove children from the classroom when issues of sexual orientation are discussed.[11] The bill's rejection, at least for now, reflects the continued tensions in the social construction of sexuality. Sexual images are ubiquitous in the culture; pornography of all stripes is readily available on the internet; lesbians and gays can legally marry, adopt children, and feature on TV; and more and more young people come out as trans or gender-nonconforming. At the same time, parents in Alberta can (and many do) ask for their children to be pulled from classrooms, so as to "protect" them from the knowledge and support that discussing sexuality and having gay and queer support groups in schools presents.

Thus while sexual images and knowledge abound in the culture and are understood as one indicator of sexual progress, there is an increasing desire to preserve children's "innocence" in all sexual (and gender) matters and not only in Alberta. Parents and adults in Canada and the United States more generally tend to be intensely uncomfortable with recognizing children and young people as sexual. Sex is generally seen as something that puts young people at risk from which they are to be protected and shielded, rather than as something that they need to learn about, experience, and practise. A common fear is that explicit sex education will incite sexual activity among teens. Such logic implies that the availability of information about sex, contraception, abortion, and sexual pleasure is the *cause* of teen pregnancies and sexually transmitted infections rather than being recognized as effective *prevention*.

Programs that teach students only to abstain from sex prevent teenagers from learning anything about sex, withholding necessary information that helps them make decisions (and communicate them) about when, how, and with whom to be sexually active. Teaching only abstinence implies erroneously that when people are ready to have sex, ideally only once they are adults and married, they will know what to do and how to protect themselves from pregnancy, infections, emotional harm, and violence. What we fail to account for when we do not educate children and teenagers on matters of the body, gender, sexuality, and pleasure is that all learning takes practise. Judith Levine (2002, p. 110) observes astutely "maturity, including sexual maturity, cannot be attained without practice, and in sex, as in skiing, practice is risky." Young people, straight and queer alike, deserve to practise with as much information at their disposal as possible. Without effective, comprehensive, and inclusive sex education, we abandon young people to learning about sex from overwhelmingly sexist, heteronormative, and transphobic mainstream and online representations of sexuality.

Endnotes

1. Androcentric means cis-male centred: the privileging and centring of the specific viewpoints and experiences of cisgendered men of the world, of culture, and of sex as if these reflected a universal viewpoint shared by everybody.
2. There is some disagreement between Lang and earlier anthropologists such as Fulton and Anderson (1992) and Roscoe (1991) about the terminology itself and whether the chosen gender or the birth sex should come first.
3. If you google ***hijra*** you will learn that large parts of South Asia socially recognize a third gender and India also does so legally.
4. The vagina is ***not*** the name for the entire genital area. The vagina is the internal orifice, the canal that extends from the exterior genitals (the vulva) to the cervix and the uterus. If you use tampons or engage in genital intercourse with a penis, a dildo, fingers, or something else, you insert these into the ***vagina***. The external genitals are the ***vulva*** and include the clitoris and the labia (majora and minora). As an aside, if women "vajazzle," they don't decorate their "vagina" as it is often claimed. Instead vajazzling involves decorating the shaven or waxed pubic area. Decorating the vagina, it being an interior canal, would be rather difficult, to say the least. But the fact that the vulva regularly gets misnamed vagina should give us pause. Also, if you have a vulva, I suggest that you take a mirror and look at it. You also might want to google vulva images to get a sense of the wide variation of what vulvas look like.
5. The Intersex Society of America describes intersex in the following way:

   a general term used for a variety of conditions in which a person is born with a reproductive or sexual anatomy that doesn't seem to fit the typical definitions of female or male. For example, a person might be born appearing to be female on the outside, but having mostly male-typical anatomy on the inside. Or a person may be born with genitals that seem to be in-between the usual male and female types—for example, a girl may be born with a noticeably large clitoris, or lacking a vaginal opening, or a boy may be born with a notably small penis, or with a scrotum that is divided so that it has formed more like labia. Or a person may be born with mosaic genetics, so that some of her cells have XX chromosomes and some of them have XY. (www.isna.org/faq/what_is_intersex)

6. Recent biological research supports the view of a wider spectrum of human sexual variation beyond XX and XY options. Indeed, this research suggests that there is a spectrum of sexual difference *within* many individuals (Aintsworth, 2015).
7. Cameron's (1992) study of male American college students' use of slang words for their genitals found, quite disturbingly, a predominant use of militaristic metaphors for the penis, such as torpedo, missile, snake, or jack hammer. Such language masculinizes a very sensitive body part and seeks to deny the penis's intense vulnerability.
8. Trans men typically were assigned female at birth or in utero, but come to identify at some point in their lives as male. Trans women on the other hand were assigned male but identify as female. Trans people choose a variety of ways to "transition" from MtF (male birth assignment to female identity) or from FtM (female birth assignment to male identity) over their life course. Some undergo full genital reassignment surgery to bring their bodies in line with their identity. Others, particularly FtMs—due to limited funds and/or lack of effective surgical solutions—might undergo top surgery and take testosterone but refrain from bottom surgery. Other trans folks might only transition socially but don't undergo any medical or hormonal interventions. Some folks identify as genderqueer and have no desire to produce any form of coherence between appearance, body, and their gender identification. Like cisgendered folks, there is an enormous diversity among trans folks.
9. For a recent study of discursive framing of trans embodiment see Edelman and Zimman (2014).
10. For a discussion of sexual antinomies in late modernity see Jackson and Scott (2004).
11. Unique to Alberta, according to the 2009 Human Rights Act, schools have to inform parents when religion, sexuality, or sexual orientation are to be discussed in class. Parents can then pull their children from these classrooms.

Discussion Questions

1. Explain the difference between the strong and weak social constructionist position with regards to sexuality. Which one do you find more convincing and why?
2. Make a list of the privileges associated with heterosexuality. Discuss what "taking responsibility" for these privileges could look like.
3. Ask your friends to draw and name the different parts of the vulva, including the location and size of the clitoris. What do you note, especially when comparing this to your friends' knowledge about the location and size of the penis?
4. Should sex education in high school entail discussions of sexual pleasure? Why or why not?

Bibliography

Abramovich, I. A. (2012). No safe place to go—LGBTQ youth homelessness in Canada: Reviewing the literature. *Canadian Journal of Family and Youth/Le Journal Canadien de Famille et de la Jeunesse*, *4*(1), 29–51.

Aintsworth, C. (2015). Sex Redefined. *Nature, 518*, 288–291.

Bersani, L. (1987). Is the rectum a grave? *October*, *43*, 197–222.

Blackless, M., Charuvastra, A., Derryck, A., Fausto-Sterling, A., Lauzanne, K., & Lee, E. (2000). How sexually dimorphic are we? Review and synthesis. *American Journal of Human Biology*, *12*, 151–166.

Blackwood, E. (2000). Culture and women's sexualities. *Journal of Social Issues*, *56*(2), 223–238.

Butler, J. (1988). Performative acts and gender constitution: An essay in phenomenology and feminist theory. *Theatre Journal*, *40*, 519–531.

Butler, J. (1990). *Gender trouble*. New York, NY: Routledge.

Cameron, D. (1992). Naming of parts: Gender, culture, and terms for the penis among American college students. *American Speech*, *67*(4), 367–382.

CBC. (2014). Teen, mother launch complaint against abstinence-based sex ed. Retrieved from www.cbc.ca/news/canada/edmonton/teen-mother-launch-complaint-against-abstinence-based-sex-ed-1.2703535

Conte, F. A., & Grumbach, M. M. (1989). Pathogenesis, classification, diagnosis, and treatment of anomalies of sex. In L. J. DeGroot (Ed.), *Endocrinology* (pp. 1810–1847). Philadelphia, PA: W.B. Saunders.

Dreger, A. D. (1995). Doubtful sex: The fate of the hermaphrodite in Victorian medicine. *Victorian Studies*, *38*(3), 335–370.

Duggan, L. (2000). *The twilight of equality? Neoliberalism, cultural politics, and the attack on democracy.* Boston, MA: Beacon.

Edelman, E. A., & Zimmerman, L. (2014). Boy cunts and bonus holes: Trans men's bodies, neoliberalism, and the sexual productivity of genitals. *Journal of Homosexuality*, *61*, 673–690.

Fausto-Sterling, A. (2000). The five sexes, revisited. *The Sciences*, *40*(4), 18–23.

Fone, Byrne (2000). *Homophobia: A history.* New: York: Picador.

Foucault, M. (1976/1978). *The history of sexuality, volume 1: An introduction*. (R. Hurley, Trans.). London: Allen Lane.

Fulton, R., & Anderson, S. W. (1992). The Amerindian "man-woman": Gender, liminality, and cultural continuity. *Current Anthropology*, *33*, 603–610.

Grant, J. M., Mottet, L. A., Tanis, J. with Harrison, J., Herman, J. L., & Keisling, M. (2011). Injustice at every turn: A report of the national transgender discrimination survey. Washington, DC: National Center for Transgender Equality and National Gay and Lesbian Task Force.

Hewlett, B. S. (1991). *Intimate fathers: The nature and context of Aka pygmy paternal infant care*. Ann Arbor: University of Michigan Press.

Intersex Society of North America. (2008a). *How common is intersex?* Retrieved from www.isna.org/faq/frequency

Intersex Society of North America. (2008b). *What is intersex?* Retrieved from www.isna.org/faq/what_is_intersex

Jackson, S. & Scott, S. (Eds.). (1996). *Feminism and sexuality.* New York: Columbia University Press.

Jackson, S. & Scott, S. (2004). Sexual antinomies in late modernity. *Sexualities*, *7*, 233–248.

Johnson, M. L. (2002). Fuck you and your untouchable face: Third wave feminism & the problem of romance. In *Jane sexes it up: True confessions of feminist desire* (pp. 13–52). New York, NY: Four Walls, Eight Windows.

Katz, J. N. (1990). The invention of heterosexuality. *Socialist Review*, *20*, 7–34.

Koedt, A. (1970). The myth of the vaginal orgasm. *CWLU Herstory Archive*. Retrieved from www.uic.edu/orgs/cwluherstory/CWLUArchive/vaginalmyth.html

Lang, S. (1990/1998). *Men as women, women as men: Changing gender in Native American cultures*. (J. L. Vantine, Trans.). Austin, TX: University of Texas Press.

Laqueur, T. (1990). *Making sex: Body and gender from the Greeks to Freud.* Cambridge, MA: Harvard University Press.

Lean, G. (2006, 2 April). Pollution: Where have all the baby boys gone? *The Independent*. Retrieved from www.independent.co.uk/environment/pollution-where-have-all-the-baby-boys-gone-472477.html

Levine, J. (2002). *Harmful to minors: The perils of protecting children from sex*. Minneapolis, MN: University of Minnesota Press.

Manalansan IV, M. F. (2005) Race, violence, and neoliberal spatial politics in the global city. *Social Text*, *23*(3–4), 141–155.

McDonald, E., Watterson, A., Tyler, A. N., McArthus, J., & Scott, E. M. (2014). Multi-factorial influences on sex ratio: A spatio-temporal investigation of endocrine disruptor pollution and neighborhood stress. *International Journal of Occupational Environmental Health,* July-September, *20*(3), 235–246.

Mead, M. (1935/1963). *Sex and temperament in three primitive societies*. New York, NY: William Morrow.

Moorhead, J. (2005, 15 June). Are the men of the African Aka tribe the best fathers in the world? *The Guardian*. Retrieved from www.theguardian.com/society/2005/jun/15/childrensservices.familyandrelationships

Nagel, J. (2000). Ethnicity and sexuality. *Annual Review of Sociology*, *26*, 107–133.

Nanda, S. (2014). *Gender diversity: Crosscultural variations* (2nd ed.). Long Grove, IL: Waveland Press.

Overall, C. (1990). Heterosexuality and feminist theory. *Canadian Journal of Philosophy*, *20*, 1–18.

Rich, A. (1996). Compulsory heterosexuality and lesbian existence. Reprinted in S. Jackson & S. Scott. (Eds.). *Feminism and sexuality* (pp. 130–143). New York, NY: Columbia University Press. (Reprinted from *Signs*, *5*, 631–660.)

Roscoe, W. (1991). *The Zuni man-woman*. Albuquerque, NM: University of New Mexico Press.

Roughgarden, J. (2004). *Evolution's rainbow: Diversity, gender, and sexuality in nature and people.* Berkeley, CA: University of California Press.

Rubin, G. (1984). Thinking sex: Notes for a radical theory of the politics of sexuality. In C. S. Vance (Ed.), *Pleasure and danger: Exploring female sexuality* (pp. 267–319). London, UK: Routledge.

Sedgwick, E. K. (1990). *The epistemology of the closet.* Berkeley, CA: University of California Press.

Segal, L. (1994). *Straight sex: The politics of pleasure*. Berkeley, CA: University of California Press.

Smith, A. (2011). Queer theory and Native studies: The heteronormativity of colonialism. In Q. Driskill, C. Finley, B. J. Gilley, & S. L. Morgensen (Eds.), *Queer Indigenous Studies: Critical Intervention in Theory, Politics, and Literature* (pp. 43–65). University of Arizona Press, AZ: Tucson.

Somerville, S. (1994). Scientific racism and the emergence of the homosexual body. *Journal of the History of Sexuality* *5*(2), 243–266.

Sullivan, N. (2003). Queering 'straight' sex. In *A critical introduction to queer theory* (pp. 119–135). New York, NY: New York University Press.

Thomas, W., and Jacobs, S.-E. (1999). '. . .And we are still here': From *Berdache* to Two-Spirit People. *American Indian Culture and Research Journal* *23*(2), 91–107.

Thomas, C. T. (2000). *Straight with a twist: Queer theory and the subject of heterosexuality*. Urbana, IL: University of Illinois Press.

Tuana, N. (2004). Coming to understand: Orgasm and the epistemology of ignorance. *Hypatia: A Journal of Feminist Philosophy*, *19*, 194–232.

Valverde, M. (1985). *Sex, power and pleasure*. Toronto, ON: Women's Press.

INTRODUCTION

The body is an important identity project for girls coming of age in Westernized cultures. As a key self-making medium, many girls and women also experience their bodies as significant obstacles and sources of distress. On the positive side, bodies are sites of agency and empowerment, primary vehicles through which individuals explore, interact with, and understand the world. On the negative side, bodies are objects of social scrutiny and sanction, fuelling girls' dissatisfaction and deprecation. In this chapter, I explore the contradictory meanings young women hold regarding their bodies. Using the concept of the "material culture of beauty" and my own research on adult women's body histories, I reveal the ways in which cultural imaginings and gazes have shaped their body self-images. Narratives of embodiment from 100 ordinary Canadian women of varying body sizes and racial backgrounds and with and without disabilities and physical differences illustrate the fact that, although women of all ages have greater freedom to play with their appearance, cultural codes of beauty have become more narrowly defined over the past few decades. The result is a curious situation in which women are told to be and look however they wish all the while experiencing social sanction and derision if they step outside narrow boundaries of acceptable bodily self-presentations.

There is an upsurge of feminist writing about beauty, both critical and celebratory. Although feminist commentary on beauty has mushroomed since the 1970s, writers continue to wrestle with the same old debate: Are beauty practices manifestations of sexist, racist, and market oppression of women? Or, do they afford women opportunities for self-expression, empowerment, and pleasure? Some critics contend that patriarchal and commercial interests push women into painful beauty work to satisfy our culturally created desires and assuage fears of difference (Clarke & Griffin, 2007; Gill, 2009; Stuart & Donaghue, 2011). Others argue that women are not cultural dupes but active agents who strategically alter their appearance in their best interests (Davis, 1995; Gimlin, 2006; Holliday & Sanchez Taylor, 2006; Scott, 2005). Body stories reveal the ways in which women of all shapes, sizes, and hues take up body ideals and identify multiple motivations for their beautifying practices, ranging from pleasure and convenience to self-esteem and economic advantage. The stories further disclose that although all women grapple with the contradictions of body practices that may oppress even as they empower, not all confront the same cultural looks and gazes. For example, young, thin, white women are more likely to be seen as the epitome of beauty; visibly disabled women as undesirable and sexless; Black women as sexually wild and aggressive; and Asian and South Asian women as meek or mysterious and exotic. The interplay of these stereotypes with body ideals calls for more intersectional understandings of the role that cultural imagery plays in women's lives. To help develop these sorts of interpretations, I explore the differing cultural gazes that diverse women confront then move to examine the body projects they take up.

THE UNEASY PRIMACY OF IMAGES

In Western culture, women are identified socially with their bodies. How the culture values or devalues physical features, sizes, and capacities has a significant impact on women's sense of body and self. In explaining why the body is so important to women's identity, French feminist Simone de Beauvoir famously wrote that "one is not born, but becomes a woman" (1974, p. 249). She argues that women's bodies are central to this process; through media, medical systems, and beauty culture we learn how to fashion our bodies to "create" our gender. Since de Beauvoir, feminist critics looking at images of female bodies have noted that women tend to be positioned as "objects" of a male gaze (Mulvey, 1975). As critic John Berger (1980) said of the ways that women and men have been depicted in Western art and advertising: ". . . men act and women appear. Men look at women. Women watch themselves being looked at. This determines not only most relations between men and women but also the relation of women to themselves" (p. 47). Many in my study experienced being looked at as an everyday occurrence in their lives: "No one verbalizes it. It becomes the norm. 'He was looking at my tits.' 'He was looking at my ass'" (Sheila, 22, South Asian Canadian). In sexist visual society, where men as a group are handed greater power to determine women's desirability and value, girls grow up with varying degrees of insecurity about the beholder's assessment: "I see girls who are competent yet they fall apart because a guy walks in the door" (Andrea, 37, white Canadian). These "gendered looking relations" not only affected how the women I interviewed surveyed their bodies but, by teaching them certain ideals and norms of femininity and femaleness, also taught them to police the boundaries of their gendered and sexed embodiment.

How did gendered looking relations emerge? For most of us, mirrors are the oldest and most ubiquitous image-making technologies in our day-to-day lives. As cultural historians have shown, prior to the Victorian period, only the wealthy could afford mirrors. In the 16th century, for example, a small glass mirror framed in precious metals and jewels cost the equivalent of a luxury car in today's currency (Melchior-Bonnet, 2001). Technological advancements in the 19th century saw massive increases in mirror production and their installation in public and private spaces. The new department stores, such as Eaton's in Canada and Macy's in the United States, used reflecting surfaces to illuminate interiors with light as a way to encourage spending (O'Brien & Szeman, 2004). At the same time, mirrors became permanent fixtures of middle-class homes as well as portable accessories for many girls and women. Thus, a majority of Western women began to subject their bodies to greater scrutiny only with the introduction of affordable image technologies—first mirrors, then photography and film (Rice, 2014).

In the 19th century, beauty was believed to derive from inner qualities such as character, morality, and spirituality. To orient female buyers toward consumption of cosmetics, marketers heightened women's image consciousness by reminding them of the critical gaze of others. For example, as one ad warns women, "Strangers' eyes, keen and critical—can you meet them proudly, confidently, without fear?" Another claims, "Your husband's eyes . . . more searching than your mirror."[1] Positioned as objects of an outsider's gaze, female viewers of commercial culture were, for the first time, invited to see themselves as recipients of evaluative looks.

Surprisingly, while today large corporations control the cosmetics market, ordinary women were industry innovators. Canadian working-class farm girl Elizabeth Arden, poor Jewish immigrant Helena Rubinstein, and African American domestic servant and daughter of slaves Madame C. J. Walker became successful entrepreneurs. Feminist social historian Kathy Peiss (1998) suggests that these socially marginalized women built their businesses by attracting other women to act as sales agents and by using stories of their own struggles to attract customers. Early entrepreneurs brought to advertising the idea that women could improve their social situation through personal transformation.

By the 1920s, the beauty business had mushroomed into a mass market overtaken by male manufacturers (Peiss, 1998). Drawing on the social permissiveness of the period, advertisers connected women's cosmetic use with greater individuality, mobility, and modernity. The caption of one ad exclaims, "The Lovely Rebel Who fought for Youth and Won!" and another reads, "Be as MODERN as you like—for you can still be lovely." While marketers sold makeup as a means for women to assert autonomy and resist outmoded gender expectations, by the end of the 1930s, messages increasingly equated beauty with a woman's "true femininity." For example, in one ad entitled "Beauty Lost—Beauty Regained," readers are told how a "lovely lady who goes to pieces" recovers her mental health by "regaining her lost youth." Ads of the time encouraged women's investment in their appearance in the name of their emotional well-being and psychological health. When image became intertwined with a woman's identity, personality, and psychology in this way, modifying the body became, for many girls and women, a principal method of caring for the self. In this way, a woman's appearance came to be read as a prime measure of her self-esteem, feminine essence, and mental health.

Throughout the 1930s and 1940s, marketers encouraged middle-class mothers to invest energy in their own and their daughters' appearance in the name of physical and emotional health (Brumberg, 1998). In one period ad from Canada, mothers are told that keeping their daughters' complexion clear is "a mother's duty" and in another that girls "are never too young" to begin their beauty routines. During the Second World War, beauty became a means for women to support the war effort, with ad copy announcing that "beauty is a duty," that "fit" bodies increased women's productivity, while "lovely" faces enhanced troop morale. It was not until the 1950s that cosmetics companies began directly targeting teenage girls—who had started to hold part-time jobs and had their own disposable income—with ads designed to appeal to their sense of generational distinctiveness and romantic desires. With copy encouraging readers to get "The 'natural' look men look for," ads for *Seventeen Cosmetics* reinforced girls' desires to attract an admiring male gaze.

Cultural norms about beauty and gendered looking relations can be difficult to question because of the ways that they are naturalized in art, advertising, and popular culture. Immersed as we are in these conventions, they appear as normal. Yet making the conventions strange can make us better able to see them. Modern-day Japanese "appropriation" artist Yasumasa Morimura (2008) remakes classical nudes by altering his features through make-up, costume, and digital-image manipulation, and then inserting himself in the place of the idealized female figures in famous paintings such as Manet's *Olympia.* (View his work at: www.luhringaugustine.com/artists/yasumasa-morimura) By putting himself, a Japanese man, in place of iconic beauty ideals, Morimura draws our attention to gendered and racialized looking relations, challenging Western conventions of seeing female bodies as objects "to be looked at" and especially of seeing *white* women's bodies as desirable objects.

Arguably, these gazes have become even more complex in today's commercial culture, as women are encouraged to find pleasure in gazing at each other's images. For example, think about the typical cover of a *Cosmo*, *Vogue*, or other fashion magazine. As you consider the cover photo, ask yourself the following questions: Who is the woman on the cover looking at? Who does she think is looking at her? Your reflections might suggest that the cover image operates not only as an object of vision for *male* but also for *female* audiences. As viewers, we might imagine ourselves to be a male or female spectator looking at the model with envy or desire. Alternately, we might imagine ourselves to be the beautiful, sexy model looking back with confidence, desire, or a conviction in our own desirability at the male and female spectators who are looking at us. In either case, through this relay of looks, the model becomes an object of desire for imagined spectators *who want her* and for those *who want to be like her*. While the idea that women find pleasure in looking at each other 's bodies may appear less sexist than that of men evaluating female bodies, media critic Rosalind Gill argues that the shift from an "external, male judging gaze" to an internal "self policing" gaze may represent deeper manipulation, since it invites female audiences to become more adept at scrutinizing their own and other women's images (Gill, 2007, p. 151).

Image culture sends powerful messages about the rejected or "abject" body, which it subjects to invasive stares, gapes, and glares. In Western culture, the fat, aged, ambiguously gendered, racially marked, disabled or diseased, and physically different body is an object of fear and fascination. The work of Polish artist Katarzyna Kozyra explores the intrusive looks and stares that women, seen as "abject," encounter such as those undergoing treatment for cancer. Rather than posing as an idealized female figure in her version of Manet's *Olympia*, Kozyra evokes the ideal's dreaded, abject Other by presenting herself lying ill and naked on a hospital bed under the insensitive ever-watchful gaze of a medic. (View her work at: http://katarzynakozyra.pl/main/10/olympia/) Julia Kristeva (1982), a Bulgarian-French philosopher, calls the abject the twisted braid of fear and fascination that people feel when they encounter bodily fluids, physical differences, disabilities, grave illness, and dying bodies. According to Kristeva, the abject is feared and rejected because it resists our drive to master and control our bodies. Physical features and processes treated as abject are those that remind us of the uncontainability of our bodies, our vulnerability to disease, the certainty of our death. A simple way to understand the abject is to see it as that which doesn't fit to body norms or ideals. Media images continually play on our fear of abjection and desire to embody norms/ideals by showing us "rejected" before and "perfected" after pictures of people who undergo cosmetic makeovers (Covino, 2004).

Rather than being an object of the gaze, abject bodies, according to disability theorist Rosemary Garland-Thomson, are subjected to "the stare" (2009). Staring is our compulsion to look at disaster, called "the car wreck" phenomenon (p. 3); the visual gape we engage in when we can't pull our eyes away from the unfamiliar, unexpected, the strange. Because people both crave and dread the unfamiliar and unpredictable, consumer culture is continuously feeding our hunger for novelty while enforcing certain notions of "normal." Women with disabilities, visible differences in particular, described the fearful and fascinated gape of non-disabled others: "There's a fascination with difference. People want the gory details of disability because they want to feel that they are better off" (Harriet, 34, WASP, chronic illness). Racialized women also reported that cultural stereotypes often informed and validated hyper-sexualizing looks onto their bodies: "From a lot of white men, I get sexual fascination: I'm the wild Black woman, with pronounced buttocks and thighs" (Marcia, 37, African Canadian, First Nation).

BODY PROJECTS TODAY

As a result of the cultural meanings given to notions of desirability and difference, many girls and women come to relate to their bodies as self-making projects. The women who participated in this study, born in the 1960s onwards, from all walks of life in Canada are among the first generation to come of age in a world replete with image technologies of mirrors, cameras, and computers. Nearly every woman I spoke with recognized the controlling influence of different cultural and gendered gazes. While the experiences of this cohort varied depending on race, size, and ability, most women I spoke to also told of how their degree of dissatisfaction increased in adolescence, a time when they encountered mounting pressure to appear as desirable. Many came to see different body sites—including skin, weight, hair, and breasts—as projects and as problems. This included the 90% who saw themselves as over- or underweight; 80% who believed their breasts were too big or small; 60% who believed their skin was too dark and/or disliked their hair colour/texture; and 100% who began to remove unwanted body hair. Body dissatisfaction increased dramatically between ages nine and 16, when all confronted a growing gap between their changing bodies and images of culturally normalized and idealized bodies. Coming of age in a consumerist, image-oriented society, they dealt with the disparity between differences and ideals by imagining, as one participant put it, their best possible bodily self: "I never had an image of me that wasn't in the [wheel]chair. But I would create images of me looking different in the sense that I would be prettier, slimmer, more popular. The most attractive

I could imagine becoming: my best possible image of myself" (Frances, 45, WASP, born with spina bifida). All navigated puberty and adolescence by envisioning or adopting diverse practices—from hair relaxing and eating disorders to dieting and cosmetic surgery—to remake their differences desirable.

The messages in today's magazines echo the efforts of the women in my study to close the gap between their body differences and desirable ideals. Fashion magazines are vehicles for delivering messages of the beauty business to female consumers; a primary purpose is to enlist readers into image enhancement through continuous consumption. Rather than advocating one ideal, magazines try to democratize beauty by convincing readers that they can achieve their "best bodies." This message enables girls' and women's expression of individuality and celebration of difference. Yet it also portrays body modification as critical to self-expression. In addition, it pulls diverse audiences into preoccupation with perpetual body improvement and purchase of products. In many ways TV shows like *America's Next Top Model* and *The Face* likewise instruct young women that they can bridge the gap between their bodily difference and images of desirability by re-visioning their differences as desirable. Such shows frequently reinforce the idea that the greatest power a young woman can wield is her sexual sway over men, and they invariably present makeovers as tickets to success. Despite purporting to represent diversity, they still promote a narrow notion of beauty and encourage body modification through consumption to achieve the desirable look.

Beauty pageants in which contestants are women with disabilities are yet another example of the idea of re-visioning differences as desirable within narrow confines. *Miss Ability* is a reality TV beauty contest from the Netherlands that started in 2006; contestants have to display a "handicap visible to the eye" (Eye2Eye Media, 2008). The winner of the first pageant, crowned by the Dutch prime minister, was a young woman named Roos who wears a cervical collar due to an acquired disability affecting her neck. The cervical collar is the only indication she has any physical disability and is not an average model. Roos manages her disability by using the cervical collar sometimes and lying prone sometimes, yet images often depict her as highly sexual. While it can't be ignored that she is disabled, the nature of her disability is socially acceptable—no dribbling, sudden movements, speech impairments, or any deviance from social protocols that make people uncomfortable. Thus, the winner is someone the non-disabled population can relate to in fundamental ways. She can look "normal," albeit for very brief periods; she is seen as sexually desirable; and she meets expectations of what is feminine. Even in a forum where it's supposedly "celebrated," disability must remain invisible (Rice et al., 2005). It is interesting to note that due to the show's surprisingly high ratings in the Netherlands, broadcasters have snapped up the rights to remake *Miss Ability* in Britain, France, Germany, and the United States. (Sherwin, 2006). In 2008, the BBC launched *Britain's Missing Top Model*, a series in which eight women with disabilities participate in a competition, with the winner appearing in *Marie Claire* (Stanley, 2009).

In what follows, I describe the various body projects that women in my study took up and consider how their motivations for engaging in bodywork varied depending on their race, ability, and size.

Weight and Eating

In contemporary Western culture, people learn to value a certain size as part of the body beautiful. For example, the thin female body is associated with health, wealth, sexiness, and success. Despite a growing dialogue about body acceptance, fat body is seen as unattractive, not physically or emotionally healthy, and lacking in control. Today's magazines criticize women's bodies, whatever their weight. Headlines such as "Battle of the Bones" and "Stars' Worst and Best Beach Bodies" regularly invite readers' criticism of famous bodies and encourage comparison based on looks and size. Coming of age in our size-obsessed culture, 66% of the women in this study came to feel their "too-big" bodies violated size standards and 24% that their "too-thin" ones failed to fit weight norms. The voices in their heads echoed messages from mainstream media: no size is acceptable or safe.

Historically and cross-culturally, fatness has been interpreted as both a sign of wealth and fertility and a signifier of disease and death. While the celebration and stigmatization of fat have fluctuated in different times among various cultures, concerns about the medical and moral risks of being overweight have intensified over the last century. In North America today, two competing frames shape the debate on overweight and obesity: Is it an "epidemic" or is it a "myth" (Lupton, 2012; Rice, 2007)? The first frame—the epidemic of obesity—dominates public debate. Global and national public health institutions have fuelled fear of fat by interpreting obesity as an escalating epidemic that threatens the health and fitness of populations and nations (World Health Organization, 2003). Beyond health problems, an increasing number of social problems are being blamed on fat, from global warming (Jacobson & McLay, 2006) to America's vulnerability to terrorist attacks (Associated Press, 2006). Despite the ubiquity of such moralistic medical messages, there is considerable uncertainty and controversy within obesity research itself about the causes, health consequences, measures, and treatment of obesity (Cogan & Ernsberger, 1999). More recently, scientists, while not dismissing health concerns raised by doctors or governments, have questioned obesity researchers' assumptions and interests and begun to explore why our society has become so alarmed about fat (Gard & Wright, 2005).

Epidemiologists now suggest that rising weights in our society may be related to people's biology combined with obesity-causing environments (Brownell & Horgen, 2004). In addition, we simply do not know the health consequences of obesity. We know that the relationship between health and weight is a U-shaped curve, meaning that health risks increase at extreme under- and overweight (Gard & Wright, 2005). While high weight is associated with hypertension and heart disease, this association does not mean there is a causal relationship—in other words, there is no evidence that being fat in itself causes these health problems (Cogan & Ernsberger, 1999). To date, there are no safe, proven treatments for "excess" weight (Ernsberger & Koletsky, 1999). The most common treatments such as dieting, pills, and surgery all have health risks and consequences (Bennett & Gurin, 1983). Finally, weight measures such as the Body Mass Index (BMI) have also been called into question. BMI was originally meant as a screening tool (to tell if someone is at risk for developing a health problem), but it is now widely misused as a diagnostic tool (to tell if someone needs to lose weight) (Ikeda, Crawford, & Woodward-Lopez, 2006; Jutel, 2006). Kate Harding (2008) developed the *BMI Slide Show* to get people to think critically about BMI. Watch the slide show to assess whether you think the categories are skewed (http://kateharding.net/bmi-illustrated/).

Some critical scholars have written about "the obesity epidemic" as a moral panic, arguing that misplaced morality and ideological assumptions underlie our "war on fat" (Gard & Wright, 2005). They argue that in obesity science the causes of and solutions for obesity invariably come back to people's health practices. This view both ignores scientific uncertainly about the causes of weight gain and blames individuals by ignoring contexts such as poverty or weight prejudice that constrain their options for eating or activity.

Recent history shows that obesity epidemic discourses dominate cultural narratives partly because they dovetail with ongoing state-sponsored efforts designed to improve the health, fitness, and competitiveness of nations. From the late 1960s onwards, many Western governments, including Canada's, initiated public education campaigns that advocated greater physical activity to prevent fatness and promote fitness in citizens (MacNeill, 1999). In response to growing concerns about excessive consumption and the sedentary lifestyles of Canadians, Prime Minister Pierre Elliott Trudeau launched the ParticipACTION Campaign in the early 1970s. It famously compared the fitness levels of a 30-year-old Canadian with a 60-year-old Swede. (See this ad at the ParticipACTION Archive Project: http://scaa.sk.ca/gallery/participaction/english/home.html.) Many ParticipACTION ads imagined the ideal Canadian citizen as a thin, fit, white, able-bodied male. They further raised the spectre of the feminized, unfit, underdeveloped, and Third-World "Other," who threatened Canada's competitiveness on the global economic stage. However, the effectiveness of interventions that link fatness prevention to fitness promotion has never been established. Studies show that fat children and adults are less likely to be physically active and more likely to have eating problems. Yet research has not revealed whether overeating and under-exercising increases weight, whether being fat increases one's susceptibility to problem eating and inactivity (Boutelle, Neumark-Sztainer, Story, & Resnick, 2002), or whether the association between behaviour and weight is mediated by other factors (such as genetics, food additives, and so on).

Some women in my research suggest that ParticipACTION ads disseminated throughout the 1970s and 1980s heightened their fear of fat and instilled the belief that their big bodies were "bad." By linking thinness with fitness and positioning fat as opposite to fit, ParticipACTION's popular "FitFat" ad conveyed the idea that fatness and fitness could *not* coexist in the same body. Those perceived as fat in childhood describe how demanding physical education programs introduced into schools often dissuaded them from participating in physical activity altogether. Adult enforcement of restrictive diets resulted in long-term struggles with food, including compulsive, binge, and secretive eating (Rice, 2007; 2009b). In other words, fatness prevention efforts contributed to producing the very behaviours and bodies that proponents were attempting to prevent!

> "I remember this feeling of dread when the ["FitFat"] ad came on TV. Once my father and I were watching, I remember a man's voice saying, "This year fat's not where it's at." This made me so self-conscious. . . ." (Maude, 27, white Canadian, blind from adolescence)

> "I wasn't doing very well in ParticipACTION or Canada Fitness. I hated gym class. I didn't like being tested in front of everybody. . . ." (Yolanda, 23, Dutch-Indonesian Canadian)

Although ParticipACTION ended in 2001, the Canadian federal government recently re-launched the campaign to stem rising levels of obesity, once again focusing on "over"weight children and adults as a high-risk group (Canadian Press, 2007). With a renewed focus on fatness prevention through fitness promotion, efforts to stem today's obesity epidemic may be leading a new cohort of large children to adopt problem eating and inactivity, possibly contributing to future problems with weight. This raises some critical questions for developing feminist-informed health and physical education policies and programs: What do you think a fat-friendly, girl-friendly and disability-friendly physical education curriculum would look like? If you had the task of designing a feminist health promotion campaign, what messages would you want to convey to promote girls' health?

Eating Distress

Although only about 3% of young women in North America have eating disorders according to medical criteria (Woodside et al., 2001), 50% admit to extreme weight control, including fasting and vomiting (Neumark-Sztainer et al., 2002). The high prevalence of problem eating notwithstanding, eating disorders are interpreted as *mental illness* (American Psychiatric Association, 2013). However, feminist critics have long noted that an eating disorder, like all diagnoses, is a social construct (Rabinor, 2004). The term *disorder* incorrectly establishes a clear dichotomy between mental illness and wellness. Yet given the pressure for women to control their appetites and weights, it is often difficult to distinguish normal from pathological eating (Cohen, 2004; Rice & Langdon, 1991).

Unfortunately, few experts consider the concept of a *continuum* of eating problems. Beyond debates about eating disorder diagnoses, there are many problems with psychiatric labelling more generally—not only do labels stigmatize people, they also tend to be applied to the least powerful groups in society (Caplan & Cosgrove, 2004). Young women's emotional struggles tend to be pathologized more than young men's, so that there are fewer diagnoses to capture the downsides of masculinity (like excessive risk taking and inability to express emotion) than of femininity (depression and eating problems). Examples of psychiatric labels that have been proposed—such as dressing disorder and compulsive shopping disorder—expose how power relations often arbitrate what is considered stereotypical behaviour and what is labelled a psychiatric condition.

Further, many feminists have been critical of psychiatric treatment for eating disorders that positions women as pathological for adopting socially induced behaviours (Fallon, Katzman, & Wooley, 1994; Rice, 1996). In her ethnographic research, Helene Gremillion (2003) has found that treatment programs tend to substitute one set of disciplinary practices that regulate women's bodies for another—disempowering female patients by replacing culturally condoned food and weight control with medically condoned surveillance of their eating and weight (LaMarre & Rice, 2015). Hospitalization can save lives, yet statistics belie the effectiveness of interventions: re-hospitalization of women with eating problems is common (Health Canada, 2002), creating a revolving-door experience that suggests that treatment often does not work.

Many of the women I interviewed described how they began dieting and disordered eating as a way of amending what they saw as their abject body fat. Some talked of starting to eat secretively in childhood as a direct response to mothers' and doctors' enforced dieting routines while others took up disordered eating during adolescence to escape their "deviant" labels and answer pressure to appear as desirable. Whether they started secretive eating in childhood to resist adult imposition of restrictive diets or later adopted disordered eating to amend size differences, it is noteworthy that *all* participants perceived as fat eventually took up problem eating.

> At least I felt normal enough and desirable enough [when bulimic] that I could actually contemplate a sexual relationship. I could actually let go of protecting myself and enter into a relationship. (Gayle, 29, English-Métis Canadian)

> The times I have felt love are times my body has been the most socially acceptable [through starving and purging]. It makes me profoundly sad that the only ways of accessing those feelings are through having a conventional body. (Sylvie, 36, Italian-Scottish Canadian)

Many people mistakenly believe that only privileged white girls have eating problems. Weight restriction became a way of life for a majority of women of *all* sizes and shapes I interviewed, whether Black, Asian, South Asian, or white. Some racialized participants told how ultra-thinness was viewed more critically in their communities, where images of attractive bodies spanned a broader range of sizes. However, most had grown up during a time when communities of colour constituted a small portion of the Canadian population, and thus many had little access to an alternative beauty aesthetic that called into question white weight standards. With stereotypic portrayals of starving African bodies circulating in Western media throughout the 1970s (such as in children's charity commercials), slenderness also became abject for Black women interviewed. According to post-colonial scholars, Western images have mythologized Africans since the colonial period as innocent yet savage; as less human than animal; as dark presence and ghostly absence (Kaspin, 2002). By portraying emaciated Africans as abused and coarsened victims of starvation and civil war, Western photography has reduced a complex continent of cultures and peoples to a few simple stereotypes. In an attempt to scare Western girls out of self-starvation, only a few years ago one eating disorder campaign unwittingly drew on these injurious associations to render the emaciated African form, faded and ghostlike, as an abject sign of strife and famine.

Growing up in a racially charged image environment, some Black women describe how they got caught between racist stereotypes of starving African bodies in mainstream media and sexist pressures to conform to conflicting feminine size ideals from both the dominant culture (thinness) and their communities (roundness). In my research, the meaning given to a woman's size depended on her race, which suggests that the emaciated brown body operates as an implicit Other against which the thin, white beauty ideal gets defined.

> A girl at school said I looked like starving kids in the World Vision commercial. That was the most hurtful thing anybody ever said to me. I thought, "I should be bigger and more normal because I look like those poster kids." (Rhonda, 32, West Indian Canadian)

> I was heavier than most girls because I was muscular. So I went on these crazy diets, where I'd only eat yogurt. I consumed so much that the bacteria started to affect my stomach. So I ended up in the hospital with "anxiety attacks." But I was just trying to make myself look the way I was supposed to look in society. (Marcia, 37, African, First Nation, Scottish Canadian)

It is significant that no medical professional identified any racialized woman in my study as having an eating problem. Instead, because clinical data in the 1970s and 1980s mostly came from white experts working with white girls (Hesse-Biber et al., 2006), health care providers interpreted the struggles of racialized storytellers as something other than problem eating. Few feminists would deny that Western culture is implicated in the global spread of eating disorders. According to Susan Bordo, the failure of medical professionals to recognize eating disorders among racialized women may be rooted in a deeper reluctance to recognize the role of culture in shaping female embodiment (Bordo, 1993, 2009). Yet some feminists, such as Mervat Nasser and Helen Malson (2009), caution against imposing Western or white meanings onto non-white and non-Western women's experiences. They argue that this denies cultural complexities and local specificities in diverse women's body practices, such as how problem eating might signal an adoption of Western feminine ideals (such as Marcia's attempts to starve away her muscularity) and rejection of racial Othering (her refusal to be stereotyped as an overly muscular Black girl through not eating). By showing how the meanings of body sizes and motivations for eating practices vary across and within Westernized contexts, this exploration reveals important differences in the meanings of experiences but leaves many questions unanswered. If eating disorders are no longer a "white girl" or "Western" problem, what challenges confront researchers in trying to explain them? How do we make meaning of problem eating without imposing Western or white understandings on non-Western and non-white women's experiences?

Skin

Historically, skin became women's first body project as they learned the power of complexion to advance or undermine their social inclusion. From ancient times, pallour was associated with high social status; women at work outdoors were tanned and aged faster, whereas women of high social status were not obliged to work in the fields but stayed indoors and were pale-skinned. From the 17th century onward, this superiority of white over dark was scientifically proclaimed, as white Europeans needed a convincing justification for systems of slavery and colonization that contradicted emerging political theories of human rights (Schiebinger, 1993). To rationalize the disenfranchisement of racialized peoples, scientists constructed a hierarchy of races based on physical traits such as skin colour and bone structure.

As a result, women of every hue attempted to improve their social standing through skin whitening, the most cosmetic procedure of the 19th century (Brumberg, 1998). In period advertisements, skin whiteners for white women promised to enhance their complexion while products for Black women pledged to remove their dark skin. For instance, one "face bleach" ad claims to "turn the skin of a black or brown person four or five shades lighter, and a mulatto person perfectly white" (St. Louis Palladium, 1901, cited in Rooks, 1996). According to Black feminist scholar Noliwe Rooks (1996), these ads persuaded African American women to purchase products by presenting dark skin as an ugly imperfection and by suggesting that skin lightening would promote women's class mobility and social acceptance in a white supremacist society.

As a result of the legacies of Western colonization, racialization, and widespread sexism, many cultures still associate light skin with female beauty, and this fuels and is fuelled by a profitable business in skin-whitening products. While some feminists have suggested that skin whitening is a practice relegated to our racist past (Peiss, 1998), they are missing the rapidly growing global trade in skin-lightening products. Feminist critical race scholar Amina Mire (2005) has called this phenomenon "the globalization of white western beauty ideals." (If you doubt Mire's claim, do an internet search for "skin lightening." It will yield over two million links!) In the West, many cosmetics companies market skin lightening to aging white women by associating light skin with youth and beauty. In ads the aging process frequently is framed as a pathological condition that can be mitigated through measures such as bleaching out "age spots." Globally, cosmetics companies also sell skin-whitening products to women of colour, often covertly via the internet in order to avoid public scrutiny or state regulation of their commodities and campaigns (Mire, 2005). This is partially because many products contain unsafe chemicals such as hydroquinone and mercury that inhibit the skin's melanin formation and are toxic. The dangers of mercury poisoning due to skin lighteners—neurological, kidney, and psychiatric damage—are well known. However, the hazards of hydroquinone, which has been shown in laboratory studies to be disfiguring in high doses and to cause cancer, are less well documented.

In Africa and other regions of the global South, skin whitening is traditionally associated with white colonial oppression. Because women who practise skin-lightening were and are harshly judged as suffering from an "inferiority complex" due to colonization, many engage in the practice covertly (Mire, 2005). Companies thus rely on covert advertising to mitigate women's secret shame about their perceived physical deficiencies, as well as their need to conceal such practices in order to avoid condemnation. Companies selling covertly also avoid public scrutiny of product campaigns. In some campaigns, explicitly racist advertisements associate dark skin with "diseases" and "deformities" such as "hyperpigmentation" and "pigmentation pathologies." In contrast, they typically associate light skin with youth, beauty, health, and empowerment. In its online ads,

L'Oréal, a leading manufacturer and marketer of skin-whiteners such as Bi-White and White Perfect, references the inferiority of dark skin and the superiority of light complexions. Bi-White features an Asian woman unzipping her darker skin. (See the ad at www.youtube.com/watch?v=l0zsVIA3x6Y.) Directed mainly to female Asian consumers, the ad uses medical language to suggest that Asian bodies produce too much melanin that Bi-White will block. As Mire (2005) writes, darkness is associated with falseness, dirtiness, ugliness, and disease. Lightness is seen as true, clean, healthy, and beautiful.

There is a growing trend for many Western-owned cosmetics corporations to rely less on covert internet marketing and more on splashy TV and print campaigns to reach customers in Asia. Since 1978, Hindustan Lever Limited, a subsidiary of the Western corporation Unilever, has sold its skin-whitening products to millions of women around the world (Melwani, 2007). Fair & Lovely, one of Hindustan Lever's best-known beauty brands, is marketed in over 38 countries and monopolizes a majority share of the skin-lightening market in India (Leistikow, 2003). One industry spokesperson recently stated that fairness creams are half of the skin-care market in India, and that 60 to 65% of Indian women use these products daily (Timmons, 2007). Ads for Fair & Lovely frequently feature depressed young women with few prospects who gain brighter futures by attaining their dream job or desired boyfriend after becoming fairer. Other commercials show shy young women who take charge of their lives and transform themselves into "modern" independent beauties. Appealing to women's dual aspirations for desirability and economic equality, ads feature taglines such as "Fair & Lovely: The Power of Beauty" and "Fair & Lovely: For Total Fairness" (Timmons, 2007). (See ads at www.youtube.com/watch?v=KIUQ5hbRHXk&NR=1.)

The accounts of racialized women in this study echo these ads' sensibilities in that all learned, often from both the dominant culture and their own communities, that lighter skin was associated with beauty, virtue, and economic opportunity.

> Being in the West Indian community I was more attractive, and with people who weren't West Indian I was more acceptable because I wasn't as dark. So I had an easier time from all groups because I am supposedly that ideal. (Salima, 30, West Indian, South Asian Canadian)

Ironically, Western psychologists and psychiatrists have framed skin whitening as a sign of mental illness, unconnected to colonial or other oppressive histories. In contrast, the experiences of informants suggest that skin-lightening practices are technologies of both oppression and opportunity, especially for racialized women who get caught between the colonizing effects of white supremacist ideals and competing desires for femininity and social acceptance (Rice, 2009b; 2009a). In their narratives, participants aspired to lighter (rather than white) ideals to straddle conflicting demands: to affirm their ethnic looks and escape being seen as Other. Many spoke of avoiding sunlight, wearing light concealer, and using skin lightening in an effort to create a desirable image that enabled them to evade demeaning racist and sexist comments while not completely erasing their embodied difference.

> I saw neither beach nor bathing suit in high school! I was already Black and with people who weren't Black. (Marcia, 37, African, First Nations, Scottish Canadian)

> We have a family friend who is a lot darker than we are. She bought Fair & Lovely and when everyone found out, they used to say, "Oh, she uses Fair & Lovely." The fact that we talked about it is mean. The fact that she feels she has to use it is terrible. (Preeta, 29, South Asian Canadian)

Many white women are well aware of the cultural associations of dark skin with devalued status. Yet in a cultural context where race is read off multiple body sites (skin colour, facial features, and so on), tanned skin may be viewed as a temporary, detachable adornment rather than an essential feature that signifies someone's racial status (Ahmed, 1998). It is in this context that white women often see skin darkening as a beauty project. After the First World War, tanning became a statement about high social status; a tan proclaimed the leisure to lie out in the sun and the money to go to tropical beaches in midwinter. White women who tan can thus connect their bronzed skin to health, wealth, and attractiveness, secure in the knowledge that they still are seen as white, regardless of the health implications (such as the increased risk of skin cancers and premature skin aging). These experiences, too, generate many questions: Why is there emphasis on white women's attainment of a sun-kissed glow while racialized women feel pressured to aspire to the glow of fairness? Is the obsession with fairness a bad case of a "colonial hangover," or is it an example of a Western cultural imperialism that uses global media to spread white beauty ideals?

Hair

Within a racial hierarchy of beauty, Black women encounter complex messages about hair due to associations of long, flowing hair with social mobility and femininity. Beauty entrepreneur Madame C. J. Walker, who is credited with popularizing the "hot" comb for straightening hair, sold such products as Black women's "passport to prosperity" (Rooks, 1996, p. 65). She saw Black women's beauty in a political light—as a "vindication of black womanhood" demeaned by slavery and as a pathway to prosperity and respectability denied by white society. Many Black feminist and critical race scholars have debated whether Madame Walker preyed on African American women's feelings of inferiority or promoted pro-Black beauty through dignifying their beauty practices (Byrd & Tharps, 2001; Rooks, 1996). In her personal letters and public talks, Walker clearly did not seek to embody white ideals. Instead, beauty was a way to challenge stereotypes of Black women as unfeminine and unattractive, and in so doing, to raise Black women's self-confidence and contribute to their collective advancement.

Today, an estimated 80% of African American women straighten their hair (Swee, Klontz, & Lambert, 2000). In 1993, the World Rio Corporation marketed a hair-straightening product on its late-night infomercials that targeted these women. In the Rio ads, good hair was equated with straightened hair and bad hair with untamed curls. Ads used the now familiar format of abject *before* and ideal *after* shots featuring women who had been given a complete makeover. As Noliwe Rooks notes (1996), models in the *before* shots were without make-up, jewellery, or accessories (p. 123). They looked unhappy and their hair was unstyled and unkempt, almost made to look primitive. The *after* shots featured women who had complete beauty makeovers. Although the manufacturers claimed Rio had low levels of acid, it actually contained harsh chemicals. Many who used it experienced hair loss, burns, blisters, and sores on their scalps. Of 340 000 people who purchased the product, over 3000 filed complaints, the largest number ever received in the United States for a cosmetic product (Swee, Klontz, & Lambert, 2000). In infomercials, women were repeatedly told that Rio would deliver them from the "bondage" of chemically treated hair (Rooks, 1996, p. 121). Rio sold itself as a product that would enhance Black women's self-worth, freedom, and social mobility. It thus sent a message designed to resonate with female consumers: that they could escape sexist and racist oppression through relaxing their hair. Many Black women in my study explained how they used hair relaxers, not because they desired whiteness, but because they wanted to avoid racial Othering, as well as aspire to desirability, acceptability, and an enhanced self.

> In high school, people would say, "What are you?" I realized if I blow-dry my hair to get it straight I might not identify as anything separate. . . . The less I try to visually look like some stereotypes from the media or their beliefs, the less I am singled out. (Ada, 27, Trinidadian Canadian, African and Chinese)

Those who think that stigmatization of natural hair is a thing of the past might consider this: in October 2007, *Glamour* magazine developed a presentation called "The dos and don'ts of corporate fashion" that showed an African American woman sporting an Afro with a caption reading, "Say no to the 'fro" (Dorning, 2007). The presenter told a women's luncheon at a Wall Street law firm that Black female attorneys should avoid wearing "political" hairstyles like dreadlocks or Afros, because these styles were seen as unattractive and unprofessional. Members of the audience were justifiably upset with the replay of stereotypes about "natural" hair as overly political, unfeminine, and unprofessional.

Not only do these attitudes have an impact on Black women's beauty perceptions but they also are linked to blocked educational and economic opportunities. Many African Canadian girls report witnessing or experiencing harassment in school arising from perceptions of their hue and hair. Some school boards in the United States have suspended African American students for wearing cornrows, dreadlocks, and other hairstyles seen as making an overly strong political statement (Rooks, 2001). Black women have even been fired from corporate jobs for styling their hair in dreadlocks and braids. Virtually all Black women I interviewed worried that if they wore their hair naturally, they would not succeed in their career or romantic aspirations. Seen in this light, it would be a mistake to interpret hair straightening as another example of women's internalization of sexism and racism. Instead, their stories suggest that managed hair could carry social benefits, including boosting status and success.

> There's a lot of anger because if I go on interviews, people have a pre-made assumption about Black women and therefore about me. When I put in a bid for a job, it is all paper. So it isn't until the interview that they meet me. So you go into a room of ten people and they're all white. Then in walks little Blackie in her braids. You can see the shock on their faces. (Sharon, 31, West Indian, English Canadian)

Along with the presence of long-flowing hair on a woman's head, the absence of body hair is a critical characteristic of the acceptable female body. Few North American women removed their underarm or leg hair before the 20th century; with the rise of beauty culture and body-baring fashions, hair removal became commonplace by the end of the Second World War (Hope, 1982). To convince female consumers to buy depilatory products, early marketers framed any hair not on a woman's head as unsightly and ugly. At the same time, physicians began to label as pathological "excess" hair on parts of the female body typically associated with hair growth in men (Herzig, 2000). However, sorting the normal from the pathological has proven to be difficult: there remains no agreed-on measure of normal amounts of hair in women and no clear markers to distinguish male from female hair growth. Men are thought to be naturally hairier, though patterns of hair growth overlap since women have the same number of hair follicles as men and, like men, produce testosterone (Ferrante, 1988). There may be more variation within than between the sexes because hair growth differs based on age, climate, lifestyle, and genes. The number of hairy women who have an endocrine problem is unknown, with rates ranging from 1 to 80% (Azziz, Carmina, & Sawaya, 2000). (The high percentages should be treated with caution since they may reflect renewed medical attempts to pathologize female body hair.) Whether or not an underlying medical condition is present, any fuzz deemed excessive is labelled "hirsutism," a word related to the Latin *hirsutus*, an adjective meaning rough, shaggy, and bristly (Barber, 2004). This suggests that in parts of the Western world, female body hair has been imagined as repellent, and the unaltered womanly body as feral and unfeminine.

From the pages of fashion magazines to illustrations in biology textbooks, the image of the hairless woman has emerged as a pervasive norm (Schick, Rima, & Calabrese, 2011). Although unshaven men are considered acceptable and their body hair removal optional, studies show that in Anglo-Western countries between 80 and 100% of women spend an average of 30 minutes per week removing unwanted face or body hair (PR Web, 2011). A strong cultural connection exists between hair and sex—the absence of body hair is interpreted as a sign of femaleness, whereas its presence signifies maleness (Toerien & Wilkinson, 2003). Despite feminist challenges to sexual dualism, Western thinking still understands femaleness and maleness as opposites that do not overlap. In this context, the vast majority of women, for whom hairlessness is not a natural state, must remove their hair or have their sex called into question. A lucrative market in hair removal products has resulted, with global sales in shaving gear topping US$25.7 billion in 2010 (PR Web, 2008). So ubiquitous is the puberty rite of shaving that Nair launched Nair Pretty, a depilatory aimed at "first-time hair removers," that is, girls 10 to 15 years old (Newman, 2007).

A majority of women in this study committed at puberty to a lifetime of hair removal, which became a routine part of the hidden work of having an acceptable female body.

The hairless norm is so ubiquitous that although pubic hair is an important marker of puberty, its discovery was horrifying and embarrassing for 25% of women, who had no prior knowledge that growing hair "down there" was typical. Many began removing leg and underarm hair to feel more attractive and a majority also told how they conformed as a way of shielding themselves from people's disapproval and their own discomfort. For some, facial hair was particularly frightening because it was read as a sign of maleness, visually undermining her sex and eliciting the scary feeling that she was not really a woman. Even though 40% of all women naturally grow facial hair (Bindel, 2010), being hirsute was emotionally and socially damaging for those in this study, such as Erum, fuelling their depression, body consciousness, and fear of relationships.

> I remember looking in the mirror thinking "Oh my God! Why are these hairs hanging out of my face?" I never thought of myself as woman. I thought of myself as a girl struggling. I didn't feel normal. I would think, "What if I really am a boy? What if I have internal male genitalia? I look like a woman on the outside but I have hair on my face. So what does that mean?" (Erum, 22, South Asian, African Canadian)

Studies of racial differences in body hair are contradictory with some researchers claiming that Black, South Asian, and "Mediterranean" women are hairier than northern European women and others, that whites are the hairiest and Asian women the least hirsute of all (Toerien & Wilkinson, 2003). A majority of South Asian women identified body hair as a problem trait, far more than any other group I interviewed. Most assumed they were naturally hairier. But their accounts point to sexual dualism and racist stereotyping as the more likely roots of their hair worries. Historically, certain groups of racialized women, including darker-skinned African and South Asian as well as Indigenous South American women from the colonized world (and to a lesser extent, those from southern Europe), have been imagined as more hairy than white northern European women. In the wake of Darwin's theories of evolution, scientists began to see body hair as a measure of racial difference and to classify amounts and thicknesses of hair according to a racial hierarchy. By the Victorian era, scientists and the lay public exhibited great interest in racialized bearded women because they were seen to represent the missing link between animals and humans. In this context Julia Pastrana, a Mexican-American Indigenous woman, became a freak show performer in Europe due to her excess facial hair (caused by a rare condition called hypertrichosis). Hypersexual advertising used to attract audiences exaggerated her female, male, and supposedly ape-like features (Browne & Messenger, 2003). Associations between race and hair haunt the stories of South Asian Canadian women today who tell how their body hair conjured up ideas about racialized women as hairier, more masculine, and hyper-sexual within white-dominated culture.

The 1970s feminist movement brought an acceptance of body hair, but hairlessness has become a thriving industry today. Consumer capitalism combined with the growing availability of free online pornography and demand for body-baring fashions have influenced where and how often women today depilate. The cohort I interviewed came of age before the popularity of pubic hair removal. Over the last several years, the Brazilian wax, which leaves behind a strip of hair above the pubic bone or takes all hair away, has gone from being a risqué novelty to a basic grooming practice. To give an indication of how popular pubic hair waxing has become, one researcher searching for the term "Brazilian wax" on the internet in 2001 yielded 133 hits (Labre, 2002); when I searched for the same phrase in 2011, I got close to 5 million. Surveys have found that 85 to 95% of Western women polled have tried removing hair from their groin area (Tiggemann & Hodgson, 2008); 50% regularly practise pubic-hair removal (Riddell, Varto, & Hodgson, 2010). Many shave or wax because they see their pubic hair as ugly and unclean. The association of female body hair with the abject is highly evident in women's descriptions of their pre-shorn bodies as disgusting and gross.

Breasts

Despite headlines to the contrary, cosmetic surgery rates in North America remain greatly skewed by gender: in 2010, over 91% of cosmetic procedures were performed on women by mostly male doctors who made up 91% of surgeons (American Society of Plastic Surgeons, 2011). According to the American Society for Aesthetic Plastic Surgery (2011), demand for plastic surgery increased by 9% in 2010 and by a whopping 155% since statistical collection began in 1997. Breast augmentation topped the list (318 123) beating out breast reduction (138 152), which placed fifth in popularity. It is difficult to get an accurate read on how many Canadian women seek breast surgery because the government does not keep track of procedures (Canadian Broadcasting Corporation News, 2008). However, it is estimated that between 100 000 and 200 000 Canadian women have implants. Little reliable data is available on the race of those undergoing reductions and augmentations, but statistics indicate that 30% of all North American procedures in 2010 were performed on non-whites, who make up a growing percentage of recipients (American Society of Plastic Surgeons, 2011). The American Society of Plastic Surgeons (2011) reports that reductions are popular among African American women, while Asian American women most commonly request augmentations. These statistics do not reflect actual numbers, however, since the rise of medical tourism means more people seek out cheap surgeries in places like India, Costa Rica, and Thailand (Morgan, 1991, 2009; see, for example, http://www.worldmedicalandsurgical.com). As surgery goes global, augmentation has become the second most sought-after procedure, with reductions coming in sixth worldwide (International Society of Aesthetic Plastic Surgery, 2010).

Techniques used in cosmetic surgery were originally developed to treat the facial burns and soft tissue wounds of male soldiers returning from the First World War. During the 20th century, doctors gradually drew a distinction between plastic surgery, aimed at restoring the body's normal appearance or functioning, and cosmetic surgery, intended to enhance features already deemed normal (Heyes & Jones, 2009). Breast augmentations involving silicone gel or sacs were introduced in the 1960s, but it was not until 1991 that controversy about the possible effects of these implants lead to a moratorium on their general use (Heyes & Jones, 2009). Almost two decades after fears that leaks could cause connective tissue diseases (such as rheumatoid arthritis), North American governments approved a new generation of "safer" implants (for more information go to www.hc-sc.gc.ca/hl-vs/iyh-vsv/med/implants-eng.php).

In the wake of this reversal, promotional pitches have escalated. Although direct-to-consumer advertising of medical drugs and devices is illegal in Canada, implant-promoting messages still trickle across our image-permeable border. Ads for the Natrelle Breast Enhancement Collection liken implants to jeans, shoes, and jewellery, framing augmentation as a fashion accessory rather than major surgery with risks. (View some examples at http://www.coloribus.com/adsarchive/prints/natrelle-breast-implants-shoes-10538005/.) On Facebook, Natrelle now gives away free "Breast Augmentation Kits" so that women considering implants can try different sizes at home. Earlier ads that used images of flowers, the word "blossom," and a just-out-of-puberty model suggest that the campaign is designed to appeal to an adolescent audience.

In makeover culture, cosmetic surgery is no longer reserved for celebrities or the super rich. Popular media and surgeons alike now promote procedures as viable solutions to ordinary image problems. Reality TV shows like Fox's *The Swan* and ABC's *Extreme Makeover* create appetites for nips and tucks in audiences seduced by the fantasy that changing bodies will transform lives (Markey & Markey, 2010). Proliferating images of medical makeovers do not in themselves enlist viewers to go under the knife (Nabi, 2009). Instead, they put surgical options on what I call viewers' "horizon of possibility"—inviting them to imagine seeking out the scalpel (where they never before had considered this as an option) to ease their image distress. For-profit medicine boosts surgical sales in similar ways. Physicians have long framed surgical breast reduction as a necessary treatment for macromastia (big breasts), an apparent disorder causing physical pain and emotional problems (Mello, Domingos, & Miyazaki, 2010). More recently, the American Society of Plastic Surgeons has also classified small breasts as a disease: micromastia (Ehrenreich, 2001). Despite efforts to establish clear lines between elective and restorative surgery, labelling small breasts as a disease indicates that the boundaries between profit-driven medicine and the beauty industry have blurred as medicine transitions into big business (Sullivan, 2001). In Canada, the medicalization of large breasts gives women access to needed surgery through our publicly funded health system. Yet medicalizing breast size can have a downside—deflecting attention away from the broader cultural and social forces fuelling dissatisfaction onto breasts themselves as the sole source of women's distress. Evidence indicates that this reframing is working: according to the American Academy of Cosmetic Surgery (2009), the number of people who approve of cosmetic surgery has climbed steadily over the last decade.

Immersed as we are in a media sea of successful transformations, it is troubling that we don't have easy access to information about surgery's downside: the health consequences of reductions and augmentations. In my role as a researcher, I have spoken with women who were satisfied with their surgeries and had no regrets. However, in my former career as a clinician, I worked with those who bitterly regretted their decision. Some felt lied to, misled, kept in the dark about the procedure's negative consequences, and angry about the long-term costs to their bodies and lives. Beyond the pain, infection, and scarring associated with any surgery, complications from reductions and implants include partial or full loss of sexual sensation in the nipple, inability or restricted ability to breastfeed, and necrosis or death of nipple tissue (Reardon & Grogan, 2011). Of women receiving implants, most will have complications requiring additional surgery or implant removal (Tweed, 2003) because of rupture, deflation, and leakage that occurs in three-quarters of recipients (Brown, et al., 2000). There is no medical consensus on how long implants last, although reputable surgeons acknowledge that *all* women with implants will require replacement at some future date (Singer, 2008). Anywhere from 25 to 100% of those with implants deal with capsular contracture, where scar tissue forms around the implant, causing implanted breasts to become hard, painful, or lopsided (Tweed, 2003). There may also be a link between silicone-gel implants and autoimmune diseases such as fibromyalgia (Brown, et al., 2001).

It is troubling that cosmetic surgery is now advocated as the only reasonable solution to girls' and women's body dissatisfaction resulting from harassment. One article in Toronto's *Globe and Mail* (MacDonald, 2001) went so far as to present surgery as the *only* viable response for adolescent girls dealing with racism and sexism at school. By promoting surgical answers to verbal abuse, the article ignored systemic solutions, such as enforcing anti-harassment policies (Larkin & Rice, 2005). In the absence of institutional policies on harassment or of the political will to enforce policies where they exist, the drive for young women to seek out individualized solutions such as surgery makes sense. The eight women in my own study who sought breast augmentations and reductions did so to avert harassing looks and hurtful comments, and to free themselves from stressful efforts to conceal their breast size and shape. As Debra Gimlin (2006) found in her research on women considering cosmetic surgery, those I interviewed described getting reductions and implants as a way to escape abjection more than to embody an ideal—as a means of alleviating negative feelings and alienation associated with being seen as an Other. Many experienced physical and psychological problems associated with too large or too small breasts that they connected to discomfort caused by looks, stares, and criticisms more than to the size of their breasts alone. At the same time, all were aware that to get Canada's publicly funded health insurance to cover the procedures they had to make the case that size constituted a serious medical, and not merely social, problem. Their accounts offer reasons for why women pursue surgical solutions without relying on the "beauty myth" as the main argument. Instead, as Holliday and Sanchez Taylor (2006) show, surgery seekers in this study exercised choice within a given set of constraints and engaged in a project of self-making using the options available.

> [Before my implants] I felt so uncomfortable hiding my breasts. I used to take off my bra, get under the covers, make sure it was dark so you couldn't see. I wouldn't let him touch the smaller one. If he did touch it, then he'd be "How come one's smaller?" (Maya, 22, Jamaican Canadian, disability from late childhood)

The surgical solution, though entirely understandable, is not without consequences that extend beyond each individual's health or wellness. In a context where the body is tied to a woman's morality and body modification is seen as a self-improvement strategy, there is a danger that what was once a difficult choice for some might become compulsory for many. Since a sizable minority of women now pursue surgery to enhance self-image or to ease emotional turmoil and, at times, physical pain, surgery's spread may create a conundrum for a majority since it contributes to a hierarchy of bodies and a narrowing of norms.

In general, cultural meanings given to women's bodies play a primary role in constructing their bodies as problem sites that need to be corrected. Women respond to these messages through diverse body modification projects that range from dieting and disordered eating to skin lightening and cosmetic surgery.

CONCLUSION: RECOVERING BEAUTY?

In my research, women report two responses to beauty standards: changing their bodies, which can lead to harmful image problems and risky body alteration practices, or changing their situations, which can lead to improved bodily self-images. Many redirected their energy into creating life circumstances where self-worth was based on things other than appearance. Significantly, the capacity of each to alter her environment emerged in each narrative as key to a woman's control and ownership of image. Beyond individuals' improvisational efforts to affirm their embodied identities, other critical ways that activists change their situations is by changing their institutional and image environments. For instance, a "body equity" approach implemented in schools, health care settings, and other institutional sites advocates accepting diverse bodies and stopping stereotyping based on size, disability, and other differences (Rice & Russell, 2002). Similarly, altering image environments entails creating representations that celebrate bodily differences and that dare to depict the abject. For example, live performances by "fat drag" troupes such as *Pretty, Porky and Pissed Off* and the *Fat Femme Mafia* poke fun at cultural stereotypes about fat while the play *'Da Kink in My Hair* explores Black women's diverse embodiments and relationships to beauty. Guerilla Girls don gorilla masks as they deliver facts and funny visuals to expose the ugly underbelly of visual culture: the sexism and racism that are rampant in art and film (at www.guerrillagirls.com/). Photographer Holly Norris and model Jes Sachse have created American Able as a spoof of American Apparel ads to reveal how disabled women are made invisible in mass media. With creativity and courage, these artists and activists imagine new possibilities for representations.

For some feminist writers, the challenge is to rethink our concept of beauty itself (Felski, 2006) so that women can reclaim notions of beauty and "ugly" in their lives. While feminists during the second wave advocated for doing away with harmful beauty standards, contemporary scholars now contend that we cannot eliminate concepts of beauty entirely (Rice, 2014). This is because judgments about what is beautiful may be universally present in societies (Holliday & Sanchez Taylor, 2006) and because there is no such thing as a "natural" body to which we can escape from imposed standards (Scott, 2005) (the natural and cultural are always shaping and transforming each other). For instance, Phoebe Farris (2013) explains that beauty has always been emphasized in Native American cultures, manifest through works of art and craft produced as well as in regalia worn and dances performed by contemporary Indigenous peoples.

Beyond recognising the futility of appealing to the "natural," some writers wonder what we would lose without beauty—without the visual and tactile, the gesture, smell, and sound, or any sensory pleasure in our lives (Colebrook, 2006). To change our image-driven, dominant conception of beauty, they argue instead for creating a feminist aesthetic—an inclusive theory of feminist beauty and sensory pleasure that incorporates the ugly. In order to reframe beauty in a way that avoids body shame, refuses to be reduced to the visual, affirms the ugly, and includes anyone who seeks it, art historian Joanna Frueh develops the concept of "monster/beauty," a condition emerging "from intimacy with one's aesthetic/erotic capacity" (2001, p. 11). Rebecca Coleman and Mónica Figueroa (2010) recast beauty in a temporal sense, saying that its past and future orientation (longing for the body we once had or hope to have in the future) needs to give way to a present orientation to make it less cruel and harmful to women. Here beauty might function in women's lives not as a visual ideal to aspire to but as an embodied feeling of aliveness or vitality recognized as it is happening in the moment.

Such theories are promising because they offer ways to rethink beauty and bodily difference so that disabled women, racialized women, fat women, and all those decreed to be unbeautiful might reclaim sensory pleasure, bodily self-celebration, and a fuller range of embodied experiences in their lives. These are only a few examples that exist for altering our image landscapes and expanding possibilities for beauty and more meaningful representation of bodies. Much work remains to be done. It is up to each of us as individuals and in our communities to give careful thought to the images and narratives we produce and consume as well as the radical ways we might transform these as we chart our pathways forward.

Endnotes

1. Unless otherwise noted in a citation, all historical advertisements discussed in this chapter were retrieved from Ad Access On-Line Project, Duke University, at http://library.duke.edu/digitalcollections/adaccess/

Discussion Questions

1. List the image-based technologies you use and the image-based media you consume in your daily life. How have technological developments increased the pressures and opportunities for body- and self-scrutiny in the 20th and 21st centuries? Applying feminist theory introduced in this chapter, explain why the proliferation of visual technologies and images has a particular significance for women. To what extent are men being similarly affected by the image system?
2. In what ways has the body become "an important identity project"? Do body modification techniques such as surgeries or fitness/beauty regimes work primarily to enhance the self-esteem of people who seek them out? Or do they conscript consumers into prescribed roles in a patriarchal, racist, and classist world? What are the possible effects of makeover shows and body modification products on diverse female and male audiences?
3. Debate the origins and implications of the "obesity epidemic" and the "epidemic" of disordered eating within Western and global contexts. Why have Western populations become so concerned about weight? Are poor countries really facing an "epidemic" of

obesity? What are the possible effects on the public of frightening messages linking over- or underweight with people's health? What's wrong with current approaches to physical education and fitness in schools, clinics, and other sites of health education? What might a "body equity approach" look like in practice?

4. What do you think girls and women really need to break free of the image system? How should we be advocating for change to restrictive norms and ideals? Will banning super-thin models from fashion shows change our ideals? Should skin-lightening, hair relaxing, and other beauty products be banned? What other changes would you like to see? What do you think "real" autonomy and liberation might look like for girls and women?

Bibliography

Adapted version of "Chapter 7: In the Mirror of Beauty Culture," which is an adapted version of Rice , C. (2009a). ***Exacting beauty: Exploring women's body projects and problems in the 21st century.*** In N. Mandell (Ed.), ***Feminist issues: Race, class and sexuality*** (pp. 131–160). Toronto: Pearson Canada. Reprinted with permission of the publisher, University of Toronto Press.

Ahmed, S. (1998). Animated borders: Skin, colour and tanning. In M. Shildrick & J. Price (Eds.), ***Vital signs: Feminist reconfigurations of the bio/logical body*** (pp. 45–65). Edinburgh, Scotland: Edinburgh University Press.

All historical advertisements discussed in this chapter were retrieved from Ad Access On-Line Project, Duke University, at http://scriptorium.lib.duke.edu/adaccess

American Academy of Cosmetic Surgery. (2009). AACS 2009 consumer survey patients' openness full report. Retrieved from www.cosmeticsurgery.org/media/position.cfm

American Psychiatric Association. (2013). ***Diagnostic and statistical manual of mental disorders: DSM-5***. Washington, DC: American Psychiatric Association.

American Society for Aesthetic Plastic Surgery. (2011). Demand for plastic surgery rebounds by almost 9%. ***Statistics, surveys & trends.*** Retrieved from www.surgery.org/media/news-releases/demand-for-plastic-surgery-rebounds-by-almost-9%

American Society of Plastic Surgeons. (2011). ***Report of the 2010 plastic surgery statistics: 2010 cosmetic demographics.*** Retrieved from www.plasticsurgery.org/x1673.xml?google=report+2010&x=0&y=0

Associated Press. (2006, March 2). Surgeon General: Obesity epidemic will dwarf terrorism threat. CBSNews.com. Retrieved from http://www.cbsnews.com/news/obesity-bigger-threat-than-terrorism/

Azziz, R., Carmina, E., & Sawaya, M. E. (2000). Idiopathic hirsutism. ***Endocrine Reviews, 21***(4), 347–362.

Barber, K. (Ed.). (2004). ***Canadian Oxford Dictionary*** (2nd ed.). Toronto, ON: University Press.

Bennett, W., & Gurin, J. (1983). ***The dieter's dilemma: Eating less and weighing more***. New York, NY: Basic Books.

Berger, J. (1980). ***Ways of seeing***. Harmondsworth, England: Penguin Books.

Bindel, J. (2010, August 20). Women: Embrace your facial hair! ***The Guardian Online***. Retrieved from www.theguardian.com/lifeandstyle/2010/aug/20/women-facial-hair

Bordo, S. (1993). ***Unbearable weight: Feminism, Western culture and the body***. Los Angeles, CA: University of California Press.

Bordo, S. (2009). Not just "a white girl's thing": The changing face of food and body image problems. In H. Malson & M. Burns (Eds.), ***Critical feminist approaches to eating dis/orders*** (pp. 46–59). New York, NY: Routledge.

Boutelle, K., Neumark-Sztainer, D., Story, M., & Resnick, M. (2002). Weight control behaviors among obese, overweight, and non-overweight adolescents. *Journal of Pediatric Psychology*, *27*(6), 531–540.

Browne, J., & Messenger, S. (2003). Victorian spectacle: Julia Pastrana, the bearded and hairy female. *Endeavour, 27*(4), 155–159.

Brown, L., Middleton, M. S., Berg, W. A., Soo, M. S., & Pennello, G. (2000). Prevalence of rupture of silicone gel breast implants in a population of women in Birmingham, Alabama. *American Journal of Roentgenology*, *175*, 1–8.

Brown, L., Pennello, G., Berg, W. A., Soo, M. S., & Middleton, M. S. (2001). Silicone gel breast implant rupture, extracapsular silicone and health status in a population of women. *Journal of Rheumatology*, *28*, 996–1103.

Brownell, K., & Horgen, K. (2004). *Food fight.* New York, NY: Contemporary Books.

Brumberg, J. (1998). *The body project: An intimate history of American girls*. New York, NY: Vintage Books.

Byrd, A., & Tharps, L. (2001). *Hair story: Untangling the roots of black hair in America*. New York, NY: St. Martin's Griffen.

Canadian Broadcasting Corporation. (2008, April 10). Cosmetic surgery: Balancing risk. *CBC News In Depth: Health*. Retrieved from www.cbc.ca/news2/background/health/cosmetic-surgery.html

Canadian Press. (2007, February 19). $5M to bring back ParticipACTION exercise program. *CBCnews.ca*. Retrieved from www.cbc.ca/health/story/2007/02/19/participaction.html

Caplan, P., & Cosgrove, L. (Eds.). (2004). *Bias in psychiatric diagnosis*. Lanham, MD: Jason Aronson.

Clarke, L. H., & Griffin, M. (2007). Becoming and being gendered through the body: Older women, their mothers and body image. *Ageing and Society, 27*, 701–718.

Cogan, J., & P. Ernsberger. (1999). Dieting, weight, and health: Reconceptualizing research and policy. *Journal of Social Issues*, *55*(2), 187–205.

Cohen, E. (2004). The fine line between clinical and subclinical anorexia. In P. Caplan & L. Cosgrove, *Bias in psychiatric diagnosis* (pp. 193–200). Lanham, MD: Jason Aronson.

Colebrook, C. (2006). Introduction. *Feminist Theory, 7*(2), 131–142.

Coleman, R., & Figueroa, M. (2010). Past and future perfect? Beauty, affect and hope. *Journal for Cultural Research, 14*(4), 357–373.

Covino, D. (2004). *Amending the abject body: Aesthetic makeovers in medicine and culture.* Albany, NY: State University of New York Press.

Davis, K. (1995). *Reshaping the female body: The dilemma of cosmetic surgery.* New York, NY: Routledge.

de Beauvoir, S. (1974). *The second sex* (2nd ed.). (H. M. Parshley, trans.). New York, NY: Vintage Books.

Dorning, A. (2007, October 10). Black hair dos and don'ts: *Glamour Magazine* can't shake fallout from bad hair advice. *ABC News Online*. Retrieved from http://abcnews.go.com/US/story?id=3710971&page=1

Ehrenreich, B. (2001, June 24). Stamping out a dread scourge. *Time Magazine*. Retrieved from www.time.com/time/magazine/article/0,9171,159040,00.html

Ernsberger, P., & Koletsky, P. (1999). Biomedical rationale for a wellness approach to obesity: An alternative to a focus on weight loss. *Journal of Social Issues*, *55*(2), 221–259.

Eye2Eye Media. (2008). *Miss Ability*. Retrieved from www.eye2eyemedia.nl/index.php?option=com_content&view=article&id=88&Itemid=27&lang=en

Fallon, P., Katzman, M., & Wooley, S. (Eds.). (1994). *Feminist perspectives on eating disorders*. New York, NY: Guilford Press.

Farris, P. M. (2013). Indigenous beauty. In P. Z. Brand (Ed.), *Beauty Unlimited* (pp. 162–174). Bloomington, IN: Indiana University Press.

Felski, R. (2006). "Because it is beautiful": New feminist perspectives on beauty. *Feminist Theory, 7*, 273–282.

Ferrante, J. (1988). Biomedical versus cultural constructions of abnormality: The case of idiopathic hirsutism in the United States. *Culture, Medicine and Psychiatry, 12*, 219–238.

Frueh, J. (2001). *Monster/beauty: Building the body of love*. Berkeley, CA: University of California Press.

Gard, M., & Wright, J. (2005). *Obesity epidemic: Science, morality and ideology*. New York, NY: Taylor and Francis.

Garland-Thomson, R. (2009). *Staring: How we look*. Toronto, ON: Oxford University Press.

Gill, R. (2007). Postfeminist media culture: Elements of a sensibility. *European Journal of Cultural Studies, 10*, 147–166.

Gill, R. (2009). Beyond the "sexualization of culture" thesis: An intersectional analysis of "sixpacks," "midriffs" and "hot lesbians" in advertising. *Sexualities, 12*, 137–160.

Gimlin, D. (2006). The absent body project: Cosmetic surgery as a response to bodily dys-appearance. *Sociology, 40*(4), 699–716.

Gremillion, H. (2003). *Feeding anorexia: Gender and power at a treatment center*. Durham, NC: Duke University Press.

Harding, K. (2008). BMI illustrated categories project. Retrieved from http://kateharding.net/bmi-illustrated/

Health Canada. (2002). A *report on mental illnesses in Canada*. Ottawa, ON: Author.

Herzig, R. M. (2000). The woman beneath the hair: Treating hypertrichosis, 1870–1930. *NWSA Journal, 12*(3), 50–66.

Hesse-Biber, S., Leavy, P., Quinn, C. E., & Zoino, J. (2006). The mass marketing of disordered eating and eating disorders: The social psychology of women, thinness and culture. *Women's Studies International Forum, 29*(2), 208–224.

Heyes, C. J., & Jones, M. (2009). Cosmetic surgery in the age of gender. In C. J. Heyes and M. Jones (Eds.). *Cosmetic surgery: A feminist primer*, (pp. 1–17). Burlington, VT: Ashgate.

Holliday, R., & Sanchez Taylor, J. (2006). Aesthetic surgery as false beauty. *Feminist Theory, 7*, 179–195.

Hope, C. (1982). Caucasian female body hair and American culture. *Journal of American Culture, 5*(1), 93–99.

Ikeda, J., Crawford, P., & Woodward-Lopez, G. (2006). BMI screening in schools: Helpful or harmful. *Health Education Research, 21*(6), 761–769.

International Society of Aesthetic Plastic Surgery. (2010). Biennial global survey. ISAPS international survey on aesthetic/cosmetic procedures performed in 2009. Retrieved from www.yourplasticsurgeryguide.com/trends/2010-isaps-biennial-study.htm

Jacobson, S., & McLay, L. (2006). The economic impact of obesity on automobile fuel consumption, *The Engineering Economist, 51*(4), 307–323.

Jutel A. (2006). The emergence of overweight as a disease entity: Measuring up normality. *Social Science and Medicine, 63*, 2268–2276.

Kaspin, D. D. (2002). Conclusion: Signifying power in Africa. In P. S. Landau & D. D. Kaspin (Eds.), *Images and empire: Visuality in colonial and postcolonial Africa* (pp. 320–336). Berkeley, CA: University of California Press.

Kozyra, K. (2008). *Olympia*. Retrieved from http://katarzynakozyra.pl/main/10/olympia/

Kristeva, J. (1982). *Powers of horror: An essay on abjection*. (L. Roudiez, trans.). New York, NY: Columbia University Press.

Labre, M. P. (2002). The Brazilian wax: new hairlessness norm for women? *Journal of Communication Inquiry*, *26*(2), 113–132.

LaMarre, A., & Rice, C. (2015). Normal eating as counter-cultural: Prescriptions and possibilities for eating disorder recovery. *Journal of Community & Applied Social Psychology. 25*(5), doi: 10.1002/casp.2240.

Larkin, J., & Rice, C. (2005). Beyond "healthy eating" and "healthy weights": Harassment and the health curriculum in middle schools. *Body Image*, *2*, 219–232.

Leistikow, N. (2003, April 28). Indian women criticize "Fair and Lovely" ideal. *Women's E-News*. Retrieved from http://womensenews.org/story/the-world/030428/indian-women-criticize-fair-and-lovely-ideal

Lupton, D. (2012). *Fat*. New York, NY: Taylor and Francis.

MacDonald, G. (2001, January 15). Girls under the knife. *The Globe and Mail*, R.1, R.25.

MacNeill, M. (1999). Social marketing, gender, and the science of fitness: A case study of ParticipACTION campaigns. In P. White & K. Young (Eds.), *Sport and gender in Canada* (pp. 215–231). Toronto, ON: Oxford University Press.

Markey, C. N., & Markey, P. M. (2010). A correlational and experimental examination of reality television viewing and interest in cosmetic surgery. *Body Image, 7*(2), 165–171.

Melchior-Bonnet, S. (2001). *The mirror: A history*. (K. Jewett, trans.). New York, NY: Routledge.

Mello, A. A., Domingos, N. A., & Miyazaki, M. C. (2010). Improvement in quality of life and self-esteem after breast reduction surgery. *Aesthetic Plastic Surgery, 34*(1), 59–64.

Melwani, L. (2007, August 18). The white complex: What's behind the Indian prejudice for fair skin? *Little India*. Retrieved from www.littleindia.com/nri/1828-the-white-complex.html

Mire, A. (2005, July 28). Pigmentation and empire: The emerging skin-whitening industry. *Counterpunch Magazine Online*. Retrieved from www.counterpunch.org/mire07282005.html

Morgan, K. (2009). Women and the knife: Cosmetic surgery and the colonization of women's bodies. In C. J. Heyes & M. Jones (Eds.), *Cosmetic surgery: A feminist primer* (pp. 49–77). Burlington, VT: Ashgate.

Morgan, M. (1991). Women and the knife: Cosmetic surgery and the colonization of women's bodies. *Hypatia*, *6*, 25–53.

Morimura, Y. (2008). *Self-portrait as art history*. Retrieved from www.assemblylanguage.com/images/Morimura.html

Mulvey, L. (1975). Visual pleasure and narrative cinema. *Screen, 16*, 6–18.

Nabi, R. L. (2009). Cosmetic surgery makeover programs and intentions to undergo cosmetic enhancements. *Human Communication Research, 35*(1), 1–27.

Nasser, M., & Malson, H. (2009). Beyond western dis/orders: Thinness and self-starvation in othered women. In H. Malson & M. Burns (Eds.), *Critical feminist approaches to eating dis/orders* (pp. 74–86). New York, NY: Routledge.

Neumark-Sztainer, D., Story, M., Hannan, P. J., Perry, C. L., & Irving, L. M. (2002). Weight-related concerns and behaviors among overweight and nonoverweight adolescents: Implications for preventing weight-related disorders. *Archives of Pediatrics & Adolescent Medicine, 156*, 171–178.

Newman, A. A. (2007, September 14). Depilatory market moves far beyond the short-shorts wearers. *New York Times Online.* Retrieved from www.nytimes.com/2007/09/14/business/media/14adco.html?_r=0

O'Brien, S., & Szeman, I. (2004). *Popular culture: A user's guide*. Toronto, ON: Nelson Education.

ParticipACTION Archive Project. Retrieved from www.usask.ca/archives/participaction/english/home.html

Peiss, K. (1998). *Hope in a jar: The making of America's beauty culture*. New York, NY: Henry Holt.

PR Web. (2008, March 5). World shaving products market to exceed US$25.7 billion by 2010 Retrieved from www.prweb.com/releases/shaving_products/razors_shavers_lotions/prweb741274.htm

PR Web. (2011, May 11). Veet® survey reveals groomed bikini lines more important to women than toned bodies. Retrieved from www.prweb.com/releases/2011/5/prweb8415224.htm

Rabinor, J. R. (2004). The "eating disordered" patient. In P. Caplan & L. Cosgrove (Eds.), *Bias in psychiatric diagnosis* (pp. 189–192). Lanham, MD: Jason Aronson.

Reardon, R., & Grogan, S. (2011). Women's reasons for seeking breast reduction: A qualitative investigation. *Journal of Health Psychology, 16*(1), 31–41.

Rice, C. (1996). Trauma and eating problems: Expanding the debate. *Eating Disorders, 4*, 197–237.

Rice, C. (2007). Becoming "the fat girl": Acquisition of an unfit identity. *Women's Studies International Forum*, *30*(2), 158–174.

Rice, C. (2009a). Imagining the other? Ethical challenges of researching and writing women's embodied lives. *Feminism & Psychology*, *19*, 245–266.

Rice, C. (2009b). How big girls become fat girls: The cultural production of problem eating and physical inactivity. In H. Malson & M. Burns (Eds.), *Critical feminist perspectives on eating disorders: An international reader* (pp. 92–109). London, England: Psychology Press.

Rice, C. (2014). *Becoming women: The embodied self in image culture*. Toronto, ON: University of Toronto Press.

Rice, C. (2015, forthcoming). Rethinking fat. *Critical Studies <=> Critical Methodologies*, *15*(5).

Rice, C., & Langdon, L. (1991). The use and misuse of diagnostic labels. *National Eating Disorder Information Centre Bulletin 6*, 1–4.

Rice, C., & Russell, V. (2002). *Embodying equity: Body image as an equity issue*. Toronto, ON: Green Dragon Press.

Rice, C., Zitzelsberger, H., Porch, W., & Ignagni, E. (2005). Envisioning new meanings of disability and difference. *International Journal of Narrative Counselling and Community Work*, *3/4*, 119–130.

Riddell, L., Varto, H., & Hodgson, Z. G. (2010). Smooth talking: The phenomenon of pubic hair removal in women. *Canadian Journal of Human Sexuality*, *19*, 121–130.

Rooks, N. (1996). *Hair raising: Beauty, culture, and African-American women*. New Brunswick, NJ: Rutgers University Press.

Rooks, N. (2001). Wearing your race wrong: Hair, drama and the politics of representation for African American women at play on a battlefield. In M. Bennett & V. Dickerson (Eds.), *Recovering the black female body: Self representations by African American women* (pp. 279–295). New Brunswick, NJ: Rutgers University Press.

Schick, V. R., Rima, B. N., & Calabrese, S. K. (2011). Evulvalution: the portrayal of women's external genitalia and physique across time and the current barbie doll ideals. *Journal of Sex Research, 48*(1), 74–81.

Schiebinger, L. (1993). *Nature's body: Gender and the making of modern science*. Boston, MA: Beacon Press.

Scott, L. (2005). *Fresh lipstick: Redressing fashion and feminism*. New York, NY: Palgrave.

Sherwin, A. (2006, December 27). Reality TV puts disabled women in beauty show. *The Times Online*. Retrieved from www.timesonline.co.uk/tol/news/world/europe/article1068730.ece

Singer, N. (2008, January 17). Do my breast implants have a warranty? New York Times. Retrieved from www.nytimes.com/2008/01/17/fashion/17SKIN.html?r=1&oref=slogin

Stanley, A. (2009, December 1). Disabled, and seeking acceptance in fashion. *New York Times Online.* Retrieved from www.nytimes.com/2009/12/01/arts/television/01model.html

Stuart, A., & Donaghue, N. (2011). Choosing to conform: The discursive complexities of choice in relation to feminine beauty practices. *Feminism & Psychology, 22*, 98–121.

Sullivan, D. A. (2001). *Cosmetic surgery: The cutting edge of commercial medicine in America*. New Brunswick, NJ: Rutgers University Press.

Swee, W., Klontz, K., & Lambert, L. (2000). A nationwide outbreak of alopecia associated with the use of hair-relaxing formulation. *Archives of Dermatology*, *136*, 1104–1108.

Tiggemann, M., & Hodgson, S. (2008). The hairlessness norm extended: Reasons for and predictors of women's body hair removal at different body sites. *Sex Roles, 59*(11–12), 889–897.

Timmons, H. (2007, May 30). Telling India's modern women they have power. *New York Times Online*. Retrieved from www.nytimes.com/2007/05/30/business/media/30adco.html?ex=1181620800&en=201bcdec2fbde98d&ei=5070&emc=eta1

Toerien, M., & Wilkinson, S. (2003). Gender and body hair: Constructing the feminine woman. *Women's Studies International Forum, 26*(4), 333–344.

Tweed, A. (2003). *Health care utilization among women who have undergone breast implant surgery*. Vancouver, BC: British Columbia Centre of Excellence for Women's Health.

Woodside, D. B., Garfinkel, P. E., Lin, E., Goering, P., Kaplan, A. S., Goldbloom, D. S., & Kennedy, S. H. (2001). Comparisons of men with full or partial eating disorders, men without eating disorders, and women with eating disorders in the community. *American Journal of Psychiatry, 158*, 570–574.

World Health Organization. (2003). *Controlling the global obesity epidemic*. Geneva, Switzerland. Retrieved from www.who.int/nutrition/topics/obesity/en/index.html

Masculinity studies have a fraught and tense history when addressing feminism, yet today they have become an important component of many women's and gender studies programs. Although later writings on men and masculinities are feminist inspired and critically oriented, too often early writers aggravated rather than advanced the project of achieving gender equality. In this chapter, we present an overview of the study of masculinities in North America as a social and historical category, distinguishing between early and later writings in the field of masculinity/ies studies. Our purpose is to show how the complexity, tensions, and contradictions within the history of the study of men and masculinity contribute to the feminist study of gender oppression.

We discuss early North American writings on men and masculinities to help contextualize and situate the later, most recent feminist-inspired, critically oriented research on men and masculinities. Next the chapter discusses the work of Australian sociologist Raewyn Connell, whose theorizing of gender has profoundly shaped contemporary academic research on men and masculinities (Beasley, 2005). We highlight and discuss the recent explosion of research on masculinities informed by Connell's work that has centred on analyses of power relations and intersectionality. Finally, to illustrate the connections between Connell's work and the everyday experiences of men and boys, we highlight a key social site for the production and reproduction of masculinities: sport. The overriding goal of this chapter is to show how a feminist perspective on men and masculinities has made significant contributions to challenging dominant models of masculinity that work against the best interests of men and boys, with a view to securing gender justice for women and girls.

THE EARLY WRITINGS ON MEN AND MASCULINITY

Until the 1970s, a distinct scholarly focus on examining "men as men," using masculinity as a primary category of analysis, was absent from academic research (Beasley, 2005, p. 179). Kimmel (2003), for example, calls masculinity during the pre-1970 period the "unexamined norm" (p. xi; for a notable early exception, see Helen Mayer Hacker, 1957). Masculinity was considered to be singular and innate—an outcome of biology or an expression of an assumed eternal quality. Critical attention by scholars to the complexity, diversity, fluidity, and plurality within masculinity (i.e., masculinities) was not paid until the late 1980s and early 1990s. However, the notion that men and boys are preordained by their biology to act and behave in certain narrow ways came under increased scrutiny by the early 1970s, triggering a wave of popular writings on men and masculinity.

Early Writings on Men and Masculinity: 1970s and 1980s

The late 1960s to the mid-1970s was marked in North America by large-scale social, political, and economic change. Set against the backdrop of the Vietnam War, Watergate, and the Cold War; and faced with the civil rights movement, the rise of the gay and lesbian liberation movement and its embrace of new racial, gender, and cultural priorities; scholars, writers, and activists began to raise questions about the "problem" of masculinity. It was second wave feminism that was key in fuelling the early writings of masculinity studies.

Beginning roughly in the early 1960s, and lasting throughout the 1970s, the second wave feminist movement was an expression of women's changing social roles. At this time, faced with structural and systemic barriers and experiencing everyday sexism, women as a group simply did not have the choices and opportunities in life available to men as a group, whether that meant access to most jobs or traditional male-dominated areas of education such as law, medicine, or engineering. As discussed extensively in Chapter 1, various types of feminist thought and action challenged patriarchal structures and everyday sexism, helping to expand social and economic possibilities for women and addressing issues of workplace inequality, salary inequity, access to better jobs, and developing anti-sexist/discrimination legislation. There was an increased social interest in challenging the social, economic, and political inequalities faced by women (Rebick, 2005).

In particular the 1970s feminist critique of the female sex role resonated with some men who began to offer a similar critique of the male sex role. Jack Sawyer's 1970 article "On Male Liberation" became a foundational text in the newly developing men's liberation movement, advising men to free themselves from the burdens of the male sex role. "Male liberation," Sawyer wrote, "calls for men to free themselves of the sex-role stereotypes that limit their ability to be human" (Sawyer, 1970, p. 32). An article published in the August 27, 1971, issue of the popular periodical *Life* quickly followed Sawyer's article. Written by Barry Farrell (1971), and titled "You've Come a Long Way, Buddy," the piece explored the views of a few "healthy and intelligent young white American" males (p. 50). Drawing on themes already being developed within the Men's Liberation literature, men spoke about how traditional masculinity was limiting as it often meant denying or suppressing emotions and limiting the types of relationships available to them, including relationships with other men. One of the men interviewed, for example, remarked that intimacy between men was a dangerous encounter in light of homophobia; simply touching another man would make them "fags" in the eyes of other men (p. 56).

Following these two works, various male writers such as Warren Farrell, Jack Nichols, and Marc Feigen Fateau began to take seriously the idea that masculinity was socially constructed and not something that was necessarily hardwired into boys and men. Warren Farrell's *The Liberated Man* (1974), Marc Feigen Fateau's *The Male Machine* (1974), and Jack Nichols's *Men's*

Liberation: A New Definition of Masculinity (1975) were inspired by feminist scrutiny of the female sex role. Male authors argued that men could benefit from their own liberation movement by challenging what they saw as an oppressive male sex role, although the call for freedom was largely directed at white, middle-class, American heterosexual males. By the mid-1980s the Men's Liberation Movement would unfortunately turn into a much more conservative, and at times stridently anti-feminist, Men's Rights movement. However, for many Men's Liberation writers of the 1970s, men's enemy wasn't women; it was the traditional male sex role.

The prevailing idea that authors forming the Men's Liberation movement wanted to convey in their books, conferences, and discussion groups (Goldrick-Jones, 2001, p. 324) was that, while sexism and the female sex role had been a significant problem in the lives of women and girls, men had also paid a high cost in their physical and emotional health and their relationships. Farrell and Nichols, for example, insisted that men were forced to conform to a standard male image that prevented them from possessing or demonstrating a broader range of ways of being men, such as being gentle, nurturing, and vulnerable human beings. The male sex role, they argued, flattened the lives of men by demanding they be physically and emotionally strong, dominating, competitive, aggressive, and of course, successful breadwinners. This set of demands was extracting a heavy toll on the emotional, psychological, and physical lives of men. In other words, "the struggle to live up to impossible standards of virility and prowess has made some [men] strangers to their own feelings and strangers to each other" (Farrell, quoted in *Life*, 1971, p. 50).

In order to help men liberate themselves from the male sex role, Men's Liberation authors borrowed a main strategy from the feminist movement—consciousness-raising. Men met together in small groups in order to raise their consciousness about the limitations and problems of the male "sex role" (e.g., Farrell, 1974, p. 207). Sessions often focused on men's hyper-relationship to work. Harry Chapin's 1974 hit song "The Cat's in the Cradle" popularized the fraught relationship between a father's hyper-commitment to work and his unfulfilled, failed relationship with his son. Echoing themes found in Chapin's hit song, Farrell and others not only reinforced the idea that men's work often came at the expense of time spent with their families, but also drew readers' attention to how some occupations were gendered differently. Farrell, for example, advised men to begin to ask themselves why a "corporation president rather than an honest salesman"; a "school superintendent rather than an elementary school teacher"; "a professor at Harvard rather than a professor at a junior college" were more respected (pp. 57–58). By raising men's consciousness, Farrell hoped to draw their attention to how their beliefs and aspirations were often heavily distorted by the expectations that marked the male sex role, including the social and cultural status afforded by certain occupations and its link to securing a socially sanctioned masculinity.

There are numerous feminist critiques of these early writings (see Messner, 1998). Little was mentioned within the Men's Liberation literature about the significant amount of structural or systemic physical, sexual, emotional, and psychological violence inflicted on women and girls by the patriarchal relations that produced the male and female sex roles in the first place. The Men's Liberation movement also failed to ask a key question when it came to gender equality, waged labour, and the work force: Why were most of these occupations male dominated? For example, they often traded in false equivalencies when it came to comparing the inequalities faced by men and women, so they promoted the idea that men were equally oppressed as women. Much of the rhetoric tended to operate from a *men as victims* framework. For instance, Nichols suggested that "women, once docile and undemanding," were now "asking for the moon" (1975, p. 11). Writing without irony and with some surprise, Nichols went on to suggest that women, in their attempt to move toward a much more equitable world, have become overly "aggressive!" (p. 11). Certainly, this form of sexist and anti-feminist rhetoric found in the Men's Liberation literature did very little to advance the cause of gender equality, despite its substantial critique of the male sex role.

Men's Liberation literature also assumed a white, heterosexual, middle-class masculinity. Little if anything was discussed about the racist or classist discrimination faced by non-white men or working class, working-poor men. The male sex role limited men's emotional range just as structural systems of oppression based on race operated to discriminate against these groups of men, but this was rarely considered. Certainly, very little was mentioned in the Men's Liberation literature about the implicit and explicit ways in which gay, bisexual, and transgendered men suffered enormous institutional and individual discrimination when it came to finding employment and housing, or facing physical violence (Carrigan, Connell, & Lee, 1985; Chenier, 2008; Kinsman & Gentile, 2010; Ramsay, 2011).

Finally, the main thrust of the Men's Liberation movement was based on the misguided notion that understanding the male sex-role better, rather than challenging gender binaries and hierarchies, would transform the broader economic and social structures that helped produce and reproduce those very roles. Early sex-role theory as practised by Men's Liberation writers was simply incapable of explaining and analyzing the complex ways different men constructed and embodied their identities in context-dependent ways. This was due to the relatively narrow social membership of this movement in the United States, and to a certain extent in Canada. White heterosexual middle-class men from the 1970s expected and operated from an unquestioned assumption that they would inherit positions of cultural, social, and economic power; find themselves in medical or law school, or working as a corporate executives or engaging with other men of power in universities; or in federal, provincial, or municipal politics. In other words, much of the Men's Liberation literature was concerned mostly with changing white, heterosexual, middle-class individual men's psychological attitudes toward gender and not questioning how gender was institutionalized through relations of power in a way that structurally and systematically oppressed and disadvantaged women and girls (Beasley, 2005, p. 179). The writers also tended to focus on the costs to individual men rather than the advantages and privileges afforded to men by being men. By the end of the 1970s, popular writing on men and masculinity remained uncritical, doing little to challenge the gender structure that entrenched male privilege and power. Popular writing on men and masculinity became increasingly conservative and antagonistic to women in general and to feminists in particular in the 1980s. It is to these writings that we now briefly turn.

The 1980s was a period of increased conservatism within the Western world. This era saw the emergence and rise of the New Right and its neo-conservative political, social, and economic agenda, including its attempt to promote (white) hegemonic constructions of masculinity for men and traditional gender roles for women. It was in this context that American writer Susan Faludi published the 1991 bestseller *Backlash: The Undeclared War Against American Women*. In *Backlash*, Faludi explored key areas of social and political culture during the 1980s as sites of anti-feminist sentiment. The response to the second wave feminism of the 1970s was the creation of a conservative counter-movement that was largely anti-intellectual and anti-feminist. The movement sought to roll back some of the real or perceived gains secured by feminist activists and others. The anti-feminist backlash Faludi describes was reinforced by a parallel rise within popular culture of a conservative, masculinist understanding of men and masculinity.

The emerging masculinist approach drew in large measure from the Mytho-Poetical Men's Movement (for a detailed discussion on the mytho-poetical men's movement, see Messner, 1997) that viewed masculinity as an eternal expression of maleness. This conservative movement was primarily shaped by the work of poet Robert Bly, in particular his 1990 national bestseller *Iron John: A Book about Men* (Kimmel & Kaufman, 1994, p. 259). In *Iron John*, Bly drew upon traditional folk cultures and Jungian psychology to provide men with a roadmap to regain their assumed "lost" masculinity. Bly argued men had lost their "true" masculinity in the face of an increasingly perceived feminized society. Fuelled by the fear of social feminization, he suggested men retreat into the wilderness and organize and perform all-male spiritual rituals that would allow them to be with other men in an all-male context. Doing this, it was imagined, would allow men to reconnect with their assumed lost "deep masculine" identity. Both the men involved and the masculinity sought were understood to be heterosexual, revealing an undercurrent of homophobia in the movement. Understandably, feminist women and some pro-feminist men termed the new Mytho-Poetical Men's Movement "patriarchy with a New Age face" (Kimmel & Kaufman, 1994, p. 260; for a critique of this movement, see also Messner, 1997).

The rise of the mytho-poetical men's movement ran alongside the emergence of the conservative men's rights movement (MRM). In fact, former 1970s men's liberation writer Warren Farrell moved away in the 1980s from feminist thinking and increasingly adopted a conservative men's rights approach to understanding and addressing issues of masculinity, ultimately becoming a leader in the conservative men's rights movement. The belief that underlay the men's right movement, which was largely made up of predominately white, middle-class men, was that it was men who were victimized by the gender order, perhaps more so than women. Much of the men's rights movement in the 1980s lobbied for greater fairness in child custody disputes, although it expanded its agenda over time to include grievances such as the ongoing struggles of boys in school (see, e.g., Biddulph, 1997; Pollack, 1998; Whitmire, 2010; for a critique of this view, see Lingard, Martino, & Mills, 2009), violence against men, false rape reporting, and alleged anti-male bias in government policies (Messner, 1997, p. 44). Despite the overwhelming evidence to the contrary, the crux of the conservative, anti-feminist Men's Rights argument rested on the perception that the world, including the legal system, was tilted in favour of women, fuelling what they would later term a perceived "war" against men and boys (see, e.g., Hoff-Sommers, 1990).

From a conservative Men's Rights perspective it was not women who were oppressed and discriminated against; it was men. A consequence of this anti-feminist, sexist perspective, which failed to recognize *patriarchy as a system of oppression* that discriminated against women and girls, was an unrelenting hostility toward feminist and pro-feminist thinking, all of which worked against efforts to create a sincere and genuine understanding of gender justice and equality for women and men.

Fortunately, during the latter part of the 1980s and the early 1990s, a feminist/pro-feminist understanding of men and masculinity emerged, one that provided a research-based corrective to the early writings of the men's movement of the 1970s and 1980s. And, although the men's rights movement remains active to this day (for recent examples, see Kay, 2014; Smith, 2013) in "mainstreaming misogyny" (Laxer & Lochwin, 2014), on university campuses, in the media, and elsewhere ("Venturing into the Male-Strom," 2014), particularly in Canada (Gheciu, 2014), and among some conservative male academics (see, e.g., Baumeister, 2010; Benatar, 2012; Mansfield, 2006); the later writings on masculinities have helped provide a critique and a corrective to this movement. It is to these the later writings on masculinities that we now turn.

Later Writings on Masculinities: The late 1980s to the Present

Later North American writing on masculinities has been feminist inspired and critically oriented, and emerged in the late 1980s, once again during a time of significant social, political, and economic change (Greig & Martino, 2012). Although a few critically oriented writings on masculinity existed (see, e.g., Hacker, 1957; Sedgewick, 1985), it was in this period that a variety of international scholars started to employ feminist frameworks in new and significant ways. They were informed by the feminist project to interrogate different masculinities based on a variety of social categories such as social class, race, and sexuality (Brod, 1987; Carnes and Griffen, 1990; Kaufman, 1993; Kimmel, 1987, 1995; Jackson, 1990; Rotundo, 1993; Segal, 1990). There has also been a growing body of work written on masculinities beyond men, manliness, or the male-identified. Some of the more important works include: Jack Halberstam's (1998) *Female Masculinity*; Lily Burana and Roxxie Linnea's (1994) *Dagger: On Butch Women*; and Bobby Noble's (2004) *Masculinities Without Men? Female Masculinity in Twentieth-Century Fictions*. Although there were certainly some differences between and among these key works when it came to theorizing masculinities they all rejected essentialist/biological notions of masculinity and shared in the larger project of challenging the structural and systemic issues that produce dominant models of heterohegemonic masculinity.

A key outcome of critical feminist informed research was the establishment of university courses and programs, associations, and a web-based database, *The Men's Bibliography*. Scholarly journals such as *Men and Masculinities*, *Journal of Men's Studies*, and *Thymos: Journal of Boyhood Studies* that focus on masculinities in a pro-feminist critical way also emerged. In this period pro-feminist campaigns to end male violence against women and girls, such as The White Ribbon Campaign (Kaufman, 2012), arose as a means to work toward the broader goal of gender justice. We turn now to several influential theories of masculinity that have helped develop a more sophisticated understanding of masculinities.

UNDERSTANDING MASCULINITIES

Over the past two or more decades, critical theories of masculinity have become very important. In this section we discuss several of these. We begin with Australian sociologist Raewyn Connell's theory of multiple masculinities, widely acknowledged as one of the most influential theories in the study of men and masculinities (Beasley, 2005; Glaser, 2004; Messerschmidt, 2000). Connell's theory of masculinities rejects the idea that there exists a fixed, monolithic, unitary, asocial, ahistorical version of masculinity (1995). Rather, Connell advances an argument that there exist many varied and competing socially and historically constructed models of masculinity at any given time; a few hegemonic, some marginalized, some complicit, some subordinated. All types are shaped and influenced by the social locations of particular men or groups of men differentiated by race, ethnicity, social class, sexuality, age, bodily abilities, and so on (Connell, 1995, 2000). As with other social identities, masculinities are continually in flux, shifting, and fluid, situated in relations of power, always in the moment-to-moment process of being made and unmade depending on the context.

Connell engages masculinities through the prism of feminist theory and thus understands them as embedded in relations of power. She theorizes that gender is a socially organized set of practices forming relationships between and among men and between men and women. Masculinities are situated in relations of power and produced together in "gender regimes." Gender regimes are patterns found within institutions such as religious institutions, families, schools, corporations, and the military that are formed through relations of power and that structure everyday experiences of gender relations. Institutionalized gender regimes are coupled with the overall gender patterns found in culture and personal life that Connell calls the "gender order" of a society (Connell, 1995, pp. 71–86). The overall structure of the current gender order found in Western societies privileges men as a group over women as a group in ways that are hegemonic, that is, dominant masculinity and its hierarchies are so normalized as to be practically invisible.

Hegemonic Masculinity

Connell's theory of multiple masculinities and its key concept of hegemony borrows from the work of scholar Antonio Gramsci (1971). In order to better understand class and class formations, Gramsci theorized that the continuing dominance of certain class formations was not secured by physical force or through ideological compulsion. Rather, Gramsci argued that dominance or hegemony was secured largely through *persuasion* by the dominant class engaged in various forms of cultural and social leadership. For Gramsci, the dominant class effectively secures key economic and political processes in society, and extends and expands its control in such a way that its interests are met, its values and beliefs internalized.

For Gramsci, it is the dominant class that establishes the standards and norms against which all other groups are measured. The success of the dominant group is principally achieved by means of winning the active *consent* of those classes and groups that are subordinated within it. Institutions such as schools and the mass media are key sites where the beliefs and values of the dominant class are "taught" to the public, in a way that will, over time, eventually lead to the securing of consent from subordinate classes. In other words, Gramsci's key theoretical insight lies in demonstrating how subordinate classes are complicit and active in their own oppression in a way that ensures the hegemony of the dominant class.

Connell borrows the concept of hegemony from Gramsci to conceptualize relations among various versions of masculinity situated in a gendered hierarchy. Connell argues that one hegemonic model of masculinity is valued and esteemed above all other versions. Within Western society today, hegemonic masculinity has been most closely associated with white, heterosexual, able-bodied, class-privileged men who are also youthful, aggressive, athletic, economically successful; and independent, a breadwinner, and physically and emotionally tough and competitive (Greig & Martino, 2012; Kimmel, 2013; Mara, 2012). This dominant form of heteronormative masculinity ensures that men and boys who come close to embodying hegemonic masculinity are culturally rewarded through the accumulation of social and cultural capital. It is important to keep in mind that hegemonic masculinity is a social and cultural product and appears differently across time and context. What becomes the idealized version of masculinity in early 21st century Canada is different than what became the idealized version of masculinity found, say, in Victorian America; what is so for white teenage boys of working-class background in Halifax, Nova Scotia, is different for Indigenous men in rural Manitoba who experienced the Indian residential schools. (For key works that compare and explore historical constructions of masculinity across time and contexts, see, for example, Carnes & Griffen, 1990; Dummitt, 2007; Greig, 2014; Horowitz, 1991; 2001; Kidd, 2004; Kimmel, 1996; Rotundo, 1993.)

Hegemonic masculinity sits atop a gender hierarchy and has been theorized to be the most valued and idealized masculine identity produced through historical and social processes. Of course, as many boys and men will know, hegemonic models of masculinity do not necessarily correspond to the actual lives of boys and men but rather express ideals. Although men and boys are persuaded to work toward living up to the ideals of hegemonic masculinity, this is simply unachievable for most boys and men. Examples, however, abound in popular culture. There are few men who are able to live up to the masculine standards set by the fictional character Tony Stark, the American billionaire, hyper-heterosexual playboy, genius industrialist and scientist, and invincible superhero recently valourized in the extremely popular *Iron Man* films. It is important to note that celebrations of a narrow hyper-masculine, white, heteronormative, able-bodied culture so central to many Hollywood action movies, comic books (e.g., *Superman, Batman, Spiderman, Wolverine, The Incredible Hulk*), and current popular television shows aimed at youth and adolescents (e.g., *Arrow, Gotham, The Flash*) play an important role in shaping and directing the desires of many young and adolescent boys to securing this particular version of hegemonic masculinity. Few, if any, men and boys can actually embody the physique and qualities of a muscular superhero, but this does not stop film makers from perpetuating hegemonic masculinity as an ideal, or millions of little boys (and some girls?) from imagining themselves as such.

It is also important to consider carefully a material example of the ways in which hegemonic masculinity manifests itself. For example, hyper-capitalism and neo-liberal globalization have more recently constructed the corporate executive as a masculine ideal. Not only has the neo-liberal offensive harmed women and girls in a variety of significant ways, including its relentless attack on the welfare state and "imposing more unpaid work on women caring for the young, the old, and the sick" (Connell, 2010, p. 33), but it has also helped promote a "transnational business masculinity" (Connell & Wood, 2005, p. 347) as the latest manifestation of a mode of hegemonic masculinity (see also Braedley & Luxton, 2010). Set against the backdrop of an increasingly neo-liberal world that endorses the so-called virtues of the free market and the valuing of hyper-competition and hyper-individualism, the image of the global corporate executive as the ideal man has emerged. This version of an ideal masculine—transnational corporate executives and chief executive officers (CEO)—is characterized by whiteness and the hyper-drive to control and dominate global markets in an effort to accumulate enormous amounts of capital and power and privilege (Connell & Wood, 2005; see also Elias & Beasley, 2009). This ideal model of masculinity promotes affluence and power as key aspirations for men. For Connell, the rise of transnational business masculinity as a mode of hegemonic masculinity legitimizes men's dominance in the global gender order (see also Greig & Holloway, 2012). Perhaps this is a good time to point out to readers the fact that of Canada's 100 top-earning CEOs, only one is female. Moreover, according to a 2012 report written by the Canadian Centre for Policy Alternatives, Canada's 100 elite CEOs make up the richest 0.01% of Canadian tax filers, indicating the nexus between masculinities, neo-liberalism, wealth, and hyper-capitalism (Mackenzie, 2012).

Dominant forms of heteronormative masculinity have been increasingly challenged in recent years by the proliferation of queer and transgender identities in pop culture and through changing legislation (e.g., Ontario's Bill 33, Toby's Act [Right to be Free from Discrimination and Harassment Because of Gender Identity]) or even the legalization of same-sex marriages in Canada (Greig & Holloway, 2012, p. 129) and the establishment of gay-straight alliances in schools. Still, to be considered a "real man" remains closely tethered to the assumption of heterosexuality. As such, the norms of hegemonic masculinity pressure boys and men to constantly work hard to have sexual relations with girls and women. Boys and men do this work in order to demonstrate to themselves and to other males that they are indeed heterosexual, to prove their masculinity, and to gain status among their male peers. In this way, women and girls become a form of commodity that men and boys acquire in order to improve their ranking on the masculine social scale.

Yet equating hegemonic masculinity with sexual power, dominance, and violence has unfortunately led to the development of powerful predatory and aggressive male heterosexuality. Within the logic of hegemonic masculinity, men must be able to possess and be successful in the area of sexual prowess and virility and be capable of sexually dominating and successfully taking charge of women. Unfortunately, a clearly harmful outcome of this misperception of male sexuality is the relatively high incidence of male violence against women, including rape and sexual harassment, in Canada and elsewhere (Sinha, 2013). Recent media attention into allegations of sexual harassment has focused on high-profile men such as Canadian radio personality Jian Ghomeshi (Bradshaw & McArthur, 2014; Kingston, 2014), American pro football player Ray Rice (Taylor, 2014), and well-known television personality Bill Cosby (Elber, 2014). One need not be reminded of an earlier incident at St. Mary's University in which male students were "celebrating" frosh week with a public chant about their intention to sexually assault underage girls (Hunter, 2015; see also, Simona, 2015).

Abiding by the premises of hegemonic masculinity also requires boys to practise homophobia. Homophobia of course refers to the fear and hatred of gay males and those who are perceived to be gay, and the prejudices and oppression that go along with that fear and hatred (Short, 2013). To be other-than-heterosexual subordinates boys and men within the dominant gender hierarchy. Homophobia keeps boys and men fixed into rigid and gendered ways of being that inhibit their creativity and self-expression. Even today, boys, for example, have to make sure that they choose the "right" words, speak them in the "right" way, walk the "right" way, and engage in the "right" sort of masculine interests or else they come under the scrutiny of other boys. However, as Christine Overall (1990) has pointed out, the threat of homophobia and homophobic violence is not limited to the regulation of masculinity. Rather, homophobic behaviour is also part of the enforcement of heteronormativity and the institution of heterosexuality, which has an impact on all people.

Within the gender order, hegemonic masculinity is constructed in relation to marginalized, subordinate, and complicit masculinities (Connell, 1995). Connell uses the term marginalization to express the relationship between masculinities in dominant versus marginalized classes. Men who are subject to marginalization in Western societies are often Indigenous or people of colour, may be dis/abled, and may come from the working-class or working-poor communities. For Connell, the intersections between and among race, class, and gender relations are significant for understanding both relations of marginalization and relations of dominance. Connell, for example, discusses well-known African American athletes in the United States (e.g., Michael Jordan) who appear to exemplify hegemonic masculinity, and yet the wealth, status, and fame of an exceptional athlete do not filter down to secure social and cultural capital for other African American men. The problem, as Connell notes, is that the increased visibility of a small number of men of colour functions in a way to position them as exemplars of racial equality; using these men as examples of racial equality actively prevents other non-white men from gaining social and cultural capital and power (see, e.g., Katz, 2011). In the same way, marginalized men or boys across racial or sexual categories may, for a brief moment, perform hegemonic masculinity but remain marginalized within a hyper-capitalist, neo-liberal world that privileges whiteness, wealth, heterosexuality; and the practice of economic, legal, and political power.

The concept of subordinate masculinity is most commonly thought to be associated with gay men or men who are perceived to be gay. Boys and men who display supposedly feminine characteristics and engage in practices and express attitudes that are not consistent with hegemonic masculinity also fall into this category (Kimmel, 1994; Mac an Ghaill,

1994). Along with hegemonic, marginalized, and subordinate, Connell also theorizes about complicit masculinity (Connell, 1995). Complicit masculinity is understood to be that version of masculinity that supports and is complicit in the propping up of hegemonic masculinity. Boys and men who adopt a complicit masculinity are not the frontline fighters for patriarchy; they are men and boys who are not violent, openly sexist, or misogynistic but nonetheless reproduce patriarchal relations of power while not appearing to be its primary enforcers. Boys and men who adopt a complicit masculinity do very little, if anything, to challenge patriarchal models of masculinity. All men, however, receive what Connell calls the patriarchal dividend. For Connell, the "patriarchal dividend" is the power and privilege that is provided to all men in a society, but is secured largely by the foot soldiers of patriarchy. In other words, not all men who benefit from this privilege are violent, sexist, misogynistic. Most men do passively benefit from those culturally engendered practices.

Masculinity As Performance

It is now common to understand gender as a performance. Conceptualizing gender as a performance emerged from the work of Candace West and Don Zimmerman in their seminal article "Doing Gender" published in 1987 in *Gender and Society*. In the paper, West and Zimmerman argued that gender is not a "property of individuals," rather gender is best thought of as an individual's *stylization* or "routine accomplishment" of gender "situated" in everyday interaction (pp. 125–126). Performing one's gender is something men and boys have to work at constantly as the project of constructing an appropriate identity is never complete but always in process. Indeed, queer theorists of the 1990s, including Judith Butler (1990/1999), convincingly argued that gender is inscribed on the body through continual performance. Butler wrote that gender was produced both within oneself and for other people as "a stylized repetition of acts" (p. 179).

A man's gender performance is assessed and evaluated by other men against socially accepted norms of what it means to be a man. Other men watch, provide surveillance, and issue the man a tentative acceptance into the realm of an assumed "acceptable" masculinity (Martino & Pallota-Chiarolli, 2003; Mac An Ghaill, 1994). For example, world champion marathon runner Alberto Salazar doggedly chased after running glory in the 1980s. In Salazar's case—he was a three-time winner of the New York City Marathon, in 1980, 1981, and 1982—he did it in order to "prove his manhood" to his father (Brant, 2006, p. 69). Masculinity then, is a homo-social enactment, a performance where other men, including fathers, function as the audience. Many men and boys test themselves, perform heroic feats, take enormous physical risks, work hard to secure enormous wealth and status, all because they want other men and boys to grant to them an "acceptable" manhood (Kimmel, 1994, p. 129).

Understanding gender as a performative act helps to explain in part why men's public and private practices of gender sometimes differ radically. Some men and boys find their actual practice of masculinity is at odds with their internal values. For instance, some men and boys may not desire or be able to engage in aggressive physical acts to demonstrate an "appropriate" masculinity. However they may do so in order to secure status among their male peers or because they feel pressure from an adult male in authority. In a similar way, some men may want to establish sensitive, caring, and non-exploitive relationships with women and other men, while others desire to engage in non-violent sports. Both groups may find it difficult to do so in light of the pressure exerted on them by standards of hegemonic masculinity (see, e.g., Messerschmidt, 2000). Along with understanding masculinity as performance, students of gender and gender relations also need to consider carefully the ways in which masculinities overlap, intersect, and interact with other important social categories such as social class, race, and disability.

Masculinities and Intersectionality

Intersectionality is an analytical tool that feminist and other critical scholars use in order to examine the relationship among identity, gender, and other systems of oppression (Crenshaw, 1989; Nash, 2008). Intersectionality rejects the single category framework (e.g., only race, only gender, only sexuality), and instead analyzes the various and complex ways in which various categories such as social class, race, age, able-bodiness, and sexuality overlap, interact, and intersect with gender to shape the multiple dimensions of all people's experiences. So the study of men and masculinities is far more complicated than many early writers and scholars first imagined. Men can be privileged in some ways and not privileged in others. For example, due to structural and systemic oppression, being born a straight, white, heterosexual middle-class, able-bodied male affords access to multiple systems of privilege that are simply not available to Indigenous and non-white boys; and/or those who are working class and/or disabled; and/or gay, bisexual, or transgendered. In many ways, being born straight, white, male, abled-bodied, and middle class is similar to "winning life's lottery," where most if not all of society's privileges are available to you (Crosley-Corcoran, 2014).

Class and Masculinities

Similar to gender, class is one of the key hierarchies within contemporary society. Class relations unequally distribute social, political, and economic benefits and life chances (Weis, 2008). An earlier work that adopted critical theoretical frameworks exploring class in the lives of working-class boys was Paul Willis's 1977 book *Learning to Labor: How Working-Class Kids Get Working Class Jobs*. In what is now considered to be a pivotal work on the relationship between class and masculinities, Willis's ethnography explored the gendered subculture of high school aged, white, working-class, disenfranchised adolescent boys from Hammertown, England. Willis demonstrated how economic, social, and cultural structures shaped the identities of working-class boys—called the "lads"—many of whom rejected the idea that school was a method to secure social and economic mobility. The lads understood that their class location and social positions would likely limit their future labour-market opportunities. Situated within a capitalist society and faced with institutional authority, the boys largely rejected schools' invitations to learn.

The lad' rejected the perceived "femininity" of mental labour in favour of the "masculinity" of manual labour. It was this strong connection between manual labour and an "appropriate" white, working-class masculinity that largely ensured the Hammertown lads' active participation in and consent to their subordinate economic and social fate. Similarly Dunk's research on working-class men from Thunder Bay, Ontario, found that real "men go to work in work clothes, work boots, and hard hats, and carry a lunchbox" (1991, p. 46). So, within the logic of the norms of white working-class masculinity in Hammertown, boys who accepted a school's invitation to learn and were academically successful were "emasculated" and ridiculed by the lads. To pursue a successful masculinity, then, in the eyes of other boys, the lads engaged in identity construction that rested on behaviours such as skipping school, fighting, drinking, and smoking. Willis's work was one of the first studies to demonstrate the relationship between the broader structure of social class and the active ongoing identity performance of masculinity by boys within the context of a capitalist society. When researchers and others begin to think more closely about men's and boys' experiences of masculinities, they also need to take into careful consideration the complex intersection of gender with social class relations, with a particular eye to how social class relations currently are being powerfully reshaped and reformed within a hyper-capitalist, neo-liberal order.

Race and Masculinities

Race has figured prominently in the configuration of masculinities. Within the current configuration of masculinities, *whiteness* privileges white men over non-white men. Because of race privilege, Indigenous men and men of colour, do not experience masculinities in the same way that white men as a group do. The high-profile examples in Ferguson, Missouri, and New York City, in which two unarmed African American men were killed by white police officers (El Akkad, 2014; Koring, 2014) provide current examples of the *politics of privilege* and the complex intersection between race as a system of oppression and masculinity. Even for non-white men, when class and other socially important properties such as sexuality are examined, there are diverse experiences within the logic of masculinities. Clyde W. Franklin II's examination of Black masculinities in *Ain't I a Man?* (1994), demonstrates the different ways of being a man that are open to differently situated Black men. In *Black Masculinity: The Black Male's Role in American Society*, Robert Staples provided one of the earliest feminist interpretations of masculinity by a Black male scholar. Staples's work was key in drawing scholars' attention to the relationship between male power and whiteness. As Staples and other scholars have noted, unlike white men, Black men constitute one of the most powerless male populations in the United States, demonstrating how some men have power based on gender, but remain oppressed due to racism.

Along with scholars such as Robert Staples and Rinaldo Wallcott, Canadian scholar Carl E. James has written extensively about the relationship between race and masculinity. James, for example, has explored race, gender, social class, and education in relation to Black male athleticism in the Canadian context. James found that race, class, gender, and location intersected in the lives of young Black men in Toronto to produce particular versions of "appropriate" masculinity. Faced with institutional racism that privileges whiteness, the young men were inclined to participate in sport because that is where they were able to exercise cultural capital, gain a sense of belonging in the school among their peers, and navigate racist structures (James, 2012). Forms of Black masculinity that became dominant within schools were grounded in a hyper-heterosexuality and the capacity to be physically strong, fearless, and athletic with a goal to becoming famous. James (2012) found that, unfortunately, living out their conception of Black masculinity through sport was not made problematic by educators and others, but rather was reinforced by the schools' teachers, coaches, and administrators; and parents, the media, and young female fans. For working-class Black males, sport, not education, became the vehicle for cultural and social mobility (see also May, 2008). The works by scholars such as those illustrate how systematic differences in the accumulation of social authority, wealth, power, and social and cultural capital are shaped in powerful ways by the structure of gender as it articulates and intersects with race, social class, and other significant social categories such as sexuality.

A critical look at whiteness has enabled feminist scholars to explore the relationship between race and masculinity. Using this approach helps us to identify and become aware of the historically and culturally dominant form of masculinity, characterized in part by whiteness, heterosexuality, and class mobility. Men who come from non-white European populations—Black, Indigenous, Métis, Inuit, Mexican, Italian, and other ethnic groups, are marginalized and "Othered." Scholars writing about the Canadian context, for example, have drawn our attention recently to the complexity of Indigenous masculinities. Kim Anderson, Robert Alexander Innes, and John Swift (2012) have explored the fraught relationship between the legacy of British Imperialism, colonization, heteronormativity, whiteness, and patriarchy on Indigenous masculinities. Their research demonstrates that how white European patriarchy was expressed in the Indian residential schools had a significant impact on Indigenous men, banning their communities' practices and rituals that had helped Indigenous boys become democratic and egalitarian men. Also consider that, in our current social, political, and historical context and best understood against the backdrop of Islamophobia, representations of Middle Eastern masculinity within the popular imagination have often been tied to a threatening "terrorist" identity (Davies & Babington, 2004). As other non-white masculinities are Othered in the popular Western media, so too are Middle Eastern masculinities which does very little to advance the goals of gender equity and equality (for a more detailed and richer discussion of race, Indigeneity, and feminism, see Chapter 2).

Masculinities and Disabilities

Early researchers (e.g., Gerschick & Miller, 1994; Hahn, 1988; Shakespeare, 1999) who studied the intersection of gender and disability found that the prevailing models of masculinity and disability were in conflict with each other. In the structure of Connell's gender hierarchy, men with disabilities fall within the category of subordinate masculinity because of the conflicting expectations placed on them as men and as people with disabilities. Consider that contemporary masculinity privileges men who are physically strong, courageous, aggressive, independent, and self-reliant (Connell, 1995). This runs in contrast to men with disabilities who are typically perceived to be, and are often treated as, weak, pitiful, passive, and dependent (Gerschick & Miller, 1994, p. 350), as men to be pitied rather than respected and admired. The image of a man with physical disabilities runs in deep contrast to all that is "embodied in the ideal masculinity: strength, power, virility and independence" (Asch & Fine, 1988, p. 3).

If this image is so persistent in North American society, how do men with physical disabilities negotiate their identities as men? Men with physical disabilities, such as quadriplegia, remain committed to negotiating their identity in relation to the standards of hegemonic masculinity in three general ways: *reformulation*, *reliance*, and *rejection* (Gerschick & Miller, 1994). According to Gerschick and Miller (1994) *reformulation* happens when "men redefine hegemonic masculinity on their own terms and along the lines of their own strengths and capabilities" (p. 187). Men who reformulate their masculinity in light of a physical disability remain committed to traditional characteristics of masculinity such as control, independence, and autonomy. Those men who reformulate their gender identity in a way that is consistent with the standards of hegemonic masculinity will also engage in traditional masculine pursuits such as an active sex life or a full-contact sport such as wheelchair rugby (Gerschick & Miller, 1994, p. 353). Men who practise a *reliance* on normative standards of masculinity do not feel comfortable with their sense of gender identity. The inability to meet society's standards of what it means to be a man leaves these men troubled and feeling "incomplete." Men who rely on dominant conceptions of masculinity tend to internalize their feelings of inadequacy and seek to compensate, or at times overcompensate, for them. This can result in increased attempts to have sexual relations with women in order to demonstrate their masculinity, or in increased attempts to engage in dangerous and risky physical pursuits or to participate in disability sports such as wheelchair rugby as ways to construct or recuperate hegemonic masculinity (e.g, see Rubin and Shapiro's 2005 award-winning documentary, *Murderball*). This model does very little to challenge the current gender order as it makes disability the problem of the individual rather than a shortcoming of the broader society.

The third method that men with physical disabilities use in relation to the standards of hegemonic masculinity is one of *rejection*. In this model men come to understand that the dominant models of masculinity are deeply problematic and begin to develop new standards of masculinity in place of the ones they have rejected. Gerschick and Miller (1994) interviewed men who rejected traditional masculinity and its emphasis on sexual prowess. The men in this category also rejected traditional notions of what it meant to be a father, placing much more emphasis on being emotionally and physically available to children. Finally, it is important to point out that men with disabilities very rarely use one method exclusively. Rather, "men often employ each of these methods at different points in their lives in complex and overlapping ways, even though they do tend to rely on one method more than others" (e.g., Mara, 2012).

An intersectional approach to understanding gender and disability accepts that not all men with disabilities experience disability in the same way. Therefore any nuanced account of the intersection between masculinity and disability needs to reject a homogeneous understanding of disability and consider how various types of disabilities intersect with gender and other factors such as class, race, age, and sexual orientation (Shuttleworth et al.,

2012). For instance, Shuttleworth et al. found that there were differences between men who acquired a physical impairment after childhood and men who experienced early onset impairments. Men who acquired impairment later in life, such as a spinal cord injury, "were more closely aligned with nondisabled normative masculinity, than men who experienced early onset impairments, such as cerebral palsy" (p. 183). In other words, men who acquired a physical impairment later in life have been perceived by other men as "real men" who lost their masculinity compared to those men who experienced an early onset physical impairment and have been considered as never having been masculine in the first place. While men with disabilities are marginalized within the logic of hegemonic masculinity, failing to differentiate between impairments overlooks types and degrees of difference in impairment as they interact with masculine expectations.

Sport: A Key Social Location for the Making of Masculinities

Individual identity construction is usefully understood and situated in relation to institutions such as education, family, and the media. Sport is a key institution for men and boys. Understanding these key cultural and social institutions such as schools, family, and organizations as gendered cultural spaces requires us to view gender as dynamic, fluid, and relational historical processes situated within complex relations of power. Although each institution is important for students of gender to examine, in the final section of the chapter we turn to the case study of sport and masculinity.

Sporting Culture and the Making of Masculinities Research on men and masculinities has consistently demonstrated how sport remains one of the key social and cultural institutions in the social production of hegemonic masculinity (Connell, 1995; Krebs, 2012; Messner & Sabo, 1994; Rand, 2012; see also Joseph, Darnell, & Nakamura, 2012). Scholars have largely agreed that boys learn at a very early age, through the institution of sport, that social and cultural capital can be secured, at least temporarily, by displaying a high level of sporting prowess (Connell, 1995, p. 54; see also Michael Buma's 2012 *Refereeing Identity: The Cultural Work of Canadian Hockey Novels*). Indeed, it almost goes without saying that demonstrating the physical and mental attributes most closely associated with athletic achievement, in particular in contact sports, is an important requirement for status in most male peer groups (Burstyn, 1999; Messner & Sabo, 1994; Pronger, 1990). Some of the more detailed work that has been completed on masculinities has demonstrated quite convincingly that boys who are considered to be competent in "appropriate" masculine sports such as ice hockey, football, basketball, or rugby acquire enormous amount of social capital and sit atop the gendered hierarchy (Burstyn, 1999; Martino & Pallota-Chiarolli, 2003; Messner, 1990, 2002). At the same time, boys who are physically small or awkward or less coordinated, and boys who are scholarly or artistic or simply have no interest in sports, are often ridiculed and marginalized and often face verbal and physical violence from other boys (Burstyn, 1999; Mac An Ghaill, 1994; Martino & Pallota-Chiarolli, 2003).

The significance of sport in contributing to gender hierarchies and to the maintenance of male supremacy should not be underestimated (Anderson, 2005; Burstyn, 1999; Lenskyj, 1986; Messner & Sabo, 1994). In fact, it has almost been taken for granted that the masculinities produced in professional men's team sports, such as ice hockey or professional football, are often the most valued and venerated in popular culture (Burstyn, 1999; Messner, 1992). The institution of sport continues to prop up hegemonic masculinity by ritualizing and embedding aggression, strength, and skill in the male body and closely connecting it with competitive achievement (Anderson, 2005). Sport is a space in which a certain definition of hegemonic masculinity has been celebrated, a version of masculinity that Burstyn termed, "a manly antifeminist warrior" (1999, p. 65). In some sports, women have gained only second-class status and have been forced to play with more "feminine" rules, positioning them as the "weaker" sex. In golf, to take one example, there exists a Ladies Tee, which suggests women should play a shorter course. Nonetheless, the distribution of wealth, power, opportunity, and authority between men and women is also connected to media coverage. Messner and Cooky (2010) demonstrated that although woman made up close to 40% of participants in sport, they received just 4% of the media coverage. Unfortunately, the researchers also found that the media coverage "of women's sport has actually declined over the past two decades" (p. 3).

Brian Pronger's (1990) early research on the relationship between masculinity and sport within the North American context also demonstrated that competitive team sports that have a strong focus on violence, such as ice hockey, were more likely to be played by hyper-heteromasculine men than sports that do not focus on violence. In *Crossing the Line: Violence and Sexual Assault in Canada's National Sport*, Laura Robinson (1998) demonstrated that young men who played junior hockey in Canada displayed a hyper-masculinity as well as demonstrated more misogynistic and sexist beliefs about women and girls than the general population. Robinson argued that within junior hockey culture, sexual assault against young women, including rape, is common. This suggests that sporting practices and cultures, which are grounded in the celebration of an aggressive, hyper-masculinity, promote sexual violence against women and girls. Certainly the growing list of high-profile domestic abuse and sexual assault cases among high school (Zernike & Schweber, 2014), university (Cohen & Bachman, 2014), and professional football players (Armour, 2014; Wilner, 2014) provides further evidence of the relationship between hyper-masculine sporting cultures and the production of a violent, hegemonic masculinity.

Sport teaches males to play through pain. This is often taken as a clear marker that a boy has adopted an "appropriate" masculinity. Don Sabo (1994) pointed out that the vast majority of male athletes in North America adopt the "pain principle," the idea that they are expected by coaches, teammates, fans, and others to ignore their body's pain. For instance, in his recent memoir, a book-length reflection on his professional hockey playing days during the 1970s and 1980s, Derek Sanderson recalls the very first lesson his dad taught him when he was just eight years old, to condition "myself to ignore pain" and "never [allow] it to intimidate me" (2012, p. 16). In a similar way, former National Hockey League (NHL) superstar Theo Fleury related in his memoir that during his time in hockey in the 1980s and 1990s, he could never be honest with other players or coaches when it came to being hurt or feeling pain. In front of other men, he always "had to be tough, never show weakness" (2009, p. 96). As these examples show, men and boys must demonstrate their manliness time and again by rejecting any supposed feminine behaviour, even though those behaviours work for self-preservation. According to Michael Messner (1990), herein lies one of the "ultimate paradoxes of organized combat sports: top athletes, who are often portrayed as the epitome of good physical conditioning and health, are likely to suffer from a very high incidence of permanent injuries, disabilities, alcoholism, drug abuse, obesity, and other related health problems" (p. 211). To put it a little differently, the norms of hegemonic masculinity teach male athletes to view their bodies as machines, which "results at times in violence against the athlete's own body" (p. 211).

To be sure, out of all the masculine attributes that fuel an elite athlete's hegemonic masculine status, sacrificing one's body in silence for the sake of sporting glory has historically been key. In a social system in which experiencing pain in silence brings so-called masculine honour, recognition, and respect, it is only natural that boys and men would strive to meet this expectation. Boys are taught at an early age that if they don't conform to the pain principle they might be labelled as "women," "fags," or "pussies" (Messner, 2004, pp. 328–329). Let's take the recent example of the National Basketball Association's (NBA) superstar Lebron James. On June 6, 2014, Game one of the NBA's final between the San Antonio Spurs and Miami Heat was played. Key to the Miami Heat's success over the season was the play of superstar forward Lebron (King) James, considered by many to be the best basketball player in the world. However, on this particular hot spring night, the air-conditioning in the San Antonio basketball stadium broke down, raising the temperature on the court to over 32° Celsius. The extreme heat appeared to have caused James to develop leg cramps late in the game. Because of the visible pain he was experiencing and the fact that he looked like he could not even walk because of the leg cramps, James made the decision to pull himself out of the game. It was James's decision to not conform to the "pain principle" that stoked controversy in the media.

The racist public backlash against James's decision to leave the game for health reasons came quickly via Twitter and other forms of media. James was ridiculed, using misogynistic and homophobic slurs for not playing through the pain: "Lebron is a woman! Having her period!" tweeted one Twitter writer (Signal, 2014). In the context of anti-Black racism, the swift public attack on James's masculinity should tell us something very important about the permeation of white heteronormative masculinity within North American culture and the cultural policing of normative masculinity. Not even Lebron James, a pro athlete who has achieved enormous athletic success and wealth in a hyper-masculine culture, is free from being unseated from the status he has earned. Denying physical and emotional weakness and playing through pain are necessary in order to maintain even pro athletes' privileged position.

Let's take a final example. In the winter of 2013, popular conservative American radio personality Glenn Beck mocked American president Barack Obama for his comments in a pre-Super Bowl interview about football safety. Obama sat down with television journalist

Scott Pelley prior to Super Bowl Sunday and was questioned by Pelley whether he would allow his son to play football. "I have to think about it," Obama said, adding that he is a "huge fan" of the sport, "but that there are concerns about safety to consider." "He's a girl," mocked Beck on the following Monday: "His man card has been revoked by me. That's saying something." Invoking a misogynist and thinly veiled racist discourse, Beck then went on to state that the president's response was typical of a woman's. Oddly, Beck then imitated a wife concerned about letting her son play football. "You're a full-fledged woman . . . I've never heard anybody but a woman say that." Beck told listeners that Obama should "[S]top being such a chick, Mr. President. You're commander-in-chief, not the chick-in-chief" (Beck, 2013). Beck's comments and the public response to James's decision clearly reveal the relationship between racism, homophobia, misogyny, and standards of hegemonic masculinity. In both cases, women are devalued, denigrated, and positioned as weak, cowardly, and passive. Even the president of the United States, often considered the most powerful man in the world, was ridiculed for not adhering to the standards of hegemonic masculinity.

For the man or boy—in particular, the athlete—who temporarily succeeds at embodying normative masculinity, its norms are often internalized to the level that violence and aggression become part of his own sense of identity. The body of these men becomes a machine that can be used to inflict pain on other men, which elevates him into the "masculine elite" (Powell, 2014) where he reaps the social, political, and economic rewards that accompany this position in all-male worlds, including professional sports. Many are willing to be involved in these sports even if it might mean acquiring early onset dementia or other cognitive and physical disorders, such as chronic headaches, memory loss, depression, and sleeplessness (Vasquez, 2014).

The recent public concern and media attention around chronic traumatic encephalopathy (CTE) and the risk of concussion for those who play professional sports such as pro football and hockey may, however, be bringing about some change. In light of the growing body of research on some sports and their relationship to the development of progressive cognitive degenerative diseases such as CTE, some parents may no longer choose to risk the long-term health of their sons for the sake of a game (see Gregory, 2014). In fact, a Canadian writer (Fitz-Gerald, 2014) recently suggested that growing public concerns over concussions could cause the death of ice hockey. Echoing a similar trend, the *New York Times* published an article that highlighted the decreasing number of boys electing to play high school football in the United States because of increased concerns over their health and welfare (Leonhardt, 2014).

Remember, however, the strong relationship among hegemonic masculinity, sport, and capitalism, in particular corporate capitalism that has historically exploited the bodies of men and women in its pursuit of greater profit (Engels, 1887/2004). The promotion of a so-called ideal masculinity needs, in part, to be understood as closely connected to the interests of those men well positioned within the corporate capitalist structure. Corporate capitalism teaches boys to develop an identity that is closely associated with physical toughness, competition, and public displays of bodily power. When it comes to major sporting leagues such as the National Football League (NFL), the National Hockey League (NHL), and the National Basketball Association (NBA) (and minor and university leagues), these corporate capitalist structures encourage boys and men to live up to the ideals of hegemonic masculinity by offering them exceptional material rewards, widespread fame, and masculine honour (Gruneau & Whitson, 1993; Howell, 2001; Whitson & Gruneau, 2006). To play in one of the professional leagues almost guarantees a man his place among the so-called masculine elite in society. Yet keep in mind that, by aspiring to live up to the so-called ideals of hegemonic masculinity within the context of sport, men and boys routinely sacrifice their bodies and minds, including experiencing the likelihood of depression, substance abuse, and premature death (for a recent example, see Branch, 2014; see also Nilan, 2013; Sanderson, 2012) for significant corporate profits. In this sense, men's (and women's) bodies are considered to be disposable and quickly discarded if they no longer serve the interests of corporate capitalism. Within the context of an increasingly corporate capitalist society, institutions such as sport adhere very closely to the principle of profit before people.

Within the logic of the hierarchy of masculinities, different sports are gendered differently. With some exceptions, the more violent the game the higher up on the gendered sport hierarchy it rests. Team sports that are gendered hyper-masculine, such as ice hockey and football, and infused with violence sit atop the gendered hierarchy, while non-violent and non-contact sports such as badminton, ballet, and gymnastics sit on the bottom. Violent, high-status sports often serve as a key zone for the expression of patriarchal practices and a place for boys to be viewed by other boys as "appropriately" masculine. Describing the North American context, Mary Louise Adams, in her 2011 book *Artistic Impressions: Figure Skating, Masculinity, and the Limits of Sport*, put it this way: "[I]n the North American sport hierarchy, hard-hitting, aggressive team activities pursued by men occupy the highest rungs, and to these sports and the athletes who participate in them accrue the highest status, the greatest profits, and most media coverage" (p. 11). As Adams suggests, many boys raised in contemporary North America rarely entertain the idea of becoming a figure skater, in part because a boy who figure skates is often viewed by other boys as effeminate, a sissy, or worse, gay (Adams, 2011). Not surprisingly, then, those men who succeed in achieving significant professional status by playing in appropriately masculine sports such as professional ice hockey are often the most popular and admired men in their national context. In our own Canadian context, and taking into serious consideration the project of whiteness, we need only consider the enormous and widespread cultural and social status afforded to former professional hockey players Jean Béliveau, Gordie Howe, Bobby Orr, and Wayne Gretzky to see the truth behind this statement (Allain, 2008; Gruneau & Whitson, 2007; for a first-hand account of race and racism in ice hockey, see Cecil Harris, 2003, *Breaking the Ice: The Black Experience in Professional Hockey*; see also Valmore James & John Gallaher, 2015, *The Val James Story: Black Ice*; for an intriguing broader discussion on race and sport in Canada see Joseph, Darnell, & Nakamura, 2012).

Sport is a key social institution in the making of masculinities. Sport remains a place of male dominance, where men and boys can live the fantasy of assumed male superiority and toughness, even if the vast majority of men and boys cannot play at the level of elite athletes. Unfortunately, some boys may also learn through organized sport to hide or repress their emotional and physical pain in order not to show perceived weakness, making sport a dangerous place for boys. Not only does this narrowing and flattening of boys' lives come at the cost of the development of their emotional life, but also the expectation to play through pain can be a source of long-term physical harm, as the recent research on CTE has demonstrated. Men and boys continue to use sport, in particular, high-status contact sports such as ice hockey, as an arena where they can prove their masculinity to other men and boys. Although sports can offer men and boys some positive benefits, such as experiencing camaraderie and mutual support from other men and boys and learning how to understand the use of their bodies, many of the values currently celebrated in sports have a negative impact on them, as well as on women and girls. Some of the key lessons boys learn through organized sport are misogyny, sexism, and violence that all work against efforts to secure gender equality. In light of the significant amount of male violence against women and girls, this is important to bear in mind because it undermines efforts by feminists and antiviolence educators to work toward gender justice.

CONCLUSION

North American writings on men and masculinity produced in the 1970s looked critically at the male sex role. These early writings began to see men as explicitly gendered rather than as innately driven to be "hard," unemotional, and driven only by work. However, early writings on men and masculinity did very little to advance the cause of gender equality between men and women. They failed to consider power relations, reducing issues of gender to individual men, rather than analyzing the systemic and structural issues that privilege men as a group over women. Moreover, the early writings on men and masculinity largely assumed a white, heterosexual, able-bodied, middle-class male as the norm. By making this assumption, early writings failed to take into consideration the complexity, fluidity, and intersection of masculinities with other significant categories such as race, social class, able-bodiness, and sexual identity.

Later writings on men and masculinity provided a much-needed corrective to popular writings produced by writers identifying with the men's liberation movement. By taking into careful consideration feminist, queer, and other critically oriented scholarship, and by understanding men and masculinities as plural, socially and historically constructed, and by understanding masculinity as performative and embodied, rather than somehow just "naturally" one way or another, the later writings on men and masculinities provided new key insights into the making of masculinities. Certainly, Connell's conceptualization of masculinity as relational between and among men has helped students of gender and gender relations understand that as a culture, we come to understand what it means to be an "appropriate" man by "setting" the definition against a group of Others, including racial minorities, differently abled, sexual minorities, and women (Kimmel, 1999, p. 4). Unfortunately, the fear of emasculation or being viewed as a sissy or gay, continues to fuel men's active and ongoing desire to meet hegemonic standards of masculinity. Relief from these forms of gender anxieties will only be achieved once we begin to help men and boys understand that it is in their own best interest and the interest of others, including those women and girls they love and care for, to begin to dismantle hegemonic models of masculinity.

Later writings on men and masculinities have pushed researchers and students of gender to think more carefully about the intersection of gender with other important social categories such as race, social class, and sexuality in the ongoing construction of men's identity. As Connell and other critical scholars of gender have noted, intersectionality analyzes the various and complex ways in which various categories such as social class, race, age, able-bodiness, and sexuality interact with gender to shape the multiple dimensions of experiences with masculinities.

Finally, the later feminist-informed and critically oriented writings on men and masculinities have helped make a contribution to the advancement of gender equality between men and women. By interrogating and working toward dismantling hegemonic versions of masculinity that are based on homophobia, misogyny, aggression, violence, and the devaluation and oppression of women and girls, men and boys can begin to work to end violence against women and girls, and promote gender equity, healthy relationships, and a new, broader understanding of masculinities. A pro-feminist research agenda that remains committed to addressing issues of gender justice for women and girls will also help men and boys live in a more socially just and meaningful way that respects a variety of healthy and respectful forms of masculinity and encourages men and boys to challenge the realities of privilege, power, and violence in their own lives.

Discussion Questions

1. What are some of the key differences between the early and later writings on masculinity/masculinities?
2. Performing masculinity is demonstrated and displayed for other men in the hope of being granted an "acceptable" masculinity. Describe examples from your own experiences where you felt a man or a boy was working hard to construct an "appropriate" masculinity for others?
3. How does the pain principle manifest itself in the everyday lives of boys and men? Give as many examples as you can think of in relation to various social institutions that you participate in (such as sports, health care, education, paid work, and others).
4. How has an intersectional approach to analyzing masculinities helped researchers theorize about overlapping systems of oppression and power? Can you think of examples from your own life in which an intersectional approach helps you to better understand a man's or boy's identity?

Bibliography

Adams, M. L. (2011). ***Artistic impressions: Figure skating, masculinity, and the limits of sports***. Toronto, ON: University of Toronto Press.

Anderson, E. (2005). ***In the game: Gay athletes and the cult of masculinity***. New York, NY: State University of New York Press.

Anderson, K., Innes, R. A., & Swift, J. (2012). Indigenous masculinities: Carrying the bones of the ancestors. In C. J. Greig & W. J. Martino (Eds.), *Canadian men and masculinities: Historical and contemporary perspectives* (pp. 266–284). Toronto, ON: Canadian Scholars' Press.

Armour, N. (2014, September 19). Devaluing of women prevalent in sports and needs to stop. *USA Today*, 1.

Beasley, C. (2005). *Gender and sexuality: Critical theories, critical thinkers.* London, England: Sage Publication.

Beck, G. (2013, 6 February). Glenn Beck to Obama: "Stop being such a chick, Mr. President." Retrieved from Huffingtonpost.com

Benatar, D. (2012). *The second sexism: The discrimination against men and boys.* Chichester, England: John Wiley and Sons.

Biddulph, S. (1997). *Raising boys: Why boys are different—and how to help them become happy and well-balanced man*. London, England: HarperCollins.

Branch, J. (2014). *Boy on ice: The life and death of Derek Boogaard*. Toronto, ON: Harper Collins Publishers.

Brant, J. (2006). *Duel in the sun: Alberto Salazar, Dick Beardsley, and America's greatest marathon.* New York, NY: Rodale.

Brod, H. (1987). *The making of masculinities: The new men's studies*. Winchester, MA: Unwin Hyman.

Buma, M. (2012). *Refereeing identity: The cultural work of Canadian hockey novels.* Montréal, QC, and Kingston, ON: McGill-Queen's University Press.

Burana, L., & Linnea, R. (Eds.). (1994). *Dagger: On butch women*. Pittsburgh, PA, and San Francisco, CA: Cleis Press.

Burstyn, V. (1999). *The rites of men: Manhood, politics, and the culture of sport*. Toronto, ON: University of Toronto Press.

Butler, J. (1990/1999). *Gender trouble: Feminism and the subversion of identity*. New York, NY: Routledge.

Carnes, M. C., & Griffen, C. (Eds.). (1990). *Meanings for manhood: Constructions of masculinity in Victorian America.* Chicago, IL: University of Chicago press.

Carrigan, T., Connell, B., & J. Lee. (1985). Toward a new sociology of masculinity. *Theory and Society 14*(5), 551–604.

Chenier, E. (2008). *Strangers in our midst: Sexual deviancy in postwar Ontario.* Toronto, ON: University of Toronto Press.

Cohen, B., & Bachman, R. (2014, October 11). Florida State defends Winston investigation. *The Wall Street Journal*, A14.

Connell, R. W. (1995). *Masculinities.* Berkeley, Los Angeles, CA: University of California Press.

Connell, R. W. (2000). *The men and the boys.* Los Angeles, CA: The University of Berkeley Press.

Connell, R. W. (2010). Understanding neoliberalism. In S. Braedley & M. Luxton (Eds.), *Neoliberalism and everyday life* (pp. 22–36). Montréal, QC, and Kingston, ON: McGill Queen's University Press.

Connell, R. W., & J. Wood. (2005). Globalization and business masculinities. *Men and Masculinities, 7*(4), 347–364.

Crenshaw, K. (1989). Demarginalizing the intersection of race and sex: A black feminist critique of antidiscrimination doctrine, feminist theory, and antiracist politics. *University of Chicago Legal Forum*, *140*, 139–167.

Crosley-Corcoran, G. (2014). Explaining white privilege to a broke white person. *The Huffington Post.* Retrieved from www.huffingtonpost.com/gina-crosleycorcoran/explaining-white-privilege-to-a-broke-white-person_b_5269255.html

Dummitt, C. (2007). *The manly modern: Masculinity and postwar Canada*. Vancouver, BC: UBC Press.

Dunk, T. (1991). *It's a working man's town: Male working-class culture.* Montréal, QC: McGill-Queen's University Press.

El Akkad, O. (2014, November 26). Missouri Gov. calls in National Guard as Ferguson braces for more violent unrest. *Globe and Mail*, A.1.

Elber, L. (2014, November 17). Cosby will not address sexual-abuse allegations, lawyer says. *Globe and Mail*, A.3.

Engels, F. (1887/2004). *The condition of the working class in England* (V. Kiernan, trans.). Toronto, ON: Penguin.

Faludi, S. (1991). *Backlash: The undeclared war against American women*. New York, NY: Doubleday, Anchor Books.

Farrell, B. (1971, August 27). You've come a long way, buddy: The repentant chauvinists of men's lib join the battle against sexism. *Life*, 11.

Farrell, W. (1974). *The liberated man*. New York, NY: Random House.

Gerschick, T. J., & Miller, A. S. (1994). Gender identities at the crossroads of masculinity and physical disability. *Masculinities 2*, 34–55.

Gheciu, A. N. (2014, July). Man down. *Sharp*, 102–107.

Gregory, S. (2014, September 29). He died playing this game: Is football worth it? *Time*, 32–39.

Greig, C. J. (2014). *Ontario Boys: Masculinity and the idea of boyhood in postwar Ontario, 1945–1960.* Waterloo, Ontario: Wilfrid Laurier University Press.

Greig, C. J., & Holloway, S. (2012). Canadian manhood(s). In C. J. Greig & W. J. Martino (Eds.), *Canadian men and masculinities: Historical and contemporary perspectives* (pp. 119–138). Toronto, ON: Canadian Scholars' Press.

Greig, C. J., & Martino, W. J. (Eds.). (2012). *Canadian men and masculinities: Historical and contemporary perspectives.* Toronto, ON: Canadian Scholars' Press.

Gruneau, R., & Whitson, D. (1993). *Hockey night in Canada: Sport, identities and cultural politics.* Toronto, ON: Garamond Press.

Hacker, H. M. (1957). The new burdens of masculinity. *Marriage and Family Living, 19*(3), 227–233.

Halberstam, J. (1998). *Female masculinity*. Durham, NC: Duke University Press.

Howell, C. (2001). *Blood, sweat, and cheers: Sport in the making of modern Canada*. Toronto, ON: University of Toronto Press.

Hunter, L. (2015, January 3). 2014 was a banner year for misogyny. *The [Hamilton] Spectator,* A.15.

Jackson, D. (1990). *Unmasking masculinity: a critical autobiography*. London, England: Unwin Hyman.

Joseph, J., Darnell, S., & Y. Nakamura. (Eds.). (2012). *Race and sport in Canada: Intersecting inequalities*. Toronto, ON: Canadian Scholars' Press.

Katz, J. (2011). Advertising and the construction of violent white masculinity: from BMWs to Bud Light. In G. Dines & J. Humez, (Eds.), *Gender, race and class in media: A critical reader* (pp. 261–269). Thousand Oaks, CA: Sage.

Kaufman, M. (1993). *Cracking the armour: Power, pain and the lives of men.* Toronto, ON: Viking.

Kaufman, M. (2012). The day the white ribbon campaign changed the game: A new direction in working to engage men and boys, In C. J. Greig & W. J. Martino (Eds.), *Canadian men and masculinities: Historical and contemporary perspectives* (pp. 139–158). Toronto, ON: Canadian Scholars' Press.

Kay, B. (2014, September 10). Giving daddy a raw deal. *National Post*, A.10.
Kidd, K. (2004). *Making American boys: Boyology and the feral tale.* London, MN: University of Minnesota Press.
Kimmel, M. S. (1987). *Changing men: New directions in research on men and masculinity*. London, England: Sage Publications.
Kimmel, M. S. (1994). Masculinity as homophobia: Fear, shame, and silence in the construction of gender identity. In H. Brod & M. Kaufman (Eds.), *Theorizing masculinities* (pp. 119–141). London, England: Sage.
Kimmel, M. S. (1996). *Manhood in America: a cultural history*. New York, NY: The Free Press.
Kimmel, M. S. (1999). Masculinity as homophobia: Fear, shame and silence in the construction of gender identity. In J. A. Kuypers (Ed.), *Men and power* (pp. 84–103). Halifax, NS: Fernwood Publishing.
Kimmel, M. (2003). Foreword. In S. Ervo & T. Johansson (Eds.), *Among men: Moulding masculinities* (pp. xi–xiii). Farnham, England: Ashgate.
Kimmel, M. (2013). *Angry white men: American masculinity at the end of an era*. New York, NY: Nation Books.
Kimmel, M. S., & Kaufman, M. (1994). Weekend warriors: The new men's movement (pp. 259–288), In H. Brod & M. Kaufman (Eds.), *Theorizing masculinities* (pp. 259–288). London, England: Sage.
Kingston, A. (2014, November 17). Why no one stopped him. *Maclean's*, 22–29.
Kinsman, G., & Gentile, P. (2010). *The Canadian war on queers: National security as sexual regulation.* Vancouver, BC: UBC Press.
Lenskyj, H. (1986). *Out of bounds: Women, sports and sexuality*. Toronto, ON: Women's Press.
Leonhardt, D. (2014, November 4). The newest partisan divide: Views on youth football. *New York Times*, A.3.
Mac An Ghaill, M. (1994). *The making of men: Masculinities, sexualities and schooling*. Philadelphia, PA: Open University Press.
Mackenzie, H. (2012). *Canada's CEO elite100: The 0.01%.* Ottawa, ON: Canadian Centre for Policy Alternatives.
Mansfield, H. (2006). *Manliness.* London, England: Yale University Press.
Martino, W., & Pallotta-Chiarolli, M. (2003). *So, what's a boy?: Addressing issues of masculinity and schooling.* London, England: Open University Press.
Messner, M. A., & Sabo, D. F. (1994). *Sex, violence and power in sports: Rethinking masculinity*. Freedom, CA: The Crossing Press.
Messner, M. A. (1990). When bodies are weapons: Masculinity and violence in sport. *International Review for the Sociology of Sport, 25*(3), 203–219.
Messner, M. A. (1997). *Politics of masculinities: Men in movements*. London: Sage Publications.
Messner, M. (1998). The limits of the "male sex role": An analysis of the men's liberation and men's rights movements' discourse. *Gender and Society 12*(3), 255–276.
Messner, M., & Cooky, C. (2010). *Gender in televised sports: News and highlights shows, 1989–2009*. Los Angeles, CA: Center for Feminist Research, University of Southern California.
Nichols, J. (1975). *Men's liberation: A new definition of masculinity*. New York, NY: Penguin Books.
Nilan, C. (2013). *Fighting back: The Chris Nilan story*. Toronto, ON: HarperCollins Publishers.
Noble, J. B. (2004). *Masculinities without men?: Female masculinity in twentieth-century fictions*. Vancouver, BC: UBC Press
Overall, C. (1990). Heterosexuality and feminist theory. *Canadian Journal of Philosophy 20*(1), 1–18.
Pollack, W. (1998). *Real boys: Rescuing our sons from the myths of boyhood*. New York, NY: Henry Holt and Company.

Powell, M. (2014, November 8). Machismo trumps safety in NFL culture. *Globe and Mail,*. S.5.
Pronger, B. (1990). *The arena of masculinity: Sports, homosexuality, and the meaning of sex*. Toronto, ON: University of Toronto Press.
Ramsay, C. (Ed.). (2011). *Making it like a man: Canadian masculinities in practice.* Waterloo, ON: Wilfrid Laurier University Press.
Rebick, J. (2005). *Ten thousand roses: The making of a feminist revolution*. Toronto, ON: Penguin Books.
Rotundo, A. (1993). *American manhood: Transformations in masculinity from the revolution to the modern era*. New York, NY: HarperCollins.
Sabo, D. (1994). Pigskin, patriarchy, and pain. In M. A. Messner & D. Sabo (Eds.), *Sex, violence and power in sports: Rethinking masculinity* (pp. 82–88). Freedom, CA: The Crossing Press.
Sanderson, D. (2012). *Crossing the line: The outrageous story of a hockey original.* Toronto, ON: HarperCollins.
Sawyer, J. (1970). On male liberation. *Liberation*, *15*(6–8), 32–33.
Segal, L. (1990). *Slow motion: Changing masculinities, changing men*. New Brunswick, NJ: Rutgers University Press.
Short, D. (2013). *"Don't be so gay!": Queers, bullying, and making schools safe*. Vancouver, BC: UBC Press.
Shuttleworth, R., Wedgewood, N., & Wilson, N. 2012. The dilemma of disabled masculinity. *Men and Masculinities 15*(2), 174–194.
Signal, J. (2014, June 6). The reaction to Lebron's cramps shows we still have some dangerously stupid views on masculinity. Retrieved from http://nymag.com/scienceofus/2014/06/macho-reaction-to-lebrons-cramps-was-stupid.html
Smith, H. (2013). *Men on strike: Why men are boycotting marriage, fatherhood, and the American dream—and why it matters*. New York, NY: Encounter Books.
Staples, R. (1982). *Black masculinity: The black male's role in American society*. San Francisco, CA: Black Scholar Press.
Taylor, P. (2014, September 15). The brutal truth. *Sports Illustrated,* 13–14.
Vasquez, T. (2014). NFL Concussion liability forecast. Analysis Research Planning Corporation. Retrieved from http://profootballconcussions.com/pdf/court_documents/Vasquez-Report-Plaintiffs.pdf
Venturing into the male-strom. (2014, November 15). *National Post,* A.2.
Weis, L. (2008). *The way class works: Readings on school, family, and the economy.* New York, NY, and London, England: Routledge.
West, C., & Zimmerman, D. H. (1987). Doing gender. *Gender & Society 1*(2), 125–151.
Whitmire, R. (2010). *Why boys fail: Saving our sons from an educational system that's leaving them behind.* New York, NY: American Management Association.
Whitson, D., & Gruneau, R. (Eds.). (2006). *Artificial ice: Hockey, culture, and commerce*. Toronto, ON: Broadview Press.
Wilner, B. (2014, September 20). Commissioner has no plans to resign. *Globe and Mail*, S.2.
Zernike, K., & Schweber, N. (2014, October 13). Arrests divide a town that lived for football. *New York Times*, 1.

INTRODUCTION

In 1982, during Question Period in the Canadian House of Commons, New Democratic Member of Parliament Margaret Mitchell asked how the government was planning to respond to a recent report on wife abuse. She was greeted with a chorus of male laughter. As Mitchell later recalled, "The uproarious and outrageous response by many male MPs . . . sent shock waves across the country." (Mitchell, 2007, p. xiii). This infamous incident was a defining moment in the Canadian women's movement. Today, we would be unlikely to hear such an open public dismissal of the issue of woman abuse. Yet well over 30 years later, the statistics do not give us reason to celebrate the end of violence against women. Women today are 5% more likely to be targets of any violence than men are, and 83% of that violence is perpetrated by males. Women are eleven times more likely to be the victims of sexual assault and four times more likely to be the target of stalking behaviour and intimate partner violence. The vast majority of violent offences (84%) were perpetrated by a man who the woman already knew rather than a stranger. Almost half (45%) were her husband or boyfriend (Sinha, 2013). In Canada, violent crime has declined overall, but sexual assault rates have remained stubbornly consistent. Statistics Canada, while reporting these figures, acknowledged that the actual rate of crimes involving male violence against women is likely much higher due to under-reporting (Sinha, 2013, p. 26). If we look at violence against women through an intersectional lens, this is compounded. Immigrant women and women of colour face particular challenges in reporting violence due to language barriers and ethnic and racial prejudices. Women with disabilities have a rate of spousal violence that is nearly double that of the general population (Brownridge, 2009). Indigenous women are estimated to suffer from a frequency of abuse that is 2.5 times than that of the general population (Sinha, 2013, p. 19). For those who do not conform to sexual and gender binaries, such as gays, lesbians, bisexuals, and gender queer and trans people, the relationship to violence is greatly multiplied (Barrett & St. Pierre, 2013, p. 5; Grant et al., 2011, p. 100). How can we understand this disturbing reality, and is there anything that can be done to change it?

IDENTIFYING THE PROBLEM

Starting in the late 1960s, with the growth of the Second Wave of feminism, women gathered to talk about the realities of their lives in what were called "consciousness-raising" groups. They soon discovered that domestic violence, sexual harassment, and rape were not uncommon. The early critics of men's violence were radical feminists who saw patriarchal society as the root cause of women's oppression, and violence against women as the key mechanism by which men exercised power and control over women. The critics worked hard to bring this to public view, which was an uphill battle. Former Liberal Member of Parliament Monique Bégin has noted that the Canadian Royal Commission on the Status of Women, which was formed in 1967 in response to feminist pressure for change, shied away from dealing with issues connected to violence. She later noted that "The commission did not even identify violence towards women—physical, sexual, and psychological—as a feminist issue" (Bégin, 1992, p. 31). Women's access to child care, abortion services, and workplace equality were the concerns that were considered the appropriate mandate of the Commission. Violence was seen as a social or criminal matter that the legal system should address. The number of charges placed and convictions gained in crime victimization data indicated that domestic violence was a problem that was thought to happen only in severely dysfunctional families at the lower end of the socio-economic order. Rape was seen as a rare event that happened in dark alleyways where predators lurked. Sensible middle-class women who stayed away from dangerous places, it was assumed, were not likely to be victimized. The Commission was criticized by many feminists who felt that the final recommendations did not adequately challenge such stereotypes or address questions of violence against women.

Unwilling to simply wait for government action, feminists moved forward to address woman abuse issues directly. In 1972 the first shelters for battered women and rape crisis centres were opened across Canada. They fought hard for government funding, which was eventually granted reluctantly, but their financial viability was precarious (Janovicek, 2007, p. 5). One of the recommendations of the 1970 Commission Report was the establishment of the Canadian Advisory Council on the Status of Women. In 1980, responding to persistent pressure from the women's movement, the Council published a study by Linda MacLeod, *Wife Battering in Canada: The Vicious Cycle*. This was the report that Margaret Mitchell had referred to in Parliament. MacLeod worked closely with battered women's shelters to obtain information about the women who used their services. Extrapolating from their records, she concluded that a conservative estimate of the proportion of Canadian women abused every year by their male partners was 10% (MacLeod, 1980, p. 21). Seven years later an update was published, also relying heavily on data from shelters. McLeod pointed to several advances since her last report, including a new law passed in 1983 that made it illegal for a husband to rape his wife. Formerly consent to sex was considered to be part of marriage. She also noted the ever-increasing number of shelters, which had tripled to 264 across Canada, as well as the corresponding increase in the number of women who used their services (MacLeod, 1987, p. 113).

Two years after this report, on December 6, 1989, a lone man with a legal hunting rifle walked into the École Polytechnique in Montreal, entered an engineering classroom, and ordered the men to leave. He accused the women of being feminists and shot them. By the time he was finished his rampage through the college and turned the gun on himself, 14 women had been killed. This is known as the Montreal Massacre and an intense and, at times, acrimonious national debate opened in its wake. Many discussions focused on gun control and mental illness as the important issues. Feminists felt that it was an example of the systemic abuse of women in a patriarchal society and the reality of male violence against women. The Montreal Massacre is commemorated on December 6 across Canada as an official day of mourning and remembrance (see also Cultural Memory Group, 2006).

Public consternation along with feminist lobbying led to the Canadian Panel on Violence Against Women that was struck in 1991, followed by public hearings across the nation. Its report, *Changing the Landscape: Ending Violence, Achieving Equality* (Marshall & Vaillancourt, 1993) was completed in 1993 and made 494 sweeping recommendations, most of which remain unimplemented today. The report argued that structural inequality was the basis of all forms of violence against women. Despite government endorsement of the report, no actual funds were allocated to implementation (Levin, 1996, p. 348).

However, at the same time as *Changing the Landscape* was released, two other positive initiatives were launched, both by Health Canada. One was the establishment of five regionally based research centres on violence against women that were funded for five years and still operate today. The second initiative was the national Violence Against Women Survey (VAWS), conducted by Holly Johnson of Statistics Canada. Since the results of the standard Canadian crime victimization surveys did not line up with the qualitative information and usage numbers being collected from front-line women's anti-violence organizations, a specialized survey was deemed necessary to get a full picture. The survey was given to a representative sample of 12 300 women across Canada. During the design of the questionnaire, Johnson consulted extensively with feminist anti-violence workers and researchers about how to ask women about male violence and specially trained the female interviewers to ask these sensitive and sometimes difficult questions.

When released, the results of the VAWS shocked Canadians. They revealed that "51 percent of Canadian women have experienced at least one incident of physical or sexual assault since the age of 16 and 10 percent had been victims of violence in the 12-month period preceding the survey" (Johnson, 1996, p. 49). As is the case now, women were three times more likely to be assaulted, either sexually or physically, by men they knew and often were in an intimate partnership with, rather than the imagined stranger in the dark alleyway.

"The VAWS captures almost twice as many incidents as the GSS [Statistics Canada General Social Survey]," Johnson reported, "3 times as many cases of wife assault as are reported to the police, and about 38 *times* as many sexual assaults as police statistics" (Johnson, 1996, pp. 50–51). One of the most striking results was women's fear for their safety when they were alone after dark: 60% of women were either very or somewhat afraid of walking in their own neighbourhoods, 76% of waiting for public transit, 83% walking to their car in a parking garage, and 40% in their own homes. As a result of the prevalence rates determined from this survey, it became possible to also calculate the economic costs to society of violence against women. Economist Tanis Day was the first to do so, conservatively estimating that based on health care alone, the cost was just under $1.54 billion annually to Canadian society (Day, 1995). A second study expanded this to cover other areas of cost and came up with an estimated cost of $4.7 billion for 1993 (Greaves, Hankivsky, & Kingston-Reichers, 1995).

The backlash to the results of the VAWS was unprecedented for a Statistics Canada survey. That it was done only on women was considered an outrage to some, who wondered why there hadn't been such a dedicated survey for men, especially in the case of spousal violence. The involvement of feminist anti-violence experts and agencies in the early stages of the survey's development was seen as inserting political bias into objective research causing the interviewers to ask "leading" questions. "Serious" and "non-serious" offences were viewed as being not sufficiently distinguished and the results about women's fear were criticized for being unnecessarily inflammatory and an attempt to cause panic among women who otherwise felt safe (Johnson, 1995, pp. 148–156). As Anthony Doob, professor of Criminology at the University of Toronto concluded, "Criticisms of the survey—couched often in 'technical' or methodological language—appear to be motivated primarily by political and social attitudes, rather than by concerns about the actual methodology" (Doob, 2002, p. 61). As a result, Statistics Canada now only conducts surveys on domestic violence that include both men and women. What shocked the public, but was no surprise to anti-violence feminists, were the variety of ways in which women experienced violence, and its deep systemic roots.

TYPES OF VIOLENCE AGAINST WOMEN

Sexual Assault

Prior to 1983 when new legislation was introduced, sexual assault was known as "rape" in Canadian law. Feminists pressed for this legal change in order to remove rape from the realm of morality and sex and make it a violent assault upon the person. Rather than see rape as only an act perpetrated by men on women, it was de-gendered so that men could be rape victims too. The intent of this change was to circumvent rape myths that had biased the behaviour of police, prosecutors, and jury members who had drawn on entrenched social attitudes that hinged on whether women meant "no" when they said "no" to sex, or whether they indicated their willingness by other, non-verbal means such as wearing skimpy clothing, drinking in public places, walking alone after dark, or having had sex previously with the assailant. Certain groups of women, such as sex workers and racialized and Indigenous women, were often considered to be more "sexual" and therefore more likely to give consent. If a woman had engaged in previous non-marital sexual relationships, it was often considered as evidence that she was more likely to have consented to sex and the accused might have reasonably assumed that she was willing. Furthermore, any delay in reporting was seen as possibly indicating that a woman had second thoughts about having sex or was seeking revenge on a man who had rejected her. Feminists protested that putting a woman's behaviour and motivation under such intense scrutiny to defend the accused in effect put the victim on trial for the crime (Du Mont & Parnis, 1999, pp. 102–109). In contrast, no one who was the target of theft was questioned about whether their behaviour had invited the crime, or to show physical injuries as proof of resistance. The new law introduced what was called a "rape shield provision" that introduced "limits on the ability of the defence lawyers to ask questions about the sexual history of the complainant . . ." (Balfour & Du Mont, 2012, p. 705). This, however, has not prevented defence lawyers from attempting to establish "inconsistent testimony or a pattern of fabrication by the complainant, thus retrenching rape myths of raped women as liars, mentally unstable, or hysterical" (p. 706).

Women who have been through the legal system and cross–examined by a hostile defence lawyer describe the process as brutal (Doe, 2003). Women who bring complaints to the police are often subjected to very rigorous interrogation to ensure that their case will be strong enough to stand up to questioning in court. This means that the victim must relive the details of a traumatic assault repeatedly throughout the whole legal process, and in front of sometimes unsympathetic and judgmental strangers. Persistent lobbying by feminist activists has resulted in efforts being made to improve the process of collecting forensic evidence immediately following a rape. There are now specially qualified Sexual Assault Nurse Examiners who not only collect evidence, but also provide support and referrals to rape victims. In many hospitals, there are sexual assault treatment centres that also aid women who have been assaulted by their partners and children who have been abused. However, as Johnson and Dawson have observed, "Despite decades of activism by feminist grassroots organizations, researchers, and legal scholars, myths and prejudicial stereotypes about sexually assaulted women persist, sexual assault remains hidden, and victims are routinely blamed and stigmatized" (Johnson & Dawson, 2011, p. 121).

Thus it is not surprising that an estimated nine out of 10 non-spousal sexual assault cases are never reported to the police. Of those who reported in 2011, 44% were unsolved either because the rapist was not identified or the police did not feel that there was sufficient evidence to lay charges (Status of Women Canada, 2013). Of the 56% that went to trial, 42% resulted in convictions (Dauvergne, 2012, p. 25). This means that in over 97% of cases of alleged sexual assault, the accused rapist walks away with few, if any, consequences. This is why many feminists call our society a rape culture that supports the sexual assault of women by not taking the issue or the women who have been subjected to such violence seriously.

A woman known only as Jane Doe has brought many of the problems with how the police and legal system deal with sexual assault to public attention. In August 1986, she was attacked in her own home at night by a serial rapist armed with a knife who had entered through her balcony door. After she reported the incident to the police, she was dismayed to learn that they were well aware of the perpetrator, who had assaulted four other women in her neighbourhood in the same manner. When she asked why she had not been warned, the police said that they did not want to alarm women, cause them to become hysterical, or scare the rapist away. In effect, Jane Doe concluded, she and other women were being used as "bait" in an on-going police investigation. Defying the police, Jane and other women postered their neighbourhood with warnings about the rapist. Ironically, this led to his arrest within 24 hours when his parole officer turned him in. He was charged with sexually assaulting Jane Doe and four other women, and the evidence against him was so overwhelming that he entered a guilty plea in exchange for a sentence of 20 years instead of indefinite incarceration as a Dangerous Sexual Offender. In an unprecedented move, Jane Doe hired her own legal representation and was granted approval by the court to be present at the entire pre-trial hearing. Previously, rape victims were only called in to testify and then required to leave. Jane did not stop there. Supported by the Women's Legal Education and Action Fund, which had been formed in 1985, she sued the Toronto Police. Eleven years later, she was awarded damages of $220 000 in a "judgment that damned the police" and found them responsible for "breaching her right to equal treatment under the law, guaranteed by the *Charter of Rights and Freedoms*; for her right to security of the person, also guaranteed by the *Charter*; and for carelessly failing to warn her that she fit this rapist's pattern of targets" (Sheehy, 2012, p. 25). This judgment made legal history. Jane continues to work to end violence against women and in support of rape victims, but she warns women to be aware of the challenges they will face as complainants in the legal system (Doe, 2003).

By 2008 in Canada, there were at least 134 rape crisis centres serving over 80 000 women every year (Johnson & Dawson, 2011, p. 119). Despite uncertain funding and constant pressure to become more professionalized and less openly feminist, they offer 24-hour crisis lines, individual and group counselling, support through all stages of the rape investigation process from the hospital to court, and are tireless in their public education efforts. They have inspired the organization of Take Back the Night women's marches held the third Friday of September since the late 1970s to protest gender-based violence. Women undertake all of this work on limited and precarious funding.

In 2011 a grass-roots action called SlutWalk developed from the reaction of young women to a Toronto police officer evoking rape myths by suggesting that women should stop dressing like sluts if they didn't want to be victimized (SlutWalk Toronto, 2015). Although he later apologized, young women responded to this with outrage, and in protest held marches where they dressed like "sluts" as an anti-rape protest and to assert their right to wear what they pleased without being assaulted. These sex-positive walks have become an international phenomenon. Some have criticized the march, arguing that "the word slut was beyond rehabilitation, and the movement was critiqued for mounting a spectacle for the male gaze in the choice by (some) participants to dress provocatively" (Teekah et al., 2015, p. 5). Some Black (Hobson, 2015) and Indigenous women and their allies (Walia, 2015) have observed that the SlutWalk ignores the daily realities of violence and racial discrimination women of colour experience in the street. In "An Open Letter From Black Women to the SlutWalk" it was pointed out that, "Although we vehemently support a woman's right to wear whatever she wants anytime, anywhere, within the context of a 'SlutWalk' we don't have the privilege to walk through the streets . . . either half-naked or fully clothed self-identifying as 'sluts,' and think that this will make women safer in our communities . . . ." (Newblackman, 2011). SlutWalk supporters acknowledge and have engaged with these critiques but still contend that the repurposing of the word is empowering and instrumental in returning popular attention to the issue of sexualized violence and victim-blaming (Teekah et al., 2015). The SlutWalk demonstrates the political engagement of a new generation of young feminists with the anti-rape movement.

Intimate Partner Violence

Canadians were very surprised to learn from the VAWS that 51% of Canadian women had been subjected to violence from a man (or men) in their adult lifetime. Almost 30% of the general sample had experienced this at the hands of their spouse and 16% from a date or boyfriend. Most Canadians believed that in a good relationship, a woman would be protected from violence in the safety of her own home. However, stranger violence was the least likely to occur, with only 23% being victimized by men they did not know (Johnson, 1996, p. 51). This was not a shock to workers in shelters and transition houses for battered women, who for years had seen spousal abuse at close hand. Rather than focusing on the violent men, however, many members of the public asked, "Why doesn't she just leave?" Looking at the abusive relationships from the outside, they wondered whether there were mental or emotional weaknesses that prevented women from leaving.

As with sexual assault, feminists objected to this victim-blaming that made women responsible for their own abuse. Researchers and activists sought to find reasons why, after fleeing to shelters in a crisis, many women kept returning to abusive relationships, sometimes a dozen times or more before finally leaving. Based on the qualitative observations of front-line workers, it was thought that battered women were trapped in a "cycle of abuse" that caused "learned helplessness" that caused them to be unable to extract themselves from the violent relationship. The cycle of abuse followed a pattern of a violent incident followed by apologies, a honeymoon period, and then a buildup of tension until the next violent episode exploded. Believing in the contrition of their spouse or boyfriend, women kept returning in the hope that things would be different next time. The constant attacks on a women's self-esteem undermine her ability to act independently for fear of invoking her partner's anger and because she may feel that she truly needs to improve to earn his approval and make her relationship work. This state of "learned helplessness" has also been called the "Battered Woman Syndrome" (BWS) (Walker, 1984/2009). The BWS has been used, first in American and then in Canadian courts, as a defence strategy in cases where women have killed their abusive husbands, especially in cases where the killing occurred during a time when the women were not immediately under direct threat of harm. The first successful case in Canada was that of Angélique Lavalee, who shot her common-law husband in the back of the head after years of abuse. He was walking away from her after just threatening to kill her later that night. In 1990 the Supreme Court of Canada acquitted her of all charges. Despite this victory, the BWS defence has rarely been used, remains controversial, and is difficult to prove in court. Some feminist analysts have objected to the use of the BWS defence because it psychologises women, making psychiatrist expert testimony more important than the woman's own words, and reduces the case to a women's individual state of mental weakness. Absent is an analysis of the political context and the systemic factors that make for an unequal society in which women can be terrorized by abusive partners.

Indeed, researchers have suggested many other reasons that women might stay in abusive relationships other than learned helplessness. One of the aspects of an abusive man's dominance over his partner is restriction and control. In Duluth, Minnesota, a model of the comprehensiveness of this abuse was made by the "Domestic Abuse Intervention Project" called the "Power and Control Wheel" (pictured on page 208). Developed by those with experience working with survivors of intimate partner violence, it graphically describes a range of inter-related controlling behaviours to which abusive partners might expose the women with whom they live. It makes the point that physical violence is only the final stage of a pattern of domination that starts out in small ways and gradually

FIGURE 8.1 Power and Control Wheel

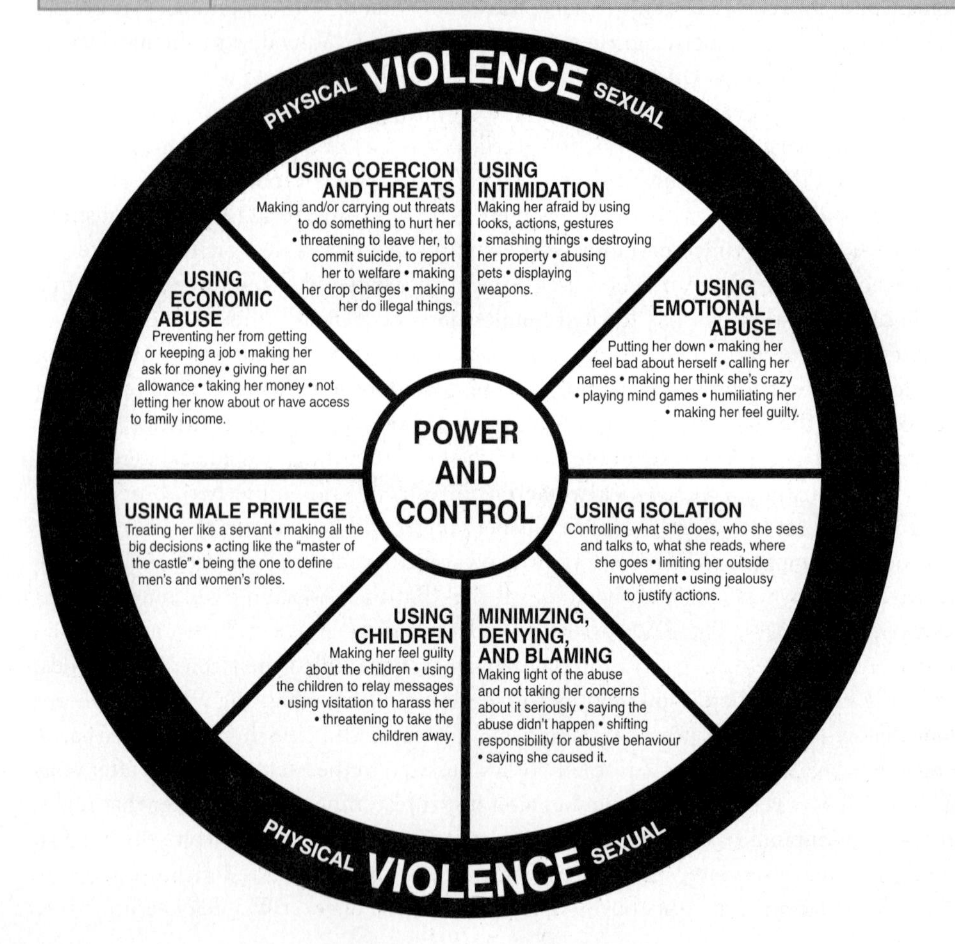

escalates. This includes such behaviours as isolating women; mocking, criticizing, and complaining; exercising male privilege to get his own way; using threats against children, pets, or the woman herself to control her; restricting and monitoring her movements; and withholding money and refusing to allow her to engage in paid work. Relationships with friends and family who could assist a battered woman are often systematically undermined, limiting the options she may have for support. Economic control and refusal to allow a woman to undertake paid work limit her ability to support herself independently.

Compounding this, welfare benefits have been cut and punitive monitoring to detect fraud increased. Thus, "research undertaken by the Ontario Association of Interval and Transition Houses shortly after a 21.6% rate cut was introduced in the mid-90's," showed that, "all of the shelters surveyed reported that women were remaining within, or returning to, abusive relationships as a direct result of the decrease in financial assistance" (Mosher & Evans, 2006, p. 163; see also Mosher et al., 2004). Women are vulnerable to negative reports to welfare agencies from vindictive ex-partners that can result in a loss of benefits. Welfare payments are so meagre that often women are unable to secure adequate housing for themselves and their children. One recent Canadian study has suggested that, "For some abused women, leaving becomes a path to homelessness" (Tutty et al., 2013, p. 1498). As a consequence of their precarious financial state, women can lose custody of their children to an ex-partner or the Children's Aid Society. Rather than face such poverty and the loss of her children, many women are forced to stay in an abusive relationship. Researchers have observed that rather than just being concerned about women's immediate safety in the wake of violence, "Adequate, non-punitive and respectfully bestowed welfare benefits must be understood as a crucial component of Canadian anti-violence policy and strategies" (Mosher & Evans, 2006, p. 162).

However, it became apparent after the VAWS that violence does not just happen to women who are economically disadvantaged. One recent study published by the Canadian Centre for Policy Alternatives, citing Statistics Canada data, asserted that, "70% of the Canadian women who report having experienced spousal violence are working women and 71% have a university or college degree" (McInturff, 2013, p. 5). Much of the information we have about women returning to their abusers is derived from the very valuable data collected by interval and transition houses that shelter abused women. Women who have alternatives might never go to a shelter. Audra Bowlus and Shannon Seitz, further analyzing the data from the 1993 VAWS, determined that the vast majority of women in abusive partnerships divorce their husbands or leave their common-law partners. The VAWS measured spousal violence both during the previous 12 months and over a women's lifetime. Over a lifetime, women who had been subjected to violence from their partners were six times more likely to have divorced or left him. On the basis of this, they challenged the model of learned helplessness that, they argued, was based on a limited, non-representative sample of abused women (Bowlus & Seitz, 2006, pp. 1113–1149). What this shows us is that the answer to "Why doesn't she just leave?" is that she *does* leave—provided that she has the economic means to do so. Women's increased educational attainment and employment is a vital systemic factor in eliminating gender-based intimate partner violence.

A final consideration deterring many women from leaving abusive relationships is that the physical violence may not start or escalate to extreme levels until the time she threatens to end the relationship. While most women leave successfully, in some cases there are increased threats to her or her loved ones' safety when the control of her partner is threatened. Johnson and Dawson, drawing on Statistics Canada data, report that 20% of women have been stalked by their partners or ex-partners. "Women stalked by a partner were more likely to experience multiple forms of stalking . . . than if the stalker was not an intimate partner. Women also faced the greatest risk of stalking by an ex-partner and were more likely than other stalking victims to be intimidated, threatened, grabbed, attacked, or to fear their lives were in danger" (Johnson & Dawson, 2011, p. 68). Indeed, women in Canada are six times more likely to be killed by an ex-spouse than a current spouse (Status of Women Canada, 2013).

It might be expected that women would turn to the police for protection and support in leaving an abusive situation, but in practice only 30% of women experiencing abuse reported police involvement. These were mainly in the most extreme circumstances of physical violence, where women would have had the greatest fear of being seriously injured or killed. In 2009, 15% of abused women obtained a restraining order against their spouses, but fully one third of those were breached (Status of Women Canada, 2013). Restraining orders mainly act as a deterrent, and the police cannot effectively enforce them on an on-going basis.

Persistent lobbying by anti-violence feminists has resulted in the police and the court system implementing a number of measures to address the issue of the safety of women in violent relationships. In the past, police had been reluctant to intervene in family disputes, because such matters were seen as private and not the proper concern of the law. Now they are mandated to respond to such complaints. As with rape myths, there were also misconceptions about domestic violence—that women stayed in such relationships because they wanted to; that they provoked men's violence; or that they were people on the lower level of society who were poor, drug abusers, or alcoholics. Although it is true that alcohol use and lower incomes are often correlated with domestic violence, the most important predictive factor found in research is the attitude of the violent men, specifically their conviction that they have the right to control their partners (Johnson & Dawson, 2011, p. 83). The education of police officers in an effort to dispel outdated attitudes has been given a high priority. In a recent report it was observed that, "In the last 30 years, Canadian jurisdictions have put into place aggressive criminal justice policies to respond to intimate partner violence, including pro-arrest policies, pro-prosecution policies, and specialized domestic violence courts" (Johnson & Fraser, 2011, p. 3). Yet in spite of this, women's rate of reporting intimate partner violence to the police has declined 6% since 2004 (Status of Women Canada, 2013). To the frustration of prosecutors, up to half of women retract their statements accusing their partners of violence when they get to court (Robinson & Cook, 2006, pp. 189–213). These women did not wish their partners to be sent to jail, rather they wanted the police to intervene to stop the violence. If a man goes to jail, the main source of family income may be removed and many women will face financial disaster. For those who leave, the on-going court process provides their ex-partner with further contact and access to information about them. If their abuser gets a light sentence or is found not guilty, he may seek revenge. Ironically, the very policies that mandate that police must charge the abuser may make women less likely to ask for police assistance.

The very high percentage of women who do not call the police (70%) when they are abused indicates that they do not feel that their safety or best interests will be served by doing so. Very often, women from particular racial or ethnic groups have had bad experiences with police and do not trust them. Many of those who did not report when asked, gave as the reason that they were afraid of retaliation, that involving the police would escalate the violence, and many women were ashamed to reveal the problems in their relationships. Some may fear that the Children's Aid Society will remove their children if violence is reported in their home. One quarter of abused women instead turned to social services such as counsellors, psychologists, crisis lines, shelters for battered women, or community centres. In a one-day snapshot survey of shelters across Canada on April 15, 2010, 4646 women were found to be seeking safety from abusive male partners (Status of Women Canada, 2013). Researchers have found that despite the efforts made to improve legal redress for women who have suffered abuse at the hands of their male partners, they remained intimidated by and dissatisfied with the results of police intervention and court proceedings. Police attitudes continued at times to be biased against abused women. In interviews with women who had been through the court system as accusers of their partners, one study found that they were "offered little protection from further violence after their partner completed his sentence. Most of these women continued to fear for the safety of themselves and their children and found little support from the legal-judicial system. . . . All women reported that they would be reluctant to involve the legal-judicial system in future domestic violence cases" (Gillis et al., 2006, 1164).

Gender Symmetry in Intimate Partner Violence? Despite the overwhelming evidence that women are the primary sufferers in abusive relationships, there are some who assert that the truth is that women are just as violent as men. Researcher Murray Straus has dedicated his career to attempting to prove this. In 1972 he developed a tool for measuring violence in interpersonal relationships called the Conflict Tactics Scale (CTS). Using the CTS, he asked men and women how they and their partners deal with conflict in their relationships. Their responses are rated on a scale of severity of violence from less severe forms, which include verbal harassment and name calling; moderately severe, which involve physical violence such as hitting, kicking, and pushing; and the most severe forms, which involve assault with a weapon such as a knife or gun. Straus and others who have used this model find that men and women have nearly equal levels of violence in their intimate relationships. As Johnson and Dawson have observed:

> The CTS has been criticized for failing to provide the context, intentions, or meanings needed to provide accurate interpretations, for equating less severe acts with more violent ones, for equating a single act with chronic on-going violence meant to terrorize, for leaving out sexual assault and violence after separation, for failing to distinguish between offensive and defensive acts, and for ignoring gendered power imbalances in intimate relations and society more generally. (Johnson & Dawson, 2011, pp. 55–56)

For example, a man who consistently terrorizes his wife with threats to harm her or those she loves would be considered equal to a women who yells a single threat in an argument. Similarly, on the CTS throwing a dish is equivalent to threatening with a gun, and shoving away an attacker is rated the same as a man hitting a women in the face with a closed fist. Isolation from family and friends, belittling, and withholding of economic resources are completely ignored by the CTS. Furthermore, research has shown that men tend to minimize and underreport their violence while highlighting what the woman may have done to "provoke" them. Women tend to do the opposite—minimize the violence done to them by men while exaggerating their own actions (Dragiewicz & DeKeseredy, 2012, p. 1012). The result is that every survey using the CTS has shown results with nearly equal amounts of male and female violence in disputes between co-habitating partners. While Straus has responded to criticism by making some modifications to his scale and has expressed concern that "the statistics are likely to be used by misogynists and apologists for male violence" (Strauss, 1997, p. 79), he feels justified in highlighting women's violence. Although he admits that male violence is more of a concern, he argues that women's violence provokes men's, and ending it is a vital component of ending men's violence. This is an example of how domestic violence myths still influence thinking today. In a 2009 article, he stated that feminist academics "have concealed, denied or hidden the evidence," given by studies using the CTS because the message is not acceptable to the front-line anti-violence workers who solely work with abused women (Straus, 2009, p. 560). He argued that this does a disservice to such women because they need to be helped to recognize their problem not only so that they will not expose their children to violence and have better relationships, but also because "it increases the probability of physical attacks by the woman's partner" (p. 563). He denies the feminist position that patriarchy is a vital causative factor in violence against women, and ignores the results of numerous surveys done around the world, which, like the VAWS in Canada, have looked at violence against women in a more complex, systemic manner, and not just in the context of current partner relationships.

The backlash to the VAWS in the mid-1990s was at least partly fuelled by those who cited Straus's work. The result was that the violence against women framework was abandoned by the Canadian government and replaced by a family violence perspective. The next round of data collection was done with the GSS in 1999 and was based on a modified version of the CTS. Unsurprisingly, the results showed far greater gender symmetry in violence that did the VAWS. Over the previous five years, the 1999 GSS found that 8% of women and 7% of men had experienced domestic violence as compared to 12% for women in the 1993 VAWS (Johnson & Dawson, 2011, p. 66). These findings seemed to fly in the face of everything scholars, policy-makers, front-line workers, and activists had been saying for the previous 25 years. Was violence against women decreasing, were women equally as violent as men, or was the design of the survey flawed? Yasmin Jiwani analyzed the results and noted that many of the flaws in the CTS, such as lack of context, the limited view of the types of violence and control women are subjected to, and the conflation of more and less severe forms of violence, had been reproduced. Additionally, the violence women experienced was much more severe:

> Some 65 per cent of the women were assaulted more than once, and 26 per cent reported being assaulted more than 10 times. Forty per cent of women compared to 13 per cent of men reported being physically injured as a result of the violence in the five years preceding the interview and women were five times more likely to require medical attention as a result of the violence. Four out of ten women are afraid for their lives, as compared to one out of ten men. (Jiwani, 2002, p. 68)

By 2012, the results were very similar, with very nearly equal rates of 6% for both men and women. However the same pattern of women experiencing more severe forms of assault, being almost four times more likely to report to police and more likely to suffer from chronic abuse, still held true (Status of Women Canada, 2013). If violence against women in intimate partner relationships is truly decreasing, this is a positive sign, but the idea that there might be parity is inconsistent with what we know from other areas of gender-based violence. As Johnson and Dawson have noted, "Given that there are no other situations in which women and men are equally violent, it would be very surprising indeed if women were violent on par with men in intimate relationships and no others" (Johnson & Dawson, 2011, p. 57).

Despite the assertions that men also suffer from domestic violence, there has yet to be any demand to have shelters established for them. Fortunately, despite government cutbacks and years of uncertain funding, the numbers of shelters for women has continued to grow. In 2010, there were 593 across Canada that had over 46 500 admissions in the previous year. Most of these abused women (60%) had not contacted the police (Burczycka & Cotter, 2011, p. 5). In a study of Canadian women's help-seeking behaviour in response to intimate partner violence, it was found that only 11% went to shelters, although 66% sought out some and often multiple types of formal support. Some contacted counsellors (39%), police or court based services (6%), crisis lines or centres (17.3%), community centres (15.5%), or women's centres (11.2%). Despite the fact that the Canadian government had adopted a comprehensive plan for gender equality in 1995, there has been little fiscal commitment to coordinating and stabilizing this patchwork of services. It is not surprising that most women who have been abused seek less formal channels of support such as family (66.5%), friends or neighbours (66.5%), co-workers (27.8%), and religious or spiritual advisors (11.5%) (Barret & St. Pierre, 2011, p. 57). For those dedicated workers who provide essential crisis support with uncertain funding to those suffering from violent partners, the task can be extremely stressful. Its effects have been called "vicarious trauma" or "compassion fatigue." Stephanie Martin, a Toronto psychologist, has pointed out, "Canadian frontline anti-violence respondents literally bear witness, on a daily basis, to the pain and suffering experienced by the victims of woman abuse." She calls for "anti-violence advocates, agency administrators, and policy-makers to prioritize the welfare of frontline anti-violence responders as an important aspect of our collective effort to eradicate woman abuse in Canada" (Martin, 2006, p. 11).

Dating Violence Less attention has been paid by researchers and activists to dating violence, but all indications are that violence against women in non-spousal intimate relationships is a serious problem as well. In fact it may be more severe than in spousal relationships. Statistics Canada reported in 2011 that unmarried women were 60% more likely to be subjected to violence from their dating partners than women in married or common-law relationships (Sinha, 2013, p. 20). In general, women ages 15 to 34 were most at risk in Canada for all kinds of violence (Sinha, 2013, p. 54; Status of Women Canada, 2013).

In 1992, Walter Dekeseredy and Martin Schwartz surveyed over 3000 randomly selected students in universities across Canada. Overall, 28% of the female participants reported having been sexually abused in the past year, while 11% of the males admitted to abusive behaviour. Since leaving high school, 45.1% of the females had been sexually abused and 35% reported physical violence. In the past year, almost 80% of the young women reported psychological abuse from their dating partner, such as insults, swearing, put-downs, threats, and jealous accusations (Dekeseredy & Schwartz, 1995, p. 62). A 2005 American study of female university students surveyed about previous relationships showed that 47% had experienced physical violence, 22% sexual violence, 57% jealousy, 58% attempts at isolating from family and friends, 54% criticism and insults, 68% monitoring of behaviour by former partners, and 36% stalking combined with physical violence post break-up (Roberts, 2005, pp. 89–114).

Drawing on Statistics Canada data, a researcher from the Canadian Centre for Policy Alternatives reported in 2013 that of the women who have been sexually assaulted in the past 5 years, 29% were students (McIntuff, 2013, p. 5). Clearly this is a significant problem, and colleges and universities across Canada have attempted to grapple with this issue with varying degrees of success. However, they are often reluctant to take aggressive action in individual cases. (For some Canadian examples, see Ikeda & Rosser, 2009/10; Quinlan, et al., 2009/10.) Adding to this is the difficulty many young women experience in recognizing and naming the violence, particularly sexual assault. If they were drinking at the time, they may feel responsible. Giving in to a dating partner's forceful sexual demands may not be recognized as rape. Thus, as we find in general population studies of sexual assault and spousal abuse of women, only a small fraction of such incidents are ever reported (Cleere & Lynn, 2013; Edwards et al, 2014; Sudderth et al., 2009/10).

Sexual Harassment

The types of sexual harassment that women experience vary greatly. In the wake of relationship break-ups, some women are stalked, threatened, or experience violence. This is called criminal harassment and is against the law. Bothersome but still frightening behaviours can include stalking on social media, harassing texts and phone calls, following or showing up in the same public places, and making threats. These may skirt the edges of illegal behaviour, but it is possible to obtain a restraining order to prevent the offender from coming into contact with his target. However, as noted earlier, restraining orders have little practical effect and mainly serve as a deterrent. Of the violent offences that women reported in 2011 to police, 7% were cases of criminal harassment and 13% uttering threats (Sinha, 2013, p. 11). How these percentages relate to the actual incidence of these behaviours is unknown.

Other types of harassment are not addressed by the law, but within the framework of human rights. Each province has a human rights commission that can deal with such complaints. In practice, these tribunals are seldom used. Since the 1970s, sexual harassment of women by men in the workplace has been recognized as a problem for women entering traditionally male-dominated job settings. (For one early Canadian example see Backhouse & Cohen, 1978.) Since 1985, it has been part of the Canadian Labour Code as constituting unacceptable workplace conditions. These behaviours include telling obscene jokes and posting or viewing pornographic images or videos at work, unwanted touching, persistent requests for dates, offering of promotions or favours for providing sex, punitive behaviours for refusing a man's advances, making comments about a woman's body, and spreading sexual rumours. At first dismissed as normal male behaviour, today most large workplaces have zero-tolerance policies and human resource departments to handle complaints. However, the deterrents to women reporting are real, and when they do complain, often the complaint is dismissed or handled privately with no penalty for the perpetrator. Often the woman is the one who suffers a second time from office backlash against her coming forward. In a 2014 report on sexual harassment in federal workplaces, the committee noted that,

> in some workplaces, sexual harassment remains under-reported because it is normalized or trivialized within the workplace culture. . . . The Committee was told that in some workplaces, victims of sexual harassment will not report the situation because they fear that they will not be believed by management or co-workers. Many victims will be concerned about the effect that reporting will have on their reputation, including being labelled as a "troublemaker," losing the trust of co-workers, or being subjected to value judgements. (Le Blanc, 2014, p. 56)

The Committee noted that this negative atmosphere was particularly accentuated when the workplace was a male-dominated one (Le Blanc, 2014, pp. 57–58). Particularly notorious are the military and the legal professions (Gill & Febbraro, 2013; Leskinen et al., 2011). Canada's federal parliament is also a well-known location for sexual harassment, both in Margaret Mitchell's time and today (Ditchburn, 2014). Ironically, having very few complaints filed does not mean that a workplace is harassment-free, but may indicate the opposite. It may be that women are afraid to come forward. A workspace where many complaints are filed may correspondingly indicate a more open and gender-sensitive atmosphere. Experiencing sexual harassment is psychologically traumatic for the victim. It may cause her to become apprehensive and fearful, undermine her confidence in her work, and cause her stress and ill health. This in turn may negatively affect her work performance (Cortina & Berdahl, 2008).

Of course, not all harassing behaviour happens in the workplace. In the VAWS, 89% of the respondents had experienced some form of sexual harassment in their lifetime (Johnson, 1996, p. 70). Women experience harassment in the streets; from landlords, police, and other officials; and in all levels of school. One study of high school students in grades 9 to 11 found that 46% of the girls had experienced sexual harassment (Wolfe & Chiodo, 2008, p. 3).

The unwelcoming atmosphere for women in universities first became known as the Chilly Climate in the 1980s and still persists (Prentice, 2000).

A new sphere for harassment that disproportionately impacts young women is the internet and all forms of social media. Studies of cyberbullying among teens show high results for both genders. One survey of over 2000 high school students in the Toronto region shows that 21% had experienced cyberbullying and 28% had witnessed it (Mishna et al., 2008, pp. 5, 7). Although there was no gendered analysis of the results, elsewhere the authors state that girls are far more likely to experience unwanted sexual comments online (Mishna et al., 2010, p. 365). The multiple means of communication, the speed with which images and gossip can be sent to many people on linked social networking platforms, and the possibility of anonymity make bullying through the internet much easier than face-to-face abuse. The internet security firm McAfee surveyed 2000 11- to 17-year-olds about cyberbullying in two consecutive years in the United Kingdom, finding that in 2013 16% reported cyberbullying compared to 35% in 2014. Similarly, 22% had witnessed cyberbullying in 2013 compared to 40% in 2014. Clearly, this is a growing problem (*The Guardian*, 2014).

Adults also report cyberbullying. Statistics Canada asked questions about internet victimization in the 2009 GSS. About 7% of all ages of adult internet users reported being cyberbullied, but younger adults ages 18 to 24 years had a much higher incidence at 17% (Perreault, 2011, p. 5). Although little systematic research has been carried out on this, some of the worst cases of internet harassment take place in anonymous postings on message boards, on Twitter, or in the responses to blogs. One university law student and feminist blogger wrote about her experiences with online harassment. "When women write about politics or technology, or when they pursue an education in a traditionally male field like law," she observed, "they are reminded of their secondary status through sexualized insults, rape threats, and beauty contests" (Filipovic, 2007, p. 303). One recent example of this was a widely publicized scandal that involved dental students at Dalhousie University, who posted sexually explicit messages about their fellow female classmates on Facebook (Hampson, 2015).

It is this chilly climate that is perhaps one of the most pervasive effects of the harassment of women—whether they are subject to disparaging sexist comments in the office, cat-calling on the street, or gossip and threats on the internet. This feeds into women's fear of violent sexual assault, which, as the VAWS showed, is a factor in their everyday existence. Women are often forced to plan their lives around avoiding situations where they might be at risk (Stanko, 1997). Some feminist scholars have gone so far as to label this "*sexual terrorism* because it is a system by which all males frighten, and by frightening, control and dominate females" (Sheffield, 2007, p. 111).

Violence Against Women and Intersectionality

In the overall statistics on violence against women, the differing experiences of many women are left out of the picture. Kimberlé Crenshaw was the first to point this out in 1991 when she wrote about Black women in America.

> Where systems of race, gender and class domination converge as they do in the experiences of battered women of color, intervention strategies based solely on the experiences of women who do not share the same class or race backgrounds will be of limited help to women who because of race or class face different obstacles. (Crenshaw, 1991, p. 1246)

One Canadian study on help-seeking behaviours of women who have been subjected to intimate partner violence indicated that women of colour faced "unique barriers" to seeking help. "Common deterrents to service utilization" included "a perceived lack of cultural sensitivity and inaccessibility of services, social isolation, distrust of service providers, and lack of specialized services" (Barrett & St. Pierre, 2013, p. 48). When interviewing women who had reported their partners to the police, one study reported that "not one woman of colour reported positive experiences within the legal-judicial system, indicating that racist stereotypes and cultural barriers were in play" (Barrett & St. Pierre, 2013, p. 1163). If all women are seen as potentially inviting sexual assault, women of colour are doubly so. Popular racial stereotypes portray women of other races as "exotic" and more animalistic. They are seen as less reliable witnesses and their testimony is given less weight. They do not fit the image of the stereotypical innocent victim to the police or in court (Pietsch, 2009/10). Very often, they also do not fit the image of the innocent "battered woman" (Goodmark, 2008) or the violence is seen to come from "the pathology of particular cultural traditions" and thus is minimized (Jiwani, 2006, p. 106).

Immigrant women also experience obstacles in seeking help. Researchers who interviewed immigrant women in Toronto found they "faced additional linguistic and cultural barriers that prevented them from contacting the police. They often did not have access to sufficient legal information and were unable to communicate their situations to English-speaking police officers" (Gillis et al., 2006, p. 1158). Many were unfamiliar with Canadian laws and what their rights were. "Some immigrant women believed that involving the police in domestic disputes could risk deportation of themselves and their partner" (Gillis et al., 2006, p. 1152). Immigrant women are also vulnerable to violence from their Canadian employers, since leaving a bad work situation may result in deportation. The live-in-caregiver provision that allows women to enter the country on work visas requires that they continue to be employed to stay in the country.

One particularly vulnerable Canadian group is Aboriginal women. In 2009, the GSS reported that Aboriginal women had a rate of violence that was 2.5 times that of the general population (Sinha, 2013, p. 19). In cases of spousal violence, more were likely to suffer severe injuries than the non-Aboriginal population (59% to 41%) and to fear for their lives (52% to 31%). "According to the 2011 Homicide Survey, between 2001 and 2011, at least 8% of all murdered women aged 15 years of age and older were Aboriginal, double their representation in the Canadian population (4%)" (Status of Women Canada, 2013). These figures do not include the high number of missing Indigenous women whose fate may never be known. In 2005, The Native Women's Association of Canada (NWAC) received $10 million in funding over five years from the federal government to investigate this issue. This was known as the Sisters in Spirit initiative. They developed a database of over

582 cases of missing or murdered Aboriginal women and girls. Most of these disappeared, not from First Nations communities, but from cities (70%) (Native Women's Association of Canada, 2010, p. ii). This information brought condemnation from such international bodies as the United Nations and Amnesty International, which embarrassed the Canadian government (see, for example, Amnesty International, 2009). At the end of the five-year period, the Sisters in Spirit initiative was terminated and the funding and responsibility handed over to the Royal Canadian Mounted Police (RCMP). However, with the addition of nationwide police resources, the RCMP were able to compile a much larger list of 1181 cases of missing and murdered Aboriginal women across Canada from 1980 to 2012. In a report released in 2014, it was admitted that this could even be an underestimate, given mistakes, difficulty in the identification of victims, and under-reporting. These new figures show Aboriginal women were 23% of all female homicides in 2012, more than five times their percentage representation in the population in 2011 (4.3%) (RCMP, 2014). A United Nations report on the situation of Indigenous peoples in Canada released in 2014 called for "a comprehensive, nationwide inquiry into the issue of missing and murdered aboriginal women and girls, organized in consultation with indigenous peoples" (James, 2014, p. 21).

The reasons for the shockingly high prevalence of violence against Indigenous women in Canada are not difficult to understand. The disadvantages experienced by all racialized and immigrant women are compounded in the case of Aboriginal women by a history of colonialism and discrimination. From the 1870s until the late 20th century, the Canadian government promoted a policy of assimilation by removing Aboriginal children from their families and placing them in residential schools where their culture and language was forbidden. Many of the children in these schools were subjected to physical and sexual abuse. The NWAC has called this "cultural genocide" (Native Women's Association of Canada, 2010, p. 8). "These schools had a profound impact on the traditional family, community and educational systems of Aboriginal nations" (Native Women's Association of Canada, 2010, p. 7).

An intersectional approach also reveals the way in which women with disabilities experience violence. This group is often ignored but is extremely vulnerable to violence, very often from those closest to them. Douglas Brownridge, in reviewing the research on women with disabilities in Canada, found that they "tended to be more likely to experience severe forms of violence and/or were more vulnerable to consequences associated with violence" (Brownridge, 2009, p. 256). The 2009 GSS collected information on women with what they called "activity limitations." It was found that although men with disabilities experienced no increase in partner violence, women "experienced rates of spousal violence in the past five years that were nearly double those without limitations" (Sinha, 2013, p. 60). Depending on the disability, it may be extremely difficult for such women to leave abusive situations because of dependency on a caregiver, difficulty in being employed, and low income. There is a severe shortage of services geared to their needs. The Disabled Women's Network of Canada reports that only one in 10 women with disabilities were able to get help at a shelter or transition house because of lack of accessibility. This is usually because of lack of funding to make the necessary renovations or purchase the required services/equipment (Disabled Women's Network of Canada, n.d.).

For those who do not fit comfortably in the stereotypical gender binary, the situation may be even more difficult. Lesbian couples or transsexual women have very few community resources available to them and may not feel welcome at agencies that were founded to support heterosexual women. Further, although scholars such as Janice Ristock have identified lesbian abuse as a significant Canadian problem (Ristock, 2002), research on partner violence in non-heterosexual communities has been sparse. Thus, "it is difficult to draw firm conclusions about the nature and prevalence of IPV [intimate partner violence] in gay, lesbian and bisexual partnerships" (Barrett & St. Pierre, 2013, p. 5). The GSS has recently started to ask questions that have allowed those who are lesbian, gay, or bisexual to identify themselves. In the 2004 GSS, 372 persons identified themselves as gay, lesbian, or bisexual and of these 186 reported current partners and so were asked questions about IPV. Researchers Barrett and St. Pierre reveal that of these, 65 people, or 34.9%, reported emotional or financial abuse and 38, or 20.4% reported physical/sexual abuse from their partners. Of these 38 persons, "38.9% identified as bisexual women, 26.4% identified as gay men, 19.6% identified as lesbian women, and 15.1% identified as bisexual males" (Barrett & St. Pierre, 2013, p. 11). Although this is a small sample, it is nationally representative. Similarly:

> The 2009 GSS indicates that women who self-identified as lesbian or bisexual were significantly more likely than heterosexual women to report violence by a current or previous spouse in the previous five years (20.8% versus 6.1%). . . . It should be noted that the sex of the abusive spouse was not asked; therefore, the prevalence rates for lesbian or bisexual women could include some opposite-sex spouses. (Sinha, 2013, p. 59)

Barrett and St. Pierre note that a 2011 American National Violence Against Women Survey found that bisexual women were most likely to be victimized by their opposite-sex partners, but warn against applying a heteronormative model to these relationships, that is, assuming that their experience is just like that of heterosexual women (Barrett & St. Pierre, 2013, pp. 17–18). The higher rate of violence experienced by bisexual women is not just because they are women in a patriarchal society. It is also because their bisexuality challenges the dominant heterosexual norm. As with other forms of intersectionality, it increases their vulnerability to relationship violence. The same has been observed of transsexual persons. An American survey found that:

> Nineteen percent (19%) of respondents have experienced domestic violence at the hands of a family member because of their transgender identity or gender non-conformity. . . . MTF [male transitioned to female] respondents endured family violence more often (22%) than FTM [female transitioned to male] respondents (15%), while gender non-conforming respondents were victimized more often (21%) than their transgender peers (19%). (Grant et al, 2011, p. 100)

A recent large Canadian internet survey on IPV found that just under 30% of those who did not identify as heterosexual were being abused in current relationships, although further details on their sexual identity were not provided (Wathen et al., 2014, p. 5).

These significant prevalence rates are regrettably not matched by services. Lesbian, bisexual, or trans women may not be "out" to some friends or family or not want to expose this information to strangers. Often they fear that they will be subject to homophobia when they approach the police or social services (Hardesty et al., 2011). If the legal system is a challenge for heterosexual women, it is even more fraught for lesbian, bisexual, or trans women. As with all others who experience the multiple oppressions of race, ethnicity, gender, or ability, IPV is a more difficult and complex problem for them.

Pornography and Prostitution

Pornography and prostitution have been areas of controversy for feminists. Those who consider themselves to be "sex positive" have argued that sexuality of all kinds should be celebrated and not subject to censorship. They point out that human self-expression and especially those areas of sexuality deemed "queer" by the heterosexual majority will be repressed. Pornography is framed more as free speech from this perspective than as a practice (see, for example, Taormino et al., 2013). Similarly, sex-positive feminists refuse to condemn the practice of prostitution and the many ways of selling sex such as by phone, erotic dancing and stripping, live streaming on the internet, videos, massage parlours, escorting, and street prostitution. They are concerned about stereotypes of "easy" women that result in "slut-shaming," which denigrates the work done by women in the sex trade. From a socialist feminist perspective, sex work is labour like any other and deserves to be treated with equal dignity and respect, with good working conditions. However, both pornography and prostitution as they exist now commercially do not meet the standard of good working conditions. Not all sex workers are at the top end of escort service, work in well-run brothels (not legal in Canada), and appear at glittering porn awards ceremonies in Las Vegas. Critics point to the dangers inherent in street-involved prostitution, the fact that many who perform in porn films are poorly paid (usually by the act with no share of the profits) and have increasingly been asked to perform painful acts involving multiple penetration, choking, and verbal and physical abuse.[1] In Canada, there are sex workers who are recruited into prostitution at very young teen ages by exploiters who lure them by a combination of seduction and coercion. This is considered human trafficking by law enforcement agencies (and is also condemned by sex worker advocacy groups) because the girls did not enter sex work of their own volition or for their own profit, in addition to being underage. Almost all of those trafficked for sexual exploitation in Canada are recruited from within our own borders (RCMP, 2010; 2013). A recent study on sex trafficking by Nicole Barrett for the Canadian Women's Foundation points out that no one knows the exact numbers of women who are trafficked in Canada. The illegality, the fact that the underage girls are rarely seen on the streets but are marketed through the internet and work indoors, the reluctance or inability of exploited girls to report their abusers, and the frequent connections with organized crime make it impossible to know the exact numbers. The small number of prosecutions and convictions recorded by the police represent only a tiny fraction of the numbers suggested by qualitative reports (Barrett, 2013).

It is also difficult to distinguish those trafficked from those who entered prostitution on their own initiative. Although a person might be lured or coerced into prostitution from all sectors of Canadian society, those who are poor or Aboriginal are significantly over-represented. Many come from violent homes or have been subjected to sexual abuse (Barrett, 2013, pp. 20–21). The Native Women's Association of Canada, in a comprehensive review of qualitative research based mainly on interviews with front-line workers in service organizations that supported sex workers, concluded that, "Human trafficking for the purposes of sexual exploitation is a serious concern in Canada. The prevalence of aboriginal women and girls who are drawn in through force and many other recruitment strategies represents a dark, discriminatory practice in this country" (Native Women's Association of Canada, 2014, p. 67; see also Sethi, 2007, pp. 37–71; Sikka, 2009).

Sex-positive feminists who acknowledge the violent realities of women's sex work argue that legalization of prostitution will allow it to be better regulated and safer. They point to the models of Australia and New Zealand where women work in legal brothels. Feminists who feel that sex work is inherently exploitative of women and girls prefer what has become known as the Nordic Model adopted in Sweden, Norway, and Iceland that makes the buying of sex illegal, but not the act of selling, and provides state support to assist women leaving sex work. Canada has recently adopted a variant of the Nordic approach that mainly criminalizes the purchasers of sex. Will this approach support women in leaving prostitution or will it expose sex workers to ever more secretive and therefore dangerous situations? Alternatively, should the state endorse the sale of sexual acts by turning pimps into respectable businesspersons? Even with legalization, there could still be an exploited group of sex workers who do not meet the requirements of brothel owners, because of physical appearance, age, race, or ethnicity, and who would be forced to work in unregulated conditions on the streets. Feminists are deeply divided on this issue, and it is clear that there are important arguments on both sides but as yet no ideal solution to the violence that sex workers in Canada experience.

VIOLENCE AGAINST WOMEN INTERNATIONALLY

In this chapter we have focused on the Canadian and sometimes North American realities of violence against women. Domestic violence against women has been recognized as a serious concern and violation of women's human rights by major international bodies such as the World Health Organization (WHO), the United Nations (UN), and Oxfam (Raab, 2012; UN Department of Economic and Social Affairs, 2010; WHO, 2010; 2013). There have been two major international surveys done on violence against women. One was a collaborative effort of the European Institute for Crime Prevention and Control, the United Nations Interregional Crime and Justice Research Institute, in partnership with Statistics Canada's Holly Johnson that took place in eleven countries worldwide from 2002 to 2005 (Johnson et al., 2008). The other was conducted by the WHO in 2000–2003 in ten other countries (Garcia-Moreno et al., 2006; WHO, 2005). Results varied considerably from nation to nation, and even in different regions of the same country. However, one systematic review of all domestic violence prevalence studies worldwide has concluded that the accumulated evidence shows that "violence against women has reached epidemic proportions in many societies" (Alhabib, 2010, p. 369). In a 2014 report on gender, the UN Statistics Division and UN Women reported that an average of 30% of women globally have experienced intimate partner violence in their lifetime (United Nations Statistics Division, UN Women, 2014). If we compare this to the almost identical result from the VAWS, it appears that Canada is consistent with the rest of the world in the amount of violence that women experience.

CONCLUSION: IS IT POSSIBLE TO HAVE A SOCIETY WHERE WOMEN ARE FREE FROM MALE VIOLENCE?

Many feminist activists, researchers, and policy-makers have sought to understand the roots of male violence against women so that effective means can be taken to end it.[2] They have found multiple causes, ranging from personal history, family context, to broad social values and influences. Particularly influential are such factors as witnessing domestic violence as a child or being abused as a child. When the broader society and a boy's peer groups support or trivialize violence, they reinforce it.

Anthropologist Peggy Reeves Sanday has surveyed studies of 95 tribal societies where it was possible to determine the presence of rape, classifying them as rape-prone or rape-free. Of these 47% were classified as free of rape, or rape was a very unusual event. They differed significantly from societies where rape was more prevalent. By far the most important indicator of a rape-prone society was the high value it placed on male dominance and control over women. The sexes were separated in such societies, with the men controlling community wealth and dominating important rituals. The rape-free societies had a much more equal distribution of power between genders and placed a higher value on women's assets, such as fertility. Sanday concluded that since the prevalence of rape is so varied in these tribal societies, it shows that it is not an act that is natural or inevitable in men. Men's violence is dependent on the social and cultural conditions men were socialized in. It follows that if we change the dominant values of a society, we should be able to also reduce or eliminate violence against women (Sanday, 1981). This is not an easy challenge, but it is possible.

Everywhere we look in the media, it seems that almost daily there is a new report of politically motivated kidnappings of girls, rapes and murders of women in both war zones and peaceful communities, gender-based internet attacks, sexual harassment, and popular male entertainment figures accused of being serial sexual assaulters. It may seem as if violence against women is increasing and out of control. However, it is also just as likely that public consciousness and the media have been sensitized to the issue by the hard work of feminists and are reporting events that would have passed unnoticed even a decade ago. What is also encouraging is that many men are now speaking out about male violence and working for positive change.[3] What was previously ignored, seen as shameful and hidden in private is now coming to light, and women are less afraid to speak out about the violence they have experienced. Viewed in this manner, these new public discussions are indicative of real positive change in social values, which bodes well for the future.

Endnotes

1. For critical perspectives on pornography and prostitution see: Gail Dines. (2010). ***Pornland: How Porn has Highjacked Our Sexuality***. Boston, MA: Beacon Press; S. Jeffreys. (2009). ***The Industrial Vagina: The Political Economy of the Global Sex Trade***. New York, NY: Routledge; and M. Tankard Reist and A. Bray (Eds.). (2011). ***Big Porn Inc: Exposing the Harms of the Global Pornography Industry***. North Melbourne, Australia: Spinifex Press.
2. For an overview of this research, see Johnson and Dawson (2011), 13–36.
3. See for example: W. S. Dekeseredy and M. D. Schwartz. (2013). ***Male Peer Support and Violence Against Women.*** Boston, MA: Northeastern University Press; J. Katz. (2006). ***The Macho Paradox: Why Some Men Hurt Women and How All Men Can Help***. Napierville, IL: Sourcebooks; M. Kaufman. (1993). ***Cracking the Armor: Power, Pain, and the Lives of Men***. New York, NY: Viking; M. Kimmel. (2008). ***Guyland: The Perilous World Where Boys Become Men***. New York, NY: Harper Collins.

Discussion Questions

1. How does the intersection of oppressions based on factors such as ability, gender, race, class, ethnicity. and sexual identity affect gender-based violence?
2. What are "rape myths"? How do they disadvantage women of many different backgrounds?
3. What is "slut-shaming"? How have different groups of women responded to this problem?
4. Why do some women stay in violent relationships? What would allow them to leave?
5. What actions have been undertaken by feminists to end violence against women?

Bibliography

Alhabib, S., Nur, U., & Jones, R. (2010). Domestic violence against women: Systematic review of prevalence studies. *Journal of Family Violence*, *25*, 369–382.

Amnesty International. (2009). ***No more stolen sisters: The need for a comprehensive response to discrimination and violence to Indigenous women in Canada.*** London, England: Amnesty International Publications. Retrieved from http://www.amnesty.ca/research/reports/no-more-stolen-sisters-the-need-for-a-comprehensive-response-to-discrimination-and-

Freeman Marshall, P., & Asselin Vaillancourt, M. (Eds.), (1993). ***Changing the Landscape: Ending Violence, Achieving Equality Ending The Final Report of the Canadian Panel on Violence Against Women***. Ottawa, ON: Minister of Supply and Services Canada.

Backhouse, C., & Cohen, L. (1978). ***The secret oppression: Sexual harassment of working women***. Toronto, ON: Macmillan.

Balfour, G., & Du Mont, J. (2012). Confronting restorative justice in neo-liberal times: Legal and rape narratives in conditional sentencing. In E. A. Sheehy (Ed.), ***Sexual Assault in Canada: Law, Legal Practice and Women's Activism*** (pp. 701–724). Ottawa, ON: University of Ottawa Press.

Barrett, B. J., & St. Pierre, M. (2011). Variations in women's help-seeking in response to intimate partner violence: Findings from a Canadian population-based study. ***Violence Against Women***, *17*(1), 57.

Barrett, B. J., & St. Pierre, M. (2013). Intimate partner violence reported by lesbian-, gay-, and bisexual-identified individuals living in Canada: An exploration of within-group variations. *Journal of Gay & Lesbian Social Services*, *25*, 1–23.

Barrett, N. A. (2013). *An assessment of sex trafficking in Canada*. Global Justice Associates commissioned by the Canadian Women's Foundation. Retrieved from http://canadianwomen.org/reports/trafficking

Bégin, M. (1992). The Royal Commission on the Status of Women: Twenty years later. In C. Backhouse & D. H. Flaherty (Eds.), *Challenging times: The women's movement in Canada and the United States* (pp. 21–38). Kingston, ON, and Montreal, QC: McGill-Queen's University Press.

Black Women's Blueprint. (2011, September 23). An open letter from Black women to the SlutWalk, Retrieved from http://newblackman.blogspot.ca/2011/09/open-letter-from-black-women-to.html

Bowlus, A., & Seitz, S. (2006). Domestic violence, employment and divorce. *International Economic Review*, *47*(4), 1113–1149.

Brownridge, D. A. (2009). *Violence against women: Vulnerable populations.* New York, NY: Routledge.

Burczycka, M., & Cotter, A. (2011). *Shelters for abused women in Canada, 2010.* Ottawa, ON: Statistics Canada.

Cleere, C., & Lynn, S. J. (2013). Acknowledged versus unacknowledged sexual assault among college aged women. *Violence Against Women*, *28*(12), 2593–2611.

Cortina, L. M., & Berdahl, J. L. (2008). Sexual harassment in organizations: A decade of research in review. In J. Barling & C. L. Cooper (Eds.), *The Sage Handbook of Organizational Behaviour. Vol. 1: Micro Approaches* (477–481). Los Angeles, CA: Sage.

Crenshaw, K. Williams. (1991). Mapping the margins: Intersectionality, identity politics and violence against women of color. *Stanford Law Review, 43*(6), 1241–1299.

Cultural Memory Group, The. (2006). *Memorials across Canada: Remembering women murdered by men*. Toronto, ON: Sumach Press.

Dauvergne, M. (2012). *Adult Criminal Court Statistics in Canada, 2010/2011*. Ottawa, ON: Statistics Canada.

Day, T. (1995). *The health related costs of violence against women: The tip of the iceberg*. London, ON: The Centre for Research on Violence Against Women and Children, University of Western Ontario.

Dekeseredy, W., & Schwartz, M. D. (1995). *Woman abuse on campus: Results from the Canadian national survey.* Thousand Oaks, CA: Sage Publications.

Disabled Women's Network of Canada. (n.d.). *Women with disabilities and violence*. Retrieved from www.dawncanada.net/issues/issues/fact-sheets-2/violence/

Ditchburn, J. (2014, November 12). MPs approved sexual harassment policy in 2001, it just didn't cover themselves. *The National Post*. Retrieved from http://news.nationalpost.com/2014/11/12/ottawa-mps-approved-sexual-harassment-policy-in-2001-it-just-didnt-cover-themselves/

Doe, J. (2003). *The Story of Jane Doe: A book about rape.* Toronto, ON: Random House.

Doob, A. N. (2012). Understanding the attacks on Statistics Canada's violence against women survey. In K. McKenna & J. Larkin (Eds.), *Violence against women: New Canadian perspectives* (pp. 55–62). Toronto, ON: Inanna Publications.

Dragiewicz, M., & DeKeseredy, W. (2012). Claims about women's non-fatal force in intimate relationships: A contextual view of Canadian research. *Violence Against Women*, *18*(9), 1008–1026.

Du Mont, J., & Parnis, D. (1999). Judging women: The pernicious effects of rape mythology. *Canadian Woman Studies*, *19*(1–2), 102–109.

Edwards, K. M., Probst, D. R., Tansill, E. C., Dixon, K. J., Bennett, S., & Gidycz, C. A. (2014). In their own words: A content-analytic study of college women's resistance to sexual assault. *Journal of Interpersonal Violence*, *29*(14), 2527–2547.

Filipovic, J. (2007). Blogging white female: How internet misogyny parallels 'real-world' harassment. *Yale Journal of Law and Feminism*, *19*(1), 295–303.

Garcia-Moreno, C., Jansen, H. A. F. M., Ellsberg, M., Heise, L., & Watts, C. H. (2006). Prevalence of intimate partner violence: Findings from the WHO multi-country study on women's health and domestic violence. *The Lancet*, *368*(9543), 1260–1269.

Gill, R., & Febbraro, A. (2013). Experiences and perceptions of sexual harassment in the Canadian Forces Combat Arms. *Violence Against Women*, *19*(2), 269–287.

Gillis, J. R., Diamond, S. L., Jebely, P., Brock, D., Orekhovsky, V., Ostovich, E., MacIsaac, K., Sagrati, S., & Mandell, D. (2006). Systemic obstacles to battered women's participation in the judicial system: When will the status quo change? *Violence Against Women*, *12*(12), 1150–1168.

Goodmark, L. (2008). When is a battered woman not a battered woman? When she fights back. *Yale Journal of Law and Feminism*, *20*(1), 75–129.

Grant, J. M., Mottet, L. M., Tanis, J., Harrison, J., Herman, J. L., & Keisling, M. (2011). *Injustice at every turn: A report of the National Transgender Discrimination Survey.* Washington, DC: National Center for Transgender Equality and National Gay and Lesbian Task Force.

Greaves, L., Hankivsky, O., & Kingston-Reichers, J. (1995). *Selected estimates of the costs of violence against women*. London, ON: Centre for Research on Violence Against Women and Children Publication Series, The University of Western Ontario.

Hampson, S. (2015, March 6). How the dentistry-school scandal has let loose a torrent of anger at Dalhousie. *The Globe and Mail*. Retrieved from www.theglobeandmail.com/news/national/education/how-the-dentistry-school-scandal-has-let-loose-a-torrent-of-anger-at-dalhousie/article23344495/

Hardesty, J. L., Oswald, R. F., Khaw, L., & Fonseca, C. (2011). Lesbian/bisexual mothers and intimate partner violence: Help seeking in the context of social and legal vulnerability. *Violence Against Women*, *17*(1), 28–46.

Hobson, J. (2011, September 27). Should Black women oppose the SlutWalk?" *Ms. Magazine*. Retrieved from http://msmagazine.com/blog/2011/09/27/should-black-women-oppose-the-slutwalk/

Ikeda, N., & Rosser, E. (2009/10). *You* be vigilant! Don't rape! *Canadian Woman Studies*, *28*(1), 37–43.

James, A. (2014). *The situation of Indigenous Peoples in Canada*. The United Nations. Retrieved from http://unsr.jamesanaya.org/country-reports/the-situation-of-indigenous-peoples-in-canada

Janovicek, N. (2007). *No place to go: Local histories of the battered women's movement*. Vancouver, BC: UBC Press.

Jiwani, Y. (2002). The 1999 General Social Survey on Spousal Violence: An Analysis. In K. McKenna & J. Larkin (Eds.), *Violence against women: New Canadian perspectives* (pp. 63–72). Toronto, ON: Inanna Publications.

Jiwani, Y. (2006). *Discourses of denial: Mediations of race, gender, and violence.* Vancouver, BC: UBC Press.

Johnson, H. (1995). Response to allegations about the violence against women survey. In M. Valverde, L. MacLeod & K. Johnson (Eds.), *Wife assault and the Canadian criminal justice system: Issues and policies* (pp. 148–156). Toronto, ON: Centre for Criminology, the University of Toronto.

Johnson, H. (1996). *Dangerous domains: Violence against women in Canada*. Scarborough, ON: Nelson Canada.

Johnson, H., & Dawson, M. (2011). *Violence against women in Canada: Research and policy perspectives*. Don Mills, ON: Oxford University Press.

Johnson, H., & Fraser, J. (2011). *Specialized domestic violence courts: do they make women safer? Community report: Phase I*. Ottawa, ON: University of Ottawa. Retrieved from http://endvaw.ca/vawreports

Johnson, H., Ollus, N., & Nevala, S. (2008). *Violence against women: An international perspective*. New York, NY: Springer.

Le Blanc, H. (2014). *A study on sexual harassment in the federal workplace: Report of the Standing Committee on the Status of Women*. Ottawa, ON: House of Commons.

Leskinen, E. A., Cortina, L. M., & Kabat, D. B. (2011). Gender harassment: broadening our understanding of sex-based harassment at work. *Law and Human Behavior*, *35*(1), 25–39.

Levin, A. (1996). Violence against women. In J. Brody (Ed.), *Women and Canadian Public Policy*. Toronto, ON: Harcourt, Brace & Co.

MacLeod, L. (1980). *Wife battering in Canada: The vicious cycle*. Ottawa, ON: Canadian Advisory Council on the Status of Women.

Martin, S. (2006). Bearing Witness: Experiences of Frontline Anti-Violence Responders. *Canadian Woman Studies*, *25*(1/2), 11–15.

McInturff, K. (2013). *The gap in the gender gap: Violence against women in Canada.* Ottawa, ON: Canadian Centre for Policy Alternatives.

Mishna, F., Cook, C., Gadalla, T., Daciuk, J., & Solomon, S. (2010). Cyber bullying behaviors among middle and high school students. *American Journal of Orthopsychiatry 80*(3), 362–364.

Mishna, F., MacFadden, R., Gadalla, T., Daciuk, J., Solomon, S., & Cook, C. (2008). Cyber bullying survey: School summary report, **5**, 7. Retrieved from https://web.archive.org/web/20150213165957/http://www.governmentevents.ca/ypo2008/presentations/634.pdf

Mitchell, M. (2007). *No laughing matter: Adventure, activism & politics*. Vancouver, BC: Granville Island Publishing.

Mosher, J. (2013). *Measuring violence against women: Statistical trends—intimate partner and spousal violence*. Ottawa, ON: Status of Women Canada. Retrieved from www.swc-cfc.gc.ca/initiatives/vaw-vff/kf-pc-eng.html

Mosher, J., & Evans, P. (2006). Welfare policy: A critical site of struggle for women's safety. *Canadian Woman Studies*, *25*(1/2), 162–166.

Mosher, J., Evans, P., Little, M., Morrow, E., Boulding, J. & Van der Plats, N. (2004). *Walking on eggshells: Abused women's experiences of Ontario's welfare system*. Toronto, ON: Woman and Abuse Welfare Research Project. Retrieved from www.cwhn.ca/en/node/24631

Native Women's Association of Canada. (2010). *What their stories tell us: Research findings from the Sisters in Spirit Initiative.* Ottawa, ON: Native Women's Association of Canada. Retrieved from www.nwac.ca/wp-content/uploads/2015/05/2010_What_Their_Stories_Tell_Us_Research_Findings_SIS_Initiative.pdf

Number of children who are victims of cyberbullying doubles in a year. *The Guardian*. (2014, November 14). Retrieved from www.theguardian.com/society/2014/nov/14/35pc-children-teenagers-victims-cyberbullying-fears-grooming-tinder-snapchat

Perreault, S. (2011/2013). Self-reported internet victimization in Canada, 2009. Ottawa, ON: Statistics Canada. Retrieved from http://statcan.gc.ca/pub/85-002-x/2011001/article/11530-eng.htm

Pietsch, N. (2009/10). 'I'm not that kind of girl': White femininity the other, and the legal/social sanctioning of sexual violence against racialized women. *Canadian Woman Studies*, *28*(1), 136–140.

Power and Control Wheel, Domestic Abuse Intervention Project

Prentice, S. (2000). The conceptual politics of chilly climate controversies. *Gender and Education*, *12*(2), 195–207.

Quinlan, E., Clarke, A., & Horsely, J. (2009/10). Countering the institutional responses to sexualized violence on university campuses. *Canadian Woman Studies*, *28*(1), 46–55.

Raab, M. (2012). *Ending violence against women: An Oxfam guide*. Oxford, England: Oxfam International.

Ristock, J. (2002). *No more secrets: Violence in lesbian relationships*. New York, NY: Routledge.

Roberts, K. A. (2005). Women's experience of violence during stalking by former romantic partners. *Violence Against Women*, *11*(1), 89–114.

Robinson, A., & Cook, D. (2006). Understanding victim retraction in cases of domestic violence: specialist courts, government policy, and victim-centred justice. *Contemporary Justice Review*, *9*(2), 189–213.

Royal Canadian Mounted Police. (2010). *Frequently asked questions on human trafficking*. Retrieved from www.rcmp-grc.gc.ca/ht-tp/q-a-trafficking-traite-eng.htm#q9

Royal Canadian Mounted Police. (2013a). *Domestic human trafficking for sexual exploitation in Canada*. 2013. Retrieved from www.rcmp-grc.gc.ca/ht-tp/publications/2013/proj-safekeeping-eng.htm

Royal Canadian Mounted Police. (2013b). *Human trafficking in Canada: A threat assessment*. Retrieved from www.rcmp-grc.gc.ca/pubs/ht-tp/htta-tpem-eng.htm

Royal Canadian Mounted Police. (2014). *Missing and murdered Aboriginal women: A national operational overview*. Ottawa, ON: The Royal Canadian Mounted Police. Retrieved from www.rcmp-grc.gc.ca/pubs/abo-aut/mmaw-fada-eng.htm

Sanday, P. Reeves. (1981). The socio-cultural context of rape: a cross-cultural study. *Journal of Social Issues*, *37*, 9–27.

Sheehy, E. A. (2012). The victories of Jane Doe. In E. A. Sheehy (Ed.), Sexual assault in Canada: Law, legal practice and women's activism (pp. 23–38). Ottawa: University of Ottawa Press.

Sheffield, C. L. (2007). Sexual terrorism. In L. L. O'Toole & J. R. Schiffman (Eds.), *Gender violence: Interdisciplinary perspectives* (pp. 111–130). New York, NY: New York University Press.

Sinha, M. (Ed.). (2013). *Measuring violence against women: Statistical trends (2012).* Ottawa, ON: Statistics Canada.

SlutWalk Toronto, 2015. Retrieved from www.slutwalktoronto.com/about/how

Stanko, E. A. (1997). Ordinary fear: Women, violence and personal safety. In P. B. Bart & E. G. Moran (Eds.), *Violence Against Women: The Bloody Footprints* (pp. 155–164.). Newberry Park, CA: Sage.

Status of Women Canada. (2013). Measuring violence against women: Statistical trends. Ottawa: Status of Women Canada. Retrieved from www.swc-cfc.gc.ca/initiatives/vaw-vff/kf-pc-eng.html

Straus, M. A. (1993). Physical assaults by wives: A major social problem. In R. J. Gelles & D. R. Loseke (Eds.), *Current controversies on family violence* (pp. 67–87). Newbury Park, CA: Sage Publications.

Straus, M. A. (2009). Current controversies and prevalence concerning female offenders of intimate partner violence: Why the overwhelming evidence on partner physical violence by women has not been perceived and is often denied. *Journal of Aggression, Maltreatment & Trauma*, *18*, 552–571.

Sudderth, L. K., Leisring, P. A., & Bronson, E. F. (2009/10). If they don't tell us. it never happened: Disclosure of experiences of intimate violence on a college campus. *Canadian Woman Studies*, *28*(1), 56–97.

Taormino, T., Parreñas Shimizu, C., Penley, C., & Young, M. (Eds.). (2013). *The feminist porn book: The politics of producing pleasure*. New York, NY: The Feminist Press.

Teekah, A., Scholz, E. J., Friedmanm, M., & O'Reilly, A. (Eds.). (2015). *This is what a feminist slut looks like: Perspectives on the SlutWalk movement*. Bradford, ON: Demeter Press.

Tutty, L. M., Ogden, C., Giurgiu, B., & Weaver-Dunlop, G. (2013). I built my house of hope: Abused women and pathways into homelessness. *Violence Against Women*, *19*(12), 1498–1517.

United Nations Statistics Division, UN Women. (2014). *Millenium development goals gender chart 2014.* New York, NY: The United Nations. Retrieved from www.unwomen.org/en/digital-library/publications/2014/3/mdgs-gender-chart-2014

United Nations, Department of Economic and Social Affairs. (2010). Violence against women. In *The World's Women 2010: Trends and Statistics* (pp. 127–139). New York, NY: The United Nations.

Walia, H. (2011, May 19). Slutwalk—To march or not to march. Racialiscious, Retrieved from www.racialicious.com/2011/05/19/slutwalk-%E2%80%93-to-march-or-not-to-march/

Walker, L. (1984/2009). *The battered woman syndrome* (3rd ed.). New York, NY: Springer.

Wathen, C. N., MacGregor, J. C. D., MacQuarrie, B. J. with the Canadian Labour Congress. (2014). *Can work be safe, when home isn't? Initial findings of a pan-Canadian survey on domestic violence and the workplace*. London, ON: Centre for Research & Education on Violence Against Women and Children. Retrieved from www.learningtoendabuse.ca/domestic-violence-work-report-release

Wolfe, D. A., & Chiodo, D. (2008). *Sexual harassment and related behaviours reported among youth from grade 9 to grade 11*. Toronto, ON: Centre for Addiction and Mental Health.

World Health Organization. (2005). *WHO multi-country study on women's health and domestic violence against women: Summary report of initial results on prevalence, health outcomes and women's responses*. Geneva, Switzerland: World Health Organization.

World Health Organization/London School of Hygiene and Tropical Medicine. (2010). *Preventing intimate partner and sexual violence against women: Taking action and generating evidence*. Geneva, Switzerland: World Health Organization.

World Health Organization/London School of Hygiene and Tropical Medicine/South African Medical Research Council. (2013). *Global and regional estimates of violence against women: Prevalence and health effects of intimate partner violence and nonpartner sexual violence.* Geneva, Switzerland: World Health Organization.

Chapter 9

Challenging Old Age: Women's Next Revolution

Nancy Mandell and Ann Duffy

FEMINISM AND AGEISM

Will 21st century feminism successfully challenge ageism? Currently, most feminist discussions of work, productivity, intimacy, body image, cultural images, and political involvement remain based on taken-for-granted notions of age-appropriate behaviour and feelings. Feminism too routinely continues to reflect society's revulsion and disgust for the elderly, shunning their aging bodies, their infirmities, and their issues. Rather than valuing their experiences as some cultures do, in North America we discount and dismiss the elderly. In turn, the elderly come to feel shame about being old, attempting to hide aging through a variety of techniques of self-management aimed at projecting health, fitness, and vitality. So unremitting is the negativity associated with being old that even young feminists will do almost anything to avoid it (Gibson, 1996, p. 434). However, recent work in critical feminist gerontology suggests the possibilities of significantly more affirmative approaches to women's aging (Freixas, Luque, & Reina, 2012).

Coined in 1975 by Robert Butler, ageism refers to:

> a process of systematic stereotyping and discrimination against older people because they are old, just as racism and sexism accomplish this with skin color and gender. Old people are categorized as senile, rigid in thought and manner, old fashioned in morality and skills . . . Ageism allows the younger generation to see old people as different from themselves, thus they subtly cease to identify with their elders as human beings. (Butler, 1975, p. 12)

Feminists have long been aware of ageism in their ranks. Barbara Macdonald, an American radical feminist of the second wave, first identified the problem of ageism in feminism. During a "Take Back the Night" march to end violence against women, one of the young feminist activists organizing the event asked Macdonald if she would be able to keep up with the other marchers. Enraged, Macdonald later reflected on her anger and concluded that for years she had put up with discrimination because she was a woman, only to find she now had to put up with discrimination from other women because she was old (Macdonald & Rich, 1991).

Feminists contribute to ageism by perpetuating a false dichotomy between the young and the old. A 20-year-old woman is frequently described as energetic, vigorous, strong, and resourceful while a 60-year-old woman is more likely to be characterized as tired, weak, feeble, and ineffective. The former describes qualities ascribed to the powerful while the latter are those traits associated with the powerless. Given that the most sought-after and desirable women are those between ages 25 and 35, the farther we drift along the life course from this standard, the less desirable we become as women. Look at who makes the red carpet on movie, television, and music award nights and you quickly see the preference for youth or, at least, a youthful facsimile (Freixas, et al., 2012, p. 54).

By seeing young/old as binary opposites, we see how the young get their meaning and power from what they are not, namely old (Bennet & Gaines, 2010). It is also easy to see why young women often side with patriarchy and male privilege since both of these structures imbue youth with feelings of power: a fleeting, but intoxicating, feeling and status that lasts as long as women remain literally young.

As women begin to approach the age of 40, the first twinges of anxiety often emerge and age management techniques take hold of many women's time and resources. By 50, women have begun to see themselves as "mature." By 60, women know they are being socially defined as the "young old" in contrast to the "old" (75 to 90) and the "frail elderly" (over 90).

Attempts to avoid ageism are generally futile. Young or old, the mandate for women is to remain small and subjugated. The belittling term "little" is applied from their earliest years as "little girls" until their oldest years as "little old ladies" (Reinharz, 1997, p. 84). Gender-specific discriminatory attitudes and behaviours are always present, even if young women feel momentarily powerful.

In this chapter we look at how ageism structures women's paid and unpaid work and their embodiment of age. Feminism seeks to increase women's involvement in societal decision-making, empower women, recognize their intrinsic value, increase their self-esteem and quality of life, and protect their right to equal treatment. Ageism has made it difficult for all women to achieve these goals. Women can begin to confront ageism by unlearning their own biases and addressing the absence of age in so much feminist analysis (Mandell, Wilson, & Duffy, 2008; Ray, 2006).

THEORIZING AGE—FEMINIST POLITICAL ECONOMY PERSPECTIVES

Until recently, feminists have neglected age relations just as gerontologists have tended to neglect both gender and feminism. If feminism is a political orientation designed to "intervene in and transform" power inequities between men and women (Hollows, 2000), then feminist age studies are a form of research and activism that similarly addresses the unequal power relations between age groups as constructed around gender. As Ruth Ray (2006) notes, feminist gerontologists study what aging looks like through a gender lens that is sensitive to power relations in order to advance knowledge and to promote social justice in the material world.

For feminists, age is a form of diversity that remains interconnected to, constitutive of, and implicated in all other forms of inequality. Using intersectionality theory (Cho, Crenshaw, & McCall, 2013), feminists pay attention to the complex relationships among social differences that socially, economically, and politically marginalize women. As Kathleen Woodward (1999) says, differences are produced by discursive formations, social practices, and material conditions. Focusing on intersections allows us to see the conjunction of old and young women's issues as articulated, for example, in material conditions such as wages, housing, and incarceration rates.

A feminist political economy perspective—our feminist "standpoint" (Armstrong, 2013)—focuses on how the material and social conditions of aging people are shaped by their positions in the socio-economic structure. This means that age, like social class, race, gender, sexuality, and other primary markers of social difference, is socially and materially constructed. For example, one significant expression of aging women's unpaid work is the concerted efforts to construct and maintain an appropriate personal front by drawing on the services and solutions provided by the consumer market (in everything from cosmetics to exercise programs) (Liechty, 2012). This work is framed by factors other than age, such as social class. Typically, major inequalities in the distribution of power, income, and property affect people's access to resources in later life, including health and body maintenance, income, assets, and access to informal and formal care (Seabrook & Avison, 2012). A feminist political economy of aging describes the role of the economy (including the consumer economy) and the state in establishing interlocking systems of domination that privilege some groups over others by structuring their access to material resources. Calasanti and Zajicek (1993) substitute the term "paradigm of domination" for the term "patriarchy" to reflect the interlocking system of oppression formed around the complex intersections of age, race, class, and gender in particular.

The state, through its social policies and ideological commitments, props up ageism. For example, pension and retirement income systems, as well as social welfare benefits and entitlements, reflect the structure and culture of advantage/disadvantage as enacted through class, race/ethnicity, gender, and age relations. Through these processes, the state promotes and reproduces the dominant institutions that render many older women vulnerable and dependent throughout their life course (McDaniel & Rozanova, 2011). The current historical context adds a crisis ideology—the notion that "greedy geezers" are going to "bankrupt" the Canadian economy—that, in turn, helps perpetuate ageism (Altman, 2014), as do economic globalization and neo-liberal ideology, which frame the actions of the state in relation to the family and the market (Estes, 2003; Philipson, 2006; Stanford, 2014). Currently these realities tend to be obscured by the hegemonic ideology of individualism—the dominant belief that individuals are and should be wholly responsible for their fate.

According to feminist political economists, there are three central processes—production, reproduction, and distribution—that shape individual life experiences. For example, the paid work you do, the amount of money you are paid, the security or insecurity of the position, and the ability to save for retirement are all features of an individual's relationship to the economy, which shapes your current and future life (Seabrook & Avison, 2012). Although Canadian feminists expanded definitions of productive work to include unpaid economic activity such as consumption work, care work, volunteerism, and domestic labour, paid labour continues to be the most valued and socially recognized form of labour (Pupo & Thomas, 2009).

Reproduction refers to the unpaid work through which life is maintained both daily and intergenerationally, including how children are socialized, how partners and the elderly are cared for, how the household is maintained and presented, and how sexual intimacy takes place. Reproduction includes, then, both the day-to-day social reproduction of dependents (children, parents, partners, friends, relatives) and the biological reproduction of children. It includes the work of producing Canadians as educated, healthy, knowledgeable, and productive citizens (Estes, 2003). Distribution refers to how services are generated and rendered: Who does what for whom?

Feminists have long pointed out that women typically perform much of this social reproductive work (care work, domestic labour, elder care) without pay, and, often, even without acknowledgement. Yet, it consumes a large portion of women's daily lives and cuts into the time they can spend earning money, accumulating pension benefits, and pursuing leisure. Often those women not in the paid workforce, despite their care work, are considered to be dependent because paid workers are the socially accepted norm of productivity. Those women under 19 and over 65 are considered to be "dependents" and thus "burdens." Interestingly, children are "light" burdens while the elderly feel "heavy," descriptions that reveal how dependence is socially constructed.

Feminists have also maintained that this privileging of paid, productive work over unpaid, reproductive work spills over into cultural ideologies and personal relationships. For example, we tend to treat social reproductive work as private matters of the household even though we recognize that it is essential to making families work. In this context, managing caregivers for senior family members or locating and liaising with seniors' residences is seen as private. In Canada, we increasingly see senior migrants moving countries in order to provide care for their adult children and grandchildren. Global domestic care chains (Hochschild, 2012) increasingly consist of old women who disrupt traditional retirement patterns to move home and country in order to provide care for others.

The fact of senior women providing essential care work for families reminds us that it is not the mere existence of reproduction and production that inevitably leads to social inequality, but rather the ways in which these functions are taken up. These profound shifts in how women are spending their senior years reminds us that feminists need to rethink traditional understandings of productivity and deconstruct outdated notions of dependency. As age, gender, and ethnicity intersect with globalization and migration, women's senior experiences are being reshaped in previously unimagined ways (Zhou, 2012).

AGING AND POVERTY

Throughout their lives, women, as a group, have greater risk of experiencing poverty than men. Higher poverty among older women reflects structural inequities experienced throughout the life course: women's lower lifetime earnings; their family and care work responsibilities; the changing nature of the labour force, and the likelihood that women will spend more time than men alone in old age. Within these overall patterns, particular senior women—immigrant women, women with disabilities, single mothers, and Indigenous women—are at greatest risk (Murphy, Zhang, & Dionne, 2012; Preston et al., 2014).

The immediate link between the risk of poverty and gender is the fact that women are less likely than men to be employed on a full-time, full-year basis throughout their working lives. Women frequently manage care work for children and other family members by taking part-time employment or by taking work interruptions. However, even full-time women workers earn a full 19% less than comparable men (Conference Board of Canada, 2013b). This pattern is reflected, for example, in the fact that licensed practical nurses, 90% of whom are women, earn a median $38 261 yearly while television service and maintenance technicians, 97% male and with comparable skill and educational assets, earn on average $51 030 (Goar, 2014; *Toronto Star*, 2014, p. A16). Higher educational credentials result in higher lifetime earnings for women, but women with university degrees still earn somewhat less than men with a university degree (Statistics Canada, 2010). Even though almost one-third of women in dual-earner households earn more than their male partners, women in general still contribute less money than male partners to their two-income households (Statistics Canada, 2010). Of course, women's "in-kind" or unpaid contribution to propping up families and partnerships are inestimable and essential.

These employment patterns and inequities obviously affect senior women's economic well-being (Turcotte & Schellenberg, 2007). Into the early 2000s, poverty among seniors, as a result of new, effective support programs for seniors, was dramatically reduced. By 1995 it had plummeted to 3.9%. However, since that time poverty among older Canadians has been slowly increasing, reaching 12.3% in 2010 (Conference Board of Canada, 2013a). Indeed, while old age poverty fell in 20 OECD countries from 2007 and 2010, it grew in Canada by about 2 percentage points. Within these patterns, elderly women remain at greater jeopardy of being poor (OECD, 2013). Escaping poverty generally requires having a male partner; widowhood and, in particular, divorce often translate into economic distress. Not surprisingly, almost 60% of the 160 000 seniors who fell into poverty between 2006 and 2010 were women (Citizens for Public Justice, 2012; Conference Board of Canada, 2013a; Turcotte 2014).

Reflecting this connection among age, single status, and poverty, research indicates that older widows experience a steady decline in their median family income in the five years after the loss of their husband (more than 15% lower) while men's income rises in the five years after their wives' deaths (5.8% higher). Similarly, single and divorced women experience a drop in income as they age compared to their married, attached female counterparts. Since more than 20% of women in their late 60s are widowed, and by age 75, widows outnumber married women, most women in Canada will face this income decline as they age (Burkhauser, et al., 2004; LaRochelle-Côté, Picot, & Myles, 2010).

This pattern is also confirmed by Statistics Canada reports. Women who remained married at age 78 to 80 had a median income that was 83% of their family income at age 54 to 56. In contrast, women widowed after age 55 saw their income drop to 79% and among women divorced or separated the drop was to 73%. Among women living at the top of the family income distribution in Canada, the impact of becoming unattached was particularly marked, with divorced women seeing their income level drop to 53% over the course of 25 years (Statistics Canada, 2012a). Most recently, with improvements in male seniors' health, there has been an overall decline in the proportion of widows in the elderly population. However, the sheer numbers of widows and duration of widowhood is increasing (Martin-Matthews, 2011, p. 340).

This prospect of poverty for senior women must be further contextualized in terms of the dramatic demographic and inequality shifts facing Canada. First, seniors, male and female, make up a growing portion of the Canadian population. For example, while centenarians were once a social oddity, by 2011 there were 4870 women and 955 men 100 and over and analysts predict that seniors 65 and older will comprise one-quarter of Canadians by 2061 (Statistics Canada, 2014a; Statistics Canada 2012c). Second, rates of divorce are dramatically increasing among seniors. From 1981 to 2011 the proportion of seniors who were divorced or separated increased from 4% to 8% and approximately one-fifth of future seniors (currently ages 55 to 64) are divorced or separated (Bazel & Mintz, 2014, p. 6; Milan, Wong, & Vezina, 2014, p. 1). Third, this growing economic precarity of Canadian senior women is occurring in the middle of dramatically increasing economic inequality.

Alarming reports from the Conference Board of Canada (2013c), the Broadbent Institute (2014), and political-economic analysts (Banting & Myles, 2013; Gill et al., 2014; Klein, 2014; Osberg, 2008) stress the rising income inequality gap in Canada across all age cohorts. Rather than declining over the past 20 years, Statistics Canada data from the Survey of Financial Security (SFS) show that income inequality has risen, with the top 10% of Canadians in 2012 now controlling 47.9% of all the wealth in Canada while the bottom 50% of Canadians together own less than 6% of all the wealth in Canada (Broadbent, 2014). Wealth is increasingly concentrated and more and more unequally distributed. Taken together, the top 20% of Canadians control 67.4% of all Canadian wealth. Put another way, the poorest 20% of Canadians had a net worth of $11 000 in 2010 while the poorest 10% had a median net worth of –$5,100, meaning they owed more in debt than they owned in assets. Rather than democratizing wealth, globalization has exacerbated inequality around the globe (Conference Board of Canada, 2013c).

In the current context, with its dramatic decline in defined benefit pensions and rapid growth in insecure employment patterns, it seems likely that growing numbers of Canadians will struggle to save enough money for their retirement. Although women's improved education and increased participation in paid employment improve their retirement prospects, significant gender differences persist (Drolet & Morissette, 2014). Most notably, women are more likely than men to head the growing numbers of single-parent families and many of these families struggle with low income (Milan, et al., 2014). Further, women, more than their male counterparts, are likely to spend a considerable portion of their senior years alone (reflecting differences in male/female longevity along with marital age patterns). Inadequate pension coverage, economic struggles during prime working years, and economic self-reliance in old age all translate into the increased risk of poverty.

Today, the longer and more intense commitment of young women to paid employment does not negate these troubling prospects. Income reports paint an alarming portrait of severe income inequality between those ages 25 to 35 compared with those ages 55 and over. Using Canada Revenue Agency tax data from 1984 to 2010, the Conference Board of Canada compared the relative employment income of older and younger five-year age cohorts for individuals, couples, and between genders. The results clearly indicate that the incomes of younger Canadians are significantly lower than those of young workers 30 years ago. These findings have important implications for social cohesion, the future growth of the Canadian economy, and, inevitably, future retirement scenarios for younger workers (Gill, Knowles, & Stewart-Patterson, 2014).

As a result, young women today face two significant challenges: not only the old problem of balancing work and family life but also the new concern about making a decent living in a structurally adjusted workplace characterized by depressed wages and employment insecurity. The rise of the precarious labour market with more part-time, temporary, and contract jobs has made it difficult to find secure, well-paying jobs with pensions and benefits, despite increased educational qualifications (Uppal & LaRochelle-Côté, 2014a). Furthermore, employed professional women continue to remain ghettoized in occupations—notably nursing and teaching—blighted by cutbacks and reduced hiring (Uppal & LaRochelle-Côté, 2014b).

OTHER UNATTACHED WOMEN

The connections among gender, being alone, and poverty have only recently received detailed research attention. In this context, consideration of the realities of aging for unattached lesbians and transgendered women is in its infancy. Preliminary investigations do suggest that lesbians (and gay men) are more likely to be single, to live alone, and to be childless in their senior years. Whether or not families (of choice) and friendship networks are able provide a viable alternative social support system for older lesbians remains unclear (Gabrielson, 2011; Gabrielson, Holston, Dyck, 2014; McGovern, 2014). However, extensive past research does suggest that older women who are "alone" are much more likely to be economically marginalized. This prospect is reflected in recent studies. The MetLife survey of lesbian and gay baby boomers—those born between 1945 and 1964—reported that lesbians' greatest retirement fear was outliving their income as they age while gay men's greatest fear is becoming sick or disabled and dependent on others (MetLife Mature Market Institute, 2010). Until research further clarifies the life conditions of senior lesbians, it is reasonable to suggest that economic struggles remain a significant issue, especially for lesbians and transgendered women who live alone as seniors.

The only group of unmarried women likely to reach old age in a materially secure position is the highly educated, professionally trained single woman, a rising trend and force changing the landscape of partnerships across the country. These never-married women who spend their entire lives in the paid labour force tend to be better off materially than previous cohorts of single women. In a recent British study, never-married women were found to have longer occupational careers and their own pension rights and were more likely than married women to own a car (Arber, 2004).

Today, the elimination of mandatory retirement at age 65 means that these women along with others who have interrupted their working lives may continue their careers and improve economic well-being well into their senior years.

RACIALIZED POVERTY AND IMMIGRANT WOMEN

Race and immigrant status are also important ingredients in senior women's impoverishment (Elgersma, 2010; Wellesley Institute, 2009). Immigrants represent an aging demographic; almost 19% of the Canadian immigrant population is over age 65 (Durst, 2005; Durst & Maclean, 2010). Except for those from Africa and Southeast Asia (Thailand, Vietnam, Laos), all other immigrant groups—Eastern Asia (Hong Kong, China, Taiwan), the Caribbean, Europe, South Asia (India, Pakistan, Sri Lanka)—have significant numbers of seniors. Currently, two-thirds of racialized persons are immigrants. It is expected that by 2031, one in three Canadians could belong to a racialized group (Statistics Canada, 2013a).

More than a quarter of all Canadian seniors were born abroad, which means that most immigrant seniors have aged in place or have lived in Canada for the past 30 or 40 years. Most of these migrants who arrived in Canada before 1960 were from Western European countries. The majority of more recent migrants, those arriving since 1981, have been racialized minorities, known officially as visible minorities (Chui, Tran, & Maheux, 2007). According to the 2006 census, 70% of the visible minority population in Canada is foreign-born (Preston & D'Addario, 2009). The three largest racialized groups are South Asian (25%), Chinese (24%), and Black (15%). These groups also have about half of all racialized persons living in poverty in Canada (NCW, 2012).

The retirement income of visible minorities—both Canadian-born and foreign-born—is lower than those of whites (Preston et al., 2013). Ethnicity and time of arrival—including both age at migration and year of arrival in Canada—affect senior economic security as census data consistently indicate that immigrant seniors who settled in Canada in 1961 or before are the least likely to be low income (16%) while those who arrived between 1991 and 2001 are most likely to be low income (24%) (Statistics Canada, 2010). Moreover, immigrant men and women who are visible minorities are more likely to have incomes below the low-income cutoff than their White and Canadian-born counterparts (Preston et al., 2013). At the time of the 2006 Census, employment incomes were a median of $22 400 for racialized persons versus $27 900 for non-racialized persons. Subsequent years have seen minimal changes in income levels.

Poverty rates among Canadian racialized groups have been rising among immigrants and falling among the Canadian-born, **a trend that** results from the steep decline in the relative earnings of immigrants between 1980 and 2000 (Creese, 2007; National Council of Welfare [NCW], 2012). Almost two-thirds of the racialized immigrants living in poverty came to Canada between 1996 and 2006, with seven out of ten arriving in the previous five years, 2001 to 2006.

Ninety percent of racialized persons living in poverty are first generation immigrants (NCW, 2012). Persons from racialized groups make up 54% of all immigrants in Canada yet they make up 71% of all immigrants living in poverty (NCW, 2012). The number of racialized families living in poverty increased between 1980 and 2000 at a rate far exceeding their population growth of 21% (NCW, 2012). Among recent immigrants, the situation is even more dire. Even though immigrants have high rates of educational achievement, their incomes remain very low. One-fifth of immigrants who arrive in Canada face low income, a rate 2.5 times higher than for Canadian-born.

It can take more than ten years for immigrants to achieve the earnings of their Canadian-born counterparts (Frenette & Morissette, 2003). If migrants arrived in the 1980s and 1990s, or even recently in the past decade, they entered a grim economy, subject to downsizing, plant closures, the rise of precarious labour, and a decrease in the creation of new jobs. Further, as extensively discussed in the media, recent immigrants have had great difficulty translating their education into well-paying work. When university credentials go unrecognized by potential employers, visible minority immigrants often face the necessity of accepting low-wage, low-skill employment. Research suggests that this pattern is particularly oppressive among visible minority women immigrants (Creese & Wiebe, 2012). These bleak economic environments have left many recent migrants economically marginalized and many have never made up the financial losses as they face retirement (Preston et al., 2013).

Racialized women face cumulative structural disadvantages. Those who experienced set-backs in economic security earlier in life too often end up in poorer health and reduced economic security later in life. Interrupted and discontinuous employment histories and/or low lifetime earnings, for example, reduce their CPP/QPP payments (McDonald, 2006a, 2006b). Their gendered life courses—occupational job ghettos, disrupted career paths, and caregiving demands—when combined with the racialized wage gap mean that, over time, racialized women are less likely to accumulate resources and more likely to end up with financial insecurity in old age.

TRANSNATIONAL SENIORS

Although most senior migrants age in place, Canada is also home to a second type of migrant senior: those who move to Canada, either permanently or for part of each year, as a senior. Globalization has precipitated this new category of the mobile aging migrant who follows the migration paths of their adult children in order to live with them or close by (Mandell et al., 2015). Recent data indicate that about 5% of seniors aged 65 and over lived with relatives in 2011—79% of women and 3% of men. About 7% of senior women and 2% of senior men live as lone parents with adult children who have no spouse, partner, or children while about 2% of senior men and women live with non-relatives such as a roommate (Milan, et al., 2014; Statistics Canada, 2012b).

Migrant seniors play a significant role in the lives of their adult children and grandchildren providing crucial financial, care, and emotional support for adult children and grandchildren. Most report gratitude to Canada for providing them with homes, pleasure in taking care of family members, and pride in their adult children and grandchildren's accomplishments (Mandell et al., 2015). Sponsored seniors play a critical role in promoting the success and survival of their extended families by providing ongoing emotional nurturing, wisdom, and material help (Mandell et al., 2015; Treas, 2008; Zechner, 2008).

Living with adult children presents its own challenges (Cook, 2010). International social security arrangements allow migrant seniors to count their work experience in other countries toward the Canada Pension Plan, which then also includes access to retirement, disability, and survivor benefits (Durst, 2005). Most transnational seniors arrive with very few resources making them financial dependent on their adult children and relatives. Their lack of English proficiency, lack of access to Canadian Old Age Security, and lack of traditional sources of social support leave many dependent seniors isolated and lonely (Mandell et al., 2015). Given that a very small number of seniors use public transportation or taxis and participation in social activities is recognized as promoting healthy and successful aging, inadequate access to transportation or difficulty in getting around represents a barrier (Turcotte, 2012).

Fortunately, ethnically diverse and responsive community groups have begun to fill this gap providing healthy living programs, retraining courses, and information sessions on available services, thus mitigating the overwhelming loneliness many experience (Din, Mandell, & Bhatti, 2012; Trask 2013).

Transnational seniors challenge traditional conceptualizations of aging by disrupting traditional life course trajectories of aging in place and diversifying family structures (Frank & Hou, 2012; Torres, 2006). When we look to emerging aging narratives, this is the group to whom we should first turn. For this group aging has turned out to be far from their youthful expectations because most never expected to move countries as seniors. Most have become significant vehicles for the transmission of transnational family connections as they stretch family ties across multiple boundaries (Arxer & Murphy, 2013). By staying connected with and influenced by more than one culture at a time, transnational senior migrants bring about a hybridization of cultures (Torres, 2006).

THE FUTURE: PRECARIOUS PENSIONS AND POSTPONED RETIREMENT

The rise in income inequality; the increase in precarious, unstable working conditions; and women's continued responsibility for care work that interrupts their paid employment all add up to a perfect storm. Younger women today remain at risk of senior poverty. From 1977 to 2011, the proportion of male workers covered by a registered pension plan declined from 52% to 37% while women's coverage increased modestly from 36 to 40% (reflecting their high levels of employment in public sectors such as education and health) (Drolet & Morissette, 2014, p. 1; Statistics Canada, 2013b). Currently 61.6% of all employees are not covered by a registered pension plan (Statistics Canada, 2014b). At the same time, fewer than one-quarter of tax-filers contribute to Registered Retirement Savings Plans [RRSP] (Statistics Canada, 2014c). The continuing impact of the 2008 economic recession and the proliferation of short-term, contract, part-time work as well as self-employment mean than hundreds of thousands of Canadian workers are unable to put aside adequate pension funds for their future retirement. Predictably, this inadequacy of pension coverage is more pronounced among not only younger workers but also women who are immigrants to Canada (Drolet & Morissette, 2014, 5–6).

In this context, governments have been shifting responsibility for senior economic support from social insurance to private investments by encouraging Canadians to invest in RRSPs and to set aside part of each paycheque for their retirement (Folbre, Shaw, & Stark, 2005; Townson, 2006). With runaway housing prices, increased educational costs, depressed wages, and high unemployment, particularly among Canadians 18 to 25, savings have all too frequently been supplanted by growing household debt. Moreover, those Canadians fortunate enough to have workplace pension plans are watching employers increasingly shift economic risk and responsibility for pensions onto employees. Specifically, defined benefit pension plans that guarantee a specified payout to retirees upon retirement are being replaced by defined contribution and blended pension plans. Among the latter, actual payouts to retirees will depend on the health of the overall economy and the financial well-being of that particular pension fund. Finally, some public and private employers, notably in cases of bankruptcy (for example, Atlas Steel [Welland, Ontario] and the City of Detroit) have successfully managed to reduce their economic obligations (and, therefore pension incomes) to retirees by pleading financial distress.

The extreme vulnerability of many senior women's pension income typically becomes apparent if they outlive their husbands (which they are likely to do). Typically, the death of the male breadwinner and workplace pension-holder results in an immediate 50% reduction in pension payouts from a workplace pension. In a 2013 global report looking at economic security among seniors, the OECD found that 61% of the gross income of Canadian seniors comes from such workplace or private pensions (OECD, 2013). The remaining 39% of gross income for seniors emanates from government support payments, which in 2012 would mean $13 079.50 in Old Age Supplement for a married couple or approximately $24 000 in Canada Pension Plan payments. These government transfer payments would similarly be reduced by approximately half since they are determined on a per person basis (Bazel & Mintz, 2014, p. 11). Given women's greater longevity and reduced labour force participation, it is not surprising that women are more dependent than men on government income security programs. In 2008, women 65 and older received 52.6 % of their total income from government transfer payments (including Old Age Security, Canada/Quebec Pension Plan, Guaranteed Income Supplement), while only 37.5% of senior men's total income came from government sources (Milan & Vezina, 2011, p. 22). Obviously, the lower your lifetime earnings (for example, as a result of work interruptions and periods of part-time employment), the more an individual relies on government transfers in their senior years. However, in the absence of private or workplace pensions, these government transfers are barely sufficient to raise a single person above the poverty line. Furthermore, home ownership is not necessarily a solution for seniors. Even though Canadians as a whole have a high rate of home ownership—around 70% of people aged 65 and over own their houses—of these, 6.5% were still repaying their mortgages in 2011 (OECD, 2013). Downsizing from a family home to an urban condo, for example, does not necessarily result (given the high cost of urban housing) in a significant influx of new capital into seniors' savings.

Given these various considerations and the current economic and employment context, it is not surprising that Canadian workers are increasingly delaying retirement. In 2009, a 50-year-old worker could expect to retire at age 66. At all education levels, compared to 20 years ago, men age 50 retired 2.1 years later and women age 50 retired 2.6 years later. Overall, retirement has been pushed back by about three years. Retiring early or involuntarily usually means less income, a lower standard of living, and higher costs for income support programs (Carriere & Galarneau, 2012; Statistics Canada, 2012c).

For most people, income declines with age (LaRochelle-Côté, Picot, & Myles, 2010). Even so, of those who are retired, the vast majority—eight in ten—report feeling their financial situation is as expected or better than before they retired; similarly, 86% say their income is sufficient to cover monthly expenses (Marshall, 2011). However, retiring with debt is increasing. One-third of those fully retired hold debt, owing an average of $19 000 compared with their non-retired counterparts who owe $40 000 (Marshall, 2011). Divorcees have the highest rate of debt followed by the never-married and widows/widowers (Marshall, 2011). Older retirees—those over age 75—are far less likely, in all categories, to carry debt.

One way that workers can seek to avoid post-retirement struggles is by returning to the labour force. Between 2000 and 2009, the percentage of women 65 and older who held a paid job increased from 3.2% to 6.4%. More than 58% of employed women were working part-time in 2009 (Milan & Vezina, 2011, 18–19). However, senior women are less likely to re-enter the paid labour force than senior men and, if they do, their employment is shorter term (Statistics Canada, 2014d). At the same time, many senior women and men remain withdrawn from paid work. Less than 3% of both women and men ages 55 plus reported returning to work in 2009. About 60% of women ages 55 plus compared to one-half of men in 2009 were fully retired and out of the labour force.

Overall, senior women are less likely to be present in paid employment and men are more likely than women to never retire fully (38% versus 30%) or to partially retire (13% versus 11%) (Park, 2011). Predictably, senior women's continued caregiving responsibilities, especially parental and senior care, means they tend to retire earlier than men, often in response to a spouse's retirement or the needs of aging parents, and they are less likely to return to paid employment post-retirement (Mandell & Wilson, 2011). Proulx and Le Bourdais (2014), for example, report from their research that women (in contrast to men) are particularly vulnerable to leaving employment when they are providing care to a parent. Men were more likely than women to never retire (38% versus 30%) or partially retire (13% versus 11%) (Park, 2011). Women's withdrawal from paid employment in the form of early retirement, full retirement, or the absence of post-retirement employment further jeopardizes their economic well-being as they age.

The move back into paid employment for both men and women is triggered by a constellation of factors including ongoing good health, opportunities to move into part-time and contract employment (often in their previous sphere of employment), and financial need. Poor health is a frequent reason for retirement (Park, 2011). Those employees who had previous jobs offering "good pay, interesting work, and few physical demands" appeared more likely to return to paid work: professionals, managers, and technicians (Uppal, 2010).

Minority and immigrant status can also influence patterns of both retirement (Honig, 1996) and timing and reasons for retirement (Bulanda & Zhang, 2009). In a 2009 study done among Canadians ages 55 plus, of the workers fully retired, the members of visible minority groups and immigrant workers retired, on average, two years later than other retirees (Park, 2011). Stobert and Cranswick (2004) found that 47% of recent Canadian newcomers who are predominantly visible minorities either did not know when they would retire or never planned to retire.

When asked if they felt financially prepared for retirement, in 2009 almost 40% of aged 55 plus never-retired workers said their financial plans for retirement were less than adequate (Park, 2011). Schellenberg and Silver (2004) found a large difference between the desired and actual financial preparation for retirement reported by recent immigrants, who were also mainly visible minorities. Forty-five percent of recent immigrants expressed concerns about their financial preparation for retirement.

Many Western nations are embarking on schemes to entice senior workers to remain in the labour force as a way to reduce the state and individual financial pressures brought about by the aging population (Carriere & Galarneau, 2012). Keeping people working allows them to save more for retirement, allows pension plans to remain sustainable, and delays skills shortages in certain sectors of the economy. Moreover, as Canadians become better educated, healthier, and live longer, they are less likely to see themselves as "old" at age 65. When they do think about retirement, many seniors ages 55 plus say they would prefer a gradual transition into retirement by way of reduced or more flexible hours while others say they are financially and psychologically unprepared for retirement (Park, 2011).

As a result of these diverse social and economic pressures, women face a variety of problematic outcomes as they age. Economic insecurity and inadequate financial resources are certainly a concern for the many women who, for diverse reasons, end up unattached and elderly. There is likely to be increasing pressure on many older women to continue their paid employment in some form and delay retirement, despite the continued likelihood that they will be expected to assume the lion's share of responsibility for caring for other family members. Government reductions in social services and health care funding typically will in all probability translate into more time spent in individualized care work by women of all ages. Given these growing caregiving responsibilities along with persistent gender inequities in paid employment, senior women turning to paid employment will often find a problematic option since they are likely to be funneled into marginal, poorly paid, and insecure work.

AGING AND CARING: GIVING AND RECEIVING CARE

A cornerstone of many women's lives is their caregiving obligations. A feminist political economy perspective understands the unpaid care work that women routinely perform is an experience of moral obligation, structured by the gender-based division of labour. On average, women spend 35 years of their lives devoted to caring for children, grandchildren, and older people (Calasanti & Slevin, 2006). Some women begin the caring process in adolescence while others do not actively begin until the birth of their first child. Regardless of when it begins, cultural scripts of femininity assume that women will take responsibility for others, care for others, and put the needs of others before their own, even if this means sacrificing employment and leisure opportunities. Neither the demands for care work nor women's feelings of obligation to perform care work lessen with age. In fact, women's caregiving actually increases as they age, peaking between the ages of 45 to 64 (Marshall, 2006; Sinha, 2012).

Data from 2012 indicate that nearly half of Canadians aged 15 and older (46%), or 13 million Canadians, provide some type of care to a family member or friend with a long-term health condition, disability, or aging need (Sinha, 2012). Of all caregivers, 54% are women, who typically spend the longest hours in caregiving. In 2012, 17% of women providing care spent 20 or more hours a week versus 11% of men (Sinha, 2012). Whether we are discussing parental care, spousal care, child care, neighbour and friendship care, or elder care, despite an increase in men's time spent in unpaid work, in each age group, women devote more of their time and more time overall in a lifetime than men to unpaid work and less time than men to leisure.

Care work is shaped by social structures and is subject to the social and material conditions within which it occurs Personal and social identities are embedded in social relationships. By accepting the cultural mandate of responsibility for care work and engaging in it, women construct their social identities as gendered, classed, and raced subjects (Twigg, 2004). By engaging in care work—mothering, grandmothering, and elder care—women produce their identities as females as well as reproduce the very structures that shape their lives. In this context, it is important to note that these "care" roles are significant in the lives of lesbians, bisexual women, and, presumably, transgendered women. Recent preliminary research into lesbians' enactment of grandmothering suggest that lesbian grandmothers often accept and perform a very similar caregiving role to that of heterosexual grandmothers (Whalen, Bigner, & Barber, 2000; Kimmell, Rose, & David, 2006).

But herein lies the dilemma. A significant investment in family care work means a lowered investment in the labour market, which results in women's reduced economic security in old age. A key barrier to labour force participation remains women's time spent in unpaid domestic and care work. In 2005, women ages 55 to 74 devoted 4.8 hours a day to unpaid work while men spent considerably less time (men ages 55 to 64 devoted 3.1 hours and those 65 to 74 devoted 3.9 hours per day to unpaid work). Currently, even in senior years the traditional domestic division of labour appears to persist with men spending more time working for pay (and in leisure) and women spending more time on unpaid work (Statistics Canada, 2012b).

Over-engagement in care work renders women poor in old age; then society blames them for their own poverty (Holstein & Minkler, 2003). Yet to ignore the responsibilities associated with caring for others leaves women open to social censure and ostracism—women are "bad women" if they do not put the needs of others before their own. Discourses of love co-mingle? with discourses of obligation, leaving many women feeling conflicted and trapped, unable to ignore care work even though the work itself remains socially undervalued and largely unrewarded.

Care work is gendered Women provide 70 to 80% of in-home care to family members at every stage of the life course (Marshall, 2006). Despite high levels of female labour force participation, many Canadians believe that home and children take precedence in women's lives over working for pay. The expectation remains that even when employed, women maintain primary responsibility for home and family. In 1995, 46% of both men and women agreed or strongly agreed that "while a job is all right, what most women really want is a home and family" (Ghalam, 1997). In the past decade, women have increased the time they spend in paid employment without a significant corresponding decrease in the time they spend on domestic labour and child care. In 1997, of all women in two-parent families, 62% of women with children under the age of 16 were employed. In 1998, employed mothers with children under the age of five spent double the amount of time on personal child-care activities than men: 91 minutes per day for mothers compared to 47 minutes per day for fathers (Hunsley, 2006).

Men are more likely than women to support aging family members financially; women are more likely to support them emotionally and in daily tasks such as household chores, shopping, and basic hygiene (Chisholm, 1999). Women take on the direct hands-on personal care duties while men generally assist in tasks such as home maintenance and financial management (Habtu & Popovic, 2006). Male and female subjectivities are thus constituted in and through gendered practices of caring (Twigg, 2004).

Care work is unevenly distributed Who receives care? Interestingly, while women are most likely to be providing care, they are also most likely to be receiving care. Since women tend to live longer than men and tend to marry men who are older than they, women are more likely to end up in need of caregiving as they age. As a result, while almost half (48%) of men turn to their spouse as their main caregiver, only 21% of women are able to do the same. Yet senior women, particularly if they are on their own and as they age, will need assistance with everyday activities (Milan & Vezina, 2011, 27, 32). Of course, as increasing numbers of women remain childless or have fewer children, family-based social support for aging Canadian women will become a problem (Penning & Wu, 2014). Of all seniors ages 65 to 74, women account for 58% of all care receivers and 65% of all care receivers among those age 75 and older (Sinha & Bleakney, 2014). Women age 65 and older represent one of the fastest growing segments of the population. Among this group, the female cohort age 85 and over is the fastest growing segment of the senior female population. This group, predictably, tends to be the most in need of social support from their communities and families as they are vulnerable to ill health and likely live alone (Milan & Vezina, 2011).

Who is providing the care and which age groups are receiving the most care? Again, not surprisingly, closest family relationships provide the primary sources of care. In 2012, 39% of Canadians were receiving help primarily from a spouse or common-law partner, while 24% were receiving care primarily from an adult child and 19% from a parent. The least common were extended family member or siblings (9%) and friends or neighbours (8%) (Sinha & Bleakney, 2014).

Ailing parents are the most common recipients of care. About 39% of caregivers look after the needs of their own parents and another 9% do so for parents-in-law. Spouses are 8% of care recipients while children represent 5% (Sinha, 2012). Caregivers of spouses and children devoted the most time to helping activities. These figures reveal that caregivers between the ages of 45 and 64 are the busiest as this is the age group most likely to be providing parental care and care to grandparents.

Seniors age 65 and older actually provide the least amount of care compared with every other age group but they also provide the longest hours in care provision. Twenty-three percent of senior caregivers provide 20 hours or more a week of care (Turcotte, 2013). Caring for their ailing partners requires an intense amount of time.

Here, once again, there are important diversities. Immigrant senior women, particularly recent immigrants, are much more likely to live with relatives than their Canadian-born counterparts. A full 40% of recent immigrant senior women who arrived in Canada between 2000 and 2006 lived with relatives, in contrast to about 7% of Canadian-born senior women (Milan & Vezina, 2011, p. 12). Similarly, low-income families facing challenging economic circumstances and with more limited support options may be choosing to turn to their families to meet their needs (McDaniel & Gaszo, 2014). Caregiving for elders is also markedly different in Indigenous communities. Issues ranging from geographic remoteness to a lack of family caregivers and limited access to health services are embedded in concerns about distinctive cultural values and community development (Habjan, Prince, & Kelley, 2012). Social support and care for the aging may also be problematic for lesbian, bisexual, and transgendered women. What happens to members of the LGBT community when they develop dementia or other needs for chronic care? Increasingly, analysts are drawing attention to innovative support and caregiving options being constructed within lesbian communities as well as the pressing need for social service agencies to also address the care needs of an aging LGBT community (Gabrielson, 2011; McGovern, 2014). Although in 2011 only a small percentage of senior couples identified as same-sex, there is every indication that same-sex couples and marriages among seniors will significantly increase in coming decades (Humble, 2014; Milan, et al., 2014).

Keeping in mind these intersectionalities, how much care is provided and by whom? While men and women report spending similar weekly amounts of time in caregiving—three to four hours a week—women spend far longer in caring than men. Women are more likely than their male counterparts to spend 20 or more hours per week on caregiving tasks (17% versus 11%). Spousal caregivers typically spend 14 hours a week on some sort of care activity while caregivers of children, including adult children, spend 10 hours per week (Simha, 2012). Caregivers of parents, the largest segment of caregivers, spend four hours a week while caregivers of grandparents and friends spend the least amount of time at two hours a week (Turcotte, 2013).

Care work is affected by global economic shifts Globalization has not brought the economic prosperity expected by middle-aged generations who increasingly rely on their families to help out. Half of contemporary three-generation households are headed by immigrants or are Aboriginal families (Che-Alford & Hamm, 1999; Milan & Hamm, 2003). Parents born in Asia and Central and South America are far more likely to live with their adult children than those in some other ethnic groups (Turcotte, 2006).

Care work is shaped by state policies Ideologies that see reproductive work as private and primarily the domain of women are used to justify minimal state involvement in long-term care and to draw old women into caring for family members (Estes, 2003). Old people, not always by choice, continue to work as unpaid caregivers in the home looking after grandchildren, spouses, and relatives (King, 2006). Grandmothers may be called upon to perform care work so that younger women can be "free" to engage in paid labour. Some 40% of American adult children with children under the age of five receive babysitting help from parents (Spitze & Logan, 1992). In Canada, in 1996, about 54% of grandparents in three-generation households helped out with household finances (Che-Alford & Hamm, 1999). Gender ideologies are also used to justify transferring care work from the formal sector of hospitals and state-run nursing homes to the informal sector of the home.

Care work is associated with quality of life Caregivers experience both objective burdens (the actual demands they experience as caregivers) and subjective burdens (feelings of worry, sadness, resentment, anger, or guilt) (Hooeyman & Gonyea, 1999). Caring obligations are thought to account in part for the poorer health and higher levels of physical disability experienced by older women, as well as their limited financial resources.

When asked in the 2002 Canadian General Social Survey to evaluate their experiences, both middle-aged and senior caregivers rate their elder care positively. Between 80 and 90% feel that helping others strengthens their relationships with the care receivers and repays some of what they themselves have received from others and from life (Stobert & Cranswick, 2004). In fact, 20.6% of men and 22.2% of women felt they should be doing more (Habtu & Popovic, 2006). Feelings of love and duty intersect across the life course.

AGING: EMBODIMENT

Our examination of paid and care work highlights the importance of the material in structuring the lives of old women. However, age is more than the sum total of material conditions. Age arises from the recursive interaction between structure, culture, and agency. In this view, age is less a biological prescription—years lived—than a social and cultural inscription. Aging is not a "natural" process but occurs within culture and history. It is through our involvement in culture that we give age meaning. Media images, representations, symbols, and metaphors offer important cultural descriptions from which women construct identities of aging.

Age is a key way in which women perform or accomplish gender. Like gender, age is not a property of individuals but rather a socially prescribed relationship, a process, and a social construction (Ray, 1996). Both aged gender identities are created and maintained through the social constructs by which we give them historical, material, and cultural meaning. We all tend to become who we are addressed as being. Gender and age identities represent ways of being in the world that take their meaning from our shared language, history, and culture (Clarke & Korotchenko, 2011).

Gender, like age, is too often presented dichotomously—male versus female, young versus old. Gender and age come together in the culture's "double standard" that pits young women against old and aging men against aging women. Defined by Sontag as a process by which women suffer scorn and exclusion as they grow old—a "humiliating process of gradual sexual disqualification" (Sontag, 1972, p. 102)—the double standard of aging represents a form of double marginality (Montemurro & Gillen, 2013). Racialized women experience a "triple jeopardy" as derogatory stereotypes of ethnicity intersect with unflattering images of women and the elderly.

Ironically, although young women are quite rightly concerned with sexual exploitation, aging women see themselves as sexual cast-offs. In fact, young women benefit from the negative sexual portrayal of old women because it enhances their social value and their opportunities with privileged men (Thompson, O'Sullivan, Byers, & Shaughnessy, 2014). Along with racism and ableism, sexual disqualification creates painful situations for some women while others welcome having outlived narrow, sexualized definitions of attractiveness.

Bodies are discursive, meaning they are shaped, represented, and constructed both materially and socially. James Paul Gee (1990) describes discourses as "ways of being in the world; they are forms of life which integrate words, acts, values, beliefs, attitudes and social identities as well as gestures, glances, body postures and clothes." Gee refers to discourses as "identity kits" because they come with complete "instructions on how to act, talk and often write, so as to take on a particular role that others will recognize" (p. 142).

Because bodies represent continuing sites of identity construction, age and gender are identities accrued over time by adhering to and performing body norms. In fact, bodies are so centrally implicated in the process of gender identity construction that Kontos (1999), following Butler, argues that bodies have no significant existence without the mark of gender. There are age- and gender-based standards by which people manage their identity kits and this management is directed toward the body. Women of all ages, races, genders, classes, and ability types mould, pressure, push, and cajole their bodies into becoming public representations of how they want to be viewed.

What is the ideal body in our society? First, the cultural ideal is the same for all women: unblemished, untainted, youthful, and vigorous bodies are considered perfect. Visible signs of impairment, disability, or aging indicate failure and reinforce fears of bodily suffering and infirmity.

Second, the ideal body is an ageless body. Successful aging means not aging at all—avoiding becoming old altogether. If a body has to age, the ideal old body is a youngish looking and acting body (Holstein & Minkler, 2003). The emphasis on youth and vitality subjects old people to a kind of cultural imperialism, a lifelong project of disciplining and managing the aging body by appearing not to age.

Third, a successful old body is an active body. Productive activity—economic, physical, and social—becomes the norm against which everyone is judged. "Staying active" becomes a type of moral obligation for the elderly, promoted as a way to avoid decline and dependency. Illness becomes a transgression of cultural rules because it prevents activity. Entire groups become marginalized when our societal vision of aging means staying economically engaged, socially active, and physically vigorous: Katz (1996) calls this emphasis on vitality a way of disciplining old age: less active elderly are considered less attractive and less socially valuable.

If bodies are public presentations of our identities, then individuals need identity kits or body practices to maintain the ideal. Wendell (1996, p. 88) calls these body practices "disciplines of normality." "Keeping up"—being active—and "passing for normal"—dressing, talking, and acting like someone who is younger—reduce the likelihood of being the target of ageist or ablest prejudice. Go into any women's clothing store and you'll find all ages trying on the same type of jeans, shirts, sweaters, and dresses. No one wants to be characterized as an "old lady" (Twigg, 2013).

Disciplinary norms generate experts who monitor and dictate how women should age successfully. Social regulation works when we all participate in the widespread conspiracy of pretending there are no impaired or aged people. Women willingly buy into the anti-aging industry by purchasing cosmetic surgery, joining gyms, and signing up for diet plans, all gendered body practices marketed as tools to help women fight aging. In 2013, Americans spent over 12 billion dollars on cosmetic procedures and 7 billion of that was spent on surgical procedures. The most common surgery in 2013 for people ages 19 to 34 was breast augmentation, for ages 35 to 50 was liposuction, for ages 51 to 64 it was also liposuction, and for ages 65 and older it was a facelift (ASAPS, 2013). These numbers will likely continue to increase as a greater percentage of the population enters their senior years.

CONCLUSION

In this chapter, we have looked at the material and social effects of the double standard of aging and the ways in which ageism is embodied. Why is it that men are "allowed" to age naturally without social penalties but the aging female body arouses revulsion? As Reinharz (1986 to 1997) reminds us, the double standard is more than a matter of aesthetics; it is the beginning of a whole set of oppressive structures that keep women in their place. And as women age, the gap between men and women, young and old, widens.

The development of feminism and ageism owes a huge debt of gratitude to disability studies (Overall, 2006). Disability, like age, is socially and materially constructed. This does not deny the reality of the aging body, but says that how we define it is socially constructed. Positive definitions of aging seem to have disappeared historically just at a time when women gained the possibility of achieving social capital by way of their own personal and professional development. The energy women could have used to affect their lower status and dependency has been re-channeled into worries about aging—worries for which the consumer economy offered resources such as makeup, surgery, and fashion literature. Ultimately, ridding the body of visible signs of aging requires spending large sums of money.

In 1921, women age 65 and older made up a scant 5% of Canadian women. By 2031, one in four Canadian women will be seniors. It is possible that this demographic bulge will translate increased engagement of older women into the creation of new age norms and social policy. The Canadian-originated activist group—The Raging Grannies—speaks to this range of new possibilities (Sawchuck, 2009). Analysts are also calling for women of all sexual orientations to advance plan for social support as they age (Boehmer, Clark, & Sullivan, 2010). The mass media encourage all boomer women to not only care for their physical health but also their financial well-being. Successful aging is, of course, in large measure dependent on being healthy enough to enjoy the benefits of retirement or reduced workload, but this is complexly intertwined with financial security.

Women who lack adequate financial resources have reduced opportunities to enjoy retirement (for example, travel, involvement in community activities, further education, and artistic endeavours) and increased pressure to take on poorly paid, marginalized employment. While public health campaigns concerning breast cancer and heart disease have drawn boomer women's attention to potential health threats, there has been less information for aging women about securing their financial well-being. Given persistent ageist and sexist patterns in the labour force, continuing pressure on aging women to assume care work, and their likelihood of becoming unattached, it is essential that older women be alerted to the financial problems of aging. However, a lifetime of caring for others continues to leave many women financially insecure in old age. Intermittent or part-time employment, combined with low-wage jobs, means far too many women face economic marginalization and, therefore, social powerlessness in old age, with racialized, immigrant, Indigenous, and low-income women particularly vulnerable.

We end by reminding our readers that feminist discourses offer us new ways to think about ourselves. Feminists, along with everyone else, have been socialized into what Reinharz (1986 to 1997) termed a geronto-phobic culture. Eliminating ageism begins by confronting our own fears and misgivings of aging. Deconstructing these derogatory narratives offers a way to begin this project.

Discussion Questions

1. An aging population "tsunami" is about to hit Canada. What are the major social issues generated by this demographic event and why is it particularly relevant to women.
2. Consider the ways in which older women are impacted by other identities such as immigrant status, race/ethnicity, social class, and sexual identity?
3. Critically examine two films about aging. What images of old women are portrayed? How is age "performed"? Are the diversities/intersectionalities in older women's identities presented?
4. What types of care work do older women perform and why? How does this vary by immigrant status, race/ethnicity, social class, and sexual identity?

Bibliography

Altman, D. (2014, June 13). The truth about those 'greedy' seniors. *The Wall Street Journal*. Retrieved from Blogs.wsj.com/washwire/2014/06/the-truth-about-those-greedy-seniors

American Society for Aesthetic Plastic Surgery (ASAPS). (2013). Quick Facts: Highlights of the ASAPS 2013 Statistics on Cosmetic Surgery. Retrieved from www.surgery.org/sites/default/files/2013-quick-facts_0.pdf

Arber, S. (2004). Gender, marital status, and ageing: Linking material, health, and social resources. *Journal of Aging Studies*, *18*(1), 91–108.

Armstrong, P. (2013). Puzzling skills: Feminist political economy approaches. *Canadian Review of Sociology*, *50*(3), 256–283.

Arxer, S. L., & Murphy, J. (Eds.). (2013). Introduction. In *The symbolism of globalization, development and aging* (pp. 1–12). New York, NY: Springer.

Banting, K., & Myles, J. (Eds.). (2013). *Inequality and the fading of the redistributive politics*. Vancouver, BC: UBC Press.

Bazel, P., & Mintz, J. (2014). Income inadequacy among Canadian seniors: Helping singles most. *The School of Public Policy SPP Research Papers*, *7*(4), 1–17.

Bennet, T., & Gaines, J. (2010). Believing what you hear: The impact of aging stereotypes upon the old. *Educational Gerontology*, *36*, 435–445.

Boehmer, U., Clark, M., & Sullivan, M. (2010). Advance care planning by unmarried women of different sexual orientations: The importance of social support. *Journal of Women and Aging*, *22*, 306–320.

Broadbent Institute. (2014). *Have and have-nots: Deep and persistent wealth inequality in Canada*. Ottawa, ON: Broadbent Institute.

Bulanda, J. R., & Zhang, Z. (2009). Racial-ethnic differences in subjective survival expectations for the retirement years. *Research on Aging*, *31*, 688–709.

Burkhauser, R. V., Giles, P., Lillard, D. R., & Schwarze, J. (2004). Income replacement among recent widows. *Perspectives on Labour and Income*, *5*(5). Retrieved from www.statcan.ca/english/studies/75-001/10504/high-2.htm

Butler, R. N. (1975). *Why survive? Being old in America.* New York, NY: Harper and Row.

Calasanti, T. M., & Zajicek, A. M. (1993). A socialist-feminist approach to aging: Embracing diversity. *Journal of Aging Studies*, *7*, 117–131.

Calasanti, T. M., & Slevin, K. F. (Eds.). (2006). *Age matters: Realigning feminist thought*. New York, NY, and London, England: Routledge.

Carriere, Y., & Galarneau, D. (2012). How many years to retirement? *Statistics Canada,* Catalogue no. 75-006-X, 1–8.

Che-Alford, J., & Hamm, B. (1999). Under one roof: Three generations living together. *Canadian Social Trends*, Statistics Canada, Catalogue no. 11-008, 6–9.

Chisholm, J. F. (1999). The sandwich generation. *Journal of Social Distress and the Homeless*, *8*(3), 177–180.

Cho, S., Crenshaw, K. W., & McCall, L. (2013). Towards a field of intersectionality studies: Theory, applications and praxis. *Signs*, *38*(3), 785–810.

Chui, T., Tran, K., & Maheux, H. (2007). *Immigration in Canada: A Portrait of the Foreign-born Population, 2006 Census.* Statistics Canada Catalogue no. 97-557-XIE. Ottawa, ON.

Citizens for Public Justice. (2012). *Poverty trends scorecard Canada 2012.* Retrieved from www.cpj.ca/files/docs/poverty-trends-scorecard.pdf

Clarke, L. Hurd., & Korotchenko, A. (2011). Aging and the body: A review. *Canadian Journal of Aging*, *30*(3), 495–510.

Conference Board of Canada. (2013a). Elderly poverty. Retrieved from www.conferenceboard.ca/hcp/details/society/elderly-poverty.aspx?pf=true

Conference Board of Canada. (2013b). Gender income gap. Retrieved from www.conferenceboard.ca/hcp/details/society/gender-income-gap.aspx?pf=true

Conference Board of Canada. (2013c). Income inequality. Retrieved from www.conferenceboard.ca/hcp/details/society/income-inequality.aspx?pf=true

Cook, J. (2010). Exploring older women's citizenship: Understanding the impact of migration in later life, *Ageing and Society*, *30*, 253–273.

Creese, G., (2007). Racializing work/reproducing white privilege. In V. Shalla & W. Clement (Eds.), *Work in tumultuous times: Critical perspectives* (pp. 192–226). Montreal, QC, Kingston, ON: McGill-Queen's University Press.

Creese, G., & Wiebe, B. (2012). 'Survival employment': Gender and deskilling among African immigrants in Canada. *International Migration*, *50*(5), 56–76.

Din, N., Mandell, N., & Bhatti, A. (2012). Healthy aging: The role of community groups in facilitating social integration. Presented at the International Conference on Aging and Community Renewal (ICACR), Kingston, Jamaica, November 18–20.

Drolet, M., & Morissette, R. (2014). New facts on pension coverage in Canada. *Insights on Canadian Society*. Statistics Canada. Ottawa: Minister of Industry. Catalogue no. 75-006-X.

Durst, D. (2005). More snow on the roof: Canada's immigrant seniors. *Canadian Issues-Themes Canadiens*, *Spring*, 34–37.

Durst, D., & MacLean, M. (Eds.). (2010). *Diversity and aging among immigrant seniors in Canada: Changing faces and greying temples.* Calgary, AB: Detselig Enterprises Ltd.

Elgersma, S. (2010). Immigrant seniors: Their economic security and factors affecting their access to benefits. Social Affairs Division, *Parliamentary Information and Research Service,* Publication No. 07-45-E. Ottawa, Canada: Library of Parliament.

Estes, C. L. (2003). Social Security privatization and older women: A feminist political economy perspective. *Journal of Aging Studies 18*(1), 9–26.

Folbre, N., Shaw, L. B., & Stark, A. (2005). Introduction: Gender and aging. *Feminist Economics 11*(2), 3–5.

Frank, K., & Hou, F. (2012). Seniors returning to Canada. *Perspectives on Labour and Income.* Statistics Canada. Ottawa: Minister of Industry. Spring, 3–14.

Freixas, A., Luque, B., & Reina, A. (2012). Critical feminist gerontology: In the back room of research. *Journal of Women and Aging, 24*, 44–58.

Frenette, M., & Morissette, R. (2003). Will they ever converge? Earnings of immigrants and Canadian-born workers over the last two decades. *Statistics Canada Analytical Studies Branch Research Series* 11F0019MIE, Working Paper No. 215. Ottawa: Statistics Canada.

Gabrielson, M. L. (2011). 'We have to create family': Aging support issues and needs among older lesbians. *Journal of Gay and Lesbian Social Services*, *23*, 322–334.

Gabrielson, M. L., Holston, E. C., & Dyck, M. J. (2014). Are they family or friends? Social support instrument reliability in studying older lesbians. *Journal of Homosexuality*, *61*(11), 1589–1604.

Gee, J. P. (2001). Reading as situated language: A sociological perspective. *Journal of Adolescent and Adult Literacy*, *44*(8), 714–725.

Ghalam, N. Zukernwick. (1997). Attitudes toward women, work and family. *Canadian Social Trends,* Statistics Canada, Catalogue no. 11-008-XPE, 13–17. Ottawa, ON: Statistics Canada.

Gibson, D. (1996). Broken down by age and gender: The "problem" of old women. *Gender and Society*, *10*(4), 433–448.

Gill, V., Knowles, J., & Stewart-Patterson, D. (2014). *The bucks stop here: Trends in income inequality between generations*. Conference Board of Canada (pp. 1–50). Retrieved from www.conferenceboard.ca/e-library/abstract.aspx?did=6510

Goar, C. (2014, April 30). Fresh insight into Canada's gender gap. *Toronto Star*, p. A23.

Habjan, S., Prince, H., & Kelley, M. L. (2012). Caregiving for elders in First Nations communities: Social system perspective on barriers and challenges. *Canadian Journal of Aging*, *31*(2), 209–222.

Habtu, R., & Popovic, A. (2006). Informal caregivers: Balancing work and life responsibilities. *Horizons*, *6*(3), 27–34.

Hochschild, A. R. (2012). *The outsourced self: Intimate life in market times.* New York, NY: Metropolitan Books.

Hollows, J. (2000). *Feminism, femininity, and popular culture*. Manchester, England: Manchester University Press.

Holstein, M. B., & Minkler, M. (2003). Self, subjectivity and the "New Gerontology." *The Gerontologist*, *43*(6), 787–797.

Hooyman, N. R., & Gonyea, J. G. (1999). A feminist model of family care: Practice and policy directions. *Journal of Women and Aging*, *11*(2/3), 149–169.

Humble, A. M. (2014). Moving from ambivalence to certainty: Older same-sex couples marry in Canada. *Canadian Journal of Aging*, *32*(2), 131–144.

Hunsley, T. (2006). Work-life balance in an aging population. *Horizons*, *8*(3), 3–13.

Katz, S. (1996). *Discipling old age: The formation of gerontological knowledge.* Charlottesville, VA: University of Virginia Press.

Kimmel, D., Rose, T., & David, S. (Eds.). (2006). *Lesbian, gay, bisexual and transgender aging: Research and clinical perspectives.* New York, NY: Columbia University Press.

King, N. (2006). The lengthening list of oppressions: Age relations and the feminist study of inequality. In T. M. Calasanti and K. F. Slevin (Eds.), *Age matters: realigning feminist thought* (pp. 47–73). New York, NY, and London, England: Routledge.

Klein, N. (2014). *This changes everything: capitalism vs. the climate.* New York, NY: Simon and Schuster.

Kontos, P. C. (1999). Local biology: Bodies of difference in ageing studies. *Ageing and Society*, *19*, 677–689.

LaRochelle-Côté, S., Myles, J., & Picot, G. (2010). *Replacing family income during the retirement years: How are Canadians doing?* Statistics Canada, Social Analysis Division, Ottawa, Catalogue no. 11F0019M — No. 328.

Liechty, T. (2012). 'Yes, I worry about my weight . . . but for the most part I'm content with my body': Older women's body dissatisfaction alongside contentment. *Journal of Women and Aging*, *24*, 70–88.

Macdonald, B., & Rich, C. (1991). *Look me in the eye: Old women, aging and ageism* (2nd ed.). Denver, CO: Spinsters Ink Books.

Mandell, N., & Wilson, S. (2011). Intergenerational care work: Mothering, grandmothering and eldercare, In C. Krull & J. Sempruch (Eds.), *A Life in balance? Reopening the family-work debate* (pp. 30–46). Vancouver, BC: University of British Columbia Press.

Mandell, N., Wilson, S., & Duffy, A. D. (2008). ***Connection, compromise and control: Canadian women discuss midlife***. Toronto, ON: Oxford University Press.

Marshall, K. (2006). Converging gender roles. ***Perspectives***, Statistics Canada, Catalogue no. 75-001-XIE, 5–17. Ottawa, ON: Statistics Canada.

Marshall, K. (2011). Retiring with debt. ***Statistics Canada*** Catalogue no. 75-001-X, 1–12. Ottawa, ON: Statistics Canada.

Marshall, L. (2006). Aging: A feminist issue. ***National Women's Studies Association Journal***, ***18***(1), vii–xiii.

Martin-Matthews, A. (2011). Revisiting widowhood in later life: Changes in patterns and profiles, advances in research and understanding. ***Canadian Journal of Aging***, ***30***(3), 339–354.

McDaniel, S. A., & Gazso, A. (2014). Liminality and low-income aging families by choice: Meanings of family and support. ***Canadian Journal of Aging***, ***33***(4), 400–412.

McDaniel, S. A., & Rozanova, J. (2011). Canada's aging population (1986) redux. ***Canadian Journal of Aging***, ***30***(3), 511–521.

McDonald, L. (2006a). Gender and family-major dimensions of retirement research. In L. O. Stone (Ed.), ***New frontiers of research on retirement*** (pp. 132–136). Catalogue no. 75-511-XIE, ISBN 0-660-19578-X. Ottawa, ON: Statistics Canada.

McDonald, L. (2006b). Gendered retirement: The welfare of women and the 'new' retirement. In L. O. Stone (Ed.), ***New frontiers of research on retirement*** (pp. 137–164). Catalogue no. 75-511-XIE, ISBN 0-660-19578-X. Ottawa, ON: Statistics Canada.

McGovern, J. (2014). The forgotten: Dementia and the aging LGBT community. ***Journal of Gerontological Social Work***, ***47***, 845–857.

Met Life Mature Market Institute. (2010). Still out, still aging: The Met Life study of lesbian, gay, bisexual and transgender baby boomers. (March). Retrieved from www.metlife.com/mmi/research/still-out-still-aging.html#findings

Milan, A., & Hamm, B. (2003). Across the generations: Grandparents and grandchildren. ***Canadian Social Trends***, ***71***(Winter), 2–8.

Milan, A., & Vézina, M. (2011). Senior women. ***Women in Canada: A Gender-Based Statistical Report***. Statistics Canada. Catalogue no. 89-503-X. Ottawa, ON: Minister of Industry.

Milan, A., Wong, I., & Vézina, M. (2014). Emerging trends in living arrangements and conjugal unions for current and future seniors. Statistics Canada. Catalogue no. 75-006-X, 1–11. Ottawa, ON: Statistics Canada.

Montemurro, B., & Gillen, M. M. (2013). Wrinkles and sagging flesh: Exploring transformations in women's sexual body image. ***Journal of Women and Aging***, ***25***, 3–23.

Murphy, B., Zhang, X., & Dionne, C. (2012). Low income in Canada: A multi-line and multi-index perspective. ***Income Research Paper Series.*** Statistics Canada. Catalogue no. 751-002M-No. 001. Ottawa, ON: Minister of Industry.

Organization for Economic Co-operation and Development (OECD). (2013). Pensions at a glance—Canada 2013. Retrieved from www.oecd.org/canada/OECD-PensionsAtAGlance-2013-Highlights-Canada.pdf

Osberg, L. (2008). ***A quarter century of income inequality in Canada: 1981–2006***. Toronto, ON: Canadian Centre for Policy Alternatives.

Overall, C. (2006). Old age and ageism, impairment and ableism: Exploring the conceptual and material connections. ***National Women's Studies Association Journal***, ***18***(1), 126–137.

Park, J. (2011). Retirement, health and employment among those 55 plus, ***Statistics Canada***. Catalogue no. 75-001-X, 1–12. Ottawa, ON: Statistics Canada.

Penning, M. J., & Wu, Z. (2014). Marital status, childlessness and social support among older Canadians. *Canadian Journal of Aging*, *33*, 426–447.

Philipson, C. (2006). Aging and globalization: Issues for critical gerontology and political economy. In J. Baars, D. Dannefer, C. Phillipson, & A. Walker (Eds.), *Aging, Globalization and inequality: The new critical gerontology* (pp. 43–58). Amityville, NY: Baywood Publishing.

Preston, V., & D'Addario, S. (2009). Recent migrants in Canadian labour markets: Exploring the impacts of gender and racialisation In S. McKay (Ed.), *Refugees, recent migrants and employment, challenging barriers and exploring pathways* (pp. 139–164). New York, NY: Routledge.

Preston, V., Kim, A., Hudyma, S., Mandell, N., Luxton, M., & Hemphill, J. (2012/2013). Gender, race and immigration: aging and economic security in Canada. *Canadian Review of Social Policy/revue candienne de politique sociale*, *68/69*, 90–106.

Preston, V., Weiser, N., King, K., Mandell, N., Kim, A., & Luxton, M. (2014). Worked to death: Diverse experiences of economic security among older immigrants. In K. Murphy Kilbride (Ed.), *Future immigration policies: Addressing challenges and opportunities during integration into Canada* (pp. 67–84). Toronto, ON: Canadian Scholars Press.

Proulx, C., & Le Bourdais, C. (2014). Impact of providing care on the risk of leaving employment in Canada. *Canadian Journal of Aging*, *33*(4), 488–503.

Pupo, N., & Thomas, M. (Eds.). (2009). *Interrogating the New Economy*. Toronto, ON: University of Toronto Press.

Ray, R. (1996). A postmodern perspective on feminist gerontology. *The Gerontologist*, *36*(5), p. 674–680.

Ray, R. E. (2006). The personal is political: The legacy of Betty Friedan. In T. Calasanti & K. F. Sleven (Eds.), *Age matters: Realigning feminist thought* (pp. 21–45). New York, NY, and London, England: Routledge.

Reinharz, S. (1997). Friends or foes: Gerontological and feminist theory. In M. Pearsall (Ed.), *The other within us: Feminist explorations of women and aging* (pp. 73–91). Boulder, CO: Westview Press.

Sawchuk, D. (2009). The raging grannies: Defying stereotypes and embracing aging through activism. *Journal of Women and Aging*, *21*, 171–185.

Schellenberg, G., & Silver, C. (2004). You can't always get what you want: Retirement preferences and experiences. *Canadian Social Trends*, *11.008*, 2–7.

Seabrook, J. A., & Avison, W. R. Socioeconomic status and cumulative disadvantage processes across the life course: Implications for health outcomes. *Canadian Review of Sociology*, *49*(1), 50–68.

Sinha, M. (2012). Portrait of caregivers, 2012. *Statistics Canada,* Catalogue no. 89-652-X-No. 001, 1–21. Ottawa, ON: Statistics Canada.

Sinha, M., & Bleakney, A. (2014). Receiving care at home, *Statistics Canada*, Catalogue no. 89-652-X — No.002, 1–18. Ottawa, ON: Statistics Canada.

Sontag, S. (1972, September 23). The double standard of aging. *Saturday Review of Society*, 29–38.

Spitze, G., & Logan, J. R. (1992). Helping as a component of parent-adult child relations. *Research on Aging*, *14*(3), 291–312.

Stanford, J. (2014, March 29). Canada's transformation under neoliberalism. *Canadian Dimension*. Retrieved from canadiandimension.com/articles/view/canadas

Statistics Canada. (2010). Economic well-being. *Women in Canada: A Gender-based Statistical Report.* Ottawa, ON: Minister of Industry. Catalogue no. 89-503-X.

Statistics Canada. (2012a). Impact of widowhood and divorce on income replacement among seniors, 1983 to 2007. *The Daily.* June 20.

Statistics Canada. (2012b). Portrait of families and living arrangements in Canada. ***Families, households and marital status, 2011 Census of Population.*** Ottawa: Minister of Industry. Catalogue no. 98-312-X2011001.

Statistics Canada. (2012c). Years to retirement, 1998 to 2009. ***The Daily***. December 4.

Statistics Canada. (2013a). Immigration and ethnocultural diversity in Canada. National Household Survey, 2011. Statistics Canada, Ottawa, Catalogue no. 99-010-X2011001.

Statistics Canada. (2013b). Study: An overview of the working lives of older baby boomers, 1983 to 2010. *The Daily.* October 3.

Statistics Canada, (2014a). Annual demographic estimates: Canada, provinces and territories, 2014. Statistics Canada, Demography Division, Minister of Industry, Ottawa.

Statistics Canada. (2014b). Pension plans in Canada, as of January 1, 2013. ***The Daily***. August 28.

Statistics Canada. (2014c). Registered retirement savings plan contributions, 2012. ***The Daily.*** March 25.

Statistics Canada. (2014d). Study: Employment transitions among older workers leaving long-term jobs. ***The Daily***. January 28.

Stobert, S., & Cranswick, K. (2004). Looking after seniors: Who does what for whom? ***Canadian Social Trends***. Statistics Canada. Catalogue no. 11-008, 2–6.

Thompson, A. E., O'Sullivan, L. F., Byers, E. S., & Shaughnessy, K. (2014). Young adults' implicit and explicit attitudes towards the sexuality of older adults. ***Canadian Journal of Aging***, ***33***(3), 259–270.

Toronto Star. (2014, October 3). Closing the wage gap. p. A16.

Torres, S. (2006). Culture, migration, inequality and 'periphery' in a globalized world: Challenges for ethno- and anthropogerontology. In J. Baars, D. Dannefer, C. Phillipson, & A. Walker (Eds.), ***Aging, Globalization and inequality: The new critical gerontology*** (pp. 231–244). Amityville, NY: Baywood Publishing,

Townson, M. (2006). ***Growing older, working longer: The new face of retirement.*** Ottawa, ON: Canadian Centre for Policy Alternatives.

Trask, B. Sherif. (2013). Locating multiethnic families in a globalizing world. ***Family Relations***, ***62***(February), 17–29.

Treas, J. (2008). Transnational older adults and their families. ***Family Relations***, ***57***(October), 458–478.

Turcotte, M. (2006). Parents with adult children living at home. ***Canadian Social Trends,*** Statistics Canada. Catalogue no. 11-008, 80, 2–10.

Turcotte, M. (2012). Profile of seniors' transportation habits. Statistics Canada. Catalogue no. 11-008-X, 1–16.

Turcotte, M. (2013). Family caregiving: What are the consequences? Statistics Canada. Catalogue no. 75-006-X, 1–14.

Turcotte, M. (2014). Canadians with unmet home care needs. Statistics Canada. Catalogue no. 75-006-X. pp. 1–12.

Turcotte, M., & Schellenberg, G. (2007). A portrait of seniors in Canada. Catalogue no. 89-519-XIE. Ottawa: Statistics Canada, February, 277.

Twigg, J. (2004). The body, gender and age: Feminist insights in social gerontology. ***Journal of Aging Studies***, ***18***(1), 59–73.

Twigg, J. (2013). Fashion and age: Dress, the body and later life. London, England: Bloomsbury Academic.

Uppal, S., & LaRochelle-Côté, S. (2015). Changes in wealth across the income distribution, 1991 to 2012. Statistics Canada, catalogue number: Catalogue no. 75-006-X ISSN 2291-0840, Ottawa, ON: Ministry of Industry.

Uppal, S., & LaRochelle-Côté, S. (2014a). Changes in the occupational profile of young men and women in Canada. *Insights on Canadian Society.* Statistics Canada. Ottawa: Minister of Industry. Catalogue no. 75-006-X.

Uppal, S., & LaRochelle-Côté, S. (2014b). Overqualification among recent university graduates in Canada. *Insights on Canadian Society.* Statistics Canada. Ottawa: Minister of Industry. Catalogue no. 75-006-X.

Wellesley Institute. (2009). *Citizenship Matters: Re-examining Income (In)Security of Immigrant Seniors*. Toronto, ON: Alternative Planning Group.

Wendell, S. (1996). *The rejected body*. London, England: Routledge.

Whalen, D. M., Bigner, J. J., & Barber, C. E. (2000). The grandmother role as experienced by lesbian women. *Journal of Women and Aging*, *12*(3/4), 39–57.

Woodward, K. M. (1999). *Figuring age: Women, bodies, generations*. Bloomington, IN: Indiana University Press.

Zechner, M. (2008). Care of older persons in transnational settings. *Journal of Aging Studies*, *22*(1), 32–44.

Zhou, Y. R. (2012). Space, time and self: Rethinking aging in the contexts of immigration and transnationalism. *Journal of Aging Studies*, *26*, 232–242.

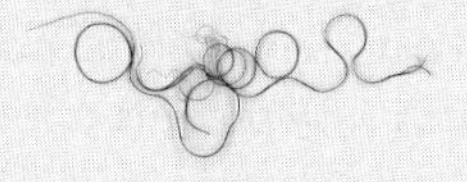

Chapter 10

Mothers' Maintenance of Families Through Market and Family Care Relations

Amber Gazso

INTRODUCTION

Since the mid-20th century, there have been significant and observable changes in the market and family care relations of Canadian families. Women have entered the labour force in ever-increasing numbers and are combining paid work with raising and caring for children, either with a partner or alone. Canadian families are also increasingly racially/ethnically heterogeneous. This diversity is reflected in differences in women's labour market participation and provisions of caregiving and is linked to changes in immigration policy. In addition, ever-growing awareness of the market and family care relations of lesbian and gay couples has coalesced with the legalization of their marriages in 2005, greater recognition of their reproductive rights, and entitlement to social programs and benefits (e.g., pension and health benefits) associated with maintaining families. Finally, for all families, there is the pressing economic need for all adult earners to be involved in some form of labour market attachment.

Intricately related to many of these changes is the neo-liberal weakening of the Canadian welfare state. As both an economic doctrine and a political ideology (Hartman, 2005), a neo-liberal agenda demands governments' increasing openness to national and international market competition and the reduced role of the state in individuals' lives. Since the 1980s, governments have spent less on social programs and more greatly prioritized individuals' responsibility for their own and their family's social and economic well-being. For example, core social policies and programs that provide much needed income support to families, such as social assistance (or welfare) and Employment Insurance (EI) have been scaled back. Families therefore have a much weaker safety net to turn to in times of need.

In the contemporary political economy, the way mothers maintain their families, including their dependent children, through their market and family care relations is a challenge. In addition to their participation in paid work, mothers who share parenting with male partners continue to perform the bulk of domestic labour and manage their child care needs with limited state support to do so. Regardless of the family structure, mothers' disproportional engagement in gender-segregated employment accompanied by few benefits (e.g., paid leaves, and health and dental coverage) translates into fewer resources to provide for their own and their children's income security. This is particularly problematic for lone mothers, who must often stretch limited resources to meet food, shelter, transportation, and child-care demands. Bringing all of these trends together, it is apparent that mothers experience a complex state-family-market nexus in the organization of their daily lives. Mothers' maintenance of families by participating in the labour market and providing care—and juggling both—is indeed the stuff of feminist concern.

In this chapter, I take these changes in Canadian families as our starting point. I focus on how families—in whatever shape or form—are maintained through mothers' engagement in and managing of market and family care relations. Whereas I use the term "market relations" to refer to the structure of the labour market and mothers' paid work experiences, "family care relations" encompasses the caregiving relationships mothers have with their children and other family members. In this chapter, I specifically outline mothers' contemporary labour market and child-care experiences, the challenges associated with these, and the strategies mothers adopt to manage them. I also show how the state, via federal and provincial social policies and programs, intersects with mothers' market and family care relations. In doing so, I assume a focus on mothers who engage in paid and unpaid work. I resist focusing on only heterosexual mothers who are part of white, middle/upper-class, nuclear families with children and instead adopt a more inclusive definition of the family, drawing attention to mothers of varying sexuality and race/ethnicity and how they engage in similar or different ways of maintaining families. I focus primarily on Canadian mothers, but where national scholarship is limited, I draw upon literature from other "liberal welfare states," such as the United States, that share with Canada these changes in market and family care relations and lesser state responsibility for citizens (see also Baker, 2006; Esping-Andersen, 1990). This chapter unfolds with a brief review of some of the ways feminists have understood the connections between women's participation in paid and unpaid work, including housework and child care.

SOME BRIEF FEMINIST INSIGHTS

Feminist scholars have long been concerned with women's (and men's) experiences of paid work and family care responsibilities. All femin*isms* at some time have shared a concern with women's experiences of inequality in one or both domains compared to men's (and other women's) and argued that these experiences are public and political issues. Although space does not permit a comprehensive analysis of the historical evolution of these feminisms, I will make brief mention of how these perspectives are applicable to a focus on mothers' maintenance of families.

Liberal feminists are concerned with women achieving equality of opportunity with men. Liberal feminists have advocated for women's equal education, employment and wage opportunities, equality before the law, choices surrounding their reproduction, and state-endorsed parental leave and child care provisions. Women's and men's equal participation in unpaid work within nuclear families has also been a concern (Garey, Hanson, Hertz, &

MacDonald, 2002). These goals and advocacy for change are intended to improve mothers' ability to balance their participation in paid work and family caregiving.

Not all feminists agree that women can better compete with men in the marketplace if more equal opportunities are available to them. Marxist feminism is cognizant of the economic and structural conditions of society and blends Marxist interests in deconstructing class-based inequalities with feminist interests in deconstructing gender-based inequalities. Of great concern to many Marxist feminists has been the creation of awareness for and among mothers that their caregiving, nurturing, and domestic activities within the home constitutes *work* and has a productive capacity much like any outside market activities. Women's unpaid housework and caregiving activities within the home produce and reproduce workers capable of participating in the labour market on a daily and generational basis (Fox, 1980; Luxton, 2006; Seccombe, 1980).

Marxist feminist scholarship also stresses how the patriarchal character of gender relations "maintain[s] and reproduce[s] the social relations of capitalism" (Weedon, 1999, p. 143). In her classic treatment of housework, for example, Hartmann (1981) argues that the nuclear family is a site of power struggles between women and men that arise over what appear to be unequal efforts at producing and redistributing. By and large, husbands' greater privilege in the labour market and dominance in the home translates into their earning for a family's survival and lesser participation in housework (Hartmann, 1981). Men's domination and power in working-class households is grounded materially in their possession of a primary wage (Seccombe, 1980). When women contribute to the household income through wage work, this does weaken the patriarchal basis of power in the home. And yet, as Fox (1980) highlights, married women's involvement in wage work is still a product of their primary responsibility for maintaining families. Managing total household income against everyday needs is part of this responsibility.

Socialist feminists also critically consider the inequality that characterizes women's and men's market and family care relations. Like Marxist feminists, socialist feminists have stressed how unpaid work performed by women is necessary for the capitalist mode of production (Luxton, 2006). They have particularly highlighted the exploitative conditions of this work. As part of heterosexual couples, mothers' primary responsibility for managing child care and the workforce attachment of their partners and themselves benefits their families. However, this same primary responsibility has a negative impact on mothers' own careers and incomes. More women than men engage in part-time work to manage these demands, a point I will return to later in this chapter.

Socialist feminist approaches also highlight how structures other than class underpin women's oppression, including gender, race/ethnicity, and sexual orientation. For example, racialized lone mothers (or "visible minority" mothers in government and policy discourse) are understood to bear greater responsibility for managing child care and market attachment than other mothers. In addition, socialist feminists have emphasized how institutionalized heterosexuality is implicated in the power relations of class and patriarchy (Dunne, 2000; Weedon, 1999); sexuality cannot be divorced from the material world. As Dunne (2000, p. 137) explains, when we understand men's labour market participation is facilitated by women's unpaid labour in the home, it is important to recognize that heteronormative assumptions about families "provide the logic that translates women's labour into men's material advantage."

Radical feminists, on the other hand, place a greater deal of emphasis on sex oppression as the root of women's and mothers' inequality in the home and labour market (Calixte, Johnson, & Motapanyane, 2005). As Hamilton (2007) explains, they do not dispute patriarchal capitalist relations, but rather argue that this sex oppression is buried far deeper historically and psychically. For some radical feminists, the family has been understood to be a site where men control women's sexuality (Nicholson, 2010/2013); women's roles within the home are created and maintained by men for their own purposes.

Since some of these feminist perspectives were largely articulated by white women for white women, they initially suffered from an inherent racism. Not all of these perspectives accurately matched the realities of racialized women and therefore marginalized women's differences (Hamilton, 2007; Harnois, 2005). Arguably, it was the work of anti-racist and Black feminists who have revealed the Eurocentric and white-centred bias of feminist scholarship from these perspectives. For example, the above feminist perspectives (perhaps with the exclusion of socialist feminism) overlooked how Black women and mothers have been historically denied fair participation in the labour market (e.g., through the practice of slavery before and during the 19th century) and/or have had a lengthier history of participating because of economic necessity (Calliste, 2003; Harnois, 2005; hooks, 1981). Anti-racist feminists therefore attempt to correct these oversights. They prioritize how overlapping and historically specific power relations, discourses, and processes—such as colonization, imperialism, slavery, and systemic racism—affect non-white and white women's social location and thus their historical and contemporary experiences of subjugation and oppression (Bannerji, 2000; Dua, 1999; Hamilton, 2007). As Lerner (1993, p. 245) observes: "Race, class, and gender oppression are inseparable: they construct, reinforce, and support one another." Some anti-racist scholarship incorporates the emphasis on material relations embedded within socialist feminism by examining, for example, how race and gender intersect in the division of paid and unpaid labour to the advantage of white women and men (Mandell, 2005). Other scholarship critiques the radical feminist emphasis on families as a site of sexual oppression. Anti-racist scholars have demonstrated that some women of color have sought the family as a place of refuge from a racist society (Dua, 1999; Mandell, 2005).

As explained by hooks (1981, p. 124): "The first white women's rights advocates were never seeking social equality for all women; they were seeking social equality for white women." Black feminist scholarship works against this feminism. Specifically, Black feminist standpoint theory assumes that Black women exist within an "intersectionality matrix" that refers to their specific location within multiple systems of oppression (Few, 2007). In any explorations of women's and men's experiences of market and family care relations, Black feminists are concerned with injecting a Black consciousness or standpoint into such studies to represent the unique experiences of Black women (Collins, 1989; Few, 2007).

Finally, feminist scholars have also approached the study of women's market and family care relations by using a feminist political economy lens. As understood by Clement (2001, p. 406), the political economy encompasses the state, including government and governance (the political), and the social, political, and cultural constitution of markets, institutions, and actors (the economy). Scholars who use this approach explore society from a materialist perspective and so are theoretically informed by Marxism; social relations are connected to economic relations of production and reproduction (Clement, 2001; Luxton, 2006). Feminists who adopt a political economy approach focus their attention on how political, economic, and cultural processes intersect to create societal conditions of inequality for women. Like other feminisms, emphasis is placed on unpaid work in households and its non-market value (Safri & Graham, 2010). Recent uses of this perspective draw upon insights from the above feminisms to show how capitalist processes of labour, exchange, and production are connected to the changing distribution of power, resources, and rights among citizens (e.g., welfare state restructuring) within households and nation states.

The inequalities that women experience within their market and family care relations are also understood as interlocked with their identities and social structures of race/ethnicity, class, gender, and sexuality (Bezanson, 2006; Danby, 2007; Vosko, 2002). For example, the insights of Marxist and socialist feminists are incorporated into analyses of how the state is not gender neutral and is instead embedded with gendered assumptions surrounding women's and men's participation in market and family care relations (Hamilton, 2005). The scholarly insights of anti-racist and Black feminists are implied in analyses that have shown that poor racialized women have the least capacity to make rights-based claims upon the state to achieve economic security and the well-being of their children. Scholarship in queer theory has sensitized feminist political economy to the need to critique heteronormative assumptions that filter into family, state, and market relationships (Danby, 2007). Finally, migration scholars have used feminist political economy to account for global family and market care relations, relations that occur across borders. Family members may reside in different countries with different political and economic contexts but participate in paid and unpaid work that benefits each other and their respective countries (Safri & Graham, 2010).

With such a myriad of feminisms, the challenge for feminists is to articulate the approach used in their own explorations of women's material everyday realities. I approach the content of this chapter using a feminist political economy lens. I show how Canadian mothers' management of their market and family experiences is shaped by gender, race/ethnicity, sexuality, and class *in relation to* the structural constraints imposed by the political and economic context in which they live. Stated more specifically, I limit my attention to the contemporary labour market and the changing structure of only some federal and provincial social policies and programs. I show how these institutions affect women's structural positions, their entitlement to government income support, and their everyday family experiences as informed by both assumptions about and actual sexuality, gender, race/ethnicity, and class.

THE CONTEMPORARY MARKET AND FAMILY CARE RELATIONS OF MOTHERS

Families, in whatever shape and form, are increasingly maintained through two key processes: market and family care relations. As lone parents or co-parents or living in extended family households, mothers intricately combine their work for pay with family care responsibilities, which include provisions for their children's emotional, physical, and material needs. Depending on the composition of their families, mothers can also provide this care to partners and other adult dependents. However, relations of production (e.g., paid work) and reproduction (e.g., unpaid work or domestic labour, including child care) are not always equally divided among family members. In this section, I explore the inequality that characterizes mothers' market and family care relations and demonstrate how it is created through individual decisions as well as economic and structural forces. To contextualize this focus, it is useful to first explore and compare the employment and income patterns of women and men more generally.

While differences in women's labour force participation have always varied on the basis of their race/ethnicity and class, women on average have steadily increased their labour force participation since the 1950s. Whereas 42% of all women over the age of 15 were part of the paid work force in 1976, 58% of all women were employed and earning wages in some capacity in 2004. During this same period, the proportion of men employed slightly decreased, from 73% in 1976 to 68% in 2004 (Statistics Canada, 2007). By 2009, the percentage of women employed remained steady; almost 60% of Canadian women were employed (Statistics Canada, 2011).

Despite these significant gains made by women, their experiences of the labour market are characterized by differences in the types of work performed and inequality in earnings compared to men (Gazso, 2004; Krull & Sempruch, 2011). Canadian men still occupy employment with higher status and higher pay than do women (Brooks, Jarman, & Blackburn, 2003), such as supervisory or administrative positions in the manufacturing or industry sectors. In contrast, women continue primarily to occupy positions in the services and sales sectors (Wilson, 2005).

Various reasons are cited for this wage inequity, including hourly commitment to paid labour, education level, and occupations chosen. Women are more likely to work part time and accounted for seven out of ten part-time workers in 2009 (Statistics Canada, 2011). Their part-time work falls into the category of non-standard jobs that are characterized by short-term contracts, low skill, low wages, and few benefits (Benoit, 2000). Men, however, are more likely to be employed on a full-time, full-year basis (Baker, 2006; Frenette & Coulombe, 2007). Although the gap between women's and men's earnings has narrowed over time (Heisz, Jackson, & Picot, 2002), 2011 data reveal that for full-time, full-year workers, the average income for women was $47 300 and $65 700 for men; women made 72% of the earnings of men (Statistics Canada, 2013).

In light of women's increasing education levels but continuing income inequality, Frenette and Coulombe (2007) examined the linkages between education and occupations chosen by using census data. They found that women ages 25 to 29 with university degrees who worked full-time for a full year still earned less money than men. Frenette and Coulombe considered that their lower earnings were because they had completed degrees in gendered fields of study (e.g., education, arts, humanities, social sciences, life sciences, and health) that are associated with lower economic returns. For example, whereas 20.6% of women completed a university degree specializing in education in 2001, only 9.4% of men did. And whereas

18.4% of men completed a university degree in engineering in 2001, only 4.3% of women did. Women's and men's choices of education and eventual earnings are also linked to labour market demands. Throughout the 1990s, the high tech sector (e.g., engineering and computer science)—predominantly the purview of men—experienced considerable growth and increased earnings whereas employment in the public sector—predominantly the purview of women—was affected by downsizing and reduced earnings (Frenette & Coulombe, 2007).

Women's unequal experiences within the labour market are further contextualized by their age, immigration status, race/ethnicity, and relationships with state policy. Immigrant women who have been in Canada for some time and are engaged in the labour market earn far less than immigrant men and slightly less than other women (Statistics Canada, 2011). Recent immigrant women are more likely to experience low income or have incomes that fall below Statistics Canada's low income cut offs (LICOs) than Canadian-born women. This is even despite the fact that recent immigrants to Canada are generally more highly educated than Canadian-born women. As well, many women who immigrate to Canada do so as dependents on their spouses (Statistics Canada, 2011) and are unable to work for pay. In general, immigrant women also experience weaker connections with education and training opportunities for future employment and a greater likelihood of being dependent on the state for income support (Statistics Canada, 2007). Like all women, immigrant women who do work for pay are more likely to experience non-standard work conditions (Zeytinoglu & Muteshi, 2000); among all foreign-born women ages 25 to 54 who were employed in 2006, the majority were engaged in non-standard employment in sales and service or in financial, administrative, and business positions (Statistics Canada, 2011).

In general, Canadian-born Aboriginal women, who make up 3% of the population, are less likely to be employed, earn less from their paid work, and are more likely to experience low income than white women. According to the 2006 Census, 51.1% of Aboriginal women over the age of 15 were employed compared to 57.7% of non-Aboriginal women (Statistics Canada, 2011). Similar to other women, Aboriginal women's work is concentrated in non-standard occupations. White, Maxim, and Gyimah (2003) found that Aboriginal women's 1996 labour force activity varied by their Aboriginal status (e.g., registered versus non-registered), education, labour force activity, and family structure. White et al. also found that unemployment among registered Aboriginal women was related to their residence on reserves, low education levels, and the presence of young children. Compared to Aboriginal women who were married or living alone, women with higher education were more likely, and lone mothers with dependent young children less likely, to be employed (White, Maxim, & Gyimah, 2003).

Regardless of their citizenship or immigration status, racialized women also experience income inequality and segregation in the labour market. They are disproportionately unemployed, underpaid, or underemployed in non-standard occupations compared to white Canadian-born women (Galabuzi, 2006; Status of Women Canada, 2005). Women who are immigrants and racialized are triply disadvantaged in the labour market (Palameta, 2004; Wilson, 2005). Age is also a factor connected to income and employment opportunities. Mandell and Wilson (2011) find that many senior women migrate to countries to perform care work for their adult children, for example, caring for their grandchildren (see Chapter 9 in this volume). Racialized, *senior* immigrant women, especially those who are sponsored to come to Canada, are more likely to have lower incomes than women who have lived in Canada for some time (Mandell et al., 2015).

Women's labour force participation is distinctly linked to their mothering and providing child care. Women with children are less likely to be employed than women without children (Statistics Canada, 2011). Generally speaking, having children is a deterrent to women's engagement in continuous full-time, full-year paid work (Statistics Canada, 2011; Wilson, 2005). Mothers are more likely to leave the workforce when rearing and caring for pre-school children. However, recent information does demonstrate that mothers with very young children and male partners have increased their labour force participation, a finding that is not surprising considering the increased cost of living and need for dual-earner families. In 2009, 64.4% of all mothers with children under the age of three participated in the labour market, whereas in 1976 only 27.5% of women did (Statistics Canada, 2011). Whereas 36.8% of women with children ages 3 to 5 engaged in paid work in 1976, 69.7% of mothers with children of these ages did so in 2004. The paid work engagement of mothers also varies by parental status. Lone mothers are less likely to be employed than mothers in two-parent families, although lone mothers' paid work participation has also increased since the mid-1970s (Statistics Canada, 2011).

In nuclear families where mothers work for pay, their experience of inequality in the labour market dovetails with their greater responsibilities for domestic labour (i.e., housework and child care) compared to their partners. Although studies over the last two decades have demonstrated that men have increased their time in domestic or household work and child care (see Marshall, 2006; Sayer, 2005), women still perform a greater amount of this unpaid work, especially when their partners are male (Gazso-Windle & McMullin, 2003; Marshall, 2006; Sayer, 2005). This greater responsibility continues for women into their later years (Krull & Sempruch, 2011).

Marshall (2006) conducted a study of the time Canadians spent in paid and unpaid work and found that the total work day amounted to 8.8 hours on average in 2005, up from 8.2 hours in 1986 (see Figure 10.1). Men's increase in total work hours is attributed to the increased time spent in daily housework, for example, food preparation and vacuuming, whereas women's increase stemmed from their greater time spent in paid work. Figure 10.1 also shows that although gender inequality appears to be slightly reduced in terms of women's and men's time spent in housework, in both 1986 and 2006, women spent more time providing care than men.

In another more recent study of paid and unpaid work, Marshall (2011) compared how the differences in time spent among those ages 20 to 29 varied by those born between 1957 and 1966 (late baby boomers), those born from 1969 to 1978 (Generation X), and those born between 1981 and 1990 (Generation Y). Among nuclear families, she found that women's time spent in housework decreased such that Generation Y women spent 2 hours and 29 minutes on housework in 2010 compared to the 3 hours spent by late baby boomers 1986. Men's time spent in housework has increased. Whereas late baby boomers spent

FIGURE 10.1 Time Spent on Paid and Unpaid Work Among Men and Women, 25–54[1]

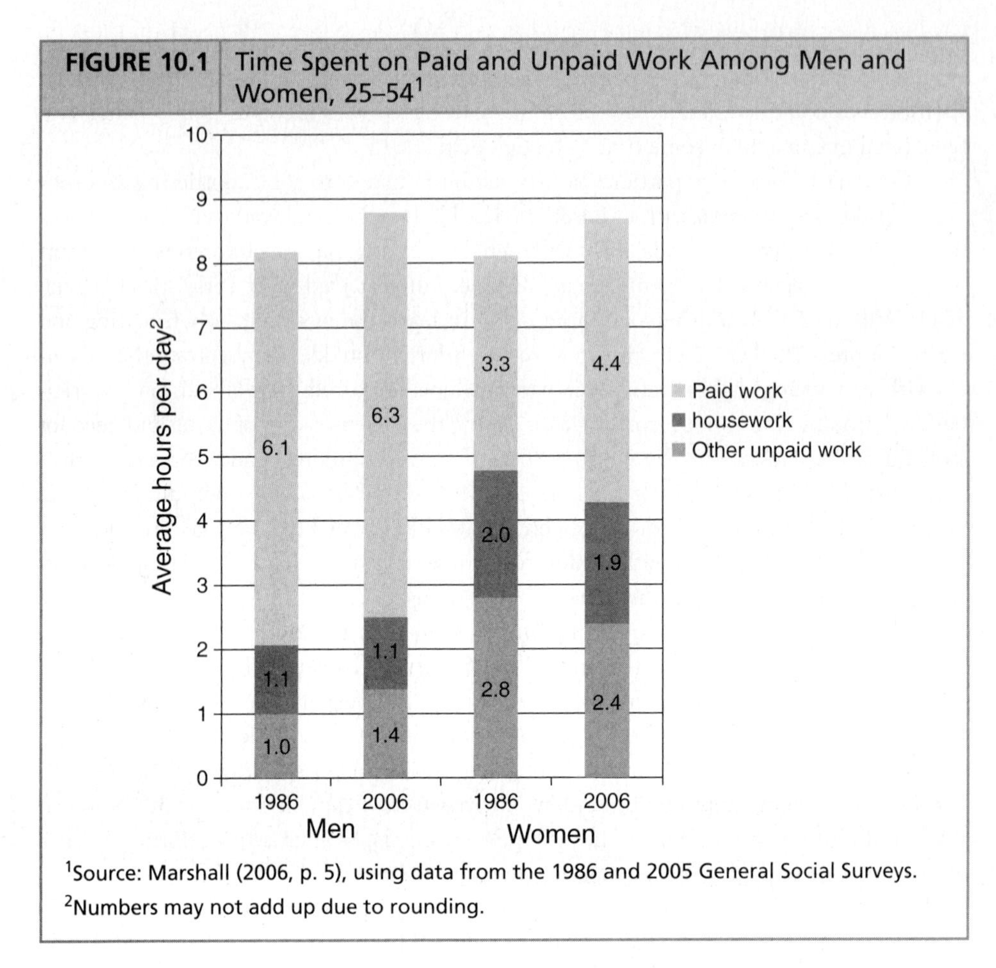

[1]Source: Marshall (2006, p. 5), using data from the 1986 and 2005 General Social Surveys.

[2]Numbers may not add up due to rounding.

1 hour a day doing housework in 1986, Generation Y men spent 1 hour and 30 minutes in 2010. What is interesting about this data is that the number of minutes spent in housework differs by only about a half hour, whether an increase or decrease. Further, Marshall (2011) observes that the presence of children had no significant effect on men's time in paid work whereas it significantly lowered the hours of paid work for women. In essence, while men in nuclear families may have increased their time helping around the home, they have not necessarily shifted their orientation to paid work as their primary responsibility.

Feminist scholars have devoted considerable energy to offering explanations for the unequal amounts of paid and unpaid work performed in nuclear families, especially given women's increased labour force participation. For example, many scholars point to women's greater family responsibilities or gendered workplace structures (e.g., glass ceilings) as contributing to their less than equal experiences compared to men (see, e.g., Cotter, Hermsen, Ovadia, & Vanneman, 2001). Other scholars argue that the gendered division of paid and unpaid work is linked to stereotypical distinctions between the types of work women and men perform as well as women's and men's "doing" of gender in everyday workplace and family activity (see, e.g., Gazso-Windle & McMullin, 2003; West & Zimmerman, 1987). Many of these explanations coalesce into a useful distinction between pragmatic strategies and patriarchal dynamics and their role in producing unequal divisions of unpaid work. Pragmatic strategies refer to time availability and resources (financial and social) and capture many of the time demands associated with managing market and family care responsibilities. Patriarchal dynamics refer to gender and gender ideology and capture how individuals' behaviours are linked to their internalization and identification with particular constructions of gender behaviour in egalitarian or non-egalitarian ways (McFarlane, Beaujot, & Haddad, 2000). Together, pragmatic strategies and patriarchal dynamics are intricately linked to the unequal amounts of time mothers and fathers spend in paid work, housework, and child care. For example, in a study of the division of domestic labour among married and common-law couples, Gazso-Windle and McMullin (2003) found that men's time spent in paid work decreased their time spent in child care, but the same was not true for women. In addition, women who believed that they are primarily responsible for domestic labour spent more time doing housework whereas women who considered paid work to be important to their families' lives spent less.

Examining the market and family care relations of lesbian couples reveals unique differences in how responsibilities for market and family relations are divided. Indeed, the experiences of lesbian couples clearly illustrate how assumptions and beliefs about gender-appropriate behaviour have less power in families where partners share genders. Scholarship on lesbian relationships suggests that a lesbian lifestyle facilitates employment experiences of both women in interesting ways. Or as Dunne (2000) puts it, a lesbian lifestyle "*necessitates* and *facilitates* lifelong financial self-reliance" (p. 138; italics in original). Based on her interviews with women, Dunne concluded that although women's dependence on men over time (often linked to women's exits and entrances into the labour market associated with child-bearing and -rearing) can vary in heterosexual couples with children, lesbian relations are based on mutual dependence. And women's relationships with women facilitate their engagement in the labour market because of the more equitable division of domestic labour within their homes.

Although Arnup's (1995) caution that not all lesbian mothers share the same view of themselves and their children is important to note, several scholars agree that lesbian couples share the quantity of tasks. The tasks are divided based on personal characteristics, each partner's capacity and availability to complete them, the material or subjective value attached to them, and the individual's satisfaction with or preference and justification for engaging in them (see, e.g., Esmail, 2010; Nelson, 2001; Sullivan, 2004). Esmail (2010), for example, interviewed 22 dual-earner lesbian couples and found that even if labour was divided unfairly, justifications that centred on time availability or higher standards of cleanliness were what enabled the couple to come to the agreement that their division of housework was fair.

This review shows that the contemporary market and family care relations of women and men are characterized by differences in occupation and income and by differences in care responsibilities for children. Variations in how mothers participate in these processes must also be understood as contextualized by broader structural forces such as the quality of the labour market and the related availability of family-friendly workplace policies (e.g., benefits). These variations are also linked to how mothers make choices and take advantage of opportunities as they are informed by their gender, racial/ethnic, and sexual identities. Given the layers of inequality that face mothers' efforts to maintain their families, it is no surprise that conflict and challenges can erupt.

MOTHERS' EXPERIENCES OF WORK-FAMILY CONFLICT

For many mothers, the challenge is to meet family needs through market and family care relations without their efforts suffering in either of these activities. When this challenge cannot be met, conflict occurs. As a sociological concept, work-family conflict generally characterizes parents' experiences of being unable, or perceiving that they are unable, to meet the challenge of juggling competing and incompatible time demands associated with their market and family relations (Duxbury, Higgins, & Lee, 1994; Tuten & August, 2006). For example, problems can arise in working mothers' relationships with their male partners and others as a result of their attempts to juggle their mothering with their roles as partners and professionals (Guendozi, 2006; Nomaguchi, 2012). Mothers' experience of work-family conflict illustrates an important feminist assumption—that the spheres of family and work life are not separate (Hammer, Neal, & Perrin, 2004; Krull & Sempruch, 2011). Although scholars do define various forms of this conflict, many also tend to agree that there are four major inter-related types: a time crunch, overload, interference, and stress.

Mothers experience a *time crunch* when the time demands associated with paid work reduce their available time for housework and child care, or vice versa. When experiencing a time crunch, mothers feel that they have insufficient time to complete any task well enough and experience stress in undertaking tasks. Using time-use data from the 1998 General Social Survey, Beaujot and Anderson (2007) found that married Canadian women ages 30 to 59 who were engaged in paid work experienced a greater time crunch if their partners spent more time working for pay than the women did themselves and if they had greater responsibilities for unpaid work within the home. Many women's perceptions of a time crunch are linked to their performance of a "double day" of work—both paid and unpaid—or a "second shift" of unpaid work after the first shift of paid work is complete. In Arlie Hochschild's (1989) oft-cited study of couples where both mothers and fathers worked for pay, she found that the performance of a second shift was distinctly gendered; more mothers performed a second shift than fathers. Among working class families in her study, tensions erupted that were related to the perceived contradiction between couples' beliefs in stereotypical gender roles (e.g., men's breadwinning, women's caregiving) and their family's economic need for two earners. Among middle- or upper-class families, tensions concerned beliefs in the importance of a family's need for care, but differences between partners in the valuation of the work that is needed to produce this care.

Sometimes the mental, physical, and emotional work involved in negotiating time spent meeting market and family care demands is so great for mothers that they experience *overload*—juggling too many demands at once (Duxbury, Higgins, & Lee, 1994). Mattingly and Sayer (2006) find that the availability of free time affects women's and men's perceptions of feeling rushed in different and gendered ways. Because women feel more overloaded and pressured in their attempts to combine a high level of paid work engagement with unpaid work responsibilities, Mattingly and Sayer call that experience a "family penalty."

Family care demands can hinder mothers' participation in paid work. For example, when a young child is ill and outside care is unavailable, a mother may have to take an unexpected day of leave. For many mothers, meeting the care needs of their children when they are engaged in paid work is a costly and precarious endeavour. High-quality child care spaces are often limited and expensive and have hours of operation that must be negotiated alongside paid work hours. In fact, since the Royal Commission on the Status of Women in Canada's recommendations for better child care resources in 1970, the lack of a universal, affordable national system of child care has been cited as a major detriment to women's balancing of market and family care relations (Hamilton, 2005). In a reciprocal manner, mothers' paid work experiences can have a negative effect on their participation in family care activities. Receiving an unexpected assignment at the end of a work day may interfere with a mother's ability to pick up her child from school on time. Not all workplaces pursue family-friendly policies such as employer-provided child care or flex-time to manage child care needs. Scholars refer to these particular time conflict dynamics as "spillover" or "interference" (Duxbury, Higgins, & Lee, 1994; Skrypnek & Fast, 1996). *Interference* can be characterized more specifically as work-to-family or family-to-work conflict (Hammer et al., 2004). Whereas work-to-family conflict stems from characteristics of the workplace, such as a parent's work role or hours, family-to-work conflict is an outcome of characteristics of family life, such as the family or gender role of a parent and having young children (Roehling, Jarvis, & Swope, 2005). These dynamics of interference are intricately inter related: "if one's work-related problems begin to interfere with the completion of one's family-related obligations, these unfulfilled family obligations will begin to interfere with one's day-to-day functioning at work and vice versa" (Hammer, Neal, & Perrin, 2004, p. 98).

Another way to see work-family conflict is as work- or family-related *stress* or psychological distress (Rosenberg, 1995). Young and Wheaton (2013), for example, conceptualize work-family conflict as a chronic stressor. Not surprisingly, mothers can experience considerable stress when they cannot be in two places at once or negotiate competing demands. In their own study of working mothers, Young and Wheaton (2013) find that mothers' work-family conflict and overall distress is linked to the perception that their experiences are unusual relative to other residents in their communities.

In essence, all of these types of work-family conflict are distinctly related to a mother's overall experience of satisfaction with her paid work and family life, and can have a significant impact on her own mental and physical well-being as well as her relationship with her partner or children. However, as Guendozi (2006) observes, although stress is a typical outcome of managing market and family care relations, it is also important to recognize that engagement in paid work often provides mothers with an outlet to express their identity in a positive manner.

The majority of scholarship on work-family conflict has focused on white professional women who are part of heterosexual, dual-earning unions (Ciabatteri, 2007; Gazso, 2007a;

Roehling, Jarvis, & Swope, 2005). Other scholars have responded by focusing on how work-family conflict is linked to parenthood/marital status, class, race/ethnicity, and sexuality. Nomaguchi's (2012) research, for example, reveals that single mothers and fathers perceive greater work-family conflict associated with job pressures than married mothers and fathers. Nomaguchi (2012) attributes this to parents having fewer child care resources, such as when asked to work overtime. Using data collected from a sample of working-class couples transitioning into new parenthood, Goldberg, Pierce, and Sayer (2007) found that mothers' and fathers' working evening or night shifts correlated with higher levels of depressive symptoms but only mothers experienced a greater deal of conflict in their relationships as a result of working rotating shifts.

Low-income lone mothers who manage paid work and family demands, particularly those who receive income support from the government, face even greater challenges. They have few economic and social resources and more time constraints, experience more barriers in the labour market, and face great pressure to exit assistance through paid employment (Crouter & Booth, 2004; Gazso 2007a, 2007b; McMullin, Davies, & Cassidy, 2002; Roy, Tubbs, & Burton, 2004). In Canada, lone-mother families constitute the greatest proportion of families on social assistance. Increasingly, social assistance policy and programs (which are managed and administered by each province) require that mothers demonstrate that they are seeking employment either by conducting job searches or participating in welfare-to-work programs in order to maintain their receipt of monthly benefits. Mothers must meet these employment expectations when their children are very young (e.g., six months old in Alberta, three years old in British Columbia) and so require greater amounts of caregiving support and in view of limited economic resources (their total welfare benefits fall below low income cut offs).

In my own past research, I interviewed 28 white or Aboriginal/Métis lone mothers on social assistance in three provinces: British Columbia, Alberta, and Saskatchewan, to see how they manage policy expectations and their caregiving responsibilities. I found that lone mothers who were expected to conduct job searches or attend programs in order to prepare for paid work experienced a time crunch and felt overloaded or overburdened trying to meet the demands of paid work and care for young children, much like that experienced by middle- or upper-class mothers who engage in paid work (see also Gazso, 2007a). Lone mothers also experienced interference when family care responsibilities hindered their employability efforts and vice versa. Indeed, mothers' experiences of conflict are linked to how they cannot afford good quality child care in order to participate in employment readiness programs. Not only do child-care subsidies provided by governments fail to provide the full costs of day care, but there is also a shortage of licensed daycare spaces (Breitkreuz, 2005). The main difference between the work-family conflict experiences of low-income lone mothers and other working mothers is that lone mothers on social assistance are under surveillance and have their efforts at managing work and family scrutinized by caseworkers in order to remain eligible for income support.

My research also revealed that compared to white mothers, Aboriginal and Métis lone mothers understood their contemporary experiences of interference as linked to their families' historical experiences of colonization and assimilation, as well as to their family composition. In particular, Aboriginal mothers from a major city in Saskatchewan acknowledged that their opportunities for good jobs were limited due to racism. They also indicated that many of their extended kin networks that could help with child care were unavailable in their urban communities; mothers' access to these networks would be greater if they lived on reserves.

Other scholarly research shows that labour market participation can interfere with racialized women's satisfaction with their marital unions. In their survey of married Black and white mothers in paid labour, Bridges and Orza (1996) found that Black women's employment in managerial or professional careers was more significantly related to marital conflict with their partners than white women's employment. Marital dissatisfaction among Black married and cohabitating women and men has, in turn, been found to be related to high levels of work-family conflict (St. Vil, 2014). However, in a study conducted on work-family spillover among diverse families, Grzywacz, Almeida, and McDonald (2002) found that Black families experienced lower forms of negative spillover from work to family compared to white families. Grzywacz et al. state that this difference is likely due to how employed Black family members can rely upon more instrumental assistance, such as caregiving support from extended families, than white families. On the basis of their study of Black, white, and Hispanic families, Roehling, Jarvis and Swope (2005) found that work-to-family interference was experienced more by Hispanic women than men, particularly when women perceived their paid work activity as inconsistent with gender role expectations of them in the family home.

Like women in relationships with men, the spillover of work life into family life can negatively affect lesbian mothers' family care relations. In their survey of lesbian mothers engaged in paid work (predominantly as managers or professionals) while in long-term relationships, Tuten and August (2006) found that their experiences of work-family conflict were linked to hours worked, job role autonomy, and elements of the workplace culture. In particular, autonomy in a mother's job did not reduce her experience of work-family conflict, leading Tuten and August to argue that a more autonomous job might be accompanied by greater responsibility and more obligations. What is significant about this study is that when coupled with the above findings it can be understood that irrespective of a mother's sexuality, the particular dynamics of her workplace are linked to her perceptions of work-family conflict and therefore her subsequent experiences of stress and overall life dissatisfaction.

To summarize, at some time or other most mothers feel that their family lives are spilling over into their paid work lives and vice versa. Their experiences of work-family conflict are contextualized by broader normative ideological assumptions about gender and caregiving and cultural assumptions specific to their membership in particular racial/ethnic groups. Whether they are lone parents or have male partners, mothers' experiences of work-family conflict are connected to their efforts to reconcile changing but often contradictory gendered and cultural expectations in what are still ideologically separate spheres of work and family. While the rigidity of gender stereotypes and ideologies appear to disappear for lesbian couples with children, they too can experience conflict in trying to manage labour market and family care relations. Mothers' experiences of work-family conflict are also linked to the structure and culture of their workplaces, their income, and their relationships with income support and child care policies. In response to their experiences of work-family conflict, many mothers rely upon one or more strategies to juggle their competing demands.

STRATEGIES FOR MANAGING AND SUSTAINING MARKET AND FAMILY CARE RELATIONS

Existing scholarship shows that mothers adopt a variety of strategies for managing work-family conflict. Although couple unions can dissolve when mothers and their partners cannot reconcile competing paid work and family demands, this section focuses on some of the strategies mothers use when parenting with a partner. I also show how low-income, lone mothers, and mothers who are domestic workers and part of transnational families use various strategies to manage their market and family care relations in light of their relationships with state policies.

Some mothers respond to work-family conflict by simply engaging in an "overload" of unpaid work, doing housework and child care on top of paid work hours to the point of experiencing exhaustion or burnout (Luxton, 2001). Other mothers will manage the competing demands of paid and unpaid work by engaging in what Hochschild (1997) identifies as a "third shift": many mothers understood the home as another workplace. On the basis of her research Hochschild argues that a cult of efficiency associated with modern workplaces has materialized in the home and creating parents' perceptions of a time bind. Parents then become compelled to schedule quality time with their children or their spouses just as they would schedule meetings at work. The efforts that are required to perform this scheduling—to manage children's resistance and their own emotions in the process—constitute the third shift.

In nuclear families, mothers also have the option of convincing their partners to share the unpaid labour. As we observed earlier, this is far more difficult than it might seem because of pragmatic factors associated with partners' workplace expectations, as well as ideological assumptions surrounding income earning and caregiving. Moreover, the fact that mothers still do more housework and child care than men, even when both are engaged in paid labour, confirms the difficulty of adopting this strategy. However, as Ranson (2010) found, there are a small number of families in which mothers and fathers go against the grain of conventional divisions of domestic labour. Ranson's study of 32 couples, including gay and lesbian couples, revealed three patterns: 1. "crossovers," where mothers work full-time, full-year and fathers take on greater homemaking responsibilities; 2. "shift workers," where mothers and fathers organized their paid work at different times of day so that one parent could be with the child at all times; and 3. "dual dividers," where both parents worked full-time and shared housework and child care. And as Doucet's (2006) research additionally shows, some fathers in nuclear families actually "mother" and it is their wives who are the primary earners.

As noted earlier, the sharing of unpaid work in an egalitarian manner does seem to be a suitable option for lesbian mothers who co-parent. Because creativity, cooperation, and the denial of gendered meanings can shape the lesbian parenting experience, couples with children will often take turns in being the main care provider for children, or the birth mother and her partner may each reduce their hours of work to part time (Dunne, 2000; Sullivan, 2004).

Lesbian mothers may also use another strategy to manage their perceptions of conflicting time demands. Tuten and August (2006) found that some lesbian mothers could reduce their work-family conflict, including perceptions of time-based and strain-based (e.g., strain in one role affects performance of another role) work-family conflict, by being "out" in their workplace. The act of making their sexual identity and family care responsibilities visible in the workplace lessened some lesbian mothers' experiences of work-family conflict.

Another way in which mothers cope with balancing market and family care relations is to change occupations or time spent in paid work. Recent American research suggests that this way of managing work-family conflict is connected to race/ethnicity. Scaling back paid work hours, for example, is more common among white and Asian mothers than Black mothers (Landivar, 2013). Mothers may also seek a workplace that is more accommodating of work-family challenges. Some workplaces are indeed successful at this. Kelly, Moen, and Tranby (2011), for example, demonstrate the positive effects of employees' participation in ROWE (Results-Only Work Environment), which shifts the workplace culture so that is normal for employees to decided when and how to work, providing the work is completed. ROWE accommodates people who want to work traditional work hours and those who would like the flexibility to work in different environments and at different hours. In a survey of employees at a large corporation, Kelly et al. (2011) found that ROWE can reduce work-family conflict and spillover and can increase mothers' perceptions of schedule control. Still other workplaces endorse "family-friendly" policies (e.g., child care provisions or flex-time [shorter or condensed time]) that can reduce mothers' levels of stress (Glass, 2004). However, the risk of these policies is that they may be used to justify mothers' lower wages, job security, and opportunities for advancement because working women with children are perceived to be on a "mommy track" (Konrad & Cannings, 1994; Mandel, 2005; Weedon, 2005).

Many mothers rely upon networks of social support to manage their market and family care relations, including formal and informal support (Connidis, 2001). "Formal support" refers to financial or material assistance provided to families by agencies and services on behalf of state programs or community organizations. The general trend toward weakening the welfare state, discussed previously, has reduced the formal supports available to families today. Mothers can turn to fewer social policies and programs to support their own and their children's material and emotional needs. Provincial governments increasingly assume that mothers will turn to support provided by community non-government and non-profit organizations, as well as relying on informal support from others (Gazso & McDaniel, 2015). Indeed, in light of these circumstances, many mothers turn to family, friends, and neighbours for "informal support" that can include expressive or emotional support—affection or intimacy—and/or instrumental support in the form of financial or physical aid (Langer, 1995).

Exchanges of informal support among family members often involve reciprocity or exchange within and across generations (Offer, 2012). As well, the amount, type, and source of informal supports exchanged within mothers' families are linked to their composition. Census data suggests that Canadian families are increasingly characterized by "cluttered nests" (Mitchell, Wister, & Gee, 2004), where more children are living at home with a parent or parents and grandparents (Milan, Vézina, & Wells, 2006). In extended and multi-generational families, mothers draw upon several family members for support in order to meet their labour market and family care relations (Gee & Mitchell, 2003). In my own research, I have found that, in addition to income support from the government in the form of social assistance, lone mothers rely on other supports. These included formal support from community organizations (e.g., food banks) and exchanges of instrumental and expressive support (e.g., child care, transportation) with parents, siblings, friends, peers, or neighbours in order to meet employment and caregiving needs (Gazso, 2007b; Gazso & McDaniel, 2013).

Racially/ethnically diverse families in Canada also involve other family members and friends in social support networks to manage paid work and family demands. Among Black families, extended family ties, involving multiple generations in care relations, play an important role in their lives (Calliste, 2003; Mays, Mays, Chatters, Cochran, & Mackness, 1998; Stack, 1974). Fiske and Johnny (2003) illustrate the importance of Aboriginal families' reliance on extended family networks for expressive and instrumental support. These families' use of support networks today are linked to history, specifically past family members' need to rely on each other in response to their experience of social and economic oppression, racism, and colonization. Penha-Lopes (2006) further argues that the historical and cultural conditions requiring Black mothers to engage in paid work demanded that they socialize their children in ways that impacted their own and their children's future market and care relations. In her study of Black men, she found that as boys they were especially socialized to be competent at housework, and this domestic independence has continued into later life.

Kobayashi's (2000) study of the support relations between generations of Japanese families shows that third-generation adult children conform to *oya koh koh*, or filial obligation, to their second-generation parents; they are more likely to provide expressive support to aging parents and more so to mothers than fathers. If adults do provide their parents with financial support, this is related to their parents' actual need for assistance rather than the children's endorsement of oya koh koh. Kobayashi maintains that, when contextualized by the support relations among generations in Japan, support relations and the traditional cultural ideas that have informed them among Japanese-Canadian families have been transformed with each successive generation.

Paying someone else to perform housework, child care, and other family care responsibilities in the home is another strategy that some mothers may use to manage competing work and family demands. In some cases, mothers hire outside domestic services to visit their home on a weekly or biweekly basis. In other cases, mothers hire live-in domestic service workers or nannies, many of whom are immigrant women. This strategy particularly highlights how the dynamics of gender, race/ethnicity, and class intersect with state policy. More than one family is affected by a Canadian mother's purchase of another mother's services to manage her market and family care relations, as we will see.

Transnational Management of Paid Work and Family Care

Many domestic workers migrate to Canada from countries such as the Philippines to take on mothering and domestic roles—or women's work—for other Canadian mothers' families. The work of domestic workers permits some Canadian mothers to engage in paid work with less tension and fewer time constraints associated with also meeting family care responsibilities. Arat-Koc (2006) argues that the Live-In Caregiver Program (LCP), the federal social policy that shapes domestic workers' lives in Canada, is based on an implicit assumption that domestic workers are single woman. The majority of migrant domestic workers who enter Canada, however, are mothers with children. They perform domestic labour for pay in order to provide for their families in their countries of origin; domestic workers usually send at least half of their earnings home. The money that domestic workers earn not only helps meet their families' social and material needs, but also contributes to the economic development of their countries of origin (Arat-Koc, 2006).

Mothers who are domestic workers are thus part of "transnational families" and so engage in trans-border management of paid work and family relations. One way that these mothers manage their paid work and their own family care demands from afar is to leave children behind in the care of another female family member. This can create tensions for mothers in their new country surrounding the affordability of family life in two places and their need to blend cultural traditions with adaptation if not full assimilation (Cohen, 2000; Gazso & McDaniel, 2015; Salazar Parrenas, 2000). Moreover, transnational mothering invokes mothers' feelings of responsibility and guilt over family separation and deprives mothers of meeting their own needs for intimacy (Arat-Koc, 2006; Cohen, 2000). Women who engage in domestic work must care for someone else's children while being unable to care for their own, as they had before they accepted overseas employment (Brigham, 2015; Salazar Parrenas, 2000). Brigham's (2015) study of undocumented Jamaican mothers who perform domestic work for others illustrates how they manage family income needs and caring from afar and find it to be an anxiety-inducing process. Often, mothers feel that their provisioning for the economic security and well-being of their children back home conflicts with the gender normative prescription that mothers best provide for their children immediately and in their presence, not from afar.

In many ways, the guilt that Canadian mothers can experience when juggling market and family care relations can be decreased by hiring another woman. Domestic workers who are mothers, however, bear a similar guilt, compounded by their desire to meet their children's needs. Moreover, other contradictions emerge along gender, race/ethnicity, and class lines when we consider this coping strategy critically. Reproductive labour is a commodity traditionally bought by class-privileged women (Salazar Parrenas, 2000), as it is predominantly middle- to upper-class white mothers who employ domestic workers (most often racialized women) to perform caregiving services (Cohen, 2000; Hodge, 2006). Although mothers in Canada might be seen as liberated because of their ability to engage in paid work and hire others to facilitate this engagement, their purchase of other women's labour power demonstrates that gendered assumptions about caregiving as a women's domain are still strong (Arat-Koc, 2006; Pratt, 2003; Salazar Parrenas, 2000) and are supported by social policy. At the same time that domestic workers benefit their families through their paid work and Canadian mothers benefit from receiving assistance with juggling multiple demands, the practice of employing domestic workers continues to effectively devalue and feminize domestic work.

Despite these contradictions, Arat-Koc (2006, p. 87) makes the significant observation that domestic workers and their female employers share a common condition. Although they may be different in race/ethnicity and class, "they both experience paid work as incompatible with their reproduction roles and responsibilities." For Arat-Koc (2006), this common condition is even more strikingly visible when we see that domestic workers are needed precisely because the Canadian state does not provide enough support, such as accessible and affordable high-quality child care, for mothers to manage their paid work and caregiving needs.

The varieties of strategies mothers use to manage their competing demands reflect the particular market and family care relations of families, total household income, family members' values and beliefs, state policies that facilitate the hiring of domestic workers, and structural and economic forces beyond families' control. While space does not permit a comprehensive analysis of how neo-liberal restructuring has affected all programs and policies that support families, the next section does specifically consider whether and federal parental leave policy alleviates the conflict associated with mothers' and fathers' management of their labour market and family care relations.

THE ROLE OF THE STATE: PARENTAL LEAVE POLICY

The list that follows outlines some federal and provincial policies and programs that support provisions of care and children's social and economic well-being. Parental leave falls under the federal government's jurisdiction, specifically Employment Insurance. The Canada Child Tax Benefit is a federal program aimed to help families with the costs of raising children under the age of 18 years; it is targeted at working families with incomes below a particular threshold. As discussed earlier, social assistance programs and some specific health benefits targeted at low-income families also fall under provincial jurisdiction.

Some Family Policies in Canada, 2014[1]

Federal

- Medicare
- Employment Insurance
- Maternity and Parental Leave
    - Compassionate Care Benefit
- Canada Child Tax Benefit
    - National Child Benefit Supplement
- Child Disability Benefit

Universal Child Care Benefit
Old Age Security

Provincial/Territorial[2]

Adult/child health benefit plans (for low-income families)
Child benefit and credit programs
Child care subsidy programs
Social assistance programs
Workers compensation boards

Structural/compositional and heteronormative assumptions about families and the way they are maintained have always been deeply embedded in Canadian federal and provincial policies and programs for families. In many ways, current family policies tend to prioritize nuclear family relations, assuming that a "family" consists of two cohabitating heterosexual partners and one or more children. In effect, policies for families can obscure and deny the diversity of families as well as the multitude of ways market and family care relations are organized.

In the final section of this chapter, my intent is to show the problematic assumptions that are embedded within parental leave policy. In doing so, I also illustrate how mothers' access to parental leave may not necessarily facilitate more equitable divisions of paid and unpaid work in Canadian families.

Some employed mothers in Canada have had access to cash benefits for maternity leave from employment since 1971. Under what was then called the Unemployment Insurance (UI) Act, mothers' eligibility for leave was based on the number of weeks worked for pay (Pulkingham, 1998). Mothers were entitled to 15 weeks of leave, whereas both parents were entitled to 10 weeks of unemployment insurance compensation (Baker, 1997). Pregnant women who decided to use both maternity and parental leave benefits could receive a total of 25 weeks of compensation, originally 60% of their previous earnings. Provisions of maternity leave (leave for childbirth) were based upon the assumption that it was necessary to compensate for the employment-related hazards, preparation, and recuperation of pregnant mothers. It was not until 1990 that adoptive parents and biological fathers were also entitled to these benefits. The availability of parental leave demonstrated the state's acknowledgement of the participation of both adoptive parents and biological fathers in childbirth and child-care responsibilities.

As part of the general trend of welfare state restructuring, Unemployment Insurance (UI) was replaced with the stricter Employment Insurance (EI) Act in 1996. With fewer funds for this program, changes were made to mothers' and fathers' eligibility. When EI was introduced, parents' eligibility for either maternity or parental leave became determined on the basis of their hours of work (as opposed to weeks of work under UI). To be eligible, parents had to work a minimum of 700 hours or 20 weeks of work at 35 hours per week in the past 52 weeks (Benoit, 2000); this change also involved an extension of the work time—35 hours per week (instead of 15) over 20 weeks. Under EI, mothers were entitled to 55% of their previous earnings for up to 25 weeks if they took both maternity and parental leave.

More recent changes to EI have extended the time parents can access benefits. As of 2001, providing mothers meet 600 hours of insured work, they can access 15 weeks of maternity leave and 35 weeks of parental leave at 55% of their earning, for a total of 50 weeks of paid leave. In addition, new opportunities exist for women to engage in some paid work while on maternity leave. According to then Human Resources Development Canada (2001) (now Human Resources and Social Development Canada, or HRSD) the changes made in 2001 ensured that maternity and parental leave benefits were more accessible, more flexible, and better adapted to families' lives. However, a more critical analysis reveals otherwise.

Expectant mothers who participate in non-standard jobs can be excluded from receiving maternity benefits simply because they may not work the 30 hours of work per week over 20 weeks that makes them eligible (Benoit, 2000). Even if mothers are able to access benefits, a drop in their monthly income may drive some mothers into poverty. As Ruhm (2012) observes, Canada provides lower wage replacement rates for maternity leave than many European countries. Moreover, race/ethnicity and class intersect and shape women's ability to access parental leave. As observed, recent immigrant women are less likely to be employed and, if they are, they are likely to work in non-standard and insecure occupations.

Upon introduction of the new policy, HRSD claimed that the new leave duration is more flexible: there is no waiting period for the second claim if parents in a two-parent family decide to share the benefits. And yet, this claim is also misleading. Leave benefits policy did and still does assume nuclear families. Flexibility may exist in terms of access, but not in terms of how leave time is divided among parents. The 55% benefit rate tends to assume that pregnant women who qualify for maternity benefits have partners who are primary income earners. If the lower income earner, usually the mother, applies for leave benefits, this thereby ensures that the family income is maintained at a higher level. This also ensures that the mother is primarily responsible for caring for children and is economically dependent on her partner for her own and her children's economic security. If we acknowledge how cultural and ideological beliefs shape mothers' and fathers' gendered identities across race/ethnicity and class, we can see how leave policy can perpetuate inequality in paid and unpaid labour.

Finally, we must question whether the new leave is better adapted to all Canadian families. Parents can now engage in paid work when they take parental leave. Although parents may benefit from the ability to earn a small income while accessing benefits, it is possible that this capability is limited. For example, it is not clear what type of employment is amenable to this provision, and not all employers would agree to a limited employment situation. Moreover, the claim that parental leave is more adaptable is questionable when we consider that the present policy assumes the availability of affordable, accessible, and high-quality child care that will enable parents eventually to return to their paid employment. Some women in two-parent families will choose to stay at home for their children's first few years because it would cost more to put children in day care than the wage they are earning. As to whether this is an actual "choice" of mothers is a matter of debate—the parameters of leave policy and the inadequate day care provisions suggest that many women's choices are actually structured and shaped in varying degrees. And yet, it may also be impossible to afford to stay at home.

To summarize, the state, via parental leave policy, supports the management of work and family demands for some but not all working mothers. Parental leave policy therefore does not universally alleviate mothers' experiences of conflicting demands associated with earning a living and providing care. This is not to discount the important role that leave policy plays for eligible mothers; it allows them temporarily to negotiate paid work and family care demands associated with having and rearing children. However, considering mothers who parent with male partners, the way leave is divided can predict mothers' future experiences of work-family conflict. If mothers in two-parent families access all available leave, their partners may expect them to continue their primary caregiving, and thus, they will be more likely to experience work-family tensions when they re-enter the labour market.

CONCLUSION

This chapter began with a brief overview of how feminist scholars have devoted considerable attention to how mothers manage their family's economic and social well-being through an intricate juggling of labour market participation and provisions of care to all members. The contemporary labour market experiences of mothers were shown to not equal those of men, reflecting structural and discriminatory barriers in workplaces and policies that inhibit their labour market participation, as well as mothers' choices about meeting their families' care needs. Mothers' experiences of a time crunch, overload, interference, and stress were strongly linked to their unequal responsibilities for meeting market and family care demands. The challenges mothers face vary with their race/ethnicity or sexuality and can be further exacerbated by low-income and ideological expectations of nurturing and caregiving, in addition to available employment, weak state support, and their own choices. Furthermore, some of the coping strategies mothers use to juggle demands and alleviate conflict may have the desired impact of relieving time pressure, while other strategies may have problematic implications, such as perpetuating gender roles in two-parent families or denying mothering to domestic workers who are part of transnational families. Still other policy-endorsed strategies, such as mothers' entitlement to parental leave, reveal how state support is not adequately available to all.

To conclude, I have used a feminist political economy lens in this chapter to highlight how mothers' maintenance of families through their market and family care relations is related to the unequal structural conditions that characterize workplaces in the capitalist labour market and the constraints imposed by social policy subject to a neo-liberal agenda. I also showed how mothers' maintenance of families is linked to their own choices and opportunities in light of these social, political, and economic forces that affect their everyday material realities. Clearly, a state-family-market nexus informs and shapes labour market and family care relations—relations that are predominantly maintained and managed by mothers and thus continue to be of feminist concern.

Endnotes

1. This list of examples is not exhaustive but includes the most common policies that families with children can access.
2. Provincial and territorial offerings of these programs vary in availability, accessibility, structure, benefit amounts, etc.

Discussion Questions

1. What is one way in which each feminist perspective reviewed in this chapter has been concerned with women's experiences of inequality in their market and family care relations, compared to men's (and other women's)? Which perspective do you think best explains this inequality?
2. How do gender, race/ethnicity, sexuality, and class intersect to influence women's and men's experiences within the Canadian labour market and of work-family conflict?
3. How are the strategies used to balance work and family demands by lesbian mothers different than those adopted by mothers in heterosexual unions? Could the strategies used by lesbian mothers be the basis for a more equitable work-family balance model adopted by mothers in heterosexual unions?
4. In what ways has the Canadian state worsened or facilitated mothers' and fathers' negotiation of their market and family care relations?

Bibliography

Arat-Koc, S. (2006). Whose social reproduction? Transnational motherhood and challenges to feminist political economy. In K. Bezanson & M. Luxton (Eds.), *Social reproduction: Feminist political economy challenges neo-liberalism* (pp. 75-92). Montreal, QC: McGill-Queen's University Press.

Arnup, K. (1995). "We are family": Lesbian mothers in Canada. In E. D. Nelson & B. W. Robinson (Eds.), *Gender in the 1990s: Images, realities, and issues* (pp. 330-345). Toronto, ON: Nelson Canada.

Baker, M. (1997). Parental benefit policies and the gendered division of labour. *Social Service Review, 71*, 51–71.

Baker, M. (2006). *Choices and constraints in family life*. Don Mills, ON: Oxford University Press.

Bannerji, H. (2000). The Paradox of diversity: The construction of multicultural Canada and "women of colour." *Women's Studies International Forum, 23*, 537–560.

Beaujot, R., & Anderson, R. (2007). Time crunch: Impact of time spent in paid and unpaid work and its division in families. *Canadian Journal of Sociology, 32*, 295–315.

Benoit, C. M. (2000). *Women, work and social rights: Canada in historical and comparative perspective*. Toronto, ON: Harcourt Brace.

Bezanson, K. (2006). *Gender, the state, and social reproduction: Household insecurity in neo-liberal times*. Toronto, ON: University of Toronto Press.

Breitkreuz, R. (2005). Engendering citizenship? A critical-feminist analysis of Canadian welfare-to-work policies and the employment experiences of lone mothers. *Journal of Sociology and Social Welfare, 32*, 147–165.

Bridges, J. S., & Orza, A. M. (1996). Black and white employed mother's role experiences. *Sex Roles, 35*, 377–385.

Brigham, S. M. (2015). Mothering has no borders: The transnational kinship networks of undocumented Jamaican domestic workers in Canada. In G. Man & R. Cohen (Eds.), *Engendering transnational voices: Studies in family, work and identities* (pp. 135–153). Waterloo, ON: Wilfrid Laurier University Press.

Brooks, B., Jarman, J., & Blackburn, R. M. (2003). Occupational segregation in Canada: 1981–1996. *Canadian Review of Sociology and Anthropology, 40*, 197–213.

Calixte, S. L., Johnson, J. L., & Maki, M. J. (2005). Liberal, socialist, and radical feminism: An introduction to three theories about women's oppression and social change. In N. Mandell (Ed.), *Feminist issues: Race, class and sexuality* (pp. 1–34). Toronto, ON: Prentice Hall.

Calliste, A. (2003). Black families in Canada: Exploring the interconnections of race, class and gender. In M. Lynn (Ed.), *Voices: Essays on Canadian families* (pp. 199–220). Scarborough, ON: Thomson Nelson.

Ciabatteri, T. (2007). Single mothers, social capital, and work-family conflict. *Journal of Family Issues, 28*, 34–40.

Clement, W. (2001). Canadian political economy's legacy for sociology. *Canadian Journal of Sociology, 26*, 405–417.

Cohen, R. (2000). "Mom is a stranger": The negative impact of immigration policies on the family life of Filipina domestic workers. *Canadian Ethnic Studies 32*, 76–89.

Collins, P. Hill. (1989). The social construction of Black feminist thought. *Journal of Women in Culture and Society, 14*, 745–773.

Connidis, I. Arnet. (2001). *Family ties and aging*. Thousand Oaks, CA: Sage.

Cotter, D. A., Hermsen, J. A., Ovadia, S., & Vanneman, R. I. (2001). The glass ceiling effect. *Social Forces, 80*, 655–682.

Crouter, A. C. & Booth, A. (Eds.). (2004). *Work-Family Challenges for Low Income Parents and their Children*. New York, NY: Routledge.

Danby, C. (2007). Political economy and the closet: Heteronormativity in feminist economics. *Feminist Economics*, *13*, 29–53.

Doucet, A. (2006). *Do men mother? Fathering, care and domestic responsibility*. Toronto, ON: University of Toronto Press.

Dua, E. (1999). Beyond diversity: Exploring ways in which the discourse of race has shaped the institution of the nuclear family. In E. Dua & A. Robertson (Eds.), *Scratching the surface: Canadian anti-racist thought* (pp. 237–260). Toronto, ON: Women's Press.

Dunne, G. A. (2000). Lesbians as authentic workers? Institutional heterosexuality and the reproduction of gender inequalities. *Sexualities, 3*, 133–148.

Duxbury, L. Higgins, C., & Lee, C. (1994). Work-family conflict: A comparison by gender, family type, and perceived control. *Journal of Family Issues, 15*, 449–466.

Esmail, A. (2010). "Negotiating fairness": A study on how lesbian family members evaluate, construct, and maintain "fairness" with the division of household labor." *Journal of Homosexuality*, *57*(5), 591–609.

Esping-Andersen, G. (1990). *The three worlds of welfare capitalism*. Cambridge, England: Polity.

Few, A. L. (2007). Integrating black consciousness and critical race feminism into family studies research. *Journal of Family Issues*, *28*, 452–473.

Fiske, J., & Johnny, R. (2003). The Lake Babine First Nation family: Yesterday and today. In M. Lynn (Ed.), *Voices: Essays on Canadian families* (pp. 181–198). Scarborough, ON: Thomson Nelson.

Fox, B. (1980). Women's double work day: Twentieth-century changes in the reproduction of daily life. In B. Fox (Ed.), *Hidden in the household: Women's domestic labour under capitalism* (pp. 173–216). Toronto, ON: Women's Press.

Frenette, M., & Coulombe, S. (2007). *Has higher education among young women substantially reduced the gender gap in employment and earnings?* Retrieved from http://publications.gc.ca/site/archivee-archived.html?url=http://publications.gc.ca/collection_2007/statcan/11F0019M/11F0019MIE2007301.pdf

Galabuzi, G. E. (2006). *Canada's economic apartheid: The social exclusion of racialized groups in the new century*. Toronto, ON: Canadian Scholars' Press Inc.

Garey, A. I., Hansen, K. V., Hertz, R., & MacDonald, C. (2002). Care and kinship: An introduction. *Journal of Family Issues*, *23*, 703–715.

Gazso, A. (2004). Women's inequality in the workplace as framed in news discourse: Refracting from gender ideology. *Canadian Review of Sociology and Anthropology*, *41*, 449–473.

Gazso, A. (2007a). Balancing expectations for employability and family responsibilities while on social assistance: Low income mothers' experiences in three Canadian provinces. *Family Relations*, *56*, 454–466.

Gazso, A. (2007b). Staying afloat on social assistance: Parents' strategies of balancing work and family. *Socialist Studies*, *3*, 31–63.

Gazso, A., & McDaniel, S. (2015). Families by choice and the management of low income through social supports. *Journal of Family Issues*, *36*(3), 371–395.

Gazso-Windle, A., & McMullin, J. A. (2003). Doing domestic labour: Strategizing in a gendered domain. *Canadian Journal of Sociology*, *28*, 341–366.

Gee, E., & Mitchell, B. (2003). One roof: Exploring multi-generational households in Canada. In M. Lynn (Ed.), *Voices: Essays on Canadian Families* (pp. 291–311). Scarborough, ON: Thomson Nelson.

Glass, J. (2004). Blessing or curse? Work-family policies and mothers' wage growth over time. *Work and Occupations*, *31*, 367–394.

Goldberg, A. E., Pierce, C. P., & Sayer, A. G. (2007). Shift work, role overload, and the transition to parenthood. *Journal of Marriage and the Family*, *69*, 123–138.

Grzywacz, J. G., Almeida, D. M., & McDonald, D. A. (2002). Work-family spillover and daily reports of work and family stress in the adult labor force. *Family Relations*, *51*, 28–36.

Guendozi, J. (2006). "The guilt thing": Balancing domestic and professional roles. *Journal of Marriage and the Family*, *68*, 901–909.

Hamilton, R. (2005). *Gendering the vertical mosaic: Feminist perspectives on Canadian society*. (2nd ed.). Toronto, ON: Pearson Prentice Hall.

Hamilton, R. (2007). Feminist theories. In N. Cook (Ed.), *Gender relations in global perspectives: Essential readings* (pp. 49–60). Toronto, ON: Canadian Scholars' Press Inc.

Hammer, L. B., Neal, M. B., & Perrin, N. A. (2004). The relationship between work-to-family conflict and family-to-work conflict: A longitudinal study. *Journal of Family and Economic Issues*, *25*, 79–100.

Harnois, C. E. (2005). Different paths to different feminisms? Bridging multiracial feminist theory and quantitative sociological gender research. *Gender & Society*, *19*, 809–828.

Hartman, Y. (2005). In bed with the enemy: Some ideas on the connections between neoliberalism and the welfare state. *Current Sociology*, *53*, 57–73.

Hartmann, H. (1981). The family as a locus of gender, class, and political struggle: The example of housework. *Signs*, *6*, 366–394.

Heisz, A., Jackson, A., & Picot, G. (2002). *Winners and losers in the labour market of the 1990s.* Ottawa, ON: Statistics Canada, Analytical Studies Branch.

Hochschild, A. R. (1989). *The second shift: Working parents and the revolution at home*. New York, NY: Viking.

Hochschild, A. R. (1997). *The time bind: When work becomes home and home becomes work*. New York, NY: Metropolitan Books.

Hodge, J. (2006). "Un-skilled labour": Canada's live-in caregiver program. *Undercurrents 3*, 60–66.

hooks, b. (1981). *Ain't I a woman: Black women and feminism.* Boston, MA: South End Press.

Human Resources Development Canada. (2001). *Changes made to maternity and parental benefits December 31, 2000.* Retrieved from HYPERLINK "http://www.hrdc.ca"www.hrdc.ca **(in November 23, 2001; no longer available on-line)**

Human Resources and Social Development Canada. (2008). *Fact sheet: The first year enhanced employment insurance (EI) Maternity/parental benefits*. Retrieved from www.hrsdc.gc.ca/en/cs/comm/news/2002/021106_e.shtml **(in February 19, 2008; no longer available on-line)**

Kelly, E. L., Moen, P., & Tranby, E. (2011). Changing workplaces to reduce work-family conflict: Schedule control in a white-collar organization. *American Sociological Review*, *76*(2), 265–290.

Kobayashi, K. M. (2000). The nature of support from adult children to older parents in Japanese Canadian families. *Journal of Cross-Cultural Gerontology*, *15*, 182–205.

Konrad, A. M., & Cannings, K. (1994). Of mommy tracks and glass ceilings: A case study of men's and women's careers in management. *Industrial Relations*, *49*, 303–322.

Krull, C., & Sempruch, J. (Eds.). (2011). *A Life in Balance? Reopening the Family-Work Debate.* Vancouver, BC: University of British Columbia Press.

Landivar, L. C. (2013). Labour force participation among Asian, Black, Hispanic, and white mothers in 20 occupations. *Advances in Gender Research*, *17*, 263–286.

Langer, N. (1995). Grandparents and adult grandchildren: What do they do for one another? In J. Hendriks (Ed.), *The ties of later life* (pp. 171–179). Amityville, NY: Baywood.

Lerner, G. (1993). Reconceptualizing differences among women. In A. M. Jagger & P. S. Rothenberg, *Feminist frameworks: Alternative theoretical accounts of the relations between women and men* (pp. 237–247). New York, NY: McGraw-Hill, Inc.

Luxton, M. (2001). Family coping strategies: Balancing paid employment and domestic labour. In B. J. Fox (Ed.), *Family patterns, gender relations* (pp. 318–338). Toronto, ON: Oxford University Press.

Luxton, M. (2006). Feminist political economy in Canada and the politics of social reproduction. In K. Bezanson & M. Luxton (Eds.), *Social reproduction: Feminist political economy challenges neo-liberalism* (pp. 11–44). Montreal, QC: McGill-Queen's University Press.

Man, G., & Cohen, R. (Eds.). (2015). *Engendering transnational voices: Studies in family, work and identities.* Waterloo, ON: Wilfrid Laurier University Press.

Mandel, H. (2005). Family policies, wage structures, and gender gaps: Sources of earnings inequality in 20 countries. *American Sociological Review*, *70*, 949–967.

Mandell, N. (2005). Making families: Gender, economics, sexuality, and race. In N. Mandell (Ed.), *Feminist issues: Race, class, and sexuality* (4th ed.). Toronto, ON: Pearson Prentice Hall.

Mandell, N., King, K., Preston, V., Weiser, N., Kim, A., & Luxton, M. (2015). Transnational family exchanges in senior Canadian immigrant families. In G. Man & R. Cohen (Eds.), *Engendering Transnational Voices: Studies in Family, Work, and Identity* (pp. 75–96). Waterloo, ON: Wilfrid Laurier University Press.

Marshall, K. (2006). Converging gender roles. *Perspectives on Labour and Income 7*, 5–17. Retrieved from www.statcan.ca/english/freepub/75-001-XIE/10706/art-1.htm

Marshall, K. (2011). Generational change in paid and unpaid work. Retrieved from http://www.statcan.gc.ca/pub/11-008-x/2011002/article/11520-eng.htm

Mattingly, M. J., & Sayer, L. C. (2006). Under pressure: Gender differences in the relationship between free time and feeling rushed. *Journal of Marriage and the Family*, *68*, 205–221.

Mays, Vicki M., Chatters, L. M., Cochran, S. D., & Mackness, J. (1998). African American families in diversity: Gay men and lesbians as participants in family networks. *Journal of Comparative Family Studies*, *29*, 73–87.

McDaniel, S., & Gazso, A. (In Press). The liminality of aging families by choice in low income. *Canadian Journal on Aging.*

McFarlane, S., Beaujot, R., & Haddad, T. (2000). Time constraints and relative resources as determinants of the sexual division of domestic work. *Canadian Journal of Sociology*, *25*, 61–82.

McMullin, J. A., Davies, L., & Cassidy, G. (2002). Welfare reform in Ontario: Tough times in mothers' lives. *Canadian Public Policy*, *28*, 297–314.

Milan, A., Vézina, M., & Wells, C. (2006). Family portrait: Continuity and change in Canadian families and households in 2006: Findings. Retrieved from www12.statcan.ca/english/census06/analysis/famhouse/index.cfm

Mitchell, B., Wister, A. V., & Gee, E M. (2004). The ethnic and family nexus of homeleaving and returning among Canadian young adults. *Canadian Journal of Sociology*, *29*, 543–575.

Nelson, F. (2001). Lesbian families. In B. J. Fox (Ed.), *Family patterns, gender relations* (pp. 441–457). Toronto, On: Oxford University Press.

Nicholson, L. 2013. [2010]. Feminism in "waves": Useful metaphor or not. In C. R. McCann & S. Kim (Eds.), *Feminist Theory Reader: Local and Global Perspectives* (pp. 49–55). New York, NY: Routledge.

Nomaguchi, K. (2012). Marital status, gender, and home-job-conflict among employed parents. *Journal of Family Issues*. *33*(3), 271–294.

Offer, S. (2012). The burden of reciprocity: processes of exclusion and withdrawal from personalnetworks among low-income families. *Current Sociology*, *60*, 788–805.

Palameta, B. (2004). Low income among immigrants and visible minorities. *Perspectives on Labour and Income*, *5*(4), 12–17.

Penha-Lopes, V. (2006). "To cook, sew, to be a man": The socialization for competence and black men's involvement in housework. *Sex Roles*, *54*(3–4), 261–274.

Pratt, G. (2003). Valuing child care: Troubles in suburbia. *Antipode*, *35*(3), 581–602.

Pulkingham, J. (1998). Remaking the social divisions of welfare: Gender, "dependency," and UI reform. *Studies in Political Economy*, *56*, 7–48.

Ranson, G. (2010). *Against the Grain: Couples, Gender, and the Reframing of Parenting*. Toronto, ON: University of Toronto Press.

Roehling, P. V., Hernandez Jarvis, L., & Swope, H. E. (2005). Variations in negative work-family spillover among white, Black, and Hispanic American men and women: Does ethnicity matter? *Journal of Family Issues*, *26*, 840–865.

Rosenberg, H. (1995). Motherwork, stress, and depression: The costs of privatized social reproduction. In E. D. Nelson & B. W. Robinson (Eds.), *Gender in the 1990s: Images, Realities, and Issues* (pp. 311–329). Toronto, ON: Nelson Canada.

Roy, K. M., Tubbs, C. Y., & Burton, L. M. (2004). Don't have no time: Daily rhythms and the organization of time for low-income families. *Family Relations*, *53*(2), 168–178.

Ruhm, C. (2011). Public policies to assist parents with children. *Future of Children*, *21*(2), 37–68.

Safri, M., & Graham, J. (2010). The global household: Toward a feminist postcapitalist international political economy *Signs, 36*(1), 99–126.

Salazar Parrenas, R. (2000). Migrant Filipina domestic workers and the international division of reproductive labour. *Gender & Society*, *14*, 560–580.

Sayer, L. C. (2005). Gender, time, and inequality: Trends in women's and men's paid work, unpaid work, and free time. *Social Forces*, *84*, 285–303.

Seccombe, W. (1980). Domestic labour and the working-class household. In B. Fox (Ed.), *Hidden in the household: Women's domestic labour under capitalism* (pp. 25–99). Toronto, ON: Women's Press.

Skrypnek, B. J., & Fast, J. E. (1996). Work and family policy in Canada: Family needs, collective solutions. *Journal of Family Issues*, *17*, 793–812.

Stack, C. B. (1974). *All our kin: Strategies for survival in a Black community*. New York, NY: Harper Torchbooks, Harper and Row.

Statistics Canada. (2007). *Women in Canada: A gender-based statistical report* (5th ed.). Ottawa: Statistics Canada. Retrieved from http://dsp-psd.pwgsc.gc.ca/Collection-R/Statcan/89-503-X/0010589-503-XIE.pdf.

Statistics Canada. (2011). *Women in Canada: A gender-based statistical report* (6th ed.). Ottawa: Statistics Canada. Retrieved from www5.statcan.gc.ca/access_acces/alternative_alternatif.action?l=eng&loc=/pub/89-503-x/89-503-x2010001-eng.pdf

Statistics Canada. (2013). Table 202-0102 – Average female and male earnings, and female-to-male earnings ratio, by work activity, 2011 constant dollars, annual, CANSIM (database). Retrieved from www5.statcan.gc.ca/cansim/a26

Status of Women Canada. (2005). *Report on Status of Women Canada's on-line consultation on gender equality*. Ottawa: Status of Women Canada. Retrieved from www.swc-cfc.gc.ca/resources/consultations/ges09-2005/finalreport_index_e.html (in April 25, 2008; no longer available on-line)

St. Vil, N. M. (2014). African American marital satisfaction as a function of work-family balance and work-family conflict and implications for social workers. *Journal of Human Behaviour in the Social Environment*, *24*, 208–216.

Sullivan, M. (2004). *The family of woman: Lesbian mothers, their children, and the undoing of gender*. Berkeley, CA: University of California Press.

Tuten, T. L., & August, R. A. (2006). Work-family conflict: A study of Lesbian mothers. *Women in Management Review*, *21*, 578–597.

Vosko, L. F. (2002). The pasts (and futures) of feminist political economy in Canada: Reviving the debate. *Studies in Political Economy*, *68*, 55–83.

Weedon, C. (1999). *Feminism, theory, and the politics of difference*. Oxford, England: Blackwell Publishers.

Weedon, K. A. (2005). Is there a flexiglass ceiling? Flexible work arrangements and wages in the United States. *Social Science Research*, *34*, 454–482.

West, C., & Zimmerman, D. H. (1987). Doing gender. *Gender & Society*, *1*, 125–151.

White, J., Maxim, P., & Obeng Gyimah, S. (2003). Labour force activity of women in Canada: A comparative analysis of Aboriginal and non-Aboriginal women. *Canadian Review of Sociology and Anthropology*, *40*, 391–415.

Wilson, S. J. (2005). Paid work, jobs, and the illusion of economic security. In N. Mandell (Ed.), *Feminist issues: Race, class and sexuality* (4th ed.) (pp. 226–246). Toronto, ON: Pearson Prentice Hall.

Young, M., & Wheaton, B. (2013). The impact of neighborhood composition on work-family conflict and distress. *Journal of Health and Social Behavior*, *54*(4), 481–497.

Zeytinoglu, I. U., & Muteshi, J. K. (2000). Gender, race and class dimensions of nonstandard work. *Industrial Relations*, *55*, 133–167.

INTRODUCTION

In this chapter I challenge the prevailing discourse of education as the great equalizer. Despite our best attempts to ensure equity, schooling continues to display gendered, raced, and classed practices that have both material and social effects. Schools, through their organization, interactions, and curricular materials, are engaged in the work of re/producing and regulating particular normative constructions of masculinity and femininity that are associated with middle-class, heterosexual, white bodies. Both the organization of schooling and people's experiences of schooling demonstrate that the privileging of masculinity, which is generally afforded an advantaged social position over femininity, continues to afford men and boys with social capital, earnings, and so forth. Through a hidden curriculum, girls still learn that they are not as important as boys, which can affect girls' self-esteem and occupational aspirations. Further, women are graduating in increasing numbers with university degrees, yet this does not seem to translate into wide occupational rewards as women still earn less than their male counterparts (with comparable levels of education) and are not well represented in the top positions of power hierarchies. Gender inequality, as it intersects with race, class, and sexuality, persists.

This chapter explores gender, race, and class in relation to both lower and higher education, predominantly focusing on Canada. First, I trace the history of the gender debate in education, beginning with a brief overview of feminist perspectives on education. I show how gender is a persistent concern for educators. Then I turn to the contemporary situation and examine what happens in schools today at both lower and higher education levels. I explore the differential treatment and experiences of girls/women and boys/men as students, teachers, and faculty at the elementary, secondary, and university level. Also examined are contemporary preoccupations and emerging areas in gender education research: the so-called crisis for boys, intersections of race and gender in schools, sexuality and schooling, and the corporatization of higher education. The development of women's studies and feminism in the academy is also considered alongside a brief discussion of feminist pedagogies.

HISTORICAL BACKGROUND

The preoccupations of researchers in the field of gender research in education have shifted. Early work in the 1970s focused on sex roles. Social relationships were seen as tied to biological differences between men/boys and women/girls. Feminist work critiqued the socializing role of schools as promoting behaviour that conformed to essentialist notions of gender distinctions (Dillabough, 2006). Critiques were launched against patriarchal language used in textbooks and calls for the equal representation of girls and women in both curriculum and the education profession itself arose (Dillabough, 2006). This early work relied on a liberal feminist framework that assumed cognizance of injustices in the educational system was sufficient motivation to engender change (Reynolds, 2001).

Wanting to expand the liberal feminist framework, British feminist scholars of sociology and education sought to highlight "larger, macro-questions of structure and their role in shaping gender relations as a historically grounded set of gender relations and codes" (Dillabough, 2006, p. 49). In this approach, which came to be known as feminist reproduction theory, schools were understood as sites for both possibilities and limits for the "democratization of gender relations" (Dillabough, 2006, p. 49). In other words, schools are sites where changes can be enacted and realized.

A more culturally oriented concern emerged in the 1990s when gender education research began to explore how culture, discourse, and identity intersect with macro concerns about men's and women's positions in education (Dillabough, 2006). In addition to critiques about the sex/gender distinction, researchers are critical of "singular or binary notions of gender identity as they have been expressed through schooling" (Dillabough, 2006, p. 53). One strand of this critique aims to disrupt the notion that there are singular categories of "girl" or "boy" (Arnot & Dillabough, 1999); multiple femininities and masculinities exist in our classrooms at any given time. Another critical strand aims to understand how colonialism, culture, race, and gender intersect for youth identity formation (Dillabough, 2006). Someone working in this area might, for example, be concerned with how colonialist and racialized discourses shape students' subjectivities.

Contemporary feminist approaches to theorizing gender and education remain diverse. We continue to see the enduring relevance of feminist reproduction theory as well as the significant increase of studies influenced by poststructuralist and culturalist approaches to the field of gender and education (Dillabough, 2006). This chapter uses a poststructuralist approach in that it deconstructs the prevailing discourse of education as the great equalizer.

LOWER EDUCATION

In this section, I explore the ways in which lower education is gendered, racialized, and classed. By examining schooling practices—including teachers' behaviour and expectations, parental behaviour and expectations, and curricular materials—I show how students remain schooled in gendered practices despite widespread acceptance of the importance of gender equality.

Teachers and Principals

Teaching at the elementary and secondary levels in Canada remains a gendered profession. Women have been overrepresented, when compared with the general population, as teachers in Canadian elementary and secondary schools since the late 1880s (Wotherspoon,

2004). More than 90% of Canadian kindergarten teachers are women (Wotherspoon, 2009). In Ontario, women represented 71% of all elementary and secondary school teachers, administrators, and early childhood educators in 2011–2012 (Ontario Ministry of Education, 2012). In Canada, the proportion of women who are both elementary and secondary school teachers has fluctuated between their lowest representation of 55.6% in 1980 to their highest proportion of teachers in 1915 (83.4%) (Wotherspoon, 2004). Women as teachers are congregated at the elementary level compared with the secondary level, a pattern also found in the United States and Western European countries (Abbott, Wallace, & Tyler, 2005; Nelson, 2006; Ontario Ministry of Education, 2012).

Women accounted for 47% of principals in Canada in 2004–2005 (Statistics Canada, 2006). However, the proportional share of women principals differs between the elementary and secondary levels. At the elementary level, women now account for 53% of principals (Statistics Canada, 2006). This is a strong improvement from the 1980s when women made up just under 20% of elementary school principals (Cusson, 1990) and the early 1990s when women accounted for only 22% of elementary school principals and only 8% of secondary school principals (Wotherspoon, 2004). We still see room for progress at the secondary level, as women only represent 42% of principals (Statistics Canada, 2006). Overall, though, these statistics represent great improvement for women's representation in the administrative ranks of Canada's elementary and secondary schools.

Women's and men's unequal distribution in the educational power hierarchy remains "one of the most salient features of the profession, one that undermines its status" (deMarrais & LeCompte, 1999, p. 191). Tyack's (1974) classification of schools as "educational harems" remains today where women predominantly teach and men predominantly supervise and administer. Such feminine teaching and masculine administrative patterns communicate to students "that men hold positions of authority and power in society while women play subordinate roles, having control only over the children in their classrooms" (deMarrais & LeCompte, 1999, p. 313).

Students

Differential Treatment Historically, Canadian educational institutions were organized to prepare boys and girls for particular societal roles (Davies & Guppy, 2006). In the mid-1800s, citizens were encouraged to commit new tax monies for compulsory schooling for girls and boys. Education leaders lobbied the public on a platform of needing a common moral education. This "common" education was not, however, to be understood as the "same" education (Davies & Guppy, 2006). Even though schooling for students in the early years was similar, by age 10 boys were directed to vocational training and higher education in preparation for the labour market and girls were streamed into domestic science courses (Davies & Guppy, 2006).

Even though boys and girls attended the same schools, they were often segregated within those schools. There were separate entrances and separate playgrounds (often with a wall between the two areas). Girls were seated separately from boys and were even required to perform different recitations (Gaskell, McLaren, & Novogrodsky, 1989; Prentice, 1977). Gendered expectations reinforced teachers', and presumably parents', notions that girls and boys were to be prepared for different occupational and social roles: girls were to be prepared to be housewives or for a limited set of nurturing occupations (nurse, elementary school teacher) while boys were prepared for vocational trades or advanced studies (Davies & Guppy, 2006). Overt gender streaming remained firmly in place until at least the 1950s (Davies & Guppy, 2006).

Contemporary studies continue to document the often unintentional differential treatment afforded to girls and boys by their classroom teachers. The difference now, though, rests in the formal assumption that schools are to educate girls and boys in the same manner. Do boys and girls receive equal classroom treatment? Regardless of whether their teachers are women or men, boys have more interaction with their teachers than do girls (Abbott, Wallace, & Tyler, 2005; deMarrais & LeCompte, 1999; Renzetti & Curran, 1999; Skelton, 1997). Boys are more likely to call out answers in class without raising their hands, and teachers typically accept their answers; however, when girls engage in the same calling out without hand-raising, teachers tend to "correct" the girls and tell them their behaviour is inappropriate (Renzetti & Curran, 1999).

Research on teacher/student classroom interactions in Canada, the United States, and the United Kingdom shows how this gendered treatment of students is also racialized (Brown, 2011; Codjoe, 2001; Dei, 2008; Sadker & Sadker, 2009; Skelton, 1997). White boys are the most likely recipients of teacher attention, followed by boys of colour, white girls, and girls of colour (Hood, 2005; Sadker & Sadker, 2009). Morris's (2007) research on working-class Black girls and their middle school classroom experiences demonstrates how teachers encourage the girls to conform to a normative model of a docile femininity. Morris argues that the predominantly white teachers hold racialized perceptions about the undesirability of the Black girls' femininity, seeing the girls as "coarse and overly assertive" (p. 91). Teachers focused on the girls' social etiquette more than their academic development (Morris, 2007). The girls drew the teachers' attention because their actions were seen as "challenging to authority, loud and not ladylike" (Morris, 2007, p. 501). Black students often report being ignored in their classes, and treated as unimportant by teachers, administrators, and fellow students (Codjoe, 2001).

Teachers' gendered, classed, and racialized notions about appropriate practices and behaviours for girls and boys affect their interactions with students. Boys are often praised by their teachers when they complete a task successfully, while girls may be applauded for their attractive appearance or quiet behaviour (Giraldo & Colyar, 2012; Nelson, 2006). Girls and boys may be afforded support for different kinds of activities—boys may receive more support for succeeding in science and math while girls may receive more support for succeeding in literacy and the arts (Eccles, 2011; Gherasim, Burnaru, & Mairean, 2013). These kinds of gendered interactions can contribute to the promotion of girls' dependence and boys' independence. Girls are praised for being "congenial" and "neat" while boys' work is praised for its intellectual quality (Giraldo & Colyar, 2012; Renzetti & Curran, 1999).

A chart of kindergarten awards that was reprinted in the *Wall Street Journal* demonstrates how gender infiltrated a kindergarten classroom: Girls were awarded with "all-around sweetheart," "cutest personality," and "best manners," whereas the boys received awards for "very best thinker," "most eager learner," and "most scientific" (Renzetti & Curran, 1999).

Teachers' differential practices have material effects. Girls learn that boys are more important than themselves, that boys are superior to girls (Bourne, McCoy, & Smith, 1998; Thompson & Armato, 2012). Teacher attention is an important contributing factor both for students' academic achievements and their sense of selves (Sadker & Sadker, 2009). Further, schools (and teachers) reinforce, and thus reproduce, narrow, restrictive normative constructions of what it means to be a girl and what it means to be a boy—what Bob Connell refers to as emphasized femininity and hegemonic masculinity (Connell, 2002).

Curriculum As early as 1970, the Royal Commission on the Status of Women took up the issue of gendered practices within schools. By examining the curricular materials used in Canadian schools to teach reading, mathematics, and social studies, the Commission argued:

> a woman's creative and intellectual potential is either underplayed or ignored in the education of children from their earliest years. The sex roles described in these text-books provide few challenging models for young girls, and they fail to create a sense of community between men and women as fellow human beings. (Quoted in Gaskell, McLaren, & Novogrodsky, 1989, p. 36)

The commission offered a liberal feminist critique of gendered schooling—boys and girls are being treated differently—and a liberal feminist solution—treat them the same. Following the commission's report, numerous studies examined curricular materials and noted the virtual absence of women and girls (Gaskell, 1977; Gaskell, McLaren, & Novogrodsky, 1989). When present, women and girls were constructed traditionally as mothers who baked cookies or girls who played with dolls. Boys were subject to equally sexist treatment as active and powerful people, playing sports while their fathers worked outside of the home, preferably as educated professionals (Gaskell, McLaren, & Novogrodsky, 1989). Clearly, liberal feminists argued, sexist images prevailed.

As a result of feminist agitation around sexist curricular materials, guidelines were developed to create non-sexist materials. Has this intervention been successful? More diverse gender images are present in contemporary materials; however, a study 20 years ago by the Ontario federation of women teachers argued that many problematic images remain (Federation of Women Teachers Associations of Ontario, 1988). The authors of the study argued that school materials need to portray an idealistic world, free from gender segregation, such that children are able to imagine a future for themselves full of possibility (Federation of Women Teachers Associations of Ontario, 1988; Gaskell, McLaren, & Novogrodsky, 1989). Gaskell, McLaren, and Novogrodsky (1989, p. 38) argue that textbooks should not go to an extreme where children are only exposed to "androgynous superpeople" but rather there should be a balance of images. An inclusive approach should show women "as secretaries as well as carpenters and girls playing with dolls as well as playing baseball" (Gaskell, McLaren, & Novogrodsky, 1989, p. 38).

Although curricular materials are no longer blatantly sexist, they nevertheless continue subtly to communicate the authority of the status quo—that of white middle-class masculinity (Arnot, 2002). For example, Bourne, McCoy, and Smith's interviews with schoolgirls in Ontario (grades 6 to 12) reveal accounts of history courses that trivialize, marginalize, or exclude women (Bourne, McCoy, & Smith, 1998). Studies also reveal how Indigenous cultures are problematically constructed in curricular materials (Archibald, 1995). Indigenous people are frequently represented as living in the distant past, before pre-European contact, which stereotypes and homogenizes Indigenous peoples (Dion, 2009). Such depictions allow teachers to skip over discussions of the impact of colonialism and Indigenous peoples' resistance to institutions such as the residential school system (Dion, 2009). Both George Dei's (1997, 2008) and Henry Codjoe's (2001) work on race, schooling, and Black Canadian students also finds evidence of racial stereotyping; the students cite a desire for courses that are more inclusive of who is in their classrooms, rather than always being exposed to a white Eurocentric curriculum that is dominated by white men with an occasional nod to a white woman or Black man, but never to a Black woman (Codjoe, 2001; Dei, 1997, 2008).

Further, lesbian students speak of an absence of any discussion in their class materials of sexualities other than heterosexuality (Bourne, McCoy, & Smith, 1998). Research on high school textbooks across a range of subject areas reveals that there is virtually no reference made to same-sex sexuality (Macgillivray & Jennings, 2008; Temple, 2005). In these texts, same-sex sexuality, when it appears, is constructed in negative contexts—in discussions of "sexually transmitted diseases, sexual abuse, and prostitution" (Macgillivray & Jennings, 2008, p. 173). Lesbian, gay, bisexual, and transgendered persons are portrayed as "hapless victims" (Macgillivray & Jennings, 2008, p. 179). Heterosexuality is a pervasive assumption running through school materials and practices (Bazzul & Sykes, 2011; deMarrais & LeCompte, 1999; Wilmot & Naidoo, 2014).

The forms of masculinity and femininity portrayed in curricular materials are ideologically driven. Many forms of masculinity and femininity exist, yet these materials generally show two dominant constructions: hegemonic masculinity and an emphasized femininity (Connell, 2002). These gendered constructions intersect with race (they are white), class (they are middle class), and sexuality (they are heterosexual); thus alternative masculinities and femininities are rendered inferior and invisible.

Contemporary Research

Crisis for Boys? Are girls outperforming boys? Some critics argue that there is widespread male underachievement in schooling. What do the Canadian statistics tell us? Every three years, Canadian students take part in the Programme for International Student Assessment (PISA) (run by the Organisation for Economic Co-operation and Development, OECD). "PISA is designed to provide policy-oriented international indicators of the skills and knowledge of 15-year-old students" (Bussière, Knighton, & Pennock, 2007, p. 9).

Students are tested on their mathematical literacy, reading literacy, and scientific literacy. Whether girls "outperform" boys depends on which levels of data are examined. For example, when looking at the overall science scale for the 2012 assessment, Canadian students showed no statistically significant gender difference (OECD, 2014). However, when examining the sub-scales within the science category, noticeable gendered differences are apparent. Canadian boys (and those in most other countries) scored higher than girls in "explaining phenomena scientifically," while Canadian girls (and those in most other countries) scored higher than boys in "identifying scientific issues" (OECD, 2014). These results are consistent with earlier test results (Bussière, Knighton, & Pennock, 2007; OECD, 2014).

The 2012 test scores are consistent with past scores for both mathematics and reading. Canadian boys score higher than girls in mathematics while girls score higher than boys in reading (Bussière, Knighton, & Pennock, 2007; OECD, 2014). There is a greater difference between boys' and girls' scores in reading than there is in mathematics. The Canadian data are consistent with the performance average of OECD countries (OECD, 2014).

The Canadian data released from the 2006 PISA tests do not analyze performance by race but do provide data based on immigrant status (second-generation immigrants and first-generation immigrants). Non-immigrant Canadian students outperformed both groups of immigrant students in the science category (Bussière, Knighton, & Pennock, 2007). The data also tell us that parental levels of education correspond with student achievement. "Youth with at least one parent who had post-secondary education outperformed their peers whose parents had high school education or less" (Bussière, Knighton, & Pennock, 2007, p. 40). Further, one's social class influences one's test scores—those students in the top quarter of socio-economic status have higher scores (equal to one proficiency level) than those whose socio-economic status is in the lowest quarter (Bussière, Knighton, & Pennock, 2007).

So what can we make of what appears to be almost a moral panic about the state of boys in Canada, the United States, and the United Kingdom? In their analysis of literature that takes up the general claim that boys are experiencing a crisis in schooling, Bouchard, Boily, and Proulx (2003) point to three arguments used in masculinist education discourses. The first argument is one of victimization or the "poor boys discourse" (Bouchard, Boily, & Proulx, 2003). To achieve equality in schools, attention must be turned toward boys as they are "in distress, losing their identity, in crisis, disoriented, guilty, lost . . . at the mercy of feminist teachers" and so forth (Bouchard, Boily, & Proulx, 2003, pp. 54–55). Michael Kimmel (2000) argues that these concerns for boys' struggles are really veiled critiques of feminism (Bouchard, Boily, & Proulx, 2003). Women are understood as the source of the boys' problems as schools are feminized spaces that promote feminine practices (Bouchard, Boily, & Proulx, 2003; Hodgetts, 2010; Lucey, 2001).

The second argument focuses on the school system itself—that schools themselves are failing boys (Bouchard, Boily, & Proulx, 2003). The logic of this line of work asserts that schools have not adapted to boys and accordingly boys develop both learning and behavioural problems that lead to poor scholastic attainment (Bouchard, Boily, & Proulx, 2003).

The third argument uses the essentialist trope of "boys will be boys" (Bouchard, Boily, & Proulx, 2003). In this discourse, boys' troubles in education are reflective of their innate characteristics. Boys are assumed to be "violent, predatory beasts; uncaged, uncivilized animals" (Kimmel, 2000, p. 8).

All of these anti-feminist arguments used in masculinist discourses about the gendered performance gap generalize an occurrence that affects boys and girls on an entire group (boys) (Bouchard, Boily, & Proulx, 2003). Further, the rhetoric that circulates about the crisis among boys fails to take an intersectional look at the data. Underachievement in schools is both classed and racialized (Hood, 2005; Skelton, 2001; Thompson & Armato, 2012). As we saw from the Canadian data, social class and immigrant status affect school performance. We do not have Canadian data by race, but similar testing in the U.K. reveals that "the highest achieving group is Chinese girls, followed by Chinese boys, while the lowest-performing are Black Caribbean girls and boys" (Abbott, Wallace, & Tyler, 2005, p. 95). Bouchard, Boily, and Proulx (2003, p. 89) conclude:

> The phenomenon of school achievement gaps between boys and girls exists only in industrialized countries, where there are co-educational and democratic public education systems that give girls (and children who do not come from well-to-do families) access to the same education as boys (and the well-to-do). In the past, each gender received differentiated—and hierarchical—training in different venues. For the first time, it is now possible to compare boys and girls enrolled in the same school programs.

Kimmel directs us not to see feminism as the root of boys' "problems"; rather he wants us to see that feminism can help us address male entitlement in such a way that we can "confront racism, sexism and homophobia—both in our communities and in ourselves" (Kimmel, 1999, p. 90, as cited by Reynolds, 2001, p. 247). The current debate about boys is really about "restabilizing power and authority that . . . has never actually been unseated" (Kehler, 2007, p. 261).

Intersections of Race and Gender Many scholars are undertaking research that recognizes the simultaneity of race and gender in the area of education. These researchers argue that education continues to be a site for reproducing racialized notions of gender (Abbott, Wallace, & Tyler, 2005; Codjoe, 2001; Kenny, 2002; Rollock, 2007; Youdell, 2003).

In her review essay, Phoenix (2001) presents results from numerous studies documenting educational performance in the U.K. by ethnicity. Bangladeshi, Pakistani, and Black Caribbean students are the most poorly performing groups, although girls from these minority groups fare better than the boys (Phoenix, 2001). As stated earlier, Chinese girls and boys are the highest achieving subgroups in the U.K. (Abbott, Wallace, & Tyler, 2005). In one Canadian study, Jun Li (2004) shows how parental expectations by Chinese immigrants strongly affect their children's school achievements. There is also much evidence documenting "a positive relationship between parental expectations and children's school achievement" among Asian immigrants in North America (Li, 2004, p. 167).

Several researchers (Codjoe, 2001; Dei, 1997, 2008; Phoenix, 2001) argue that students from racialized groups are treated differentially from white students, and that students themselves actively contribute to reproducing gendered and racialized disadvantage.

Phoenix (2001) cites studies demonstrating Black girls' willingness to "forgive" the racist practices at their schools because they need their schooling credentials for future success. Mac an Ghaill (1988) calls this "resistance within accommodation." Young Black men do not appear to engage in such accommodation strategies (Phoenix, 2001).

Mirza and Reay's (2000) research aims to redefine "citizenship" in relation to education and illustrates the possibilities for challenging the white hegemony of schools. They outline how Black African Caribbean U.K. communities (specifically, Black women educators in supplementary schools) developed a "third space"—a space of "strategic engagement." "It is in the 'third space,' a de-essentialised but invisible counter-hegemonic space, where the marginal and the excluded—those situated as such through their gender and radicalized construction—find a voice" (Mirza & Reay, 2000, p. 70). The work of these women educators destabilizes fixed constructions of citizenship (distinction between private and public spheres) and demonstrates new inclusive forms of citizenship (Mirza & Reay, 2000).

Closer to home, Canadian teacher Alnaaz Kassam reflects on his approach to teaching English and challenges the Eurocentric biased curriculum in light of the multiple and heterogeneous identities of his students, and the insistence by many of his students that "there is no racism in Canada" (Kassam, 2007, p. 356), despite research that shows otherwise in the sphere of education (Codjoe, 2001; Dei, 2008). Through the poem "The Hijabi Girl," written by one of his students outlining the racism she experiences daily as a Muslim girl wearing the hijab in Canada, Kassam explores how students' identities are negotiated through curriculum, media, and global politics and signals the importance of creating classroom spaces that enable students to deconstruct the social relations around them.

Sexuality and Schooling Researchers are finally turning their attention to how schools work to reproduce gendered sexualities. A main focus in this area examines how schools (through both social and curricular practices) are heterosexualized institutional spaces. Further, schools' assumed heterosexuality often goes unchallenged.

Louisa Allen's 2007 research in New Zealand schools demonstrates how schools both produce and regulate students' sexual identities. Allen points to the "official culture" of schools as a discursive strategy for producing students as "non-sexual." Allen traces how a discourse of sexual "risk" and an absent discourse of desire in sexual education simultaneously produce students in contradictory ways as both "childlike" and as "sexual decision makers" (Allen, 2007, p. 231). Allen encourages schools to change their official culture such that student sexuality is understood as "legitimate and positive." Understanding students' sexuality in this way "may open up more spaces for young people to be the kinds of sexual subjects desired by the Health and Physical Education curriculum" (Allen, 2007, p. 232).

Michael Kehler's research on young men in Canadian high schools demonstrates that male students are expected to perform a "coherent heterosexual masculinity" (Kehler, 2007, p. 262). Those youth who attempt to resist practices associated with masculine heteronormativity often find themselves cast to the periphery—subject to homophobic taunts. Kehler argues that as a result of such practices, young men avoid developing close friendships with other male youths for fear of being labelled homosexual.

Research on men teachers also reveals the connections between gender and sexuality in educational contexts. Martino and Frank (2006) document how male teachers in a single-sex school negotiate their masculinities. For example, like the students in Kehler's study, the teachers speak of having to establish a "normalized heterosexualized masculinity" (Martino & Frank, 2006, p. 22). The teachers perceive the male students as policing their masculinities—that as an art teacher, one teacher has to somehow demonstrate strong masculine traits to assure the students of his heterosexual identity. The art teacher in this instance drew on his position as a football coach to reaffirm his heterosexual masculinity (Martino & Frank, 2006).

Lesbian and gay teachers are also subject to regulation in school contexts (Ferfolja, 2008; Jackson, 2006; Khayatt, 1994). Despite harassment, these teachers are hesitant to report abuse for fear of losing their jobs and experiencing further harassment, ostracism, and even violence (Ferfolja, 2008; Jackson, 2006; Khayatt, 1994). By keeping silent about such harassment, teachers contribute to the institutional invisibility of a range of sexualities (Ferfolja, 2008).

Rebecca Raby's (2005) Canadian research on student codes of conduct also takes up schools' regulation of students' sexuality. Raby argues that school rules about displays of affection aim to restrict adolescent sexuality while simultaneously developing academic settings that are "separate from the body, rational and self-disciplined" (Raby, 2005, p. 81). Emma Renold's U.K. research similarly explores schools as settings that aim to reproduce compulsory heterosexuality. Renold (2006, p. 504), drawing on Judith Butler, argues that schools are key spaces for the production of children's gendered identities that "are performed within a constraining and regulatory hegemonic heterosexual matrix." When sexuality is addressed, it is situated within a heteronormative framework such as passing around condoms (Taylor, 2006). This presumed heterosexuality often goes unchallenged, rendering alternative sexualities problematic.

HIGHER EDUCATION

We now shift our attention to higher education, which also remains gendered, racialized, and classed. Women are graduating with university degrees in increasing numbers, yet this has not yet translated into wide occupational rewards as women continue to earn less than men (with comparable education) and are not well represented in the top positions of power hierarchies in their respective fields (Abbott, Wallace, & Tyler, 2005; Hogan, Perucci, & Behringer, 2005; Mandell & Crysdale, 1993). Despite popular sentiment, education does not appear to be the great equalizer.

In this part of the chapter I look at contemporary trends in student enrolment and the professoriate as well as people's experiences of higher education. I then turn to address the development of women's studies and feminist pedagogies in the academy, which both spatially and practically challenge the masculinism of the university. Lastly, I examine the rise of the McUniversity and how such corporate challenges are problematic for women and feminism on campus.

Students

Statistical Overview Gendered trends exist of women students' concentration in particular disciplinary areas in higher education. In Canada, the late 1980s marked the shift from men comprising the majority of undergraduate students to women being the majority. By 1988 women's and men's enrolment as undergraduates were the same in Canadian universities and 1989 was the first year that women's enrolment exceeded the enrolment of men as undergraduates (Drakich & Stewart, 2007). In undergraduate programs overall, women now account for 57% of full-time students (2010–2011) (Canadian Association of University Teachers [CAUT], 2013). However, when women's participation as undergraduates exceeded men's, rather than hearing celebration about equal participation we heard concerns "of equity for men and the feminization of universities" (Drakich & Stewart, 2007, p. 6).

We see the highest proportional representation of undergraduate women in health, parks, recreation, and fitness (71.3%) and in education (76.4%) while the lowest proportion of women undergraduates are in mathematics and computer and information sciences (24.9%) (CAUT, 2013). Currently, women represent 54% of master's level students and 47% of doctoral level students (CAUT, 2013). At the master's level, education again has the highest proportion of women students (72%) with health, parks, recreation, and fitness having the second-highest concentration of women (64%). There are fewer graduate women students in architecture, engineering, and related technologies (27%) (CAUT, 2013).

When we further subdivide graduate enrolment to differentiate between master's and doctoral students, we continue to find greater categories of gender divide. Women account for 47% of doctoral students (CAUT, 2013). Again, this is a significant improvement from the early 1970s when women accounted for only 19% of PhD students (Drolet, 2007). The 1980s also saw tremendous improvement in women's representation at the graduate level, with women representing 40% of master's students and 30% of PhD students (Association of Universities and Colleges of Canada [AUCC], 2007). Education once again has the largest proportion of women doctoral students (69%) whereas the field of architecture, engineering, and related technologies have the lowest proportion of women doctoral students (22%) (CAUT, 2013).

There are little systematic data on visible minority students in Canada. From survey data, 16% of undergraduates self-identified as a member of a visible minority, while 24% of first year undergraduates in 2010 self-identified as a member of a visible minority (AUCC, 2007; CAUT, 2013). This percentage representation mirrors the proportion of the general Canadian population who identify as visible minorities. However, for Aboriginals, the picture is not as encouraging. The proportion of Aboriginals ages 25 to 64 with a university degree is 6%, compared to 20% of the general Canadian population and only 5% of first year undergraduates in 2010 self-identified as Aboriginal (CAUT, 2013). Aboriginals are significantly under-represented in their participation as students and as faculty in higher education in Canada (AUCC, 2007).

The continued gendering of particular subject areas leads to differences in career options and salaries for women and men, with men continuing to earn higher annual salaries than women with the same levels of education.

The Professoriate

Statistical Overview In the realm of higher education we can celebrate gradual improvement in women's presence as academics in Canadian universities. Recent Canadian statistics (2010–2011) illustrate that women represent 36.6% of all full-time faculty in our universities (CAUT, 2013). This representation is a strong improvement from 11% women faculty in 1960–1961 and 20% in 1989–1990 (AUCC, 2002; Sussman & Yssaad, 2005). However, women are disproportionately represented in lower academic ranks. In 2010–2011, women accounted for only 22.8% of full professors (the highest academic rank in Canada), 38% of associate professors, 46.4% of assistant professors, and 53% of lecturers (CAUT, 2013).

Figures for academic women's participation change little when we look at other Western countries. In OECD countries, collapsing college and university level teaching into one category, women represent 47.7% of teachers in Canada and 47.1% in the United States. The highest representation of women teachers in post-secondary education in OECD countries is found in New Zealand (51.5%) and the lowest representation of women is found in Japan (18.5%) (CAUT, 2013).

The numbers above demonstrate a definite accomplishment in women's increasing presence as full-time faculty in the academy. This change in presence is due in part to the increased hiring of women into full-time appointments. For instance, women represented 39.4% of all new full-time Canadian university appointments in 2004–2005 and 44.2% of new hires in 2011 (CAUT, 2007a; 2013). However, a puzzling scenario comes from the social sciences, where women doctoral graduates have outnumbered men since 1997, yet only 40% of new appointments were awarded to women between 1999 and 2004 (Drakich & Stewart, 2007). Another factor contributing to women's increasing presence among university faculty is the retiring of older male faculty (Acker & Webber, 2006; AUCC, 2002).

Despite such appearances of improvement, we still see a persistence of gendered trends. Women in universities continue to be concentrated in the lowest academic ranks, are more likely than men to be employed in part-time (non-secure) academic appointments, are concentrated in particular subject areas (such as the humanities and education), and earn lower salaries than men faculty (Acker & Webber, 2006; CAUT, 2007a; 2013). Further, Canadian research demonstrates that women are less likely to be promoted from associate professor to full professor than men, and when they are promoted, they are promoted to the position more slowly than men (spending more time at the rank of associate professor) (Drakich & Stewart, 2007; Dusseault, 2007). In the United States, women are less likely than men to be awarded tenure (Mason, Wolfinger, & Goulden, 2013). As Baker (2012) notes, in Western countries, "male academics are more likely to work full-time with fewer career interruptions, to publish more peer-reviewed articles, and to be promoted to higher ranks with higher salaries in a promotion system that often favours research over teaching and service" (pp. 8–9).

The racial and ethnic representation of women is also not evenly dispersed (Gaskell & Mullen, 2006). It is difficult, though, to provide a statistical profile of the racial and ethnic representation of Canadian university faculty as there is virtually no systematic reporting or collecting of such data (CAUT, 2007b). However, it is clear that the growing diversity of Canadian universities' student population is not yet matched in the professoriate as both people of colour and Aboriginals are under-represented (Henry & Tator, 2007). In 2006 only 14.9% of all university faculty members identify as visible minorities, which represents a small increase from 11.7% in 1996 (CAUT, 2007b; 2013). Aboriginal Canadians are significantly under-represented in faculty positions, and account for only 1.0% of total faculty appointments, compared with 2.3% of positions in the Canadian labour force (CAUT, 2013; Gaskell & Mullen, 2006). In 2013 in the United States, 79% of full-time faculty positions are occupied by whites, yet whites represent only 69% of the total United States population, leaving Blacks, Hispanics, and American Natives under-represented among faculty ranks (Gaskell & Mullen, 2006; NCES, 2015).

There is also gender segregation in the academy in disciplinary areas. Overall in Canada 36.6% of full-time faculty (all ranks) are women, however only 14.2% of architecture, engineering, and related technologies faculty; and 20.4% of mathematics, computer, and information sciences faculty are women. On the other side, there is greater overall representation of women in the health, parks, recreation, and fitness (47.1%), visual and performing arts (42.8%), humanities (44.2%), and education (57.4%) (CAUT, 2013).

A prestigious government initiative, the Canada Research Chairs Program (CRC), awards research faculty positions to outstanding faculty in an effort to both attract and retain exceptional faculty. The strongest criticism against the CRCs is one of gender discrimination. After the first four rounds of CRC appointments, just under 15% of the 532 chairs were awarded to women (Kondro, 2002). In 2003, eight women academics filed a complaint against the CRC Program alleging discrimination against women and other minority groups (Birchard, 2004; Tamburri, 2007). In 2004, women accounted for 20% of all CRCs and 26.6% in 2014 (Birchard, 2004; CRC, 2014), still well below their overall representation in Canadian universities. A "theoretical victory" occurred in 2006 when the CRC Program reached an agreement with the eight women complainants (Tamburri, 2007). Universities are now compelled to develop targets for appointing women, Aboriginals, visible minorities, and people with disabilities to the CRC Program (Tamburri, 2007).

While women are increasingly taking up administrative posts in Canadian universities, they remain a minority in senior positions (Drakich & Stewart, 2007; Grant, 2005). In 2004–2005, 30% of senior administrative posts in universities were held by women, a number unchanged since a survey in 2000 (Grant, 2005). The largest concentration of women in administration is at the level of chair or head of department, which is considered a junior administrative position (Drakich & Stewart, 2007). Experiences in these positions tell us that gendered expectations follow women even in these senior administrative posts; women administrators experience expectations to be "wife to the dean and mother to the faculty" (Acker, 2007, p. 10). Overall, as Drakich and Stewart (2007, p. 8) argue, there is considerable growth in terms of women's presence in Canadian universities, yet women have "failed to penetrate the still largely male world of academic prestige." The same pattern prevails in United States universities, a problem that Mason (2011) refers to as "the pyramid problem" (cited in Castaneda & Isgro, 2013, p. 4).

A worrisome trend in the contemporary academy, connected to the growing corporatization of universities, is the increasing reliance on part-time faculty. Hiring part-time faculty (also called contingent or non-permanent faculty) is an effective fiscal strategy for universities (Bauder, 2006; Mason, 2011). Curtis (2005) argues that the reliance on contingent faculty members symbolizes the most definitive change in the past 20 years in higher education. Part-time women academics proportionately outnumber their full-time counterparts, as almost half (42%) of part-timers (1997–1998) are women (Omiecinski, 2003). In the United States, women are overrepresented in non-tenured appointments (Mason, 2011; Mason, Wolfinger, & Goulden, 2013). As Muzzin (2003, pp. 6–7) notes, contingent academic workers are a "feminized (and somewhat racialized, though still mostly white) group supporting the still largely white male academic enterprise." Such a trend raises important questions with respect to the working conditions and career prospects in terms of job security, wages, and academic freedom, as well as opportunities for promotion for women employed in these positions.

Persistent patterns of segregation or lack of representation have profound effects on the academy. When we see an under-representation of groups from the general population (in the case of university faculty, it is members of equity-seeking groups), the academy lacks equity. Lacking equity in our universities may mean that the range of pedagogical approaches may be diminished, particular areas of research may go unexplored, the kinds of questions that should be asked may not be posed, and the range of research methodologies may be narrowed (CAUT, 2007b). The university is still a masculinist, Eurocentric organization (Henry & Tator, 2007). Feminist faculty and faculty of colour both argue that only certain forms of knowledge are legitimized in the contemporary academy (Henry & Tator, 2007; Webber, 2005).

Faculty Experiences Much of our information about the diverse experiences of women academics comes from personal narratives. The narrative approach seems especially suited to highlighting the complexities of the intersection of gender with other processes such as racialization (Carty, 1991; James & Farmer, 1993; Lewis, 2012; Medina, 2011; Medina & Luna, 2000; Monture-Angus, 2001; Rios, 2013), generation (Looser & Kaplan, 1997), ableism (Chouinard, 1995/1996), or sexuality (Bensimon, 1997; Lewis, 2012; Renn, 2010). In some cases (e.g., Bannerji, 1991; Chavez Silverman, 2000) the impact of a person's identity on pedagogy as well as career is discussed.

Canadian research on women of colour and Aboriginal women academics outlines the constant inhospitable environment of the white-dominated, male culture of the academy (Henry & Tator, 2007). These faculty members point to the hostility and tension of their white colleagues and students "as a minefield through which they constantly have to navigate" (Henry & Tator, 2007, p. 25). Students' racist behaviour toward them is not considered problematic by their colleagues, department chairs, or deans. The "culture of whiteness" remains dominant in Canadian universities (Henry & Tator, 2007, p. 25).

There is considerable tension for women academics who combine career and family (Baker, 2012; Castaneda & Isgro, 2013; French & Baker-Webster, 2013; Wolf-Wendel &

Ward, 2003). Research demonstrates that (heterosexual) women academics in full-time tenured positions in the United States are significantly less likely to be married and have children than full-time tenured men (Mason & Goulden, 2004). Further studies in Canada and the United States document higher rates of childlessness for younger women academics. For those considering children, women wrestle with how to synchronize progressing in their academic careers (tenure and promotion) with having children (Acker & Armenti, 2004; Baker, 2012; French & Baker-Webster, 2013; Meyers, 2012; Ward & Wolf-Wendel, 2004; Williams, 2000; Wolf-Wendel & Ward, 2003). Women academics with young children find it difficult to balance the demands of their careers alongside the demands of their children (Acker & Armenti, 2004; Dillabough, 2007; Raddon, 2002; Wajcman & Martin, 2002). These women speak of high levels of pressure, anxiety, exhaustion, and sleeplessness, and those at research-intensive institutions worry about the effect of taking maternity leaves on their research productivity and colleagues' perceptions about their commitment to their scholarship (Baker, 2012; Conley & Carey, 2013; Mason, Wolfinger, & Goulden, 2013; Wolf-Wendel & Ward, 2006). As a result of this thinking, many women opt not to take advantage of leaves available to them (Wolf-Wendel & Ward, 2006). As Dillabough (2007, p. 14) argues, "the traditional model of the independent scholar, autonomous and unencumbered, is a fraught one for any whose goal is to become a learned female in the academy. To embrace this powerful, inherited image is to inflict high levels of guilt upon women academics who are also parents."

The Chilly Climate In the United States, Roberta Hall and Bernice Sandler (1982) wrote the first report that documented faculty members' often unintentional differential treatment of men and women students in their classes, coining the phrase "the chilly climate" when representing women's experiences on university campuses. Hall and Sandler demonstrate that small instances of inequity exert a cumulative effect when experienced constantly. Some examples of differential interactions between faculty members and women and men students are calling on the men students more than the women (even when women have their hands up), and engaging more with the men in classroom interactions (praising, criticizing, giving feedback). Further, women's issues (such as violence against women) are often downplayed or trivialized. The chilly climate concept illuminates the micro processes of power—the little things that may seem insignificant really do matter.

Canadian research documents that the chilly climate also exists in our universities. A group of faculty members from the University of Western Ontario, calling themselves the Chilly Collective, published a collection called *Breaking Anonymity: The Chilly Climate for Women Faculty* (1995). In the preface to this collection, the Chilly Collective point to Sheila McIntyre's experiences in the Faculty of Law at Queen's University and subsequent publication (McIntyre, 1988) of her infamous memorandum ("Gender Bias within a Canadian Law School") as impetus for putting the anthology together. In this memo, McIntyre details "the patterns of stereotyping, sexualization, overt harassment, exclusion, and devaluation" (Chilly Collective, 1995, p. 1) she experienced in her first year as a faculty member.

Following this publication a group from York University published *York Stories: Women in Higher Education* (York Stories Collective, 2001). The *York Stories* collection includes chapters from undergraduate and graduate students and faculty members. The majority of chapters are interviews with women students and faculty and detail horrific experiences of sexism, racism, elitism, heterosexism, and homophobia.

Women's Studies and Feminism in the Academy

Women's studies is heralded as a "site of promise for social and intellectual transformation" (Braithwaite, Heald, Luhmann, & Rosenberg, 2004, p. 10). It became an institutional support for feminism in Canada in the early 1970s (Eichler with Tite, 1990). Individual women's studies courses were first offered in 1970 at the University of British Columbia, University of Toronto, McGill University, University of Waterloo, York University, Université de Montréal, University of Guelph, and Sir George Williams (later renamed Concordia) University (PAR-L, 2008). The first formalized program in women's studies came in 1973 at the University of British Columbia (PAR-L, 2008). In the United States, California State University at San Diego (1969) housed the first women's studies program while Cornell University followed suit the following year (Bracken, Allen, & Dean, 2006). The Royal Commission on the Status of Women (1970) "stated that Women's Studies courses indicated the necessity for change, helped show the ways this could be accomplished, and suggested that such courses could improve the conditions for women in future educational systems" (Reynolds, 2001, p. 248).

Prior to the formal institutionalization of women's studies in universities, some individual faculty members introduced students to the topics of women's liberation and sexism in their classrooms. Women's studies offers a challenge to the masculinist regime that operates in the academy (Smith, 1992) and brings with it the promise of using liberatory pedagogies in its classes. Feminist faculty are supposedly able to "do" academia differently: use feminist perspectives in their research and publications, employ feminist pedagogies in their classrooms, and draw upon feminist principles in their contributions to university governance. The National Women's Studies Association of the United States (NWSA) describes women's studies as

> the educational strategy of a breakthrough in consciousness and knowledge. The uniqueness of Women's Studies has been and remains its refusal to accept sterile divisions between academy and community, between the growth of the mind and the health of the body, between intellect and passion, between the individual and society. (NWSA, 2002, p. xx)

The field of women's studies is now firmly entrenched in Canadian universities, with over 40 institutions across the country offering programs or housing women's studies institutes. Around the globe, there are over 700 women's studies programs, departments, institutes, and/or research centres (Korenman, 2007).

Women's studies is not a static monolith; rather, vigorous debate among feminists pushes its boundaries and landscape (HCWSC, 2005). We have seen how women students and faculty of colour, lesbians, bisexuals, and trans* people have criticized feminist theories and projects that only seem to account for white, middle-class, heterosexual women's lives (HCWSC, 2005). We have seen how these debates have changed feminist theories, research agendas, and preoccupying questions. We have also seen how these debates have affected university programs—as we now see many programs changing their names from "Women's Studies" to "Women's and Gender Studies" or "Gender Studies" (WGSRF, 2012). After much dialogue, the professional association changed its name too—from the Canadian Women's Studies Association to the Women's and Gender Studies et Recherches Féministes (WGSRF, 2012).

Women's studies (and gender studies) also offers opportunities "to challenge the most egregious effects of a masculinist culture, both within the university and beyond" (Webber, 2006a, p. 62). Women's and gender studies continue to be a key space for engendering feminist identities and encouraging feminist agency (Webber, 2006a).

Feminist Pedagogies

The impetus for addressing the importance of pedagogical practices came not from theoretical deliberations on feminism (or education or teaching) but from practical concerns of both feminist academics and schoolteachers who wanted strategies to be able to attend to gender, as well as other equity issues, in their classrooms (Weiner, 2006). Interest in feminist pedagogy surfaced from a dissatisfaction with masculinist schools and universities as well as dissatisfaction with non-existent analysis of gender in pedagogic theory (Luke & Gore, 1992; Weiner, 2006).

Building on Paulo Freire's critical pedagogy as developed in *The Pedagogy of the Oppressed* (Freire, 1972), feminist pedagogies revolve around intentions to understand and make visible gender relations/gender oppression (also, as connected to race, class, sexuality, and so forth), value the realm of experience, be aware of and attempt to reconstruct power relations in classrooms, interrogate the status quo, and engender social change/social transformation (Bignell, 1996; Briskin, 1994; Fisher, 2001; hooks, 1988; Hornosty, 2004; Lewis, 2012; Morley, 2001; Pereira, 2012; Rinehart, 2002; Welch, 2002). In her work on queer pedagogy, Deborah Britzman (1995; 2012) calls for pedagogies that go beyond binary constructions of "the tolerant and the tolerated and the oppressed and the oppressor" (Britzman, 1995, p. 164) in order to have pedagogies that make "all bodies matter" (p. 165). Such an approach requires an engagement with "difference as the grounds of politicality and community" (Britzman, 1995, p. 152).

Feminist pedagogies are not above criticism. One of the core tenets of feminist approaches to teaching is the inclusion of personal experience in the classroom (of both faculty/teacher and student) (Briskin, 1994; Welch, 1994). Yet in these prescriptive writings, the use of experience is rarely troubled; there is rarely a discussion that takes up how expressions of experience are discursively constructed (Webber, 2006b). Another goal of many feminist pedagogues is to create "safe" and "respectful" classroom spaces (Lewis, 1992; Shrewsbury, 1998). While a laudable goal, classrooms "like all social spaces are imbued with spoken and unspoken assumptions about sexuality, gender and 'race'" (Nairn,

Archibald, J. (1995). Locally developed Native studies curriculum: An historical and philosophical rationale. In M. Battiste & J. Barman (Eds.), *First Nations education in Canada: The circle unfolds* (pp. 288–312). Vancouver, BC: UBC Press.

Arnot, M. (2002). *Reproducing gender? Essays on educational theory and feminist politics*. London, England: Routledge Falmer.

Arnot, M., & Dillabough, J. (1999). Feminist politics and democratic values in education. *Curriculum Inquiry*, *29*, 159–189.

Association of Universities and Colleges of Canada (AUCC). (2002). *Trends in higher education*. Ottawa: Publications and Communications Division, Association of Universities and Colleges of Canada.

Association of Universities and Colleges of Canada (AUCC). (2007). *Trends in higher education: Volume 1: Enrolment*. Ottawa: Publications and Communications Division, Association of Universities and Colleges of Canada.

Association of University Teachers (AUT) (UK). (2004). *The unequal academy*. Retrieved from www.ucu.org.uk/media/pdf/aut_unequalacademy.pdf

Baker, M. (2012). *Academic careers and the gender gap*. Vancouver, BC: UBC Press.

Bannerji, H. (1991). Re: Turning the gaze. *Resources for Feminist Research*, *20*(3/4), 5–11.

Bauder, H. (2006). The segmentation of academic labour: A Canadian example, *ACME*, *4*(2), 228–239.

Bazzul, J., & Sykes, H. (2011). The secret identity of a biology textbook: Straight and naturally sexed. *Cultural Studies of Science Education*, *6*, 265–286.

Bensimon, E. M. (1997). Lesbian existence and the challenge to normative constructions of the academy. In C. Marshall (Ed.), *Feminist critical policy analysis: A perspective from post-secondary education* (pp. 141–155). London, England: Falmer.

Bignell, K. (1996). Building feminist praxis out of feminist pedagogy: The importance of students' perspectives. *Women's Studies International Forum*, *19*(3), 315–325.

Birchard, K. (2004). Women make gains in getting Canadian research chairs. *Chronicle of Higher Education*, *51*(14), A38.

Bouchard, P., Boily, I., & Proulx, M. (2003). *School success by gender: A catalyst for masculinist discourse*. Ottawa: Status of Women Canada.

Bourne, P., McCoy, L., & Smith, D. (1998). Girls and schooling: Their own critique, *Resources for Feminist Research*, *26*(1/2), 55–68.

Bracken, S., Allen, J., & Dean, D. (2006). Introduction: The past, present and future—women's studies, higher education and praxis. In S. Bracken, J. Allen, & D. Dean (Eds.), *The balancing act: Gendered perspectives in faculty roles and work lives* (pp. 1–8). Sterling, VA: Stylus.

Braithwaite, A., Heald, S., Luhmann, S., & Rosenberg, S. (2004). "Passing on": Women's studies. In A. Braithwaite, S. Heald, S. Luhmann, & S. Rosenberg (Eds.), *Troubling women's studies: Pasts, presents and possibilities* (pp. 9–42). Toronto, ON: Sumach.

Briskin, L. (1994). Feminist pedagogy: Teaching and learning liberation. In L. Erwin & D. MacLennan (Eds.), *Sociology of education in Canada: Critical perspectives theory, research and practice* (pp. 443–470). Toronto, ON: Copp Clark Longman.

Britzman, D. (1995). Is there a queer pedagogy? or, Stop reading straight. *Educational Theory*, *45*(2), 151–165.

Britzman, D. (2012). Queer pedagogy and its strange techniques. In E. Meiners & T. Quinn, *Sexualities in education: A reader* (pp. 292–308). New York, NY: Peter Lang.

Brown, A. (2011). Descendants of "Ruth": Black girls coping through the "Black male crisis." *Urban Revue*, *43*, 597–619.

Bussière, P., Knighton, T., & Pennock, D. (2007). *Measuring up: Canadian results of the OECD PISA study, the performance of Canada's youth in science, reading and mathematics*. Statistics Canada, Catalogue no. 81-590-XWE2007001. Ottawa, ON: Minister of Industry.

Canadian Association of University Teachers (CAUT). (2004). Closing the equity gap: A portrait of Canada's university teachers, 1996–2001. *CAUT Education Review*, *6*, 1–5.

Canadian Association of University Teachers (CAUT). (2006). Women in the academic work force. *CAUT Education Review*, *8*(1), 1–6.

Canadian Association of University Teachers (CAUT). (2007a). *CAUT almanac of post-secondary education in Canada*. Retrieved from www.caut.ca/docs/almanac/2007_caut_almanac_en.pdf?sfvrsn=2

Canadian Association of University Teachers (CAUT). (2007b). A partial picture: The representation of equity-seeking groups in Canada's universities and colleges. *CAUT Equity Review*, November 1.

Canadian Association of University Teachers (CAUT). (2013). *2013-2014 CAUT almanac of post-secondary education in Canada*. Retrieved from www.caut.ca/docs/default-source/almanac/almanac_2013-2014_print_finalE20A5E5CA0EA6529968D1CAF.pdf?sfvrsn=2

Carty, L. (1991). Black women in academia: A statement from the periphery. In H. Bannerji, L. Carty, K. Dehli, S. Heald, & K. McKenna (Eds.), *Unsettling relations: The university as a site of feminist struggles* (pp. 13–44). Toronto, ON: Women's Press.

Castaneda, M., & Isgro, K. (2013). Introduction. In M. Castaneda & K. Isgro (Eds.), *Mothers in academia* (pp. 1–14). New York, NY: Columbia University Press.

Chavez Silverman, S. (2000). Tropicalizing the liberal arts classroom. In S. Geok-Lin Lim, M. Herrera-Sobek, & G. M. Padilla (Eds.), *Power, race and gender in academe: Strangers in the tower?* (pp. 132–153). New York, NY: Modern Languages Association.

Chilly Collective, (Eds.). (1995). *Breaking anonymity: The chilly climate for women faculty.* Waterloo, ON: Wilfrid Laurier University Press.

Chouinard, V. (1995/1996). Like Alice through the looking-glass: Accommodations in academia. *Resources for Feminist Research*, *24*(3/4), 3–11.

Codjoe, H. (2001). Fighting a "public enemy" of black academic achievement—the persistence of racism and the schooling experiences of Black students in Canada. *Race Ethnicity and Education*, *4*(4), 343–375.

Conley, S., & Carey, D. (2013). Academic mothers on leave (but on the clock), on the line (and off the record): Toward improving parental-leave policies. In M. Castaneda & K. Isgro (Eds.), *Mothers in Academia* (pp. 200–212). New York, NY: Columbia University Press.

Connell, B. (2002). Hegemonic masculinity. In S. Jackson & S. Scott (Eds.), *Gender: A sociological reader* (pp. 60–62). New York, NY: Routledge.

CRC. (2014). *Canada Research Chairs*. Retrieved from www.chairs-chaires.gc.ca/about_us-a_notre_sujet/statistics-statistiques-eng.aspx

Currie, J., & Newson, J. (Eds.). (1998). *Universities and globalization: Critical perspectives*. Thousand Oaks, CA: SAGE.

Curtis, J. (2005). Inequities persist for women and non-tenure-track faculty. *Academe*, *91*(2), 20–98.

Cusson, S. (1990). Women in school administration. *Canadian Social Trends*, *Fall*, 18.

Davies, S., & Guppy, N. (2006). *The schooled society: An introduction to the sociology of education*. Don Mills, ON: Oxford University Press.

Dei, G. (1997). Race and the production of identity in the schooling experiences of African-Canadian youth. *Discourse: Studies in the Cultural Politics of Education*, *18*(2), 241–257.

Dei, G. (2008). Schooling as community: Race, schooling, and the education of African youth. *Journal of Black Studies*, *38*(3), 346–366.

deMarrais, K., & LeCompte, M. (1999). *The way schools work: A sociological analysis of education* (3rd ed.). New York, NY: Longman.

Department of Education, Science, and Training (Australia). (2004). *Staff 2004: Selected higher education statistics*. Retrieved from http://education.gov.au/selected-higher-education-statistics-1997-2007-staff-data

Dillabough, J. (2006). "Education feminism(s)," gender theory and social thought: Illuminating moments and critical impasses In C. Skelton, B. Francis, & L. Smulyan (Eds.), *The SAGE handbook of gender and education* (pp. 47–62). London, England: SAGE.

Dillabough, J. (2007). Parenting and working: A model change needed. *Academic Matters*, *February*, 14.

Dion, S. D. (2009). *Braiding histories: Learning from aboriginal peoples' experiences and perspectives.* Vancouver, BC: UBC Press.

Drakich, J., & Stewart, P. (2007). Forty years later, how are university women doing? *Academic Matters*, *February*, 6–9.

Drolet, D. (2007). Minding the gender gap. *University Affairs*, *October*, 9–12.

Dusseault, C. (2007). UBC confronts gender-related differences in Faculty of Science. *University Affairs*, *October*, 34–35.

Eccles, J. (2011). Gendered educational and occupational choices: Applying the Eccles et al. model of achievement-related choices. *International Journal of Behavioral Development*, *35*, 195–201.

Eichler, M., & Tite, R. (1990). Women's studies professors in Canada: A collective self-portrait. *Atlantis*, *16*(1), 6–24.

Federation of Women Teachers' Associations of Ontario (FWTAO). (1988). *The more things change . . . the more they stay the same*. Toronto, ON: FWTAO.

Ferfolja, T. (2008). Discourses that silence: Teachers and anti-lesbian harassment. *Discourse: Studies in the Cultural Politics of Education*, *29*(1), 107–119.

Fisher, B. (2001). *No angel in the classroom: Teaching through feminist discourse*. Lanham, MD: Rowman and Littlefield.

Freire, P. (1972). *The pedagogy of the oppressed*. London, England: Penguin.

French, S., & Baker-Webster, L. (2013). Tales from the tenure track: The necessity of social support in balancing the challenges of tenure and motherhood. In M. Castaneda & K. Isgro (Eds.), *Mothers in academia* (pp. 170–180). New York, NY: Columbia University Press.

Gaskell, J. (1977). Stereotyping and discrimination in the curriculum. In J. D. Wilson & H. Stevenson, (Eds.), *Precepts, policy and process: Perspectives on contemporary education* (pp. 263–284). Calgary, AB: Detselig.

Gaskell, J., McLaren, A., & Novogrodsky, M. (1989). *Claiming an education: Feminism and Canadian schools*. Toronto, ON: Our Schools, Our Selves.

Gaskell, J., & Mullen, A. (2006). Women in teaching: Participation, power and possibility. In C. Skelton, B. Francis, & L. Smulyan (Eds.), *The SAGE handbook of gender and education* (pp. 453–468). London, England: SAGE.

Gherasim, L., Bunaru, S., & Mairean, C. (2013). Classroom environment, achievement goals and maths performance: Gender differences. *Educational Studies*, *39*, 1–12.

Giraldo, E., & Colyar, J. (2012). Dealing with gender in the classroom: A portrayed case study of four teachers. *International Journal of Inclusive Education*, *16*, 25–38.

Grant, B. (1997). Disciplining students: The construction of student subjectivities, *British Journal of Sociology of Education*, *18*(1), 101–114.

Grant, K. (2005). Women in senior university administration in Canada in 2005: Where do we stand? *Senior Women Academic Administrators of Canada E-News*, *September*, 2–5.

Hall, R., & Sandler, B. (1982). *The classroom climate: A chilly one for women*. Washington, DC: Project on the Status and Education of Women.

HCWSC. (2005). *Women's realities, women's choices: An introduction to women's studies*. New York, NY: Oxford.

Henry, F., & Tator, C. (2007). Through a looking glass: Enduring racism on the university campus, *Academic Matters*, *February*, 24–25.

Hodgetts, K. (2010). Boys' underachievement and the management of teacher accountability. *Discourse: Studies in the Cultural Politics of Education*, *31*, 29–43.

Hogan, R., Perrucci, C., & Behringer A. (2005). Enduring inequality: Gender and employment income in late career. *Sociological Spectrum*, *25*(1), 53–77.

Hood, S. (2005). Addressing boys' achievement in school. *ETFO Voice*, (Winter), 25–27.

hooks, b. (1988). *Talking back: Thinking feminist, thinking Black*. Toronto, ON: Between the Lines Press.

hooks, b. (1994). *Teaching to transgress: Education as the practice of freedom*. New York, NY: Routledge.

Hornosty, J. (2004). Corporate challenges to academic freedom and gender equity. In M. Reimer (Ed.), *Inside Corporate U: Women in the academy speak out* (pp. 43–66). Toronto, ON: Sumach Press.

Jackson, J. (2006). Removing the masks: Considerations by gay and lesbian teachers when negotiating the closet door. *Journal of Poverty*, *10*(2), 27–52.

James, J., & Farmer, R. (Eds.). (1993). *Spirit, space and survival: African American women in (white) academe*. New York, NY: Routledge.

Kassam, A. (2007). Locating identity and gender construction in a post 9/11 world: The case of the hijabi girl. *Intercultural Education*, *18*(4), 355–359.

Kehler, M. (2007). Hallway fears and high school friendships: The complications of young men (re)negotiating heterosexualized identities. *Discourse: Studies in the Cultural Politics of Education*, *28*(2), 259–277.

Kenny, C. (2002). *North American Indian, Metis and Inuit women speak about culture, education and work*. Ottawa: Status of Women Canada. Retrieved from http://publications.gc.ca/collections/Collection/SW21-90-2001E.pdf

Khayatt, D. (1994). Surviving school as a lesbian. *Gender & Education*, *6*(1), 47–61.

Kimmel, M. (1999). What are little boys made of? *MS Magazine*, *October/November*, 88–91.

Kimmel, M. (2000). What about the boys? *Women's Educational Equity Act Digest, November*, 1–2, 7–8.

Kondro, W. (2002). Few women win new academic chairs. *Science*, *296*(5577), 2319.

Korenman, J. (2007). *Women's studies programs, departments and research centers.* Retrieved from http://userpages.umbc.edu/~korenman/wmst/programs.html

Lewis, M. (1992). Interrupting patriarchy: Politics, resistance and transformation. In C. Luke & J. Gore (Eds.), *Feminisms and critical pedagogy* (pp. 167–191). New York, NY: Routledge.

Lewis, M. M. (2012). Pedagogy and the sista' professor: Teaching black queer feminist studies through the self. In E. Meiners & T. Quinn (Eds.), *Sexualities in education: a reader* (pp. 33–40). New York, NY: Peter Lang.

Li, Jun. (2004). Parental expectations of Chinese immigrants: a folk theory about children's school achievement. *Race Ethnicity and Education*, *7*(2), 167–183.

Looser, D., & Kaplan, E. (Eds.). (1997). *Generations: Academic feminists in dialogue*. Minneapolis, MN: University of Minnesota Press.

Lucey, H. (2001). Social class, gender and schooling. In B. Francis & C. Skelton (Eds.), *Investigating gender: Contemporary perspectives in education* (pp. 177–188). Buckingham, England: Open University Press.

Luke, C., & J. Gore. (1992). Introduction. In C. Luke & J. Gore (Eds.), *Feminisms and critical pedagogy* (pp. 1–14). London, England: Routledge.

Mac an Ghaill, M. (1988). *Young, gifted and Black*. Milton Keynes, England: Open University Press.

Macgillivray, I., & Jennings, T. (2008). A content analysis exploring lesbian, gay, bisexual, and transgender topics in foundations of education textbooks. *Journal of Teacher Education*, *59*(2), 170–188.

Mandell, N., & Crysdale, S. (1993). Gender tracks: Male-female perceptions of home-school-work transitions. In P. Anisef & P. Axelrod (Eds.), *Transitions: Schooling and employment in Canada* (pp. 21–41). Toronto, ON: Thompson.

Martino, W., & Frank, B. (2006). The tyranny of surveillance: Male teachers and the policing of masculinities in a single sex school. *Gender & Education*, *18*(1), 17–33.

Mason, M. (2011, March 9). The pyramid problem. *Chronicle of Higher Education*. Retrieved from chronicle.com/article/the-pyramid-problem/126614

Mason, M., & Goulden, M. (2004). Marriage and baby blues: Redefining gender equity in the academy. *Annals of the American Academy of Political and Social Science*, *596*, 86–103.

Mason, M., Wolfinger, N., & Goulden, M. (2013). *Do babies matter? Gender and family in the ivory tower*. New Brunswick, NJ: Rutgers University Press.

McIntyre, S. (1988). Gender bias within the law school: "The memo" and its impact. *Canadian Journal of Women and the Law*, *2*(1), 362–407.

Medina, C. (2011). The value of a multidimensional lens: A Puerto Rican professor negotiates academic systems of power. In M. Meyers (Ed.), *Women in higher education: The fight for equity* (pp. 119–134). New York, NY: Hampton Press.

Medina, C., & Luna, G. (2000). Narratives from Latina professors in higher education. *Anthropology and Education Quarterly*, *31*(1), 47–66.

Meyers, M. (2012). Women in higher education: the long, hard road to equality. In M. Meyers (Ed.), *Women in higher education: The fight for equity* (pp. 3–18). New York, NY: Hampton Press.

Mirza, H. S., & Reay, D. (2000). Redefining citizenship: Black women educators and "the third space." In M. Arnot & J. Dillabough (Eds.), *Challenging democracy: International perspectives on gender, education and citizenship* (pp. 58–72). London, England: Routledge.

Monture-Angus, P. (2001). In the way of peace: Confronting whiteness in the university. In R. Luther, E. Whitmore, & B. Moreau (Eds.), *Seen but not heard: Aboriginal women and women of colour in the academy* (pp. 29–49). Ottawa: CRIAW.

Morley, L. (2001). Mass higher education: Feminist pedagogy in the learning society. In P. Anderson & J. Williams, *Identity and difference in higher education: "Outsiders within"* (pp. 28–37). Aldershot, England: Ashgate.

Morris, E. (2007). "Ladies" or "loudies"? Perceptions and experiences of Black girls in classrooms. *Youth and Society*, *38*(4), 490–515.

Muzzin, L. (2003). Report of the professional practice, ethics and policy subcommittee. *The Canadian Sociology and Anthropology Association Annual Report 2002–2003*. Ottawa, ON: CSAA.

Nairn, K. (2003). What has the geography of sleeping arrangements got to do with the geography of our teaching spaces? *Gender, Place and Culture*, *10*(1), 67–81.

National Center for Education Statistics (NCES) (US). (2015). Fast Facts: Race/ethnicity of College Faculty. Retrieved from https://nces.ed.gov/fastfacts/display.asp?id=61

National Women's Studies Association (NWSA). (2002). National Women's Studies Association constitution. *NWSA Journal*, *14*(1), xix–xx.

Nelson, A. (2006). *Gender in Canada* (3rd ed.). Toronto, ON: Pearson Prentice Hall.

OECD. (2014). *PISA 2012 Results in Focus*. Retrieved from www.oecd.org/pisa/keyfindings/pisa-2012-results-overview.pdf

Omiecinski, T. (2003). Hiring of part-time university faculty on the increase. *Education Quarterly Review*, *9*(3), 9–15.

Ontario Ministry of Education. (2012). *Quick Facts: Ontario Schools 2011-2012*. Retrieved from www.edu.gov.on.ca/eng/general/elemsec/quickfacts/2011-12/quickFacts11_12.pdf

PAR-L. (2008). *A chronology of the development of women's studies in Canada: The 1970s*. Retrieved from www2.unb.ca/parl/chronology.htm

Pereira, M. dM. (2012). Uncomfortable classrooms: Rethinking the role of student discomfort in feminist teaching, *European Journal of Women's Studies*, *19*, 128–135.

Phoenix, A. (2001). Racialization and gendering in the (re)production of educational inequalities. In B. Francis & C. Skelton (Eds.), *Investigating gender: Contemporary perspectives in education* (pp. 126–138). Buckingham, England: Open University Press.

Prentice, A. (1977). *The school promoters: Education and social class in mid-nineteenth century Upper Canada*. Toronto, ON: McClelland & Stewart.

Raby, R. (2005). Polite, well-dressed and on time: Secondary school conduct codes and the production of docile citizens. *Canadian Review of Sociology and Anthropology*, *42*(1), 71–91.

Raddon, A. (2002). Mothers in the academy. *Studies in Higher Education*, *27*(4), 387–403.

Reimer, M., (Ed.). (2004a). *Inside Corporate U: Women in the academy speak out*. Toronto, ON: Sumach.

Reimer, M. (2004b). Will women's studies programs survive the corporate university? In M. Reimer (Ed.), *Inside Corporate U: Women in the academy speak out* (pp. 118–137). Toronto, ON: Sumach.

Renn, K. (2010). LGBT and queer research in higher education: the state and status of the field. *Educational Researcher*, *39*, 132–141.

Renold, E. (2006). "They won't let us play . . . unless you're going out with one of them": Girls, boys and Butler's "heterosexual matrix" in the primary years. *British Journal of Sociology of Education*, *27*(4), 489–509.

Renzetti, C., & Curran, D. (1999). *Women, men and society* (4th ed.). Boston, MA: Allyn and Bacon.

Republished with permission of John Hopkins University Press, from National Women's Studies Association (NWSA), National Women's Studies Association constitution. *NWSA Journal* 14(1), 2002; permission conveyed through Copyright Clearance Center, Inc.

Reynolds, C. (2001). The educational system. In N. Mandell (Ed.), *Feminist issues: Race, class and sexuality* (3rd ed.) (pp. 242–259). Toronto, ON: Prentice Hall.

Rinehart, J. (2002). Feminist education: Rebellion within McUniversity. In D. Hayes & R. Wynyard (Eds.), *The McDonaldization of higher education* (pp. 167–179). Westport, CT: Bergin and Garvey.

Rios, D. (2012). A southwest Chicana in the Connecticut Yankee realm: A cross-cultural feminist critique on gender, ethnic, and racial inequities in higher education. In M. Meyers (Ed.), *Women in Higher Education: The Fight for Equity* (pp. 97–118). New York, NY: Hampton Press.

Ritzer, G. (1998). *The McDonaldization thesis: Explorations and extensions*. London, England: SAGE.

Rollock, N. (2007). Why Black girls don't matter: Exploring how race and gender shape academic success in an inner city school. *Support for Learning*, *22*(4), 197–202.

Sadker, M., & Sadker, D. (2009). Missing in interaction. In E. Disch (Ed.), *Reconstructing gender: A multicultural anthology* (5th ed.) (pp. 362–368). New York, NY: McGraw-Hill.

Shrewsbury, C. (1998). What is feminist pedagogy? In M. Rogers (Ed.), *Contemporary feminist theory* (pp. 167–171). Boston, MA: McGraw-Hill.

Skelton, C. (1997). Women and education. In D. Richardson & V. Robinson (Eds.), *Introducing women's studies: Feminist theory and practice* (2nd ed.) (pp. 303–323) Basingstoke, England: Palgrave Macmillan.

Skelton, C. (2001). *Schooling the boys: Masculinities and primary education*. Buckingham, England, Philadelphia, PA: Open University Press.

Smith, D. (1992). Whistling women: Reflections on rage and rationality. In W. Carroll, L. Christiansen-Ruffman, R. Currie, & D. Harrison (Eds.), *Fragile truths: Twenty-five years of sociology and anthropology in Canada* (pp. 207–226). Ottawa, ON: Carleton University Press.

Statistics Canada. (2006, June 26). Education matters: Profile of Canada's school principals. *The Daily*.

Sussman, D., & Yssaad, L. (2005). The rising profile of women academics. *Perspectives on Labour and Income*, *6*, 6–19.

Tamburri, R. (2007). Mediated agreement reached in CRC dispute. *University Affairs January*, 40.

Taylor, Y. (2006). Intersections of class and sexuality in the classroom, *Gender and Education*, *18*(4), 447–452.

Temple, J. (2005). "People who are different from you": Heterosexism in Quebec high school textbooks. *Canadian Journal of Education*, *28*(3), 271–294.

Thompson, M., & Armato, M. (2012). *Investigating Gender*. Malden, MA: Polity Press.

Tyack, D. (1974). *The one best system*. Cambridge, MA: Harvard University Press.

Wajcman, J., & Martin, B. (2002). Narratives of identity in modern management: The corrosion of gender difference? *Sociology*, *36*(4), 985–1102.

Ward, K., & Wolf-Wendel, L. (2004). Academic motherhood: Managing complex roles in research universities. *Review of Higher Education*, *27*, 233–257.

Webber, M. (2005). "Don't be so feminist": Exploring student resistance to feminist approaches in a Canadian university. *Women's Studies International Forum*, *28*, 181–194.

Webber, M. (2006a). "I'm not a militant feminist": Exploring feminist identities and feminist hesitations in the contemporary academy. *Atlantis*, *31*(1), 55–63.

Webber, M. (2006b). Transgressive pedagogies? Exploring the difficult realities of enacting feminist pedagogies in undergraduate classrooms in a Canadian university. *Studies in Higher Education*, *31*(4), 453–467.

Weiner, G. (2006). Out of the ruins: Feminist pedagogy in recovery. In C. Skelton, B. Francis, & L. Smulyan (Eds.), *The SAGE handbook of gender and education* (pp. 79–92). London, England: SAGE.

Welch, P. (1994). Is a feminist pedagogy possible? In S. Davies, C. Lubelska, & J. Quinn (Eds.), *Changing the subject: Women in higher education* (pp. 149–162). London, England: Taylor and Francis.

Welch, P. (2002). Feminist pedagogy and power in the academy. In G. Howie & A. Tauchert (Eds.), *Teaching and research in higher education* (pp. 113–124). Aldershot, England: Ashgate.

Williams, J. (2000, October 27). How the tenure track discriminates against women. *Chronicle of Higher Education*, B10.

Wilmot, M., & Naidoo, D. (2014). "Keeping things straight": the representation of sexualities in life orientation textbooks. *Sex education*, *14*, 323–337.

Wolf-Wendel, L., & Ward, K. (2003). Future prospects for women faculty: Negotiating work and family. In B. Ropers-Huilman (Ed.), *Gendered futures in higher education: Critical perspectives for change* (pp. 111–134). Albany, NY: State University of New York Press.

Wolf-Wendel, L., & Ward, K. (2006). Faculty work and family life: Policy perspectives from different institutional types. In S. Bracken, J. Allen, & D. Dean (Eds.), *The balancing act: Gendered perspectives in faculty roles and work lives* (pp. 51–72). Sterling, England: Stylus.

Women's and Gender Studies et Recherches Féministes (WGSRF). (2012). Our New Name! Retrieved from www.wgsrf.com/blog/our-new-name

Wotherspoon, T. (2004). *The sociology of education in Canada: Critical perspectives,* (2nd ed.). Don Mills, ON: Oxford University Press.

Wotherspoon, T. (2009). *The sociology of education in Canada: Critical perspectives* (3rd ed.). Don Mills, ON: Oxford University Press.

York Stories Collective (Eds.). (2001). *York stories: Women in higher education*. Toronto, ON: TSAR Publications.

Youdell, D. (2003). Identity traps or how Black students fail: The interactions between biographical, sub-cultural, and learner identities. *British Journal of Sociology of Education*, *24*(1), 3–20.

Chapter 12

Health As a Feminist Issue

Carrie Bourassa

With contributions from Mel Bendig, Eric Oleson, Cassie Ozog

INTRODUCTION

Feminism and health are inexorably linked. Historically, feminist movements have grappled with diverse views on women's health, health care, health policy, sexuality, and the role that medicine (particularly biomedicine) plays in women's lives. Even when they disagree about the movement's goals, values, ideologies, and strategies, feminists are united in their attempts to understand how gender and sex are implicated in our understanding and treatment of women's health. Moreover, many feminists recognize that social constructions of race and class intersect with other social determinants of health to contribute to different health outcomes for women around the globe.

This chapter examines the intersection of feminism and health. It defines "health" and examines social determinants of health—emphasizing the role social environments play in generating and maintaining health, and the connections between oppression and health. The theory of intersectionality demonstrates how identities and lived experiences intersect to create both inequity and opportunities (Cho, Williams Crenshaw, & McCall, 2013). We argue that race is a social construction and that Indigenous people, in particular, but also racialized minorities experience poorer health outcomes than their white Canadian counterparts because gender, race, and class combine in complex ways with socio-economic determinants of health in producing health outcomes. In order to help us understand gender inequities in health in relation to other social identities and circumstances, we provide a brief overview of international and national health trends as well as specific information pertaining to Canadian immigrant and Indigenous women. The chapter concludes by examining women's health policy, contemporary women's health activism in Canada, issues of cultural safety, and women-centred health care.

DEFINING HEALTH

As early as 1948, the World Health Organization (WHO, 1948) defined health as "a state of physical, mental, or social well-being, not merely an absence of illness or disease."[1] Definitions of health continually evolve and are influenced greatly by individual and societal values, experiences, and worldviews. Individuals and communities understand health and well-being differently as culture, geography, and time shape our interpretations. Even though people have individual definitions of health, commonalities exist across regions and groups of people, confirming that our perspectives on health are partially developed, maintained, and altered socially by both history and culture. As an example of a cultural influence on health, many Indigenous populations in the Canadian plains traditionally held eco-centric views of health. In these communities, the environment (Mother Earth, plants, animals, the air) is inextricably connected to both an individual's and a community's well-being. Another example can be found in manifestations of mental illness. In the United States, Asian Americans are more likely than other Americans to express psychological distress as physical complaints (Kramer, Kwong, Lee, & Chung, 2002). Symptoms of mental illness and depression are reported as physical complaints and pain, rather than as emotional or mental distress. Although common discourse outlines health and ill health as objective, consistent, and diagnosable, we see that, in fact, how we understand health and how illness manifests itself is subjective and influenced by who we are and the environments in which we live.

For much of the 20th century, a biomedical model of health dominated the health field, focusing largely on physical illness, symptoms, and cures. In this model, individual genetics and behaviour were seen as causes for ill health. It wasn't until the mid-1970s that mainstream health discussions began to acknowledge the impact of environment on well-being. Contemporary conceptualizations of health often extend beyond a biomedical illness-based model to include holistic elements, which encompass emotional, spiritual, and social aspects of health (Smylie, 2013). In this way, everyday life is seen as intertwined with producing health and well-being.

In 1974, Marc Lalonde, then minister of National Health and Welfare in Canada, authored a paper for Canada's Department of Health entitled "A New Perspective on the Health of Canadians." This influential document shifted perspectives of health from a focus on biomedical care to consideration of the social and environmental determinants of health (Groff & Goldberg, 2000). Focusing on four main areas of health determinants—lifestyle, health care organization, human biology, and the environment—the report acknowledged the complexities affecting health, and argued for the conceptualization of health beyond that of medical care (Glouberman, 2001). By moving conversations of health promotion beyond individual risky behaviour, the report discussed the role of communities as advocates for social and economic change, and encouraged policy that generates "good" health. The report's overemphasis on lifestyle did, unfortunately, limit comprehensive consideration of the social environment.

In 1980, this deficit was addressed by the *Black Report*; published in the United Kingdom by the Department of Health and Social Security (McIntosh Gray, 1982). This report outlined that even though the overall health of the United Kingdom's population had increased with the introduction of the welfare state, significant health inequalities still existed. These health inequalities and differences in disease rates were associated largely with economic inequities. The *Black Report* initiated global consideration of the effect of income and socio-economic status on health.

The most recent phase in health discussions has extended ideas discussing social impacts on holistic health and the importance of physical and social environments. The *Ottawa Charter of Health Promotion* was produced as a result of the first International Conference on Health Promotion, held in Ottawa in 1986 (WHO, 1986). The Charter outlines prerequisites for health that include peace, shelter, education, food, income, a stable eco-system, sustainable resources, social justice, and equity. It acknowledges that health status is directly connected to the social environment.

It is important to understand that these discussions on the shifting perspectives of how health is understood focus on mainstream, dominant, Western discourses of health. An understanding of holistic health and the environmental influences on health have existed within many North America Indigenous communities for many years. This is true for many communities in other regions around the globe. Although these ideas have infiltrated into some mainstream health documents and conversations, health care systems in many countries, including Canada, remain rooted in biomedical models of health. However, these frameworks that see health inequities as a result of limited income, resources, and social injustice do set the scene for discussions to evolve and acknowledge the impacts that social environments have on health, creating ideological space for collaborations between those working in social justice and health delivery.

SOCIAL DETERMINANTS OF HEALTH

The social determinants of health model provides us with a framework for understanding health and the factors that influence it. Social determinants of health acknowledge that social structures govern people's experiences as individuals and populations. This model has gained increasing attention in the last decade. Many local and national health agencies throughout Canada have incorporated a social determinants of health model. In 2011, the World Health Organization convened the World Conference on Social Determinants of Health (WHO, 2011), validating the model at an international level and encouraging action from member states to address social determinants.

Various social determinant models exist within Canada, and depending on the source, different social determinants of health will be outlined in the model. Some determinants of health presented throughout these models are income, education, employment, working conditions, social security, food security, social supports, social exclusion, class, housing, early childhood development, access to health care, culture, gender, race, ability, Aboriginal status, and colonization. This model does not deny that there are biological and genetic influences on health. These models instead acknowledge that the many social structures impacting physical and biological health have, for many years, been neglected in health discussions.

As an example, let us look specifically at socio-economic status. It is well established in the literature that income is positively correlated with many health indicators—as income increases, so does health and well-being. The same applies for education, a correlation demonstrated continually in population level data. Even at a surface level, these claims seem reasonable. Individuals living with lower incomes have fewer resources with which to purchase healthy food, participate in recreation, or purchase health care or products not covered by public health insurance. Income also intersects with other determinants of well-being such as food security; decent housing; and access to health care, employment, and education. A higher level of education means that people are more likely to have the ability to secure continuous employment opportunities, which increase lifetime earnings and increase their likelihood of living long and healthy lives. Critically investigating the social determinants of health furthers our understanding of how many health inequalities and disease disparities result from economic inequalities.

However, some theories of the social determinants of health fail to provide a critical analysis and often overlook the underlying factors that cause social inequality in the first place. What factors contribute to income inequality between and within populations? Why do certain populations in Canada not experience the same health as other groups? Ill health results from both individuals' health choices and differential access and opportunity to make good health choices. There are concrete social factors limiting individual choices and opportunities that are connected to social values and systems that privilege some groups of people over others. Health models need to acknowledge the role of social structures in creating unjust and avoidable differences in well-being. It is in this acknowledgement that the social determinants of health model and feminism converge. Acknowledging gender as a social construct, the arbitrary societal importance it receives and its ability to shape relationships connects feminist ideologies to this model. Gender, class, race, religion, culture, ability, and sexual preference are examples of factors that affect the position of groups and individuals in the hierarchy. Social location or positionality shapes experiences, opportunities, and, subsequently, health.

A model outlining the social determinants of the health of Aboriginal peoples in Canada organizes determinants of health into proximal, intermediate, and distal categories that create a framework for a more in-depth analysis. It outlines proximal determinants of health as those that have direct impact on health (physical, mental, emotional, or spiritual). Examples include: health behaviours (such as smoking), physical environments (such as overcrowding), income, employment, education, and food insecurity (Loppie Reading & Wein, 2009).

Intermediate determinants delve further into understanding the structural influences underlying the inequalities that exist within the proximal determinants, such as community infrastructures and institutions (Loppie Reading & Wein, 2009). Take for example education and the institutions of education that historically have limited education among Aboriginal populations, while simultaneously utilizing education to repress Aboriginal culture and identity. These features were not only detrimental to past but also future generations since well-educated parents pass on social mobility opportunities and the value of education to their children. These historical contexts have intergenerational effects. Partnered with contemporary schooling in which education does not genuinely focus on Indigenous knowledge systems or ways of learning (and potentially negating interests and skills of Indigenous children), the result is a significant barrier to educational mobility. Lastly, the distal determinants of health outline historic, political, social, and economic contexts within which the intermediate determinants are generated. This includes determinants such as colonization, self-determination, racism, and social exclusion.

The above model demonstrates the necessity to look beyond individual health behaviours and understand that socially generated circumstances that surround the construction of identity create circumstances that influence health. Reading Loppie and Wein focus on racism within their distal determinants of health (as their model pertains particularly to Aboriginal peoples); however, it also extends to include sexism, classism, homophobia, ableism, among other forms of oppression. For example, there are clear connections between oppression, stress, and health outcomes. Chronic stress has been connected not only to mental and emotional health, but also physical health. With limited self-determination and continual everyday acts of oppression (including exclusion), non-dominant populations are often subjected to related stresses that contribute to chronic disease (Cohen et al., 2012).

Discussions put forth by Loppie Reading & Wein focus on oppression as a social determinant of health. However, other discussions within the fields of medicine, nursing, and public health often label the identity of a person as a determinant of health, or a risk factor for ill health. For example, Aboriginal status has been labelled as a social determinant of health and a risk factor for various diseases. Although this presentation (of identity as a risk factor) may correctly identify groups that are at a greater risk, and likely overrepresented in reported cases, it becomes dangerous to oversimplify a risk factor to a socially ascribed identity. Labelling an identity as a risk factor insinuates that there is something inherent with the identity that underlies ill health. Without adding historical and social contexts to this conversation, this discussion becomes reminiscent of historical race and gender theories that incorrectly assumed a person's gender or race was the root causes of disease. "Infected" groups were thought to be biologically and genetically inferior and therefore more susceptible to disease. Throughout history, "hysteria" (or mental illness) was associated, incorrectly, with various aspects of women's biology or sexuality and femininity was pathologized as a precedent for disease (Tasca et al., 2012). In regards to race, infectious disease (smallpox, tuberculosis, influenza) among Canada's Indigenous populations in the late 19th and early 20th centuries was attributed to "racial weakness." Although politically motivated policies of starvation and relocations and the stresses associated with colonization contributed significantly to the high rates of infectious disease, the prevailing scientific and medical experts attributed them solely to a racial, biological inferiority (Green, 2006; Lux, 2001).

It is imperative that models emphasize that identities are socially constructed, changed, reaffirmed, or challenged dynamically. Health emerges within certain groups because of their social status and experiences. If social contexts change, then so too do the social determinants of health. Let us now look specifically at gender and the ways in which health is a feminist issue.

HEALTH AS A FEMINIST ISSUE

Feminism has had a long history of trying to understand how gender, class, race, sexuality, and other systems of inequality intersect to create health inequities. Though deeply problematic in their proposed solutions, early liberal and maternal feminists made direct links between poverty and the health of women and children (Mann, 2012). Early Canadian feminists advocated for birth control as a solution to the unending state of pregnancy that plagued many women's lives; most women wanted some control of their fertility (as both biomedical and "country" methods of birth control and abortion had been illegal since the 1890s). This call was disproportionately directed at growing immigrant populations in urban areas and later at Indigenous populations in various parts of Canada. For example, Dr. Helen MacMurchy (1862–1953) and her contemporaries advocated for birth control as much out of concern for women's ability to control their own fertility, and by extension their overall health, as she did out of concern for the growing population of non-Northern European immigrants in Canadian urban areas (Valverde, 1992). By extension, though, the work of feminists in some communities did bring attention to the connections between poverty, poor housing conditions, education, gender, and poor health outcomes (Valverde, 1992). This work contributed somewhat to the basis for Canada's early public and community health care systems.

A focus on women's health emerged with the second wave of feminism in the 1960s and 1970s that pushed to acknowledge the role of gender in shaping health and well-being and to fill gaps within the health care field (Varcoe, Hankivsky, & Morrow, 2007). With a much wider base of diverse women contributing to it, the Canadian women's health movement of the 1960s and 1970s took a different approach than its forebears at the turn of the 19th to 20th centuries. In this later period, systems of inequality were acknowledged as socially constructed, many were ideologically driven, and they have become pervasive in our everyday lives (Weber & Castellow, 2012). For example, feminists see gender as a structural driving force for health inequities (Connell, 2012). Certainly, when we are discussing health, there are biological differences underlying some health disparities exhibited between males and females. Sex, in mainstream discourse is regarded as a biological truth, whereas gender and its meanings are socially constructed and ever-changing (Juschka, 2014).

Feminists define gender as a social and ideological construction in which social roles, opportunities and limitations, and social status are shaped by gender identification. Women's bodies are differentially valued depending on geography and social and historical context. Socially, gender categorizes humans into roles and "life limitations" based on genitalia, ideology in terms of social relations with others, with nature, with deities, which were used to legitimize roles and assert limitations on behaviours, roles, and statuses (Juschka, 2014). In short, depending on geography, social context, and time, gender roles and their related social expectations play a direct role in how women and their bodies are valued in both health care and society. While the second wave of feminists achieved many successes for women in general—equal pay for work of equal value, legislation against sexual harassment, educational achievement for women, the emergence of women's studies programs, and a range of sexual assault services—the second wave was criticized for being mainly a white, middle-class women's movement that excluded many women of colour, Indigenous women, lesbian women, minority women, poor women, and women with disabilities (Biggs, 2011). Those who felt marginalized and excluded began to explore how race, class, dis/ability, and sexuality intersect to produce or compound various forms of oppression and offer sites for resistance and opportunities for change.

Third wave feminists extend ideas about the social construction of gender (Biggs, 2011) by focusing on intersectionality and poststructionalist theories, often incorporating post-colonial narratives (Mann, 2012). Not only is gender a source of inequity, but race, class, migration, nationalization, cultural movements, colonization, and decolonization must also be taken into account (Biggs, 2011). Third wave feminists, sometimes referred to as "Generation X," often focus on reproductive rights including subsidized fertility treatments and freedom from sterilization abuse; reduction of sexually transmitted infections (STIs) among women; eliminating violence against women; equitable access to health care for women regardless of income; and liberating women and youth from "slut"-bashing, sexual harassment, and bullying (Mann, 2012).

Intersectionality looks at the simultaneous connections that exist among multiple social determinants of health, aspects of social identity, or multiple forms of oppression. These intersections happen on a variety of levels and are complex and interdependent (Browne, Varcoe, & Fridkin, 2011; Dhamoon & Hankivisky, 2011). Intersectionality attends to manifold identities (e.g., gender, race, ethnicity, sexual orientation) and lived experiences (i.e., sex work, homelessness) that produce both inequity (e.g., sexism, racism) as well as opportunity (i.e., social support, resistance, resilience) (Logie, 2014; Logie et al., 2011). American critical race theorist Kimberlé Crenshaw popularized the concept of intersectionality, but the analysis of multiple oppressions and their complex relationships has been crucial to anti-slavery and anti-colonial work for a long time (Dhamoon & Hankivsky, 2011). As discussed in Chapter 2, feminist critical race theorists have even fine-tuned these theories to underscore that gender is embedded in complex relations of power. Razack's (1998) discussion of "interlocking oppressions," for example, acknowledges that there are multiple forms of oppressions and that they are connected to interrelated social identities that are forever evolving. When applied to health studies, intersectionality reminds us that while a single social determinant of health can have a drastic effect on an individual's ability to generate and maintain health, when two or more social determinants intersect, they can have an even more complex outcome (McGibbon, 2011).

Intersectionality is often utilized to deconstruct categories and focus attention on the relationships between and within groups (Connell, 2012). For example, so-called marginalized populations have, within them, smaller subsets of marginalized groups. Within the Indigenous community in Canada, low-income Indigenous women may be faced with challenges associated with ethnicity, such as discrimination and cultural differences in how health is perceived, as well as barriers created by poverty, such as the inability to take time off of work or to travel for care. Taken together, all these obstacles limit women's access to health care (McGibbon, 2011). In contrast, a white man of average income might face barriers and obstacles in accessing care, but discrimination, sexism, cultural differences, and lack of resources inherent in belonging to the three previous groups would not factor into his ability to access and utilize health services. The intersection of social determinants compounds the barriers faced by those outside of the majority.

Though many Indigenous women have raised issues of gender inequality within their communities as well as in relation to the Canadian state and its health care system,

Indigenous feminism has more recently emerged as a body of activism and scholarship. A highly debated issue within many Indigenous communities and academia, Indigenous feminism is the preferential designation with which many Indigenous women identify. Indigenous women experience "multiple oppressions" of race, class, gender, and colonization, both within and outside of Indigenous communities. These obstacles intersect in complex ways to create multiple oppressions that result in inequities and produce poor life chances for Indigenous women.

As Joyce Green (2007, p. 23) notes:

> Aboriginal feminism brings together two critiques, feminism and anti-colonialism, to show how Aboriginal people, and in particular Aboriginal women, are affected by colonialism and by patriarchy. It takes account of how both racism and sexism fuse when brought to bear on Aboriginal women by Indigenous men and Indigenous governance practices. Aboriginal feminists are the clearest in linking sex and race oppression. They are identified as political adversaries not only by colonial society but also by male Indigenous elites whose power they challenge. And they are also criticized by some Aboriginal women, who deny their analysis and question their motives and authenticity.

Kim Anderson (2010) explains that Indigenous feminism is rooted in our traditional understandings and responsibilities as Indigenous women. Indigenous women are, after all, the carriers of our culture and the strength of our nations. We are the mothers of our nations and honoured for our abilities to give birth and nurture our children and female authorities within families. Gender roles, traditionally equitable until colonization, forced patriarchal notions onto Indigenous communities. "Feminism of all stripes," Anderson says, "can help us to tease out patriarchy from what is purportedly traditional and to avoid essentialist identities that are not to our advantage as women" (p. 86).

Like gender, Indigenous feminism also sees race as a social construction. Race and ethnicity, or rather, racism and ethnic discrimination, have an impact on the well-being of both immigrant and Indigenous women. Race is not seen as biologically innate or inevitable. Rather, it is a tool, a social construction, an arbitrary classification of persons into categories based upon real or imagined characteristics. Without empirical validity or scientific merit, race is a concept used to manipulate people and "reinforce unequal relations between dominant and subordinate groups" (Fleras & Elliott, 2003, p. 386). Race in society permeates our political, economic, and social structures. It is found in our institutions including the state, justice, health care, business, work, and education, to name but a few (Bourassa, 2004) and complicates even basic discussion about its definition.

Terms such as race, "immigrant," and ethnic or "visible minority" are often used interchangeably in problematic ways. We do not intend to further this error but note that the use of these words in a great deal of health and statistical literature should be made visible and critiqued. For instance, the term "immigrant" simply means one who has recently moved to a new country, such as Canada. It says nothing directly about whether a person is white or a person of colour. Likewise, the term "ethnicity" may or may not refer to someone who happens to be a person of colour, and has more to do with national membership, language, and, possibly, religion. In both these cases Valverde notes that in different historical periods the term might nearly guarantee one was speaking of one of these groups or another within Canada's restrictive immigration policies (Valverde, 1992). Although the term "visible minority" has been challenged by many, including the United Nations Committee on the Elimination of Racial Discrimination, it is still used by the Canadian government throughout policy and data collection. Therefore, most discussions surrounding the health experiences associated with race or ethnicity must rely on data that is collected utilizing the term visible minorities. The term, as defined by the Employment Equity Act, refers specifically to "persons, other than Aboriginal peoples, who are non-caucasian in race or non-white in colour" (Statistics Canada, 2015).

Race and racism serve the interests of the most advantaged groups (Cherland & Harper, 2007, pp. 109, 117). Albert Memmi (2013) argues that racism is ingrained in actions, institutions, and the nature of colonialist methods of production and exchange (p. xxiv). As an ideology, race emerged from the imperial and colonialist efforts of Europeans, and in Canada's case, specifically, the British and French. Colonial racism is built from three ideological components (Memmi, 2013, p. 71):

1. The gulf between the culture of the colonialist and the colonized;
2. The exploitation of these differences for the benefit of the colonialist; and
3. The use of these supposed differences as absolute fact.

Race and racism, like class and gender, are social constructions used to oppress those who are not in power within capitalist societies. Operationalized through ideology (Smedley & Smedley, 2005, p. 19), race continues to be used to justify class inequality. Critical race theory argues that white privilege is reinforced as both race and class privileges intersect and strengthen each other (Cherland & Harper, 2007, p. 109). Race reinforces white privilege, and as Peggy McIntosh explains, white people are taught to not recognize their unearned privileges (McIntosh, 1988). Whether one welcomes privilege or not, privilege is a societal norm reinforced daily by societal structures and practices.

Race is a relatively modern concept. It arose not only out of a need to exert control over people, land, and resources, but also to justify such actions. With the collapse of the feudal system in Europe in the late 15th century and the rise of capitalist economies, new systems were needed to enforce privilege at the individual, local, national, and international levels. Europeans spread a specific worldview that was required to uphold and justify European dominance and expansion:

> The expropriation of property, the denial of political rights, the introduction of slavery and other forms of coercive labor, as well as outright extermination, all presupposed a worldview which distinguished Europeans—Children of God, human beings, etc.—from "others." Such a worldview was needed to explain why some should be free and others enslaved, why some had rights to land and property while others did not. Race and the interpretation of racial differences, was a central factor in the worldview. (Omi & Winant, 2004, pp. 13–14)

While concepts of patriotism, ethnocentrism, and Eurocentrism existed prior to capitalism, the concept of race and the effects of this concept (such as racism and discrimination) did not exist (Liggio, 1976). Ethnocentrism is defined as a tendency to see reality from a specific cultural perspective, which believes in the superiority of one culture over all other cultures. Eurocentrism is a specific form of ethnocentrism, which advocates the moral superiority of European thoughts and practices as the standard by which others should be judged. These concepts existed prior to the rise of capitalism but were not based on skin colour, height, brain size, or other elements common to the concept of "race" (Bourassa, 2004).

Race and racialization lend legitimacy to the actions of the dominant power. Historically, it allowed the dominant power, European colonizers in the case of Canada, to exert control over "other" racial groups. Race became a societal norm and an unquestioned privilege. Pittz (2005, p. 7) argues that health disparities can be attributed to "racism and its social and institutional manifestations." Structural racism is the normalization and legitimization of the domination of one group over another. Structural racism lies beneath social and economic inequities that are at the root of a vast majority of health disparities (Pittz, 2005; Smedley & Smedley, 2005).

While examining social and health disparities on a societal level for women, visible minorities, Indigenous groups, and others, it is essential to situate these trends in their wider social and historical contexts. In exploring the concept of intersectionality further, we will break down the effects of the social constructs of gender in creating inequality, and then apply these concepts to discussions of health trends for different populations of women in Canada.

GENDER EQUITY AND BIAS

Gender inequity is rooted in social structures, in particular, power structures. For example, gender intersects with economic inequality, class inequality, differences in sexual orientation, racial or ethnic differences, and other social markers including ability or disability or geographical location (Sen & Ostlin, 2008). Like other constructions, gender is governed by and exists in relation to social structures. Sen and Ostlin (2008) note that sex and society interact to determine who is well and who is not.

Ultimately, women and girls around the globe have less land, have less wealth and property, have lower social status, have higher burdens of work in the economy, have higher health burdens, have lower educational attainment, have higher rates of violence perpetrated against them, are often viewed as less capable compared to boys or men, are often seen as objects in their own homes or communities; and often have lower participation rates in political institutions (Sen & Ostlin, 2008). Although we have seen some improved trends for women over the past several decades, global illiteracy rates among women have remained unchanged over the past twenty years. Women still represent two-thirds of the world's illiterate adult population (United Nations Department of Economic and Social Affairs, 2010). Globally, women and girls are burdened more by poverty than are men and boys. Although regional variances exist, at a household level, most often female-headed households face higher rates of poverty than male-headed households (United Nations Department of Economic and Social Affairs, 2010).

Furthermore, women tend to be caregivers for both young and old; have poorer access to health care/services; and experience a societal bias that often expects women to sacrifice their own health, happiness, and well-being for the betterment of their families, communities, and husbands (Sen & Ostlin, 2008). Globally, women are predominantly responsible for maintaining and caring for families (United Nations Department of Economic and Social Affairs, 2010). These caregiving responsibilities create unique experiences for women and their health.

CANADIAN DEMOGRAPHICS

Although Canada continues to experience economic growth, one in seven women live in poverty (CRIAW, 2006). Furthermore, 38% of lone female parents had after tax incomes that were less than the low-income cut-off (LICO) compared to only 13% of lone male parents and 7% of two-parent families (CRIAW, 2006). In Canada, according to 2006 census data, visible minority women were generally more susceptible to unemployment than their male counterparts as well as non-visible minority women. In the week prior to the 2006 census, 8.4% of visible minority women ages 25 to 54 were in the labour force but unemployed compared with 5% of non-visible minority women and 6.2% of visible minority men. In fact, there was a bigger gender gap in unemployment rates between visible minority women and men (2.2%) than between non-visible minority women and non-visible minority men (0.1%). Finally, there was an earnings gap between men and women. The median employment income of visible minority women ages 25 to 54 who worked full-time, full-year was close to $7000 less than that of visible minority men, whose median earnings were $40 800. This difference revealed that visible minority women of core working age earned about 83% of their male counterparts' earnings (Statistics Canada, 2010–2011). According to the Canadian Research Institute for the Advancement of Women (CRIAW), visible minority women are also overrepresented in precarious (part-time and temporary) work and often have to live in substandard and segregated housing. They are also more vulnerable to violence and other health risks (CRIAW, 2005, p. 2).

GENDER EQUITY, SOCIAL DETERMINANTS OF HEALTH AND INTERSECTIONALITY—LET THE DATA SPEAK

How do the theoretical concepts discussed above translate into health disparities? How do they play out in health practices and in the daily lives of girls and women, in particular? As outlined, sex and society interact to determine who is well and who is not, and as a result, health outcomes can be significantly different for men and women. Gender inequity affects millions of women and girls: transgendered, gay, lesbian, bisexual, queer, and two-spirited individuals. Gender inequity impacts the social capital of women and girls around the globe and therefore impacts the abilities of individuals and communities to gain and maintain holistic health. Additionally, other determinants of health intersect with gender inequity to produce varying health disparities across different populations. This section will first look at some general health trends of women, both globally and within Canada, and then will move to look at specific health trends for immigrant women, and Indigenous women to highlight the health impacts of multiple, intersecting oppressions.

TRANSNATIONAL HEALTH CONCERNS

Although there is significant regional variance when we discuss health trends among women, several patterns are consistent. We suggest that many of these patterns are interconnected transnationally because local experiences of health can be affected by global events and vice versa. For example, the availability of a new drug for HIV/AIDS treatment, which is subsidized by a national health care plan in one part of the world might be detrimental to the life expectancy of those in another part of the world if that drug's availability is beyond the means of most people in most countries without a national health care plan. The availability of the drug can also be artificially managed by a variety of players whose influence extends beyond the reach of individual countries, such as hospitals that accept international medical travellers, national governments, multi-national corporations, and insurance companies, making the wellness of people who need the drug a cross-border transnational issue, not just a local or individual problem. Economic and political disparities between nations, not just between individuals, necessarily complicate discussions of gender and health.

Life expectancy is a standard, although sometimes simplistic, indicator of health that bears scrutiny from a transnational perspective. In all regions of the world, women live longer than men (United Nations Department of Economic and Social Affairs, 2010; Stevens, Mathers, & Beard, 2013). This difference is partially accounted for by a natural biological advantage; however, in some countries, this advantage is diminished by social and economic factors. For example, if we look at low-income countries, the complications associated with pregnancy and childbearing significantly impact women's life expectancy (United Nations Department of Economic and Social Affairs, 2010).

Globally, between 2005 and 2012, maternal deaths decreased approximately 3.1% each year (WHO, 2013). All regions saw a decrease in maternal deaths; however, some regions saw a greater decrease than others. Unfortunately, it was the countries with the highest maternal mortality rates that saw the least progress when it came to decreasing rates (WHO, 2013). During the same year span, 81% of women had at least one prenatal care visit. The statistics drop significantly to only 55% of women who had the recommended four prenatal visits (WHO, 2013). Births attended by skilled professionals were above 90% in three of the six WHO regions. In the WHO African region, this rate dropped to under 50% (WHO, 2013). Maternal health issues significantly impact the health of adolescent women in low and middle-income countries, and complications from pregnancy and childbirth are the leading cause of death for this age group. It is also estimated that this age group is highly exposed to unsafe abortions. In 2008, it was estimated that 3 million abortions were performed on adolescent women in unsafe conditions (WHO, 2013). Globally, in 2014, more than 140 million women had unmet family planning needs, which significantly impacts maternal health, child health, and community health (United Nations Entity for Gender Equality and the Empowerment of Women, 2014).

Although deaths associated with maternal health do influence life expectancy discrepancies between men and women, if we look at high-income countries, we see regionally consistent low rates of maternal mortality but variant gaps in life expectancy. In 2011 the gaps in Malawi, Canada, Japan, and the Russian Confederation consisted of 1, 4, 7, and 12 years respectively (WHO, 2013). The one-year variant in Malawi provides an example from a low-income country where maternal deaths likely play a significant role in decreasing the life expectancy gap. Canada, Japan, and Russia are all deemed high-income countries with relatively low maternal death rates, but here there is significant variance. These regional variations outline the fact that although there is a biological component to life expectancy variations between males and females, it is also affected by behavioural and environmental factors shaped by social factors.

As a result of women living longer than men, there are more elderly women than men. As maternal mortality rates decrease globally, this demographic difference is growing larger. Although we have seen that maternal mortality and reproductive health are significant issues in some parts of the world, there are other health needs surfacing, particularly in regards to non-communicable disease. Despite the continually growing health needs of middle-aged and elderly women, the global health response to women's needs remains largely concentrated on reproductive matters (Stevens et al., 2013). As the detection, prevention, and management of non-communicable diseases has received less focus globally, there is a need to shift broader health systems to accommodate women's health issues that extend past reproductive health (Stevens et al., 2013).

Another universal global health trend is women's increased exposure to violence. Although rates do very from region to region, statistics continually demonstrate that violence against women is a universal phenomenon. This violence takes a variety of forms and can include physical, sexual, psychological, and economic violence that is perpetrated both by intimate partners and others outside the home (United Nations Department of Economic and Social Affairs, 2010).

Other global trends for women's health include an over-representation of HIV cases and higher mortality from cardiovascular disease. Women constitute the majority of HIV cases in sub-Saharan Africa, North Africa, and the Middle East, where there are social and cultural factors that often increase women's vulnerability to HIV (United Nations Department of Economic and Social Affairs, 2010). Lastly, women, on a global scale, are more likely than men to die from cardiovascular disease—especially in Europe (United Nations Department of Economic and Social Affairs, 2010).

CANADIAN HEALTH TRENDS

Within Canada, there are a variety of health indicators, largely focused on morbidity and mortality that outline health disparities between males and females. For some indicators, such as cancer, we see shared disparities where the mortality rates are higher for one sex depending on the specific type of cancer (Health Canada, 2012). Reports from 2012 show that women are disproportionately affected by the following: chronic obstructive pulmonary disease, asthma, arthritis, osteoporosis, chlamydia, high blood pressure, and self-reported stress (Health

Canada, 2012). These trends are very general and don't allow for detailed understanding of how various social determinants of health intersect and influence health. To better understand how gender, race, class, and other social positioning and circumstances shape well-being, we will now examine some health trends among immigrant and Indigenous women of Canada.

Immigrant Women's Health

When examining the health of immigrant women, we need to consider structural inequalities associated with immigration. Often, race and ethnicity are considered as factors in studies of immigrant health; however, is it essential to look at how *racism* intersects with other forms of marginalization to influence immigrant health (Viruell-Fuentes, Miranda, & Abdulrahim, 2012). Not only does discrimination based on gender, race, ethnicity, and class intersect to create health challenges for immigrants, but also cultural integration and social inequity associated with immigration policies influence health outcomes (De Maio & Kemp, 2010; Viruell-Fuentes et al., 2012).

In 2011, 20.6% of Canada's population was foreign-born. Of the foreign-born population, 17.2% are recent immigrants, having arrived in the last five years. The majority of immigrants come from Asia and the Middle East (approximately 60%), followed by Europe (approximately 15%), and Africa (approximately 9%). Nearly 6 264 800 people identified themselves as a member of a visible minority group. They represented 19.1% of the total population. Of these visible minorities, 30.9% were born in Canada and 65.1% were born outside the country and came to live in Canada as immigrants (Statistics Canada, 2011b).

Varying circumstances surround immigration. Although it is not the experience of all newcomers to Canada, many immigrants have low socioencomic status, live with limited economic means in low resource communities, and face residential segregation (Viruell-Fuentes et al., 2012). Results from a Canadian-wide longitudinal study demonstrated that 34.4% of recent immigrants did not have enough money to meet their basic needs, and only 9% of immigrants reported having more than enough money (De Maio & Kemp, 2010). Additionally, new immigrants to Canada may experience culture shock, reduced autonomy, loss of previous social supports, social isolation, exposure to violence, and additional caregiving responsibilities resulting from language and cultural barriers.

Based on immigration policies, the health of immigrants upon migration to Canada is often better than that of Canadian-born populations. However, health status usually decreases once people have settled in Canada. Some have termed this the "healthy immigrant effect" (De Maio & Kemp, 2010). Declines in health status occur as early as the first two years after immigration (Newbold, 2009). Immigration to Canada has been associated with unhealthy levels of weight gain, increased risk for chronic disease, and increased rates of depression (De Maio & Kemp, 2010). The highest levels of health were reported among immigrants with high economic status. Refugees report the lowest levels of health and are more likely to transition into poorer states of health (Newbold, 2009).

Some studies have shown drastic decreases in health status. One Canadian longitudinal study found that at six months after immigration, 43% of immigrants reported their health as excellent, but after two and four years this rate fell to 30% and 23% respectively. The study also found that at six months only 5.1% of recent immigrants reported persistent feelings of sadness or depression, but after two years the rate increased to 30% (De Maio & Kemp, 2010). Women were most likely to experience increasing persistent feelings of sadness, depression, and loneliness as their time spent in Canada increased (De Maio & Kemp, 2010).

Immigrant women in British Columbia and Quebec reported higher rates of diabetes than their Canadian-born counterparts. In Quebec this trend was not found in immigrant men. Rates varied by birth region and language ability (Wang et al., 2012). Diabetic immigrants had lower rates of physician visits in comparison to Canadian-born diabetics; however, this trend did not appear to be related to language ability (Wang et al., 2012).

One study from California speaks directly to the health effects of discrimination on visible minority women, many of whom are immigrants. Although this study is not Canadian, national borders do not limit social perceptions of race and ethnicity, and Canada and the United States are similar in many cultural ideals and norms. The study explored birth outcomes of Arabic-named women during the six months following 9/11. Elevated risks for preterm and low-weight births were found for Arabic-named women but not for other groups (Lauderdale, 2006). This study further supports the connection between discrimination and health impacts. It demonstrates how larger social understandings influence our behaviours, perceptions, and subsequently our health.

INDIGENOUS WOMEN'S HEALTH

In Canada's Indigenous population (referred to as Aboriginal in census data), Aboriginal women face multiple health disparities. As noted earlier, this is due to multiple oppressions. According to Statistics Canada's four-year estimates (2007–2010), 47.2% of First Nations women living off reserve, 54.1% of Métis women, and 53.7% of Inuit women reported their health as very good or excellent. The share of Aboriginal women describing their health in these terms was smaller than the percentage of women in the total Canadian population who reported their health as excellent or very good (62.4%). If we look specifically at First Nations women living on reserve (for the years 2008–2010), we see 41.7% of females reporting very good or excellent health in comparison to 46.4% of males (Health Canada, 2012). Rates of diabetes on reserve were 17.9% among women. This rate is higher than the rate for men living on reserve (14.5%), as well among non-Aboriginal women (4%) in the following years (Health Canada, 2012; Statistics Canada, 2010). Women living on reserve have significantly higher rates than other women living in Canada. Unfortunately, there are significant lags in the analysis of health statistics. The most recent Aboriginal Peoples Survey from 2012 has only released information pertaining to Inuit health even though it does outline a higher rate of chronic conditions among Inuit women in comparison to Inuit men (Wallace, 2014). Although data collection and survey methods for Indigenous health information are complicated by jurisdictional issues that limit the comparability of information (different years, age ranges, and so on), we can still identify trends that outline varied health trends between Aboriginal men and women as well as between Aboriginal women and non-Aboriginal women.

Most health statistics and health indicators in Canada demonstrate disparities between Aboriginal and non-Aboriginal populations. Let's take a look at that information with a specific focus on female health trends. For example, between 2007 and 2010 rates for arthritis were 16.7% for First Nations women, 15.3% for Métis women, and 14.8% for non-Aboriginal women. Asthma rates demonstrate a similar disparity, where rates were 16%, 15%, and 9.7% respectively (Statistics Canada, 2010). In regards to mental health, Aboriginal women do not experience the same levels of health as non-Aboriginal women. Between 2007 and 2010 perceived rates of excellent or very good mental health were recorded for 74.6% of non-Aboriginal women in comparison to 61.7%, 64.1%, and 67% respectively for Inuit, First Nations, and Métis women (Statistics Canada, 2010). Food security is another indicator of health directly connected to the prevention and management of both physical and mental health conditions. The rates of food insecurity are significantly higher among Aboriginal women (26.4% and 16.8% among First Nations and Métis women in comparison to 8% of non-Aboriginal women), and result in diminished physical health as well as additional stress for Aboriginal women (Statistics Canada, 2010).

Métis specific health data is sparse, particularly mortality and morbidity rates; however, a recent study revealed that mortality rates for Métis were much higher compared to non-Aboriginal Canadians particularly for women. In addition, Métis women were more likely to have higher rates of circulatory, digestive, and respiratory system diseases compared to non-Aboriginal Canadians. Finally, for both Métis and First Nations people socio-economic indicators (income, education, occupation) explained two-thirds of the excess mortality in men and almost 30% of excess mortality in women (Tjepkema, Wilkins, Senécal, Guimond, & Penney, 2009).

Aboriginal people are also over-represented in HIV cases. Between the years of 1989 and 2009, Aboriginal people represented 24% of HIV cases, although Aboriginal populations represented only 4.3% of the Canadian population in 2011 (PHAC, 2014). This over-representation is even more significant for Aboriginal women who account for 47.3% of HIV cases reported among Aboriginal people (between 1998 and 2012) in comparison to women of other ethnicities who make up 20% of cases (PHAC, 2014). Aboriginal women are also more likely to be diagnosed late and present with AIDS in comparison to non-Aboriginal women (PHAC, 2014). Aboriginal women have had, and continue to have, distinct experiences with colonialism, and these experiences can manifest themselves in adverse determinants of health. Intergenerational impacts of assimilation, acculturation, sexist policies in the Indian Act, and residential schools, have created environments ridden with poverty, violence, and social immobility for Indigenous women. These environments of risk influence Aboriginal women's susceptibility to HIV.

Global trends clearly outline that women are significantly more likely than men to be victims of violence. When we review rates of violence against Aboriginal women, we see how gender, race, and colonization intersect to create health disparities. Aboriginal women aged 15 and older are three and a half times more likely to experience violence (defined as physical and sexual assault and robbery) than non-Aboriginal women (Amnesty International Canada, 2004; Statistics Canada, 2006). According to the 2006 census data, 36% of Aboriginal women were living in poverty compared to non-Aboriginal women in Canada (Statistics Canada, 2010). According to the Canadian Research Institute for the Advancement of Women, "Aboriginal women face interconnected disadvantage due to the intergenerational legacies of racism, colonization, residential schools, and cultural devaluation that contribute to vulnerability to intimate partner violence, sexual violence, femicide, and the normalization of this violence" (CRIAW, 2013, p. 6).

CRIAW notes that Aboriginal women in Canada "also experience racially-motivated attacks and are harassed on the streets by the public and police more so than non-Aboriginal women." (CRIAW, 2002, p. 2). In 2013 the Royal Canadian Mounted Police (RCMP) released the *Missing and Murdered Aboriginal Women: A National Operational Overview* report. The report documented 1181 missing or murdered Aboriginal women. The report also indicated that this was an over-representation, most of the women knew their perpetrators, and many of the murders were intimate partner violence situations. While the solve rate was the same for Aboriginal and non-Aboriginal women, the over-representation of Aboriginal women is of concern. Between 1980 and 2012, there were just over 20 000 homicides in Canada. Females represented 32% of the victims. There were just over 1000 female Aboriginal homicide victims during this same time period, which represents 16% of all female homicides—a much higher representation of Aboriginal than non-Aboriginal women. Further, the number of Aboriginal female homicides has remained constant while the number of non-Aboriginal female homicides has been decreasing (RCMP, 2014). For example, in 1984 Aboriginal women accounted for 8% of all female victims and 23% in 2012. Keep in mind the total national Aboriginal population in Canada according to the 2006 census was 3.8% (Statistics Canada, 2010). Unfortunately the risk factors listed in the report were not very insightful. The risk factors cited in the report that made Aboriginal women more "vulnerable" included employment status, use of intoxicants, and involvement in the sex trade. Other determinants not discussed included gender, race, class, education, and the experience of colonization. Further, Aboriginal women experience racism both within and outside of their communities (Kubik et al., 2009).

RELEVANT POLICY ANALYSIS

In 1995 the Fourth United Nation's Conference on Women was held in Beijing. The *Beijing Declaration and Platform for Action* revealed at the conference had the goal of empowering women around the globe. The Platform for Action outlined a number of goals aimed at removing barriers to women's full participation and equal share in economic, social, cultural, and political decision-making. Changes were to occur by 2000 with achievable targets to improve women's health, economic prosperity, education, and legal reforms to reduce discrimination against women. Participants included 189 governments and 2100 non-governmental organizations from around the world (United Nations Entity for Gender Equality and the Empowerment of Women, n.d.).

The Beijing Declaration sets the stage for *Canada's Women's Health Strategy* in 1999. In keeping with the Beijing Declaration, the main goal of the Women's Health Strategy was to improve the overall health of women in Canada by improving the health system particularly through policy and program restructuring including gender-based analysis; increasing knowledge and understanding of women's health needs; supporting the delivery of appropriate women's health services; and women's health promotion, prevention, and reduction of risk factors (Hankivsky, 2006).

In Canada, efforts by grassroots organizations to close the inequality gap between Indigenous and non-Indigenous women have been obstructed by many policy barriers. Notably, the cutting of funding for the Native Women's Association of Canada (NWAC), particularly their Sisters in Spirit project that focused on the issue of missing and murdered Indigenous women in Canada, demonstrates the urgent need for the experiences of Indigenous women to be taken seriously in social policy development, not only for the continued use of gender-based analysis (GBA), but to advance culturally relevant gender-based analysis (CRGBA) in policy development and programming in Canada (see Health Canada n.d.; NWAC, n.d.).

The goal of GBA is to create inclusive approaches in policy development that respond to inequities faced by women in all aspects of society by viewing women in relation to men as opposed to examining women's issues separately (NWAC, n.d.). While great improvements have been made by utilizing GBA in challenging contemporary inequities faced by women, utilizing only this process still isolates Indigenous women's experiences in all aspects of society from health care to economic development. Though both Indigenous and non-Indigenous women face ongoing personal and structural experiences of sexism in Canada, Indigenous women face multiple forms of oppression through both sexism and racism (NWAC, n.d.). Thus, there is a need for CRGBA in order to properly consider the unique circumstances of Indigenous women, and incorporate Indigenous ways of knowing, historical circumstances and experiences, and contemporary realities in Canada into public policy analysis and development (NWAC, n.d.).

In response to the lack of culturally relevant policy development and to improve the knowledge of the experiences and realities of Indigenous women with policy makers and stakeholders, NWAC developed a tool to apply the principles of CRGBA, the Culturally Relevant Gender Application Protocol (CR-GAP) (NWAC, n.d.). This tool is guided by four key principles:

- The CR-GAP will revitalize the value of Aboriginal women's roles within Aboriginal and non-Aboriginal society and reconnect race and gender to positively impact health and healing;
- The CR-GAP reflects cultural values and practices, highlighting the principles of balance and equilibrium, with gender being one component of balance;
- The CR-GAP complies with the laws of the Creator, Aboriginal world view and law, inherent right, Constitutional and International law; and
- The CR-GAP captures the diversity and different circumstances of Aboriginal women based on their distinctive cultures and cultural practices (NWAC, n.d., p. 5).

Though GBA is an effective tool in analyzing and developing good public policy and programming, it is ultimately limited in scope because it does not take into account the needs of Indigenous women and could potentially silence these needs through homogenous assumptions about all women's experiences in Canada. CRGBA, and the CR-GAP tool developed by NWAC, can aid in breaking down barriers in understanding the experiences and needs of Indigenous women through deepening the understanding of colonization and its impacts, recognizing both the historical effects of trauma and the current, ongoing impacts in our contemporary society and the intersectionality of multiple oppressions experienced daily by Indigenous women in Canada. This tool could also arguably be adapted for other cultural and ethnic populations.

INTERSECTIONAL FEMINIST FRAMEWORKS

The Canadian Research Institute for the Advancement of Women (CRIAW) developed policy frameworks called Intersectional Feminist Frameworks (IFFs). The goals of the IFFs are to promote understanding of the complex and often discriminatory social practices that produce inequality and exclusion. IFFs examine systems of discrimination including colonialism and globalization and how these affect a person's social and/or economic status, race, class, gender, and sexuality (CRIAW, 2006). IFFs

- promote the use of tools for analysis that consider the complexities of women's lives (i.e., GBAs);
- ensure policy analysis is focused on those who are most marginalized;
- promote holistic thinking when developing policies;
- promote and value self-reflection of how we are all part of a system of privilege and power;
- are specific to people's experiences of history, culture, politics, geography, and ecology;
- are based on women's specific locations and situations rather than generalizations;
- focus on many types of discrimination;
- are locally and globally interconnected;
- incorporate worldviews that have historically been marginalized;
- understand that women are diverse with varied histories and social identities which place them in different positions of hierarchical power;
- make efforts to challenge binary thinking that sustains inequities (gay/straight, white/Black, etc.);
- and recognize that binary thinking is a result of unequal power relations (CRIAW, 2006).

IFFs in policy and practice can be difficult and complex work. They can result in tensions and pressures as one oppression emerges and is pitted against another. For example, if an organization employs a GBA, will that address the needs of say, Indigenous women? Or immigrant women? As noted, the GBA was critiqued for not being inclusive to Indigenous women and CRIAW acknowledges that this can occur. This is why they encourage IFFs as a framework so that organizations can understand that there are no magic tools that can be implemented. Organizations must make serious commitments to the principles of social justice and realize that change will take time. They note, "The process of implementing IFFs has brought about tensions and struggles both internally and externally. People have had to set aside focusing on one existing framework to learn to open up to multiple perspectives and different voices" (CRIAW, 2006, p. 19). Ultimately, attempting to eradicate sexism alone will not address the myriad issues faced by women—racism, ageism, disabilities, poverty, discrimination, poor health—and the list goes on. As argued in this chapter, IFFs promote the idea of addressing those issues that intersect with gender.

Current human rights approaches to addressing and mitigating discrimination do not incorporate intersectional discrimination into their tools. Therefore, generalizations about discriminatory actions are placed into a larger category of gender or racial discrimination, when in fact, the discrimination may lie at the intersection of race and gender. For example, problems or circumstances known to affect women who are newly landed immigrants might be framed as a women's issue, ignoring the discrimination faced by newly landed immigrants in general. Because of this approach to human rights, the experiences of subsets of people within a larger group are often painted with as broad a brush as possible, thus limiting the ability to identify and address the full scope of the discrimination (Ontario Human Rights Commission, 2001). Any efforts made to mitigate the discrimination can, at best, be considered incomplete, as the process by which the analysis of the problem was undertaken was in itself flawed by design.

WOMEN'S HEALTH ACTIVISM IN CANADA

The women's health movement in Canada has focused on three primary issues:

1. the health care delivery system;
2. the development and analysis of the social determinants of health;
3. a commitment to increase participation of all women in all aspects of health care (Boscoe et al., 2006).

The women's health movement was founded on an understanding of the intersections of racism, sexism, and paternalism, as key social constructions and sources of power shaping health outcomes and delivery (Boscoe et al., 2006). The movement had some success, lobbying for the creation of women's health bureaus or departments within provincial and federal governments and the establishment of women's health research centres across Canada. They also advocated for women-centred programs and services within the health care system, which included equity in hiring practices and promoted the idea that women were the experts in terms of their bodies and their health needs (Boscoe et al., 2006). In 1993 the Canadian Women's Health Network (CWHN) was launched. After years of networking and consultation, and in spite of funding challenges, the network still exists (www.cwhn.ca/en/node/44838) with a mandate to improve the health of women and girls through research and information sharing, education, and advocacy (Boscoe et al., 2006). In recent years, there have been massive cuts to women's programs and services, including the CWHN. Boscoe et al. (2006) note that despite evidence that understanding women's health has more to do with social determinants, health care systems still place heavy emphasis on a biomedical model and invest substantially in the medicalization of women's health. Women's lives are more likely to be medicalized in comparison to men's, particularly in the areas of mental health and reproduction (Boscoe, et al., 2006; Lippman, 2004; McGibbon & McPherson, 2013). Often, serotonin uptake inhibitors are prescribed for depression and mental health issues. McGibbon and McPherson (2013) point out that depression and stress among women are often associated with violence, oppression, and structural systemic problems (for example poverty and housing). Although oppression associated with gender (or other social identities connected to marginalization) is often a root cause of mental illness and stress among women, current models of health care tend to over-medicalize women's mental health and fail to address structural change or even alternative therapies or interventions (Boscoe, et al., 2006; McGibbon & McPherson, 2013). Another example is the continued funding of breast cancer screening through mammography, but limited funding for prevention programming such as smoking cessation/awareness or addressing food insecurity (Boscoe et al., 2006). Although mammography is an essential tool in diagnosing many cases of breast cancer, it is limited by over diagnosis (Marmot et al., 2013) and is often the sole focus of breast cancer prevention funding (Boscoe et al., 2006).

In 2012, Health Canada eliminated the Women's Health Contribution Program, which funded both the CWHN and the National Network on Environments and Women's Health. The cuts also severely impacted the Native Women's Association of Canada, the Pauktuutit Inuit Women of Canada, the Prairie Women's Health Centre of Excellence in Winnipeg, and the Atlantic Centre of Excellence for Women's Health. In 2012, sweeping cuts to funding for many Aboriginal wellness programs were made by the federal government. This came just six years after the same government had made drastic cuts to Status of Women Canada (SWC), forcing most of their offices across the country to close. The Native Women's Association of Canada (NWAC) faced further budget cuts a year later in 2013, effectively shutting down many of their operations. In 2010, funding for the Sisters in Spirit project, a database created by NWAC that documented missing and murdered Indigenous women was terminated. The project had only begun to receive federal funding in 2005. Continued funding cuts limit research, advocacy, and ultimately women's health.

Race and class create multiple oppressions and cause more maltreatment for women of different races or ethnicities and in lower classes (Govender & Penn-Kekana, 2008). Bias and inequity are engrained within our institutions—including the health care system. Govender and Penn-Kekana (2008) note that health care providers end up perpetuating societal biases and discrimination in health care settings on the basis of class, gender, and ethnicity/race, and thus the cycle continues. Unfortunately, this bias can also result in blatant abuse of patients. Govender and Penn-Kekana (2008) document several experiences of verbal and physical abuse of young women in childbirth or while trying to access contraception. They found that women who were socio-economically marginalized were particularly vulnerable to abuse. Therefore, they recommend more gender sensitization training for health care professionals and women-centred programs (Govender & Penn-Kekana, 2008).

CULTURAL SAFETY

Cultural safety is a concept that originated in the 1980s in New Zealand and is rooted in the strength of Maori self-determination and decolonization as a response to their unpleasant experiences with nursing care (National Aboriginal Health Organization, 2006). While transcultural nursing promotes the idea that nurses (and other health practitioners) should provide the same care to everyone regardless of differences, cultural safety espouses that that nurses become respectful of differences including nationality, culture, age, sex, and political and religious beliefs (NAHO, 2006).

Cultural safety is a post-colonial approach to interactions between subjects and researchers or patients and health care practitioners (Anderson, et al., 2003). Recognizing the power differentials that exist among cultural groups is the key to ensuring fair and equitable care and research. Reflecting on the political, social, cultural, and historical relationship between the groups reduces the risk of re-victimization, oppression, and power imbalances. Cultural safety is most commonly used in the health care field, where providers are encouraged to reflect on historical relationships in order to eliminate their own prejudices that might impede their ability to treat and care for a patient (Anderson et al., 2003).

While cultural safety opens the dialogue on power imbalances based on race, some may argue that it does not address class, gender, or sexuality, all of which affect the treatment and care of patients. Although in theory cultural safety does expand to address these points, often a unilateral focus is placed on culture when it is implemented. The importance of acknowledging all of the power imbalances that exist between patients and health care providers is critical to ensuring the safety of clients (Anderson et al., 2003).

Many health practitioners are being made aware of and applying the concept of cultural safety. The Royal College of Physicians and Surgeons of Canada include the concept in their *Indigenous Health Values and Principles Statement* released in 2013. They note that cultural safety can reveal the underlying causes of health inequities for Indigenous people—oppression and a legacy of colonization. Through critical thinking skills and self-reflection, physicians can nurture cultural safety and better understand upstream barriers (e.g., structural racism, discriminatory laws, historical legacies, uneven distribution of economic opportunities, and so on) and their connection to downstream effects (e.g., person-to-person mediated racism, classism, cycle of poverty, and so on) influencing the health and healing of those defined as under threat (Royal College of Physicians and Surgeons of Canada, 2013).

In 2009, the Indigenous Physicians Association of Canada (IPAC) produced a curriculum framework entitled *First Nations, Inuit, Métis Health Core Competencies: A Curriculum Framework for Undergraduate Medical Education.* The curriculum framework was developed based on a joint IPAC and Association of Faculties of Medicine of Canada (AFMC) meeting in 2005 to increase the content of Aboriginal curricula. Strategies include content that is culturally safe and engaging in patient and community-centred approaches.

They note: "Taking a cultural safety approach to dealing with inequities enables physicians and other care providers to improve healthcare access for patients, aggregates, and populations; acknowledge that we are all bearers of culture; expose the social, political, and historical context of healthcare; and interrupt unequal power relations" (IPAC, 2009, p. 10).

Similarly, in 2009 the Canadian Nurses Association (CNA), the Aboriginal Nurses Association of Canada (ANAC), and the Canadian Association of the Schools of Nursing (CASN) released their curriculum document entitled "Cultural Competence and Cultural Safety in Nursing Education—A Framework for First Nations, Inuit and Métis Nursing." Their focus was on recruitment and retention of Aboriginal nurses in Canada.

They remind us that cultural safety takes us beyond cultural awareness (acknowledgement of difference), cultural sensitivity (respecting difference), and cultural competence (focus on skills). Cultural safety is about addressing inequities through education and power disparities and understanding that cultural safety is actually defined by those accessing care (Aboriginal Nurses Association of Canada, 2009).

Two essential aspects of cultural safety are challenging privilege and addressing power imbalances. This is accomplished primarily through self-reflection and critical thought that aims to disrupt oppression, discrimination, and racism within the health care system. Self-reflection is the first step for the practitioner in creating culturally safe care. In particular, a person must self-reflect on her or his privilege as a practitioner and the power infused in that position alone, as well as any other privileges that individual may have. The practitioner then moves from critical self-reflection into active practice that challenges racism and stereotypes and addresses inequities (Lavallée, et al., 2009).

An excellent example of incorporating cultural safety into a clinical practice is Dr. Mona Loutfy's HIV/AIDS clinic for women in Toronto.[2] The clinic's health questionnaire for HIV-positive patients includes a checklist of the patients' main concerns outside of direct health-related concerns, including personal finances, support systems, housing, mental health, relationship health (which opens the door for discussions of intimate partner violence), parenting, and food security. These practices are adapted to the unique setting and marginalized situation of clients being served. Recognizing that their clients are not a single group with homogeneous beliefs, experiences, and values, Dr. Loutfy's cultural safety model allows for the clients to explain their own experiences and challenges to accessing and sticking to their health care interventions. By enabling the clients to identify the barriers they may have to access, the clinic is able to customize their services to better meet the needs of their client base.

According to Dr. Loutfy and her team, women's experiences of HIV are unique and health services must be adapted to their needs. Many women who are HIV positive or who have AIDS experience stigma in the health care system and need appropriate supports by health care providers; however, women-centred care is still very rare in Canada (Carter, et al., 2013). Based on her team's recent literature review, they found that women will access holistic, safe, welcoming environments where they feel respected and involved in the decision-making (Carter et al., 2013). In particular, women want and need to be involved in the planning, delivery, and evaluation of the service. This may require health care providers to provide childcare, transportation, care for other family members, or honoraria. However, women-centred programs have an empowering effect on women and challenge systemic racism, sexism, power, and privilege.

Dr. Loutfy's clinic is one of only six in Canada that is women-centred and she regularly provides childcare, honoraria, and transportation to ensure HIV-positive women or women living with AIDS access much needed culturally safe programming. As you can see from her digital storytelling video,[3] she is addressing particular social determinants of health, understanding that they interact in complex ways to produce poorer outcomes for women particularly those whom also are racialized, poor, or experience stigma because of their health status. She also provides sample exercise and nutritional plans for her patients as well as a checklist of issues that she discusses with her patients, which includes everything from the flu vaccine to bone density testing to housing and intimate partner violence. Dr. Loutfy sees many diverse women including Indigenous women, visible minority women, poor women, wealthy women—they all have one thing in common—they live with HIV and AIDS and experience stigmatization. By using a model of cultural safety, holism, and women-centred care she adapts her practice to meet the needs of her patients.

CONCLUSION

This chapter has provided an overview of important discussions within the feminist movement regarding health. We have argued that feminism and health are linked and that all feminist movements have grappled with the concept of health. Important theories and frameworks including intersectionality, the social determinants of health, gender-based analysis, culturally relevant gender-based analysis, cultural safety, and intersectional feminist frameworks. All of these are important when either examining or addressing the health disparities among women in Canada and around the world. We argued that it is critical to look beyond biology when examining both individual and community health and examining root or systemic factors including gender, race, class, sexual orientation, and a whole variety of social determinants of health that interact in complex and multiple ways to create a variety of health outcomes for women. These different health outcomes were measured using socio-demographic data to demonstrate these complex interactions.

Endnotes

1. Preamble to the Constitution of the World Health Organization as adopted by the International Health Conference, New York, June 19–22, 1946; signed on July 22 1946, by the representatives of 61 States (Official Records of the World Health Organization, no. 2, p. 100) and entered into force on April 7, 1948.
2. Dr. Loutfy provided the authors with permission to discuss her work. More about her work can be read at www.mlmedical.com. See also Loutfy, Dr. Mona. "They Call Her Dr Mona." Retrieved from an online video clip. Youtube, January 2, 2014.
3. http://youtube/4Mbak_e8fBA

Discussion Questions

1. What do theories of intersectionality add to the social determinants of health model?
2. How do race, class, and sexuality intersect to affect an individual's health?
3. What are some examples of obstacles in accessing health care services that might be faced by members of different genders, classes, races/ethnicities, and sexual orientations?
4. Discuss social and ideological constructions and the ways in which these constructions affect health and well-being.

Bibliography

Aboriginal Nurses Association of Canada. (2009). *Cultural competence and cultural safety in nursing education*. Ottawa, ON: Aboriginal Nurses Association of Canada.

Amnesty International Canada. (2004). *Stolen sisters: A human rights response to discrimination and violence against indigenous women in Canada*. Toronto, ON: Amnesty International.

Anderson, J., Perry, J., Blue, C., Browne, A., Henderson, A., Khan, K. B., Kirkham, S. R., ... Smye, V. (2003). "Rewriting" cultural safety within the postcolonial and postnational feminist project: Toward new epistemologies of healing. *Advances in Nursing Science, 26*(3), 196–214.

Anderson, K. (2010). Affirmations of an indigenous feminist. In C. Suzack, S. M. Huhndorf, J. Perreault, & J. Barman (Eds.), *Indigenous women and feminism: Politics, activism and culture* (pp. 81–91). Vancouver, BC: UBC Press.

Biggs, L. (2011). Cheryl Krasnick Warsh, Prescribed norms: Women and health in Canada and the United States since 1800. *Social History of Medicine*, *24*(2), 529–530.

Boscoe, M., Basen, G., Alleyne, G., Bourrier-LaCroix, B., & White, S. (2006). The Canadian women's health movement: Looking back and moving forward. In A. Medovarski & B. Cranney (Eds.), *Canadian woman studies: An introductory reader* (pp. 503–513). Toronto, ON: Inanna Publications & Education Inc.

Bourassa, C. (2004). Colonization, racism and the health of Indian people. *Prairie Forum*, *29*(2), 207–224.

Browne, A., Varcoe, C., & Fridkin, A. (2011). Addressing trauma, violence, and pain: Research on health services for women at the intersections of history and economics. In O. Hankivsky (Ed.), *Health inequities in Canada: Intersectional frameworks and practices* (pp. 295–311). Vancouver, BC: UBC Press.

Canadian Research Institute for the Advancement of Women. (2002). *Women's experiences of racism: How race and gender interact*. Ottawa, ON: Canadian Research Institute for the Advancement of Women.

Canadian Research Institute for the Advancement of Women. (2006). *Intersectional feminist frameworks: A primer*. Ottawa, ON: Canadian Research Institute for the Advancement of Women.

Canadian Research Institute for the Advancement of Women. (2013). *FACT SHEET: Violence Against Women in Canada*. Ottawa, ON: CRIAW.

Carter, A., Bourgeois, S., O'Brien, N., Abelsohn, K., Tharao, W., Greene, S., Margolese, S., Kaida, A., ..., and on behalf of the CHIWOS Research Team. (2013). Women-specific HIV/AIDS Services: Identifying and defining the components of holistic service delivery for women living with HIV/AIDS. *Journal of the International AIDS Society*, *16*, 17433.

Cherland, M. R., & Harper, H. J. (2007). *Advocacy research in literacy education: Seeking higher ground*. New York, NY: Routledge.

Cho, S., Williams Crenshaw, K., & McCall, L. (2013). Toward a field of intersectionality studies: Theory, applications, and praxis. *Signs*, *38*(4), 785–810.

Clark, S. (2013). Intersectionality: "The Promise & the Challenge." *QScience Proceedings*. Retrieved from http://dx.doi.org/10.5339/qproc.2013.fmd.8

Cohen, S., Janicki-Deverts, D., Doyle, W., Miller, G., Franks, E., Rabin, B. & Turner R. (2012). Chronic stress, glucocorticoid receptor resistance, inflammation, and disease risk. *Proceeding of the National Academy of Sciences of the United States of America*, *109*, 5995–5999.

Connell, R. (2012). Gender, health and theory: Conceptualizing the issue, in local and world perspective. *Social Science & Medicine*, *74*(11), 1675–1683.

Daly, T. (2012). The politics of women's health equity: Through the looking glass. *Canadian Woman Studies*, *29*(3), 84–95.

De Maio, F., & Kemp, E. (2010). The deterioration of health status among immigrants to Canada. *Global Public Health: An International Journal for Research Policy and Practice*, *5*, 462–478.

Dhamoon, R. K., & Hankivsky, O. (2011). Why the theory and practice of intersectionality matter to health research and policy. In O. Hankivsky (Ed.), *Health inequities in Canada: Intersectional frameworks and practices* (pp. 16–52). Vancouver, BC: UBC Press.

Engler, S., & Stausberg, M. (Eds.). (2015). Gender. In *The (Oxford) handbook of the study of religion*. Oxford, England: Oxford University Press. In press.

Fleras, A., & Elliott, J. L. (2003). *Unequal relations: An introduction to race and ethnic dynamics in Canada*. Toronto, ON: Pearson Prentice Hall.

Fyfe, C. (1994). Using race as an instrument of policy: A historical view. *Race & Class*, *36*(2), 69–77.

Glouberman, S. (2001). *Towards a new perspective on health policy*. Ottawa, ON: Renouf Publishing.

Govender, V., & Penn–Kekana, L. (2008). Gender biases and discrimination: A review of health care interpersonal interactions. *Global Public Health*, *3*(S1), 90–103.

Green, A. (2006). Telling 1922s story of a national crime: Canada's first chief medical health officer and the aborted fight for Aboriginal health care. *The Canadian Journal for Native Studies, 2*, 211–228.

Green, J. (2007). Taking account of Aboriginal feminism. In J. Green (Ed), *Making space for indigenous feminism* (pp. 20–32). Black Point, NS: Fernwood Publishing—Zed Books.

Groff, J., & Goldberg, S. (2000). The health field concept then and now: Snapshots of Canada. A document of the health network, *Canadian Policy Research Networks Towards a New Perspective on Health Policy*. Background Paper. Retrieved from http://cprn.org/documents/18420_en.pdf

Hankivsky, O. (2006). Reflections on women's health and gender equality in Canada. *Canadian Woman Studies*, *25*(3/4), 51–56.

Health Canada. n.d. Gender-based analysis. *Health Canada*. March 2003. Web. 24 March 2015. Retrieved from http://www.hc-sc.gc.ca/hl-vs/pubs/women-femmes/gender-sexes-eng.php

Health Canada. (2012). *Healthy Canadians 2012: A federal report on comparable health indicators*. Ottawa, ON: Health Canada.

Hesse-Biber, S. N. (Ed.). (2012). *Handbook of feminist research: Theory and praxis*. Thousand Oaks, CA: Sage.

Hull, J. (2001). *Aboriginal People and Social Classes in Manitoba*. Winnipeg: CCPA–Manitoba. Retrieved from www.policyalternatives.ca/publications/reports/aboriginal-people-and-social-classes-manitoba

Indigenous Physicians Association of Canada. (2009). *First Nations, Inuit, Métis Health Core Competencies: A Curriculum Framework for Undergraduate Medical Education,* Retrieved from www.afmc.ca/pdf/CoreCompetenciesEng.pdf

Juschka, D. M. (2014). Fixed geomorphologies and the shifting sands of time. *Failure and Nerve in the Academic Study of Religion*, *50*, 50–61.

Kramer, E., Kwong, K., Lee, E., & Chung, H. (2002). Cultural factors influencing the mental health of Asian Americans. *Western Journal of Medicine, 176*(4), 227–231.

Kubik, W., Bourassa, C., & Hampton, M. (2009). Stolen sisters, second class citizens: The legacy of colonization in Canada. *Humanity and Society*, *33*(1) 8–34.

Lauderdale, D. (2006). Birth outcomes for Arabic-named women in California before and after September 11. *Demography*, *43*, 185–201.

Lavallée B., Neville A., Anderson M., Shore B., Diffey L., Indigenous Physicians Association of Canada, The Association of Faculties of Medicine of Canada. (2009). *First Nations, Inuit and Métis Health Core Competencies: A Curriculum Framework for Undergraduate Medical Education*. Retrieved from www.afmc.ca/social-aboriginal-health-e.php

Liggio, L. (1976). English origins of early American racism. *Radical History Review*, *3*(1), 1–36.

Lippman, A. (2004). Women's cycles up for sale. *Canadian Women's Health Network*. Retrieved from www.cwhn.ca/en/node/39520

Logie, C. H. (2014). Where do queer women belong? Theorizing intersectional and compulsory heterosexism sexism in HIV research. *Critical Public Health*. Retrieved from http://dx.doi.org/10.1080/09581596.2014.938612

Logie, C. H., James, L., Tharao, W., & Loutfy, M. (2011). HIV, gender, race, sexual orientation, and sex work: A qualitative study of intersectional stigma experienced by HIV-positive women in Ontario, Canada. *PLoS Med*, *8*(11), e1001124. doi:10.1371/journal.pmed.1001124

Loppie Reading, C., & Wien, F. (2009). *Health Inequalities and Social Determinants of Aboriginal Peoples' Health*. Prince George, BC: National Collaborating Centre for Aboriginal Health.

Lux, M. (2001). *Medicine that walks: Disease, medicine, and the Canadian Plains Native People, 1880–1940*. Toronto, ON: University of Toronto Press.

Marmot, M., Altman, D., Cameron, D., Dewar, J., Thompson, S., & Wimcox, M. (2013). The benefits and harms of breast cancer screening: An independent review. *British Journal of Cancer, 108*, 2205–2240.

Mann, S. (2012). *Doing feminist theory: From modernity to postmodernity*. New York, NY: Oxford University Press.

McGibbon, E. (2011). Applying intersectionality & complexity theory to address the social determinants of women's health. *Women's Health and Urban Life*, *10*(1), 59–86.

McGibbon, E., & McPherson, C. (2013). Stress, oppression, and women's mental health: A discussion of the health consequences of injustice. *Women's Health and Urban Life, 12*, 63–81.

McIntosh, P. (1988). *White privilege: Unpacking the invisible knapsack*. Retrieved from www.michelepolak.com/WMST100fall10/Weekly_Schedule_files/mcintosh.pdf

McIntosh Gray, A. (1982). Inequities in health. The Black Report: A summary and comment. *International Journal of Health Services, 12*(3), 34980. DOI: 10.2190/XXMM-JMQU-2A7Y-HX1E

Memmi, A. (2013). *The colonizer and the colonized.* New York, NY: Routledge.

National Aboriginal Health Organization. (2006). *Fact Sheet: Cultural Safety*. Retrieved from www.naho.ca/documents/naho/english/Culturalsafetyfactsheet.pdf

Native Women's Association of Canada. (n.d.) *A Culturally Relevant Gender Application Protocol*. Retrieved from www.nwac.ca/wp-content/uploads/2015/05/2010-NWAC-What-is-a-Culturally-Relevant-Gender-Application-Protocol.pdf

Nazroo, J. Y. (2003). The structuring of ethnic inequalities in health: Economic position, racial discrimination, and racism. *American Journal of Public Health*, *93*(2), 277–284.

Newbold, B. (2009). The short-term health of Canada's new immigrant arrivals: Evidence from LSIC. *Ethnicity and Health, 14*, 315–336.

Omi, M., & Winant, H. (2004). Racial Formations in Rothenberg, P. (Ed.), *Race, class and gender in the United States: An integrated study* (pp. 13–22) (6th ed.) New York, NY: St. Martin's Press.

Ontario Human Rights Commission. (2001). *An Intersectional Approach to Discrimination: Addressing Multiple Grounds in Human Rights Claims.* Retrieved from www.ohrc.on.ca/sites/default/files/attachments/An_intersectional_approach_to_discrimination%3A_Addressing_multiple_grounds_in_human_rights_claims.pdf Website: www.ohrc.on.ca/en/intersectional-approach-discrimination-addressing-multiple-grounds-human-rights-claims

Pittz, W. (2005). *Closing the gap: Solutions to race-based health disparities*. Oakland, CA: Applied Research Center and Northwest Federation of Community-Based Organization. Retrieved from: http://accessalliance.ca/wp-content/uploads/2015/03/ClosingGap.pdf

Public Health Agency of Canada. (2008). *Population-Specific HIV/AIDS Status Report: Aboriginal Peoples*. Retrieved from www.phac-aspc.gc.ca/aids-sida/publication/ps-pd/aboriginal-autochtones/chapter-chapitre-3-eng.php

Razack, S. (1998). *Looking white people in the eye: Gender, race, and culture in courtrooms and classrooms*. Toronto, ON: University of Toronto Press.

Royal Canadian Mounted Police. (2014). *Missing and Murdered Aboriginal Women: A National Report*. Ottawa, ON: RCMP.

The Royal College of Physicians and Surgeons of Canada. (2013). *Indigenous Health Values and Principles Statement.* Ottawa, ON: Royal College of Physicians and Surgeons of Canada.

Sen, G., & Ostlin, P. (2008). Gender inequity in health: Why it exists and how we can change it. *Global Public Health*, *3*(S1), 1–12.

Smedley, A., & Smedley, B. D. (2005). *Race in North America.* Boulder, CO: Westview Press.

Smylie, J. (2013). Health professionals working with First Nations, Inuit and Metis consensus guideline. *Journal of Obstetrics and Gynaecology Canada*, *35*(6), 1–50.

Statistics Canada. (2010). Table 105-0513—Health indicator profile, by Aboriginal identity and sex, age-standardized rate, four year estimates, Canada, provinces and territories, occasional (rate), CANSIM (database). Retrieved from www5.statcan.gc.ca/cansim/a26?lang=eng&id=1050513

Statistics Canada. (2010). Aboriginal peoples' survey—health indicator profile, by Aboriginal identity, age group and sex, four year estimates, Canada, provinces and territories. Retrieved from www5.statcan.gc.ca/cansim/a05?lang=eng&id=1050512&pattern=1050512&searchTypeByValue=1&p2=35

Statistics Canada. (2010–2011). *Women in Canada: A gender-based statistical report* (2010–2011, 6th Edition). Retrieved from www.statcan.gc.ca/pub/89-503-x/89-503-x2010001–eng.htm

Statistics Canada. (2011a). Aboriginal peoples in Canada: First Nations people, Metis and Inuit. Retrieved from www12.statcan.gc.ca/nhs-enm/2011/as-sa/99-011-x/99-011-x2011001-eng.cfm

Statistics Canada. (2011b). Immigration and ethnocultural diversity in Canada. Retrieved from www12.statcan.gc.ca/nhs-enm/2011/as-sa/99-010-x/99-010-x2011001-eng.pdf

Statistics Canada. (2015). Visible minority of a person. Retrieved from www.statcan.gc.ca/eng/concepts/definitions/minority01

Stevens, G., Mathers, C., & Beard, J. (2013). Global mortality trends and patterns in older women. *Bulletin of the World Health Organization, 91*, 630–639.

Taska, C., Rapetti, M., Giovanni Carta, M., & Fadda, B. (2012). Women and hysteria in the history of mental health. *Clinical Pratice in Epidemiology in Mental Health, 8*, 110–119.

Tator, C., & Henry, F. (2006). *Racial profiling in Canada: Challenging the myth of "a few bad apples."* Toronto, ON: University of Toronto Press.

Tjepkema, M., Wilkins, R., Senécal, S., Guimond, E., & Penney, C. (2009). *Mortality of Metis and Registered Indian adults in Canada: An 11-year follow-up study*. Ottawa, ON: Statistics Canada.

United Nations Department of Economic and Social Affairs. (2010). *The World's Women 2010 Trends and Statistics*. New York, NY: United Nations.

United Nations Entity for Gender Equality and the Empowerment of Women. (n.d.). The Beijing platform for action: Inspiration then and now. Retrieved from http://beijing20.unwomen.org/en/about

Valverde, M. (1992). 'When the mother of the race is free': Race, reproduction, and sexuality in first-wave feminism. In F. Iacovetta & M. Valverde (Eds.), *Gender conflicts: new essays in women's history* (pp. 3–26). Toronto, ON: University of Toronto Press.

Varcoe, C., Hankivisky, O., & Morrow, M. (2007). Introduction: Beyond gender matters. In M. Morrow, O. Hankivisky, & C. Varcoe (Eds.), *Women's Health in Canada* (3–32). Toronto, ON: University of Toronto Press.

Viruell-Fuentes, E., Miranda, P., & Abdulrahim, S. (2012). More than culture: structural racism, intersectionality theory, and immigrant health. *Social Science & Medicine*, *75*, 2099–2106.

Wallace, S. (2014). Inuit health: Selected findings from the 2012 Aboriginal Peoples Survey. Statistics Canada. Retrieved from www.statcan.gc.ca/pub/89-653-x/89-653-x2014003-eng.htm

Wang, F., Stewart, M., McDermott, S., Kazanjian, A., Vissandjee, B., DesMeules, M. De Groh, M., & Morrison, H. (2012). Migration and diabetes in British Columbia and Québec: Prevalence and Health Service Utilization. *Canadian Journal of Public Health, 103*, 59–64.

Weber, L., & Castellow, J. (2012). Feminist research and activism to promote health equity. In S. N. Hesse-Biber (Ed.), *The Handbook of Feminist Research Theory and Praxis* (2nd ed.) (pp. 434–454). Los Angeles, CA: SAGE Publications.

World Health Organization (WHO). (1986). *The Ottawa Charter for health promotion*. Geneva, Switzerland: WHO.

World Health Organization. (2011). World conference on social determinants of health. Retrieved from www.who.int/sdhconference/en/

World Health Organization. (2013). World Health Statistics 2013. Retrieved from www.who.int/gho/publications/world_health_statistics/EN_WHS2013_Full.pdf

Index

D

E

F

G

H

I

J

K

L

M

N

O

P

Q

R

T

U

V

W

Y